SECOND-CLASS SAINTS

SECOND-CLASS SAINTS

BLACK MORMONS AND THE
STRUGGLE FOR RACIAL EQUALITY

MATTHEW L. HARRIS

OXFORD
UNIVERSITY PRESS

Oxford University Press is a department of the University of Oxford. It furthers
the University's objective of excellence in research, scholarship, and education
by publishing worldwide. Oxford is a registered trade mark of Oxford University
Press in the UK and certain other countries.

Published in the United States of America by Oxford University Press
198 Madison Avenue, New York, NY 10016, United States of America.

© Oxford University Press 2024

All rights reserved. No part of this publication may be reproduced, stored in
a retrieval system, or transmitted, in any form or by any means, without the
prior permission in writing of Oxford University Press, or as expressly permitted
by law, by license, or under terms agreed with the appropriate reproduction
rights organization. Inquiries concerning reproduction outside the scope of the
above should be sent to the Rights Department, Oxford University Press, at the
address above.

You must not circulate this work in any other form
and you must impose this same condition on any acquirer.

Library of Congress Cataloging-in-Publication Data
Names: Harris, Matthew L., author.
Title: Second-class saints : Black Mormons and the struggle for
racial equality / Matthew L. Harris.
Description: New York : Oxford University Press, [2024] | Includes index.
Identifiers: LCCN 2023051088 (print) | LCCN 2023051089 (ebook) |
ISBN 9780197695715 (hardback) | ISBN 9780197695739 (epub) |
ISBN 9780197695746
Subjects: LCSH: African American Latter Day Saints. |
Race relations—Religious aspects—Church of Jesus Christ of Latter-day
Saints—History. | Race—Religious aspects—Church of Jesus Christ of
Latter-day Saints—History. | Priesthood—Church of Jesus Christ of
Latter-day Saints—History.
Classification: LCC BX8643.A35 H37 2024 (print) | LCC BX8643.A35 (ebook) |
DDC 289.3089/96073—dc23/eng/20231122
LC record available at https://lccn.loc.gov/2023051088
LC ebook record available at https://lccn.loc.gov/2023051089

DOI: 10.1093/oso/9780197695715.001.0001

Printed by Sheridan Books, Inc., United States of America

To Newell Bringhurst, my dear friend
To Michael Harris, my brother, who loves books
And to Linda Morgan, my beloved mother

Contents

Preface	ix
Acknowledgments	xvii
A Word about Terminology	xxi
1. From Policy to Doctrine, 1830–1949	1
2. Racial Passing, 1949–1954	28
3. Segregation, 1954–1962	62
4. Civil Rights Resistance, 1962–1967	93
5. Investigations and Protests, 1968–1970	127
6. Lobbying for the Priesthood, 1970–1973	159
7. Lifting the Ban, 1973–1978	192
8. Debris in the Streets, 1978–1985	227
9. The Stigma Still Goes On, 1985–2000	258
10. Hard Doctrine, 2000–2013	285
Epilogue: Black (Mormon) Lives Matter, 2013–2023	307
Abbreviations	321
Notes	327
Index	437

Preface

Mormon Revelation

On June 9, 1978, the phone lines in Salt Lake City jammed when thousands of people called into the headquarters of the Church of Jesus Christ of Latter-day Saints because they could hardly believe what they had heard. Reporters for the AP and UPI had broken the story first, sending ripples of anticipation through the Mormon community. The news was so shocking that some Latter-day Saints traveling that day pulled off to the side of the road when they heard the news on the radio and quietly sobbed in their cars. Those who listened to the radio while they worked in their yards dropped their garden tools and rushed inside to call family and friends. Still others left work early, unable to focus.[1] LDS church president Spencer W. Kimball said that the phone "rang continuously" all day from people all over the world who wanted confirmation. Black Mormons were especially interested in confirming the news for they had the most at stake.[2]

What was the news that gripped hundreds of thousands—perhaps millions—of people that day? Kimball, the church's "prophet, seer, and revelator," announced a revelation. The church's 126-year-old policy banning Black men from holding the priesthood and Black couples from attending the temple would be lifted. Black couples could now be admitted into the sacred spaces of Mormon temples and Black men could enjoy the privileges of holding the priesthood. The revelation also meant that Black Latter-day Saints could qualify for the Celestial Kingdom—the highest degree of status in the Mormon afterlife. Kimball's revelation was the most important policy change since the end of polygamy almost one hundred years earlier. The church would never be the same. The end of the priesthood and temple ban meant that the church could now expand into Sub-Saharan Africa and other predominantly Black regions of the world. With

X   PREFACE

this policy change, it could truly be the global church that Kimball and his predecessors had envisioned.

★ ★ ★

The policy was colloquially known as the "priesthood ban," but it was more far-reaching than that. It meant that Black Latter-day Saints couldn't hold the priesthood, solemnize their wedding vows in Mormon temples, marry someone of another race, sermonize in worship services, bestow priesthood blessings on their children, give Sunday School lessons, offer pastoral counsel, count church tithes, or serve church missions. They were the only racial minorities designated for these exclusions, and, not surprisingly, their pain has been acute and long-lasting.[3] Black Latter-day Saint Melodie Jackson, still bearing the trauma of the ban, reflected, "The Church refused to grant the black body whole recognition and divinity. To Nephi, I was not fair and delightsome. To Joseph, I was a violator of the most sacred principles of society, chastity, and virtue. To Brigham, I was Cain's curse. To McConkie, I was an unfaithful spirit, a 'fence-sitter.'"[4]

The reasons the church excluded Black Latter-day Saints from full inclusion are controversial. Mormon leaders claimed that Black people bore a biblical curse, the result of sins committed in a pre-earth existence. By the 1960s, however, as critics vilified the church during the civil rights era, church leaders took a different position: they said the reasons for the ban were unknown. By the twenty-first century, the church's position shifted again as leaders branded Mormon racial teachings "folklore." Some church leaders still assert that they don't know why the ban existed; others acknowledge the racist impulse behind it.[5]

If the rationale for the ban's origins remains murky, so too does the story of its demise. How Kimball ended the exclusionary practice has never been told in all of its complexity because the church hasn't made available the appropriate records to tell it. Nor has the church itself told the story reliably, for official accounts are shrouded in faith-promoting narratives that do little to explain this significant event in Mormon history. Its Sunday School manuals, for example, gloss over key events and pivotal moments that culminated in Kimball's historic revelation.[6] And the apostles' official biographies haven't fared much better. Most address the revelation only briefly, and some not at all. The standard narrative is that Kimball had a revelation to lift the ban in the Salt Lake Temple, which caught the general

PREFACE   xi

membership and church leaders off guard. In this triumphant moment, the
Mormon prophet was joined by his two counselors in the First Presidency
and members of the Quorum of the Twelve Apostles. They were all unified,
the story goes, and all felt divine grace as they made arguably one of the
most consequential decisions in the church's history.[7]

All of this may be true, but it's a woefully incomplete explanation of
what occurred. Kimball's revelation was not unexpected to the high church
leadership. It was the result of many months of intense discussions between
President Kimball, the apostles, and close friends and advisers. Apostle
Bruce R. McConkie provided the only detailed account from a high
church leader when he published a brief essay titled "The New Revelation
on Priesthood." He called lifting the ban "the long-promised day" and predicted its demise as if it was fated.[8] The LDS *Church News* enthusiastically
echoed McConkie, commenting, "Prophets tell of promise to all races."[9]
These faith-promoting accounts, however, do not consider how the ban
ended or the bruises and wounds that some church leaders incurred trying
to end it. In fact, McConkie's quasi-official account, and the church's official characterization of the revelation, ignores the plot twists and turns and
contingent moments when the story didn't have to turn out the way that it
did. Rather, as I argue in *Second-Class Saints*, the inclusion of Black people
in the church was as much the product of human agency as it was divine
revelation. Kimball and others made the decision to lift the ban because
it posed a major deterrent to spreading the gospel globally, which is a key
element in Mormon theology.

The full story, told here for the first time, explores such contingent moments and provides an illuminating backstory to Kimball's revelation. In the
three decades before he lifted the ban, Mormon leaders were engaged in a
vigorous debate about whether to keep it in light of the apostles' ambitious
attempt to globalize the church. Their clashes were lively, fraught with emotion, and bitterly contested. These took place behind closed doors, leaving
Latter-day Saints largely unaware of what was transpiring. On one side of
the debate were church liberals, namely Apostle Hugh B. Brown, Apostle
Adam S. Bennion, general authority Marion D. Hanks, and Mormon intellectuals Lowry Nelson, Sterling McMurrin, and Lowell Bennion. Opposing
them were the ultraconservatives, whom I call hard-liners, whose most important spokespersons include Apostle Joseph Fielding Smith, his son-in-
law Apostle Bruce R. McConkie, and Apostles Ezra Taft Benson, Mark E.

xii PREFACE

Petersen, and Harold B. Lee. In the middle stood the moderates: church president David O. McKay, his counselor J. Reuben Clark, and then-Apostle Spencer W. Kimball.

★ ★ ★

The revelation occurred on June 1, 1978, in the Salt Lake Temple, was announced to the church on June 9, then formally codified into the Mormon canon on September 30, during the faith's semi-annual general conference. Kimball's revelation, however, has been misunderstood by members and outsiders. The term "revelation"—which Latter-day Saints use often in their discourse—sometimes implies or assumes that LDS church presidents see and speak with God, just as founding prophet Joseph Smith Jr. claimed in his widely known epiphany called the First Vision.[10] After all, the highest-ranking leaders of the church are known to the faithful as "prophets, seers, and revelators." What is most widely taught in the church is that revelation is a spiritual impression or prompting that one receives after meditation, study, and prayer. Mormon scripture and Mormon leaders both describe revelation as "a still, small voice" or "sudden strokes of ideas" that enters one's mind when influenced by the Holy Spirit.[11] However, institutional revelation is more nuanced than this, particularly when the church hierarchy produces new doctrine or announces important policy changes. Apostle Hugh B. Brown provided the most candid and succinct definition of revelation:

> When a question arises today, we work over the details and come up with an idea. It is submitted to the First Presidency and Twelve, thrashed out, discussed and re-discussed until it seems right. Then, kneeling together in a circle in the temple, they seek divine guidance, and the president says, "I feel to say this is the will of the Lord." That becomes a revelation. It is usually not thought necessary to publish or proclaim it as such, but this is the way it happens.[12]

Here we get right to the heart of the matter. Mormon revelation isn't the dramatic thunderbolt observers might imagine. There was no burning bush, no angels telling Kimball what to do, no cosmic force scripting it for him. Rather, Kimball, his counselors, and the Twelve Apostles, "thrashed out, discussed, and re-discussed" the church's race doctrine until they reached a consensus that it needed to be changed. Then, after a prolonged period of debate and discussion, punctuated with prayer, church leaders concluded that it was time to admit Black people into their ranks as full, functioning members.

PREFACE

xiii

That Kimball achieved a revelation to lift the ban was nothing short of extraordinary given the hard-liners' deeply held prejudices. Yet his revelation—known in the Mormon canon as "Official Declaration 2"—provided more questions than answers.[13] The revelation lifted the ban, but it didn't address the doctrine that had sustained it. This oversight proved catastrophic for the postrevelation church as Latter-day Saints continued to teach that Black people bore a divine curse.[14]

At no time was this more evident than in 2012, when BYU religion professor Randy Bott gave an interview to a *Washington Post* reporter. In that fraught interview, Bott spoke openly and approvingly of the church's race teachings, including his support for biblical curses and demeaning racial tropes, seemingly unaware of how it might affect Mitt Romney's presidential campaign, then underway.[15] On blogs and websites, dozens of Latter-day Saints exploded in rage, demanding that church leaders address the institution's long history of systemic racism.

In 2013, the church published a brief essay titled "Race and the Priesthood," in which leaders dismantled the theological scaffolding that had anchored the ban. In that seminal document, the First Presidency and Quorum of the Twelve Apostles repudiated the curse and related teachings, signaling a rare acknowledgment that Mormon racial teachings had damaged the lives of thousands of Black and biracial Latter-day Saints.[16]

★ ★ ★

This book is about Mormonism's priesthood and temple ban—its stormy beginnings, its dramatic ending, and its painful legacy. Although I provide context to the origins of the ban, my principal focus is on the critical fifty-year period leading up to the revelation, a turbulent time during which the church opposed civil rights for African Americans. Next I discuss the revelation itself—how it came to be, who resisted it, who supported it, and how church president Spencer W. Kimball reached a consensus with church apostles to grant Black people full inclusion in the church. As I explain in detail throughout the book, a number of interlocking factors led Kimball to lift the ban, including the fact that it clashed with his desire to globalize the church. In the final third of the book, I focus on the postrevelation church, a neglected yet critical period in LDS church history. I argue that, after 1978, Black Latter-day Saints pressured the Brethren— members of the First Presidency and Quorum of the Twelve Apostles, the church's two highest governing bodies—to repudiate the theology that fueled the ban.

PREFACE

In researching this story, I have had unprecedented access to the personal papers, meeting minutes, and diaries of influential church presidents and apostles. I have also had access to dozens of oral histories, which, like the personal papers of the prophets and apostles, provide never-before-seen glimpses into how Latter-day Saints both embraced and subsequently rejected the church's race theology. One of the most valuable collections I reviewed was the Spencer W. Kimball Papers at the LDS Church History Library in Salt Lake City—a restricted collection that proved essential to this book. Edward Kimball, President Kimball's son and biographer, made these papers available to me, and I reviewed them only because of his generosity and trust. Edward also gave me a cache of documents that he didn't donate to the church. These documents are sensitive and controversial, and he didn't feel at liberty to include them in his own previously published work of his father's presidency.[17] I have utilized them in this book and have tried to follow Edward's counsel to treat them with care.

Before moving forward, it's important to state what this book is and what it isn't. It isn't a definitive history of the Mormon priesthood and temple ban. It focuses on international developments within the church insofar as these affected Mormon racial policies and practices, but it doesn't purport to be a history of the ban in the international church. Nor is it a history of Mormon racism in general or a comprehensive examination of the origins of the ban during the nineteenth century. Indeed, that story has been superbly told by other scholars of Mormonism.[18]

My focus, rather, is on racism as it affected Black and biracial people in the Church of Jesus Christ of Latter-day Saints. Readers will see that I include a wide variety of voices and perspectives. Some of these people are well known to Latter-day Saints and to outsiders; others are obscure. They include bishops and stake presidents, newly baptized converts, college professors, LDS religion teachers, disaffected Latter-day Saints, believing Latter-day Saints, politicians and government figures, dark-skinned Africans and light-skinned Brazilians, Motown singers, former Black Panthers, and civil rights organizations like the NAACP. Because the priesthood and temple ban affected Black and biracial Latter-day Saints so profoundly, I have privileged their perspectives as much as the sources would allow.

Readers will also see that I have tried to place Mormon racial teachings in the larger U.S. social, political, and cultural context. Ralph Waldo Emerson perceptively noted that "the ideas of the time are in the air and infect all who breathe it," and so it is with Latter-day Saints.[19] To that end, I juxtapose Mormon teachings with Catholic, mainline Protestant, and evangelical perspectives on segregation, racism, and civil rights and point out where Mormons hold similar views and where they differ. For instance, when religion scholar Anthea Butler wrote that evangelicals "believed African Americans were inferior to whites, supported Jim Crow, and avidly opposed civil rights, busing, and interracial marriage," she could have been talking about Mormons.[20]

Some readers might take offense at the book's unvarnished account of the LDS church's history with antiblack racism, but in my defense, I believe that readers will appreciate the story more if all the artificial preservatives and sweeteners are left out. Honesty is the only way to heal faith communities from the devastating effects of racism, and if people of goodwill can learn from the Latter-day Saint experience, it might prompt them to excavate their own racial assumptions, wipe them clean of apologetics and rationalizations, and begin anew.

Acknowledgments

This book took nearly fifteen years to research and write, and I'm glad to finally see it in print. During the course of my work, I have accumulated debts too numerous to repay. Nevertheless, I want to give a shout-out to people who have aided me in this long and delightful journey. Those who read the manuscript in part or in full or offered sage advice through email or phone conversations or at conferences or over meals include Newell Bringhurst, Armand Mauss, Matthew Bowman, Paul Reeve, Patrick Mason, Kif Augustine-Adams, Stirling Adams, Steven Epperson, Scott Abbott, Darius Gray, Bruce Van Orden, Gary Bergera, Ron Priddis, Curt Bench, Rebecca de Schweinitz, Mel Johnson, Bryan Buchanan, Becky Roesler, Edward Kimball, Cameron McCoy, Greg Christofferson, Mark Grover, Bill Russell, Darron Smith, Max Mueller, Sam Brunson, Kevin Barney, Rich Hanks, Lester Bush, Greg Prince, Alice Faulker Burch, Eugene Orr, Jonathan Stapley, Paul Harvey, Margaret Young, Mike Quinn, John Turner, Chris Kimball, John Seidel, Barbara Jones Brown, Craig Foster, David Jackson, Chris Thomas, Taylor Petrey, Ben Park, Jana Riess, and Kristine Haglund.

From this distinguished group, I must recognize five people in particular. First and foremost is Newell Bringhurst, to whom this book is dedicated. When I called Newell many years ago to introduce myself, he quizzed me about my research interests and immediately realized, as I did, that we had much in common. We formed a friendship that has flourished ever since. Newell has read virtually everything I have written about Mormon history, including this book—some chapters multiple times. His wisdom and knowledge shadow every page.

The late Armand Mauss—also a dear friend—bears special recognition too. In the last year of his life, when his health (but not his mind) was rapidly failing, we exchanged emails almost every day. We discussed Mormon leaders, Mormon theology, and, most of all, our shared interest in Mormon

xviii ACKNOWLEDGMENTS

racial history. Frequently I sent Armand documents to read that served as the basis for our discussions. At one point, thinking it was too onerous for me, he said, "You don't have to keep feeding the beast," to which I replied, "If the beast appreciates it, I'll keep feeding it." Needless to say, he appreciated the steady stream of documents, and I appreciated his penetrating and witty insights. I count myself fortunate that the last thing Armand read before he died was one of the chapters in this book. I only regret that he didn't live to see the finished product.

The two readers for Oxford University Press offered marvelously helpful critiques. I owe thanks to Paul Reeve of the University of Utah and Patrick Mason of Utah State University. They read the manuscript with a critical eye and offered the perfect blend of criticism and praise. Matthew Bowman of Claremont Graduate University also read the manuscript in full and provided a thoughtful appraisal. I am grateful to these gifted scholars.

Likewise, Mel Johnson read the manuscript with characteristic sensitivity and made a number of suggestions to improve it. Thanks also to the indomitable Steve Mayfield, the Mormon photographer extraordinaire. Over a span of six years, Steve sent me a stream of documents relating to race issues in Utah and the LDS church. I told Steve that if he kept sending me material I'd keep writing because the material was so good.

A number of scholars and laypersons shared material with me as well. These generous souls include Edward Kimball, Greg Prince, Rich Hanks, Cory Bangerter, Camille Fronk Olson, Mark Grover, Gary Bergera, Matthew Bowman, David Cook, Stirling Adams, Bryan Buchanan, Reid Moon, Catherine Beitler Humphrey, David Jackson, Kristine Haglund, Sandra Tanner, Armand Mauss, Mike Marquardt, Ernie Lazer, Mary Kimball Dollahite, Ross Boundy, Curt Bench, Jonathan Stapley, Darius Gray, Robert Greenwell, Barbara Jones Brown, George Rickford, Mel Johnson, Max Mueller, Dennis Gladwell, Steven Epperson, and Newell Bringhurst.

Thanks also to the journal editors who allowed me to use material from my previously published articles. These include "A Tale of Two Religions: RLDS and LDS Reponses to the Civil Rights Movement," *John Whitmer Historical Association Journal* 43, no. 1 (Spring–Summer 2023): 114–32; "Confronting and Condemning 'Hard Doctrine,' 1978–2013," *Mormon Studies Review* 7 (2020): 21–28; "Joseph Fielding Smith's Evolving Views on Race: The Odyssey of a Mormon Apostle-President," *Dialogue: A Journal of Mormon Thought* 55, no. 3 (Fall 2022): 1–41; and "Mormons and Lineage:

The Complicated History of Blacks and Patriarchal Blessings, 1830–2018," *Dialogue: A Journal of Mormon Thought* 51, no. 3 (Fall 2018): 83–129.

No work of history is possible, of course, without the support of libraries and archives. At my home institution, Colorado State University, Pueblo, Kenneth McKenzie, our inimitable interlibrary loan librarian, made it a personal challenge to track down every book and article I ordered. When Kenny encountered obstacles, he refused to quit until he achieved the intended result. Thank you, Kenny, for your persistence and dedication. Thanks also to the archivists at the LDS Church History Library, especially Bill Slaughter and Ben Whisenant, who have been enormously helpful. Archivists at the University of Utah, especially Betsey Welland and Elizabeth Rogers, always make work there memorable. Archivists at BYU have been equally attentive and helpful, notably Gordon Daines, Cory Nimer, and Cindy Brightenburg. Gary Bergera, the former director at the Smith-Pettit Foundation, granted me unlimited access to his rich trove of Mormon documents, for which I am grateful. I'm also grateful for the professionalism and expertise of the archivists at the University of Chicago, Stanford University, Wisconsin Historical Society, University of Arizona, Utah State University, Yale University, Utah State Historical Society, the Library of Congress, and the Utah Division of Archives and Records, especially Anthony Castro.

This is my second book with Theo Caldera, editor-in-chief of humanities at Oxford University Press. My thanks to Theo for his sage advice and professionalism and his counsel about what to keep in the manuscript, what to cut, and what to streamline. That's what great editors do, and Theo is one of the best.

I have received generous funding over the years from Colorado State University, Pueblo, and Brigham Young University, Provo. CSU–Pueblo has funded my research excursions to numerous archives. BYU awarded me research funds from the Charles Redd Center that allowed me to investigate the incomparable African American oral histories that Jessie L. Embry and Alan Cherry conducted back in the 1980s. I could not have completed this book without the generous assistance of these two institutions.

And finally, my family. My in-laws, Lind and Meridee Williams, hosted me too many times to count during my research visits to BYU and provided a loving and peaceful environment after a long day's work. My sister Trina Hammond and her husband Chris performed a similar function when I traveled "up north" to work at the LDS Church History Library and the University of Utah. My mother, Linda Morgan, loaned me her LDS books, but most of all listened patiently as I worked through knotty issues relating to Mormon racial history. She even read some of my chapters for tone and effect and encouraged me to remove certain words or phrases when I got carried away. My father, Lawrence Harris, has likewise been a great support. My brothers—Michael, Aaron, and Jason—and my brother-in-law Chris Hammond discussed many of the topics in this book with me, often with humor and insight. My wife, Courtney, was unfailingly patient when I was distracted during the final stint of the revision stage. She has always encouraged me in my professional work, and I have benefited enormously over the years from her wisdom and love. Our children—Madison, Taylor, and Jackson—have been just as supportive. Madison read parts of the manuscript and emerged as a skilled critic and invaluable interlocutor. Taylor drew me away from the manuscript to shoot hoops and hike. Jackson, my autistic son, frequently disrupted my writing by bolting into my office to ask for a hug. After I squeezed him for a few precious seconds, he would disappear. My loved ones remind me of all that is good in life and that what famed basketball coach John Wooden said is undeniably true: "The most important thing in the world is family and love."

A Word about Terminology

I use the term "Brethren" throughout the book. It refers to members of the First Presidency and Quorum of the Twelve Apostles, the two highest governing bodies in the Church of Jesus Christ of Latter-day Saints. The Quorums of the Seventy, the third highest tier in the church hierarchy, rank just below the First Presidency and Quorum of the Twelve Apostles. Cumulatively, they comprise the general authorities of the church—all members of a full-time church ministry who set doctrine and policy for the church and regulate its 16-million-member body throughout the world. Most of these leaders bear the title "President" or "Elder," but I refer to them as apostle or general authority to avoid confusion. The only person I call president is the church president, whom Latter-day Saints sustain as a "prophet, seer, and revelator."

As for Latter-day Saint congregations, they are divided into geographic regions comprised of "stakes" under which are included "wards" and/or "branches." These congregations are run by local lay leaders: stake presidents preside over stakes, and bishops and branch presidents preside over wards and branches, respectively. Two other important lay positions include mission presidents and relief society presidents. Mission presidents preside over LDS church missions throughout the world, while women preside in their stakes, wards, and branches to oversee LDS women who coordinate philanthropic, service, and educational activities. All of these leaders answer to the general authorities in Salt Lake City, Utah, the headquarters of the church.

And finally, because most outside observers recognize the Church of Jesus Christ of Latter-day Saints as the "LDS church" or "Mormon church," I have chosen to use the more familiar names in this book. When possible, I use the full name of the church, but in most instances I use "LDS," "Latter-day Saint," "Mormon," and "Mormonism" synonymously and interchangeably.

I

From Policy to Doctrine, 1830–1949

The Church of Jesus Christ of Latter-day Saints didn't always ban persons of African ancestry from the priesthood and the sacred rituals of Mormon temples. Under founding prophet Joseph Smith Jr., who led the church from 1830 to 1844, a handful of Black men held the priesthood, and some performed limited temple rituals. Today these Black Latter-day Saints have been removed from the pages of Mormon history, their voices lost, their stories untold. In an era that privileged histories of White people over histories of slaves, women, and Indigenous populations, their stories have simply been forgotten. But in the nineteenth century many members in the fledging Latter-day Saint movement were likely familiar with the names of Elijah Abel, Q. Walker Lewis, and Joseph T. Ball, each of whom held the priesthood and at least one of whom (Abel) received temple blessings, while another (Ball) served as a presiding minister in a Mormon congregation. And there's good evidence (though inconclusive) that three other Black men—William McCary, Enoch Lovejoy Lewis, and Peter Kerr (also known as "Black Pete")—also held the priesthood.[1]

Priesthood ordination for Black men came to an abrupt halt under Brigham Young, the second prophet-president of the church, who governed with an iron fist for some thirty years.[2] In 1847, the visionary Mormon colonizer led the Saints westward to the Great Basin, where three Black Latter-day Saints—Green Flake, Oscar Crosby, and Hark Lay—were part of the vanguard pioneer company. Within three years of settlement, however, Young began to support race-based slavery and instituted a number of policies designed to stifle Black participation in the church. First and foremost, he established the priesthood and temple ban in 1852. He cited no direct decree from God nor any revelation from Joseph Smith Jr. to justify the bold measure.[3] Instead, Young asserted that because Cain murdered his brother Abel, God marked him with a "flat nose and black skin," proclaiming that "any man" with African ancestry "cannot hold the priesthood."[4] When Young died in 1877 the ban had been in effect for nearly twenty-five years and his successors were not inclined to change it.

During the first century of the church, however, Mormonism's exclusionary racial policies garnered little notice. After the Second World War, as the church began to expand internationally, critics emerged demanding to know why Black people were denied sacred priestly rites. In response, the First Presidency produced a statement in 1949 canonizing its racial teachings, moving what had been a policy and a practice to a firm and entrenched doctrine. Designed to answer critics, the First Presidency drew on the writings of Apostle Joseph Fielding Smith, whose influential book *The Way to Perfection* (1931) laid the groundwork for the authoritative 1949 statement.

★ ★ ★

We don't know the precise number of Black members in the church during Joseph Smith Jr.'s tenure as founding prophet, but scholars estimate that it was somewhere around one hundred. Most were enslaved or formerly enslaved; some were free.[5] We do know that by the 1850s at least eighty slaves and thirty free Black people had migrated west to the Utah Territory. Included among them were Jane Manning James and Elijah Abel—both converts and committed members of the LDS church.[6]

If anyone deserved special consideration to receive the full privileges of the church it was Jane Manning James. She was in her early twenties when she converted to Mormonism in 1842, and during the next sixty years until her death in 1908 she became one of the church's most devout and loyal members. The church-owned newspaper, the *Deseret Evening News*, said that her fellow Latter-day Saints respected "her undaunted faith and goodness of heart."[7]

Baptized into the New Canaan Congregational Church at age fourteen, James joined the Church of Jesus Christ of Latter-day Saints some six years later and soon thereafter converted her family, including her mother, three brothers, and two sisters. All were mesmerized by the charismatic teachings

Jane Manning James, a Black Latter-day Saint convert and admirer of church founder Joseph Smith Jr. Courtesy of Zuri Swimmer/Alamy Stock Photo.

of early Mormon church leaders.[8] The Saints' speaking in tongues, unique healing practices, and claims of angelic visitors excited James, as did another exciting feature: the church was interracial. It didn't segregate by race.[9]

James's new religion was founded in 1830 in upstate New York, where Joseph Smith Jr. proclaimed a divine epiphany. In a cluster of trees not far from his home in Palmyra, Smith declared that God and Jesus had appeared to him in a vision and told him to start his own church, for the others were "all wrong."[10] With the divine epiphany came responsibilities and within a few years Smith was informed that he would restore ancient

4 SECOND-CLASS SAINTS

priesthood rituals, establish a godly church in preparation for the End Times, and translate hundreds of pages of ancient records, resulting in sacred scripture.[11]

This origin story fascinated James. Shortly after her baptism she left her home in Wilton, Connecticut, and with her family trekked hundreds of miles to Nauvoo, Illinois, the hub of church activity in the early 1840s. There she met the Mormon prophet and became enchanted by his charisma and kindness and with his fascinating new religion. Smith, in turn, invited her to live in his home as his servant. He allowed her to see the church's most cherished artifacts, including the Urim and Thummim, the special instrument that Smith used to translate Mormon scripture.[12] Years later "Aunt Jane," as Mormons called her, described what Smith meant to her: she saw him in a vision "and knew that he was a prophet."[13]

James's affection for the Mormon prophet motivated her to petition church leaders to be sealed to him as a member of his family. This bold request, which occurred years after Smith's death in 1844, affirmed James's longtime desire to experience a Mormon temple sealing. The sealing ritual was designed to bind families together for eternity.[14] Prior to that, church leaders had granted James and a handful of other Black Latter-day Saints permission to perform lesser temple rituals such as proxy baptisms for deceased ancestors, but church officials excluded them from one of the most important Mormon rituals—the endowment—which prepared Mormons for the afterlife.[15]

James probably wasn't surprised when church leaders denied her request to be sealed to Smith or to receive her endowment. After all, they deemed her cursed. She bore a "mark," they said, that tainted her skin. James learned of her alleged curse in a "patriarchal blessing"—a Mormon rite in which all faithful Latter-day Saints learn their Israelite lineage.[16] The patriarch who issued James's blessing told her that she descended from the cursed lineage of "Cainaan, the son of Ham," and thus was excluded from God's covenant with the house of Israel, which made her ineligible to receive the church's most sacred rituals. Furthermore, the patriarch told James that she would be whitened in the resurrection—a bold claim—given James's dark skin. The whitening would occur at Jesus Christ's Second Coming, when the Messiah returned in all his glory.[17]

James's status in the church changed drastically after Smith died. Brigham Young had a much harsher view of Black people than Smith did, and he passed a number of measures to stifle their spiritual growth. Whereas Smith linked the plight of Black people to environmental factors—"[C]hange their situation with the white [and] they would be like them," he famously said—Young attributed their plight to biology.[18] He called them "black, uncouth, uncomely, disagreeable and low in their habits, wild, and seemingly deprived of nearly all the blessings of the intelligence that is generally bestowed upon mankind." His views about interracial marriage weren't any kinder. He said that if White and Black people married it would lead to "death on the spot." Most notably, while Smith opposed slavery, Young called it a "divine institution." In further contrast to Smith, Young audaciously claimed that God's curse on Black people made them fit only to be servants to White people. In another sermon Young talked about the "superior wisdom" of White people "to the descendants of Cain."[19]

Smith, however, was far from progressive on race. He shared many common assumptions about Black people and, like dozens of Protestant clergymen from his era, he called Black people the "sons of Cain."[20] Nor did he support interracial marriage. "Had I anything to do with the Negro," Smith said, "I would confine them by strict law to their own species." But what must be remembered here is that Smith allowed Black men to be ordained to the priesthood, whereas Young didn't.[21]

In 1852 Young made the bold announcement to the Utah Territorial Legislature barring Black members from the priesthood and temple. According to Apostle Wilford Woodruff, Young told lawmakers that anyone with "one drop" of African blood would be barred from the full rites of the church, meaning that the slightest trace of African ancestry would deem them cursed. Young added that the curse would be lifted only after all the other races had the opportunity to receive the priesthood.[22] He didn't explain why he made such an abrupt announcement, but there were rumors swirling throughout the church that a Black Latter-day Saint named William McCary had taken a polygamous White wife, which angered Young. The Saints had been practicing polygamy in secret since the 1830s, but by the time of Young's presidency the practice was openly acknowledged. What was challenging about a Black man taking a White woman for a plural wife was that the practice appeared to be confined mostly to White members. We don't know all the details of McCary's interracial relationship, but shortly after Young learned of it, he told the legislature that "if any man mingles his seed with the seed of Caine, the ownly way he could get rid of it or have salvation would be to come forward & have his head cut off & spill his Blood upon the ground."[23]

Brigham Young, the second president of the Church of Jesus Christ of Latter-day Saints and originator of the priesthood and temple ban, 1850. Courtesy of Utah State Historical Society.

Some three decades later Young's "racial venom" influenced the Utah Territorial Legislature when it passed a statute in 1888 barring Black, White, and Asian ("Mongolians") people from intermarrying. In 1939, the legislature expanded the law to prevent "a mulatto, quadroon, or octoroon" from marrying a White person.[24] As in other states, Utah lawmakers defined a mulatto as anyone with one White and one Black parent (one-half Black), a quadroon with one Black grandparent and three White grandparents (one-fourth Black), and an octoroon with one Black great-grandparent and seven White great-grandparents (one-eighth Black).[25]

Unquestionably, these human-invented legal constructions made it difficult for Americans to define race, because race doesn't have a biological basis.[26] In 1918, Relief Society leader and women's suffragist Susa Young Gates, Brigham Young's daughter, shed light on this when she published a six-hundred-page book that attempted to link genealogy to the world's racial history.[27] Drawing on history textbooks and research from nineteenth-century physicians and anthropologists, Gates asserted that only three races existed: Black ("Ethiopian"), Yellow ("Mongolian"), and White ("Caucasian"). Much of her book focused on global migrations and interracial encounters, giving inadvertent support to the idea that race is socially constructed. But Gates didn't understand this concept, nor did she understand how her research undercut the one-drop rule or challenged notions of "racial purity." She claimed that each race had a distinctive "strain" or lineage that became blurred over time through interracial marriage.[28]

Gates's book became an immediate topic of interest in the church. Amy Brown Lyman of the church's Relief Society general presidency said that it possessed a "wide interest for every person in the church," which proved to be the case for both high-ranking church leaders and rank-and-file members. Apostles Joseph Fielding Smith, Anthon Lund, and Charles Penrose studied it very carefully, as did the women in the Relief Society, who adopted it as part of their curriculum.[29] However, Gates's work didn't

Susa Young Gates, Brigham Young's daughter and a prominent Mormon writer, n.d. Courtesy of Utah State Historical Society.

8　　　　　　　　　　　SECOND-CLASS SAINTS

convince church leaders to abandon the one-drop rule. The apostles didn't understand that Gates's work crashed head-on with the concept of a "pure white race." As Gates (and others) demonstrated, Africans, Europeans, and Indigenous peoples had crisscrossed the globe for centuries, during which they had married interracially, had had mixed-race children, and had forged new racial identities.[30]

But there was another fundamental flaw with the one-drop rule. As Gates implied, you couldn't tell whether someone had African ancestry simply by looking at them. In the nineteenth century, when Brigham Young and other Mormon leaders defined a "negro" as anyone having one drop of African lineage, there were no reliable ways to identify bloodlines. DNA tracing through the Human Genome Project was decades in the future, which made determining lineage imprecise and often wrong.[31]

All of this is to say is that the one-drop rule underscored a brutal reality that neither Mormon leaders nor Americans in general could grasp. The racial boundaries they sought to enforce were built on fiction.

★ ★ ★

No one in the church generated more discussion of racial identity and inclusion than Elijah Abel, a Latter-day Saint who was one-eighth Black. His light skin and short-cropped hair placed him in a racial no-man's land, not unlike tens of thousands of other mixed-race individuals in the United States, which the 1850 census defined as "mulattos."[32] Abel's grandmother was purportedly "half White" and half Black, his grandfather White, and his parents, Andrew Abel and Delilah Williams, purportedly White. Born in 1810 in Hancock, Washington County, Maryland, Abel was baptized in 1832 in Kirtland, Ohio, and ordained an "elder" in the LDS church in 1836. He advanced to the rank of "seventy"—an office in the Melchizedek priesthood—and served a number of church missions. Also in 1836, Abel was given his "washings and anointings" in the Kirtland Temple—a precursor to endowments and sealings.[33]

Following Smith's death in 1844, Abel's status in the church quickly changed. He became subject to scrutiny by Smith's successors. Sometime during Brigham Young's tenure as prophet-president, Abel asked to receive his endowments and be sealed to his wife and children, but this was "a privilege that President Young could not grant," recalled Apostle Joseph F. Smith.[34] Abel made the same request to church president John Taylor,

Gravestone of Elijah Abel, a Black Latter-day Saint missionary and priesthood holder, Salt Lake City, Utah, n.d.

Young's successor, and again was told no. Despite this, Taylor allowed Abel to keep his priesthood, declaring him to be an exception to the rule. The fact that Abel had light skin undoubtedly played to his advantage, as did his patriarchal blessing, which conspicuously omitted a lineage designation.[35] Abel's years of devout service in the church must have also played a role. He had been a faithful member and a loyal follower of Joseph Smith Jr. and had served honorably in the church's Third Quorum of Seventy. Still, none of that was enough to grant him full inclusion.

One might conclude that Abel's death in 1884 would have made his status in the priesthood moot, but that wasn't the case. After Abel died, then–church president Joseph F. Smith found it implausible that his uncle, Joseph Smith Jr., would have allowed the ordination to stand. In 1908, Joseph F. Smith declared, without evidence, that Abel was ordained to the priesthood by mistake and that when the founding prophet learned about it, he nullified the ordination.[36] Not only did Joseph F. Smith disagree with John Taylor, but he wanted to undo an ordination that his uncle had permitted.

Joseph F. Smith proclaimed that the priesthood and temple ban had originated with Joseph Smith Jr. Abel's ordination didn't quite fit the emerging narrative that the ban had existed since the church's founding.

★ ★ ★

The cases of Jane Manning James and Elijah Abel demonstrate that the church didn't have a consistent policy that governed Black and mixed-race Latter-day Saints during the first century of the church. Both of these devout Latter-day Saints participated in some church rituals despite their alleged cursed status, and both enjoyed certain privileges in the church denied to other Black members during Joseph Smith Jr.'s tenure as church president, but both were also subject to the fickle, often contradictory whims of Smith's successors.[37]

Most troubling to Mormon leaders was that Mormon scriptures offered few insights to guide them on the status of Black people. In the four books of scripture that Joseph Smith Jr. produced—a revised version of the Bible, the Book of Mormon, the Doctrine and Covenants, and the Pearl of Great Price—very little is said about Black and mixed-race people, although the church's "Standard Works," by inference or direct corollary, comment extensively on Native Americans ("Lamanites"), Polynesians ("Hagoth"), and other racial and ethnic groups.[38]

What little is said about Black people is only by inference. Like many Protestant Christians, LDS church apostles cited two critical passages in the Bible to affirm a divine curse. In one, God places a "mark" on Cain for murdering his brother Abel. In the other, when Ham mocks his father, Noah, for being naked, God curses Ham's son Canaan and his posterity.[39] Neither of these verses designated the "mark" as Black skin per se; nonetheless, many people in antebellum America interpreted these verses to mean that the mark or curse on these individuals destined Black people for a lifetime of servitude and bondage.[40]

The Book of Mormon was also awash in curses. In this seminal text, which Joseph Smith Jr. claimed to produce from golden tablets in 1830, God cursed the sinful Lamanites with dark skin and blessed the righteous Nephites with white skin.[41] This racial binary was most prominent in 2 Nephi, which states that God

> had caused the cursing to come upon [the Lamanites], yea, even a sore cursing, because of their iniquity. For behold, they had hardened their hearts against

FROM POLICY TO DOCTRINE

him, that they had become like unto a flint; wherefore, as they were white, and exceedingly fair and delightsome, that they might not be enticing unto my people the Lord God did cause a skin of blackness to come upon them.[42]

Nineteenth-century Protestant ministers embraced a similar racial binary, equating whiteness with purity and wholesomeness and blackness with sin and savagery, but perhaps no Christian sect had racialized its theology as thoroughly as did the Latter-day Saints.[43] The Book of Mormon promoted a racial fluidity, with prophets declaring that the curse would vanish through moral probity and righteous living—the same promise that Jane Manning James's patriarch made to her. When the Lamanites repented of their sins, the Book of Mormon states, their "curse [would be] taken from them and their skin [would become] white like unto the Nephites."[44]

Paradoxically, the Book of Mormon also contains a message of inclusion, one obscured by the church's exclusivist racial theology. God "denieth none that come unto him, black and white, bond and free, male and female," a prominent verse notes. "All are alike unto God."[45]

The Pearl of Great Price was even more explicit in depicting racial curses. The Pearl of Great Price contains two parts: the Book of Moses and the Book of Abraham. The Book of Moses links the "seed of Cain" with blackness and Cain's progeny with the devil. Its most suggestive passage warns that mixing the "seed of Cain" with "the seed of Adam" will incur God's wrath, providing fodder for twentieth-century Mormon leaders to oppose civil rights. The Book of Abraham was the church's most widely cited proof text in defending the priesthood and temple ban.[46] A notable passage states that God had cursed Pharaoh's descendants, who were thought to be the ancestors from the "loins of Ham." This divine curse originated from a "war in heaven" before the creation of the earth, during which the followers of Jesus Christ clashed with the devil and his followers. The devil and his minions, the text states, sought to overthrow Jesus and were therefore thrust from heaven, causing God to curse them "as pertaining to the priesthood."[47]

Over the next half-century Mormon leaders would clash with each other over the meaning of the "war in heaven," especially as it applied to Black people. After the Pearl of Great Price was canonized in 1880, a number of Mormon leaders began to link "cursed lineages" to a pre-earth life, fundamentally changing the way the church hierarchy understood Black and biracial people within Mormonism's evolving racial theology. At least two church apostles—Orson Hyde and Orson Pratt—had already made this connection in the mid-nineteenth century, but their teachings were not uniformly accepted until after the Pearl of Great Price became canonized.[48] At the turn of the twentieth century, Mormon leaders began to read race and lineage into the Book of Abraham, finding an innovative justification for the priesthood and temple ban.[49] They interpreted Abraham chapter 1 to mean that Black and biracial Latter-day Saints were disqualified from the church's most sacred rituals because they had committed some unspecified misdeed or sin before they were born.

The most vocal proponent of this position was general authority B. H. Roberts, one of the most influential LDS theologians of his era. "Negroes," he wrote in a widely publicized church magazine, followed the devil and were therefore cursed and cast out of God's presence. They "were not valiant in the great rebellion in heaven," he explained, adding that "their indifference or lack of integrity to righteousness rendered themselves un-worthy of the Priesthood and its powers and hence it is withheld from them to this day."[50] Most apostles echoed Roberts's view that Black people had been "less valiant" during the "war in heaven," but some, like church president Wilford Woodruff, speculated that they were "neutral" in the war in heaven and refused to take sides. Woodruff said that they "were 'astride the fence.'"[51]

These contrasting viewpoints were not just meaningless theological quibbles among high church leaders. Differences between Roberts and Woodruff sent confused messages to the Mormon laity about the status of Black members and also raised questions about Mormon racial theology. Some LDS periodicals published Roberts's views, some Woodruff's, but what is most instructive is that the "war in heaven" typology created a new nomenclature in the church and added a layer of theological complexity to Mormon racial teachings. Beyond being cursed, Black people were now deemed "less valiant" or, more colloquially, "fence-sitters." Just as significant, this hypothesis became firmly embedded in LDS culture, giving it a staying power well into the twenty-first century.[52]

The preexistent hypothesis was Mormonism's unique theory on why Black people occupied an inferior status to White people. It's what made the church's race theology different from that of Protestants, Catholics, Evangelicals, and Jews who merely asserted that Black people were cursed.

★ ★ ★

FROM POLICY TO DOCTRINE 13

As this thinking spread throughout the church, some of the Brethren felt uncomfortable with the direction that Mormon racial teachings had taken, and there was a fair amount of confusion in terms of when the ban started and by whom. At roughly the same time that leaders debated Abel's and James's status in the church, then–church president Lorenzo Snow noted in 1900 that he didn't know whether the curse-of-Cain teaching originated with Joseph Smith or Brigham Young. He couldn't determine whether this teaching was the product of revelation or whether Young "was giving his own personal views of what had been told to him by the Prophet Joseph."[53] Snow's successor, Joseph F. Smith, and his counselors were even more frank in admitting that "there is no written revelation" to "show why the negroes are ineligible to hold the priesthood." Nevertheless, they opined that the ban began with "the Prophet Joseph Smith."[54]

Church leaders also expressed uncertainty about the rationales for the ban, particularly the preexistence hypothesis that B. H. Roberts and Wilford Woodruff advanced. In a candid admission in 1912, church president Joseph F. Smith and his counselors confessed that they didn't know of any "revelation, ancient or modern," supporting the teaching that "negroes" were "neutral in heaven."[55] Such uncertainty also prompted Apostle Orson F. Whitney to write in 1918 that "Ham's sin, which brought the curse upon Canaan . . . may not be fully known; but even if it were, there would still remain the unsolved problem of the punishment of a whole race for an offense committed by one of its ancestors." Apostle Melvin J. Ballard expressed concern as well, sermonizing in 1922 that Black people had committed some egregious act in a pre-earth life to disqualify them from the priesthood in mortality, but he couldn't say what it was: "It is alleged that the Prophet Joseph said—and I have no reason to dispute it—that it is because of some act committed by them before they came into this life."[56]

Predictably, some Latter-day Saints questioned the various racial theories circulating throughout the church. The apostle who typically answered them was Joseph Fielding Smith, the church's most important twentieth-century writer.[57]

Born in 1876 in what was then the Utah Territory, Joseph Fielding Smith came from royal Mormon stock. He was the grandnephew of Mormon founder Joseph Smith Jr., grandson of high-ranking church leader Hyrum Smith, son of apostle and church president Joseph F. Smith, and cousin, brother, or relative to several other apostles, including leaders in the Reorganized Church of Jesus Christ of Latter Day Saints (today the Community of Christ). In 1910, when Smith was thirty-four, his father called him to the Quorum of the Twelve Apostles, and thereafter he served in a number of capacities in the church, including church historian, president of the Genealogical Society, president of the Salt Lake Temple, president of the Quorum of the Twelve Apostles, First Presidency counselor, and church president.

Tall, slender, and gruff, Smith had a directness about him that irritated his fellow Latter-day Saints. "We always knew where he stood," one of Smith's acquaintances said. He always "called a spade a spade." Smith's direct style, combined with an overbearing sense of Puritan morality and strictness, also tested the patience of his fellow apostles, who occasionally clashed with him over the meaning of scripture.[58]

Smith had a reputation among his colleagues for his ability to recite long passages of scripture and to find answers to questions about church doctrine

Joseph Fielding Smith of the Quorum of the Twelve Apostles and author of *The Way to Perfection* (1931), the most important book on the priesthood and temple ban, ca. 1930s. Courtesy of Utah State Historical Society.

in the Standard Works. Church president Heber J. Grant called Smith the "best scriptorian of the General Authorities of the Church." Fellow apostle J. Reuben Clark said that all the tough questions on church history and doctrine went to Joseph Fielding Smith.[59]

Besides his family, Smith drew inspiration from his patriarchal blessing, which promised him that his "counsels will be considered conservative and wise." This was consistent with something his father allegedly told him. The younger Smith was to be the "conservative element" in the Quorum of the Twelve Apostles and "preserve the doctrines of the church."[60] To that end, Apostle Smith published a variety of books and articles, offering his opinions on an astonishing range of topics relating to church history and doctrine. Two of his published works were *Doctrines of Salvation* and *Answers to Gospel Questions*, appropriately titled given how he positioned himself as the church's doctrinal expert.[61] But it was his spirited defense of Mormon racial theories that were his most important contribution to church policy and doctrine.

In 1907, three years before he was called as a church apostle, Smith expressed discomfort with the rationales justifying the priesthood and temple ban. He had heard them his entire life from his father and other church leaders and knew that there wasn't a written revelation affirming the ban, which is why he initially believed that it was more a tradition than a fixed doctrine. "Tradition states that the Prophet Joseph Smith declared that the reason why the children of Cain cannot receive the Priesthood is that Cain cut his brother Abel off from the earth before he had seed," Smith speculated in a letter to a concerned member. But then Smith went on to denounce other rationales for the ban, namely that Black people had been "neutral" in the "war in heaven." This position lacked scriptural support, Smith asserted, echoing his father. He called this teaching "the opinion" of earlier leaders.[62]

By 1924, however, some fifteen years after he became an apostle, Smith cast a decidedly new tone. In the church's magazine, the *Improvement Era*, the precocious apostle wrote that Mormon racial teachings were "doctrine," that Joseph Smith Jr. taught them as doctrine, and that under no circumstances could Black members hold the priesthood. Like his father, he cited no specific revelation in the scriptures supporting the ban, but asserted that Joseph Smith Jr. implemented it because Black people were not "obedient to the first principles of the gospel" in a prior life.[63]

Smith's most spirited defense of the ban came in 1931, when he published *The Way to Perfection*, one of his most influential books.[64] The First Presidency had asked him to write it, and Smith himself recognized its potential when he proudly noted that it would be used "for general use throughout the church." He touted his book as "a faith-promoting discussion of doctrinal principles and historical themes . . . in the life of every Latter-day Saint."[65]

The book furnished answers about the meaning of life that Smith believed had eluded Western theologians and philosophers. He wrote extensively about the LDS concept of the premortal life, agency, and mortality, explaining why God created the earth and its inhabitants and how, if they lived worthy lives, they could return to live with God in eternal glory. In this sweeping teleological account, he characterized premortal individuals as "spirit children" and proclaimed that they had agency that allowed them to take sides in the "war in heaven." This agency, he wrote, dictated whether they would choose Jesus over Satan, piety over sin, righteousness over rebellion. Bestowed with different talents, aptitudes, and intellectual abilities, spirit children made decisions in the premortal life that governed which lineage they would be born into. The most meritorious lineage, what Smith called the "favored" or "birthright" lineage, was that of Ephraim. Smith claimed that each lineage in the house of Israel had a unique role to play in history, with Ephraim assigned the most significant one. Ephraim's descendants would bring the Mormon gospel to the world, introduce converts to the "saving" rituals found only in Mormon temples, and lead the church in its governing councils.[66]

Black and mixed-race individuals had a curious place in Smith's grand narrative. He wanted to explain how Black people had become a fallen race and how they might be redeemed to win God's favor.[67] But there were other reasons why Smith wrote the book. He wanted to provide a theological framework for the priesthood and temple ban and systematize the church's race teachings.[68]

Smith insisted that because God had placed a curse upon "negroes," they were a "less favored lineage," which barred them from the "holy priesthood." They had committed an unspecified sin in the preexistence, he claimed, and were being punished. From that logic, Smith reasoned that because Black people had descended through a cursed lineage, God had excluded them from full inclusion in the church. Smith asserted that only "choice spirits" from a "better grade of nations" could receive the church's sacred temple ordinances and hold the priesthood. Quoting Brigham Young, Smith also said that anyone with "one drop" of African ancestry was ineligible for the priesthood. But Smith didn't stop there: he claimed that Black people were an "inferior race," forever doomed to be the servants of God's covenant people.[69]

This was Smith's most brazen claim. Years later, in a letter to BYU religion professor Sidney Sperry, he elaborated what he meant when he called Black people an "inferior race." Smith said that they were entitled to mortal bodies, could hear the gospel and receive patriarchal blessings, but because they followed Satan in the preexistence their "bodies had to be of an inferior class."[70]

Smith's claim that the priesthood restriction began with Joseph Smith Jr. was similarly audacious, given that there wasn't a definitive revelation linking the ban to his great uncle. Smith was aware that some Black members, like Elijah Abel, had been ordained to the priesthood during the early days of the church, but he never acknowledged this fact in his book.[71] Furthermore, Smith noted that the curse would be lifted in the future after "the seed of Adam"—White people and non-cursed lineages—had the chance to receive the priesthood first. In God's due time, he wrote, Black skin would revert back to its primitive state of whiteness, making Black people eligible for all of the church's salvific ordinances. He meant this in a literal, physical way. He also claimed that if Black people were to receive "exaltation"—the highest level of salvation in the Mormon afterlife—the curse would have to be purged.[72]

Smith gleaned his antiblack ideas from several sources. Beyond the familiar verses in Genesis and Abraham, he quoted Brigham Young freely and uncritically. Smith also embraced secular theories that privileged hierarchies of race. He supported a strange ideology called British Israelism, which had begun in England in the nineteenth century. In the early to mid-twentieth century, the LDS church frequently published the core ideas of this ideology in its books and magazines.[73] Proponents claimed that Anglo-Saxons were the "lost tribes of Israel" descended through Abraham, the Hebrew patriarch. These "lost tribes of Israel," the theory went, derived from Great Britain, Scandinavia, and Germany—all White European countries—through which the chosen lineages descended.[74] Smith eagerly embraced these ideas and incorporated them in *The Way to Perfection*. One idea that he found helpful came from his father-in-law, general authority George Reynolds, who wrote a pamphlet called *Are We of Israel?*, a work steeped in British Israelism. Smith touted it as a "valuable little work" because it articulated beautifully why Latter-day Saint leaders "were of the blood of Israel" and why God's favorite lineage, Ephraim, bore a privileged place "in all the races of mankind."[75]

★ ★ ★

When Smith published *The Way to Perfection*, White supremacy was endemic in the nation's churches. In the 1930s, scores of Protestant and Catholic clergy asserted that Black people were inferior to other races, and some even plunged into eugenics to prove the point. Others touted antiblack theologies from the pulpit, branding Black people cursed and therefore unfit to worship with White people. Some ministers even donned the robes of the Ku Klux Klan, cloaking themselves in the Bible to preserve White hegemony.[76] The larger, secular American culture wasn't any more accepting of Black people. Dozens of states implemented segregation and antimiscegenation laws, and scores of African Americans were lynched. Moreover, high school and college history textbooks glorified White supremacy, and popular histories that unabashedly promoted racial hierarchies rose to best-seller lists. The publication of Smith's book also coincided with racial oppression in Germany, culminating in the notorious Nuremburg Laws that proved lethal to Jews.[77]

When Smith published *The Way to Perfection*, then, American culture was soaked in White supremacy ideology. Black people, in particular, suffered in excruciating ways. American magazines and music portrayed them as childlike, promiscuous, and ignorant. Writers and producers created a new visual rhetoric of "Sambo Art" that framed blackness by stereotyping African Americans: Aunt Jemima "flipped pancakes," glutinous Black men and women gorged themselves on watermelon, and shoeless Black children danced merrily in the streets.[78] Latter-day Saints also participated in this racist discourse. The *Improvement Era*, the church's most prominent magazine, published stories about "Little Black Sambo," "Rastus," and "Uncle Remus"—prominent Disney characters portrayed in Mormon advertisements as happy and content during their time as chattel slaves. No less egregious, church magazines advertised minstrel shows in which White Mormons donned blackface to satirize Black people. This provided cheap entertainment at church fundraisers and "roadshows," which lasted well into the 1960s.[79]

Similarly, Mormon publications referred to Black people as "darkies," "niggers," and "coons," exaggerating their features and mocking their habits.[80] One poem, "Little Nigger Baby," began, "Little nigger baby with your curly, kinky hair."[81] This was the period in which Smith spent his early years as an apostle, and his book absorbed the racism that pervaded American and Mormon culture.

It didn't take long for the Brethren to recognize the book's genius, for Smith had neatly summarized the rationalization for the priesthood and temple ban. Recognizing its value, the First Presidency commissioned *The Way of Perfection* for study in the church's adult Sunday School programs. In 1936, for example, the church devoted an entire year to Smith's magnus opus, calling it "an advanced course in Gospel doctrines." The manual carefully dissected each chapter, offering "study thoughts" or questions at the end of each section. As one might expect, the study questions for Smith's teachings on race were the most controversial. After telling students that Cain was the "father of an inferior race," a "servant of servants," the manual asked members, "What portion of Cain's curse was inherited by his posterity?"[82]

Another question, just as pointed, asked, "How do we know the negro is descended from Cain through Ham?" Yet another asked readers to "[n]ame any great leaders this race has produced." Perhaps the most dramatic directed, "Discuss the truth of the statement in the text, p. 101 that Cain 'became the father of an inferior race.'"[83] Six years later Smith's teachings on race still formed the basis of LDS Sunday School lessons. A manual in 1942 titled one of the lessons "Cain and His Posterity," asking Latter-day Saints to consider why a "mark" was put on Cain and why "the Negro . . . may not hold the priesthood." The manual derived all of its questions from *The Way to Perfection*.[84]

As Smith's ideas circulated through the church, the prolific apostle became the church's most influential authority on Mormon racial theology. The feverish excitement that *The Way to Perfection* generated thrilled Smith, as it did his colleagues who urged Latter-day Saints to read it.[85] Members had used their hard-earned money during the throes of the Great Depression to purchase the book, making it a best-seller within the church. Over the course of Smith's lifetime, *The Way to Perfection* went through eighteen reprint editions and sold tens of thousands of copies; it continued to amass royalties even after his death in 1972. That it was translated from English into German, Dutch, French, Portuguese, Danish, Finnish, and Japanese only widened its appeal and solidified the apostle as a prominent church spokesman.[86]

Years later, Nigerian American author Tope Folarin reflected on the scope and power of Smith's ideas when he described his experience living in Utah as a young Black kid in the late 1980s. In his novel *A Particular Kind of Black Man*, Folarin recounted how a White Mormon neighbor walked him to school each day and told him he'd be a servant to her in the next life if he behaved properly:

> She would often pat my head as we walked together, and a penetrating silence would cancel the morning sounds around us. I felt comfortable, protected somehow, in her presence. . . . Her parting words were always the same: "Remember, if you are a good boy here on earth, you can serve me in heaven." I was 5 years old. Her words sounded magical to me—vast, and alluring.

Folarin continued, "[Y]ears later I learned that Mrs. Hansen was referencing an old notion of the Mormon church, th[at] black people, sons and daughters of Cain, could only get to heaven as servants."[87]

★ ★ ★

While Smith's teachings on race and lineage became mainstream throughout the church, at least two apostles countered them. John A. Widtsoe, an immigrant from Norway and a prolific author of LDS books, was one of Smith's critics, despite considering him a good friend. Like Smith, Widtsoe had connections in the church, having married one of Brigham Young's granddaughters. He was a distinguished-looking man, with oval glasses, a short mustache, and sparkling gray hair. His friends said that he was "very personable, very friendly and warm," with "a great intellect and a broad point of view." A chemist by training with BA and PhD degrees from Harvard and the University of Göttingen, respectively, Widtsoe had served as the president of Utah State Agricultural College and the University of Utah prior to his call into the Quorum of the Twelve Apostles in 1921. And yet, despite praising Smith's *The Way to Perfection* as a "fine piece of work" when it was published in 1931, Widtsoe rejected Smith's major points on race.[88] More precisely, Widtsoe didn't believe that people of African ancestry were cursed. He came to that conclusion after a detailed study of the scriptures.[89]

Widtsoe had been wrestling with the "negro question" for quite some time and told a friend in 1947, "The Negro problem within the Church is a puzzling one to me." He fussed that "the old idea that Negroes were neutral in heaven is not supported by anything in the scriptures." What also concerned Widtsoe was something church president Heber J. Grant said to him while he was editing the *Discourses of Brigham Young* for publication. The president told Widtsoe to omit Young's statement that Black people would receive the priesthood at some unspecified time because "no one knew how soon the spirit might move on the brethren to give the Negro full privilege in the Church." In private, Grant confided to his diary that he wanted some parts of Young's sermons left out because he believed that they "would create a great deal of discussion" among Latter-day Saints.[90]

Yet, despite Grant's unease in discussing the church's race teachings, Widtsoe made his views known in quorum meetings. He recommended that a "sister having [one-]thirty-second of negro blood in her veins" be permitted to marry in the temple, even though he knew that this contradicted the one-drop rule.[91]

Nor was Widtsoe afraid to challenge Apostle Smith. In 1944, he published a short piece in the church's *Improvement Era* titled "Were Negroes Neutrals in Heaven?" Widtsoe wrote that there was no evidence that Black people were "neutral" in the preexistence or cursed, which put him fundamentally at odds with Smith. "The cause of the black skin of the negro is not known," Widtsoe stressed. "A mark was placed upon Cain because of his skin. The negroes are *supposed* to be his descendants." After musing further on the topic, Widtsoe confessed that "it is very probable that in some way, unknown to us, the distinction harks back to the pre-existent state," but he was clearly skeptical of that claim.[92]

Three years later Widtsoe wrestled with race again, this time in a book he published called *Gospel Interpretations*. With the shadow of World War II hovering over him, the apostle condemned Hitler's belief in a "master race" of White Anglo-Saxons. He found it infuriating that the German Fuhrer appealed to White supremacy to justify murdering millions of Jews. Widtsoe called these ideas subversive and evil and branded them "sheer poppycock" because they didn't comport with biblical teachings about grace and love,

22   SECOND-CLASS SAINTS

but also because he claimed that racial hierarchies were based on "sheer delusion." For Widtsoe, all races enjoyed equal standing before God, but it's not clear if he understood the irony of his writing—that his fellow apostles also advanced racial hierarchies similar to Hitler's. The Brethren called Anglo-Saxons God's "favored lineage," while Hitler deemed them the "master race."[93]

Widtsoe also expressed skepticism in private. When Apostle George F. Richards stated in general conference that the "negro race" was "indifferent perhaps, and possibly neutral in the war [in heaven]," Widtsoe complained to a friend that he didn't know where Richards "obtained the authority for his statement that Negroes were not valiant in the life before this." Widtsoe asserted, "We know that the old idea that Negroes were neutral in heaven is not supported by anything in the scriptures or the utterances of modern prophets."[94]

Another apostle conflicted by Mormon racial teachings was David O. McKay, Heber J. Grant's counselor in the First Presidency. A tall handsome man with wavy blond hair, a gregarious personality, and a robust stature— his secretary called him "a remarkable specimen of physical manhood"— McKay didn't have the church connections of Smith and Widtsoe.[95] When McKay was called into the Quorum of the Twelve in 1906, he was relatively unknown. Born in the Huntsville, Utah Territory, to parents of Welsh and Scottish descent, McKay played football at the University of Utah, was a class president and valedictorian, and taught high school religion and literature classes at the LDS Weber Academy before his call into the church ministry. He would serve for some sixty years—one of the longest tenures in LDS church history.[96]

Like Smith, McKay hadn't encountered many Black people in the Utah Territory, but he favored allowing mixed-race Latter-day Saints of African ancestry to be ordained to the priesthood and sealed in the temple. On more than one occasion after he became the church president, McKay overrode the decisions of local leaders who denied others access to the priesthood or the temple.[97] The independent-minded McKay didn't hesitate to flout church policies when he felt the circumstances warranted it. To those closest to McKay, it was clear that he didn't hold the same views as the other apostles. His son Edward stated that his father was "much more liberal" on race and priesthood "than many of the brethren," which is why he sometimes allowed mixed-race Latter-day Saints to receive their priesthood and temple ordinances. Years later the elder McKay told one of his good friends that the ban was a policy and a practice, not a revealed doctrine enshrined in scripture.[98]

McKay's first encounter with the church's race teachings came in 1921, when he embarked on a mission tour to the South Pacific and met a "worthy man" from a "cursed lineage." McKay promptly wrote President Grant and asked if he could ordain the man to the priesthood, but the president said no. Grant expressed sympathy with McKay's position but told the concerned apostle, "[U]ntil the Lord gives us a revelation regarding the matter, we shall have to maintain the policy of the church."[99]

McKay's most important exposition on the priesthood and temple ban occurred in 1947 in a letter to a church educator named Lowell Bennion, who expressed deep misgivings about the church's race teachings. In it, McKay attempted to convince Bennion that God would one day make it right with "the negro." There was nothing original in the letter; McKay had simply drawn on LDS teachings that he felt comfortable with, while ignoring others. He quoted several biblical verses that focused on God's justice and mercy, couching them in the familiar language of the LDS concept of the preexistence. He explained to Bennion that the ban was part of "some eternal law" in heaven where "spirits come through parentages for which they are worthy—some as Bushman of Australia, some as Solomon Islanders, some as Americans, as Europeans, as Asiatics." McKay concluded, "Of this we may be sure each was satisfied and happy to come through the lineage to which he was attracted and for which, and only which, he or she was prepared."[100]

Noticeably missing from the letter were appeals to *The Way to Perfection* and Smith's other writings on race and priesthood. McKay studiously avoided quoting the popular apostle because he didn't share Smith's views on race. In fact, of the hundreds of pages that survive of McKay's diary and private correspondence, not once did he call Black people cursed, although he opposed interracial marriage and civil rights. McKay told Bennion that there was "no scriptural basis for denying the Priesthood to the Negroes other than one verse in the Book of Abraham (1:26)."[101]

One might conclude that, given their strong views on the church's race teachings, McKay and Widtsoe would press to lift the priesthood and temple ban, but they didn't. Although they felt uneasy about denying the church's rituals to faithful Latter-day Saints—especially those of mixed-race

24   SECOND-CLASS SAINTS

ancestry who looked White—they weren't crusaders or agitators. They held firm in their convictions but were fully aware that their colleagues didn't share them. They also knew that there was a variety of opinions among the Brethren whether Black people had been "less valiant" in the preexistence or "neutral" when it came time to choose sides between Jesus or Satan. By midcentury the church's race teachings were held together by a fragile consensus.

★ ★ ★

In 1947, as the Brethren quibbled among themselves about the church's race theology, an explosive letter arrived at church headquarters. Addressed to church president George Albert Smith, it was from Lowry Nelson, a brash middle-aged college professor who had left BYU years earlier under a cloud of controversy. Nelson had told a colleague that he didn't believe in the church's teachings on the trinity, which led to his dismissal from the university.[102]

Nelson caused a ruckus at church headquarters when he told George Albert Smith that he didn't believe Black people were cursed. A letter from an old friend had set him off. A week before he wrote Smith, Nelson had received a "disturbing letter" from Heber Meeks, an acquaintance from college, who was then the president of the LDS church's southern states mission in Atlanta, Georgia.[103] Meeks wanted to know if it was feasible to open an LDS church mission in Cuba and believed that Nelson, a sociologist who had written a book called *Rural Cuba*, was the right person to assist him. The ambitious mission president asked his friend if "there [were] groups of pure white blood in the rural sections, particularly in the small communities," and, further, whether those areas were segregated from "the Negroes."[104]

Meeks's question disturbed Nelson. He thought it was foolish to open a mission in Cuba given the island's long history of slavery and race-mixing. How could the church in good faith seek out only converts of "pure white blood" when Cuba had a robust mixed-race population? But Nelson was also affected by this personally. He told President Smith that he had many mixed-race friends in the Caribbean, and they "would be shocked . . . if I were to tell them my Church relegated them to an inferior status." It "would be far better that we not go into Cuba at all than to go in and promote racial distinction." Nelson also told the president that he hoped "there is no irrevocable doctrine on this subject."[105]

FROM POLICY TO DOCTRINE

Smith didn't write the professor back; the entire First Presidency did, in what was as much a show of unity as of force. Although no one ever claimed authorship, it is likely that counselor J. Reuben Clark wrote it. We can say with certainty that George Albert Smith didn't write it because he was in poor health; he suffered from multiple nervous breakdowns after he became the church president in 1945 and delegated many of his responsibilities to his counselors.[106] Nor was it likely authored by counselor David O. McKay. McKay had his own distinctive style: warm, personal, and devoid of dogma. That left Clark, the most intellectually savvy member of the First Presidency and its dominant personality. Besides, he had written most of the First Presidency's statements since he joined it in 1933 and had a reputation throughout the church as a skilled writer and shrewd leader. A Columbia-educated lawyer, former State Department official and ambassador to Mexico, Clark was a larger-than-life figure in the church. He was brash, confident, and certain—all of the things the two church presidents under whom he served, Heber J. Grant and George Albert Smith, were not.[107]

The letter read like Clark. It was punchy and brief and steeped in dogma. It answered Nelson's concerns with an assurance that only Clark could give: "Some of God's children were assigned to superior positions before the world was formed. We are aware that some Higher Critics do not accept this, but the Church does." The First Presidency then rebuked Nelson for embracing interracial marriage between Cubans and White people, calling such marriages "most repugnant to most normal-minded people from the ancient patriarchs till now." The letter continued, "We are not unmindful of the fact that there is a growing tendency, particularly among some educators, as it manifests itself in this area, toward the breaking down of race barriers in the matter of intermarriage between whites and blacks, but it does not have the sanction of the Church and is contrary to Church doctrine."[108]

The First Presidency's rebuke angered Nelson. Some three months after their initial exchange, he wrote them again. He didn't hold back. Nelson told the First Presidency that during his boyhood a church leader told him that "negroes" sat on the "fence" during "the Council in Heaven" because they lacked courage to "take a stand." Nelson found this teaching dubious and offensive. He believed that it was based on racial ignorance, not scripture. The idea that God would curse an entire race of people didn't make sense to him. He hoped that the curse and preexistence stories he heard as a boy had not assumed "an aura of the sacred."[109]

Nelson's blunt language caught the First Presidency off guard. Their terse, one-paragraph response indicated their displeasure. They brushed aside Nelson's concerns and told him to accept church teachings: "We feel very sure that you understand well the doctrines of the Church. They are either true or not true. Our testimony is that they are true." The presidency then cautioned Nelson not to be "led off from the principles of the Gospel by worldly learning." He was "too fine a man" for that.[110]

But underlying the First Presidency's letter was a sense of unease. If Nelson didn't understand that the church's race teachings were doctrine, then others might not either. The Brethren made immediate plans to address the issue.

In August 1949, the First Presidency produced a three-paragraph statement likely authored by J. Reuben Clark that drew on all the church's race teachings to justify the priesthood and temple ban. Both President Smith and counselor McKay signed it, the latter signaling a dramatic change from the position he had taken two years earlier in his letter to Lowell Bennion. Undoubtedly, pressure and the need to present a unified presidency forced him to sign. Regrettably, McKay's diaries and private correspondence offer no clues about his feelings on the matter.[111]

It was a bold statement. In it, the First Presidency made several claims not supported by evidence or past church practice. The statement declared that the ban was a "direct commandment from the Lord on which is founded the doctrine of the Church from the days of its organization," but it ignored the fact that Black men had been ordained to the priesthood during Joseph Smith Jr.'s tenure as founding prophet, and it didn't acknowledge that at least one of them had participated in limited temple rituals. It also claimed that the "position of the Church regarding the Negro may be understood when another doctrine of the Church is kept in mind, namely, that the conduct of spirits in the premortal existence has some determining effect upon conditions and circumstances under which these spirits take on [in] mortality." The statement didn't affirm whether Black people had been "less valiant" or "neutral" in the preexistence—the Brethren didn't want to take sides in this theological thicket—but simply noted that Black people had agreed to take on bodies of flesh and blood and come to earth accepting the "handicap" of not holding the priesthood. And finally, the First Presidency, quoting Brigham Young, stated that Black people were cursed, further noting that the curse would be lifted one day, after "all the rest of the children have received their blessings in the holy priesthood."[112]

The statement also affirmed three important principles that had gnawed at the Brethren over the years. First, it enshrined into doctrine the divine curse and the preexistence hypothesis, making it clear that Mormon racial teachings were not merely the "traditions" of earlier leaders, as Joseph Fielding Smith had once called them. Second, Black men would get the priesthood at some unspecified time in the future, but they would have to be patient. And third, the statement called the church's race teachings "a direct commandment from the Lord," refuting any notion that the priesthood and temple ban was man-made.

That the entire First Presidency signed the statement gave it heft and provided fodder to stifle critics like Lowry Nelson who found the church's racial teachings repugnant. The statement also raised a host of other issues, especially in light of what Marion G. Romney, an assistant to the Quorum of the Twelve Apostles, had said in 1945 at the church's semiannual general conference. When the First Presidency speaks, he proclaimed, it "is what the Lord would say if he were here himself." Romney even likened the collective voice of the First Presidency to scripture.[113] That prompted the question: Was the 1949 statement scripture?

The Brethren never answered that question, nor did they publish the 1949 statement in the church's magazines or newspapers or broadcast it over the pulpit in general conference. It was simply a document that would supplement *The Way to Perfection* when Latter-day Saints had questions about the ban.[114] They also wanted a statement to clarify the church's race teachings in light of some of the Brethren calling them theories and opinions and in light of Nelson's skepticism that the ban was doctrinal. In addition, the Brethren hoped that the statement would provide guidance when mixed-race and Black Latter-day Saints asked to be permitted into the faith's temples. In that context, George Albert Smith and his counselors took the bold step of codifying the church's race teachings into doctrine. It was the first time that the First Presidency had ever done this, and it was a transformative moment, the import of which was not lost on the Brethren. When Apostle Widtsoe read the statement, he immediately recognized what the First Presidency had done. He studied it carefully, then wrote at the top of his copy, "Church doctrine regarding Negroes."[115]

2

Racial Passing, 1949–1954

In 1948, Brigham Young University student David Lloyd made a start-ling admission to church president George Albert Smith: he was wor-ried that one of his children might "unknowingly" marry someone "with Negro blood." He told Smith he had read a report that "over fifty-thousand Negroes" had "crossed the color line each year" and feared that with the church growing "in all sections of the Nation," it would increase the like-lihood of his son or daughter marrying someone with African ancestry. Lloyd had several questions for the president:

1. Who is a Negro?
2. Does the Church accept the South's definition that a Negro is a person who has from 1/64 percent to 100 percent Negro blood?
3. If "yes" to question 2, then is a person with 1/65 percent Negro blood a white individual?
4. Are Negroes only those persons who have been so designated by revelation?
5. Is there any explanation in the case of Elijah Abel?
6. How does the Church determine who and what a Negro is?

Lloyd also wanted to know how bishops and stake presidents dealt with in-dividuals with "cursed" lineages who "appeared white" but were ordained to the priesthood. Were they relieved of their priesthood duties when their African blood was discovered?[1]

No one at church headquarters wanted to answer Lloyd's pointed ques-tions, but President Smith's secretary, Joseph Anderson, was asked to re-spond. He ducked most of them. He wasn't sure how the church detected persons with "drops of Negro blood" or how church leaders handled cases when a man's African ancestry was discovered after his priesthood ordination. In fact, of the seven questions that Lloyd asked George Albert Smith, Anderson answered only one of them. He said that Elijah Abel's ordination "was due to an inadvertence, and since then it has never been knowingly repeated."[2]

Questions like Lloyd's flummoxed the Brethren because they didn't have good answers. J. Reuben Clark, Smith's counselor in the First Presidency, wrote that the "First Presidency received some pretty tough questions; and they don't always agree in the Quorum." His fellow counselor, David O. McKay, also expressed frustration: "The Negro question . . . seems to be coming up frequently."[3]

As Clark and McKay knew, "race" was difficult to discern, and racial passing was common. They feared that as the church opened missions in South Africa, Brazil, and the Caribbean, converts of African lineage would unwittingly be ordained to the priesthood. They also feared that this had already occurred in the United States, where light-skinned individuals passed as White. Racial passing was happening everywhere in the United States and throughout the world, and the church wasn't immune to this larger societal practice.[4] In 1954, three years after David O. McKay became the president following George Albert Smith's death, he commissioned a secret committee of apostles to investigate the problem of the color line. But racial passing wasn't the only problem that McKay and the church faced. Internal dissent was rife within the Church Education System as a number of Mormon intellectuals rejected the church's race teachings. Some became vocal in their protests; others left the church silently.

★ ★ ★

Evan Wright was nervous, but excited, when church president George Albert Smith called him to be the mission president in South Africa in 1948, a position he would hold for five years.[5] Smith was nervous too. Both were aware of the challenges that previous mission presidents had faced in this racially divided country. Determining lineage in South Africa had always been fraught—a point that mission president Ralph Badger experienced firsthand.[6] When Badger arrived in 1906 the mission had been open for only three years (following an aborted attempt a half-century earlier), and he had the impossible task of policing racial boundaries in a country that was only 18 percent White. Frustrated, Badger wrote the First Presidency: "What are we to do with the people who embrace the Gospel who have intermarried with colored people or who themselves are [a] mixture of blood?" He stated that the "colored race, or people of part negro-blood, are quite numerous in the south of South Africa" and many were members of the church. Badger also raised another problem. He told the presidency that a number of White South African Latter-day Saints didn't want to sit at church next to light-skinned or Black South Africans who bore "the curse."[7]

These problems became more complicated in 1948, when South African leaders introduced apartheid. New laws banned mixed-race marriages, segregated Black people from White, and imposed stiff penalties for violations of the law, making compliance essential for the church.[8] Especially difficult under apartheid was that the South African government created four new racial classifications that were enshrined into law: "native," "coloured," "Asian," and "white." According to the Population Registration Act of 1950, South African law designated "a white person" as anyone who looked "white," "a coloured person" as anyone known to be "coloured," and a "native person" as anyone "generally accepted as a member of any aboriginal race or tribe of Africa." South Africans looked to skin tones, facial features, hair color, socioeconomic status, friends and relatives, and other factors to determine race, making it nearly impossible to classify South Africans with any degree of precision or certainty.[9]

So when Evan Wright was appointed to lead the mission in 1948, President Smith and his counselors were worried. Perhaps they had the new apartheid laws in mind, or perhaps they knew from experience the perilous waters that Wright would soon navigate. Whatever the case, Smith gave him a "particular blessing," telling him that the "problem [of racial detection] is very complex and the Lord himself must clarify it." He added that individuals "with Negroid blood are entitled to all of the blessings except the priesthood" and that "no man was to be ordained or advanced in the priesthood until he had traced his genealogy out of Africa."[10]

Smith's counsel proved most problematic for Wright and his missionaries. The Brethren had long counseled members to trace their ancestral lines so that they could perform proxy ordinances in temples for their ancestors. This is one of the reasons the church established the Genealogical Society of Utah in 1894; it was supposed to assist in this task.[11] Now the

Brethren counseled Wright to follow a similar method by asking his mission to research ancestral lines to determine whether South Africans bore Black African ancestry. The venture was fraught with challenges and tinged with uncertainty. This difficult task fell to nineteen- and twenty-year-old missionaries who had little or no training in genealogy. "Our greatest problem in this work," noted one, "is that we are amateur genealogists and our methods are primarily those of an amateur."[12]

With inadequate resources, scanty training, and spotty records, Wright didn't think that his missionaries were up to the task. And yet he concealed his frustration from the First Presidency. Instead, he invited them to visit South Africa so they could see firsthand how difficult it was trying to keep the bloodlines "pure" in a nation that was full of Black and light-skinned people.[13]

The Brethren wrote back and counseled Wright to be "most careful" and "discreet" in how he evaluated prospective converts who might have "the blood."[14] They didn't agree to visit. A few weeks later, they followed up with a letter reaffirming church dogma. They told him that the priesthood ban came from "the Lord" and that it applied "to every person whose veins are but slightly tainted with the blood of Cain, as well as to the full-blooded negro." They told him, "People whose veins are but slightly tainted with the blood of Cain must be classed as negroes, for the reason that while they may distribute the taint in their blood among the white races by intercourse with them, it never can be eliminated while the curse placed on Cain stands unsatisfied." The Brethren further explained that dark skin by itself was not a determining factor in priesthood eligibility; it was only African lineage that mattered: "A person's complexion has no bearing upon his standing in the church except where that color is the result of an intermingling of negro blood. The American Indian, Hawaiians, Spaniards of dark complexions, and other Orientals such as Chinese and Japanese are entitled to hold the Priesthood."[15]

The First Presidency's counsel didn't satisfy Wright, and he wrote them again in frustration. He told them that he knew lineage detection was a problem before he accepted the call, but he had no idea just how difficult it would be. But he didn't just complain—he proposed a solution: what if, instead of missionaries trying to trace bloodlines, they relied on church patriarchs to declare lineage? If a patriarch "gives them a [patriarchal] blessing and tells them of their lineage through the House of Israel," didn't that "automatically give them the privileges of receiving the Priesthood, temple endowments, and eternal marriage"?[16]

The First Presidency rejected Wright's idea. They stated that "a man's lineage is not sufficient justification for ordaining him if there exists any evidence of negro blood in his veins." It was probably too much pressure to place on patriarchs to declare lineage in a country as racially diverse as South Africa, but it also spoke to the fact that the church had never established guidelines for declaring lineages of persons of African descent.[17]

Despite his misgivings, Wright remained loyal to the Brethren. After all, he considered them "living oracles." So he counseled South African Latter-day Saints to follow their instructions. He told local priesthood leaders not to ordain anyone to the priesthood "until the necessary research has been done." Furthermore, he practiced what he preached. He assigned six missionaries who spent "much of their time doing genealogical work" to determine whether light-skinned converts were free of Black African blood. And yet, despite his best efforts, Wright knew that individuals with "cursed" lineages were being ordained to the priesthood.[18]

None of these problems was new to President Smith or to his counselors. Smith's private papers contain dozens of examples of Latter-day Saint mission presidents like Wright who asked the Brethren for advice about how to detect mixed-race lineages and what to do about them when they were discovered. Moreover, Smith participated in discussions about Jane Manning James and Elijah Abel and knew the hardships they experienced because of their race. And as an apostle he decided the fate of mixed-race Latter-day Saints when their ancestry was discovered.[19] For example, a Hawaiian man named John Pea, an elder in the priesthood, discovered that he was "one-eighth negro." After pondering the matter, Smith told Pea that he must relinquish his priesthood. Smith continued to receive these inquiries as church president and he struggled to answer them. He couldn't find words of comfort or advice to give Wright or other church leaders who struggled with lineage detection. All Smith could do was turn to *The Way to Perfection*, his cousin's book, trying to make sense of the curse and the timing of when it would be lifted.[20]

After Smith died in April 1951, his son, George Albert Smith Jr., claimed that his father believed "the Church's position on the negro question was one of custom and not of revelation." If this is true, it suggests that Smith wasn't as committed to the church's race teachings as his signature in the 1949 First Presidency statement might indicate. But he upheld them nonetheless.[21]

★ ★ ★

When David O. McKay took the reins after Smith's death, the church embarked on an aggressive missionary campaign to fulfill the Book of Mormon's injunction to take the gospel into "every nation, kindred, tongue and people." Under McKay's direction, the church established scores of new temples and began proselytizing in dozens of new countries.[22] U.S. membership swelled from 1.1 million to 2.8 million during his presidency, and international membership increased dramatically under his direction. Thirty-four new stakes were created outside of North America. Near the end of his nineteen-year tenure, McKay told a *New York Times* reporter that his greatest accomplishment was transforming the church into "a worldwide organization."[23]

David O. McKay, the ninth president of the Church of Jesus Christ of Latter-day Saints, Salt Lake City, n.d. Courtesy of Utah State Historical Society.

34 SECOND-CLASS SAINTS

But expanding the church into majority-Black and -mixed-race countries brought McKay and his counselors considerable grief. The question of lineage bedeviled them. In December 1951, McKay approved the "South African Mission Proselytizing Plan," compiled by missionary Gilbert G. Tobler. Under the plan, missionaries would prep their prospective converts by teaching them that God had "cursed Cain" as an "inferior race," culminating in "restrictions concerning the holding of the Priesthood." "Since Africa is the traditional home of the seed of Cain," the lesson stipulated, "the Lord through modern prophets has required that prospective priesthood bearers in this land establish the purity of their lineage by tracing their family lines out of Africa through genealogical research."[24] The missionaries would inform prospective converts that they had to produce a "cursed-free" genealogy for men to move forward with priesthood ordination or families to be sealed in Mormon temples. It was not an easy task.

Some six months after President McKay approved the plan Wright wrote the First Presidency an anguished twenty-page, single-spaced letter detailing his frustration. Three years into his mission, he knew that what he and his missionaries were doing was not working. Wright complained that the genealogy work was slow, cumbersome, inaccurate, and most of all humiliating. He asked the Brethren "to have a highly trained genealogist come here from Salt Lake City." Many branch presidents and district presidents, Wright noted, "haven't traced their own lines. The sons of some of these men haven't been ordained to the priesthood which is causing bitter disappointment."[25]

All of this was troubling enough, but Wright faced what seemed to him to be a bigger problem. Mixed-race South Africans had been passing as White to achieve upward mobility and privilege in the church. They researched their genealogy and had run into "slave lines," Wright explained, which caused them tremendous grief. Rather than accept their cursed status, they moved to Canada or the United States, where it wasn't necessary to prove your racial purity—as long as you looked White. Wright told the First Presidency about a light-skinned family whose daughter passed as White. "The mother is one of the most outstanding Latter-day Saints I have ever known," he explained. "The father is a very good man, and I wouldn't hesitate on points of faithfulness or activity to recommend these people for temple blessings." But they had traced their genealogy back to slaves, he noted, which abruptly halted their advancement in the church. Wright explained that the daughter had kept their cursed lineage a secret

RACIAL PASSING   35

and traveled to Utah, where she married a man in the Salt Lake Temple. "Now the problem arises if the young woman was worthy to go to the temple to receive her endowment and blessings, may not her parents also be privileged to enjoy the same blessings?"[26]

He also told a story about his "good friends" whose genealogy "hasn't been cleared." This created an immediate crisis, and despite Wright's urging them to remain patient while it was addressed, the anxious couple packed up their belongings and moved to Salt Lake City. There they passed as White and received a temple recommend from their new ecclesiastical leaders. In Wright's mind, this was a clear double standard. "Apparently this is the only mission in the Church where it is necessary for a man to trace his genealogy," he grumbled to the First Presidency. "As a result, the members of the Church in this country feel that that are penalized."[27]

Letters like Wright's kept McKay up at night because the president didn't know how to advise him. McKay and the other Brethren had agonized over these questions for years. Minutes of their council meetings show them struggling with the one-drop rule, especially as the church expanded globally. Take the example of one young Dutch convert who immigrated to Utah with his family. His father and brothers held the Melchizedek Priesthood, regarded as the highest priesthood and required to enter the temple. All of his older siblings had married and been sealed in the temple to their spouses. Just a few days before the young man was to be married in the temple, however, his sister made a startling discovery: "a paternal ancestor had served in the Dutch colonial army in the West Indies and had there married a woman who was part negro and part native American." That made the young man "probably one-thirty-second or one-sixty-fourth negro." This untimely discovery created insurmountable angst for the young man, and he struggled to know if he should disclose his cursed ancestry to his church leaders and to his fiancée. Grief-stricken and ashen-faced, he sought the advice of Edgar Lyon, a one-time mission president in Holland. The young man saw three options. According to Lyon, he could

1. Hide the information and go ahead and marry the L.D.S. girl to whom he is engaged.
2. Break off the engagement and refrain from marrying any L.D.S. girl.
3. Tell his bishop, with the result that his brother will lose his priesthood, the temple marriages of both his brother and sister will be declared invalid and their children deprived of the priesthood.

He explained that he couldn't "fit in with the 'colored' race nor would he have any interest in marrying a negress." His church placed him in a racial no-man's land, bereft of his "Nordic" race and bereft of a spouse he could marry in the temple—all of which could impact his status in the church and jeopardize his fate in the afterlife.[28]

With the stakes high, and the young man's anguish great, Lyon consulted with Apostle Joseph Fielding Smith at the beginning of a church meeting about the young man's predicament. Lyon explained that the boy had been active in the church, served a church mission, and was scheduled to be married in the temple. His family was also active. His brothers had served in several positions within the Mormon priesthood: one brother served as a stake president, another as a high councilman, and another in a bishopric. Then Lyon explained the problem: despite having "blond hair and blue eyes," the young man discovered that he was "cursed."[29]

What did all this mean? If the young man disclosed his "cursed" ancestry, Lyon knew that it would affect the young man's brothers and trigger a release from their church callings; he also knew the disclosure would dash the couple's plan to marry in the temple.

As Smith listened to the story, he appeared impervious to the young man's plight. He told Lyon to instruct the young man to tell his fiancée about his cursed lineage, which meant, of course, that there would be no temple wedding. "Our doctrine is very clear on that," the apostle stated. But as he pondered the situation further Smith had a sudden and swift change of heart. At the close of the meeting, he whispered to Lyon to see him in private. There, Smith did something dramatic and uncharacteristic. He told Lyon to tell the boy to keep the matter to himself. Smith explained that if the boy disclosed his "cursed" ancestry, it would harm himself and his brothers. "All of these [men] have been married in the temple and have participated in Church ordinances," Smith noted. This disclosure "would ruin their lives." Smith further instructed Lyon to inform the boy not to explain his circumstance to either his fiancée or his bishop. "This is something between him and the Lord, and if the Lord ratifies the sealing in the Temple, who are we to question it?"[30]

The one-drop policy was just as devastating for women. Mormon historian Juanita Brooks told a friend about a devout Mormon woman who discovered that she was "1/8 or 1/16 negro." The woman was "the most ardent temple worker," Brooks explained. She had done "more than

RACIAL PASSING 37

2000 endowments" in the temple, and her husband an equal number. The woman considered herself a mix of Indian and White, but then learned a startling and agonizing fact: "[d]oing genealogical work she discovered that her grandfather brought his wife," a slave, to the United States, where they married. Once she disclosed her African roots to her priesthood leaders, they banned her from the temple.[31]

These weren't isolated incidents. Stories circulated in the church about priesthood men of cursed lineages who had to stay their hand when their curse was disclosed. President McKay himself experienced the difficulty of the one-drop rule as both an apostle and a church president. During one difficult incident, he had to decide the fate of a "blue-eyed, blond, and wholesome" student whose family, the Marshalls, allegedly bore the curse. The young man wanted to serve a church mission.[32] His sister wanted to marry in the temple but had been "unable to obtain a recommend as it is rumored that she has negro blood in her veins." According to McKay's private notes, he was vexed because there was "no evidence of negro blood in the parents, grandparents, or great-grandparents." All of them "had blue eyes and blond hair."[33]

The Brethren discussed the family's plight on numerous occasions. Rumors that the family had African ancestry were enough, apparently, to convince the Brethren that the family was cursed, so in 1944 they repeated the policy "that a person with any negro blood in his veins may not receive the Priesthood," stipulating "that the question will continue to stand thus until another ruling is made."[34] When the matter was brought to McKay's attention years later as church president, he was now in a position to do something about it. After Lowell Bennion, a friend of the Marshalls, convinced him that there was insufficient evidence that that family had African ancestry, McKay permitted the boy to serve a mission and his sister to be married in the temple. With one stroke, the president overturned the 1944 ruling of the apostles, seemingly unconcerned about how his colleagues had viewed the matter.[35]

As these cases indicate, the Brethren knew that light-skinned Latter-day Saints of African descent had been passing below the color line. It was an open secret, Edgar Lyon remarked to a friend, that in Salt Lake City "several cases" existed in which "people of negro blood—one-thirty second and one-sixty-fourth negro—hold the priesthood, have been married in the temple," and "in one case a man is functioning as a member of a bishopric."[36] The Brethren also knew that Elijah Abel's son and grandson, whose family was listed as "mulattos" in the 1860 census, passed as White and were ordained to the priesthood.[37] The Brethren further knew that some church leaders flouted the church's racial policies. Evan Wright informed them that some local leaders counseled their flock to pass quietly as White. In contrast, some church leaders encouraged dark-skinned members of African descent to move to majority Black countries that were not deemed to have ties to Africa, which meant they could blend in and receive the priesthood. The church's presiding patriarch, Eldred G. Smith, the great-great-grandson of Hyrum Smith, told a faithful African American Latter-day Saint from Colorado, "If you were to go over to Fiji and take up citizenship, I bet in a little while you'd have the priesthood."[38]

Smith's advice undoubtedly didn't sit well with the Brethren, but this wasn't the most challenging issue they faced. Over the years, they fielded numerous queries from Latter-day Saints who looked White but were classified as Black by the church. Unlike the cases in South Africa, however, they didn't try to pass as White. They wanted to be obedient to the church's teachings and follow the Brethren's counsel to maintain racially pure bloodlines. These sensitive cases always frustrated the Brethren because the individuals in question wanted to serve missions, marry in the temple, and hold the priesthood, but the church's restrictive racial boundary made this difficult. The simplest answer was to get rid of the one-drop rule and cut through the bureaucratic gauze that prohibited full church participation. But the Brethren couldn't see themselves changing decades of tradition. On at least three occasions in their council meetings the apostles discussed—and reaffirmed—that they would keep the one-drop rule.

In 1879, when questions arose over whether to ordain a biracial Latter-day Saint to the priesthood, the Brethren vigorously defended the policy. In 1908, they reaffirmed it.[39] Three decades later, in 1940, the matter was discussed during a council meeting when a bishop in Hawaii wanted to ordain to "two [light-skinned] boys" to the Aaronic Priesthood, an appendage to the higher and more powerful Melchizedek Priesthood. J. Reuben Clark expressed sympathy for the young boys and pushed for their ordination, despite their "having Negro blood in their veins." He told the Brethren that local leaders were conferring priesthood ordination on persons of African ancestry throughout the church, specifically in Brazil, South Africa, the Pacific Islands, and the Southern states where "negro ancestry" was difficult to detect. He asked the apostles to form a subcommittee to evaluate "whether or not one drop of Negro blood deprives a man of the right to receive the priesthood." Apostle John A. Widtsoe seconded Clark's proposal.[40]

Joseph Fielding Smith and George F. Richards—two apostles on the subcommittee—scoffed at the idea of ordaining "part Negroes"; the other apostle on the subcommittee, Charles Callis, supported it. The majority of the Twelve agreed with Smith and Richards, and the one-drop rule stood. None of the Brethren appeared to share Callis and Clark's pragmatic views. Callis had presided over the Southern states mission for nearly two decades and knew firsthand the challenge of discerning African ancestry in the slaveholding South. As for Clark, though he had never been a mission president, he was pragmatic and recognized the difficulty of maintaining the status quo when the church was expanding internationally.[41] The one-drop rule also affected him personally. Clark sympathized with biracial Latter-day Saints who were "faithful in the Church" yet who had "some Negro blood in their veins." Denying them the faith's rituals didn't seem to be a good way to build the church.[42]

Still, Clark didn't propose lifting the ban completely. He only wanted biracial Latter-day Saints ordained. He chafed at the one-drop rule and in 1947 urged the Brethren to reconsider the 1940 ruling.[43]

Clark also made another dramatic proposal that year. He recommended to the Brethren that Afrikaners in South Africa be allowed to run their own meetings, which was controversial since these Dutch-speaking natives were thought to have Black African ancestry.[44] Clark suggested that these "negroes" be "duly authorized" to "preside and conduct meetings or through membership gatherings, where the Priesthood is not present." To underscore his request, he proposed that "Negro men be organized into Preparatory Deacon Groups, Preparatory Teacher Groups, [and] Preparatory Priests Groups." He didn't request priesthood ordination for them, but his proposal portended a time in the not so distant future when they might be ordained to the Aaronic Priesthood.[45]

The Brethren rejected both proposals.[46] They didn't want mixed-race individuals to serve even in limited functions in the church. The one-drop rule was here to stay.

★ ★ ★

South Africa wasn't the only place where racial boundaries were difficult to police. The Brethren struggled in Brazil too. In 1940, J. Reuben Clark informed the Brethren that "it was impossible with reference to the Brazilians to tell those who have Negro blood and those who have not."[47] Larry Storrs, a missionary in Brazil, concurred; within two weeks of his arrival in the country he noted, "[W]e can't be positive which are Negroes." "There are many Negroes and much intermarriage," he wrote. Policing racial boundaries made his missionary experience all the more difficult, he confided to Lowell Bennion, because it seemed "intolerant, unreligious, and also judgmental . . . on my part" to determine which Brazilians had cursed lineages.[48]

Clark's and Storrs's concerns about racial detection had merit. Brazil's long history of slavery and interracial marriage blurred color lines, which is why Apostle Mark E. Petersen privately grumbled that the church had no business establishing a mission in Brazil. After visiting and seeing "the low numbers of converts, complicated by the ban on ordaining Blacks," Lola Timmins, David O. McKay's secretary, observed, Petersen "returned to Salt Lake with a recommendation that the mission be closed."[49]

When missionary work began in Brazil in 1928, church leaders instructed missionaries to proselytize only in the southern part of the country where German-speaking peoples resided. Their European ancestry made their ethnic origins appear certain, and the Brethren reasoned that they were more likely to convert than Portuguese-speaking Brazilians in other regions of the country.[50] But that policy became difficult to maintain in the late 1930s, after Portuguese-speaking Brazilians began moving to southern Brazil, where they lived among German immigrants. "Over thirty-five percent of the population . . . has Negro blood," mission president Rulon Howells explained. Or, as the First Presidency bluntly put it, "[n]ormally the dark skin and kinky hair would indicate" African ancestry, but in Brazil "the races are badly mixed."[51]

In Brazil's 1950 census, White people comprised 61.7 percent of the population, Brown, 26.5 percent, and Black 11 percent. Racial designation was further complicated by the Brazilian government's liberal use of Brown or *pardo* as a catch-all label for disparate groups of people such as "mulattos," "assimilated Indians," and "persons of mostly indigenous ancestry."[52] This made it difficult, if not impossible, for church leaders to discern potential converts with one drop of African ancestry—a point that McKay knew all too well. Years earlier he had informed President Howells that the First Presidency had "been somewhat concerned about the negro problem" in South America and that it "is not an easy problem to handle."[53]

Like his predecessors, McKay didn't offer much guidance. He supported Howells's proposal for Brazilians to "trace their genealogy out of the country," but he offered little support beyond that. As Howells noted, "when the [First Presidency] sends a mission president out, [they] leave him on his own. They bless him with help from the Holy Ghost and let him direct the affairs of the mission."[54] Unlike in South Africa, however, in Brazil the genealogy requirement was applied haphazardly. Missionaries were instructed to simply avoid teaching light-skinned or Black-skinned Brazilians if they suspected them of having "negro" ancestry, so that's what they did. Asael T. Sorensen, who succeeded Howells, noted, "[W]e carefully instructed our missionaries that we are called to gather in the remnants of the House of Israel." He added, "[O]ur calling is not to the Negro."[55]

Sorensen lacked both confidence in lineage detection and clear guidelines from church headquarters in how to discern African ancestry. As a consequence, Brazilian church leaders took matters into their own hands. They looked to church patriarchs to discern if church members had the "lineage of Cain." As Mark Grover, a Latin American specialist, perceptively noted, patriarchal blessings were "a very simple method to dispose of the difficult administrative problem of determining lineage in questionable cases."[56]

With the exception of Joseph Fielding Smith, the Brethren didn't approve of using patriarchs in this fashion, but Brazilians did it anyway.[57] They reasoned that it was more efficient than doing genealogy work. Brazilian mission presidents struggled with lineage detection as well and prayed to know if an individual had a cursed lineage. William Grant Bangerter, who succeeded Sorensen, explained that he sought God's guidance for such difficult tasks: "As I made these decisions, I prayed to Heavenly Father and told Him that in the various cases before me I had decided to ordain them to the priesthood and that if it was not approved, He should let me know in order that I would not make a mistake."[58]

Missionaries in Brazil also employed "lineage lessons," refined and developed from techniques used in South Africa. They were instructed that if they discovered someone with African ancestry when they tracked door to door, they were to apologize and state that they must have found the wrong home to "avoid teaching the gospel to them." When missionaries encountered someone of uncertain ancestry, they would ask to enter the person's house and discreetly evaluate their nose, hair, face, and other physical features for clues to whether they had "negro blood." They might also ask to review the family's photo album for further clues of African ties.[59]

If the person appeared interested in the church, missionaries asked a series of carefully scripted questions, after which they had prospective converts study the Cain and Abel story. They explained that God had withheld certain privileges from some of his children because of their unworthiness in the preexistence. Missionaries also informed the prospective convert that God led the church through divine revelation with the expectation that the investigator would accept the priesthood ban as God's will. Then the missionary got to the heart of the matter, asking, "Do you know if any of your ancestors were Negro or descendants of Negroes? . . . If in the future you discover that one of your ancestors was Negro, will you tell your Branch President?"[60]

Another lineage lesson outlined the dangers of interracial marriage. Missionaries were instructed to read the following aloud to prospective converts:

> By marrying a descendent of Cain, we would not only curse ourselves, but all of our posterity which follows us. Anyone who married into the cursed race must take the curse upon himself, therefore the children of such a marriage would be cursed, and they would not be able to hold the priesthood. Any man had better think twice before he takes a step that will rob him of the greatest blessings of the Lord.[61]

When, despite all this, Black or biracial Latter-day Saints still wanted to be baptized, their records were often marked "colored" or "B" for Black, "C" for Cain, "N" for negro, or simply "Cain," "blood of Cain," or "seed of Cain." This was not official church policy, but it was done frequently.[62] In Guatemala, for instance, a woman's baptismal certificate marked her "the descendency of Cain." In the United States a record simply noted that a Black couple was "colored."[63]

Brazil and South Africa weren't the only places where the church struggled with these issues. Questions about race and lineage flooded into church headquarters from mission presidents eager to receive instruction about whether to proselytize and confer priesthood ordination on Indigenous populations within their mission boundaries. Typically, McKay and his counselors turned to Joseph Fielding Smith, the church's doctrinal authority on race and priesthood, to answer such questions. In 1951, as McKay was considering expanding the church's missionary program in the Pacific Islands, First Presidency counselors Stephen L. Richards and J. Reuben Clark asked Smith if he could determine whether "the inhabitants of the Melanesian and Micronesian Islands" were of "the seed of Cain." After researching the matter in the *Encyclopedia Britannica* Smith claimed he didn't know.[64] The Brethren had similar questions about ancestry relating to Māori, Fijians, Philippine Negritos, Australian Aborigines, and other Indigenous populations: they wanted to know whether they derived from Africa.[65]

There was nothing precise or scientific about any of this. Smith's hasty research in the *Encyclopedia Britannica* notwithstanding, the Brethren did try to determine ancestry according to the best available methods of the day. They instructed mission presidents and missionaries to visit local history museums and speak with native anthropologists to determine the origins of the Indigenous populations. They also consulted with native Latter-day Saints to gauge their knowledge about where the Indigenous population might have originated.[66]

But these inarticulate methods were fraught with problems, which made McKay cautious about establishing missions in regions with predominantly mixed-race populations or where ethnic origins were unknown. Expansion into these countries occurred in fits and starts, accompanied by a lot of mistakes and many prolonged discussions among the First Presidency and Quorum of the Twelve. McKay knew that if the church grew in the Caribbean, South America, and South Africa, biracial individuals would inevitably be ordained to the priesthood, and he often asked himself, "What will my Father in Heaven say to me about this when I see him?" His friends told him that God would "forgive" him, that he would "err on the side of mercy."[67]

This live-and-let-live approach governed McKay's decisions where lineage was ambiguous. After initially rejecting dark-skinned Fijians for priesthood ordination, for example, McKay concluded, after speaking with a local Fijian named C. G. Smith, that they "were in no way related to African negroes." He therefore "reclassified" them "Israelites" and authorized church leaders to ordain them.[68] He followed the same course of action with Australian Aborigines. Initially they were thought to be "of the

Negro race," but after considering the matter, McKay changed his mind and permitted their priesthood ordination. This also happened with Philippine Negritoes. After deeming them cursed, McKay reversed himself and said they could be ordained to the priesthood.[69]

By contrast, Solomon Islanders, Egyptians, Nigerians, Jamaicans, Ghanaians, and other dark-skinned peoples were deemed cursed, and the McKay administration instructed mission presidents to avoid proselytizing in those countries. In regions where the church already had a presence, such as Brazil, South Africa, New Zealand, Mexico, the United States, Papua New Guinea, and the Caribbean, McKay continued the policy established by his predecessors to avoid teaching individuals believed to have African ancestry. Kent Brown, a missionary in Papua New Guinea, recalled, "Basically, when we went in there, we were told that we were sent there to proselyte the white people." Joseph Fielding Smith echoed that instruction, telling Brazil mission president William Grant Bangerter to have his missionaries avoid teaching Black people "whenever possible, in view of the problems which generally arise."[70]

★ ★ ★

At the same time, McKay was dealing with critics in the Church Education System who rejected the church's race teachings. Lowry Nelson boasted to his friends that he "was the first Mormon to protest the church policy with regard to Blacks," but this wasn't entirely true. For years, a number of the church's institute and seminary teachers had expressed strong reservations about the church's race theology. They just didn't air their grievances publicly.[71] Even so, Nelson's critical exchange with the First Presidency endeared him to dozens of Mormon educators, who praised him for confronting a troubling dogma in the church. "Your letter[s] to the First Presidency . . . should be included among the important documents in Church history," Mormon philosopher Sterling McMurrin enthusiastically wrote years later.[72] Another admirer, BYU religion professor Gustive Larson, jubilantly reported that he and his wife had stayed up until 1:30 a.m. reading Nelson's correspondence with the Brethren and "were entertained, amused, delighted and disappointed alternately." Larson admired Nelson's "frankness and [envied] his relative position of freedom." The BYU professor said he was "shocked to see the Brethren take such a definite stand on something I had hoped we were outgrowing."[73]

RACIAL PASSING   45

Nelson's admirers circulated, without his knowledge, his correspondence with the First Presidency. Nelson was astonished at the rapid spread of the letters and noted years later that "many hundreds if not thousands" of copies had circulated "sub rosa," creating what he called "the Mormon Underground."[74] Dozens of people within the Church Education System had copies, as well as, he suspected, "every member of the BYU faculty." An enterprising Latter-day Saint even shared copies with the BYU library and the Utah State Historical Society. The material even reached Mormon faculty at the University of Michigan, including Apostle Spencer W. Kimball's son LeVan.[75]

But Nelson's frustration with Mormon racial teachings didn't end with his testy exchange with the First Presidency. A few years after writing the Brethren, Nelson decided to go public. It wasn't a knee-jerk response, nor was it a calculated attempt to embarrass the Brethren. Rather, Nelson thought he could do the church some good. He reasoned that outside pressure might force the Brethren to change course. He wrote a carefully crafted letter to President McKay to inform him of his intention to publish his views in a national magazine. The professor found it "inconceivable," he explained to McKay, "that in this enlightened age the Church can continue to hold this doctrine" of Black inferiority. Years later Nelson ruminated that what he wrote was "simply polemical." It was "an expression of my disgust with the whole business."[76]

Nelson's essay "Mormons and the Negro" was published in *The Nation*, a popular magazine in the United States.[77] In his personal copy of the article Apostle Spencer W. Kimball underlined the most controversial part, when Nelson called the ban a "source of embarrassment and humiliation to thousands of its members (the writer among them) who find no basis for it in the teachings of Jesus, whom all Mormons accept as the Savior." Nelson's article angered church leaders, including McKay and Kimball. McKay instructed his secretary, Joseph Anderson, to respond to Nelson. The hard-fisted secretary informed the professor that he was sliding into apostasy: "[W]hen a member of the Church sets himself up against doctrines preached by the Prophet Joseph Smith and by those who have succeeded him in the high office which he held, he is moving into a very dangerous position for himself personally."[78]

Why did Nelson's article anger Kimball and McKay? Besides the obvious point that Nelson called Mormon racial teachings a "source of embarrassment and humiliation to thousands of members," he took dead aim at the Mormon concept of the preexistence—specifically the "war in heaven"—claiming that it violated all of the basic concepts of human decency and fairness. Nelson wrote that there was no scriptural precedent for the notion that Black people "sat on the fence" during the war in heaven, and he characterized Mormonism's preexistence hypothesis in unflattering terms—as "a twilight zone between the Satanic hosts and those who were ready to be counted on the side of Michael" the archangel.[79]

Nelson meant the article to be direct and frank even if it skirted the edges of being disrespectful. But he also wanted to offer "constructive criticism" on a policy that he believed had plagued the church. The Brethren didn't take it that way, though, and neither did orthodox BYU professors. Besides Kimball and McKay, BYU religion instructor Roy Doxey also took issue with Nelson's article and published a spirited response in *The Nation*. Doxey, a junior faculty member, lacked the status and the experience of some of the more erudite members of the religion faculty, namely Hugh Nibley and Sidney Sperry—PhD-trained scholars in ancient history and ancient languages from Berkeley and Chicago, respectively. Rather than give a historical or theological response, as Nibley and Sperry might have done, Doxey, who lacked a doctoral degree and was something of a fundamentalist, responded with dogma. He quoted liberally from Joseph Fielding Smith's *The Way to Perfection*.[80] Doxey accused Nelson of "grossly" misrepresenting Mormon teachings, citing, in particular, Nelson's characterization of the war in heaven. Nelson had declared that the church taught that Black people "sat on the fence" in the pre-earth life, echoing Wilford Woodruff's position he learned as a boy. Doxey, in contrast, endorsed Joseph Fielding Smith's view—now mainstream in the church—that Black people had been merely "less valiant" in the preexistence.[81]

Predictably, Nelson strongly refuted Doxey's claim that Black people enjoyed a number of blessings in the church. What "self-respecting Negro is going to seek fellowship with a church which permits him only limited participation," he asked. And what Negro would join a church that denies him "the crucial blessing of holding the priesthood" and tells him that "his blood is 'tainted' and that the color of his skin represents a curse of the Almighty?" "If blessings are available to Negroes why hasn't the church brought those blessings to the Negro? Why have they deliberately avoided doing so?"[82] Nelson published a critical rejoinder to Doxey in a subsequent

RACIAL PASSING 47

edition of *The Nation*, in which he called Doxey's position disingenuous. He chided Doxey for giving the impression that the church sought out Black people to teach and convert when the opposite was true. "They just are not welcome" in the church, Nelson scoffed.[83]

The public dispute between these two passionate Mormons reflected, as much as anything, that Mormon racial teachings were hotly contested by some members of the church. Nelson boasted that his article "was the first [time] the non-Mormon world knew of [the priesthood and temple ban]. . . policy," and he was delighted that "it was widely publicized throughout the Negro press."[84] He also boasted to a fellow Mormon scholar, "Quite a number of people have written me, all of them favorable to my point of view except one Roy W. Doxey of the BYU who wrote me a five page, single-spaced letter attempting to set me right on my theology." Nelson found his skirmish with Doxey strangely amusing, but the Brethren didn't. They recognized almost instinctively that a problem existed within the church, particularly among the "thinking people"—educated professionals, college professors, and instructors in the Church Education System and at the flagship university, BYU, where reports trickled back to BYU president Ernest Wilkinson that many on the conservative campus were unorthodox on the "Negro question."[85]

Wilkinson reported to the First Presidency that "a number of teachers in our Church School System . . . have departed from our beliefs as it respects the Negro Question." He admitted to BYU religion professor Sidney Sperry that "one of the most delicate subjects to handle is the attitude of the Church towards the Negro." Wilkinson wasn't quite sure how to deal with liberal faculty who didn't believe in the church's race teachings. For a church that prided itself on conformity and obedience to authority, this was an unusual problem. To bring the faculty into line, Wilkinson proposed giving them copies of the 1949 First Presidency statement, which he shared with each academic department. Privately, however, he doubted that the statement would do any good. He claimed it wasn't scholarly enough.[86] That belief prompted him to ask a trusted faculty member to produce something erudite—something hefty and substantive that the faculty could get behind.

The obvious choice of writer for such a statement was BYU professor Hugh Nibley, the church's chief apologist and the university's most respected scholar. In Wilkinson's judgment, Nibley was the right person to do "exhaustive research" and the scholar most likely to "come up with a real scholarly treatment on the matter." After all, Nibley had mastered several languages, authored dozens of books and articles on a variety of Mormon and secular topics, and had a national and international reputation in his field of classics and ancient history. (After hearing Nibley spontaneously quote thirty lines from an ancient text, Harvard Divinity School dean George MacRae covered his eyes and said, "It is obscene for a man to know that much.") But not even Wilkinson, the man the faculty called "Little Napoleon," could persuade the venerable scholar to take on a research project as explosive and contentious as the priesthood and temple ban.[87]

In 2009, when Nibley's papers became available at BYU, it became clear why he spurned Wilkinson's request: he was one of the dissenters. Nibley, for instance, scoffed at the notion of a "pure white race" and claimed it didn't make sense to prohibit priesthood ordination based on a fictional one-drop rule. Nor did he accept LDS teachings on "the curse of Ham." God cursed land, not people, Nibley posited years later in an influential book called *Abraham in Egypt*.[88] Wilkinson then asked BYU religion dean David Yarn to produce a statement, but he too declined, though he didn't provide a reason. Frustrated, the president then asked his deputy, William Berrett, to write a statement, and he agreed, but it took him several years to finish it. His twenty-three-page statement, "The Church and the Negroid People," was published in 1960 as a supplement in John J. Stewart's book *Mormonism and the Negro*.[89]

Even if Berrett's statement had appeared in a timely manner, it's unlikely it would have had the desired effect. Many professors—including some of BYU's most distinguished faculty—were firmly opposed to Mormon racial teachings. Several confided to Lowry Nelson that they agreed with him, and others circulated letters among themselves in which they praised Nelson for his criticism of the ban.[90]

The Church Education System was rife with doubters too. The most vocal critic was Lowell Bennion, a highly regarded teacher at the University of Utah Institute of Religion, where he had taught since 1934.[91] During the course of his career, Bennion taught thousands of Mormon students and was a towering intellectual and spiritual influence in their lives. His student admirers included future Pulitzer Prize–winning author and Harvard University historian Laurel Thatcher Ulrich, who said Bennion's teachings were "a landmark experience in my life," and historian Douglas Alder,

Lowell Bennion, an influential LDS religion teacher at the University of Utah Institute of Religion, 1956. Courtesy of Utah State Historical Society.

who called Bennion "the most exemplary, moral, human being in Church history and also the greatest mind in the Church, even today." He was a "Mormon hero."[92]

The Brethren too recognized Bennion's unique talents. President McKay once asked him to speak about marriage in general conference because he had built a reputation with "our young people." "They don't listen to us old fuddy-duddies," the church president said, "but they might you." McKay also asked Bennion to write lesson manuals for the church's Sunday School program.[93] Apostle Hugh B. Brown paid him the highest compliment by seeking his advice on sensitive church topics. "We had many fine discussions," Bennion remembered.[94]

What endeared Bennion to his students and certain members of the upper church leadership? The affable teacher wasn't afraid to challenge church teachings that he believed contradicted scripture. As early as 1943 Bennion confided to McKay that he thought church teachings on race were unscriptural and said that "he couldn't explain with satisfaction why the negro should be excluded from holding the priesthood."[95] McKay wasn't the only one with whom he shared his grievances. Bennion once gave a "fireside" talk—a supplementary monthly meeting among Latter-day Saints—in which he titled his remarks, "Why I Cannot—without Further Light—Be Content and Happy and Complacent about the Traditional and All-Too Official Attitude of the LDS Church towards the Negro." He also made his views known to his students and close friends, including his "Black friends" in the church.[96]

Bennion claimed that the "negro doctrine destroys faith" and "produces unchristian feelings, attitudes and practices in the lives of our saints everywhere." He told McKay, "This negro teaching does not bring the fruit or spirit of the Gospel [because it] breeds hate, envy, pride, humiliation, and rules out mercy, love, and kindness." Just as troubling, many of his students lost "faith in the mission of the Church," Bennion lamented, "because ... of the practice of the Church toward the Negro."[97]

Some of Bennion's colleagues in the Church Education System were equally critical of the race doctrine. George Boyd of the University of Southern California Institute of Religion (Spencer W. Kimball's brother-in-law) and Lewis Max Rogers, his colleague, didn't air their grievances in public, but they voiced their displeasure all the same. Rogers lost his cool on one occasion when he told Wilkinson's assistant, William Berrett, that he "never took the word of the Authorities on the Negro question as final," to which Berrett became "very angry."[98] Edgar Lyon, a colleague of Bennion's at the Salt Lake Institute of Religion, and biblical scholar Heber Snell at the Utah State University Institute of Religion also criticized the church's race teachings.[99]

A number of these dissenters formed a group called "the Swearing Elders" that met at the University of Utah. Organized by Mormon philosopher Sterling McMurrin and his colleague William Mulder, the group met regularly from 1950 to 1955 and engaged in lively discussions on race and priesthood, evolution, the Book of Mormon, Joseph Smith's golden plates, and more.[100] Their discussions were often critical of church theology, and some even mocked the general authorities for positions they had taken on the age of the earth, "negroes," and scripture. Participants included a range of Mormon academics from the University of Utah, BYU, and the Church Education System, mixed in with faculty from nearby Utah State and Weber State. Occasionally out-of-town scholars, such as Lowry Nelson and acclaimed western historian Wallace Stegner, were guests. Apostle Adam S. Bennion spoke to the group on at least one occasion, and general authorities Levi Edgar Young and Bruce R. McConkie attended a session or two to monitor the free-spirited professors.[101]

As one might suspect, the "Swearing Elders" repulsed Joseph Fielding Smith, who tried to fire a number of them from their church employment. In his most audacious attempt, he tried to get two of them excommunicated, but President McKay wouldn't allow it. Heber Snell, one of the men in question, had been in Smith's crosshairs for quite some time. He had written a book on the Old Testament that Smith strongly disliked; the apostle claimed there wasn't enough Mormon orthodoxy in it. Snell also incurred Smith's wrath when he taught his students that "God may be either white or black," which prompted one student to report Snell to his local ecclesiastical leaders, who threatened to excommunicate him.[102] McMurrin was also on the chopping block. When Smith and Apostle Harold B. Lee heard that he and the "Swearing Elders" had challenged Smith's views "on some of the fundamental doctrines of the church," he called the philosopher in for a private meeting. Later, word trickled back to McMurrin that Smith wanted him cut off from the church. McKay told McMurrin that if local officials tried to excommunicate him at a church court, he'd be a "witness on his behalf."[103]

But McKay's influence stretched only so far, and Smith and his allies in church leadership were determined to hold the line on the race doctrine. They were angry with the church's intellectuals. And they had their hands full with students in the Church Education System, some of whom became restless over the ban. When eighteen-year-old Ardis Westwood decided to write a research paper on the church's race teachings for her BYU freshman English class, she wrote President McKay indicating her topic, which she titled "The Curse on the Negro regarding the Priesthood." Westwood wanted to know when the curse would be lifted, if "Negroes" would receive the priesthood, and if "the descendants of Cain" were cursed "because they were his descendants," or because they came "through Cain's lineage" and "were not valiant in the war in heaven?"[104] Questions like these irritated McKay, and he didn't answer her directly; instead, he asked Ernest Wilkinson to politely steer Westwood and other students "away from subjects such as this."[105]

Westwood wasn't the only Latter-day Saint college student puzzled by Mormon racial teachings. J. W. Monroe asked Apostle Joseph F. Merrill where he could "find that it is church doctrine that the Negro cannot hold the Priesthood of God." He had searched the scriptures in vain; the only place he found such answers was in *The Way to Perfection*. Monroe informed the apostle that the "young people of the Church are very interested in finding an answer to this question, both in Sunday School and Priesthood."[106] Even future First Presidency counselor Dallin H. Oaks expressed frustration with the policy. As a law student at the University of Chicago in the 1950s, he recalled that the ban "was deeply troubling to many," himself included, "and an increasingly awkward position for the Church." Edgar Lyon, who taught thousands of college-age students during his tenure in the Church Education System, said that "Negroes and the Priesthood" was the most difficult subject to teach. Especially troubling, as Lowell Bennion noted, was the one-drop rule. Students asked, "When is a person a Negro? Why should one drop of Negro blood make him such? Or does it?" They also asked, "If [the Negro] had done wrong in the pre-existence, why wouldn't a just and loving Father let him know and give him an opportunity to repent?"[107]

With difficult questions like these, students turned to their teachers in the Church Education System for guidance. Typically, teachers gave them handouts of assorted church statements defending and affirming the ban. Sometimes apostles would visit the church institutes to allay student concerns and reassure them of church teachings.[108] Joseph Fielding Smith, for example, visited the University of Utah Institute in the spring of 1952 and informed students that "negroes have just exactly what they deserve." He warned that "a white person who marries a negro becomes thereby himself a literal descendant of Cain."[109]

Few students, however, were as unsettled about the priesthood ban as Boyd Mathias, a recently returned missionary, student at the Agricultural College at Logan (now Utah State University), and admirer of Lowry Nelson. Troubled over how the church consigned Black people to an

RACIAL PASSING 53

inferior status, Mathias had a "long interview" with Apostle Spencer W. Kimball and informed him of his heterodox views. As Kimball observed, Mathias was "much disturbed over the Negro question," as well as "other matters which affect those who begin in their apostasy." Kimball tried to "help him and get back to correct thinking," but it was too late; Mathias's faith was already "shattered." The grieved apostle found the meeting deeply troubling and recorded in his diary that it made him feel "depressed all day." Kimball felt that he "had done little" to assuage Mathias's concerns and informed the young man that he was "disturbed greatly for his future."[110] Kimball had reason to be concerned. Mathias eventually left the church and became a zealous critic of LDS racial teachings.[111]

Besides disgruntled students and church-employed faculty, the Brethren also had to deal with skeptics outside of BYU. Prominent University of Chicago scholar Chauncy Harris, one of the world's leading authorities on Soviet and Russian geography, was an unlikely critic. He achieved prominence in 1933 as BYU's first Rhodes scholar, served an LDS church mission, and had married a well-connected LDS woman in a Mormon temple. His father, Franklin Harris, moreover, was in close contact with the First Presidency and Quorum of the Twelve Apostles, having served as president of BYU. His wife Edith's connections were even more impressive. Her father was general authority Clifford E. Young—a great-grandnephew of Brigham Young—and her maternal grandfather was the late church president Heber J. Grant.[112]

In the early 1950s, however, Chauncy and Edith had a crisis of faith and slipped away from church activity. The family's departure had drastic consequences for their daughter Margaret, then a young child. When the Harrises visited their relatives in Utah and attended church with them, Margaret went "into a panic" any time Mormon-related topics came up. Her cousins were astonished that she didn't know the basic primary songs that all Mormon children were expected to sing at church and couldn't recite basic Book of Mormon stories that all good LDS children typically knew. Margaret recalled years later that they just assumed "I was slightly slow and pitied me." Little did they know that Margaret didn't attend church in Chicago, and neither did her parents. The Harris family kept it a secret.[113]

The race doctrine is what pushed Chauncy Harris and his family out of the church. Chauncy was asked to give an adult Sunday School lesson on the "Children of Cain," but he found its portrayal of Black people demeaning

54   SECOND-CLASS SAINTS

and insulting. Eventually, he confided his doubts to his father-in-law, who was predictably unsympathetic. Young gave Harris a copy of Apostle Harold B. Lee's address "Youth of a Noble Birthright," which leaned heavily on the notion that Black people were cursed. Neither his father-in-law nor Apostle Lee were "very helpful," Harris lamented to Lowell Bennion.[114] To another friend Harris was just as vocal in expressing his frustration: "I must confess that the Negro question is one that troubles me." "The stand of the Church on the Negro and the position of Joseph Fielding Smith on evolution," he explained to another friend, outraged his "moral and intellectual sensibilities that yearn for a brotherhood of man and an honest quest for truth."[115] For years Harris kept his heresies to himself, confiding his anguish to only a few close friends and family members, but after seeing the courage of his friend Lowry Nelson, Harris decided to speak out.

He coordinated with Nelson. Both agreed that "the church might be most sensitive to outside pressures and publicity," and though, unlike Nelson, Harris didn't air his grievances publicly, he pressured the Brethren privately to lift the ban.[116] He wrote a long letter to President McKay about eight months after Nelson's article was published. Harris poked holes in just about every justification that Joseph Fielding Smith provided in *The Way to Perfection*. He postulated that there was no scriptural proof for Smith's theory that Black people had been less valiant in a pre-earth life. Harris also wanted to know how Joseph Smith could be the originator of the ban if Elijah Abel held the priesthood during the early days of the church and had served as a "Traveling Elder." Harris closed the letter with a plea to lift the ban on the negroes "before great harm is done to the good name of the Church."[117]

A month later McKay replied in a terse letter that sidestepped Harris's concerns. Not wanting to engage in a theological dispute with the sharp-tongued professor, the elderly president simply informed Harris that it would take a revelation to lift the ban. McKay's response left Harris frustrated and confused, so he decided to write the president again. Also prompting the second letter was a newspaper article Harris had read that mocked Mormon racial theology and criticized Mormon apostle Ezra Taft Benson, then serving as the secretary of agriculture in Dwight D. Eisenhower's administration. Benson had been in Washington less than a year when newspapers began skewering his farm policies—and his church. The article sneered that Mormons believe Black people were cursed and could become White again through moral probity and righteous living.[118]

An embarrassed Harris sent another letter to church headquarters, this time to the entire First Presidency. "Newspaper reporters," he wrote, "already have harassed Church members in the area for an explanation of the Church attitude [toward Negroes]. Any public official now identified in the press as a Mormon, whether he be a cabinet officer, congressmen, college president, or governor, is potentially vulnerable to a barrage on this subject which could become detrimental to the church, the individual or both." He closed with an earnest request: "Unless the Church intends to face the searchlight of widespread publicity and public disapproval on an issue in which it will appear in an extremely unfavorable light—and to many in an immoral and un-Christian position—it needs to re-examine its statements and policy on the race question without delay."[119]

It took the First Presidency several weeks to reply. Joseph Anderson, their secretary, responded on their behalf and again ignored the issues that Harris raised.[120] Harris's letter must have rankled the First Presidency, however, because a few days later someone in the governing hierarchy produced another statement on the race and priesthood question—one that similarly ducked the issue. It proclaimed that God loved all of his children equally "without regard to the race or color of their mortal bodies" and noted that African Americans were entitled to "full civil rights and liberties." The statement further affirmed that Black people could "attend all general meetings of the Church, partake of the sacrament," "participate in testimony meetings," and "engage in recreational activities." The statement closed by noting that "there is no segregation in any Church gathering or activity, but that under the revelations so far received negroes may not, at the present time, receive the Priesthood . . . in the Church."[121]

★ ★ ★

In 1954, President McKay decided that he had had enough. He traveled to South Africa in January to make a dramatic statement that had profound consequences for missionary work there. In a surprise announcement, McKay said that South Africans no longer had to trace their genealogy out of Africa. There were "worthy men in the South African Mission who are being deprived of the Priesthood simply because they are unable to trace their genealogy out of this country." McKay asked, "Why should every man be required to prove that his lineage is free from Negro strain especially when there is no evidence of having Negro blood in his veins?" Henceforth, if a South African man had "no outward evidence of a Negro strain, even though he might not be able to trace his genealogy out of the country, the President of the Mission is hereby authorized to confer upon him the Priesthood."[122]

After McKay left South Africa, he traveled next to Rio de Janeiro, Brazil, where he met with Asael Sorensen, the mission president. Sorensen was thrilled that McKay visited his mission and "gave [him] a lot of good counsel and advice."[123] Whatever that advice was, it didn't lead to a policy change, because eleven years later, in 1965, Apostle Spencer W. Kimball visited the mission and found that there were "2,400 men and boys who hold no Priesthood." They couldn't prove that they didn't "have any colored blood in them," the apostle noted dourly. This prompted Kimball to explain that McKay had reversed the policy of tracing genealogy in South Africa, which meant that it should end in Brazil too.[124]

Why McKay didn't make this explicit to Sorensen can only be a matter of speculation. The best explanation is that it was probably a function of his missionaries avoiding teaching Black people and mixed-race individuals, which meant that they didn't bother to do the genealogy required to ordain them. Or it could have been a function of Brazilians looking to church patriarchs to pronounce lineage before they were ordained to the priesthood. Or it might have been that Sorensen didn't complain about the issue like Wright did and therefore didn't get the correction from the church president.[125]

In any event, when McKay returned to Utah in February 1954, he informed the Brethren about the new policy change in South Africa. His counselor, Stephen L. Richards, enthusiastically called the new policy "a marvelous statement." The apostles asked why McKay made the sudden change, and he told them that it was unfair to make South Africans trace their genealogy to prove that they weren't Black when such a policy wasn't required in South Carolina, Washington, New York, Salt Lake, or the Hawaiian Islands. "Unless there is evidence of negro blood," he informed the Brethren, "you need not compel a man to prove that he has none in his veins." The apostles unanimously approved the change.[126]

★ ★ ★

Less than two months after McKay returned from South Africa and Brazil, he convened a special committee of apostles to look into the possibility of lifting the ban. Never before had a church president considered such a drastic move.[127]

Apostle Adam S. Bennion chaired the committee, and he asked his cousin, Lowell Bennion, to help assess the feasibility of ending the restriction.[128] In preparation for the task, Apostle Bennion compiled a thick packet of meeting minutes from the First Presidency and Quorum of the Twelve Apostles, including council deliberations dating all the way back to the earliest days of the church. This meant that Bennion and the committee had at their disposal prior rulings by church leaders on a range of issues, mostly on questions dealing with conferring priesthood ordination on light-skinned Latter-day Saint men with African ancestry to questions about whether they should have full access to the faith's temple rituals.

Not much is known about this secret committee. We don't know which apostles served on it, other than Bennion, or what conclusions they drew after discussing the matter. Spencer W. Kimball considered the committee's work, including the meeting minutes that Apostle Bennion compiled from the Quorum of the Twelve Apostles and First Presidency, top secret. In his

Adam S. Bennion of the Quorum of the Twelve Apostles and chairman of the committee that produced the influential "Bennion Report," n.d. Courtesy of Utah State Historical Society.

copy of the minutes, Kimball wrote in all caps what should be done with them when he died:

TO MY FAMILY AND ANY OTHERS, UNDER NO CIRCUMSTANCES, NONE, ARE THESE PAPERS AND THIS BOOK AND ALL EXCERPTS FROM THE MINUTES OF THE MEETINGS OF THE BRETHREN IN THE TEMPLE OR OTHERWISE TO BE APPROPRIATED FOR THE LIBRARY OR OFFICE OR POSSESSION OF ANY OF FAMILY FRIENDS OR OTHERS. THESE ARE TOTALLY PERSONAL AND PRIVATE AND MUST BE TURNED IN TOTAL TO THE BRETHREN—THE FIRST PRESIDENCY OF THE CHURCH OR COUNCIL OF THE TWELVE. NO DELETIONS, NO COPIES, NO XEROX. OR ANYTHING LIKE UNTO IT. I HAVE PLEDGED TO MYSELF THAT I WOULD HOLD ALL THESE PAPERS INVIOLATE.

He closed the request by signing his full name: Spencer W. Kimball.[129]

Apostle Bennion provided a few clues about the nature of this secretive body. In May 1954, he met with the "Swearing Elders" and listened to their concerns about "the failure to give the priesthood to the blacks and similar matters." In response, Bennion told them that "the Church leadership" was "now undertaking a careful reevaluation of our doctrine in this respect." He said that a special committee had produced a report, concluding that "the denial of the Priesthood to Blacks had no sound scriptural basis."[130] But the "Swearing Elders" weren't the only members privy to the existence of Apostle Bennion's secret committee. In July of that year, Utah State University professor George Ellsworth, a close friend of Lowell Bennion's, told one of his students, Boyd Mathias, about the committee's work. Mathias, in turn, contacted Lowell Bennion and wished the committee well. "If nothing else," Mathias wrote, "I hope [Apostle Bennion] can resolve the position of part Negroes."[131]

Lowell Bennion drafted the report, but it's unclear whether he was an official member of the committee or just assisted his cousin. Regardless, his close friendship with President McKay and his outspoken opinions on the "negro question" made him a key figure to reassess the doctrinal underpinnings of the ban. Across six single-spaced pages, the outspoken church educator wrote a critical, unvarnished account of LDS racial policies and practices.[132] He scoured the meeting minutes of the First Presidency and Quorum of the Twelve for clues about how past church presidents and apostles approached the ban. Was it based on revelation? Did it have sound scriptural support? Did it address practical problems discerning who had "negro ancestry"? Could the preexistence hypothesis be reconciled with other scriptures suggesting that people would be judged on their own merits, not that of their ancestors?

To each of these questions Bennion answered no. There was nothing in the scriptures to justify priesthood denial, including Abraham 2 in the Pearl of Great Price, which Bennion alleged "is not a statement of theological belief, but is a record or narration of the historical situation in which [Black people were] believed to be cursed." Bennion then dissected each scripture commonly used to defend the ban, refuting them so as to puncture a gaping hole in the church's proof texts for the ban. None of the scriptures in question—not in Genesis, Moses, or the Book of Mormon—addressed the theology underlying the ban, he asserted. Rather, the scriptures spoke of "all the blessings and privileges of the Gospel of Jesus Christ." Bennion also raised practical issues relating to the ban. There was no science to indicate bloodlines, and he flatly rejected the notion of a "pure white race": "There has been so much inter-mixture of 'races' and peoples in human history through the ages, who can be sure of the blood of his ancestors." Bennion then offered proof: "Negroes in the Southern States have crossed with Indian tribes and with whites in extra-marital relations for generations. 'Negroes' become 'whites' continually in America, Brazil, France, and North Africa."[133]

Bennion next challenged Mormonism's preexistence theology. "The trouble with the pre-existence," he stated, is that it was "a catch-all for the unanswered questions." It "becomes the answer for too many and too much. Every unanswered question relative to the conditions of man," he affirmed, "can be thrown into this hopper with the result that we neglect our religious and moral responsibility in relation to these problems." Bennion also asserted that the ban was "contrary to Christian morality." The preexistence hypothesis robbed a Black person of the fundamentals of Christian theology because it didn't allow him to repent of the sin that he was allegedly guilty of. "The Negro cannot even learn what his sin is," Bennion wrote.[134]

Bennion also undercut the notion that founding prophet Joseph Smith Jr. had instituted the ban, thus challenging both the 1949 First Presidency statement and *The Way to Perfection*. "Joseph Smith's attitude toward the Negro is not clear," Bennion insisted, in what was sure to provoke a fight with Joseph Fielding Smith, who repeatedly claimed that the ban began with his great-uncle. The founding prophet "received no revelation on the subject, of which we are aware," Bennion wrote, and he "seems to have dealt with it as a practical, political and social issue rather than as a moral issue." Furthermore, Bennion implied that church leaders themselves had conflicted views about Mormon racial teachings. "B. H. Roberts, Joseph Fielding Smith, and John A. Widtsoe have in more recent times offered explanations of why the Negro cannot hold the priesthood."[135]

The report further stated that the ban was pushing away the church's best and brightest people. On this point, Bennion couldn't have been clearer: "We are alienating many of our most intelligent and morally sensitive members of the Church. We have had students leave the Church and others not wish to be baptized on account of this practice." Bennion added that the ban had stymied church growth because it prevented the church from fulfilling its mission to globalize "the gospel." The ban, moreover, contributed to the hardships that Black people faced. He regretted that the church contributed "to animosity, hatred and division among men instead of increasing love, respect for human dignity, and democracy." Bennion thus drew a powerful, unmistakable conclusion: the priesthood and temple ban had to end. "There was no basis in our theology to deny the Negro the Priesthood."[136]

Little is known about the submission of the report. The record isn't clear whether the Brethren discussed it in their council meeting, voted on it, or scrapped it altogether. We do know, however, that the report influenced President McKay, for in the days after the report was issued the church president shared some of its major points with his friend Sterling McMurrin. McKay said that Black people were not under a divine curse and that the ban was not a fixed and irrevocable doctrine. For McKay, the ban was simply a practice. The church president's unusual candor prompted McMurrin to press McKay to share his views with the church body. But the president declined. When McMurrin pressed him again, McKay replied, "All I will say is that there is no such doctrine in this church. [The priesthood ban] is simply a practice, and that's all there is to it."[137]

McMurrin immediately recognized that McKay's statement was "historic," yet he couldn't persuade the elderly president to make "an official statement on [the] matter." As both men knew, strong headwinds worked against them; there were too many apostles who opposed ordaining Black men to the priesthood.[138] Joseph Fielding Smith had spent the better part of his ministry defending the ban, and few in the church hierarchy had the

RACIAL PASSING

temerity to challenge him, much less the inclination to disassemble the theological scaffolding he had crafted in *The Way to Perfection*. At the same time, the 1949 First Presidency statement had elevated the policy to doctrine, making it less likely that the Brethren would alter the ban. Of the Twelve, only Adam S. Bennion and John A. Widtsoe would have changed it, but Widtsoe had died in 1952 and Bennion didn't have the support of his colleagues—as McKay certainly knew. McKay himself might have lifted the ban in 1954, but the hard-liners in the Twelve would have opposed him. Sterling McMurrin put it bluntly: "McKay wanted to reverse the policy excluding Blacks from the priesthood, but . . . he was unable to sway the rest of the Brethren."[139]

Still, even as the status quo remained, the Bennion Report was not without value. The meeting minutes compiled by Apostle Bennion made it clear that there was no revelation to justify the ban, which is why Apostle Kimball warned his family that his copy of the Bennion Report should be carefully guarded. Years later, when the meeting minutes leaked, Kimball remarked that the minutes "allegedly proved total lack of revelation past or present" on "the negro question."[140] Kimball was savvy enough to know what that meant. What the Brethren defended all these years in their books and sermons, what they defended as doctrine to church educators, what they said to mission presidents—it could all be challenged with the words of the apostles themselves. As Kimball rightly feared, the Bennion Report showed that the foundation for the priesthood and temple ban was built on sand.

3

Segregation, 1954–1962

The year 1954 was a pivotal one for the church. Earlier that year President McKay returned from South Africa and made an important ruling that South African Latter-day Saints no longer had to disprove their African lineage to hold the priesthood. The Bennion Report, likewise, forced the church president to grapple with the reality that the priesthood and temple ban had a dubious origin. And now, in June 1954, exactly one month after he commissioned the secret Bennion committee, McKay and his colleagues faced another difficult situation when the U.S. Supreme Court struck down segregation in the nation's public schools in *Brown v. Board of Education of Topeka, Kansas*. The Court ruled that segregation was unconstitutional, overturning an earlier ruling affirming that segregation was permissible as long as schools and public institutions were "separate but equal."[1]

The Brethren responded to the Court's ruling with a mixture of alarm and uncertainty. They didn't know how it would affect Utah, church-owned properties, or the church's teachings on interracial marriage. The ruling provoked a wave of opinions from concerned church members and a variety of responses from the Brethren. J. Reuben Clark approached the *Brown* decision cautiously, President McKay preferred to ignore it and keep silent, while Apostle Mark E. Petersen attacked the ruling viciously. In an address to the church's religion teachers, Petersen not only rejected integration but, most egregiously, said that Black people would be servants to White people in the afterlife. This was likely the most controversial address that a church apostle had ever given in the twentieth century, because of its patronizing tone and the fact that it resembled the rhetoric of the White Citizens' Councils and Ku Klux Klan—the two most prominent White supremacist groups in the United States in the 1950s. Like many southern

SEGREGATION 63

Protestant clergymen, Petersen grounded his opposition to *Brown* in the Bible. "I think the Lord segregated the negro," he famously said.

The church's support for segregation met fierce criticism from the NAACP, which complained that Utah's record on civil rights was abysmal. Indeed, as the civil rights movement surged during the late 1950s, critics— both internal and external—assailed the Brethren for not doing more to fight racial inequality. Under siege, the Brethren adopted a strategy to remain silent on civil rights while concurrently cracking down on dissenters within their ranks.

In 1962, they fired Lowell Bennion and his colleague Edgar Lyon from their teaching assignments at the University of Utah Institute of Religion, sending a strong warning that educators who opposed the church's race teachings would be punished. No one in the Church Education System was safe, not even the church's most beloved religion teachers.

★ ★ ★

When acclaimed African American sociologist W. E. B. Du Bois wrote, "The problem of the twentieth century is the problem of the color line," he could have been talking about the Mormons.[2] The church's problem with the color line was laid bare in the summer of 1950, when the Korean War erupted, hastening J. Reuben Clark's efforts to collaborate with an LDS doctor named Albin Matson to segregate blood banks. Clark's intentions were transparent. "We want to protect the purity of the blood streams . . . of this church," he informed Matson, and he wanted to know if the doctor could scientifically determine blood lines. Clark first made this inquiry in 1948, as lineage questions in South Africa and Brazil arose, but with the Korean War escalating he felt a sense of urgency. Clark and his colleagues feared that if LDS servicemen received a blood transfusion from an unsegregated blood bank, they would inherit cursed blood.[3]

Matson wasn't successful locating hereditary blood factors, but it wasn't for lack of trying. He went to conferences, conducted extensive research, and kept Clark apprised of his progress throughout the war.[4] Meanwhile, as Matson's work stalled, Clark used his influence in the First Presidency to see that LDS-affiliated hospitals in Utah segregated their blood banks. Clark didn't think of this on his own. The American Red Cross segregated blood banks during World War II to avoid giving White soldiers "inferior hemoglobin and plasma"—a policy that drew the ire of experts in the

64   SECOND–CLASS SAINTS

medical community, including a medical researcher writing in the *Journal of the American Medical Association* who called it "not only unscientific but a grievous affront to the largest minority in our country."[5]

Clark's ambitious effort to segregate blood banks demonstrates how deeply entrenched segregation was in the United States and in the LDS church. When the Supreme Court issued the *Brown* ruling, Utah was deeply segregated. Though Jim Crow laws didn't govern Utah's schools—the state had few African Americans—school districts seldom hired Black teachers. Indeed, nearly 40 percent of the state's employers refused to hire African Americans. In addition, segregation was rampant throughout Salt Lake City, the state's largest and most racially diverse city. Zoning laws forbade "any person not of the Caucasian race" to enter certain sectors in the city. Utah's bowling alleys prohibited Black families from entering, and movie theaters excluded them from the main floor, forcing them to sit in the upper balcony, where it was often uncomfortably hot.[6] Similarly, the vast majority of hotels and restaurants refused to serve Black people, and two prominent amusement parks, Lagoon and Saltair, denied them entry. Adding further humiliation, the infamous "Green Book," distributed by the Chamber of Commerce and other outlets, indicated which businesses would patronize Black travelers. There weren't many.[7]

All of this is to say that Utah's segregation laws were governed by custom, not by law, but their pernicious effect was all the same.

In 1954, the National Urban League published a report stating that "in large areas of Utah, Nevada, and southern Arizona, and in most of the smaller towns, the discrimination is almost as severe [as] in the south."[8] Indeed, at the time of the *Brown* ruling Utah was a microcosm of the deeply segregated nation. A number of states segregated bus terminals, restaurants, movie theaters, swimming pools, zoos, and schools. Now Mormon leaders feared that the *Brown* ruling would spark a backlash against other Jim Crow laws. Their fears were not unwarranted. Even before *Brown*, the Supreme Court had struck down restrictive covenants, which denied Black people the right to live in White neighborhoods.[9]

These changes came suddenly, causing the Brethren tremendous anxiety as they struggled to reconcile the church's race teachings with the wave of antisegregation sentiment sweeping across the country. Like many White southern evangelical and Fundamentalist Christians, the Brethren supported segregation. In 1945, Apostle Harold B. Lee gave a spirited radio

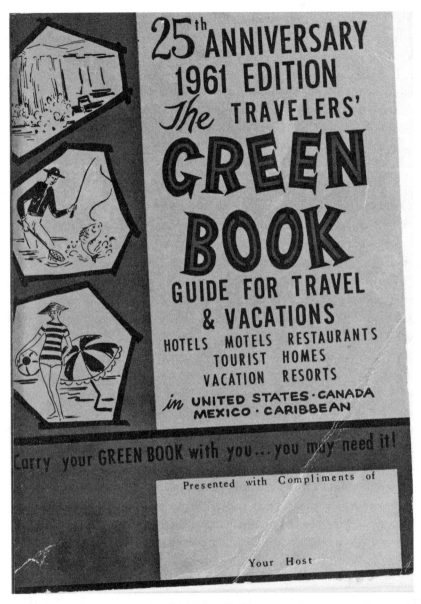

Cover of the 1961 *Green Book*, which identified hotels and restaurants that would serve Black people in Utah. Courtesy of New York Public Library.

address to the youth of the church, affirming that the "seed of Cain ha[s] been separated from the rest of mankind." Lee issued a strong warning that race-mixing offended God, claiming that it would lead to interracial marriage. "Surely no one of you who is an heir to a body of the more favored lineage would knowingly intermarry with a race that would condemn your posterity to penalties that have been placed upon the seed of Cain by the judgments of God."[10] That same year George Albert Smith and other church leaders explored the possibility of using LDS meetinghouses to discuss ways "to prevent Negroes from becoming neighbors." The previous year J. Reuben Clark had urged church leaders in Salt Lake to participate in "a civic organization whose purpose is to restrict and control negro settlement." President McKay, also a staunch segregationist, opined that "colored people" were better off in the segregated South than anywhere else in the country because "the South knows how to handle them."[11]

Given the church's small African American membership, the Brethren didn't have a lot of direct experience with segregation. Nevertheless, in 1942 Ezra Taft Benson, then the stake president in Washington, D.C., asked the First Presidency for guidance on what to do about "two colored sisters" who were "faithful members of the Church." Their presence in the Relief Society offended the White sisters, and Benson didn't know how to handle it. The First Presidency instructed Benson to tread carefully. "If the white sisters feel that they cannot sit with them or near them, we feel very sure that if the colored sisters were discreetly approached, they would be happy to sit at one side in the rear [of the room] or somewhere where they would not wound the sensibilities of the complaining sisters." They told Benson they trusted him to make the right decision.[12]

This wasn't the first time that Black Latter-day Saints experienced segregation in Mormon pews. A decade earlier, an ecclesiastical leader in Cincinnati, Ohio, told Len and Mary Hope, a Black couple, that they couldn't worship alongside White Latter-day Saints. This obviously alienated them from fellow Latter-day Saints, but they weren't ignored. Marion D. Hanks, then a missionary in Ohio and later a general authority, brought them communion each week in their home, in a desperate attempt to make them feel welcome.[13] Despite Hanks's best efforts, however, the Hopes were devastated and in 1947 they moved to Salt Lake City. They were astonished to find that it too was segregated.[14]

Some Latter-day Saints were puzzled to learn that the Brethren segregated church properties. A concerned church member from New Jersey asked Clark why "traveling colored artists" couldn't stay at the Hotel Utah, a church-owned property, and Clark's secretary, Rowena Miller, replied that "since they are not entitled to the Priesthood, the Church discourages social intercourse with the negro race, because such intercourse leads to marriage."[15] Occasionally, the Brethren made exceptions. When acclaimed African American singer Marian Anderson gave a recital at Utah's Kingsbury Hall, for example, the First Presidency allowed her to stay at the church hotel "on condition that she use the freight elevator." The distinguished diplomat Ralph J. Bunche, the first African American to win a Nobel Peace Prize, experienced a similar humiliation when he visited Utah. President McKay allowed him to stay at the Hotel Utah provided he eat his meals in his room. In another instance, a desk clerk at the Hotel Utah refused a room to Adam Clayton Powell, a Black congressman from New York, upon which Powell demanded to speak with McKay. The two had an "animated [phone] conversation," recalled a bystander, resulting in the Mormon president permitting the congressman to lodge at the hotel.[16] But such exceptions were rare.

While the church was firmly committed to segregation, Latter-day Saints outside of the South began to challenge it. Apostle Joseph Fielding Smith ruefully acknowledged that a "wave of non-segregation" had "arisen in this country," which "brought a flood of correspondence from all parts of the Church asking how it is that the Church of Jesus Christ of Latter-day Saints stands out in opposition and teaches a doctrine of segregation denying the Negro the right to hold the Priesthood. Some of these letters border on a spirit of resentment," he lamented, "and claim that the Church is guilty of a great injustice since 'all men are created equal.'"[17]

★ ★ ★

No one expressed greater concern about the church's segregationist policies than liberals in the Church Education System—the men with the most influence over the youth of the church. Their concern was evident in the summer of 1954, when the Brethren held a series of classes with church religion instructors, which the *Church News* touted as "graduate courses in religion"—"firsthand instruction from . . . General Authorities." But that upbeat description belied the purpose of the meeting. Years later Apostle Harold B. Lee described why they held the seminars. The Brethren provided instruction to church teachers on "theological problems with which they were having some difficulty."[18]

68   SECOND-CLASS SAINTS

None of the Brethren wanted to admit it publicly, but the religion seminars were a subtle attempt to rein in the liberal faculty at the Salt Lake Institute of Religion, whose main teachers—Lowell Bennion, Edgar Lyon, and George Boyd—had "difficulty" with church teachings on race and lineage, which prompted Church Education Chancellor Ernest Wilkinson to keep a secret file on them.[19] On tap to lead the seminars were several members of the Church Board of Education: Apostles J. Reuben Clark, Adam S. Bennion, Harold B. Lee, Marion G. Romney, Henry D. Moyle, Mark E. Petersen, and Joseph Fielding Smith. They aimed to set the errant teachers straight.

The gathering wasn't the faith-promoting experience that it was billed to be, at least for the liberals who attended. Several had preconceived notions about Apostle Lee. They found him "narrow minded" and were annoyed that he wanted to offer graduate courses for credit when he didn't have a PhD. Still, his addresses on the "Godhead" and "The Church and Divine Revelation" didn't incite controversy.[20] That was left to Smith, then the second most senior apostle in the church, and Petersen, who had been an apostle for some ten years. Smith gave a controversial address on the "origins of man and the fundamentals of the gospel," based on his equally controversial book *Man, Origin and Destiny*. His sermon upset the liberal educators, who scoffed when he tried to get his anti-evolution views into church manuals.[21]

But it was Apostle Petersen who aroused the most controversy, which was surprising given that he had been in the Quorum of the Twelve only since 1944 and had never sermonized on the church's race doctrine. The *Brown* ruling fired him up, and for nearly two and a half hours he gave a sermon on the "negro problem," followed by an intense Q-and-A exchange with the church's religious educators. Edgar Lyon recorded the event in his diary: "Mark E. Petersen—Race Issue," which tersely implied his intense dismay.[22]

Petersen, a journalist by profession, had previously served as the managing editor for the church-owned *Deseret News*. He wasn't a deep thinker nor a particularly inspiring speaker. A gruff man with a prickly personality, he wanted to be taken seriously by those who thought and spoke deeply about Mormon doctrine. But it was an elusive effort, undermined by his pithy books, which demonstrated neither a profundity of Mormon doctrine nor a theological richness that captured the writings of B. H. Roberts

SEGREGATION 69

and John A. Widtsoe. In fairness, his books were billed as devotional works, but that didn't stop Petersen from commenting on issues that deserved more than perfunctory treatment.[23]

On a warm August day in Provo, before a crowd of nearly two hundred church educators, Petersen condemned the *Brown* ruling. He called his address "my little talk on the race question," but the official title was "Race Problems—As They Affect the Church."[24] The address demonstrated how much he loathed civil rights. The apostle explained that "[t]he discussion on civil rights, especially over the last twenty years has drawn some very sharp lines. It has blinded the thinking of some of our own people," and he didn't want them to "be led astray by the philosophies of men on this subject any more than another subject."[25]

Petersen quoted extensively from an interview with Congressman Powell, a Baptist minister–turned politician from Harlem, who favored full "social equality," including interracial marriage. In Powell's words, "an increasingly large number of Negro leaders are marrying whites of extremely stable and respected families." He predicted that it would soon happen all over the United States. An anxious Petersen claimed that interracial marriage was "what the Negro is after."[26]

That was the warm-up. Petersen then unleashed a verbal barrage condemning integration. Carefully and methodically, he weaved scriptures into the address and quoted liberally from Joseph Fielding Smith's *The Way to Perfection*:

> We cannot escape the conclusion that because of performance in our pre-existence some of us are born as Chinese, some as Japanese, some as Indians, some as Negroes, some as Americans, some as Latter-day Saints. Is it not a reasonable belief that the Lord would select the most choice spirits to come to the better grades of nations? Is it not reasonable to believe that the less worthy spirits would come through [a] less favored lineage? Does this not account in very large part for the various grades of color and degrees of intelligence we find in the earth?[27]

The educators had heard all of this before. Even so, Petersen continued unabated. Quoting further from *The Way to Perfection*—"this very wonderful book"—he explained that God had engaged in acts of segregation throughout history. When "the Lord chose the nations to which the spirits were to come, determining that some would be Japanese and some would be Chinese and some Negroes and some Americans, He engaged in an act of segregation." "When He permitted the banishment of Hagar and Ishmael . . . He indulged in segregation." "When He preserved His people Israel in Egypt for 400 years, He engaged in an act of segregation." "When He cursed the descendants of Cain as to the Priesthood, He engaged in segregation."[28]

But Petersen didn't want his audience to think that segregation was cruel and unkind. It was all a manifestation of "the mercy of God." "Negroes" got what they deserved because of poor choices they had made "in the pre-existence life," which "justified the Lord in sending [them] to the earth in the lineage of Cain with a black skin." However, Petersen remarked, not all was grim for Black people. They could receive "the blessings of baptism and the gift of the Holy Ghost" and even "enter the Celestial Kingdom," but they "will go there as a servant." Here Petersen quoted again from *The Way to Perfection*, showing little awareness of the controversial nature of this radical theology.[29] In 1954, on the cusp of a civil rights movement, only two months after the Supreme Court's historic decision in *Brown*, Petersen was astonishingly unaware of which way the winds were blowing.

Concerning "the removal of the curse," Petersen took a different stance from Joseph Fielding Smith and some of the other apostles. "I know of no scripture," he stated, "having to do with the removal of the curse from the Negro," and he cautioned the religious educators not to speculate. He said that previous general authorities had given their own opinions on the matter, but Petersen wasn't sure if Black people would be whitened in the resurrection.[30]

Petersen finished the talk where he began: with interracial marriage. He reminded the educators, "If there is one drop of Negro blood in my children . . . they receive the curse." He insisted, "We must not intermarry with the Negro." He explained that if the "50 million Negroes" living in the United States all intermarried with White people it would destroy the church, for the descendants of these mixed-race families couldn't hold the priesthood. "Think of what that would do to the work of the Church!" Petersen protested. To end the sermon on a positive note, he said that the church was

> generous with the negro. We are willing that the Negro have the highest kind of education. I would be willing to let every Negro drive a Cadillac if they could afford it. I would be willing that they have all the advantages they can get out of life in the world, but let them enjoy these things among

themselves. I think the Lord segregated the Negro and who is man to change that segregation?"[31]

"Race Problems—As They Affect the Church" was Petersen's most controversial address in his forty years as an apostle, and, predictably, it sparked a blizzard of questions. Because it was a private meeting, the transcript wouldn't be published. That provided space for educators to ask sensitive questions and the apostles to provide them with frank answers. The attendees included a veritable who's who of religious educators in the LDS Church Education System.[32]

Their questions were broad and far-reaching. Hugh Nibley wanted to know whether the curse of dark skin that applied to the Lamanites in the Book of Mormon also applied to Black people. The Brethren had taught that through righteous living and moral purity the curse on the Lamanites would vanish, making them White again, but they couldn't determine if that transformation would occur during mortality or in the resurrection. Apostle Smith answered the question cautiously, noting, "The Lord did put a mark on Cain" and "[W]e know of cases where it really has disappeared."[33] But the crux of Nibley's question was when the curse might be removed. On that point, Smith was ambivalent. That particular question, he confessed, "plagued me more than anything I ever wrote."[34]

The questions then turned to segregation. Eugene Campbell asked Petersen point blank if he believed in or advocated for "the Jim Crow law." It was a strange question to ask; the apostle had made it clear in his address only minutes earlier that he did. Petersen didn't mince words answering Campbell: "I believe strongly in segregation." He said that if he had his way and he was the mayor of a town or on the city council he'd have negroes "live in one area." They could have "their Cadillacs and beautiful homes and all that, but [he] would have them live in their own area" with their own schools.[35]

Probing further, Campbell asked Petersen if he'd put a wall around Black communities. The apostle seemed taken aback by the directness of the question. "I wouldn't, of course not," he shot back. But the "Lord did draw a line" between the races, and "the more we mix with them, the more chance there is for inter-marriage," he stammered. The only exception was at church, where Black members could worship with White members—notwithstanding the Hopes' experience in Cincinnati, which Petersen said he regretted.[36]

Another questioner wanted to know whether church missionaries should preach "to the negro." Petersen stated that it was church policy, as he understood it, that "the missionaries go out and preach to the white people." They were "not sent to proselytize among the negroes," but "if a negro comes to the meeting, we don't bar him," and if he "applies for baptism" and is converted, then "we give him baptism." Petersen was unusually frank: "We're sort of in a situation where they come to us, we don't go to them."[37]

Then the issue of lineage came up. Sidney Sperry recounted an experience he had while transcribing patriarchal blessings for his grandfather, Orson Sperry, an ordained patriarch. His grandfather gave a blessing to a young couple about to be married in one of the faith's temples. Neither the young man nor the young woman looked like they had a cursed lineage. "They looked like anyone else," Sidney noted. But when his grandfather laid his hands on the young man's head, he couldn't proceed with the blessing. "He told [the young man] that he had the blood of Cain flowing in his veins." Sidney explained, "Ever since that case with grandfather, I have understood, and have never doubted what the Church Authorities have been teaching about the negroes." He closed his remarks expressing support for Petersen. Sperry thought the church "ought to have segregation," not because he had prejudice "for the negro, but just as Brother Petersen said, if we get mixed up among us, I'm telling you we're going to be in a pretty bad position."[38]

Smith and Petersen nodded in agreement with Sperry's impromptu remarks, and Smith commented that there was no reason why Black people couldn't have patriarchal blessings, but they were forbidden from receiving "the blessings of Abraham, Isaac, and Jacob"—a euphemism for priesthood and temple blessings. Petersen echoed Smith's point, reminding educators that even if Latter-day Saints had some of the "blood of Israel" in them but also had "a drop of the blood of Cain," they'd still be cursed.[39]

Lowell Bennion found all of this very troubling, and he sat silent for a long time. Finally, when he couldn't remain silent any longer, he took aim at Apostle Petersen. "If the Negroes sinned [in the preexistence]," he asked, "what sin could they commit for which 'a merciful God'—as you speak of, Brother Petersen—'would not be willing to forgive, if they repented with a contrite heart and a broken spirit?'" Bennion pressed further. He wanted to know how Petersen could brand Black people less valiant in a pre-earth life if Mormon scriptures taught that all men were born innocent. And finally,

SEGREGATION 73

he poked the apostle on the unjustness of the one-drop rule. Bennion re-counted the story of a student of his at the University of Utah of supposed mixed-race ancestry. The boy was "blue-eyed" and "fair in complexion,"[40] but his bishop wouldn't ordain him to the priesthood and his sister was able to marry in the temple only after President McKay personally intervened.[41]

At this point, Ernest Wilkinson interjected with a pointed question. "Would you advise the boy in question to marry a negro girl or a white girl, or would you advise him not to marry at all?" he asked Apostle Smith.[42] Neither Smith nor Petersen wanted to answer. After pausing for what seemed like several seconds, Smith replied, "[I] would not like to give [the young man] any advice at all in regards to marriage. I would not like to be involved."[43]

That troubling exchange was followed by Paul Dunn, a future general authority, bluntly asking, "Students are constantly asking about situations where evidently negroes have received the Priesthood and they've func-tioned in Church ordinances, what happened?" Assistant Church Historian Andrew Jenson stoked the controversy in 1920 when he published the *Latter-day Saint Biographical Encyclopedia*, in which he wrote that early church leaders had conferred priesthood ordination on Elijah Abel. The Brethren fielded this question often from concerned Latter-day Saints, and it perturbed them to have to answer it.[44]

President McKay responded this way: "In the days of the Prophet Joseph Smith one of Negro blood received the Priesthood. Another in the days of Brigham Young received it and went through the Temple. These are authen-ticated facts but exceptions." On other occasions, Apostle Smith claimed, without evidence, that there were actually two Elijah Abels in Nauvoo in the 1840s—one a Black man and one a White man—and that it was the White Abel who was ordained.[45] On this occasion, though, Smith ac-knowledged the Black Abel's ordination but said it was an accident. When Joseph Smith learned about it, the apostle insisted, "he said it is wrong." An educator then asked a challenging follow-up question. He wanted to know what would "become of the validity of the ordination" when mixed-race Latter-day Saints slid behind the color line and achieved ordination. Did the Latter-day Saints for whom they performed the priesthood or-dinances require a legitimate priesthood holder to perform the ordinances again? Smith couldn't answer that question; it was "too deep" for him, he claimed.[46]

74 SECOND-CLASS SAINTS

Petersen's address, along with the Q and A, gobbled up most of the morning, and the teachers had to be in the Salt Lake Temple that afternoon to worship. Still, a burning question lingered. An educator wanted to know if "the negro as a whole is inferior to the white race." The answer to that question was clearly implicit in all that had come before, but the inquiring educator wanted clarity. The question annoyed Petersen, who hotly responded that when Latter-day Saints turn away from the counsel of church leaders "they become disobedient and then the spirit of rebellion develops within them until eventually they apostatize." After lecturing the man for a few minutes, Petersen offered a barely coherent response: "I don't know exactly where you are going to draw the line on this matter of inferiority, because everybody is his own agent and can determine his own life, and some may develop more spirituality than others, depending upon their love for it."[47]

The meeting ended with a thud.

The next day, Edgar Lyon wrote Lowell Bennion and described what he had observed: "I looked at the faces of the men in the room while you were speaking [and] your words were heresy of the first [order]." In contrast, Lyon said, some teachers relished the fact that Bennion stood up to Smith and Peterson. It was something they didn't have the courage to do. "Your words fell like manna from heaven on a starving people," Lyon gushed to Bennion. "You said everything that I had thought, but said it ten time[s] more pointedly and in a nicer spirit that I could have said it."[48]

★ ★ ★

It took courage for Bennion to publicly criticize Smith and Petersen, and it immediately put a bull's-eye on his back. Church Education teachers were not supposed to correct, challenge, or criticize the Brethren, and Bennion had violated all of those sacrosanct rules. Two weeks after the conference, Wilkinson wrote Bennion asking him to provide more details about "the negro question" that he had raised. This put Bennion on the defensive, and he told Wilkinson, "It was not my intention to give offense to anyone, least of all to President Smith." He went on to explain that he was "deeply concerned with the effect of our teaching and manner of teaching [on] the lives of students." Bennion's rejoinder was gutsy: he continued to reiterate that the church's race teachings had harmed the church.[49]

Bennion's tussle with the apostles, along with Petersen's forceful defense of segregation, made the talk a hot commodity among the church's intellectuals and general authorities. Orthodox teachers at BYU circulated the address, touting it as an authoritative statement on segregation, race, and priesthood.[50] Petersen's colleagues in church leadership also found the address instructive. Apostle Spencer W. Kimball marked it up in red ink, underlining phrases he found helpful. Apostle N. Eldon Tanner called it "the Church's position on the negro question." Harold Hillam, a future general authority, found it "very enlightening."[51]

Yet other Latter-day Saints found the address disturbing. "Elder Petersen's view is shocking," an LDS law student complained. "Petersen's whole argument is based on conjectures, which don't follow at all. And he doesn't even try and explain the case of the negro that Joseph Smith ordained." J. D. Williams, an outspoken Latter-day Saint professor (and later LDS bishop), called the address a gross misreading of Mormon scripture. Petersen, Williams scoffed, "overlooks the most important point" in scripture: "that segregation is plainly and simply anti-Christ." *New York Times* journalist Wallace Turner, meanwhile, belittled Petersen for suggesting that God favored segregation.[52]

Petersen's claim that God favored segregation wasn't unique, as Turner must have known. Southern Protestant clergymen had preached a biblical defense of segregation for years. One of the most well-known segregationist clergymen was the Reverend Jerry Falwell Sr. who pastored at the Thomas Road Baptist Church in Lynchburg, Virginia. Falwell detested the *Brown* ruling as much as Petersen did and declaimed, "If Chief Justice Warren and his associates had known God's word and had desired to do the Lord's will, I am quite confident that the 1954 decision would never have been made. The facilities should be separate. When God has drawn a line of distinction, we should not attempt to cross that line."[53] Another clergyman, Reverend James F. Burks, pastor of the Bayview Baptist Church in Norfolk, Virginia, claimed that the "issue of segregation or non-segregation has been turned into a major problem because of the tactics and brainwashings by liberal clergymen, the National Council of Churches." He rejected their position that segregation lacked biblical support. Like Petersen, he appealed to Ham and "Canaan's curse" to bolster his conviction that God didn't intend for the races to integrate.[54]

76   SECOND-CLASS SAINTS

While it's tempting to think that most conservative Christians believed that the Supreme Court was poised to "destroy race distinctions which God [had] ordained," some Protestant clergymen supported the *Brown* decision and viewed it as a way to achieve racial harmony.[55] The Presbyterian Church Council on Christian Relations prepared a statement expressing hearty support for *Brown*. The "oneness of mankind" and the "equal value" of "every person," it declared, was firmly grounded in scripture. The Southern Baptist Convention also supported *Brown*. At the same time, the immensely popular Billy Graham, a preacher from the Southern Baptist tradition, praised integration. He initially "waffled" on segregation, but after the Court's decision, and after many nights on his knees in prayer, he integrated his crusades.[56]

If sides had to be drawn, Apostle Petersen followed not the path of Reverend Graham but that of Reverends Falwell and Burks—a choice he'd later regret. Years later the apostle distanced himself from his controversial address after critics excoriated him for his extremist views. He was upset when someone leaked a copy of the address. In the early 1950s, a Salt Lake City barber named James Wardle, a member of the Reorganized Church of Jesus Christ of Latter Day Saints (now Community of Christ) obtained an illicit copy and shared it with Jerald and Sandra Tanner, former Mormons and indefatigable critics of the faith. Both had deep-rooted Mormon ancestry. Jerald's great-great-grandfather, John Tanner, had given money to church founder Joseph Smith when the church was mired in debt, and Sandra was the great-great-granddaughter of Brigham Young, Mormonism's second prophet-president.[57] When the Tanners received a copy of Petersen's speech, they authenticated it at the church archives and declared that Wardle's copy matched the original. Shortly thereafter, they published it as a twenty-eight-page pamphlet titled "The Negro in Mormon Theology." They sold the pamphlet for $1.00 and claimed that it contained information "not usually found in Mormon publications about the Mormon doctrine concerning the Negro."[58]

BYU religion professor Richard Anderson informed the apostle of the Tanners' mischievous deed. Petersen was furious, not only for the tantalizing way in which the Tanners advertised the pamphlet but because he assumed that someone from the conference had leaked the address. He demanded that BYU president Ernest Wilkinson find the culprit. He also wanted Wilkinson to exert pressure through the university's legal department to

SEGREGATION 77

force the Tanners to cease publication.[59] But Wilkinson refused to pursue such measures. He thought trying to suppress the speech would just bring more attention to it. The Tanners would "certainly shout to high heaven about this," he snarled.[60]

Wilkinson's inaction frustrated the apostle, who decided to take matters into his own hands. He wrote a forceful letter to Jerald Tanner threatening legal action if he didn't cease publication. Tanner refused.[61]

The speech would haunt Petersen for years. BYU graduate Craig Hanson read it in 1968 and wrote the apostle an unusually strident letter condemning him for writing a speech that bore a strong resemblance to Hitler's book *Mein Kampf* and the literature produced by the American Nazi Party.[62] Lowry Nelson, a former BYU professor, used it as fodder to antagonize the apostle. He told Petersen that he wanted to give him "a little preachment" from "a favorite theme" of his: "ETHNOCENTRISM." Nelson then lectured the apostle for perpetuating a myth that a pure White race existed. "In the course of a few more centuries," Nelson adamantly insisted, "bloods of whites and blacks will continue to mix, but it will be gradual." The professor thought it was futile to support segregation on account of interracial marriage. It was only a matter of time, he told Petersen, before interracial marriages would be ubiquitous, making LDS racial teachings look foolish.[63]

The Brethren typically ignore grumblings from the rank and file, but on this occasion Petersen wrote back. The two men had known each other in their earlier years at BYU—Nelson as a professor and Petersen as a student. After brief pleasantries, Petersen denied ever giving the talk: "You referred to a copy of an address that I am supposed to have given at BYU in late 1954. I have heard from other people that copies of such an address are being passed around. I have never seen the copy and I do not know whether it is authentic or not."[64] Nelson had written to a friend that "Bro. Petersen is a little embarrassed about his address, and does not like to have it circulated."[65] This proved it.

As Petersen's talk circulated on the underground, a number of allies rushed to his defense. BYU religion professor James R. Clark, nephew to J. Reuben Clark, offered a bizarre if creative defense. He wrote—and had his students perform—"a drama with a prologue and five acts" reinforcing segregation as God's will.[66] Another defender, Arthur M. Richardson, wrote, "Segregation of the Blacks and Whites, has a very ancient, honorable and authoritative history behind it." Richardson wanted Latter-day Saints to understand that God's "Living Oracles [would] hold to the color line drawn by God."[67]

Another ally was Emma Petersen, the apostle's wife, who vigorously defended her husband's segregationist views. She published a novel in 1956, *Choose Ye This Day*, which a church magazine called a work "carefully based upon fact."[68] The story features Milo Peterson, a Black athlete from Los Angeles, who plays football at the local college, along with several White LDS athletes. When the LDS athletes learn that they will be playing with Milo, they threaten to quit the team, putting the season in jeopardy. Two of the LDS athletes on the team debate the merits of integration. "Even the Church holds out against the Negroes," one asserts. To resolve their differences, the boys seek counsel from Hank Weston, a hamburger store owner, staunch Latter-day Saint, and "friend to nearly all the students on the campus." Hank says that his feelings on the subject are guided by his religious views, which hold that Black people are cursed because of their cowardice in a pre-earth life. He has "heard some of our [Church] leaders teach that even the Negro can go to the celestial kingdom if he is faithful. However, he can be only a servant there." Hank concludes his homily by cautioning the boys not to integrate with Black students. "Each race may develop within itself. So far as the Negroes are concerned, we will give them every right and privilege within their race that we claim for ourselves within our own race, but will not become intimate with them in any way, and we will not intermarry with them." Hank calls this a "fair position to take"—one that "squared with the word of God."[69]

Other apostles also endorsed segregation. J. Reuben Clark, for one, took a more moderate position on segregation and civil rights.[70] Perhaps he felt inclined to soften Petersen's extreme views, or perhaps he wanted to broaden the discussion to include all Latter-day Saints. In any event, he wrote a carefully crafted sermon on the subject, which he planned to deliver in general conference in October 1954. He penned three drafts and had Apostles Petersen and Kimball read one of them. Petersen thought that Clark had addressed segregation exceptionally well. He gushed, "I think the manner of treatment of this subject is wonderful. It will offend no one, it is kindly and fair, and yet it gets the point of view over in a forceful way." Kimball expressed approval too.[71]

Clark's address was a mishmash of LDS racial teachings, filled with curses and promises. Black men would eventually hold the priesthood, he insisted, but he couldn't say when. "Modern prophets have declared that in the due time of the Lord, the great burden the colored folk now bear will be removed from their shoulders and they will be permitted to enjoy the Priesthood, to the full extent to which they are heirs. But until the Lord again speaks, the situation will be as it is." Then Clark switched gears and focused on civil rights. He claimed that the church was willing to grant "colored folk" civil rights—"all the rights, privileges, liberties, and protection guaranteed them by the Constitution of the United States and the laws in this country." But, he added, "for biological and Priesthood reasons, the Church is opposed to intermarriage of the races." Then Clark made another startling admission: "There was one and possibly two colored men upon whom the Priesthood was confirmed in the very early days of the Church before the Brethren understood the scriptures on the subject. A few since then have inadvertently received the Priesthood."[72]

Whereas Smith and Petersen reluctantly acknowledged Abel's ordination at the BYU teacher's conference, Clark didn't hesitate. He wanted the church to know the truth. He also took a much different tone on civil rights than Petersen, striving to keep his address upbeat and positive. He didn't fixate on interracial marriage like Petersen or make condescending remarks that it was okay for Black people to own Cadillacs, nor did he discuss Black people becoming servants to White people in the afterlife. Rather, he told the Saints that the church fully supported civil rights, though he didn't specify exactly what those rights were.

Clark never gave the address. President McKay prevented it as just too risky. Discussing segregation, and especially admitting that the church had ordained a handful of "colored men" to the priesthood, even inadvertently, would only invite scorn from the church's critics. Clark surely wasn't happy about the president's decision, but he had the good sense not to press the matter. He understood the wisdom of remaining silent on LDS racial teachings during a national movement promoting racial equality. However, that posture didn't stop him from expressing his views in private—views that were much harsher than the ones he had planned to share publicly. As a lawyer, he had strong opinions about the *Brown* ruling and groused that the Court would "hand down a decision from above that the people are preponderately against." Clark declared that the "[c]olor line won't be erased suddenly by law" and that discrimination wouldn't end for Black Americans until they showed "themselves worthy of equality and respect." That line

80 SECOND-CLASS SAINTS

reflected the sentiment of a number of prominent southern politicians, who also believed that the government couldn't force Americans to accept Black people. Even so, Clark was ill-informed. He said that "many intelligent Negroes don't want integrated schools" and asked why they would want to "leave good schools where the children are prominent and popular," held office in student government, and had good grades. Of course, most Black people supported *Brown* precisely because they didn't have good schools.[73]

Ironically, though, even though Clark disliked the *Brown* ruling, he concluded that it was in the church's best interest to support civil rights—at least with lip service. This explains why he had planned to endorse it. Joseph Fielding Smith and David O. McKay arrived at the same conclusion, not out of principle but because it was politically expedient.

An unlikely person pushed the Brethren in this direction. University of Utah librarian L. H. Kirkpatrick wasn't a Latter-day Saint, but he worked with them, lived among them, and cared deeply about civil rights. More important, he recognized that LDS racial theology was a barrier to getting civil rights legislation passed in Utah. As early as 1952, he began corresponding with Clark, McKay, and Smith about an article he was writing that would show that "it's possible for members of the L.D.S. Church to do a good deal for civil rights for the Negro and at the same time work within church doctrine."[74]

This was a clever strategy. Kirkpatrick managed to convince McKay, Clark, and Smith that civil rights aligned with Mormon theology, or at least didn't pose a threat. After discussing the matter with Kirkpatrick, Sterling McMurrin enthusiastically reported that Smith, Clark, and McKay "[e]ach insisted that the negro should have full civil rights."[75] Kirkpatrick's article appeared in the *Pen Magazine* in the winter of 1954, two months after Clark's aborted conference address and four months after Petersen's address to LDS religion teachers. Kirkpatrick wrote that McKay, Smith, and Clark had read and approved his address. The perceptive librarian informed his readers "that there is nothing in Mormon doctrine to prevent any member working to combat prejudice among men here on earth." He continued, "There is actually official doctrine in favor of earthly rights for the Negro." Kirkpatrick closed by proudly declaring that "scores of Latter-day Saints whole-heartedly agree with the views of this article."[76]

The devil was in the details, though, and the article didn't say anything about segregation or the *Brown* decision. Nor did it discuss various civil

SEGREGATION   81

rights bills in Utah that had failed to pass in four legislative sessions, in 1945, 1947, 1949, and 1951.[77] Thus, it wasn't clear what specific civil rights issues the Brethren supported—certainly not interracial marriage and certainly not integration. Did they support a bill to bar discrimination in jobs? Housing? The Brethren didn't say. But Kirkpatrick's clever maneuvering put the hierarchy on record, and that's what he wanted. Lowry Nelson praised the strategy as a harbinger of things to come. He hoped that the church's endorsement of civil rights, as tepid as it was, would be the first step toward removing the priesthood restriction. "I think you are very wise in getting any civil rights issue into the picture and with the possibility of getting a formal commitment by the Church authorities," he told Kirkpatrick.[78]

★ ★ ★

While the church's position toward potential Black converts may have been "They come to us, we don't go to them," they did not totally ignore them. In the early 1950s, the church's presiding bishop, LeGrand Richards, asked Abner Howell, a Black Latter-day Saint convert, to travel to the South with his wife to gauge the feasibility of establishing a segregated congregation for Black members. Howell was the perfect choice for the mission. Everyone loved "Abe," recalled Frances Fleming, a close friend. Not only was he "very heavy in the LDS Church," but he had a personality that was warm and infectious.[79] Moreover, he was loyal to the church, despite the racism he experienced at the hands of his fellow Latter-day Saints. When he was a young boy, White Mormon boys told him that, because he "was cursed," he "could not go to heaven when [he] died, but was doomed to go to hell ... and burn forever." Howell wept. The insults didn't stop there. When he led the Salt Lake High School football team to a victory over Colorado's East Denver High in 1900, he suffered the indignity of being told that he couldn't celebrate with the team at a local restaurant; the owner informed him that he'd have to dine alone in the kitchen.[80] Howell experienced further humiliation at church, where the bishop required the Howell family to listen to the sermons in the church foyer by themselves.[81]

Howell must have known, therefore, what he was getting himself into when he accepted Richards's invitation "to call upon our people" in the South to establish a Black congregation. Howell knew that Mormons could be mean, and most of all he knew that the South was a vicious place, with frequent lynchings of Black men and stifling Jim Crow laws designed to

82   SECOND-CLASS SAINTS

"keep Black people in their place." Apostle Spencer W. Kimball warned Howell that a mission to Old Dixie could be dangerous: "Be *very* careful what you say and where you go. . . . Say nothing [and] you will then get along."[82] Of course, Kimball was talking about Mormons, who were really not that much different from segregationist Southerners in their hostility toward Black people. LDS religion educator William E. Berrett provided some context to the challenges the Howells faced when he noted that it was futile to preach to Southern "negroes" because "the whites will not mix with them in church and they won't mix with the missionary if he goes among the negroes."[83]

Thus, it probably didn't shock the Brethren when Howell and his wife, Martha, returned to Utah without success. They had gone to Georgia, Louisiana, and Mississippi, and while Howell said that the Saints treated them with respect, none had an interest in helping establish a Black congregation.[84] Racism ran too deep in the South and was too deeply embedded in Mormon culture.

Be that as it may, the Brethren weren't finished with Howell. Four years later, Apostle Kimball asked him to assist the First Presidency with a survey in the Salt Lake Valley to see who among "the Negroes" was active in the church. He had done this before, in 1947.[85] This time, after consulting with Howell, Kimball concluded that approximately 144 Black Latter-day Saints lived in the Salt Lake area, "few of them . . . active." There was no program for them, he lamented, which accounted for their lack of enthusiasm in the church. Kimball's suggestion was to create "some kind of program" for them, which would not involve "the Priesthood." Specifically, he called for a "central place" for them to "attend Mutual, Relief Society, Primary"—the primary programs for LDS adults, teenagers, and children.[86]

Apostle Joseph Fielding Smith took Kimball's recommendations and added details of his own. In a letter to the First Presidency, Smith proposed that "all the Negro members in the [Salt Lake] area be organized into an independent unit which would function somewhat the same as the Deaf Branch or the Spanish-American Branch." This could be done, he reasoned, by having White priesthood holders administer the sacrament and conduct their services under the careful eye of the stake president, the ecclesiastical officer with oversight over LDS congregations in the Salt Lake Valley.[87] In other words, Smith believed that White priesthood holders could run worship services for Black people, administer their communion, and listen

SEGREGATION 83

to their confessions when they sinned. He even promised to build Black members their own chapel if they remained loyal to the church.[88]

J. Reuben Clark favored Smith's proposal, as did several other Brethren, but President McKay nixed it. With racial tension engulfing the country, the timing wasn't right.[89] When the Brethren met in the summer and winter of 1955 to work out the details of Kimball and Smith's proposal, two White supremacists brutally murdered Emmett Till, a fourteen-year-old African American boy in Mississippi, who allegedly whistled at a White woman. Four months later Rosa Parks's arrest unleashed a wave of protests in segregated Alabama when authorities apprehended her for violating a Jim Crow law on a city bus. With the Till and Parks injustices hovering over the country like a thundercloud, President McKay didn't think it was prudent for Smith and Kimball to move the proposal forward. The president reasoned that it would be difficult to establish a segregated unit within the church during a national outcry against segregation. The optics would be bad.[90]

The Brethren instead adopted a strategy of silence in the face of questions about the church's position on civil rights. They reasoned that the less they said about the matter, the better, and they instructed high-profile Latter-day Saints to follow similar counsel. J. Reuben Clark, for example, told Belle Spafford, the general president of the Relief Society, before she attended a meeting of the National Council of Women, that "this was no time to stir the negro question in the United States." Clark was emphatic that she not endorse civil rights or even discuss it. He also urged her to use her influence on the National Council to keep them "from going on record in favor of what . . . would be regarded as negro equality."[91]

The following year the First Presidency cautioned Utah senator Arthur Watkins not to serve on a committee that would evaluate "racial intermarriage." His participation, they warned, would bring "confusion and probably irritation of our local situation."[92] At the same time, when a White school district asked to hold segregated classes at an LDS meetinghouse in Charlottesville, Virginia, the First Presidency refused. They reasoned that "on the question of integration or disintegration . . . the Church had better not take sides, especially on the question of segregation."[93]

The First Presidency applied the same strategy to the federal civil rights bill of 1957, the first voting rights bill passed since Reconstruction. The bill ensured voting protections for African Americans by creating a civil rights commission, prompting the Brethren to remain silent on a bill of such major importance. The bill came amid a wave of racial unrest. President Eisenhower signed it into law at roughly the same time that nine African American students in Arkansas were denied entry into Little Rock High School, forcing the president to send federal troops to the embattled school to ensure that the students could attend school safely and peacefully. The only LDS official to comment on the bill was Apostle Ezra Taft Benson, who was well into his second term as Eisenhower's secretary of agriculture. He told President Eisenhower that he was moving too fast on civil rights legislation. In a private meeting with Latter-day Saints, however, Benson was more direct, criticizing the president for sending federal troops to Little Rock.[94]

Also in 1957, the First Presidency refrained from supporting a pending civil rights bill in the Utah state legislature. General Authority Marion D. Hanks hand-delivered a copy of the bill, authored by his good friend Adam Duncan, a Republican lawmaker from Salt Lake, to the First Presidency, hoping to get the church's support before introducing it in the legislature. After waiting for a period, President McKay declined to offer support. If a bill passed granting racial equality to Black people, he felt it "could conceivably be very embarrassing to some [LDS] church institutions."[95]

At the same time, critics panned Utah's poor record on civil rights and linked it to the priesthood ban. In 1958, an LDS seminary teacher named John Fitzgerald wrote to President McKay and complained that the "church's policy of discrimination against all negroes is very embarrassing" as well as "unjust and unfair." That same year, Roy Wilkins, the executive secretary of the NAACP, said that the church's race doctrine was the main factor thwarting civil rights legislation in Utah: "The "[Mormon] church is further behind than even the bigoted white churchmen in Mississippi or Alabama."[96] The following year, the Utah State Advisory Committee to the U.S. Commission on Civil Rights issued a scathing report on Utah's poor civil rights record. Utah's "predominantly white (98.2%, 1950 Census) population" was "prone to respond to a question on Civil Rights" by asserting that the state didn't have a problem. The report further stated that Jews, Greeks, and Japanese were treated well in Utah, but that Indians, Mexicans, and especially "the Negroes" were routinely discriminated against in housing and education. "The Negro is the minority citizen which experiences the most generally widespread inequality in Utah," the report stressed, adding "that the Negro is simply not given any kind of equal chance to compete for the

SEGREGATION 85

jobs for which he is qualified, and irrespective of his personal habits or his ability to pay he simply will not be allowed to buy a decent home."[97]

The report was candid about the reason for the rampant discrimination against Black people in the state:

> The Mormon interpretation of the Curse of Canaan in the Old Testament and Latter-day scriptures, together with unauthorized, but widely accepted statements by leaders in years past have led to the view among many adherents that birth into any race other than the White is a result of inferior perform-ance in a pre-earth life, and that by righteous living dark-skinned races may again become "white and delightsome."

The report then stated, "The Mormon practice of excluding the Negro from their universal priesthood does not extend to any other race and interracial marriages have been extensively performed in that Church's Temple elsewhere."[98]

Time magazine obtained a copy of the report and issued a scathing re-buke of Mormons. Its conclusions were unusually critical for a magazine that sought to reach a broad audience. "Whatever they may do or leave un-done about their Negro brethren, most U.S. churches hold that all men are created equal before God," the article began. "One notable exception: the Church of Jesus Christ of Latter-day Saints."[99]

The Brethren read the article carefully and approved a response: a terse, one-page editorial in the *Deseret News* that showed a stark indifference to the issues the NAACP raised in its report. Most notably, the editorial insisted that the "Negro race is certainly treated no worse in Utah than elsewhere, and most whites and Negroes would mutually agree that treat-ment here is generally much better." The editorial noted, "There is no ra-cial segregation in schools, employment or elsewhere in our communities," which may have been true as a matter of law, but was demonstrably false as a matter of fact.[100]

Failing to acknowledge this distinction was a clever way for the Brethren to defend themselves against critics. NAACP leaders, in particular, pointed out the disingenuousness of the *Deseret News* editorial. The *Time* article, they said, exaggerated by assigning all blame for the poor treatment of Black people in the state to the Mormon church. But at the same time, the *Deseret News* editorial did "as much harm as the article in *Time* magazine" because it didn't recognize Mormon racial teachings as a stumbling block to racial equality in Utah.[101]

The *Time–Deseret News* tiff was the first time that the church defended itself publicly against criticism of its exclusionary practices, and it prompted a number of devout Latter-day Saints to speak out. Several wrote letters to the *Deseret News* editor strongly defending Mormon racial practices.[102] A number complained that the church defended itself *too* well. A member identifying herself as "Mrs. Petersen" called the First Presidency's office and left a long, rambling message with J. Reuben Clark's secretary, Rowena Miller. Petersen groused "that there is a large group of people who are very much upset at the *Deseret News* editorial—because this will invite negroes into the area—and all they are interested in is intermarriage."[103]

Disgruntled Latter-day Saints also made their voices heard with regard to interracial marriage. In a letter to President McKay, an anonymous writer, identifying herself only as a Latter-day Saint woman, complained, "Many of us are becoming confused at recent trends in some of our church literature. Namely, the publication of pictures depicting negroes mingling with whites socially." She objected to two pictures published in church magazines: one depicting "a little white girl and a smaller Negro boy" and another showing "young people lounging [in] picnic fashion on the grass, a Negro among them."[104]

The anxious woman piled on. "Too many of us are being led astray," she rued. "Recently I assisted in a hospital with the delivery of a baby to a beautiful blond white girl. Soon into her room walked a tall Negro. I tried to usher him from the room. She assured me that he was her husband. Within a few days her little baby acquired the deepening grey of his father's race. The girl knew no shame. She felt that moderns are above race differences." The woman then wrote in all caps, "PERHAPS SHE WOULD HAVE KNOWN BETTER HAD SHE BEEN TAUGHT!" She followed that story with another one of equal drama, saying that a stake president she knew had a daughter who married a Black man. She wondered if the stake president didn't "grieve for his error in failing to teach" his daughter "that each race has a different destiny."[105]

The woman's blunt criticisms jolted President McKay—so much so that he shared a copy of the letter with his counselors and asked them to share it with all the auxiliary officers of the church, accompanied by a letter signed by the First Presidency asking them to read the letter carefully and avoid printing anything in church magazines that would give the appearance that the church favored "interracial mingling."[106] In the spring of 1960,

SEGREGATION

87

J. Reuben Clark reiterated this counsel to mission presidents. He wanted his audience to know that he was "unalterably opposed to the amalgamation of the negroes, both on religious and biological grounds." These were strong words coming from a Mormon leader who expressed sympathy for "part-negroes" and had tried to get them ordained to the priesthood some ten years earlier.[107]

If Clark had his way, the church would ordain men of mixed-race ancestry to the priesthood so as to avoid the challenges of lineage detection. But on segregation, he held the line, as did a number of Latter-day Saints in the South. When one-third to one-half of Latter-day Saints walked out of a church service in 1959 when a "Negro from the Fiji Islands" visited a Mormon meetinghouse in Memphis, Tennessee, it spoke to the strong racial prejudices of the era.[108] And when President McKay considered lifting the ban in the 1950s, it wasn't just the hard-liners in the Quorum of the Twelve he had to worry about. As general authority Paul Dunn stressed years later, if McKay would have ended the priesthood restriction in the 1950s, there would have been "a break in the Church. I think you would have lost the South."[109]

★ ★ ★

Nothing rankled the Brethren more than when Latter-day Saint intellectuals criticized the church, especially in public, and especially over the church's race teachings. In March 1960, the Brethren learned that Sterling McMurrin was scheduled to address the NAACP at Trinity Baptist Church in Salt Lake, just a few blocks from church headquarters. McMurrin didn't look like the kind of person who would make the Brethren nervous. He wore a cowboy hat, a bolo tie, and scuffed cowboy boots, none of which indicated that he was the church's most respected philosopher of religion. Lowell Bennion described him as "brilliant," armed with "a vast sum of knowledge in the whole fields of religion and philosophy." President McKay "admired McMurrin's intellectual power and integrity."[110]

Having earned a PhD in philosophy at the University of Southern California, with postdoctoral work in philosophy and religion at Columbia, Princeton, and Union Theological Seminary, McMurrin was a formidable presence among Mormon intellectuals. His first major publication on Mormonism, a slim book titled *The Philosophical Foundations of Mormon Theology*, garnered stellar reviews from Mormon and non-Mormon scholars alike. The Brethren didn't know what to make of the book, but they had plenty of opinions about his lack of orthodoxy. In 1952, McMurrin informed them that he didn't believe in the divine origins of the Book of Mormon ("[Y]ou don't get books from angels and translate them by miracles," he famously said years later), nor did he believe in Joseph Smith's First Vision or the divinity of Jesus Christ.[111]

It's not surprising, then, that McMurrin made the Brethren nervous. Fearing what he might say to the NAACP, they sent First Presidency secretary D. Arthur Haycock to keep an eye on him. Joseph Fielding Smith, who also doubled as the church historian, sent Thomas Romney of the Church Historian's Office to monitor McMurrin as well. Haycock and Romney took careful notes of McMurrin's address, then reported back to the First Presidency.[112]

Approximately 150 people attended the event.[113] The philosopher spoke extemporaneously for almost an hour, followed by questions from the audience. He left no doubt how much he despised Mormon racial theology: "I feel very keenly the situation in which the Mormon people find themselves, entertaining a religious doctrine of racial discrimination, which certainly is unworthy of a Church and unworthy of a religion and, I believe myself, unworthy of what is in many respects the praiseworthy and great tradition of the Mormon Church." McMurrin explained the origins of Mormon racial discrimination, as he understood it from reading a controversial biography of Joseph Smith by Fawn McKay Brodie, David O. McKay's niece. McMurrin explained, echoing Brodie, that the ban began in Missouri after Latter-day Saints migrated there in the 1830s, "when the slave question was very intense" in that state. The Saints had to convince Missourians that they didn't oppose their pro-slavery policies. To accomplish this, they instituted a priesthood ban for people of African heritage and incorporated harsh rhetoric toward "negroes" into their theology.[114]

McMurrin closed the address with a tantalizing detail that must have greatly unnerved the First Presidency and Apostle Smith. The philosopher said that "there is far more of a liberal attitude" on the Mormon race question than most people would suspect, and he cryptically noted that a general authority had explained to him "not very long ago that he did not believe that the Negroes were under any kind of curse and as far as he was concerned this was not a doctrine of the Church, and never was." He didn't say who the general authority was, but he teased the audience that it wasn't a bishop or stake president but a high-ranking leader. Few, if any, in the room could have known that McMurrin was talking about church president McKay as his source. That disclosure would come years later. But for now, McMurrin was simply content to let his audience know that not everyone in the high church leadership believed in the sanctity of the ban.[115]

McMurrin's address electrified the audience, about half of whom were Black. The NAACP enthusiastically reported that McMurrin gave an "enlightened" and "very inspiring message." Mormon intellectuals too raved about the address. Others who didn't attend heard about the address and asked McMurrin for copies, which he enthusiastically provided.[116] However, the address flustered Lowell Bennion, who heard about it from a friend. "You purportedly called our refusal to give the negro the priesthood a doctrine," he wrote McMurrin, asking for a copy of the address. "It occurs to me that we should call it a practice. If we could call this thing . . . a practice, it would be much easier to change." After quibbling a bit, McMurrin concurred and admitted that Bennion had made a "very good" point.[117]

How did the First Presidency respond? The meeting minutes record that McMurrin's talk "was under consideration," but they didn't elaborate further.[118]

★ ★ ★

Sterling McMurrin wasn't the only Mormon intellectual the Brethren kept close tabs on. Lowell Bennion had been in the hard-liners' crosshairs ever since he challenged Apostles Smith and Petersen at the teachers' conference. In the spring of 1962, matters heated up when the Brethren received reports that Bennion had told his students the ban would be lifted at the April general conference. He had it on good authority: Hugh B. Brown, the newly called counselor to the First Presidency, informed him that a change was coming.[119] When word circulated among Bennion's students that the ban would be lifted, the Brethren transferred a church employee named Melvin Tagg to the Institute to spy on Bennion. Merle Bennion, Lowell's wife, didn't take the subterfuge lightly. She scoffed that Tagg was "planted at the Institute to report to the Brethren." Bennion's colleague Edgar Lyon was also under surveillance. Lyon confided to "family and close friends" that a "new, young faculty member had been sent as a 'mole' or spy to discover heterodoxy and report it to Commissioner Wilkinson."[120]

It didn't take long for Tagg to find the evidence he was seeking. Bennion and Lyon, who comprised the "liberal wing" at the Institute, were not shy about expressing their views; they told Tagg that the church's race teachings were immoral. That disclosure triggered a chain of events that would ultimately get them fired. After learning of their views, Tagg snitched to Lauritz Petersen of the Church Historian's Office and to Apostle Smith. Troubled by the disclosure, the vigilant apostle asked Petersen to interview students to marshal additional evidence against Bennion and Lyon. After a hasty investigation, Petersen declared that "[f]alse teachings were being taught," the "Church was . . . being attacked from within." He identified the culprits as not only Bennion and Lyon but also their colleague Albert Payne, who complained at a recent faculty meeting that, "by denying the priesthood to the Negro, we discriminate against the colored race."[121] Petersen then compiled his observations in a report to Apostle Smith. The most striking aspect of the report is not just that these men opposed the ban, but the fact that the trio taught that the Brethren are susceptible to "social pressure," which meant, of course, that if other Latter-day Saints pressured them, they'd lift the ban.[122]

But Tagg and Petersen weren't the only ones bothered by Bennion and Lyon's liberal views. In July 1962, another damaging report came to Apostle Smith, this time from Boyd K. Packer and Theodore Tuttle, two lower-ranked general authorities on the Board of Education. Their report made it personal. Both men had taught in the Church Education System with Bennion and Lyon before their call as general authorities. They were all friends. Now Packer and Tuttle had turned on them. They complained to Smith that Bennion and Lyon taught that "the Church would give the priesthood to the worthy Negro" and "that the policy at present of denying them the priesthood was unfair and not in accordance with the justice of God."[123]

Petersen's report, along with Packer and Tuttle's, proved fatal to Bennion and Lyon. The Board fired them from their teaching positions in 1962—but offered them a reassignment writing church manuals. (Only Lyon accepted.) The Board never said why they took action against the popular instructors, and both men were understandably distraught over losing their teaching positions. Bennion took the news especially hard. He had worked for the Church Education System for nearly twenty-eight years and no one had the decency to tell him why he had been terminated. The fact that President McKay and Hugh B. Brown failed to protect him from the hard-liners added to his grief. McKay never provided a reason to Bennion, but given his advanced age and frail health it's possible that he couldn't muster the energy to fight them.[124] Brown, by contrast, was quite vocal in his support for Bennion, but he lacked the clout on the Board to save his friend's job.[125]

In any event, the ouster humiliated Bennion, and he confronted Wilkinson's deputy, William Berrett, demanding answers. When Bennion asked why the Board had dismissed him, Berrett gave him an "uncertain, ambiguous answer." Bennion then turned to Chancellor Wilkinson, who did the same. Neither wanted to tell him why he had been fired; it was clear they were protecting the Board. Even so, they offered a hint when they told Bennion that he "might be too liberal," which was a dramatic understatement.[126] Years later Merle Bennion attributed her husband's ouster to Smith and Packer. "I just can't be forgiving," she bitterly reflected. "When [Packer] talks [in general conference], then I turn off the TV. I'm not very forgiving." She had similar feelings about Smith.[127]

Because Berrett and Wilkinson wouldn't reveal why the Board fired them, Bennion and Lyon demanded an opportunity to ask the Board directly.[128] Initially, the Board agreed to grant them a hearing, but they changed their minds after Packer "vigorously" protested. He didn't want to have to answer for his actions. Nothing good would come of it, he told the Board.[129]

A stunned Lyon called Packer's rationale a "weak excuse," but it wasn't a secret who had fired them. Bennion and Lyon rightly suspected that Apostle Smith was behind the purge.[130] George Boyd said that Smith was "the most exercised over the liberal attitude of the Institute faculty on the Negro issue." Another colleague, George Tanner, explained, "The way it looks to me is that the Brethren have suddenly become worried that there is a little too much liberalism among some of our better trained men and they are trying to stamp it out."[131]

When the news trickled out that Bennion and Lyon had been fired, their supporters exploded in anger. Hundreds of current and former students sent protest letters; some even marched outside of church headquarters to show their displeasure.[132] One former student and colleague, Marion D. Hanks, now a general authority, was "deeply disturbed" by the firing and "let it be known." Another former student, David W. Bennett, wrote a pointed letter to the First Presidency, ending it, "May God forgive those men who know not what they do by letting [Bennion and Lyon] go." Meanwhile, a frustrated Wilkinson tried to do damage control. He drafted a public statement that he distributed to news outlets in a desperate and disingenuous attempt to assure critics that Bennion and Lyon had been promoted by being reassigned. But Wilkinson knew this wasn't true, and Bennion and Lyon knew it too. The reassignment was simply a ruse to remove the liberal instructors from the classroom.[133]

Apostle Smith also called Bennion's termination a reassignment, informing an inquisitor, "We needed him somewhere else." He echoed the same talking points about Lyon.[134] In private, though, Smith responded to Bennion and Lyon's predicament with a cold indifference, writing in his diary that he "received a number of letters of protest because of the release of Drs. Bennion and Lyon who [had] been at the Institute for a number of years. I have also interviewed some students who were taught by them and reached the conclusion that the change and release was in order."[135]

News of the terminations shocked Bennion and Lyon's colleagues, and many feared that they might be next. Amplifying their concerns was Apostle Mark E. Petersen, who fired a warning shot across the bow. In July 1962, he told Church Education System teachers that the Brethren only wanted teachers of "fundamental orthodox doctrine and truth." Petersen pledged that any teacher who is "in the least opposed to Church doctrine" would be dismissed. With the civil rights movement gaining steam, and with critics carping at them over civil rights, the Brethren didn't want unorthodox teachers like Bennion and Lyon adding fuel to the fire.[136]

4

Civil Rights Resistance, 1962–1967

If the hard-liners intended to stifle critics by harassing church liberals, they failed spectacularly. Soon pressure to lift the ban was coming from within the First Presidency itself. Hugh B. Brown became a general authority later in life, but rose quickly through the ranks. Called as an assistant to the Quorum of the Twelve Apostles at the age of seventy, then into the Quorum of the Twelve itself at age seventy-eight, it took him just eight years to become David O. McKay's counselor in the First Presidency.[1]

Brown didn't quite fit the profile of a typical LDS general authority. He was a liberal Democrat in a church hierarchy dominated by conservative Republicans, and a Canadian surrounded by men from the American West—an outsider.[2] Brown was beloved by Mormon intellectuals—including his good friends Sterling McMurrin and Lowell Bennion—but distrusted by the hard-liners. That distrust intensified when Brown began lobbying McKay to end the ban. As Charles Brown, the apostle's son, explained, "Dad had a very decided view on the Negro in the Priesthood and he stood almost alone among the Brethren in that."[3]

Brown's ambitious effort to end the ban occurred during a precarious time. The Brethren believed that it was imprudent of Brown to push to end the ban when George Romney, a Mormon governor from Michigan, emerged as a presidential candidate just as the civil rights movement gained momentum. If the ban was lifted, they believed, it would signal to members that they had caved from outside pressure. Apostle Ezra Taft Benson's right-wing extremism also posed a challenge. He linked Martin Luther King Jr. to communism and sought to undermine Hugh B. Brown's and N. Eldon Tanner's negotiations with the NAACP as they discussed civil rights.

94   SECOND-CLASS SAINTS

The friction between the NAACP, Benson, and Brown might have vanished had the Brethren lifted the ban and supported civil rights. But the hard-liners couldn't bring themselves to do it, so Brown pressured them.

★ ★ ★

The Brethren kicked off 1962 with exciting news. On January 3, they received word that four thousand Nigerians "had converted to the truth of the gospel and are appealing for baptism and membership in the Church."[4] Letters from Nigerians interested in baptism had been pouring into church headquarters. In the fall of 1961, McKay had sent LaMar Williams, a church missionary employee, to visit Nigeria to determine whether they were sincere. The Brethren knew that creating a Nigerian mission wouldn't be easy. Hugh Brown observed that it would be "a precedent establishing decision."[5] The church had never successfully established a mission in a predominantly Black country before. In 1853, four White missionaries from Utah made an ill-fated attempt to preach to Black Jamaicans, but after proselytizing for a short period on the balmy island they concluded that Jamaica was "[a] verry poor place for our doctrine."[6] After the struggles in South Africa and Brazil, few church leaders seemed ready to take on what could be an even more difficult challenge in Nigeria. Underlying it all was the priesthood ban. As McKay nervously explained, "white men" would have to go into "Nigeria to preside over a Branch of the Church if and when one is organized."[7]

And yet President McKay felt compelled to push ahead in Nigeria. He believed that the time was right to "preach the gospel unto every creature." The sheer number of letters coming into church headquarters had given him a sense of exuberance that he hadn't experienced in years.[8]

Following months of intense discussions with the apostles, and after a recommendation from Williams, in March 1962 the First Presidency decided to open a mission in Nigeria. It would operate under the West European Mission, headquartered in England, with Apostle N. Eldon Tanner as the inaugural president; Williams would assist him. The First Presidency didn't want "any public announcement or fanfare." Everyone in the upper leadership knew the operation was risky.[9] With the civil rights movement in full swing, they worried how it would look to have White missionaries running all-Black churches. At the same time, George Romney, a practicing Latter-day Saint, was running for governor of Michigan—a state with "a very large negro population."[10] The First Presidency instructed Williams not to depart until after the election in November, fearing that "certain politicians might take the view" that the church had established a Nigerian mission "to influence the negro vote in favor of Romney."[11]

There were other difficulties too. The logistical challenges of establishing churches when so many Nigerians wanted to be baptized were daunting. The Brethren also feared that after Nigerians joined the church, they might migrate to Utah, increasing the risk of interracial marriage. And they feared that if word got out that they were baptizing Nigerians, it would invite criticism of the church's race doctrine from "southern negroes" aligned with the NAACP.[12]

Hugh Brown saw an opportunity. Lifting the priesthood and temple ban would solve two problems. It would allow Nigerians to run their own churches but also quell criticism from civil rights groups back home. In a First Presidency meeting in January 1962 with McKay and counselor Henry

Hugh B. Brown, David O. McKay's counselor in the First Presidency and staunch advocate for overturning the priesthood and temple ban, 1960s. Courtesy of Utah State Historical Society.

D. Moyle, Brown proposed giving Nigerians the Aaronic Priesthood, or "lesser priesthood"—a proposal that J. Reuben Clark had considered years earlier with Afrikaners. (Clark had died the previous year.) LaMar Williams had made the same recommendation.[13]

Brown gave the proposal a lot of thought and concluded that, while they couldn't serve in leadership positions, holders of the Aaronic Priesthood would be able to "administer the Sacrament and baptize" fellow Nigerians. McKay, intrigued by Brown's proposal, weighed it carefully. He knew it made logistical sense to have Nigerians run their own congregations, but he feared that if the Brethren gave them the lesser priesthood, they'd demand the higher priesthood. "You do that and you give them the [Melchizedek] Priesthood," the president warned Brown. That was precisely what Brown had in mind.[14]

As the Brethren debated, Brown confided to a church member in March 1962 that the priesthood ban "is having more constant and serious attention by the First Presidency and the Twelve than at any time, I think, in the history of the Church."[15] A few weeks earlier he had summoned Lowell Bennion to his office at church headquarters to inform him that a change "was coming" at the April general conference. He said that President McKay would lift the ban and ordain Nigerians to the Aaronic Priesthood.[16]

The meeting lasted thirty-five minutes. Afterward, Bennion rushed to tell his close friend Edgar Lyon the good news. Lyon scribbled down notes as fast as he could:

> President Brown told [Lowell] that President McKay had discussed the Negro question with the Presidency and the Twelve within the past week or two; everyone spoke. "Almost to a man," they agreed that a change would have to take place. President McKay said a change must come, but he didn't know when it would be. Said this Negro question was the greatest issue the church had faced since plural marriage.[17]

Bennion also told two African American Latter-day Saints, Abner Howell and Ruffin Bridgeforth, that a change was imminent.[18] And he informed George Romney as well: "I have it on good authority that the brethren are deeply concerned and most of them feel that something must be done" on "the Negro problem."[19]

Last, Bennion shared the news with his students. Frederick Buchanan recorded the exciting news in his diary: "The priesthood will be given to the Negroes sooner than we think."[20] Two weeks later he wrote again: "Lowell

CIVIL RIGHTS RESISTANCE 97

Bennion mentioned this week that the General Authorities are agreed that the Negro should have the priesthood—the only thing is when? They're afraid of the effect on the Southern States and South Africa."[21]

As anticipation mounted among Bennion and his friends, the April general conference came and went without a change. What happened? Brown seems to have engaged in some wishful thinking. McKay hadn't agreed to grant Nigerians the Aaronic Priesthood; he only considered it. The president didn't give any indication in quorum meetings that he supported Brown's proposal. McKay believed that lifting the ban would require a revelation and that all the apostles would have to be onboard with such a drastic move. The hard-liners wouldn't allow it.

Even so, Brown didn't give up. During another meeting with the First Presidency, on October 11, the counselor pushed again to confer priesthood ordination on Nigerians. He had "hoped that the time would come when we could give them the Aaronic Priesthood." Brown told McKay that it was "one of the saddest things in the policy of the Church. In years past we have baptized the negro. They have been faithful and just as faithful as any human beings can be and their children have attended Sunday School and Primary and they have associated with our children in Primary." McKay listened to his counselor's plea but wasn't convinced. He denied him again.[22]

The following year Brown pressed the issue a third time, now much more forcefully. Violating an unspoken quorum rule by disclosing sensitive deliberations, he told *New York Times* reporter Wallace Turner, "We are in the midst of a survey [now] looking toward the possibility of admitting Negroes." Turner took the quote and ran with it, writing, "The top leadership of the Mormon church is seriously considering the abandonment of its historic policy of discrimination against Negroes." The *Times* ran the piece under the headline "Mormons Weigh Negro Stand: May End Ban on Complete Membership in Church." Two days later the *Chicago Tribune* republished it as "Negro Is Considered by Mormons: Church May Abandon Its Discrimination."[23]

Brown's leak rattled church headquarters. McKay angrily declared that Brown should "straighten the matter out," while Apostle Spencer W. Kimball observed that "the First Presidency are much disturbed and embarrassed by the N.Y. Times article."[24] Exasperated with the outspoken counselor, the Brethren confronted Brown, demanding an explanation. Brown replied that he had been "misquoted." But this wasn't true. A church public relations employee had heard the entire interview and confirmed its accuracy, as did Turner himself, who stated that the "quotes that appeared in the story were precisely the words spoken by Mr. Brown."[25]

Especially flustered by Brown's brazen act was Joseph Fielding Smith, a rock-ribbed institutionalist, who zealously protected the Brethren's private discussions from his position as president of the Quorum of the Twelve. In an interview published in *Look* magazine just a few months after Brown's interview with the *New York Times*, the senior apostle bluntly declared, "The Negro cannot achieve the Priesthood in the Mormon Church." Smith didn't give even the slightest hint that the Brethren had been discussing the topic in their meetings.[26] But behind the apostle's calm demeanor was frustration that one of their own had violated the quorum's secrecy rule. Not only had Brown disclosed deliberations that should have remained private, but he also undercut a public relations strategy that Smith himself had devised the previous year. Smith told a *Time* magazine journalist that "the [LDS] Church does and can do more for the Negro pertaining to his salvation than any other Church in existence." Smith reiterated this strategy with the LDS *Church News*, asserting that the "Negro who accepts the doctrines of the church and is baptized by an authorized minister of the Church . . . is entitled to salvation in the celestial kingdom of the highest heaven. . . . What other Church can make a better promise?" he asked. In a private letter to an inquisitor, he acknowledged that other "so-called Christian churches" could place Black people in ministerial positions, but they didn't have the "Divine Priesthood."[27]

Brown's interview with the *Times* revealed that Smith's comments were both erroneous and misleading, given that Mormons needed the priesthood and temple ordinances to achieve "Exaltation" in the Celestial Kingdom.[28]

Meanwhile, as the Brethren dealt with the fallout from Brown's interview, Jeff Nye, a former BYU student, wrote an article for the popular magazine *Look* that also embarrassed the church. Nye portrayed Apostle Smith as the mastermind behind the church's race doctrine and characterized him as an out-of-touch rube who couldn't adjust to the times. He singled out the apostle's controversial statement from *The Way to Perfection* that "negroes belonged to an inferior race." Nye sneered, "The Negro is a junior partner in my Church" and declared that "he cannot hold the priesthood and the priesthood is the foundation of the Church."[29]

Called for comment, Smith didn't help his cause when he denied that he ever said demeaning things about African Americans, which his own writings demonstrated to be untrue.[30] He informed the magazine, "The Mormon Church does not believe, nor does it teach, that the Negro is an inferior being." Instead, Smith expressed a favorable view of African Americans, noting that they are "capable of great achievement," even more so in some cases than "the white race." They can become doctors, scientists, lawyers, whatever they want, Smith said, which sounded eerily similar to Apostle Mark E. Petersen's condescending remarks to the Church Education System (CES) educators some ten years earlier. Smith's most memorable line, however, would come back to haunt him in the years ahead. He told *Look*, "I would not want you to believe that we bear any animosity toward the Negro. 'Darkies' are wonderful people, and they have their place in the Church."[31]

★ ★ ★

Hugh Brown had a stubborn streak that didn't always fly at church headquarters. He insisted that the ban was a "policy," while his colleagues proclaimed it "doctrine." But what was at stake here was more than a finely spun theological dispute. The hard-liners insisted that it would require a revelation to lift the ban, while Brown believed that it could be lifted at the president's discretion. Brown didn't appeal to a particular scripture to justify his position, but the hard-liners believed that the scriptures, particularly the Doctrine and Covenants, justified theirs. It stipulated that a revelation required unanimity among the Quorum of the Twelve and First Presidency, which, of course, underscored the challenges Brown faced. Brown knew he didn't have a consensus. The only apostles besides him who supported overturning the ban—John Widtsoe and Adam Bennion— were now dead.[32]

Brown became increasingly isolated from his colleagues. The hard-liners resented his activism, but more important, they resented his certainty that the ban didn't align with Mormon scripture or the revelations of Joseph Smith. When Brown pestered President McKay about lifting it, the president tried to calm him by assuring him that a change would come at some point. That was McKay's subtle way of saying that he wasn't certain when the hard-liners would agree to lift the ban, or whether they would agree to lift it at all. Like Brown, McKay knew that it would be difficult to convince them, for the hard-liners had fixed, rigid views of Mormon scripture. Apostle Smith was the most formidable holdup. He was next in line for the church presidency and had just published, or was in the process of publishing, two multivolume books—*Doctrines of Salvation* and *Answers to Gospel Questions*—that reaffirmed the church's antiblack teachings.[33]

But Smith wasn't the only hard-liner with entrenched views. Harold B. Lee and Bruce R. McConkie, Smith's son-in-law, shared a similar commitment to preserving the priesthood and temple ban. Next to Smith, Lee was the most influential apostle during the 1950s and 1960s. Latter-day Saints knew him as the chief architect of the church's correlation program, designed to maintain doctrinal orthodoxy. He was also known for his innovation in creating a church welfare program meant to combat poverty during the Great Depression.[34] Fellow apostle Marion G. Romney said that Lee "was the most influential man in the Twelve" during the post–World II years. "He was like the Prophet Joseph [Smith]."[35]

With his sharp jawline and deep baritone voice, Lee exuded confidence. He was ordained an apostle in 1941 at the age of forty-two, making him the youngest apostle in the quorum at the time. His daughter Helen said he had a "very quick" temper, and his associates commented that he couldn't seem to "accept criticism." But perhaps more important, Lee couldn't entertain the thought of lifting the ban, which he told a group of CES teachers was "silly" to even consider.[36] The only sermon he had ever given on Mormon racial teachings was forceful and hard-hitting. He talked about "enlightened races" and "favored lineages," audaciously claiming that God would lift the curse on Black people in the resurrection to make them "white and delightsome"—all of which drew a polite, but gentle, rebuke from J. Reuben Clark, who complained that Lee "was just a little severe in [his] treatment of the negroes and the curse placed upon them."[37]

McConkie, a member of the First Quorum of the Seventy and a future member of the Quorum of the Twelve, was another leader with strong opinions about the ban. At six foot five inches, he was an imposing man who looked more like a drill sergeant than a churchman. He had a tight-cropped crew cut and unusually large hands and feet and spoke and wrote in a manner reflective of his training in the law. Rigid and dogmatic, McConkie had a reputation in the church for his pulpit-pounding sermons and fiery jeremiads.[38] Some members deplored his style. Others condemned his unrelenting aggressiveness in calling members to repentance.[39]

McConkie's magnum opus was *Mormon Doctrine*, a massive, encyclopedic work that sold tens of thousands of copies and went through several editions over a fifty-year period. The LDS *Church News* called it "one of the

Bruce R. McConkie, member of the First Quorum of Seventy (later a church apostle) and author of the best-selling book *Mormon Doctrine* (1958), ca. 1946. Courtesy of Utah State Historical Society.

most complete reference works ever published"; another report said it was "[a] must for every L.D.S. library."[40] In it, McConkie made a number of statements about Black people that shaped how generations of Latter-day Saints would view the ban. He asserted that Black people "are not equal with other races" and unabashedly claimed that Cain was "the father of the Negroes." He also declared that segregation was God's will and warned obsessively against interracial marriage, proclaiming it a sign of "racial degeneration."[41]

Another firebrand was Ezra Taft Benson. A solemn man seldom inclined to laugh or joke, he sometimes began his sermons by stating, "The message I bring is not a happy one." Benson, who served as secretary of agriculture in the Eisenhower administration, never authored a theological work and seldom sermonized on theological matters. Instead, he preached a radical brand of Cold War conservatism. For example, he declared that he felt "no compunction to make the Church popular with liberals, Socialists, or Communists," and he railed incessantly against the Democratic Party, labor unions, and government welfare programs—all of which he decried as precursors to communism.[42] Benson embraced the far-out conspiracy theories of FBI director J. Edgar Hoover and John Birch Society founder Robert Welch, two figures who convinced him that the civil rights movement had been hijacked by communists. Just as important, Benson associated with White supremacists, stumped with them at segregationist rallies, and counted them as friends and advisers. He called Black people the "seed of Cain" and church members "apostates" when they complained that the Brethren were not "at the forefront of the so-called civil rights movement."[43]

Then there were so-called moderates, including President McKay, Apostle Spencer W. Kimball, and general authority Marion D. Hanks. Perhaps no one was more conflicted over Mormon racial teachings than Kimball. He told his son Edward that the ban may have been a "possible error." He visited South America in the 1950s and was moved by the number of "negro" Latter-day Saints he met who anguished over the ban.[44] Kimball knew that the exclusionary policy affected Black Mormons deeply, both spiritually and emotionally, and yet he wanted to uphold the teachings of the church. He once told a Latter-day Saint that there was "no scripture to prove that the negroes were neutral in the War in Heaven," but he recommended *The Way to Perfection* when inquisitors asked about the ban, noting that Smith's discussion of Abraham chapter 2 would answer any questions about the church's race doctrine.[45] Kimball rejected these views years later when he became the church president, but in the 1960s he affirmed them.

Hanks was another moderate. Before he was called into the First Quorum of the Seventy in 1953—a rank just below the Quorum of the Twelve—Hanks taught in the LDS Seminary and Institute program, where he worked with Lowell Bennion, Edgar Lyon, and other liberals. In fact, he fondly quoted the late Apostle John A. Widtsoe, who declared that "negroes are *supposed* to be [Cain's] descendants." Like Widtsoe, Hanks found scriptural support for neither this claim nor the widely held hard-line belief that the scriptures spoke of a divine curse. His son Richard recalled years later that his father "never felt comfortable with the priesthood ban." Just as significant, Hanks told President McKay that he opposed the ban and even tussled with Apostle Lee over it: "I told Elder Lee, I can't believe that . . . blacks are inferior to whites. I don't believe that."[46]

CIVIL RIGHTS RESISTANCE

But moderates and liberals were far outnumbered. And it wasn't just the leadership that opposed them. Most Latter-day Saints accepted the church's racial theology as essential doctrine. Some even criticized those who questioned the ban. "When a man raises the Negro issue," noted Glenn Pearson, a conservative BYU religion professor, "he really means that he does not believe we have prophets and are guided by God through divine communication." Other Latter-day Saints defended the ban in highly popular books. John J. Stewart's *Mormonism and the Negro* and John L. Lund's *The Church and the Negro* sold thousands of copies and went through multiple editions, demonstrating that a robust market existed for apologetic defenses of Mormon racial teachings.[47]

All of these factors conspired to thwart Hugh Brown.

★ ★ ★

In December 1963, an agitated George Romney gave a press conference. "He was visibly upset," according to one report. His "voice trembled," and he "slapped his desk repeatedly with his palm." What had set him off? Basil Brown, an African American state senator from Detroit, had given a pointed speech in the state senate the previous day excoriating Romney for belonging to a church that embraced racist teachings. Brown had read Jeff Nye's *Look* article and was appalled to find that Mormon Apostle Joseph Fielding Smith didn't "regard Negroes as human beings on an equal basis with whites." The senator demanded a response: "We Negroes have a right to know whether the major leader of our state submits to this philosophy. Are we and our ancestors branded with the curse of Cain? Someone owes an answer to me."[48]

Romney angrily defended himself. "I have never been taught the inferiority of Negroes and I don't believe in it," he stammered. "I have been taught that every person on this earth is a child of God and thus is entitled to full and complete civil rights." He sidestepped the question about curses and focused instead on his civil rights record: "I ask Senator Brown and others to judge me on the basis of what I have done." In his twenty-three years in Michigan he had spent his time "working to eliminate discrimination and injustice in the fields of housing, employment, education and public accommodations."[49]

Romney wasn't truthful when he said that he had never been taught that Black people were inferior to White people. He was born in 1907 and came of age in the church when *The Way to Perfection* was taught in Mormon Sunday School classes. Thus, he would have learned about Smith's teachings at church and probably at home. But Romney wasn't about to admit that, so he resorted to a line that he developed during his gubernatorial campaign calling attention to his support for civil rights, while ignoring questions of his church's position on race. It was an effective strategy.[50]

The Brethren had been anxiously watching Romney's rise in politics for quite some time. They held him in high esteem. Not only had he served honorably as a stake president in Michigan, but he was well-connected in the church. His first cousin was Apostle Marion G. Romney, and he came from a prominent polygamous family from the Mormon colonies in Mexico.[51] "We count you as one of our most devoted and most respected [members] in the church today," Apostle Lee told him. In 1974, Apostle LeGrand Richards nominated him to fill a vacancy in the Quorum of the Twelve, demonstrating how respected the Mormon governor was in high church circles. In the nomination letter, Richards praised Romney as "one of the great Missionaries of the Church," a man with a "strong testimony" of the gospel.[52]

Nevertheless, even though the Brethren liked and respected Romney, they were nervous when he announced his gubernatorial bid in 1962 and were even more nervous the following year when Republican Party operatives urged him to run for the presidency. The Brethren knew the church's race doctrine would be a major talking point in the media. Journalists had criticized the church's race teachings during Benson's tenure in Eisenhower's cabinet, and that would surely intensify during a presidential campaign.[53] Apostle Kimball lamented "that nearly every time George Romney is mentioned in the press, the Negro question is tied to him." Apostle Smith grumbled that should Romney become a candidate, "enemies will play up the Negro question to the very limit."[54]

Romney understood that a campaign could be perilous for the church, which is why he sought the First Presidency's blessing when he ran for governor. They considered telling him not to run, but ultimately President McKay advised him to "make his own decision without any feeling that if he decides to run it will be detrimental to the church."[55] Clearly, their concerns were justified, not only because of Senator Brown but also because of the Associated Negro Press, whose reporter P. L. Prattis took delight in mocking Romney for deflecting questions about his church's race teachings. Prattis pointed out that Romney always turned these questions into statements about how he personally supported civil rights, and the reporter wasn't having it. "Now isn't that quite something," Prattis jeered. "In essence, he is telling us that wherever it is politically desirable he is prepared to ignore the mandates of his church. This is what is known as blatant hypocrisy."[56]

No one, though, stoked the flames more vigorously than syndicated columnist Clare Boothe Luce, billed as "one of America's most brilliant women." A former congresswoman, ambassador, author, playwright, and managing editor of *Vanity Fair*—as well as the wife of Henry Luce, the most powerful magazine publisher in the United States—Luce had an international reputation.[57] Millions of people read her columns, which is why the Brethren winced when she published a critical assessment of Romney as the potential 1964 Republican nominee for president. "Romney, as well as his church," holds "the human dignity of the Negroes in low esteem," she noted acidly, adding, with Hugh Brown's recent *New York Times* interview in mind, "A hopeful sign for Gov. Romney's candidacy is that his co-religionists seem to be having second thoughts on the subject, and there are indications that the Mormon doctrine on Negroes may soon be repealed."[58]

Luce's tone angered the First Presidency, and President McKay asked his counselor, Henry D. Moyle, to rebut her. Moyle was well-equipped for the task. A lawyer by training, he was an aggressive personality, a blustery man full of opinions.[59] He was also arrogant, brash—and rich. Before his rise to the apostleship in 1947 and the First Presidency in 1959, he had made a fortune in the oil and railroad businesses using his training in the law to negotiate deals that netted him millions of dollars. He was also known in the Mormon community for his controversial "baseball baptism" program and for investing church funds in a variety of businesses and properties that nearly bankrupted the church.[60] But in this instance Moyle didn't display his considerable rhetorical talents nor demonstrate the pugnaciousness for which he was known. Perhaps McKay and Brown toned him down after they read a draft; perhaps Moyle himself recognized the futility of writing a combative response.[61]

In any event, Moyle assumed a defensive posture to convince Luce that Mormon racial teachings were not as harsh on the "negro" as she claimed. He acknowledged that Luce was correct in that the church didn't ordain

106 SECOND-CLASS SAINTS

Black members to the priesthood, but he noted that they could be baptized and even qualify for the "Celestial or highest Kingdom of God" if they were worthy. "We therefore, may be pardoned," he wrote, borrowing a line from Joseph Fielding Smith, "when we say that we have more to offer the negro than any other church." Moyle also made clear that the church had no intention of lifting the priesthood and temple ban until the Mormon president received a revelation. "When or if such a revelation is to be received, obviously we do not know."[62]

Luce's piece also infuriated Romney, and he, too, pushed back. In a strongly worded letter he told her that she misrepresented his "religious views" and harbored "religious bias and prejudice" against his church. What rankled Romney the most was that Luce claimed Mormonism "teaches that Negroes have souls inferior to souls of men of all other races." Romney knew, of course, that Luce was correct. Even so, he wasn't about to concede that point to a prominent journalist like Luce because he feared it would doom his chances for national office.[63]

Luce wasn't the only critical writer during the fall and winter of 1963. Scores of journalists published sharp criticisms of Mormon racial teachings, specifically condemning the church's silence on civil rights. The *Montreal Gazette* reported, "The Mormon Church had remained aloof from a current drive for equal rights, and integrationists feel this is hurting their cause." The *Daytona Beach Morning Journal* in Florida noted, "It's bad enough being a Negro any place, but in Utah you're told that you're bearing some damned curse to boot."[64]

★ ★ ★

As Romney and the church came under heavy fire from Basil Brown, Clare Boothe Luce, and others, they also took heat from one of their own, a liberal Mormon bishop named J. D. Williams, who detested the church's race doctrine.[65] An influential political science professor at the University of Utah, a lifelong Democrat, and a member of the NAACP, Williams wasn't afraid to criticize the Brethren on the race issue or any other matter. He had already pointed out the flaws in Mark Petersen's pro-segregationist address, and years later he would lampoon Apostle Benson's right-wing extremism in a salty article called "The Separation of Church and State in Mormon Theory and Practice." But in 1962, Williams reserved his most forceful salvo for Mormon lawmakers. That year, as the civil rights movement surged, he

CIVIL RIGHTS RESISTANCE

wrote a scathing article in *Pen Magazine* lamenting that "minority rights in Utah" weren't any better than in Mississippi. Williams didn't admit this lightly. He knew that Utah was one of only two western states without civil rights protections, and he believed that the LDS church was largely responsible.[66] He based his conclusions on a 1960 national civil rights report, which noted that Black people were confined through zoning laws to "the least desirable areas of Salt Lake City and Ogden"; they were not "admitted to barber shops, beauty parlors," and other public spaces; and they suffered because of a Mormon tenet equating their skin color with sin.[67]

Williams, however, took some satisfaction the following year, when Utah lawmakers struck down the state's antiquated interracial marriage laws—about four years before the U.S. Supreme Court decision in *Loving v. Virginia.* LDS church leaders worked with prominent community members to initiate this change.[68] Mormon men had been marrying "nisei girls" (women of Japanese ancestry) in violation of the statute, and both church and community leaders wanted these unions to be recognized. Apostle Gordon B. Hinckley was quite candid about this, as was Alice Kasai, a Japanese American activist in Utah, who lobbied for the bill. Kasai was relieved that Hinckley and his colleagues supported the bill, but she knew they had reservations about it. The Brethren feared that Black and White couples could now marry, which would "curse" their offspring and disqualify them from the priesthood and temple. President McKay wondered whether the church "had better put up with a little inconvenience regarding interracial marriage to avoid greater troubles" later.[69]

As the legislature quietly repealed Utah's interracial marriage statute, the NAACP seized on the results of the 1960 civil rights report to press the LDS church to fight racial injustice.[70] They demanded that the Brethren lobby Mormon lawmakers to support two civil rights bills then up for debate in the legislature. Albert Fritz, president of the Salt Lake branch of the NAACP, hand-delivered a letter to the "church heads" at LDS headquarters apprising them of the NAACP's intentions to protest at the October 1963 general conference if the Brethren didn't support the bills. Joining them, he said, would be dozens of students from the University of Utah, who also opposed the church's inaction on civil rights. "Some of the University students already had placards, picket signs made to picket the church conference," Fritz noted. He further explained, "Negro citizens [and] other minorities are denied their rights along with foreign students, and Negro

108   SECOND-CLASS SAINTS

tourists are insulted by being refused service in public places of accommodations. We feel that now is the time to end these indignities to human
beings."[71]

Fritz's letter caught the Brethren off-guard, and they scrambled to secure
a meeting with him. Sterling McMurrin, a member of the NAACP and
the newly appointed commissioner of education in the Kennedy administration, arranged for Hugh Brown and Eldon Tanner, McKay's counselors,
to meet with NAACP leaders. "I remember [Brown]," Fritz recalled years
later, "because I met with him personally. He was a wonderful man."[72]
Three other members of the NAACP branch in Salt Lake—Danny Burnett,
Charles Nabors, and Florence Lillian Dahl—joined Fritz at the meeting.
Burnett recalled, "We didn't ask them to change the church doctrine [on
Black members]. We didn't attack the church doctrine. We went down and
told them about all the discrimination in the Mormon mecca right here.
We asked the Mormon officials to speak out against it," but they refused.
"We don't know of any discrimination," they reportedly said. The group
persisted and gave Tanner a "list of proclamations" they wanted him to
issue at the conference. Neither counselor agreed to it, prompting a heated
rejoinder from Burnett: "This is your city, your town. This is happening
here, in your city and we're sure that it [would have] a tremendous impact
if [you] would speak out against these things. They refused to do it."[73]

After nearly two hours the meeting ended with no assurances. Both
counselors knew they would have to obtain permission from President
McKay to make such a bold statement—and it was unlikely that permission would be forthcoming. After some coaxing, however, McKay agreed
to let Brown read a statement in general conference endorsing civil rights.
Brown asked his good friend McMurrin to write it. Out of deference to
the apostles who opposed civil rights, McKay instructed Brown to present
the statement as his own, not an official pronouncement of the church.
Brown, however, ignored the president's instructions. As he stood at the
podium, he paused, read the statement, then began his address "giving the
impression," McMurrin later explained, "that this was . . . an official statement of church policy from the First Presidency."[74]

By Mormon standards, it was a bold statement:

During recent months both in Salt Lake City and across the nation considerable interest has been expressed in the position of the Church of Jesus Christ
of Latter-day Saints in the matter of civil rights. We would like it to be known
that there is in this Church no doctrine, belief, or practice that is intended to

deny the enjoyment of full civil rights by any person regardless of race, color, or creed. We again say, as we have said many times before, that we believe that all men are the children of the same God and that it is a moral evil for any person or group of persons to deny to any human being the right to gainful employment, to full educational opportunity, and to every privilege of citizenship, just as it is a moral evil to deny him the right to worship according to the dictates of his own conscience. We have consistently and persistently upheld the Constitution of the United States, and as far as we are concerned that means upholding the constitutional rights of every citizen of the United States. We call upon all men everywhere, both within and outside the Church, to commit themselves to the establishment of full civil equality for all of God's children. Anything less than this defeats our high ideal of the brotherhood of man.[75]

McKay didn't comment on what he thought of Brown's stunt, but Spencer Kimball recognized it as an "official statement." Brown himself called it "the Church's stand on this subject."[76]

How did the NAACP respond to Brown's statement? They were divided. Although they called off the march when they heard Brown speak on the radio, some members "said that [Brown's] statement was flimsy. It wasn't strong enough." Others characterized it as "adequate" but not impressive.[77] They balked that Brown's statement didn't endorse "any stand on any bill," as Brown himself admitted, and this led the Brethren to speculate that the protests would intensify in the coming months unless the church supported specific civil rights bills. Some of the Brethren even predicted that the NAACP would resort to violence until they got what they wanted.[78]

Events outside of Utah heightened their anxiety. The Brethren were alarmed when earlier that year, Birmingham, Alabama, Commissioner of Public Safety Eugene "Bull" Connor unleashed police dogs and fire horses on Black men, women, and children as they marched peacefully to protest the segregationist policies of Birmingham, "the most thoroughly segregated city in the United States." Moreover, Martin Luther King's march on Washington in August 1963, which drew a quarter of a million people, also alarmed them, as did a Klan bombing in September at a Baptist church in Birmingham, where four African American girls were murdered.[79] Apostle Kimball, like millions of Americans, learned about these shocking events from news reports and told his son Edward that civil rights

will become hotter. It would not surprise me to see bloodshed. When you get millions of colored plus the numerous millions of whites marching for freedom "here and now," where will they stop? Will they be satisfied with civil rights? Or will they with power in their hands exercise more than "equal civil rights." Will they move into inter-marriage? Will they be satisfied in the civil area?[80]

That fall brought uncontrollable angst for the Brethren. No one at church headquarters believed that Brown's statement would satisfy critics. Yet the Brethren feared that if the church supported civil rights it would lead to interracial marriage, which J. Reuben Clark had earlier characterized as a "wicked virus."[81] Anxiety turned to gloom in November 1963, when a gunman assassinated President Kennedy, prompting many frantic discussions at church headquarters. Hugh Brown called his death a "shocking tragedy," while Ezra Taft Benson, echoing a Birch line, claimed that communists had killed the president because he wasn't aggressive enough in pursuing civil rights. At the same time, Apostle Delbert L. Stapley irrationally claimed that Kennedy died like other presidents because they "were very active in the Negro cause."[82] No apostle, however, was as unnerved and unsettled at Kennedy's death as Apostle Kimball. Barely able to control his emotions, he feared that violence would befall the Brethren, just as it had the president. "How do you know," Kimball asked his son Edward, "but that some white or black person inflamed by the ever-growing prejudice and persecution complex could do for the President of the Church or some of the Apostles the same act which ended the life of Mr. Kennedy, the President of the United States?"[83]

As the Brethren agonized over civil rights protestors, the national media continued to condemn the church's race teachings. Most significant, the church's tepid endorsement of civil rights posed a serious problem for Governor Romney.[84] After interviewing the governor in 1964, journalist Wallace Turner came away convinced that Romney "deeply regrets his church's position on Negroes," yet he "never said this or hinted it with words. But the impression was inescapable as he talked of the problem."[85]

Disagreeing with his church on civil rights must have been frustrating for Romney. He wanted to be loyal to the Brethren, yet knew that if he didn't support civil rights it would harm his ambitions for national office. But to his credit, Romney continued to affirm support for racial equality. He forged "a bond" with Martin Luther King Jr. and marched at various civil rights rallies, making his views on civil rights "well known and well publicized." Some of the Brethren couldn't tolerate his openness in expressing views they wished he'd keep silent.[86]

CIVIL RIGHTS RESISTANCE

Nowhere was this frustration more vividly illustrated than when Romney spoke at a January 1964 Republican fundraiser in Salt Lake City. Nearly fourteen hundred people attended this event at the Hotel Utah on a brilliant, snowy evening. Among them were Apostle Richard L. Evans, who served as master of ceremonies, First Presidency counselor N. Eldon Tanner, who gave a prayer, and Apostle Delbert L. Stapley. Romney gave a "fiery talk urging equal rights for all citizens," the *Salt Lake Tribune* reported. His most pointed criticism was aimed at so-called patriotic groups like the John Birch Society. "They offered no constructive solutions to the problems of our nation," Romney thundered. "They pledge allegiance to rigid creeds and dictatorial leaders. Theirs is a heritage of brown shirts and of black shirts, of massed flags and massed drums."[87]

Romney had an uphill battle in trying to convince his party to support the Civil Rights Act of 1964. The GOP's most influential voices—Republican presidential nominee Barry Goldwater and prominent conservative pundit William F. Buckley—both opposed it. They stressed personal choice and states' rights and said that business owners should be free to associate with anyone they wanted.[88] By contrast, moderates within the party emphasized that antidiscrimination laws superseded a business owner's right to freedom of choice in who they would serve and do business with. George Romney, Nelson Rockefeller, and Richard Nixon were the most prominent Republicans taking this position.[89]

As these ideological battles fractured the Republican Party, they also affected the LDS church. Lowell Bennion and Hugh Brown both called Romney's presentation "first-rate," in obvious agreement with the moderates.[90] But President McKay and Apostle Benson sided with the hard-right conservatives, as did Apostle Stapley, who called the Civil Rights Act of 1964 "vicious legislation." Romney's position on the historic act so frustrated Stapley that he wrote the governor a pointed letter trying to dissuade him from supporting racial equality. "It wasn't right," he told Romney, for the federal government "to force any class or race of people upon those of a different social order or race classification." "People are happier," the apostle said, "when placed in the environment and association of like interests, racial instincts, habits, and natural groupings."[91]

Romney ignored him.

★ ★ ★

In July 1964, Congress passed the Civil Rights Act, prompting President McKay to remark that "the Negro will now have to prove himself."[92] The act mandated that all public facilities be desegregated and provided protections in housing and employment. But in Utah questions still lingered over the LDS church's commitment to racial equality. In the spring of 1965, Adam Duncan, an LDS lawyer and congressman from Salt Lake, with support from Marion D. Hanks and the NAACP, introduced two bills in the Utah legislature that would protect against discrimination in jobs and housing. Church leaders remained silent. N. Eldon Tanner stated, "[C]ivil rights legislation is not a moral question and therefore not a church matter."[93]

Here, quite predictably, the Brethren diverged sharply from Presidents Kennedy and Johnson—as well as Martin Luther King and other Black leaders—who proclaimed civil rights a "moral issue."[94] And yet, Black people in Utah were routinely discriminated against in employment and housing by Latter-day Saints who couldn't seem to untether themselves from the church's race teachings. Noted Mormon historian William Mulder found it "ironic that a church professedly with religious values should be silent on civil rights and seek exemption from fair employment legislation. Both of these are eminently religious concerns because they touch human dignity. The right to vote and the right to work without social discrimination or legal disability are ultimately spiritual concerns." Bennion concurred, claiming that he too couldn't understand why his church didn't support civil rights. "If we had faith in Christ," he professed, "we would be anxiously and voluntarily engaged in seeing that Hawaiians, Indians, Negroes, Orientals, and every other ethnic group of people in our midst had equal opportunity for education, culture, employment, and housing as we who are Caucasian." For civil rights leader Albert Fritz, the issue wasn't a lack of faith—it was racial prejudice. He explained that church leaders feared that all-White Mormon neighborhoods would be "invaded by Blacks" if the legislature passed the "fair housing" and "fair employment" bills.[95]

Fritz and his colleague Johnie Driver learned of the church's intention to remain silent on both bills at a March 1965 meeting with Brown and Tanner. Fritz and Driver felt especially aggrieved because most Christian churches in the Salt Lake Valley—the Methodists, Presbyterians, Baptists, United Church of Christ, and the Episcopal churches, along with the "Utah Council of United Church Women"—supported the bills. But Mormons

CIVIL RIGHTS RESISTANCE 113

comprised 90 percent of the legislature, so the bills wouldn't pass without LDS church support. Brown and Tanner wouldn't budge; they had strict orders from President McKay. Fritz and Driver told the counselors the NAACP had no choice but to make good on their threat to protest.[96] On March 10, three days after state troopers beat dozens of African Americans as they marched across the Edmund Pettus Bridge in Selma, Alabama, in what became known as "Bloody Sunday," the Ogden and Salt Lake City branches of the NAACP, along with students at the University of Utah, gathered in downtown Salt Lake. Among the participants was Roy Jefferson, the star of the University of Utah football team, who stood defiantly on the steps of the LDS church administration building with his wife, Camille, and their eleven-month-old son, Marshall, and related that they couldn't find housing because they were Black. Jefferson's testimony deliberately rebutted Eldon Tanner, who told a newspaper reporter that "he knew of no incident where Negroes have had housing problems in Salt Lake City."[97]

The protests spanned three days and drew crowds of up to 350 people. Protestors sang "We Shall Overcome" and prayed. Dr. Palmer S. Ross, minister of the Trinity A.M.E. Church in Salt Lake, asked God for "justice and equal rights," which triggered a rapturous "Amen."[98] Perhaps the most notable speech was by Albert Fritz, who declared, "Much of the difficulty which Negroes . . . face in gaining access to decent housing and securing adequate employment in Utah exists because of the official L.D.S. Church doctrine of exclusion of Negroes from the priesthood." A large poster adorned the backdrop as he spoke. It read, simply, "L.D.S. Church leaders should speak out for moral justice."[99]

The Brethren were astonished at the passion and energy of the protestors and appeared determined to miss the substance of Fritz's speech. In a desperate attempt to quell tension, the church-owned *Deseret News* published an editorial, "A Clear Civil Rights Stand." It merely repeated Brown's statement in general conference, and it didn't fool anyone.[100] Driver, indignant at the church's failure to take the NAACP's concerns seriously, strongly criticized the editorial for ignoring the housing and employment bills. "Again, we call upon the Church of Jesus Christ of Latter-day Saints to put itself on record for fair housing, as many other churches have done, and to begin work to make fair housing *real*, as other churches and organizations are beginning to do."[101]

NAACP members and University of Utah students protest the LDS church's inaction on civil rights at the headquarters of the Church of Jesus Christ of Latter-day Saints, Salt Lake City, March 1965. Courtesy of Special Collections, J. Willard Marriott Library, University of Utah.

John Driver, president of the Salt Lake City Chapter of the NAACP, marching at the headquarters of the Church of Jesus Christ of Latter-day Saints, March 1970. Courtesy of Special Collections, J. Willard Marriott Library, University of Utah.

CIVIL RIGHTS RESISTANCE   115

It was day 3 of the protests, and the Brethren watched nervously from their offices as protestors continued marching, getting more animated and exuberant with each passing day. Apostle Kimball recorded in his diary:

> At 5:00, I went down to deliver a letter to President Tanner and saw through the doorway the picketing of the Negroes and their associates. There were about 60 of them walking back and forth in a circle in front of the Church Office Building, picketing the church. This is the third day. They had done it on Sunday and on Monday and again today. Their chief complaint was that the Church was silent [on civil rights]. They said they were not well treated in Utah, that they were discriminated against in housing and in jobs, and that the Church discriminated against Negroes because they would not give them the priesthood. I jokingly said to Brother Tanner, "Your friends are still marching." And he said, "Yes, what would you do with them?" And I said, "I would ignore them." And as I went to his door, quite a large group of our people were inside the building watching them and I said to them, "Your rapt attention is exactly what the Negroes appreciate."[102]

Three days after Kimball recorded his observations, Sterling McMurrin published a provocative editorial in the *Salt Lake Tribune* calling the church's opposition to civil rights a "moral failure." "The time is running out," he wrote, "when the church will be able to exert any kind of leadership or even positive influence in this greatest moral struggle of our time."[103] The Utah legislature, clearly affected by the NAACP's relentless pressure, passed the hotly contested employment bill, but only after lawmakers assured the Brethren that the church itself, and its university, BYU, would be exempt. The other civil rights bill—commonly called the "fair housing" bill or more generally the public accommodations bill—failed. It isn't clear whether the Brethren instructed lawmakers to kill the bill or they did it on their own.[104]

The church's failure to support the fair housing bill troubled the NAACP, and they continued to criticize the Brethren over the next couple of years until the federal government passed the Civil Rights Act of 1968, which superseded state law. NAACP leaders were also troubled by Apostle Benson, who delivered an impassioned sermon at the April general conference proclaiming that "communists were using the Civil Rights movement to promote eventual take-over of the country"—a phrase the First Presidency struck from the published record. A year later Benson told BYU students that Martin Luther King was "the most notorious liar in the country."[105] Benson's anti–civil rights position revealed cracks in the church hierarchy. A reporter from the *San Francisco Chronicle* observed that there were "sharp and bitter differences" over civil rights among LDS church leaders. Asked which position on civil rights represented the church's, Brown "tartly said that Benson 'speaks strictly for himself.' My statement is the official Church position." Brown's brusque retort to the reporter's question demonstrated his anger. And he had good reason to be angry. Benson's extremism undermined everything Brown was trying to achieve. "I think the stand of the Church on the civil rights issue is clear and definite," he told McMurrin, "although some of our associates still lead the attack in the opposite direction."[106]

Caught up in Cold War hysteria, Benson became fixated on Birch founder Robert Welch's explosive claim that communists had infiltrated the civil rights movement. Benson called Welch and FBI director Hoover, who made a similar claim, "the two best informed men in America . . . on the threat of this most dangerous Conspiracy."[107] Hoover asserted that King was a tool of international communists, while Welch took it a step further, claiming that King had a secret plan to create a "Negro Soviet Republic."[108]

Neither of these claims had any basis in fact, but Benson accepted them uncritically, not realizing that they could damage the church.[109] He didn't seem to anticipate that there'd be a backlash to his extremist views, particularly from people he'd least suspect. Leon Johnson, a Mormon student at the University of Utah, excoriated Benson for telling "a damned lie" when he branded civil rights leaders communists. BYU students also challenged the apostle, drawing a swift rebuke from Ernest Wilkinson, who accepted the fringe view that King was "a top Kremlin agent." Other Latter-day Saints, just as frustrated with Benson, sought guidance from Dr. King on how to combat the apostle's extremism. BYU professor Larry Wimmer, along with a Mormon woman named Edris Head, asked King what they could do to rebut "questions of communist involvement in the civil rights movement."[110]

Of course, King had heard these charges before and went to great lengths to refute them. He called communism "evil" and claimed that it undermined individual freedom and responsibility. As a Baptist minister, King rejected communism's secular and materialist aims, though he also expressed concern over capitalism's inability to bridge the gap between the rich and the poor.[111] And he was quite aware of the risks involved when he quoted from or associated with prominent African American intellectuals, artists, and poets—men like Langston Hughes, W. E. B. Du Bois, Ralph Ellison, and

CIVIL RIGHTS RESISTANCE

Richard Wright—who were either affiliated with the Communist Party or expressed sympathy with its egalitarian goals. King lamented that Birch sympathizers like Benson had used their affiliation with the Communist Party to stain the entire civil rights movement as "communist inspired." He complained, justifiably, that Birchers thrived on "half-truths and outright lies" to denigrate himself and his followers.[112]

There's no evidence that King ever took note of Benson himself. Nevertheless, the NAACP refused to let Benson's blustery rhetoric or the church's lackluster support for racial equality go unchallenged. Weary of fighting Mormon leaders over civil rights, they retaliated by targeting the church's vaunted missionary program. In July, some three months after Benson's controversial April 1965 general conference address, the NAACP leadership passed a unanimous resolution asking countries in "South America, Asia, and Africa to refuse to grant visas to missionaries and representatives of the [LDS] church" until it changed its "doctrine of white superiority" and produced "a positive statement of civil rights."[113] Eldon Tanner, visibly frustrated, groused that the NAACP "have decided they will correspond with every government of black people and try to persuade them not to allow our people in." The counselor knew what this meant: if the Nigerian government acceded to the NAACP's demands, it would end the church's proselytizing efforts there.[114]

Tanner's worst fears were soon confirmed. The NAACP contacted the Nigerian government, which responded by halting Mormon missionary visas. This was the beginning of the end for the Nigerian mission.[115]

★ ★ ★

Perhaps it will come as no surprise that the LDS church was out of the mainstream on civil rights. While it's true that the Brethren supported an employment bill, they did so only after lawmakers assured them that they didn't have to hire Black people at church-owned businesses and schools. This was hardly a ringing endorsement for racial equality. Other churches, including two of the South's oldest and most prominent regional churches—the Presbyterian Church in the United States and the Southern Baptist Convention—called for protections in jobs and housing. Likewise with Catholics. Dozens of Catholic clergymen marched with Dr. King to support legislation for "interracial justice," and the pope himself met with King to express support.[116] Even the Reorganized Church of Jesus Christ of

Latter Day Saints (RLDS), the biggest offshoot of mainstream Mormonism, took a moderate position on civil rights. In a 1963 editorial published in the *Saints' Herald*, an official RLDS publication, assistant editor William Russell urged members to support Dr. King. What's more, the RLDS First Presidency encouraged Black members to join the NAACP.[117]

The only Christian denominations that opposed civil rights were pockets of loosely affiliated southern Baptists, evangelicals, fundamentalist Christians, and Mormons.[118] The Brethren were terrified that civil rights protections could complicate the church's teachings on interracial marriage. They weren't willing to take that risk.

In the meantime, Hugh Brown tried a new tack in his efforts to overturn the ban. To the media, he soft-pedaled the church's stance, claiming the reason for the ban was that Black people were not "in sufficient numbers in the Church and not advanced in the position where [they] could assume leadership."[119] Brown knew this wasn't true. Church hard-liners had deep-rooted prejudices that prevented them from lifting the ban—the number of Black people in the church had nothing to do with it. But as Brown sought to reassure the media that the church wasn't prejudiced toward Black people, he privately lobbied President McKay again to lift the ban. Ongoing friction with the NAACP, coupled with the lingering problem of having White missionaries run Nigerian Mormon worship services, compelled Brown to push again to ordain Black men to the Aaronic Priesthood. In a June 1965 meeting with McKay, he suggested that "the time has come when the Negro should be given the Lesser Priesthood." The president, however, quickly dismissed the idea. He stood "with all former Presidents of the Church that these boys having Negro blood cannot have the Priesthood."[120]

Whereas he may have considered lifting the ban in 1954 when he read the Bennion Report, now McKay was too tired, too feeble, and too cognitively impaired to consider such a move. He was in a wheelchair, recovering from a stroke the previous year, and simply didn't have the energy to fight the hard-liners.[121] There were other reasons too. Granting Black men the priesthood during a national civil rights movement would have signaled that the Brethren caved to outside pressure. General authority Paul H. Dunn perceptively understood that if the Brethren had lifted the ban in 1965, the "Church would have come apart. I think they would have seen that as strictly a response to the pressure." Brown used more colorful terms to characterize the president's refusal to lift the ban: "President McKay is a Scot and does not like to have a gun pointed at his head."[122]

CIVIL RIGHTS RESISTANCE   119

An exasperated Brown threw up his hands and conceded defeat. He confided to his friend George Tanner that lifting the ban "has been discussed again and again with different [apostles] taking different positions, but while President McKay is alive, I think perhaps the matter will remain dormant and then the new president, whoever he may be, will be at liberty to take such action as he may be inspired to take."[123]

★ ★ ★

No one was more frustrated with Brown's crusade for racial equality than Ezra Taft Benson and his son Reed. Radicalized into right-wing extremism by his father, Reed had been the John Birch Society's regional coordinator since 1964. In a September 1965 memo to the Utah JBS chapters, he claimed that Black militants, supported by the NAACP, were planning to disrupt the October LDS general conference. Recent events had put the Bensons on edge. On August 11, riots had erupted in a Black neighborhood in Los Angeles called Watts, after police clashed with members of a Black family. More than thirty people were killed.[124] The Watts riots led Reed to start a "whispering campaign" in Utah to capitalize on the publicity, claiming that the same rioters would come to Salt Lake City to disrupt the conference:

> [A] few well-placed comments will soon mushroom out of control and before the conference begins there will be such a feeling of unrest and distrust that the populace will hardly know who to believe. The news media will play it to the very hilt. No matter what the Civil Rights leaders may try to say to deny it the seed will have been sown and again the Civil Rights movement will suffer a telling blow.[125]

The NAACP condemned the rumors as "malicious," but they were persistent enough and sensationalist enough that a number of Latter-day Saints believed them.[126] More important, Reed's antics demonstrated how far he and his father were willing to go to promote their conspiracy theories and to undermine those in the church who supported civil rights. Moreover, Reed's memo, which his father likely supported given that the two were close confidantes, revealed that the Bensons had put their right-wing political agenda ahead of unity in the church.[127]

Militants didn't come to Salt Lake City as Reed had maliciously predicted. But his memo still caused alarm among the Brethren.[128] Concerned for their safety, they held a "long meeting" in the Salt Lake Temple in

November 1965. With the stakes high and emotions raw, the Brethren voiced their concerns about the Nigerian mission, the NAACP's relentless criticism, and perceived threats from Black militants. Apostle Gordon B. Hinckley said that he had received a phone call from LaMar Williams's wife, who claimed that Monroe Fleming, a Black Latter-day Saint employee at the church-owned Hotel Utah, had joined the NAACP and wasn't to be trusted. She implored the Brethren to be "very careful regarding the information you give him." Other apostles expressed concern about the missionary work in Nigeria. Apostle Mark E. Petersen said that LaMar Williams should be recalled home and the mission aborted. He believed that it would do the church "great damage" if the mission remained open while critics back home vilified the church's race teachings. Harold B. Lee concurred and said that he wasn't going to let the NAACP pressure the Brethren into lifting the ban. They would fail in their demand "that the Church bring [Black people] in as full-fledged members with the priesthood."[129]

Apostle Benson spoke next. He told his fellow apostles that "he was confident in his own mind from a study he had made of the negro question that we are only seeing something being carried out today that was planned by the highest councils of the communist party twenty years ago." He punctuated his remarks by claiming, "Martin Luther King is an agent if not a power in the communist party." Then he took a jab at the NAACP, saying they "are largely made up of men who are affiliated with one of the communist-front organizations, and he thought they would do anything in their power to embarrass the church." From that reasoning, Benson believed that the apostles "ought to be very careful what we do in the negro field, whether it be Nigeria, here, or any other place in the world. He also thought that Williams's work in Nigeria "should be terminated."[130]

The Nigeria mission came to an end in the fall of 1965, even though seven thousand Nigerians had joined the church and formed their own branches.[131] With the visas shut off, the Brethren had no choice but to call Williams home. It was a sober warning of the NAACP's influence and a stark reminder that as long as the ban remained in effect and as long as the church continued to oppose racial equality, it would face limits on its expansion.

★ ★ ★

CIVIL RIGHTS RESISTANCE

In January 1967, George Romney declared that he would seek the 1968 Republican nomination for president.[132] The Brethren had prepared for this day for some time, and now that it was upon them they were worried. A spate of newspaper stories put Romney and the church on the spot, shining a bright light on the church's antiblack teachings. The *New York Times* provided the headline "Romney Denies Mormon Policy Curbs His Fight for Civil Rights." The *Minnesota Star* intoned, "Most burdensome for Romney ... is the position of the Negro in Mormon theology."[133]

As in his gubernatorial campaign, Romney deflected questions about Mormon racial theology by shifting the discussion to his support for civil rights. Even Lenore Romney, his wife, tried to ward off critics. She told *Look* magazine, "If my church taught me anything other than that the Negro is equal in every way to any other person, I could not accept it."[134] The governor, of course, appreciated his wife's support, but he knew that it wasn't enough to dispel criticism from those—both outsiders and fellow Mormons—who blanched at the church's teachings on race.

This was certainly true of Stewart Udall, one of the most prominent Latter-day Saints in the 1960s. In the spring of 1967, Udall, the secretary of the interior in the Johnson administration and a lifelong Mormon, wrote an article for the liberal Mormon journal *Dialogue* calling on the Brethren to lift the ban. The piece didn't mention Romney, but anyone reading it would know that it might cause trouble for Romney's presidential campaign. As a courtesy, Udall sent advance copies to President McKay, Apostles Spencer Kimball and Delbert Stapley, and Governor Romney.[135]

What provoked Udall's demand? He had long been troubled by the church's race doctrine. But now, he thought, "I occupy a national office. They'll have to listen."[136]

The title of Udall's piece, "An Appeal for Full Fellowship for the Negro," was meant to show that it was born out of his concern for a genuine brotherhood with African Americans.[137] It wasn't as blunt or provocative as Sterling McMurrin's 1960 address to the NAACP. Udall didn't chastise anyone or throw out tantalizing teasers that he had had private conversations with the Brethren. Instead, he couched the problem as a moral crisis. "How different have been our associations with the American Indians, the Spanish-speaking peoples, the Japanese and Polynesians," he rued, acknowledging that Black members received worse treatment. Joseph Smith had ordained Black men to the priesthood, he argued, and he couldn't fathom

SECOND-CLASS SAINTS

122

why the church had changed its policies. He closed with an emotional appeal: "Every Mormon knows that his Church teaches that the day will come when the Negro will be given full fellowship. Surely that day has come."[138]

The Brethren were furious. So were conservative Latter-day Saints, who sent the secretary a blizzard of angry letters—some bordering on hate mail. Newspapers fueled their rage by running stories on the piece.[139] Even *Dialogue* editor Eugene England received dozens of testy letters from Latter-day Saints, angry that the journal had published Udall's statement. "We didn't really sense that [Udall's article] would cause the reaction it did" was England's naive response.[140]

In an attempt at damage control, Mormon radio broadcaster Rex Campbell and Lowell Bennion asked Hugh Brown if the church could "make an official declaration." But the First Presidency, which now included Joseph Fielding Smith, declined to issue a statement or reply to Udall directly.[141] They left that task to Apostles Kimball and Stapley, both of whom knew Udall well since all of them hailed from Arizona. In sharply worded letters, the apostles condemned Udall for pressuring the prophet. Kimball chastised him for daring "to make a command of a Prophet of God." Stapley told him that his "statement has done the church a great disservice" and predicted that it would be "a stumbling block to George Romney if he decides to run for President."[142]

Udall's statement also unnerved Romney. When Udall sent the governor a draft, he remarked in a cover letter that the race doctrine "has long been an issue that has troubled my conscience" and hinted that Romney should join him in condemning Mormon racial theology.[143] Udall knew that he and Romney were the church's most prominent political figures and a statement from both men would have been difficult for the Brethren to ignore. Yet, unlike Udall, who had drifted away from church activity, Romney remained a loyal member and wasn't about to tell the Brethren how to run the church. The governor's public relations team rebuked Udall, saying that he didn't speak for the church and that demanding change "cannot serve any useful religious purpose."[144]

* * *

As the criticism mounted that summer and fall, Mormon sociologist Armand Mauss decided that he had had it with critics taking swipes at the

CIVIL RIGHTS RESISTANCE 123

Brethren. He, too, took to the pages of *Dialogue*: "My plea . . . to civil rights organizations and to all critics of the Mormon Church is [to] get off our backs!"[145] Apostle Lee also grew weary of criticism, especially from Latter-day Saints, and exasperatedly noted that when members asked "What does the Church think about Civil Rights legislation?" he always gave them the same curt answer: "Be loyal to the General Authorities."[146]

No church leader, however, was as troubled by the civil rights movement as Apostle Benson. By 1967, his ferocious opposition to civil rights had intensified to the point of hysteria. His fears were whipped up by right-wing talk radio. He listened devoutly to populist firebrands such as Clarence Manion, Billy James Hargis, and Dan Smoot—all Birchers—who convinced him the civil rights conspiracy was better planned and further along than he had ever imagined. Benson also stumped with them on the John Birch Society speakers' circuit, where he warned Americans about King's supposed ties to the Kremlin.[147] Benson even accepted an invitation to run on the 1968 presidential ticket with Republican senator Strom Thurmond of South Carolina, a prominent segregationist. The ticket didn't materialize, but the fact that Benson even considered running with a White supremacist demonstrates how much he loathed civil rights.[148]

Benson's angst reached a stunning climax at the October 1967 general conference, when he delivered the most controversial address of his ministry. With the Watts riots fresh in his mind, Benson fretted about "Black Marxists," whose strident denunciations of police brutality, racism, and poverty, and incessant chants of "Black Power," shook him to his core. The apostle claimed that Black Marxists "had spent two years in Watts agitating for the uprising." Then, during the summer of 1967, violence erupted in Newark, Boston, Detroit, and dozens of other cities, creating flashes of Watts all over again for the worried apostle.[149] Benson's colleagues worried too. President McKay was "disturbed over [the] racial riots which have broken out in the country," and Hugh Brown shared that concern. They feared that the church's properties—Temple Square, the Hotel Utah, and church headquarters—would be subject to a "Negro Disturbance." In August 1967, as protests raged across the country, Brown received a phone call from the Salt Lake City police chief indicating that "four carloads of Negroes armed with machine guns and bombs were reported coming to Salt Lake City for the purpose of inciting a riot, and particularly to destroy property on the Temple Bloc." This was probably another baseless allegation from the John Birch Society, but Brown took it seriously.[150]

124 SECOND-CLASS SAINTS

Accordingly, the Brethren arranged for snipers to be placed on the rooftops of buildings around Temple Square at the October general conference, and the governor placed the National Guard on high alert. Tension soared even higher when a prophecy by former church president John Taylor began circulating in Salt Lake City, which reportedly said that "the Negroes will march to the west and that they will tear down the gates to the [Salt Lake] temple, ravage the women therein, and destroy and desecrate the temple. Then the Mormon boys will pick up deer rifles and destroy the Negroes and that's when blood will run down the street."[151]

Fear gripped Latter-day Saints. It didn't help that the Brethren talked about a "race war," sometimes publicly, though it isn't clear whether they actually believed that one was coming. Still, violence roared in American cities throughout the spring and summer of 1967, buttressed by news reports that Black Power advocates were committed to defending themselves "by any means necessary" against overzealous law enforcement.[152]

Against these alarming events, Ezra Taft Benson decided to address the topic in general conference. He wanted to prepare the Saints for what lay ahead. Recognizing that his sermon would invite controversy, Benson sought—and received—McKay's support. But he didn't tell the elderly president what exactly he was going to say. He gave no indication that he would unload a fulsome attack on the civil rights movement or its leaders. Rather, he told the president that he would discuss "the plight of the Negroes in this Civil Rights issue" and address the "subject from the viewpoint of bringing peace in our country instead of the uprisings of the Negroes in riots."[153]

The title seemed innocent enough: "Trust Not the Arm of Flesh." But Benson's address was hardly innocent.[154] He unleashed a twenty-minute barrage of invective proclaiming that Black Marxists, masquerading as civil rights activists, would "create hatred," then "trigger violence," then "overthrow the established government." The apostle provided gruesome descriptions of how Black revolutionaries would sabotage power grids, take over government buildings, and murder law enforcement officers. Because Benson believed that Black Marxists had provoked a wave of violence across the country, he felt compelled to "expose the secret communists who are directing the Civil Rights Movement." Remarkably, he didn't even attempt to hide who influenced him. Scattered throughout the text were references from prominent Birchers. Reed Benson proudly sent a copy of his father's address to Robert Welch.[155]

Two months after Benson's dystopian address, the *Improvement Era*, the church's most prominent magazine, published it, and the following year the LDS-owned Deseret Book company issued it as a book titled *Civil Rights—Tool of Communist Deception*.[156] Jerreld Newquist, a Mormon Bircher, republished the address in a conspiracy-themed book called *An Enemy Hath Done This*. The address was so controversial and so inflammatory that Benson's authorized biographers refused to even discuss it.[157]

Nevertheless, it rippled throughout the Mormon community and shaped how thousands of Latter-day Saints viewed the civil rights movement. Ultraconservative members, in particular, found Benson's apocalyptic warnings prophetic and his conspiracy theories credible.[158] His address offered unambiguous proof that right-wing extremism had seeped into the church and that neither President McKay nor Hugh Brown had the power to stop it.

Most of the Brethren couldn't seem to grasp how the church's race doctrine, coupled with Benson's radical views of civil rights, were damaging the church. The Brethren should have learned that the ban would keep the church in the spotlight until it was lifted. Indeed, one of the tragedies of the

Apostle Ezra Taft Benson (center), his son Reed Benson (right), and John Birch Society founder Robert Welch (left) at a Birch Society meeting, Salt Lake City, April 6, 1966. Courtesy of Utah State Historical Society.

126   SECOND-CLASS SAINTS

LDS church of the 1960s is that no one in the hierarchy, except for Hugh Brown and Marion Hanks, pressed the church to support racial equality. Protestant and Catholic clergy reinterpreted their theology in response to the civil rights movement. But LDS church leaders remained stubbornly defiant, which put them out of touch with much of the nation. This was strikingly illustrated in 1964, when a reporter asked President McKay if the ban would end and he replied, "Not while you and I are here." Three years later nothing had changed. "The church has no intention of changing its doctrine on the Negro," Eldon Tanner remarked.[59]

As 1967 careened to a close, it was clear that the Brethren weren't going to lift the ban anytime soon. Their obstinance would cost the church dearly in the days ahead. The following year, two events would plunge the church into its greatest public relations crisis of the twentieth century. First, federal authorities investigated BYU for civil rights violations. Then dozens of universities boycotted BYU athletic competitions in protest against Mormon racial teachings. While the hard-liners wanted to double-down, Hugh Brown saw another opening.

He had to seize the moment while President McKay was still alive.

5

Investigations and Protests, 1968–1970

April 1968 was an unusually difficult month for BYU president Ernest Wilkinson. The man known by his faculty as "Little Napoleon" could scarcely control the events swirling around him. The first blow was struck on April 11, when he received notice that BYU was under investigation for alleged violations of the Civil Rights Act of 1964, which prohibited "discrimination on the basis of race, color, or national origin in any program or activity that receives Federal funds or other Federal financial assistance."[1] In 1968, only three Black students attended the church-owned school, and there were no Black faculty. Wilkinson panicked.

The second blow came two days later, when athletes at the University of Texas–El Paso track team refused to compete against BYU. The UTEP protest was the spark that ignited an inferno. Over the next three years, student-athletes at dozens of universities refused to compete against BYU, loudly condemning the school and the church for discrimination against Black people.[2] "You've got to understand how we feel," protested one Black athlete. "Those Mormons say we're the mark of Cain and that we can't go to heaven because we're black. Man, I just don't want to associate with those people in any way."[3]

These twin crises put the Brethren on edge. The widespread exposure of these events forced the Brethren to grapple with the church's race policies in a way they had never experienced. For Hugh B. Brown, the civil rights investigation and the athletic protests provided leverage to lift the ban. For

128   SECOND-CLASS SAINTS

the hard-liners, it was a chance to reaffirm that they wouldn't yield to external pressure.

* * *

Nestled within the majestic Rocky Mountains in Provo, Utah, is Brigham Young University, the Mormon church's flagship institution. It was established on October 16, 1876, and named after Mormonism's second prophet-president, who died the following year. By the time Ernest Wilkinson was selected as the school's seventh president in 1951, it was poised to become one of the largest private universities in the United States. During his twenty-year tenure, enrollment would grow sixfold, to more than twenty-five thousand students. Under Wilkinson's careful watch, the school instituted several master's and PhD programs and aggressively recruited Latter-day Saint students from outside the Intermountain West. Shortly into his tenure the Board expanded his job to include oversight of the church's junior colleges, a new four-year university in Hawaii, and the church's seminaries and institutes for high school and college students.[4]

Wilkinson had close ties with First Presidency counselor J. Reuben Clark and Apostle Ezra Taft Benson, both of whom shared his extreme conservative views and both of whom had lobbied President George Albert Smith and the Board of Trustees to appoint him as BYU's president.[5]

Wilkinson imposed his conservative values on the institution. He prohibited student activism against the Vietnam War, even forbidding students to place peace signs in their dorm windows, and barred left-wing speakers from campus. He imposed an "honor code" that strictly forbade students from alcohol, premarital sex, and interracial dating. This wasn't just a matter of following church strictures.[6] Wilkinson was a strict believer in LDS racial teachings and a strong opponent of interracial relationships. Of Apostle Mark E. Petersen's controversial 1954 BYU address on segregation, Wilkinson declared that it represented "the truth."[7]

BYU's Black student population never exceeded more than one or two at any given time in the mid-twentieth century. In 1953 Wilkinson wrote to a Latter-day Saint parent from Florida who expressed concern about sending his daughter to a university where Black students were admitted. Wilkinson assured the anxious father that he had nothing to worry about. "We have had only two colored students in our Student Body over the last ten years or so," he explained, adding that at the current time only "one

BYU president Ernest L. Wilkinson, 1964. Courtesy of Utah State Historical Society.

colored person out of 7,500 students" was on campus. Wilkinson further assured the father that the university "discouraged social relations between the races.... We are just as emphatic as the Church in our teaching that there should be no intermarriage."[8]

BYU's recruitment policies strongly resembled the church's posture toward proselytizing Black people. They wouldn't seek them out, but neither would they turn them away. But although that was the policy, none of the Brethren wanted Black students at BYU. Joseph Fielding Smith, the president of the Executive Committee of the Board of Trustees, made this abundantly clear in 1952. When Wilkinson asked him if BYU should admit a "one quarter negro" from California, the apostle balked. Light-skinned Black people were the most dangerous kind, Smith reasoned, because no one could tell if they bore the curse.[9] He wasn't alone. Fellow apostle Harold B. Lee expressed outrage when, in November 1960, Wilkinson attended a Board of Trustees meeting and informed the Board about a "colored boy"

130   SECOND-CLASS SAINTS

at BYU who was running for the vice presidency in student government. The announcement stunned Lee, who looked Wilkinson straight in the eye and proclaimed, "[If] a granddaughter of mine should ever go to BYU and become engaged to a colored boy there I would hold you responsible." The strong-willed president, however, didn't shrink from the apostle's threat. Wilkinson told Lee that he should hold himself responsible since he was one of the Board members who created the policy in the first place.[10]

The truth is, the Brethren were not unlike many Americans in the 1960s who feared Black sexuality. It governed their views about civil rights, segregation, interracial dating and marriage, and whether or not to admit Black students at BYU.[11] The Board's reluctance to admit Black students was also rooted in their unfamiliarity with Black people. With the exception of Hugh B. Brown, who spent his formative years in Canada, the most influential Mormon apostles in the post–World War II years were born and raised in overwhelmingly White Mormon communities in Utah, Idaho, and Arizona. Apostles Benson and Lee, for example, hailed from agricultural communities, and even those raised in comparatively cosmopolitan Salt Lake City, like Mark E. Petersen, Bruce R. McConkie, and Gordon B. Hinckley, came of age in the 1920s and 1930s when less than 1 percent of Utah's population was Black.[12]

What little the apostles knew about African Americans came largely from their church and probably from the "white media," neither of which depicted Black people favorably. Perhaps this explains why Black music made them uncomfortable and why some of the Brethren used racial slurs to characterize Black people. Under the Board's direction, Wilkinson denied students permission to perform the "negro twist" at BYU dances, fearing that it would sully the morals of the predominantly White student body. Apostle Smith called Black people "Darkies"; First Presidency counselor J. Reuben Clark referred to them as "nigger."[13] When Spencer W. Kimball attended a Broadway play in New York City with his wife, he was uncomfortable sitting next to people from diverse backgrounds. "The show itself was very good and entertaining," he mused, "but the people that surrounded us made us wonder if we were in America—the colored people and the foreign element, the Puerto Ricans. It was almost unbelievable."[14]

Future apostle and church president Thomas S. Monson likewise felt out of place among African Americans. When "minority elements" began moving into the neighborhood where he lived, he sought counsel from Apostle Petersen, who told him to move. (Monson heeded his advice.)

INVESTIGATIONS AND PROTESTS   131

Apostle McConkie referred to Black people as the "seed of Cain" and Apostle Benson vilified them as communists for supporting civil rights. Admittedly, few in the Mormon hierarchy held Benson's radical views— Hugh Brown said that "most of the Brethren" opposed the John Birch Society, the extremist group from which Benson derived his ideology—but a number of them were steeped in racist literature.[15] Apostles Benson and Kimball and counselor Clark, for example, had thick files of marked-up racist magazine articles in their private papers, in which the authors asserted that Black people were determined to destroy the White race through "mongrelization."[16]

The Brethren could see their worst fears realized at rival Utah State University, some 126 miles to the north of BYU. There, Black athletes openly boasted about dating "white girls," which deeply scandalized the community of Logan. Wilkinson followed this development very closely, as did the Brethren, and both concluded that if BYU recruited Black student-athletes, the school would experience a similar fate.[17]

Fear of interracial dating forced the Board of Trustees to tighten up BYU's admission policies. Though BYU's promotional literature said that the school welcomed all races, this wasn't true. William Berrett, Wilkinson's vice president, issued instructions to guide admissions officers on how to discourage "Negroes" when they applied. It was a strange document, full of contradictions, half-truths, and innuendos. It claimed that Mormonism "is for all peoples, black and white, bond and free," but tried to discourage Black students from enrolling if they were admitted. Berrett didn't have the courage to tell Black students outright that they weren't welcome. He feared the negative publicity that an exclusionary admissions policy might create. If BYU "closed its doors to students of known Negro blood," he confessed privately, it "would arouse a great deal of adverse publicity both as to the Church and its schools." Light-skinned "Negroes" particularly concerned Berrett: "The real danger is intermarriage with those of limited Negro blood, who are difficult to identify and which cannot therefore be excluded."[18]

Berrett attempted to thread the needle. He asked, "How can the door of the university be left open and still attract few Negroes?" He had an uncommonly frank five-step plan:

1. Do no proselytizing of Negro athletes.
2. Discourage undue publicity of the Negro who is on campus.

3. Watch moral standards carefully.
4. Quietly counsel students against dating a known Negro. (Call in any boy or girl seen with a Negro.)
5. Send a prepared letter to answer inquiries of Negroes regarding admittance to B.Y.U. or other Church school. (Sample attached.)[19]

The "Proposed Letter to Be Used for Non-L.D.S. Negro Students Who Inquire about Attendance at Brigham Young University" would attempt to dissuade prospective students. The letter said that the overwhelming number of students and faculty at BYU were White, and so Black students would feel uncomfortable. "Non-church members are often unhappy here regardless of race," the letter noted. The letter cautioned Black students that they should "take into consideration the social difficulties and disappointments you would encounter on entering an Institution where all the students are of the white race, save a mere dozen or so." They were also warned that they couldn't date White students, not because of prejudice but because of the challenges the couple would face if the courtship culminated in marriage. The "differences in family and cultural backgrounds" would be difficult to endure. The letter closed with a bitter reality: Black students would most likely incur prejudice at BYU: "You are welcome to come, but if you do so, it should be with your eyes open to realities so that you do not develop bitterness or frustration while you are with us."[20]

Berrett also compiled a list of questions and answers that the BYU admissions office could circulate when critics inquired about the school's recruitment policies. "Why are no blacks on the BYU football team right now?" the first question asked. They would have to ask the Black student-athletes why they chose not to come, carefully adding that they were welcome at BYU just as any other student. The second question asked, "Why so few Negroes at BYU?" "This is the result of their decision," he replied, "not of our policy." He wanted critics to understand that if Black students rejected BYU because they perceived the school was racist toward Black people, that was a case of Black students "judging us without knowing the facts." Another question asked, "To what extent are other minorities represented on the BYU campus?" Here Berrett floated a softball claiming that the university actively recruited minorities, making BYU "one of the most cosmopolitan campuses in America." The university actively sought students from South America, Asia, and the Hawaiian Islands, and they had a robust Native American population, "representing 48 tribes and 16 blends." To our knowledge," Berrett asserted, "few, if any, universities in the United

INVESTIGATIONS AND PROTESTS   133

States . . . have tried harder to make minority-group and foreign students more welcome."[21]

There was nothing true in either the letter or the question-and-answer document. The fact is that BYU didn't recruit Black students and they were most emphatically not welcome, despite BYU aggressively recruiting other races and ethnicities. And this wasn't even a secret. In 1962, a year after Berrett established the policy, BYU athletic director Eddie Kimball bluntly told a reporter, "We do not actively recruit Negro athletes and will not in the foreseeable future." This "is not a matter of discrimination," he said. "We simply feel Negroes would not be comfortable on our campus. . . . [There] is not a single Negro family living in Provo. . . . This creates quite a social problem for Negroes wishing to come to our school."[22]

Berrett and Kimball both knew the *real* reason the school didn't recruit Black students—they just wouldn't admit it. Unlike Native Americans, Polynesians, Pacific Islanders, and other students of color, whom the school recruited and touted in its promotional literature, Mormon theology deemed Black people cursed.

★ ★ ★

The context for the twin crises at BYU was the much larger crisis in the nation. On April 4, 1968, Martin Luther King Jr. was assassinated. Hundreds of African Americans took to the streets to protest, resulting in waves of violence and millions of dollars in property damage. Riots broke out in 196 cities in thirty-six states.[23]

This fueled the right-wing extremism that had begun to permeate the church. Two days after King's murder, Apostle Benson circulated a scurrilous memo to all the general authorities branding the slain leader a communist and urging his colleagues not to celebrate his life or acknowledge his death at the April general conference. Hugh Brown was furious. He ripped up the memo and read a brief statement honoring King at general conference. President McKay said that he did this on his "own accord."[24]

The violence sparked by King's death so unnerved Benson that six days later, he wrote the First Presidency and Quorum of the Twelve Apostles an urgent letter warning of "dangers ahead." He didn't want to be considered an "alarmist," he wrote, but then he proceeded to ring the alarm: "Great dangers are rapidly developing which will likely result in a series of serious crises between now and 1970." The Russians were plotting to destroy American democracy. Communists had killed King because he wasn't radical enough; they got rid of him "to make room for more vigorous leadership." Benson predicted that in the coming months Marxists would incite "racial violence in a hundred or more cities," leading to chaos and lawlessness. They would collapse the nation's financial institutions and plunge the United States into "the possible outbreak of World War III."[25]

At general conference the week before, Benson preached his apocalyptic, doomsday message in public: "We live in a time of crisis. Never since the period of the Civil War has this nation faced such critical days. Americans are destroying America." He implied that it was Black Americans who were destroying America, specifically Black-militant types like "the Stokely Carmichaels and H. Rapp Browns," who terrified Benson.[26]

That spring, Benson continued sounding the alarm. In May, he delivered an address at BYU laced with conspiracy theories about Black people, government welfare programs, and Marxism. He titled it "The Book of Mormon Warns America" in a brazen effort to link his conspiracy theories to sacred scripture. This was a strange kind of genius, as thousands of Latter-day Saints accepted the fantastical claim that Book of Mormon prophets predicted the apocalyptic scenarios that Benson had warned about.[27] The apostle's antics, however, angered the First Presidency. They not only refused to publish the address but went one step further: President McKay instructed Brown to speak at BYU the following week to rebut Benson's racist remarks. The counselor accepted the assignment. He had always punched back hard against right-wing extremism, and now he had the president's support. Not mincing words, Brown warned the student body to "avoid those who preach [the] evil doctrines of racism." It was a devastating rebuke to Apostle Benson.[28]

As Brown and Benson feuded, the UTEP boycott rocked the church.[29] With the nation still reeling from the assassination of Dr. King, and the Black students' own racial grievances at UTEP bubbling up (they, too, couldn't date White girls), the athletes informed their coach that they would boycott the meet in Provo. "There were about a dozen reasons" why they refused to go, declared athlete Dave Morgan in an interview with *Sports Illustrated*. "The Mormons teach that Negroes are descended from the devil. ... [W]ho the hell wants to go up there and run your tail off in front of a bunch of spectators who think you've got horns?"[30]

Morgan's colorful language angered Ernest Wilkinson, and he responded, "We do not discriminate because of race, and we have Negro students in our student body." Left unmentioned was the number of such

INVESTIGATIONS AND PROTESTS 135

students (three) and the fact that BYU didn't recruit them. Wilkinson also wrote to UTEP president Joseph Ray, informing him, "The charge that we believe the Negroes are emissaries of the devil is completely ridiculous." But Ray was unmoved. "I think your institution," he frankly noted, "will be a thorn in the side of the Conference until such time as you recruit at least a token [Black] athlete. Until you do, all explanations that the charges are not true will not carry weight."[31] Ray wanted BYU removed from the Western Athletic Conference. Wilkinson's assurances that BYU "had a policy against discrimination" and had always welcomed "all Negroes" were hollow.[32] Wilkinson clearly knew that BYU discriminated against Black students, but he wasn't about to admit that in the midst of a public relations fiasco.

Wilkinson's cagey efforts to convince Ray that Mormons weren't racists was undermined by John Fitzgerald, a former LDS seminary teacher. In an article in the *Salt Lake Tribune*, BYU athletic director Floyd Millet said that the church didn't teach that "Negroes are inferior and disciples of the devil."[33] But Fitzgerald, who was well-versed in LDS theology, couldn't let that slide. He wrote Millet a strongly worded letter laced with quotations from Joseph Fielding Smith's *The Way to Perfection* reminding him that Black people are indeed "considered inferior and a cursed race in Mormon Theology." And that was just the tip of the iceberg. "There are many, many other references in Mormon literature stating or inferring and teaching that Negroes are inferior, if not actual representatives of the devil." Fitzgerald's letter might have faded into obscurity had he not also sent a copy to UTEP track coach Wayne Banderberg. Now evidence of Wilkinson's duplicity was plain to see.[34]

Fitzgerald's stunt angered Wilkinson and the Board of Trustees. Wilkinson sulked to Apostle Kimball that Fitzgerald's letter "is just another example of where jack Mormons cause us more trouble than outsiders." Likewise, First Presidency counselor Alvin R. Dyer complained in a First Presidency meeting that Latter-day Saints like Fitzgerald were taking "constant pot-shots at Church leaders."[35] He was angry that critics kept dredging up statements by past and current church leaders that put the church in an unfavorable light.

The timing of the UTEP boycott couldn't have been worse. The church's race policies had been under scrutiny during George Romney's presidential campaign. (He had ended his bid in February.) At about the same time, and

136   SECOND-CLASS SAINTS

about a year after Benson's ticket with Strom Thurmond failed, national reports emerged that Benson was exploring the possibility of joining the presidential candidacy of segregationist George Wallace on the American Independent Party ticket.[36] Mercifully, this didn't come to fruition. President McKay denied Benson's request to join Wallace, knowing that allowing a senior apostle to run on a ticket that attracted support from the Ku Klux Klan, American Nazi Party, John Birch Society, and White Citizens' Councils would validate outsider perceptions that the church was a racist institution. Plus, it would have undermined a recent First Presidency decision not to bring attention to the church's race doctrine. In April 1968, the First Presidency determined that when "inquiries . . . come to the Church regarding the Negroes holding the Priesthood," all replies should be upbeat. There should be no mention of the preexistence, or curses, or any other rationalizations of the priesthood restriction. The Brethren wanted all statements about LDS racial teachings to "be clear, positive, and brief."[37]

This decision supplemented an ongoing public relations effort to bolster the church's image with Black people. For example, the First Presidency removed offensive chapters from the Portuguese edition of *The Way to Perfection*.[38] They denied permission for BYU religion professor James Clark to publish the 1949 First Presidency statement on race and priesthood in a multivolume edition called *The Messages of the First Presidency*. They refused to print a controversial address dealing with race and lineage by church patriarch Eldred G. Smith "because of the present turmoil over the Negro question." They forbade BYU students from writing on "the Negroes position in the Mormon church," questioning why students would choose "this subject, particularly at the present time." Moreover, they instructed the Brethren not to publish the church's interracial marriage teachings, affirming "that any instruction should be of an oral nature." And finally, Apostle Smith denied that he had ever taught that Black people were an inferior race.[39]

It was clear that the Brethren were attempting to deflect attention from the priesthood and temple ban.

★ ★ ★

When civil rights investigators visited BYU on a wet day in May, the Board was ready for them.[40] About three weeks before the site visit, the Board passed a resolution stating that the university didn't discriminate in admissions standards with respect "to race, color or national origin." This was an obvious attempt to preempt accusations of racism. The Board authorized that the resolution be sent to local businesses and area offices, as well as the Bi-City Urban League and the NAACP. The Board also authorized Wilkinson to hire Robert Barker, his friend and former law partner in a Washington, D.C., firm, to negotiate with federal investigators. There were a lot of questions that needed to be resolved. Could BYU be compelled into compliance of the Civil Rights Act of 1964 if it received federal contracts? Did "federal assistance" that BYU received permit government oversight of the university's recruitment policies? What if the school were to terminate its contracts with the government?[41]

As expected, the investigation didn't go well for the school. While the five-member committee was "friendly," they went right to the heart of the matter, demanding to know why BYU didn't recruit Black students, athletes, or faculty when they aggressively recruited Native Americans, Polynesians, Māori, Brazilians, Mexicans, people from the Caribbean, and other people of color.[42] This penetrating question flummoxed Wilkinson and put him on the defensive. We "practice no discrimination of any kind," he stammered. Wilkinson boasted that hundreds of students from the Pacific Islands, Native Americans from reservations, and Spanish-speaking students from South America and Mexico attended the university, which was foolish to admit since it only proved that the school discriminated against Black students. Black students didn't enroll at the university by their own choice, he argued, not because of BYU's recruitment policies.[43]

When Wilkinson intuited that the investigators didn't believe him, he changed tactics. Drawing on his years as a lawyer, he offered a spirited legal defense of BYU's right to discriminate. He explained that the federal government's meddling into BYU's recruitment practices was a violation of the LDS church's right to freedom of religion. If "the Government feels that BYU is discriminatory because of this theological concept of the Church," Wilkinson groused, "we think that would be in violation of the Bill of Rights, which prevents abridgement of religion."[44]

As the investigators were wrapping up, Wilkinson asked BYU religion dean David Yarn to explain to them "the revelatory basis for the Negro not being permitted to hold the Priesthood." Wilkinson reported afterward, "He made it pretty plain."[45]

What would happen next was anyone's guess. Wilkinson must have known that BYU faced an uphill battle in trying to claim an exemption from the Civil Rights Act. Title VI of the act vested executive agencies with authority to deny federal monies to universities and high schools that practiced racial discrimination. The Johnson administration, in fact, had instructed the Justice Department to target universities and high schools that had discriminatory policies. In 1968, some fifty school districts in the South still refused to integrate, and a fair number of private Christian universities, including Bob Jones University and Grove City College, drew the attention of federal authorities.[46] Wilkinson also must have known that there was a mounting body of case law affirming the government's ability to penalize religious institutions. While the administration recognized the right of private religious institutions to practice their religion, that right had to be carefully balanced against federal law, especially when institutions received federal assistance. Simply put, the Johnson administration declared that religious institutions like BYU couldn't hide behind the First Amendment to discriminate against Black students.[47]

Hollis Bach, the civil rights official leading the investigation, didn't take long to produce his report. Less than two weeks after visiting Provo in May 1968, he sent Wilkinson a damning letter informing him that BYU was not in compliance with the Civil Rights Act of 1964. BYU, he stressed, had to do eight things to comply with federal law:

1. The university catalogue had to "contain in the admissions policy a positive statement of nondiscrimination."
2. The university handbook had to contain a similar statement.
3. BYU had to recruit in "population centers where minority students are significant in number," which the committee "deemed to mean 25% or more."
4. Alumni had to be informed of BYU's "nondiscriminatory policy."
5. BYU had to recruit Black athletes.
6. BYU had to inform "off-campus employers" that it would refer students of color for employment.
7. BYU student housing had to accept all students regardless of "race, color, or national origin."
8. Placement of student teachers had to be "made without regard to race, color, or national origin."

Bach gave BYU one year to comply with the law and informed Wilkinson that civil rights investigators would do another site visit in 1969 to ensure compliance.[48]

Bach's letter stunned the Board. They held "a very long meeting" with Wilkinson and his top assistants mostly to complain about Bach's letter. "It was a very rough meeting," Wilkinson confessed. Most disturbing to the Board was that no other university in the Intermountain West was under investigation. The Board felt that BYU had been unduly targeted because of the church's race doctrine, and some Board members expressed frustration "that the committee was 'out to get us.'" They may have had a point. In the fall of 1968, some four months after the investigation commenced, Black students constituted about 0.03 percent of the student body at BYU. At the University of Utah, they totaled 0.4 percent; at the University of Wyoming 0.5 percent; at the University of Colorado 0.5 percent; and at the University of Arizona 1.0 percent.[49] None of these schools was under investigation. But none of them had a Board that openly supported an anti-black theology. Adding to the Board's grief was that some members feared UTEP would use the civil rights investigation as a pretext for removing the university from the Western Athletic Conference. Some Board members sought a quick fix: they wanted to decline all federal assistance, both research grants to faculty and aid to students. Wilkinson urged the Board not to consider such drastic measures until he received word from Robert Barker about their legal rights.[50]

Barker's report came in June. It was a hefty legal analysis totaling some thirty-eight pages. In a document marked "privileged and confidential," Barker carefully weighed the merits of the government's case against BYU, zeroing in on *Jones v. Mayer* (1968), in which the U.S. Supreme Court ruled that Congress had the power to prohibit "private acts of racial discrimination in the sale and rental of residential housing." He wasn't sure if the government could deny BYU faculty research grants, claiming he needed more information about the nature of the contracts. But as to the government's mandate that BYU hire "Negro faculty," he was quite sure that BYU was within its rights not to comply.[51]

For Barker, a practicing Latter-day Saint, the government's case against BYU was nothing more than a shameful attempt to "embarrass the church." But his personal feelings aside, he took the charges seriously; he knew the government wasn't going to back off. Some two months after Bach's initial report, lawyers from Barker's office met with members of Bach's team to discuss the specifics of the investigation. It was at that meeting that the civil rights team outlined the penalties BYU would face if they didn't comply with federal law. Members of the military wouldn't be able to use the GI bill to enroll at the school. Students would be ineligible for federal Pell grants. Faculty would be barred from federal research grants. In short, the government wanted "equal access at BYU" for students of color.[52]

The charges were serious, but the Board of Trustees didn't seem to be in a hurry to address them. They were away from their offices during much of the summer of 1968 and didn't have an opportunity to consult with Wilkinson about how to address Bach's letter. Besides, many of the Brethren were still reeling from an acerbic address that Sterling McMurrin had given to the NAACP in June—a speech that made national headlines. As the Brethren knew, McMurrin wasn't to be taken lightly. His clout within the Mormon intellectual community had only increased since his previous address to the NAACP. In that period, he published another well-received book on Mormon philosophy and theology and had been appointed commissioner of education in the Kennedy administration.[53] And the fact that he remained close personal friends with David O. McKay and Hugh B. Brown made him a formidable foe to the hard-liners in the Twelve.

Before a packed audience in Salt Lake, McMurrin chastised the church for its failure to support civil rights and condemned the Brethren for refusing to give up a race doctrine that he called "crude, immoral nonsense." Unlike in his previous appearance to the NAACP, this time he focused on the current church leadership, condemning their inability to change with the times. McMurrin brusquely noted that previous Mormon leaders "had a vital, prophetic, revolutionary message that called for a just society" and were "willing to run great risks in advocacy of its principles," while current leadership was "quiescent and conservative and has lost much of its capacity to dream new dreams and chart new paths." They honor the church's "prophets and pioneers of the past but have lost the art of prophecy and pioneering for the future."[54]

McMurrin reiterated that the "divine curse" wasn't church doctrine. He didn't think it was his place to disclose that President McKay was the source of this statement, so he skirted around the edges, cleverly implying to his audience that there was a division in the highest ranks of church leadership on the "negro question."[55]

NAACP national president Roy Wilkins received a copy of the address and told McMurrin that he was impressed by his "thoughtful presentation." Dozens of well-wishers praised him. He heard from orthodox Latter-day Saints too, but they branded him a heretic.[56] Newspapers, similarly, commented on McMurrin's address, focusing on his claim that unless the Mormon leadership "abandoned its crude superstitions about Negroes" people would leave the church. "Mormon says church to lose 'thousands' over Negro stand," the *Palo Alto Times* reported.[57]

As one might suspect, the Brethren were in no mood to be lectured to about their moral courage by a lapsed Mormon. The First Presidency minutes clearly show their anger: "Some of the Brethren are very upset over Dr. McMurrin's attitude toward the Church and feel that he should be tried for his membership."[58]

The person most exercised over the address was Apostle Joseph Fielding Smith, the man with whom McMurrin had feuded since the "Swearing Elder" days. Smith wanted him cut off from the church. He had tried to excommunicate him in 1952, only to be thwarted by President McKay. What saved McMurrin this time was the cool head of First Presidency counselor Alvin R. Dyer.

In 1965, McKay, now in his nineties and in need of further assistance with the duties of running the church, called Thorpe Isaacson and Joseph Fielding Smith, McKay's likely successor, to the First Presidency as additional counselors. But the most consequential counselor proved to be Alvin Dyer, who replaced an ailing Isaacson in 1967.[59] Dyer was a bulldog in defending the church's race teachings. He had worked in the air-conditioning business prior to his call as an assistant to the Quorum of the Twelve Apostles in 1958, but dabbled in theology and church history, having written several books on a range of LDS topics.[60] He wrote about the "negro question" in some of these books and occasionally spoke with missionaries about the ban. In 1961, he gave an impassioned defense of LDS racial teachings to church missionaries in Oslo, Norway, in which he declared that Black people had "rejected the Priesthood of God."[61] McMurrin called Dyer "an authentic lightweight," but ironically it was Dyer who saved the outspoken philosopher from excommunication after his well-publicized NAACP address. When Apostle Smith asserted that McMurrin should be "tried for his membership," Dyer calmly suggested that it would be unwise to cut him off given the tremendous criticism the church had been receiving over "the

142   SECOND-CLASS SAINTS

Negroes holding the Priesthood." Besides, Dyer reasoned, such a drastic step seemed unnecessary since McMurrin had already "cut himself off from the Church" with his pointed criticisms of its teachings.[62]

What did McKay think about McMurrin's address? The First Presidency minutes simply state that he was "disturbed over Dr. McMurrin's statements and attitude" but "made no commitment concerning the matter"—meaning, presumably, that he didn't weigh in on whether or not McMurrin should lose his church membership. Though the two were friends, critics like McMurrin made McKay uncomfortable.[63]

Behind the scenes, though, McMurrin was preparing bolder moves. In August, as Bach's report lay unanswered, McMurrin devised a scheme to disclose President McKay's true views to the church body. He wrote to McKay's sons Llewelyn, David, and Edward and informed them about his conversation with their father back in 1954. He told the McKays that their father didn't believe in the divine curse, and he claimed that "withholding the Priesthood from the Negro" was a practice, not a doctrine—one that needed to be changed. McMurrin hoped to nudge the McKay sons to pressure their father to disclose his views to the church. "I frankly wish I could feel free to make President McKay's statement to me on this subject a matter of public record." It "would be a very good thing for the Church and would help to clear up a great deal of confusion in the minds of many of its members."[64]

At McMurrin's prodding, Llewelyn read the letter to his father, who confirmed McMurrin's account of their meeting some fourteen years earlier: "That is exactly what happened and that is exactly what I said."[65] The crucial question was how to disseminate President McKay's views to the church body. Time was of the essence. McKay's health was rapidly declining—he had suffered a stroke and had only rare moments of lucidity—so McMurrin felt a sense of urgency. This is why he sent copies of the letter to McKay's counselors—Hugh B. Brown and N. Eldon Tanner—as well. He wanted their help. But this put Brown in an awkward position. He had been lobbying the president to lift the ban for years, and the two had had a falling out of sorts over that issue and others. Indeed, as Ernest Wilkinson had speculated just a few months earlier, McKay had "lost confidence" in Brown.[66]

The counselor clearly sympathized with McMurrin's position but didn't want to badger the president further, or at least he didn't want to do it alone.

INVESTIGATIONS AND PROTESTS 143

He told McMurrin that he shared President McKay's belief that the ban was a policy, not a doctrine, and he even predicted that "in the not-too-distant future" the church would accept this fact. He wasn't sure exactly when, but he told his friend, "I confidently expect the time will come during your lifetime when this somewhat controversial matter will be clarified."[67]

Brown's optimism encouraged McMurrin, but there was work to be done to lay the groundwork to lift the ban. Getting the word out that it was merely a policy would be a start. An even bigger feat would be to convince McKay that ending the ban didn't require a revelation—that it could be done by administrative fiat. As McMurrin ruminated on how best to move forward, an unexpected opportunity emerged. Stephen Taggart, a former student of his, asked him to review a draft of an article he had written called "Mormonism and the Negro." Taggart, now a PhD student in sociology at Cornell University, was inspired by McMurrin's 1960 NAACP address in which he argued that the ban wasn't rooted in doctrine or revelation but was simply a policy that originated to appease pro-slavery Missourians in the church's early days.[68]

When McMurrin read a draft of Taggart's manuscript in the spring of 1968, it occurred to the crafty philosopher that his former student should be the one to disclose McKay's position on the ban. The young graduate student seemed to be the ideal person. He was a practicing Latter-day Saint, a returned missionary, and his father was the president of Utah State University, making him well connected within the Mormon community and with LDS general authorities. In other words, Taggart had credibility, unlike the brash professor who was widely known for his searing criticisms of the church. McMurrin's plan would require permission from the McKays to disclose their father's views, which Llewelyn happily granted. For the next year and a half, Taggart would continue to tinker with the article. For the time being, McKay's secret lay buried in an unpublished manuscript.

★ ★ ★

Meanwhile, in the fall of 1968, Ernest Wilkinson became increasingly anxious about the investigation into BYU's racial policies. The clock was ticking, and Hollis Bach demanded a response to his May letter. Wilkinson expressed frustration at the Board's dithering and confided to BYU legal counsel Clyde Sandgren, "[T]he Board does not have any idea of the need for speed on this matter, but you and I do."[69] It had been nearly three months since federal investigators visited BYU, and Bach demanded a response. By November, Bach had run out of patience and sent Wilkinson a blunt letter urging the Board to make the civil rights issues raised by the investigation the highest priority at the next Board meeting.[70]

Deciding which of Bach's recommendations to adopt was difficult, in part, because BYU alumni, faculty, and students had different views about the recruitment of Black students. Esther Petersen, a prominent labor advocate and 1927 graduate of BYU, told Alumni Director Leslie Stone that she wouldn't make any additional financial contributions to the church or the university "as long as its racial policy remains unchanged."[71] BYU professor Merlin Brinkerhoff wrote a pointed letter to football coach Tommy Hudspeth and asked a simple question: "Why do we not actively recruit Negroes for our football team?" The professor found it difficult to explain to his professional colleagues why BYU gave scholarships "to many non-members of the Church, but not to black non-members of the Church." At the same time, a student survey in the school newspaper revealed that some "students favor Negro recruitment," though a number of them strongly rejected the idea. When asked "Should Brigham Young University actively pursue the recruitment of Negro athletes?" one student emphatically answered, "No! If you are going to have Negro athletes you've got to have Negro girlfriends. I have been at other schools and have seen the problems of integration—Negroes dating white girls—and this is bound to happen."[72] That is precisely what the Board feared.

As pressure from Bach mounted, Wilkinson had to deal with another troubling event that occupied his attention. In November, rumors circulated that Black Power student-advocates at San Jose State planned to boycott the football game against BYU that fall. Harry Edwards, an outspoken African American sociologist at San Jose State, and leader of the boycott, made it clear how much he detested racism and, by extension, BYU. "We're going after them," Edwards said of BYU to the *San Francisco Chronicle*, "and if they don't change their ways, we'll close them up."[73]

Edwards wasn't to be trifled with; he had a history of bringing attention to racial injustices. He had helped to organize the UTEP protests against BYU, and he inspired the highly publicized Black Power salute that track stars Tommie Smith and John Carlos had given during the 1968 Summer Olympics in Mexico City.[74] BYU officials thus took the alleged boycott seriously and dispatched their own security team to San Jose State to ensure the safety of coaches and players. A police convoy escorted the BYU football team to their hotel. On the night of the game, someone phoned the hotel threatening to blow it up. During the game itself dozens of students, both Black and White, held up protest signs outside the stadium condemning "the Mormon Church and its 'sub-human' treatment of Negroes."[75]

In December, the Board finally responded to Bach's letter. The school would follow five of its recommendations, but on the sticky issue of recruiting Black faculty, BYU wouldn't budge. And Wilkinson made it known that the school wouldn't follow "any general program of recruitment," though it would seriously consider "any qualified Negro member" of the church who applied.[76]

The response troubled BYU Vice President of Academic Affairs Robert Thomas, who urged Wilkinson to stand up to the Board. "I think you will need to point out to the Brethren that we can't escape the explicit question 'Do you recruit Negroes?' [and] as long as our answer is negative or ambiguous, we will be under increasing pressure."[77] Thomas also informed Wilkinson what would happen if the university didn't change its recruitment policies: "Few universities would associate with BYU"; BYU would lose qualified faculty if the school lost federal funds; and the school "would be almost sure to lose accreditation." Other considerations too weighed on Thomas. He told Wilkinson, "[I] would like to believe that there is no discrimination at BYU because we fully practice the principles of Christian love and brotherhood rather than because of the practical necessity to obtain funds from federal agencies that prohibit discrimination."[78]

Thomas's concerns, however, went unheeded. In early January 1969, during another contentious Board meeting, Board member Marion D. Hanks said that "[a] number of the Brethren were again in favor of hiding their heads." Few seemed to know what counsel to give Wilkinson as he pleaded for direction on how to deal with the athletic protests and the civil rights investigation. Harold B. Lee walked out in the middle of the meeting, "having said nothing." Apostle Richard L. Evans urged the Board to resist producing a statement indicating that the school recruited all students of "whatever race or creed." Why state it if it wasn't true? The majority of the Board agreed with Evans. By contrast, First Presidency counselor N. Eldon Tanner opined, "We could not long run away from this or refuse to face it." Hanks agreed. He didn't think it was fair to Wilkinson "to keep

146   SECOND-CLASS SAINTS

him silent in the face of all the attacks."[79] After a meeting the following month, Apostle Spencer W. Kimball noted that the Board "had a long and protracted discussion of the Negro question as it relates to Brigham Young University." Nothing was resolved.[80]

That spring brought more protests. In February, over one hundred protestors stormed the floor during the BYU–University of New Mexico basketball game. A few weeks later California State College at Hayward canceled a baseball game against BYU, and Stanford announced plans to cancel a basketball game against BYU in December. Most troubling, UTEP students asked the Western Athletic Association to investigate BYU for its racist practices. All of this angered Wilkinson. He asserted in a Board meeting, "No active recruiting program of Negro athletes has taken place at BYU because of the advice of the Executive Committee." Wilkinson resented the fact that the Board had hung him out to dry as he faced relentless criticism from the media and his peers in the Western Athletic Conference. Apostle Kimball called the Board meeting "a stormy one."[81]

The Board, seemingly indifferent to Wilkinson's frustration, returned to a strategy they had earlier dismissed. They told Wilkinson that faculty "should not even enter into contracts with the Government for research" and that university employees must "be completely free" of government entanglements. Apostle Lee also "questioned the right of the Government to tell BYU which teacher to employ." He was adamant that "we would run our school as we wanted to without regard for accreditation agencies." Apostle Benson, likewise, thumbed his nose at the federal government and told Wilkinson that Bob Jones University, an ultraconservative fundamentalist school in South Carolina, should be commended for refusing federal funds.[82]

Nor would the Board grant BYU permission to recruit "Negro athletes." Lee informed Wilkinson that "he would close BYU if we ever had a colored athlete on our teams."[83] But the Brethren were far from unified on the subject. Apostle Evans confided to Wilkinson that "not having Negro players on our teams" would jeopardize BYU's standing in the conference and only "intensify criticism" against the school and the church. Others, like First Presidency counselors Brown and Tanner, and Apostle Kimball, expressed sympathy with Evans's position. Brown brazenly stated that the only way to satisfy the investigators was to grant Black men the priesthood.

Still others—Apostles Stapley, Benson, Petersen, and Smith—joined Lee in rejecting the government's request for BYU to recruit Black athletes and faculty.[84]

Wilkinson was caught between the conflicted Board and the demands of federal investigators. Nor could he look to President McKay for assistance. The prophet's poor health prevented him from attending Board meetings that spring, and he seemed largely unaware of the trouble that BYU and the church were facing. Marion Hanks informed him about the athletic protests, the canceled games, and "the pamphlets being passed out of ancient stuff written by President Smith and others." McKay was "astonished and sorrowed by all of this," Hanks reported in his diary.[85]

Some of Wilkinson's closest associates were not much help, either. As Wilkinson stewed over the Board's hasty and ill-conceived plan to cut off all federal assistance, William Berrett admitted what the civil rights investigators suspected but couldn't quite prove: that BYU and the church harbored racist policies. The previous month Berrett had offered guidance to church religious instructors. "What can we tell students as they are confronted with the charges that our Church is discriminating against the Negro?" he asked. "Tell them it is true. We are prejudiced, but so is every other white group."[86]

Prudence might dictate that Berrett stop before he made BYU's plight worse, but he wanted the teachers to know that all the pressure in the world would not force an end to the ban. "No teacher should give apologies for the fact that Negroes cannot hold the priesthood," he proclaimed. "All the prophets from Joseph Smith to President McKay have had the same response to their prayers. We have people who think that if enough social pressure is brought to bear, then there will be a revelation of convenience to do away with the Negro not holding the priesthood." Such people were essentially apostates, he said.[87]

Certainly, it was unwise of Berrett to give such a talk in the midst of a federal civil rights investigation. Neither was it wise to claim that the church "was prejudiced" or admit that no outside pressure would force the church to abandon its race teachings. Berrett's entire address reeked of stubborn defiance, of desperation, and of an unwillingness to read the room and keep quiet. One imagines that this is the kind of poor judgment that kept Wilkinson up at night—causing him to fret that his associates should have been working with him and not against him.

SECOND-CLASS SAINTS

In any event, what convinced Bach to exonerate BYU was Wilkinson's insistence that the school had been recruiting Black students since the investigators deemed BYU out of compliance with federal law. Wilkinson decided to tell Bach that BYU had been recruiting "negro students" in Utah and Wyoming—a dubious claim given the paucity of Black people in those states. His strategy was disingenuous at best, unethical at worst. The crafty president could say that BYU was making an effort to recruit Black students, even though he knew that it wouldn't yield the results the investigators demanded. Wilkinson informed Bach that "negro students" in the fiftieth percentile on aptitude tests in those states would receive "a letter inviting their further consideration of BYU."[88]

Wilkinson was playing a dangerous shell game with federal investigators. He insisted that BYU was recruiting minority students when the school wasn't, as he later admitted. Only three Black students enrolled at BYU in 1969—unchanged from 1968—and all of them felt out of place among the predominantly White student body. One Black BYU student took his grievances public: "We are spectacles here. We feel uncomfortable."[89] Nevertheless, Bach took Wilkinson at his word and informed him in a letter that BYU was now in compliance with the Civil Rights Act of 1964.[90] But that wasn't the end of it. Bach still demanded that BYU recruit Black faculty, and he asked Wilkinson to participate "in a Talent Search program" to identify qualified instructors. He also wanted to know if BYU would recruit "minority guest lecturers." And finally, Bach wanted evidence that "negro recruitment" was paying off. He vowed to visit campus again in October 1969 and demanded a list of minority students "by race."[91]

Bach's letter clearing BYU of civil rights violations provided Wilkinson with fodder to counter his critics, but Wilkinson knew that if the university didn't boost Black student enrollment federal investigators would come after them again. Moreover, Bach's unambiguous demand that BYU recruit Black faculty forced Wilkinson, once again, to navigate between the whims of the Board and the demands of federal law. Apostle Lee told an anxious Wilkinson "to sit tight and it will take care of itself," but Wilkinson knew that further inaction would only cause more trouble for the beleaguered school.[92]

As the investigators prepared for another visit, Wilkinson grew increasingly anxious—an anxiety compounded by "thousands of stories" that

INVESTIGATIONS AND PROTESTS   149

journalists had published on student protests, which had now spread to dozens of other schools.[93] Between October 1967 and May 1969, he explained to the Board, "there were 471 student disturbances or riots on campuses throughout the country, 25 bombings, 46 arsons or suspected arsons, and 67 incidents of general destruction, involving injuries to 589 persons."[94] Black Power advocates like Harry Edwards, anti–Vietnam War activists, and other provocateurs had made their positions known on dozens of college campuses, and it was only a matter of time, Wilkinson feared, before they found their way to Provo.[95]

★ ★ ★

It was in this hothouse atmosphere of paranoia and uncertainty that First Presidency counselor Hugh B. Brown intensified his efforts to lift the ban. Clare Middlemiss, David O. McKay's secretary, said that Brown couldn't "sleep at night because of the condition of the church."[96] The eighty-six-year-old counselor was simply overwhelmed by the negative publicity. In September 1969, he worked with Lawrence and Llewelyn McKay, the president's sons, to pressure the prophet to ordain Black men to the priesthood. The previous month Brown had dinner at the Hotel Utah with prominent Mormon liberals who favored such a move, including Marion Hanks, Lowell Bennion, Sterling McMurrin, and Obert Tanner. Whether McMurrin shared Taggart's manuscript with Brown at this meeting is not known, but it is clear that Brown knew about it and was determined to make use of it.[97]

On September 10, the McKay sons met with their father at his apartment. Lawrence McKay had approached his father "several times" before about ending the ban, but each time his father had said that he "never had a revelation on that."[98] Now, realizing that their father was in the final stages of his life, Lawrence and Llewelyn decided to pressure him. Lawrence brought a copy of Taggart's manuscript, which Brown had given him. First Presidency counselor Dyer also attended the meeting, suspecting that something sinister was about to take place. Lawrence immediately began thumbing through the manuscript and asked his father a point-blank question that few others had the temerity to ask: "[W]hat proof do we have that Negroes are descendants of Cain?" Lawrence reasoned that Taggart's article brought "the whole Negro question regarding the right to hold the

Priesthood into focus," and he asked, "[I]f this truly was a practice and not a doctrine, as Sterling McMurrin had inferred ... then why was this not time to drop the practice[?]"[99]

Dyer panicked. He hadn't heard of the Taggart manuscript and demanded to see a copy. Lawrence handed it over and, after hastily thumbing through it, Dyer abruptly proclaimed, "[I]t has many erroneous statements and concepts in it." Most troubling to Dyer was Taggart's insistence that the ban wasn't doctrinal and therefore could be lifted at the president's discretion. Dyer responded by claiming that the ban "could be changed only as the Lord would direct through His Servant," the prophet. Dyer then went on to lecture the McKay sons about the curse of Cain and the preexistence.[100]

It must have been humiliating being lectured by Dyer about a teaching the McKays had heard their entire life. Nevertheless, Dyer feared that the Taggart manuscript had pried open a door he wished to slam shut. The president was obviously frail and was certainly vulnerable. Dyer feared that the sons and Brown would manipulate him into reversing the ban. He insisted on a revelation, because that meant the entire Quorum of the Twelve would have to support it, and Dyer clearly knew that Brown and the McKays didn't have the support of the hard-liners.

The following week Dyer began laying the groundwork to preserve the ban. During a meeting on September 17, he informed the First Presidency that he would make a thorough study of Taggart's manuscript, but he prefaced his remarks by saying that he "considered it one of the most vicious, untrue articles that has ever been written about the Church." It was full of "untruths and vilifications."[101] Two weeks later Dyer completed his assessment of the Taggart manuscript and shared copies of this report with the First Presidency. He began with a bold statement, directed squarely at counselor Brown: "Any effort to force the Church to alter the program of the Lord as it is now understood and is a part of our religious beliefs, unless sanctioned by Him, would be ineffectual." He then proceeded to ignore most of Taggart's claims and reaffirmed all the traditional dogma that Joseph Fielding Smith and others had used through the years to justify the ban.[102]

Brown refused to read the report. He had "a very strong ego" and wasn't about to be lectured to by someone for whom he had minimal respect.[103] Dyer and Smith both strongly opposed Brown's effort to lift the ban, but the other counselor, N. Eldon Tanner, appeared to support Brown. Tanner told the counselors about a letter he received from a Reed Wahlquist, a tithe-paying Latter-day Saint, who claimed that the late George Albert Smith had said "the negro question was one of custom and not of revelation." When Joseph Fielding Smith heard this, he exploded in anger: "He is wrong on that[!]"[104]

Undaunted, Brown and the McKay sons pressed further. Using Taggart's manuscript as leverage, they convinced the president that lifting the ban didn't require a revelation. They had a sense of urgency because Brown believed that if the ban wasn't changed "while President McKay is alive . . . we'll be set back several years . . . as long as Joseph Fielding Smith and Harold B. Lee are in control."[105] Tanner supported the move, as did Apostle Kimball, but it appears that few other apostles knew Brown's intentions. Apostle Lee certainly didn't. He was in the hospital with an undisclosed illness. Apostle Benson was away on church business. The record isn't clear on whether the rest of the Twelve understood what was about to transpire.[106]

Sometime in late September, Brown and the McKay sons convinced President McKay to ordain Monroe Fleming, "a faithful Negro member," to the Melchizedek Priesthood. Fleming was a safe choice. The Brethren all knew and liked him; many considered him a friend. He had worked at the church-owned Hotel Utah for thirty years, was a loyal Mormon, and loved the church despite enduring humiliating taunts from critics who called him an "Uncle Tom" for belonging to a church that treated him as an inferior.[107] Plus, he always said the right things in public about the ban, having affirmed many times over the years that the ban would end according to God's timetable. Privately, however, he was anguished that he couldn't hold the priesthood. It pained him that he was excluded from the church's rituals, and he informed Jerald Tanner, the ex-Mormon critic of the church, that "most of the members of the Negro race" wanted the priesthood, himself included.[108]

When Apostle Lee learned of McKay's intention to ordain Fleming, he marshaled his allies and mounted a vigorous protest. Lee's daughter Maurine said that as long as her father was alive Black people would "never have the priesthood," and Lee's opposition to Fleming's ordination made that prediction true. Wilkinson observed that Lee "would not consent to any change of policy as respects the Negro problem."[109] The details are scant on which apostles assisted him and what their reactions were to Fleming's anticipated ordination, but all joined with Lee to oppose McKay's unilateral decision to lift the ban.

152   SECOND-CLASS SAINTS

Predictably, Brown was devastated. His failure to end the decades-old restriction plunged him into a deep depression. "Some of the other Brethren got wind of it and put a stop to it," Brown bitterly noted.[110] Worse, he knew that time was running out. McKay, who had just turned ninety-five, was in no condition to fight the hard-liners. Deteriorating health had muted his voice.[111] Apostle Kimball was equally crestfallen. He was in favor of Fleming's ordination, but Lee forced him to rescind his support. "I fear Brother Lee," Kimball is reported to have said. Wilkinson said Kimball had "soft feelings" and that "he will not dare oppose Brother Lee on any matters." Kimball had good reason to fear Lee. Lee was the most influential member of the Twelve and was widely considered to be the future church president.[112] None of the Brethren wanted to cross him.[113]

Despite Lee's formidable authority, though, it was Lee's ally Alvin R. Dyer who dealt with Brown. Dyer didn't have much luck convincing the stubborn Canadian to abandon his crusade. During a private meeting with Brown on October 8, Dyer asked him if he had read his critique of Taggart, and Brown said no. Brown had made up his mind: "We should give the Negro the Priesthood." Brown also repeated what N. Eldon Tanner said in a previous meeting—that George Albert Smith said the ban was a policy. Dyer didn't dispute that critical fact but insisted that it was "a practice based upon principles that have been revealed from the Lord." The meeting ended without any resolution but with a reservoir of distrust and a whole lot of ill will between Brown and Dyer. That night, Dyer wrote about the meeting in his diary, unable to control his disdain for his fellow counselor: "[Brown] had tried twice of late to get President McKay to withdraw the withholding of the Priesthood from the Negro, but President McKay had refused to move on it." Brown didn't even mention the meeting in his diary.[114]

Two days later, on October 10, the forlorn and defeated Brown spoke to a "large crowd" of Mormon students at the University of Utah.[115] It must have troubled him when a student asked if there was "a consensus among the First Presidency and the Council of the Twelve that the Negro ought not to hold the Priesthood." Brown couldn't quite bring himself to answer the question truthfully. His emotions were too raw to allow him to reveal what had just transpired. Choosing his words carefully, he said that the Brethren were "all united as of *now*, that the time has not come until the

INVESTIGATIONS AND PROTESTS 153

President speaks on it. When he does, we will be united in our response to his expressed wish."[116]

All of Brown's behind-the-scenes maneuvering occurred during an extremely contentious period. On October 11, a day after Brown's visit to the University of Utah, students at Arizona State staged "an anti-BYU demonstration" at a football game. The school's African American students paraded around the stadium with signs that read "Brigham Young University is an institution of both overt and covert racism."[117] A week later, fourteen Black football players at the University of Wyoming informed their coach that they would wear black armbands in an upcoming contest against BYU. Their coach, Lloyd Eaton, dismissed the athletes from the team, sparking a firestorm that captured the attention of *Sports Illustrated*, as well as *Jet* magazine, an African American publication, and dozens of newspapers across the country.[118] A national wire service report noted that the Black athletes were not protesting BYU per se, but the "racist policies" of the Mormon church. Wilkinson rightly feared that the "anti-BYU movement" had now extended to a full-throated critique of the church's priesthood policy. Also that month, representatives from UTEP asked BYU to resign from the Western Athletic Conference. There were even rumors that University of Utah president James Fletcher, a practicing Latter-day Saint, wanted BYU out of the conference. "BYU is going to have to actively recruit black athletes if they expect to stay," he said bluntly. Paul James, a BYU radio broadcaster, put it in even more stark terms: "[I]f these protests continue to grow and if we do nothing to take some of the pressure off the opposing schools . . . within six months we would be out of the 'athletic business.'"[119]

★ ★ ★

With events spiraling out of control, and anxiety at a fever pitch, Ernest Wilkinson sent the Board of Trustees a thirty-five-page memo titled "Charges of 'Racism' and 'Bigotry' against BYU and the LDS Church." Marked "private and confidential," the memo acknowledged that he had lied to federal authorities and stated that he couldn't do so any longer. Wilkinson told them that BYU treated Black athletes like White athletes, but he knew that was false.[120] "We . . . discriminate against the Negro in two particulars in relation to the athletic program," he told the Board. "We don't affirmatively recruit Negro athletes . . . [nor] do we offer athletic grants-in-aid to Negro students, as we do the whites." "Our policy," he grudgingly admitted, "would be considered highly discriminating by the NCAA and would cause us to lose their support." Recognizing the seriousness of the issue, Wilkinson provided the Board with several options: BYU could resign from the Conference; "pull out of athletics entirely"; continue its "present policy with respect to Negro athletes"; or "stop discriminating as a matter of policy" and recruit Black athletes. He implored the Board to allow BYU to recruit Black student-athletes, but he assured them that the university would keep the numbers low: "We do not intend to have many [Black students] at BYU," he frankly admitted, trying to preempt concerns about interracial dating and marriage.[121]

Wilkinson's forceful memo pushed the Board to reverse course and permit BYU coaches to recruit Black athletes and award them scholarships. The timing was crucial. In November 1969, commissioners in the Western Athletic Conference were scheduled to vote to remove BYU. Apostle Gordon B. Hinckley approached Harold B. Lee and expressed his concern, as did other Board members. The apostle listened to his colleagues and determined that BYU had to change course, lest the school—and the church—suffer irreparable damage.[122] Wilkinson marveled at the about-face. "At one time [Lee] said that he would close the BYU if we ever had a colored athlete on our teams. He has now given his consent to have a colored athlete." Wilkinson later reflected, "On many occasions before becoming a member of the First Presidency, he indicated his contempt for accreditation agencies. Since becoming a member of the First Presidency he has been very, very concerned that we do nothing to offend these accrediting agencies."[123]

BYU began recruiting Black athletes immediately after the Board changed the policy, but they were not out of the woods. The possibility of a racially inclusive university lay in the future, not the present, and although the university had made modest progress in recruiting Black student-athletes, the Board refused to budge on recruiting Black faculty. BYU would hire qualified Black Latter-day Saints for faculty positions, but they wouldn't recruit them.[124] The question then centered on whether BYU had a legal right to discriminate against non-Mormons in hiring practices.

INVESTIGATIONS AND PROTESTS

Could non-Latter-day-Saints teach at BYU, and, more specifically, could non-Latter-day-Saint Black faculty teach at BYU? These were all questions that had to be resolved.[125]

★ ★ ★

As if BYU's legal challenges weren't troubling enough, the school continued to be hounded by bad publicity. In November 1969, Stanford president Kenneth Pitzer dealt the university a severe blow when he announced that Stanford would discontinue all athletic relationships with BYU.[126] Pitzer explained, "[It] is the policy of Stanford University not to schedule events with institutions which practice discrimination on a basis of race or national origins or which are affiliated with or sponsored by institutions which do so." A California newspaper put it even more bluntly: "Mormon racial doctrine was the cause of Stanford University . . . severing relations with . . . Brigham Young University."[127]

Pitzer's announcement alarmed the Brethren. Apostle Hinckley wrote Stanford's vice provost Howard Brooks trying to convince him to get Pitzer to reverse his decision. And Wilkinson invited Pitzer to visit campus. "Such a visit I am sure would convince you that we practice no racial discrimination of any kind," he insisted. "Our Negro students are given the full rights of all other students and have no feeling of being inferior." Pitzer, however, refused to budge, which made the Brethren angry.[128] Their meetings that month were uncommonly long, their tempers short. The Board was as agitated as Wilkinson had ever seen them. They were "cantankerous as hell," he observed.[129]

The Brethren feared that other universities in the conference would follow Stanford's lead, which would leave the school without a conference. In recognizing the gravity of the decision, Stanford officials had called Hugh Brown before announcing that the school would sever ties with BYU. They wanted to make sure that they understood the church's teachings. They asked Brown if "Negroes" could be baptized into the church, and he said yes. They asked if "Negroes" could receive the priesthood, and he said no. But Brown then made a bold prediction that the church would lift the ban soon.[130]

Brown's prediction got back to Lee and infuriated him. Lee informed Brown that he would organize a committee to draft a statement that the First Presidency would sign reaffirming the doctrinal status of the ban. Lee was essentially demanding that Brown sign a statement that was contrary to his beliefs.[131]

In a memorandum marked "ULTRA CONFIDENTIAL," N. Eldon Tanner told Wilkinson what Lee was up to: a "special committee was to report on the Negro situation."[132] Lee, church education commissioner (and future apostle) Neal A. Maxwell, and Arizona State University president (and future general authority) G. Homer Durham, along with Apostle Hinckley, comprised the committee. According to Lee's instructions, Maxwell and Durham would join him in writing individual statements defending the church's racial theology. Hinckley would then meld them in what his biographer described as a "delicate and mentally exhausting" task. Others offered to help as well. Wilkinson sent Hinckley a list of suggestions to include in the statement. He called attention to President McKay's 1947 letter to Lowell Bennion and the First Presidency statement of 1949 (which he misdated 1951). Marion Hanks gave Lee a document stating his views about the priesthood ban and wrote in his diary that his views wouldn't please Lee. Hanks was right. Lee ignored him.[133]

The mélange that Hinckley patched together was a bold affirmation of the ban. Yet, unlike the 1949 First Presidency statement, it didn't attribute the ban to a divine curse or the preexistence. Rather, it stated that God didn't reveal why Black people were banned from the priesthood, adding that at a future date they would receive all the same blessings as the favored lineages, including the priesthood. Furthermore, the statement quoted liberally from President McKay's past teachings without acknowledging his recent attempt to ordain a Black man to the priesthood.[134] What are we to make of the statement? It was a public relations stunt designed to clear up the confusion that Brown had generated by speaking to Stanford officials about lifting the ban. Predictably, Brown initially refused to sign it, but he relented under "great pressure" from Lee. When Hanks saw Brown leave Lee's office after discussing the statement, he observed that Brown looked "very grey and red in the face and very subdued."[135]

Brown had only one card left to play, and he played it. As a precondition for his signature, he told Lee that a statement endorsing civil rights needed

INVESTIGATIONS AND PROTESTS   157

to be included. Lee reluctantly complied. Even that concession didn't make it any easier on Brown. He wept as he signed it, lamenting that the ban wouldn't be lifted in the foreseeable future. Tanner was no less dispirited. He read the statement and commented, "[W]e are all helpless until the Lord tells the Prophet." Hanks lamented that none of his ideas made it into the document.[136] President McKay didn't sign it; he was too ill.

Brown remained defiant. Two weeks after he signed the statement, he told Lester Kinsolving of the *San Francisco Chronicle* that the ban would soon end "since human rights are basic to the church.""The church's denial of its priesthood to Negroes of African lineage 'will change in the not-so-distant future,'" Brown predicted.[137] He had nothing to base this on, other than raw emotion and optimism, but it didn't matter: Brown was determined to see the policy go.

When Brown's interview with Kinsolving was published on Christmas Day 1969, the hard-liners exploded in anger. Lee fumed that Brown was "talking too much." Wilkinson opined that Brown had "very little support among his associates."[138] Sterling McMurrin, a loyal friend, recalled that Brown "faced intense opposition from some [of] the apostles."[139] Brown's interview with Kinsolving pushed the Brethren into releasing the statement before they were ready. They wanted the timing to be right so as not to give "the impression" that there was conflict between "President Brown" and the Quorum of the Twelve. Their plan was foiled, however, when *New York Times* reporter Wallace Turner received a copy of the statement and said he planned to publish it. It appears that Brown himself leaked it, but that is not clear from his private papers. On January 10, 1970, the Brethren preempted Turner and published it in the *Deseret News.*[140]

Brown paid a high price for his activism. When President McKay died in January 1970, Joseph Fielding Smith, the new church president, dropped him from the First Presidency, where he resumed his place of seniority within the Quorum of the Twelve. Brown was devastated.[141] To his friends, he shrugged off the demotion as a change that "will relieve me of many irksome duties which I have carried for quite some time."[142] In private, however, he lashed out. When an interviewer asked him if he "had a renewal of . . . feeling with President Smith as he has taken over from Pres. McKay," Brown angrily replied, "No comment. [Smith] is 93. He is worn out. He is done." While Brown reaffirmed his commitment to the church, he bitterly admitted that he had "had some experiences that were hard to take."[143]

Brown's dismissal from the First Presidency marked the end of an era and a "great loss to the Church," lamented McMurrin. Brown had "become the symbol of authentic liberality among the leaders of the Church," and now he was silenced, or at least severely muted.[144] Another supporter, Grant Ivins, son of the late First Presidency counselor Anthony Ivins, stated that "Brown represented their only hope for any progressive changes in the organization."[145]

With McKay gone and Brown at bay, the church's racial problems were now in the hands of ninety-three-year-old hard-liner Joseph Fielding Smith. He faced the daunting task of trying to burnish the church's image in the face of relentless protests.

6

Lobbying for the Priesthood, 1970–1973

Following David O. McKay's death in January 1970, all eyes in the church turned to Joseph Fielding Smith. He would be ordained the next president at the April general conference and sustained by the faithful as the "prophet, seer, and revelator." In the meantime, as Smith waited to be ordained, a rumor circulated that spring that he would be bypassed in favor of Apostle Ezra Taft Benson, whose right-wing views were embraced by some sectors of the church. Nothing ever came of the rumor, and Apostle Harold B. Lee debunked it in conference, but it spoke to an issue that many Latter-day Saints feared but didn't dare speak: Could Smith, given his advanced age, perform his duties?[1]

Smith had been sleeping through many of the meetings, which prompted Hugh B. Brown to note that the new president was "worn out." Many feared that Smith didn't have the stamina to fulfill his obligations as church president.[2] They needn't have worried. His two counselors—Harold B. Lee and N. Eldon Tanner—were skilled administrators, and most of the responsibilities of running the global church fell to them as well as the Quorum of the Twelve. Among the most pressing issues was the ongoing civil rights investigation. The ongoing athletic protests also consumed them. At the same time, a group of outspoken Black Latter-day Saints demanded the priesthood. After meeting with Apostles Gordon B. Hinckley, Thomas S. Monson, and Boyd K. Packer, Eugene Orr, one of the participants, stated bluntly, "The cards were laid on the table and the Apostles were told that Blacks in the Church want the Priesthood."[3]

This was a dramatic request, but it didn't sway Smith. Throughout his ministry, Smith made it clear where he stood on the ban, and no one in the high church leadership believed that he would lift it. In January 1970, a journalist from the *Honolulu Star Bulletin* published an interview in which Smith reaffirmed his position. When he asked Smith about the ban, the Mormon leader gave his characteristic reply: "Young man, Joseph Smith did not decide that the Negro should not have the priesthood. Brigham Young did not decide it. David O. McKay did not decide it. . . . God did." After hearing Smith's conviction, the journalist concluded, "There is no indication that [Smith] will sway under pressure."[4]

And yet Smith had every reason to lift the ban. It would have eased tension with civil rights investigators, quelled the protests, and satisfied liberal Mormons. Instead, the Brethren launched a massive public relations blitz to burnish the church's image. This effort consumed Smith's presidency and that of his successor, Harold B. Lee, and it would dog them even as the Nixon administration announced that it would revoke the tax exemption of churches and universities that harbored discriminatory policies.

★ ★ ★

On a chilly winter day in January 1970, as David O. McKay lay dying in his apartment at the Hotel Utah, Apostle Spencer W. Kimball told his son Andrew about a prophecy that the elder Kimball's grandfather had made many years earlier. "Grandfather said," the apostle explained, that a "test" would be coming and that Latter-day Saints had to be prepared. Spencer told his son that he believed the test was "the negro." "Our enemies will increase and present a formidable opposition. I expect that numerous of the spiritually weak will fall by the wayside and some of them will even join the enemy."[5]

Little did Apostle Kimball know of "the tests" that lay ahead. Four days later, the apostles received a letter from Howard Marsh, the regional representative to the Twelve, informing them that White Mississippians were protesting school busing policies. Marsh said that a "good number of members of the Church are considering moving from the state of Mississippi" rather than integrate.[6] The next day the Brethren received word that a stake president in Jacksonville, Florida, had been complaining about "[b]using children into Negro ghetto areas," which he feared "would endanger [White Mormon children] spiritually, physically, mentally and socially."[7]

If those problems weren't enough, the athletic protests had now spread from football to basketball. A journalist from *Sports Illustrated* astutely observed, "As much as the [BYU] Cougars would like to ignore them, the protests have grown in intensity to the point where they have almost transcended all else."[8] Even more alarming, the protests had devolved into violence. On February 5, the BYU basketball team played against Colorado State University in Fort Collins. Tensions at the university had been mounting for weeks. Students from Colorado's Black Student Association (BSA), defiant over the Vietnam War and racial injustices, met with university administrators. The BSA students failed to get the game canceled but secured permission from university president Adrian Chamberlain to "stage a peaceful demonstration in conjunction with the contest."[9] President Chamberlain informed Ernest Wilkinson of the plan prior to the game, explaining that he would allow students "to stand in protest against policies of . . . BYU and the Mormon Church." Wilkinson seethed. Allowing students to protest was not only foolish, he believed, but also "discourteous." Plus, it would only invite "further trouble."[10]

Wilkinson's premonitions proved accurate. A faculty adviser to the BSA, who was supposed to be offering a "special invocation," launched into "a tirade against . . . BYU and the Mormon Church." Wilkinson called it "a very inflammatory speech."[11] Following the prayer, as the BYU basketball team warmed up, raucous student protestors unleashed a verbal barrage on the BYU players, spewing obscenities at them and calling them racists. Student protestors held up signs that read "Bigot Young University."[12]

At halftime, as BYU's "pom-pom girls" were doing a routine, about 150 students stormed the floor, plunging the arena into hysteria. The BYU cheerleaders, unable to process what was happening, continued their routine until a student protestor exposed himself to them, after which they scurried off the floor. Fistfights broke out between protestors and "indignant fans." Someone in the upper level hurled a Molotov cocktail to the floor, narrowly missing BYU sports broadcaster Paul James and splashing gasoline everywhere. Fortunately, there was no fire.[13] Moments later someone threw a tire iron from the same upper stands, hitting a reporter from the *Rocky Mountain News* in the head, leaving him unconscious, lying motionless in a pool of his own blood. For Paul James, it was an evening never to be forgotten. Years later he rued, "I was almost a victim . . . of one of the ugliest incidents ever to take place on a basketball floor."[14]

The ordeal in Fort Collins caused Wilkinson inexpressible grief. The beleaguered president searched for answers and struggled to make sense of

Students from the Black Student Association at Colorado State University giving the Black Power salute during a basketball game against Brigham Young University, Fort Collins, Colorado, February 5, 1970. Courtesy of Special Collections, Colorado State University Libraries.

it all. He asked BYU religion dean Daniel Ludlow if he knew "of any revelations that are specific as to what we might expect by way of disorders in the near future. Anything you can give me will be helpful in this time of crisis."[15] The violent outburst at Colorado State affected others as well, in equally dramatic ways. BYU basketball coach Stan Watts bitterly complained that "these people" aren't "after us. They're after America." Dean Ludlow lashed out at the demonstrators as well, asserting that they "are not really demonstrations against the racial policies of this University ... but against The Church of Jesus Christ of Latter-day Saints." They are against the "freedom of religion" and the "constitutional government of the United States." Unconsciously echoing Kimball, Apostle Lee told students later that fall, "This is a time of testing, the likes of which the Church has never gone through."[16]

Just three days after the incident in Colorado, activist Jerry Rubin, one of the nation's most militant anti–Vietnam War protestors and cofounder of the Youth International Party, a radical offshoot of the antiwar movement, gave a fiery speech at the University of Utah, in which he declared, "We

LOBBYING FOR THE PRIESTHOOD 163

will either integrate the Mormon Church or we will destroy it."This incendiary language alarmed the Brethren. Rubin was known as a fire-breathing radical who associated with a number of left-wing causes. Authorities in Chicago wanted to arrest him for fomenting a riot there, and some of the antiwar rallies he led had devolved into violence. He was a vocal and unabashed supporter of Black Power and a friend of Black Panther leader Eldridge Cleaver.[17] Adding fuel to the fire was an LDS Vietnam veteran named William Koerner, a devotee of Cleon Skousen's and Ezra Taft Benson's conspiracy theories, who was going around to LDS congregations and predicting that militant activists like Rubin would return to Salt Lake to make good on his threat to destroy the church. Koerner, Lee grimly noted, had aroused "people to a fever pitch, with scare stories about impending doom." The Brethren instructed Koerner's bishop to excommunicate him, which stifled his ability to speak in LDS meetinghouses.[18]

In this highly charged environment, Lee and his associates decided to beef up security at church headquarters. They feared not only activists like Rubin and his Black Power allies, but also fellow Latter-day Saints whom Lee called "Judases within the church."[19] On February 14, some nine days after the Colorado State game and about a week after Rubin's address, Lee asked the Presiding Bishopric to devise enhanced security measures that would protect the upper leaders of the church. They increased the number of armed security personnel around church headquarters, replaced night watchmen with trained security professionals, installed riot-proof glass on the main floors of the church headquarters, and assigned a personal security detail to Lee himself and the other top leaders. "President Lee even had a police escort when he went to the barbershop," according to one account.[20]

★ ★ ★

The ongoing protests continued to convulse the church, and the Brethren recognized that they needed a coordinated response to the negative publicity. To improve the church's image, they developed a two-pronged approach with both BYU administrators and church officials playing a role. Black and White students would sing together at halftime of the BYU basketball games to give the impression of "brotherhood." Heber Wolsey, the assistant to the president for communications, would write a public relations piece and distribute it to newspapers. Wilkinson instructed him to stress three critical points: (1) that the Mormon "Priesthood is merely a particular assignment not involving civil rights"; (2) that the priesthood ban could be lifted only through a revelation to the church president; and (3) that BYU was sensitive to the needs of "minority groups, including blacks."[21]

The Brethren also launched a PR campaign. First Presidency counselor Lee called for an urgent meeting of apostles and prominent LDS business-men. Apostle Mark E. Petersen explained that the committee would "take in the direction of public relations to help combat some of the unfavorable publicity that we have been having."[22]

Apostles Richard L. Evans, Spencer W. Kimball, Ezra Taft Benson, and Gordon B. Hinckley and counselor Lee led the meeting, and J. Willard Marriott, Lee Bickmore, and Robert Sears—three LDS businessmen—joined them. Two well-connected LDS lawyers, George Mortimer and Robert Barker, also attended. Apostle Kimball explained that the com-mittee had "a long discussion about all the problems of the Church," adding that the "persecution was beginning to pile up[:] the negro question, the [Vietnam War] draft status and many other areas."[23]

Out of this meeting emerged the "formal genesis" of the church's public relations department. The Brethren believed that this would help to combat what they perceived were false stories about the church in the press. Because "newspapers and other news media" were "making light and picking on us," Apostle Kimball lamented, the committee decided "that we should de-velop a very strong, positive position and program and feed the news media with successful stories."[24]

How did BYU students respond to all the negative publicity? They were devastated. "The students are hurt and angry," the New Yorker noted. "There's probably not a higher type of student body in the United States," a BYU official told the magazine. The campus was squeaky clean, he stressed, and the students were clean-cut, well-groomed, and intensely patriotic: "When the flag goes up, the students come to attention. On other campuses, the students burn the flag. Our students are patriotic and they're well dressed, and these are the people who are being persecuted. The kooks, the hippies, the filthy people—they're not persecuted." The official continued, "There is a feeling among students and administrators that the press had not fairly presented the University's position that the restriction on Negroes holding the priesthood is purely a religious matter and has no connection with the University's policies on race."[25]

BYU students and staff weren't the only ones who claimed to be vic-tims in the protests against the university and the church. Popular BYU religion teacher Cleon Skousen, a close friend of Apostle Benson's, wrote a conspiracy-laced screed declaring that communists had fomented the student protests. The "Negro issue [was] a smokescreen," he claimed. "The negro-priesthood issue means absolutely nothing to the Communists or to the protestors. How could it?" Skousen asked. "They don't even know what it is! This entire attack is but a vehicle to further their ulterior objectives." Skousen's conspiracy-fueled tirade showed just how desperate he was to make sense of a troubling reality that no one in the church could seem to control. His speech even made the *New York Times*, stoking racial tensions at the same time the church was trying to ease them through an aggressive public relations campaign.[26]

Indeed "The Communist Attack on the Mormons," as Skousen titled his address, was precisely the kind of right-wing extremism that the church didn't need in such an explosive environment. Counselor Lee and President Smith once called Skousen's writings "B.S."[27] Nevertheless, his conspiracy theories captivated Latter-day Saints. Next to Bruce R. McConkie and Joseph Fielding Smith, Skousen was the most popular Latter-day Saint author of the time, having sold hundreds of thousands of copies of *The Naked Communist*, in which he claimed without evidence that communist spies lurked within the U.S. government, churches, universities, and businesses. Skousen's insatiable desire for publicity propelled his outlandish claims, and many Latter-day Saints, like so many other Christians, embraced conspiracy theories in the midst of Cold War hysteria.[28]

Skousen peddled his conspiracy theories on the speakers' circuit of the ultraconservative John Birch Society, as well as in LDS meetinghouses; for the latter he drew a stern rebuke from the First Presidency.[29] "The Communist Attack on the Mormons" had merely expanded on conspiracy tropes that he'd been preaching for years. Not surprisingly, given that the two were neighbors and close friends, "The Communist Attack on the Mormons" drew extensively from Apostle Benson's controversial general conference sermon "Civil Rights: Tool of Communist Deception."[30]

Just a couple of weeks after Skousen published "The Communist Attack on the Mormons," the Brethren received word from Roy Fugal, a prominent LDS businessman, that "the less responsible of the Black element may try to disrupt sessions of General Conference" in April. Fugal said he had contacts with a number of Black leaders—including Whitney Young of the National Urban League, the Rev. Leon Sullivan of Zion's Baptist Church, and Hobart Taylor of President Nixon's Committee on Equal Employment

166   SECOND-CLASS SAINTS

Opportunity—implying that he heard the rumors from one of them.[31] In 1965, and again in 1967, the Brethren placed armed guards around Temple Square and snipers on the roof at the Salt Lake Temple in response to such rumors. This time, they took even more drastic measures.[32]

On April 2, church security personnel received a bomb threat against the Tabernacle as the Mormon Tabernacle Choir rehearsed. There was another bomb threat that night during a rehearsal of the Utah Symphony Orchestra.[33] Apostle Kimball captured the mood: "We go into Conference with some apprehension for many weeks. We have been increasing the security around the buildings because of threats being made that there would be bombings and demonstrations and possible riots, and some veiled threats against the Brethren. We have had uniformed police in the front office of the lobby and at the backdoor and near the temple" as well as "plain clothesmen" security officers who guarded "our building."[34]

Kimball and his fellow apostles were relieved when the first day of the conference "went off well" with "no untoward incidents."[35] But during the Sunday afternoon session of the conference, as Theodore Tuttle, a lower-level general authority, delivered an End Times sermon promising Latter-day Saints, "[I]f ye are prepared, ye shall not fear," a police officer delivered an urgent message to Harold B. Lee. A bomb was about to go off, the note read. According to Lee's biographer, the counselor calmly replied, "There is no bomb in here; relax." The conference went on unabated.[36]

Despite three bomb scares in less than forty-eight hours, the Brethren managed to maintain an aura of confidence and normalcy at the conference. But the threats of violence did not end. After the general conference, when Joseph Fielding Smith visited Los Angeles to install a new temple president, Black Power militants made "a number of threats against his life and on his safety," a Latter-day Saint from Los Angeles remembered, prompting church officials to build a robust fence around the temple prior to his visit.[37] Also that month, a militant group called the Black United Front Organization threatened to commandeer a "Mormon Ward Chapel" in the Washington, D.C., area. Rev. Douglass Moore, the leader of the group, angrily announced that Mormons "are the most rabid racists. They can go back to Utah, go to hell or wherever they want to go." Apostle Kimball noted the ordeal in his diary: "It was an ugly threat—it looks bad."[38]

★ ★ ★

As the Brethren dealt with threats—real and perceived—BYU president Ernest Wilkinson continued to be dogged by the athletic protests. Students at the University of Arizona threatened to cancel all games with BYU, as did those at Wyoming, New Mexico, and other schools. The most significant threat, however, came from the University of Washington. Energized by the Seattle Liberation Front (SLF)—a "radical coalition" of anti–Vietnam War protestors from the community—who worked in concert with the Black Student Union (BSU) at the University of Washington—activists demanded that the university condemn the Mormon church for its anti-black teachings, brand BYU a racist institution, and sever all ties with the Utah school. One of their placards read, "Off BYU" and depicted the Black Power salute.[39]

Their anger toward BYU took an unfortunate turn when, prior to a competition with BYU gymnasts in January 1970, activists from the SLF and BSU smeared oil all over UW's gym mats, turned over tables and chairs, and dumped heaps of garbage everywhere, infuriating the gymnastics coach, who confronted the protestors. They threw a bucket of water in his face and cursed at him. Within days, African American UW gymnast Lynn Hall circulated a petition to sever all athletic contests with BYU, amassing over fifteen hundred signatures. One report stated that the SLF convinced "a majority of UW athletes" to sign "a pledge to not compete against BYU. At least three athletes said later they signed the statement under threat."[40]

Over the next several weeks protestors occupied UW campus buildings, disrupted classes, and were a general nuisance to the university community. University administrators sought—and received—a court injunction to quell "further disturbances and riots on their campus."[41]

In this caustic environment, John Hogness, UW's executive vice president, who was serving as acting president while President Charles Odegaard was on vacation, issued a statement proclaiming that the university would sever all ties with BYU. It was clearly a hasty concession to mollify militant activists. "The University," Hogness said, "intends to honor its existing schedule of athletic events with BYU, but it has no plans to schedule other events in the future." The news hit Wilkinson like a punch to the gut. At first, he was hurt; then he was furious. After the Stanford debacle and countless other threats to sever ties with BYU, his patience had run thin. Wilkinson and his PR assistant, Heber Wolsey, wrote letters to President Odegaard, pleading with him not to discontinue the relationship. The two schools had always

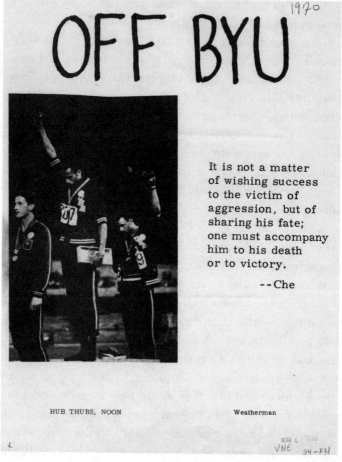

Advertisement by the Black Student Union at the University of Washington organizing a protest against Brigham Young University, Seattle, Washington, March 1970. Courtesy of Special Collections Division, University of Washington Libraries.

had a "fine relationship," Wolsey reminded him. For his part, Wilkinson denied that BYU was a racist institution and asked President Odegaard if BYU could send a representative to the University of Washington to clarify any misperceptions about "BYU's policy concerning blacks."[42]

When Odegaard returned from vacation he read Wolsey's and Wilkinson's letters and agreed to receive their emissary. The BYU president promptly dispatched Darius Gray and Heber Wolsey, for the first of many such trips the pair would make.[43] Gray was a wise choice. He was charming and witty, immensely likeable, and noticeably confident but not overbearing. Most important, he was Black—and a BYU graduate. Wilkinson hoped that this would give him instant credibility with militants and perhaps allay criticism that BYU harbored racist policies. Wolsey was also a fine choice. He was skilled in public relations, affable and approachable, and had a quick laugh and a keen sense of humor.[44]

Gray and Wolsey traveled to the Seattle campus on a cold, wet day in February 1970. It didn't go well. When they met with BSU students and leaders from the Black community they were treated with contempt. "We don't hate you Mormons from BYU," a community member told Wolsey, "but you represent the establishment, the white establishment that has kept us in bondage and as second-class citizens for generations, and I will fight you with every power I have."[45] Critics saved their worst invective for Gray, calling him an "Uncle Tom" and shouting obscenities at him as he tried to explain the priesthood restriction. A reporter was shocked at what he witnessed. That Gray should have been "subjected to such an inquisitorial form of abuse by such shallow, small persons under the banner of 'dialogue' is a disgrace."[46]

After this humiliating encounter, Wilkinson nudged Wolsey to finish a tract he had asked him to write weeks earlier. As both men knew, the tone had to be right. The Board of Trustees carefully reviewed the work, as did Wilkinson. The BYU president praised it, but he wanted an addendum attacking the militants, a clear sign that he was tired of enduring insults from what he perceived to be insufferable student activists. Wolsey, though, thought it unwise to denigrate their critics and let Wilkinson know it. The addendum was too caustic, Wolsey suggested, which made the BYU president angry. "You wouldn't make a very good lawyer," Wilkinson snapped, to which Wolsey retorted, "And you'd make a worse PR man." Alfred Schweppe, a local Seattle attorney and non-Latter-day-Saint, whom Wilkinson hired to advise BYU, settled the matter, siding with Wolsey. There was nothing to be gained by the addendum. Of all things, the lawyer noted, it was too "argumentative!"[47] With the full support of the Board of Trustees, they published it in newspapers in Washington, Oregon, and Utah.[48]

They may have dropped the most caustic part, but it was hardly a soft piece. In "Minorities, Civil Rights, and BYU," the LDS school went on the offensive. The tract made a distinction between civil rights and Mormon

Statement signed by BYU president Ernest L. Wilkinson, "Minorities, Civil Rights, and BYU," published in newspapers in Washington, Oregon, and Utah, 1970. Courtesy of L. Tom Perry Special Collections, Harold B. Lee Library, Brigham Young University.

LOBBYING FOR THE PRIESTHOOD

racial theology, implying that the two were entirely separate matters. What the church believed and taught about Black people was its own business, separate from the admissions policies of BYU. In other words, the former didn't influence the latter—or so the tract alleged. The tract also appealed to the Bible to justify the church's race policies, claiming that God had established a precedent in biblical times for denying certain groups of people privileges. Next, it explained that the federal government had cleared BYU of all civil rights violations. And, finally, it emphasized that BYU had successfully registered its first "Black football player" and added that the university had a long history of inviting Black speakers to Utah, including singer Marian Anderson, who was "barred from singing in Constitution Hall [in Washington, D.C.] because of her race."[49]

The tract attempted to give the impression that the university had a history of racial inclusion, but this was highly misleading. BYU didn't welcome Black students, and the tract failed to mention the federal government's ongoing investigation into BYU's hiring practices. Moreover, it was disingenuous to suggest that the church's racial teachings didn't affect BYU's admissions policies. The week before the tract was published, for example, Wilkinson wrote in his diary that "intermarriage" would be "one of the tragedies that will inevitably result if we have a sizeable number of Negro students at BYU."[50] Such words were hardly welcoming. None of that mattered to Wilkinson, though. What was important was that the tract placed the church and BYU in a positive light by offering a robust defense of LDS racial teachings. Wilkinson received dozens of congratulatory letters from people in the Seattle area, none of whom were Latterday Saints. They praised him for publishing the tract; some even sent the university money. One local Seattle resident captured the sentiment of the well-wishers, stating, "Your recent full-page advertisement in newspapers in this State has been extremely well received. I have had many people comment to me how unjust it was for your fine university to be attacked by a militant minority."[51]

This feedback pleased Wilkinson and the Brethren, of course, but BYU was still in a pinch. That spring, the Faculty Senate at the University of Washington voted to terminate all athletic relationships with BYU.[52] This drew a swift response from UW president Odegaard, who was trying to work with Wilkinson on a solution. Wilkinson fed him a steady diet of documents to ease his concerns that BYU and its sponsoring church harbored racist policies, and Odegaard, in return, delivered a blistering address rebuffing the BSU and SLF. The local newspaper published Odegaard's hard-hitting address.[53]

In the midst of all of this, the University of Washington sought "a judicial determination" in court to prove that it couldn't legally terminate its contract to compete against BYU "because of the religious beliefs of the Mormon Church."[54] Odegaard believed that this would bolster his cause against militant activists. He found the support he was looking for in the state's Attorney General's Office. Assistant Attorney General James Wilson wrote a preliminary analysis, concluding that the school "cannot determine its policies or its relationships on the basis of race or creed." That would constitute discrimination against BYU.[55]

As expected, the BSU rejected the attorney general's position and vowed to fight it in court. They wanted to prove that BYU and the Mormon church held racist policies toward Black people, and they found fodder in Mormon scriptures. In an interview with a local newspaper, BSU attorney James McIver provided a glimpse of the strategy he planned to pursue in court. He would target the faith's most cherished scripture—the Book of Mormon—to prove that racism was structurally embedded in Mormon theology. And he would demonstrate this by proving that all BYU students had to take religion classes that taught Mormon racial theology. "The Utah university has a requirement that all students take two courses in religion to receive a bachelor's degree," McIver stated, and that one of the courses was "an introduction to the Book of Mormon and its teachings." This "religious course," he stressed, "is discriminatory against black people." He asked the court to issue a "permanent injunction preventing any further athletic events with B.Y.U. until the teaching and practices of the institution [are] terminated or instructions in religion are removed from the mandatory curriculum." In this effort, McIver was aided by the Commission of Human Rights, comprised largely of faculty from the University of Washington. They also asked the courts to permit the university to sever all ties with BYU. Neither the BSU nor the Commission of Human Rights believed that the University of Washington was required by law to associate with an institution that blatantly discriminated against Black people. Now they claimed to have the goods to prove it.[56]

Throughout it all, Wilkinson kept Apostle Kimball and the Board of Trustees updated. The Brethren, predictably, were aghast at the recent turn of events and held a long Board meeting in April. Most of it was focused "on our relations with other athletic teams and relations with other universities resulting from the Negro-Priesthood doctrine of the Church," Wilkinson wrote.[57] Adding to Wilkinson's anxiety was Lowry Nelson, who had been following the athletic protests from afar. He sent the harried BYU president a flurry of letters that month. There was, in his view, no easy solution to the mess in which BYU and the church found itself, short of giving Black men the priesthood, a point Wilkinson ruefully acknowledged in a return letter. Both men knew that the ban wouldn't be lifted as long as Joseph Fielding Smith and Harold B. Lee were in charge. All Wilkinson could do, then, was to put Mormon racial teachings in the best possible light.[58]

Wilkinson's PR campaign wisely included students. In May, Heber Wolsey gave a spirited devotional address to the BYU student body imploring them to counter what he deemed were misperceptions and half-truths about Mormon racial teachings. "We need to use the mass media of communication more widely, and that means all of them—newspapers, television, radio, magazines, and so forth," Wolsey intoned. "[W]e need to utilize you Brigham Young University students more fully." He asked students not to be "spectators" in the fight against critics, but to "let people know what our beliefs are," even at the risk of being misquoted by the media.[59]

As BYU's media blitz unfolded, Wilkinson became more anxious with each passing day. He faced the daunting task of explaining alleged racism in Mormon scripture—something he felt ill-equipped to do. He was a lawyer, not a theologian, and wasn't comfortable pontificating on the finer points of Mormon scripture. Thus, visibly frustrated, Wilkinson asked BYU religion dean Daniel Ludlow for help. He wanted to know what scriptures could be deemed racist and whether students were tested on them.[60] BYU Academic Vice President Robert Thomas also contacted Ludlow, informing him, "We are . . . under increasing pressure from our critics concerning our curriculum at BYU. Recently, the Commission on Human Rights at the University of Washington took direct aim at the religion courses which are listed in our catalog." Thomas continued, "I'm sure the President is feeling unusual pressure from agencies which are accusing us of discriminating on the basis of creed. Would you please prepare something that I could take to him as soon as you can get around to it?"[61]

Ludlow surveyed his faculty with great dispatch.[62] He asked them what courses they offered in the College of Religious Instruction in which they taught "the Negro-Priesthood doctrine," and whether or not they asked

174   SECOND-CLASS SAINTS

questions about it on examinations. Three days later he produced a report that included ten pages of quotations from the Book of Mormon. These scriptures "might be used on either side of the questions of racial and/or religious discrimination," but he wanted to make the list comprehensive so that Wilkinson would be prepared if the university's legal counsel, Albert Schweppe, had to rebut the charges in court.[63]

Ludlow's report specified that the university required two Book of Mormon courses and that only a few professors asked students questions about the "Negro-Priesthood doctrine" in their classes. Only one professor discussed it in his Book of Mormon class. Other faculty taught the church's race teachings in classes called the "Teachings of Joseph Smith," "LDS Church History," and the "Pearl of Great Price"—the last of which was the main proof text for Black priesthood denial. Most of the faculty admitted to discussing the "Negro-Priesthood doctrine" only when students asked questions about it. Only one acknowledged asking questions about it on an exam.[64]

Wilkinson failed to disclose these critical facts to Schweppe, informing him that, while it was true that students were required to take a two-sequence course on the Book of Mormon, none of the church's race teachings was taught in those classes. Wilkinson conveniently ignored the fact that one faculty member said that he taught the "Negro-Priesthood doctrine" in his Book of Mormon class, and the president certainly didn't volunteer that the church's race doctrine was taught in other religion classes.[65] He had enough trouble to worry about, as he was still grappling with federal investigators. In June, Hollis Bach sent him a letter inquiring about recruiting Black faculty. It had been three months since Bach informed him that BYU was not in compliance with President Johnson's Executive Order stating that institutions that received federal funding couldn't discriminate in employment on the basis of race, color, or religion. Bach made three demands. First, the university had to remove all barriers "on the hiring of non-Mormons," which meant changing their application procedures to not privilege LDS applicants. Second, they had to discontinue lists the school compiled targeting potential LDS applicants. And third, BYU needed to "institute a program to overcome the effect of the past policy of excluding non-Mormons from faculty and employment."[66]

Bach's demands shocked and angered the Brethren. They scoffed at the federal government telling them who to hire at the Mormon-run school.

LOBBYING FOR THE PRIESTHOOD 175

Apostle Kimball, who was the chairman of the Board at the time, reported that the Board had a very "stormy session" at the June meeting.[67]

★ ★ ★

That summer brought the Brethren yet more angst. In July, Elmo Smith, a stake president from California, notified his uncle Joseph Fielding Smith about a bill working its way through the California legislature that could put the church in jeopardy. Although the bill was "directed towards the Elks Club and would require them to admit Negroes to membership or lose their tax exemption status," the stake president opined that it could affect the church if it passed.[68] The bill's sponsor, California lawmaker Fern Ellery, called for "any organization that institutionalizes racial inequality" to lose its tax-exempt status. He had the LDS church in his sights. The church's "policy banning Negroes from holding the priesthood is 'socially unacceptable and a racist doctrine,'" the fiery lawmaker said. The Brethren followed the bill's progress very closely.[69]

The Brethren had every reason to be concerned. In the late 1960s the Nixon administration vowed to crack down on churches and private Christian universities that engaged in discriminatory practices.[70] In addition, in January 1970, the U.S. Supreme Court ruled in *Green v. Connally* that religious schools that discriminated against Black students were not entitled to tax exemption. Wilkinson breathed a sigh of relief when he read the ruling and eagerly informed the Brethren that "it is clear . . . we made the proper decision to permit Negroes and other minorities to attend" BYU. He wasn't sure, however, whether "the failure to grant the priesthood to the Negro could conceivably be held to be a denial of civil rights." Wilkinson tried to separate the two issues, but he was keenly aware that critics wouldn't make the distinction.[71]

BYU did manage to avoid IRS scrutiny. The fact that they started recruiting Black students was surely one reason. Another might have been Nixon's secretary of the treasury, David Kennedy, a practicing Latter-day Saint, who had authority over the IRS. It's tempting to think that he might have used his influence to get the agency to give his church a pass, but there's no evidence for this.[72] Still, he would at least have been aware that BYU might be in legal jeopardy. Kennedy certainly knew that the IRS had targeted Bob Jones University. The fundamentalist Christian school refused to admit Black students, or allow interracial dating until 1971. They were

176   SECOND-CLASS SAINTS

stripped of their tax exemption in 1976. The LDS church filed a friend of the court brief arguing that private religious institutions had the right to establish their own racial policies under the Free Exercise Clause of the First Amendment.[73]

Even as BYU managed to steer clear of the IRS, civil rights investigators continued to hound them. With an accreditation review scheduled for the following spring, Wilkinson and his fellow administrators feared that the school would be penalized for its failure to recruit Black faculty or invite Black speakers to campus. In 1968, the Board passed a resolution allowing BYU to invite Black speakers as long as they did "not malign the church." The faculty had been pressuring Wilkinson for quite some time, and he reluctantly agreed to the request but said that speakers had to be "the right kind" of "negro" with the right kind of temperament. The BYU president told the faculty that the school didn't want crusaders or agitators or anyone who would "discuss the Negro question."[74]

The Brethren agreed to Wilkinson's criteria and limited the number of Black speakers to two per year, often rejecting them after careful scrutiny. Among the denied were NAACP spokesman Julian Bond, entertainer Bill Cosby, and acclaimed author Alex Haley. But as the civil rights investigation of BYU tightened, Wilkinson and his vice president Robert Thomas decided that it would be good PR to invite at least one prominent civil rights activist to campus. This was a deliberate strategy to appease federal investigators.[75]

They invited Thurgood Marshall, the nation's first Black Supreme Court justice and a key contributor in *Brown v. Board* (1954)—but he declined.[76] Next, Wilkinson and Thomas invited Roy Wilkins, the president of the NAACP. They were impressed with an article that Wilkins had written for the *Los Angeles Times*, "The Mormons and Negroes."[77] But he too declined. In subsequent years, a range of impressive Black leaders and public figures came to BYU, among them, poet and civil rights activist Maya Angelou, Olympian Jesse Owens, and Republican senator Edward W. Brooke. In 1977, just a few years after denying him a chance to speak, BYU even gave Alex Haley an honorary degree and asked him to give the commencement address.[78] But in 1970 the Board struggled to find someone who would agree to speak and would also win them points with investigators and the accreditation review team. That they continued to resist demands to recruit faculty of color certainly didn't help their cause.

In September 1970, Wilkinson wrote a lengthy rebuttal to Bach's June letter refuting point by point many of the charges against BYU. It would be impossible to recruit qualified Black Latter-day Saint faculty, Wilkinson insisted, because they didn't exist. In addition, Wilkinson resisted the government's demands to recruit non–Latter-day-Saints of color. This was not inconsequential, for as Wilkinson explained, BYU faculty had a special mandate to teach Mormon theology, and non–Latter-day-Saints couldn't do that. Wilkinson spent much of the letter discussing how the Humanities, Social Sciences, Family Living, Fine Arts, Business and Commerce, and even Physical Education departments taught their subjects through the lens of Mormonism. BYU's unique mission, Wilkinson explained, went back to founder Karl Maeser, who famously said that faculty "should not teach even the alphabet or the multiplication tables without the Spirit of God." Wilkinson also challenged Bach's legal analysis, contending that the government didn't have the authority to require BYU to hire non-LDS faculty. President Johnson's Executive Order, he stressed, didn't comport with Title VII of the Civil Rights Act of 1964, nor did it allow the government to dictate which faculty a private university should hire. In that context, he asked Bach to reconsider his "factual and legal conclusions."[79]

Wilkinson knew he was fighting an uphill battle. The Board had already given permission for Wilkinson to recruit "any qualified Negro member" of the church, but that was much different from actively recruiting non–Latter-day-Saints.[80] With so few Black Mormons, staffing BYU with qualified faculty of color was virtually impossible. Wilkinson laid out the stakes at the October meeting with the Board of Trustees. If they failed to comply with the government's demands, there would be a "disallowance of tax deductions for contributions to the University," BYU's status with "accrediting committees" would be jeopardized, and the university would lose "all research contracts." This was on top of the ongoing athletic protests—including new ones at San Diego State, the University of Arizona, and Western Michigan—and the University of Washington's threat to terminate its relationship with BYU.[81]

These were the most serious issues that Wilkinson and the Board faced in the fall of 1970. But there were other issues that continued to gnaw at them. They were losing the battle in the court of public opinion. Almost daily, it seemed, critics published stories calling attention to the church's racist policies. Some of these critics couldn't be brushed aside so easily.

178   SECOND-CLASS SAINTS

They had stature in the church; some were even related to general authorities. Grant Ivins, the son of the late First Presidency counselor Anthony
Ivins, published a hard-hitting editorial in the *Salt Lake Tribune*, chastising
Ernest Wilkinson for his "insistence that the church policy of denying
the priesthood to the Negro does not infringe on the civil rights of 'minority groups.'" This argument, Ivins claimed, "shows a complete lack of
understanding of the issue." Ivins went on to debunk the preexistent hypothesis and the curse of "Cain and Ham" teachings. He scoffed that "ten
thousand missionaries are spreading this doctrine and it is being taught in
auxiliary organizations and the seminaries and religious institutes of the
church."[82]

Fawn Brodie, David O. McKay's outspoken niece, added her voice to the
cacophony of critics. Since the publication of her Joseph Smith biography,
No Man Knows My History, in 1945, she had kept a low profile in Mormon
affairs, but the church's acquisition of Egyptian papyri in 1967—the basis
for part of the Pearl of Great Price—had plunged her back into Mormon
studies.[83] In October 1970, before a packed crowd of over five hundred people at the Hotel Utah, she gave a rousing address, in which she accused the
Mormon church of reinventing its racial history. There was nothing divine
about the priesthood ban or the way the church defined Black people as
cursed, Brodie asserted. Rather, she characterized Mormon racial teachings
as "Jim Crowism" and reaffirmed what she had written in *No Man Knows
My History*: the ban was the direct result of conflict in Missouri that had
nothing to do with God. Brodie's address riveted the audience. They were
"most sympathetic," she gushed to a friend.[84] The enthusiastic response led
the University of Utah Press to publish the address as a pamphlet. While
the *Salt Lake Tribune* covered the address in some detail, the church-owned
Deseret News ignored it completely.[85]

Another critic, Sharon Pugsley, an LDS graduate student, publicly
shamed the general authorities when she published an ad in the *Salt Lake
Tribune* calling for Latter-day Saints to donate money to Black charities to
account for the "psychological hurt" that Black children had "suffered while
growing up among people who believe and teach" that Black people "have
been cursed by God." The ad was forceful and direct. Across the top it read,
"Attention L.D.S." Below the caption Pugsley provided instructions on how
to donate to the Coretta Scott King Educational Fund in Washington, D.C.,
and the Meharry Medical College Fund in Nashville—both institutions

LOBBYING FOR THE PRIESTHOOD

that served African American communities. Pugsley sent a copy of the ad to general authorities and told them that the priesthood doctrine was "immoral because it is degrading to human beings."[86] Former CES instructor Heber Snell congratulated Pugsley on her fine work and expressed his wish that her "protest will not fall on deaf ears."[87]

But it wasn't just critics of the church who expressed concerns. The news stories condemning LDS racial teachings alarmed even believing Latter-day Saints. Many sought answers from the First Presidency. An earnest member from Kentucky was "concerned about the Negro question." Another from Chicago asked hard questions "regarding the Negro." A brother from Hawaii wanted his questions answered "about the position of the Church in regard to the Negro."[88] Not all of the letters were civil in their tone. In an anonymous letter addressed to Joseph Fielding Smith, Hugh B. Brown, N. Eldon Tanner, and Robert L. Simpson, the writer assailed church leaders for the "stand the Church is taking on the Negro-priesthood situation," which "makes the Church look foolish and its leaders ignorant." The writer pointed out the absurdity of proselytizing in South America, a region filled with people of African descent, and bluntly told the Brethren that they were "alienating" the "young people" of the church by proselytizing there: "They see the absurdity of the Church granting the Priesthood to people of one continent or area, without worrying about Negro blood, and refusing it to people of another area. . . . Ethnically, medically, morally, sociologically, and historically this position is indefensible."[89]

As these criticisms escalated in the fall of 1970, the Brethren made a pivotal move. In December, at the end of an extremely difficult year, the BYU Board of Trustees agreed to hire Wynetta Martin, the school's first African American professor. Not much is known about Martin or the circumstances in which she was hired. But what we do know is that the Board had previously refused to hire Black faculty. In 1960, for example, Ernest Wilkinson, under the Board's direction, rejected a Latter-day Saint candidate when it was discovered that the man was Black. "I wish we could take him on our faculty, but the danger in doing so is that students and others take license from this, and assume that there is nothing improper about mingling with other races," Wilkinson explained. "Since the Lord, himself, created the different races and urged in the Old Testament and other places that they be kept distinct and to themselves, we have to follow that admonition."[90] This was also the sentiment of Apostles Lee, Benson, Smith,

180   SECOND-CLASS SAINTS

and Stapley, as well as racist southern clergymen who declared that God had "created the races" and then segregated them. But the civil rights investigation had put significant pressure on BYU. The government's threat to revoke federal funds forced the university into compliance. The Brethren wisely concluded that it was better to hire Black Mormon faculty than to fight the federal government.[91]

Not much is known either about Martin's brief tenure at BYU, other than what she wrote in her memoir, *Black Mormon Tells Her Story*, published two years after she joined the faculty. Her memoir depicts a spunky woman with a delightful sense of humor and a zest for life. She learned about Mormonism in the unlikeliest of places: a hospital. Barbara Weston, a White LDS woman, introduced Martin to her faith as both women lay in adjacent hospital beds recovering from surgery. Martin, who was raised a Baptist, had never heard of Mormons prior to meeting Weston. As the two women talked, Martin became intrigued by Mormon teachings, specifically the idea of family ties in the afterlife. The more the two women talked, the closer they became, and soon Martin expressed interest in becoming a Mormon. In 1966, she was baptized into the LDS church, and four years later she moved to Utah, where she auditioned for, and subsequently joined, the Mormon Tabernacle Choir.[92]

Martin's hiring seemed to have paid off. In March 1971, investigators informed Wilkinson that BYU had "the right to give preference to members of the Church in hiring faculty." In what Wilkinson called "the long-awaited letter," investigators implied that BYU could hire whom it wanted. But this was short-lived. By the mid-1970s, the investigators had reversed course and increased pressure on BYU to recruit Black faculty—and also women. This was driven by Congress, which extended the Civil Rights Act of 1964 to include protections against sex discrimination. Title IX, as it was known, gave the government broad authority to examine hiring practices at private schools like BYU, exacerbating the school's already existing challenges. The government wanted BYU to address its hiring deficiencies through an Affirmative Action program, which required "sexual balance" and "balance for Blacks."[93] BYU sought an exemption to this requirement, tussling with the federal government for much of the decade. Demands that BYU hire women, they argued, conflicted with the church's teachings that women remain in the home to raise their children. The feud ended in 1979 when the parties reached a compromise: BYU agreed to adopt some of the

LOBBYING FOR THE PRIESTHOOD   181

government's guidelines for recruiting women and minorities, and the government agreed to leave them alone.[94]

★ ★ ★

In 1971, the protests against BYU's athletic teams came to a halt after the civil rights movement ended.[95] But after three devastating years of protests, riots, bomb scares, lawsuits, and federal investigations, the church was battered. The athletic protests and the sheer intensity of the news coverage condemning Mormon racial teachings had simply overwhelmed the church.

A pivotal moment occurred in the spring of 1971, when three African American converts—Ruffin Bridgeforth, Darius Gray, and Eugene Orr—demanded to meet with President Smith. They wanted the priesthood.

This wasn't the first time that African Americans had made such a request, of course. As recently as 1967 Black Mormon convert David Gillispie had written a sobering letter to President McKay lamenting that neither he nor his family could participate in Mormon temple ordinances. If that wasn't painful enough, Gillispie also complained that he couldn't give his children a father's blessing, something all White priesthood holders did. "As these truths dawn on me," he wrote to President McKay, "I find myself shocked out of this nightmarish day dream with the realization that it is not merely a bad dream, but it is the truth. . . . One question stands foremost in my mind. Is this the will of God or the will of man?"[96] McKay's secretary, Hamer Reiser, acknowledged the letter but could do very little to assuage Gillispie's pain. McKay and Hugh Brown didn't know what to say to him either, so they wrote Gillispie's bishop and instructed him to give "encouragement" to Gillispie.[97]

It's difficult to know whether Gillispie's case was typical among Latter-day Saints, but some Black members defended the ban or at least didn't appear to be troubled by it. When students at the Olympus LDS seminary in Salt Lake asked Abner Howell how he felt about not holding the priesthood, he answered, "I'm too busy getting into the Celestial Kingdom that I'm not worried about the priesthood." John Lamb expressed a similar position. In the *Improvement Era*, the official church magazine, he wrote that not all "negroes" want the priesthood, and when questioned about it, Lamb gave a simple yet direct answer: he believed in the "restored gospel of Jesus Christ" and was content to patiently wait until God saw fit to lift the ban.[98] His article angered fellow Black Mormon Edgar Whittingham, who challenged Lamb for implying "that the Negro was contented with his lot." Whittingham was anything but content. He hoped that the church president "might have a revelation to give the Priesthood to worthy Negroes." Another Black Latter-day Saint, Carey Bowles, concurred, expressing his views in a self-published book called *A Mormon Negro Views the Church*.[99]

Gillispie, Whittingham, and Bowles weren't the only Black Latter-day Saints frustrated with the priesthood and temple ban. Bridgeforth, Gray, and Orr each anguished over the ban and had personal stories to share. They were an unusual group from different walks of life. Bridgeforth was a forty-nine-year-old truck driver from Louisiana. He had light skin with "thin," "wispy" hair. Gray, who "wore a proud Afro," was a twenty-six-year-old reporter from Colorado. His skin bore a "copper tint," and he had Native American as well as Black ancestry. Orr, age twenty-five, was from Georgia. He had dark skin and short cropped hair. He often teased Bridgeforth and Gray for "not being real black men."[100]

In 1961, some seven years after Bridgeforth converted to the LDS church, he confessed his anxiety about the priesthood ban in an unpublished autobiography. John Fitzgerald, the former CES teacher who had pressured President McKay to lift the ban, asked Bridgeforth to tell his story, and Bridgeforth agreed. In vivid detail, he recounted how the ban had pained him and his family, especially when Latter-day Saints discussed the priesthood and temple at church. Bridgeforth would try to ignore them and "go on as though nothing happened." Especially stressful was explaining to his young son Ronald why he couldn't hold the priesthood or pass the sacrament like other boys at church. It was awkward telling his son that his church deemed him cursed. Adding to Bridgeforth's anguish, the boys at church asked Ronald repeatedly why he attended deacon's quorum when he couldn't hold the priesthood. "This really hurt [my son]," Bridgeforth lamented. And yet Bridgeforth remained an active believer, yearning for the time when the ban would end. "I have faith in the Church, but it will take men like you, Brother Fitzgerald, to stop this dogma."[101]

Gray's story was just as unsettling. He had joined the church in Colorado Springs in 1964, attended BYU, and went to work for the church's radio station KSL in the late 1960s. During the athletic protests he had traveled with Heber Wolsey to hot spots around the country to counter negative perceptions about BYU and the LDS church. He was a terrific ambassador for the church, as both Wolsey and Wilkinson readily admitted. Yet hidden beneath Gray's genial exterior was a man who anguished over the priesthood restriction, which was compounded by racism he experienced at church. At his first worship service in a Mormon chapel a little girl greeted him by calling him the "n-word."[102] At BYU, the dean of student life instructed him not to interact with White girls. Gray suffered further indignity when he married a White LDS woman and couldn't solemnize his wedding vows in a Mormon temple—a rite that was open to all faithful Latter-day Saints, of all races and ethnicities, except Black members.[103]

Eugene Orr was the most outspoken of the three men and seemed to relish condemning Mormon racism.[104] During a road trip to Salt Lake City in 1968, Orr met a White Mormon woman named Lei at a Greyhound bus station. "Are you a Mormon?" he brusquely asked when they first met. "Yes," Lei replied. Orr then asked, "So you guys have the only true religion? Yes," came her reply. "And you don't like blacks?" he asked. "Who said we don't like blacks?" Lei retorted. They eventually married. Over the next few years Orr became deeply immersed in Mormon racial theology, trying to understand how a church claiming to be Christian could teach that Black people bore a divine curse. Just as troubling, he agonized over the reception, or lack thereof, that he and his wife received at church. Orr recalled, "We could be standing, we could be sitting; they were all around us, [yet] nobody [said] one word to us."[105]

Racism covered the three men like a suffocating blanket. They decided to confront the priesthood ban head-on. Orr initiated a meeting at the University of Utah Library, where he worked. The trio was anxious about where it might lead. Only Bridgeforth had been a Mormon for long (a little over twenty years), and none had ever challenged the church president. They knew that convincing President Smith to lift the ban would be difficult, especially considering that he "was from the old school and had ... said some harsh and unkind things about people of color," Orr reflected years later.[106] Yet in a private room at the University of Utah, just a few miles from LDS church headquarters, they knelt in prayer, after fasting for three days. It was a defining moment for each of them. "Back then, having three black Mormons together was like having a quorum," Gray recalled. "There weren't many of us."[107]

As the men huddled together in prayer, they decided to bring a letter to President Smith outlining "all those things we specified of what we wanted to see happen and changed" in the church. Orr said they added "quite a bit" to the list. We had "just been frustrated," Gray explained, "and often times when we got together, we'd talk about our common problems" in the church. "The bits of discrimination and the paternalism that we found and we'd share it with each other and we got sick of it."[108]

In early May, Orr took the bold step of contacting President Smith. He went to church headquarters alone to set up an appointment with Smith and to hand-deliver the letter. "I'd like to meet with the Prophet," Orr stated, as D. Arthur Haycock, Smith's secretary, greeted him outside Smith's office. Haycock asked what the purpose of the meeting was, but Orr wouldn't tell him. Haycock then informed Orr that Smith wasn't in his office, upon which Orr delivered the letter and Haycock promised that he would speak to the church president and then call Orr to set up an appointment.[109]

Haycock never called. Nearly three weeks elapsed before Orr anxiously contacted Haycock demanding to know why he couldn't get in to see President Smith.[110] The nervous secretary sniffed trouble; he didn't like Orr's tone. He had read Orr's letter and knew that the three men weren't happy with the church's race teachings. Most troubling, Haycock became alarmed when the trio demanded to meet with the president together. "Why three," Haycock asked Orr defensively, "and what do you want to talk to him about?" Orr provided a "very brief overview" of what the men wanted to discuss. They'd talk about racism in the church, Orr informed Haycock, but he said nothing about the priesthood "so as to not frighten Smith."[111]

Perhaps it isn't surprising that President Smith didn't want to meet with them. Mormon racial teachings were clearly a touchy subject for the Brethren, and especially for Smith, since many critics blamed him for the ban. In 1963, for example, a non-Mormon man from New York wrote a pointed letter to Smith, who was then the president of the Quorum of the Twelve Apostles, asking him why Black men were denied the priesthood. The letter triggered a sharp response from Smith, who informed his interrogator that he was "getting a little fed up on the idea that so many people think I am responsible for the Negro not holding the priesthood."[112] Smith's hypersensitive response left little doubt about his unwillingness to

LOBBYING FOR THE PRIESTHOOD

discuss the ban. He had said all that he wanted to say about the topic in his books and articles. Discussing it further would serve no good purpose.

Haycock claimed that President Smith wasn't feeling well and couldn't accept appointments. That might have been convincing had the *Church News* not reported on his activities. Gray frustratingly noted that Smith "was well enough to do everything except to see us." Calling Haycock's bluff, the men persisted in their demands to meet with Smith. They were encouraged by LaMar Williams, who years earlier pushed the Brethren to open a mission in Nigeria. Williams told Bridgeforth, "Until you and your people want something and make it manifest and carry the burden and show some responsibility, you will not be recognized by the Church. You've got to do something on your own. You've got to let them know that you desire a place in the Church." Bridgeforth internalized this urgent message, which is what motivated the trio to keep calling and asking for an appointment with the prophet. "Our conversations over the phone with [Haycock] became a bit more heated," Gray remembered, "and all of a sudden there was a committee of three [apostles] assigned to . . . deal with us."[113] For Gray, Bridgeforth, and Orr, the pressure paid off. They didn't secure an appointment with the church president, but now they had a direct line to the apostles.

It was an unusual committee. Two of the apostles—Gordon B. Hinckley and Thomas S. Monson—had worked for the church in public relations prior to their call to the Quorum of the Twelve and were good choices for outreach. Both were warm and affable and both had the capacity to put people at ease. But the third apostle—Boyd K. Packer—seemed an unlikely choice. He was prickly and gruff and, like his close friend Bruce R. McConkie, overbearing and doctrinaire. Packer was also the person who worked behind the scenes to get Lowell Bennion fired.[114] In any event, the First Presidency tasked the three apostles with resolving the concerns of Bridgeforth, Gray, and Orr. Apostle Monson cautioned that the apostles had to tread carefully: "We should extend to our black brethren every blessing up to the holding of the priesthood, then the Lord will show us the next step."[115]

On June 8, 1971, the six men met in Apostle Hinckley's office at church headquarters in downtown Salt Lake. It was "very interesting," Gray mused.[116] The meeting began promptly at 8:00 a.m. with a prayer. Packer and Monson joined Hinckley behind his desk while Orr, Bridgeforth, and

Gray sat directly across from the apostles.[117] Typically, Latter-day Saints show great deference to the Brethren, but on this occasion, Orr didn't hold back. "Let's not beat around the bush," he blurted. "Let's go straight through the bush. Why can't black men have the priesthood?" This is precisely what Haycock feared would happen, and it's precisely why he wouldn't let the trio meet with President Smith. Hinckley floundered as he struggled to answer Orr. He reiterated all the usual talking points, including the one about preexistence, to which Orr bluntly asked, "How is it that white people know we've been less valiant but black people don't know this?"[118]

Orr continued his fusillade, getting more animated with each passing minute. "Make no mistake about it we want the priesthood," he thundered.[119] Gray then asked a pointed question that few Latter-day Saints had the courage to ask but to which many certainly wanted the answer: Had the Brethren ever prayed about lifting the ban? That bold question unnerved the apostles, catching them off guard. They sat silent for what must have been several seconds and then tried to change the subject. Gray wouldn't let them; he pressed further. "Have you really prayed?" he asked. "What does the Lord say on this issue?" "There was no answer." Again, he pressed. "Still no answer."[120]

Bridgeforth sat stunned as Orr and Gray worked over the apostles. The tension in Hinckley's office was palpable—so much so that the meeting ended without a prayer. The apostles decided to meet again with their interrogators a few weeks later. (Gray was unable to attend.) This time the apostles were ready. Almost immediately after the prayer was said, the apostles preempted Bridgeforth and Orr by informing them that on June 24, the entire Quorum of the Twelve and First Presidency had met in the Salt Lake Temple and prayed about the priesthood ban. The apostles told them that the answer was no; the time was not yet right for Black men to have the priesthood. The apostles explained that it was the "first time to their knowledge in the history of the church" that the Brethren had prayed about it.[121] Orr recounted that the Brethren "were not in agreement on the question," which was a vast understatement given Hugh Brown's very public attempts in recent years to pressure the Brethren to lift the ban. Bridgeforth and Orr were troubled by the apostles' admission that they hadn't prayed about the ban before. Gray, who learned about the results of the meeting later, was bothered by the apostles' focus on the "negative consequences" of giving Black men the priesthood—that it would cause problems for the church, as Apostle Hinckley explained. Gray incredulously asked: Do the Brethren "ever really look at the positive side?"[122]

Another area of concern was patriarchal blessings. Bridgeforth, Gray, and Orr didn't receive a lineage pronouncement in theirs, and neither did scores of other Black Latter-day Saints. There wasn't a church-wide policy on this. Some Black members were told that they were of the lineage of Cain and Ham; some had the blessings of Abraham, Isaac, and Jacob pronounced on them; and some were given no lineage at all. Not surprisingly, Black Latter-day Saints were frustrated when church patriarchs proclaimed a cursed lineage on them or when they were denied a lineage altogether.[123] In 1970, the Brethren spent two quorum meetings discussing the issue, but both meetings ended with nothing resolved.[124]

But the group did make progress in one area of common concern: the desire to reactivate disaffected Black Latter-day Saints. Of the 250 Black members in the Salt Lake area, only about 40 were active.[125] To entice them back to church, Lee counseled Hinckley, Monson, and Packer to "go as far as [they] could in providing opportunities for our black brethren, short of the priesthood, and then seek the inspiration of Heavenly Father for further light and knowledge."[126] The apostles proposed a "social unit" for Black Latter-day Saints—essentially the same one that Joseph Fielding Smith and Spencer Kimball had proposed some fifteen years earlier. Bridgeforth, Gray, and Orr were shocked when Apostle Hinckley apprised them of the plan. He called Bridgeforth to be the inaugural president and Gray and Orr his counselors. This special support group, known formally as the "Genesis Group," signaled a new beginning for Black Latter-day Saints; more important, it reenergized Bridgeforth, Gray, and Orr and strengthened their faith in the church. Eager to thank the prophet, Gray enthusiastically explained, "We tried to get in to [see] President Smith and Brother Haycock [said he'd] been ill. We never had anything really that positive, and all of a sudden here we were with something positive to tell them."[127]

One of the first things the new Genesis presidency did was organize a "fireside"—a supplementary church meeting—with local Black members to share the good news. They also asked Mary Bankhead, a Black woman of pioneer Mormon stock, to serve as the inaugural Relief Society president.[128]

On a crisp fall day in October 1971, some 175 Black Latter-day Saints attended the inaugural meeting. Genesis member James Sinquefield recalled that the purpose of the Genesis Group was to provide a place to worship for Black members where they could "identify with each other" and bear each other's burdens. The First Presidency authorized them to hold testimony meetings once a month as well as weekly Relief Society meetings for women and weekly Primary meetings for children.[129] They were also authorized to do limited rituals in Mormon temples for their deceased ancestors, in a Mormon ordinance called "baptisms for the dead."[130]

The Genesis Group met in the Third Ward Chapel in the Liberty Stake in Salt Lake on the last Sunday of the month—the same building where Norwegian and Danish Latter-day Saints met. All of this would be under the watchful eye of the Liberty stake president, who would report to Apostles Hinckley, Monson, and Packer. The apostles were cautious. None of them knew whether the men would use the Genesis Group as a platform to lobby for the priesthood, or if they would be content to fulfill their charge to reactivate Black Latter-day Saints in the area. Recognizing the need for caution, Apostle Packer counseled the Genesis leadership to keep a "low profile." They were not to talk to the media. This "was not a tourist attraction," he warned. Apostle Monson said, "This is a small beginning; it has the hand of approval from the First Presidency and the Twelve Apostles." In other words, Packer and Monson warned, "don't blow it."[131]

The *New York Times* ran a story about the Genesis Group, noting that "those who attend the [Genesis] meetings will need to go to their home wards to receive the sacrament from the white men who are ordained priests." A *Times* reporter asked Bridgeforth if he would like to hold the priesthood, and he gave a cautious, yet unambiguous response: "Certainly, I'd like it. Quite a responsibility goes with this, and I'm not going to demand something if it could destroy me. So I'll live with the commandments of the Lord."[132] That was the most that Bridgeforth had to say publicly about the ban. He didn't want to make waves with the Brethren or make them regret organizing the Genesis Group. He was the most circumspect of the trio and the most senior of the group. In Orr's candid assessment, Bridgeforth "was not the type of person to rock the boat." He was simply a "yes man."[133]

Gray too was cautious, but he wasn't quiet. He pressed the Brethren to address racism in the church and became frustrated when they didn't. "We asked for things like a conference address because it's not a Negro question or a Negro problem," Gray stated. "It deals with the Black man not having the priesthood, and it deals with, in my case, the racist attitudes of a lot of members of the church." Gray was even more frustrated with the attitude of many Latter-day Saints. They would "sit back and say, 'I'm White, you're Black, you're cursed. I don't have to have anything to do with you,' and that's what needs to be dealt with," he informed Apostle Packer. Gray lamented that White Latter-day Saints didn't "really want to accept the Black man as being an equal." Yet Gray rarely discussed the priesthood in public after his call into the Genesis presidency. He knew that it would take time to get the priesthood, but even more, he knew the Brethren wouldn't be pressured. Privately, though, Gray expressed discontent with Mormon racial teachings. The ban gnawed at him. He rejected the notion that Black people were less valiant, and he stoutly opposed the teaching that they were cursed. None of that made sense to him. He didn't know why Black men were denied the priesthood. All he could muster is that it must have begun "because of social pressures in the 1800s when the saints were in Missouri"—which is precisely, of course, what Fawn Brodie, Sterling McMurrin, and Hugh Brown believed.[134]

Orr, on the other hand, bubbled over with enthusiasm and didn't feel the need to proceed with caution like Bridgeforth and Gray. Gray characterized him as a "young firebrand." Orr was uncommonly vocal in expressing contempt for Mormon racial theology, especially teachings from the Book of Mormon that dark skin would gradually lighten over time when Black people converted to Mormonism and remained faithful. Orr found these teachings absurd and took particular delight in mocking them. "So if I had kids when I was righteous my genetics [will] have changed, now [are] all my kids going to be white?" he asked with a chuckle years later. "[What if] I decided not to be righteous anymore? . . . Now [would] my skin color . . . change back?" he asked, again chuckling. "What kind of God is that?" God doesn't "change colors" of people.[135]

When asked years later if he "pressed for the priesthood," Orr's response was honest and straightforward: "Oh, yes, I was asking for the priesthood." But, he added, that "was not part of [Bridgeforth and Gray's] agenda."[136] All three men clearly wanted the priesthood; the issue was whether they should lobby for it. Bridgeforth and Gray said no; Orr said yes. "Look," Bridgeforth told Orr, "you knew before you came in the Church how we stood on the priesthood, so you can't push this. . . . You knew what was up before you came in the Church, and you are just going to have to wait."[137]

Bridgeforth's plea for restraint failed to temper Orr. To Bridgeforth's dismay, Orr had been traveling around the Salt Lake Valley giving firesides predicting that Black members would get the priesthood. To bolster his

190   SECOND-CLASS SAINTS

crusade, Orr apprised Latter-day Saints of Elijah Abel's priesthood ordination, clearly implying that it was an injustice to deny Black men the priesthood when an early Black member had been ordained. When Hinckley
learned of Orr's antics, the apostle told him to cool it. Frustrated, he asked
Hinckley if he was teaching "false doctrine," and the apostle said he wasn't.
But Hinckley asked him if he would "feed a baby meat before he can
crawl," and Orr replied no, unable to grasp Hinckley's larger point that
Black men weren't ready for the priesthood. "Just because you were right
doesn't always make it right," the apostle counseled. In another act of defiance, Orr claimed that his twelve-year-old son would one day receive the
priesthood—this in the presence of Apostle McConkie in the home of
one of McConkie's relatives. The apostle sat stoically as Orr spoke. He said
nothing in response.[138]

All of this came to a head when Orr formed a faction within the Genesis
Group, which infuriated Bridgeforth. Orr called it the Special Interest
Group. Comprised of a number of "male black members," the faction co-
alesced around one salient and burning issue: to lobby the Brethren for the
priesthood. This was precisely what the three apostles feared might happen.
Orr produced a petition requesting the priesthood; dozens of Genesis members signed it. Bridgeforth tried to stop it, but couldn't. He fretted that Orr's
antics might destroy the Genesis Group and jeopardize the goodwill that
Black Latter-day Saints had mustered with the Brethren. Joseph Freeman,
an early Genesis member, candidly noted, "The entire incident encouraged
some of the Genesis members to get their grievances off their chests by
openly criticizing the leaders of the Church for their failure to acknowledge equality of its black members by revoking the priesthood restriction."
He went on to say, "Most . . . would not sign this petition; but quite a few
did—enough to cause a damaging split in the group."[139] Bridgeforth characterized it this way: "We had dissention, and we had people who were
dissatisfied. 'Why can't we do this?' and 'Why can't we do that?' And trying
to keep them calm was a constant challenge."[140]

To quell the commotion, Bridgeforth invited Apostles Hinckley, Monson,
and Packer to speak with the dissenters. "They need our help, they need
our prayers and our blessings," Packer observed. "They really need our attention."[141] But nothing seemed to work. The divisions in the Group were
too stark and the emotion too raw to calm the dissenters. Exhausted and
thoroughly fed up when the Brethren wouldn't give in to his demands, Orr

LOBBYING FOR THE PRIESTHOOD 191

quit the Genesis Group in protest and moved to Canada. Gray eventually left as well, as did a number of others. All of this pained Bridgeforth, who tartly observed that the "controversy over Blacks holding the priesthood" had pushed them away.[142]

In this tragic moment, the Brethren learned two important and incontrovertible facts: first, Black people would never be happy in the church as long as they were denied the priesthood; second, they would struggle to remain in the faith as long as the church denied them full access to sacred Mormon rituals. The Brethren knew that no public relations campaign could ever change this, and they knew that a support group couldn't assuage the pain they felt from being treated like second-class citizens. Recognizing this, the Brethren held several intense meetings in the years ahead to determine how to lift the ban. This would require a revelation, and it would require unanimity among the Quorum of the Twelve Apostles and the First Presidency. Mormon racial theology would have to be reimagined in a way never thought possible by earlier prophets and apostles.

7

Lifting the Ban, 1973–1978

July 1972 was a stressful month for seventy-three-year-old Harold B. Lee. On July 2 he received word that church president Joseph Fielding Smith passed away at the age of ninety-five. That put Lee in line for the presidency. It also put him on the hot seat. All throughout July, journalists asked repeatedly: Will Lee lift the priesthood ban?

Lee knew this question was coming. He told a *Newsweek* reporter, "[I]f you believe in revelation as we do, you will see that [equal status for Black people] is a matter of the Lord telling us." To a *New York Times* journalist, he claimed that "sometime in God's eternal plan the Negro will be granted the priesthood."[1]

None of these answers satisfied journalists, much less critics. Lee had given no timetable. And he was emphatic that neither critics nor naysayers would change what "only God could change."[2] In fact, Lee took a number of steps to retrench. First, he republished his controversial 1945 sermon "Youth of a Noble Birthright," affirming the doctrinal rationale for the ban.[3] Second, Lee's administration upheld the excommunication of former LDS Seminary instructor John Fitzgerald, who had long been critical of the ban. Fitzgerald made the fateful mistake of airing his grievances in several letters published in the *Salt Lake Tribune*. And third, Lee called doctrinal hard-liner Bruce R. McConkie into the Quorum of the Twelve Apostles. McConkie, the son-in-law of Joseph Fielding Smith, had fiercely defended the ban in his best-selling book *Mormon Doctrine*, which had recently been released in a second edition. McConkie was the least inclined apostle to lift the ban.[4]

And yet, despite sending a strong message that he would maintain the status quo, Lee also took some steps in the opposite direction. He knew the ban was damaging the church and hindering its efforts to expand. So he asked his secretary, D. Arthur Haycock, to report on what the Reorganized Church of Jesus Christ of Latter Day Saints was doing to welcome the African Americans into their worship community.[5] At the same time, Lee reached out to general authority Marion D. Hanks—a well-known critic of the ban—for advice on how to answer questions about the ban from non-Latter-day-Saints. There was even a report that Lee spent three days and three nights in the Salt Lake Temple fasting and praying about lifting the ban, to which God allegedly responded "Not yet."[6]

Next to polygamy, Lee had deemed "the negro" the most "sensitive area" of the church, but he couldn't bring himself to change the church's race doctrine.[7] But fate would intervene. In December 1973, after just over a year as president, Lee died after a short illness. Into his shoes stepped Apostle Spencer W. Kimball. He made lifting the ban the focal point of his administration.

* * *

Spencer W. Kimball seemed like an unlikely president. He was unassuming and unpretentious, precisely the sort of man who would avoid the lime-light.[8] At five-feet-six-inches tall and weighing about 170 pounds, he wasn't an intimidating-looking man. He once referred to himself as a "pygmy" compared to his "giant" of a predecessor. Kimball was also something of an introvert. He was a sensitive a man—a man with "soft feelings," Ernest Wilkinson observed.[9]

But the church president also had a fierce temper and could lash out when something bothered him. An article by Fawn Brodie once sent him into a spasm of anger. "I was so angry when I looked through this PEN [magazine] that I rebuked [the editors] with all my power [though] my poor relatives had to sit and listen." Reading the article "was almost more than I could bear."[10]

And then there was his health. When Kimball became Mormonism's twelfth prophet-president, no one expected him to be in the role for very long. He had suffered a heart attack a few years earlier, survived throat cancer, and had numerous other ailments that impaired his health and threatened his presidency. Most Latter-day Saints thought he'd be a "caretaker presi-dent," at best, yet Kimball turned out to be "one of the most innovative presidents" in the history of the church, according to LDS church historian Leonard Arrington.[11] In April 1974, Kimball provided a glimpse of where he wanted to take the church when he delivered a sermon that would both define his presidency and change the course of LDS church history. In his groundbreaking address, "When Will the World Be Converted?," the church president outlined a plan to globalize Mormonism. Delivered to "regional representatives," apostles, and midlevel general authorities, Kimball promised that if they would "lengthen their stride," God would open up new missionary possibilities in the Soviet Union, China, India, and elsewhere—countries that were closed off to Mormon missionaries. "We need to enlarge our field of operation," Kimball declared. "We will need to make a full, prayerful study of the nations of the world which do not have the gospel at this time, and then bring into play our strongest and most able men to assist the Twelve to move out into the world and to open the doors of every nation as fast as it is ready."[12]

Everyone had a role to play in this vast and far-reaching vision. Diplomats had to secure access to countries behind the Iron Curtain; church leaders had to utilize the latest technologies to teach Mormonism; and young men and women had to prepare themselves spiritually, emotionally, and financially to serve church missions. "Every member a missionary," Kimball memorably said, which became the "catchphrase" of his administration.[13]

Kimball's address electrified the general authorities; they talked about it for months and even years afterward. Apostle Gordon B. Hinckley told Kimball that his sermon was "the greatest talk ever given in these seminars. You thrilled us. You challenged us. None of us can ever be quite the same after that. The missionary work will now move as it has not moved in years."[14] General authority William Grant Bangerter agreed. As President Kimball delivered his address, he said, listeners

> became alert to an astonishing spiritual presence, and we realized that we were listening to something unusual, powerful, different from any of our previous meetings. It was as if, spiritually speaking, our hair began to stand on end. Our minds were suddenly vibrant and marveling at the transcendent message that was coming to our ears. With a new perceptiveness we realized that President Kimball was opening spiritual windows and beckoning to us to come and gaze with him on the plans of eternity.

Bangerter continued, "I doubt that any person present that day will ever forget the occasion."[15]

Kimball's bold vision to take the Mormon gospel into new nations became the guiding light for his presidency and set the tone for what lay ahead. Simply put, it mesmerized the church.

Kimball's enthusiasm soon collided with reality. He appointed former Nixon official David Kennedy to be a "special ambassador" to help carry out his global vision.[16] The president sought Kennedy's advice, and the retired ambassador gave it to him, unvarnished and unfiltered. In a private conversation in April 1974, just after Kimball's landmark address, Kennedy informed the Mormon leader that he couldn't truly globalize the church as long as the priesthood ban existed. Then he did something that caught the church president off guard: Kennedy walked up to a globe on Kimball's desk and placed his hand over the African continent. Forget about proselytizing there, he told Kimball. It was foolhardy to establish a mission in Africa when Black members couldn't hold the priesthood. White priesthood holders from the United States simply could not go to Africa to run churches. It wouldn't work. Nor should it. Black people had to run their own churches.[17]

Kennedy wasn't the only Latter-day Saint to recognize this brute fact. After reading Kimball's seminal talk, a disgruntled LDS man from Pennsylvania wrote the church president a pointed letter criticizing his globalist vision for omitting Black Africa. "Where is Africa on the missionary map?" the man asked. "When will the Church abandon its racist position on blacks, since careful research has shown that position is based on tradition, not revelation?" He continued, "Must a policy rooted only in tradition wait for direct revelation in order to change? . . . When will you act, so that I can in conscience reclaim my Mormon heritage and testimony?"[18]

★ ★ ★

Hovering over Kimball's universalist vison was an explosive article published in 1973 in the liberal Mormon journal *Dialogue*, which the Pennsylvania man called to Kimball's attention. Kimball was already familiar with it. The article was written by a Latter-day Saint medical doctor named Lester Bush, who fancied himself an amateur historian. Few could predict that Bush's would be the most important article ever published in the journal or the most heralded article ever produced on the priesthood and temple ban. Bush titled it "Mormonism's Negro Doctrine: An Historical Overview." The work spanned sixty pages and had over two hundred footnotes.[19] What

196   SECOND-CLASS SAINTS

made the article intriguing were the sources he used. Bush drew principally from the private papers of Apostle Adam S. Bennion, which included extensive meeting minutes from the Quorum of the Twelve Apostles and First Presidency—a record that spanned 1830 to 1954. Bush was the first LDS author to get access to these highly confidential meeting minutes, which allowed Latter-day Saints to see the decision-making that lay behind the ban.

It was purely by accident that Bush stumbled on Bennion's collection. His brother, a BYU student, learned about Apostle Bennion's papers from BYU librarian Chad Flake, a free-spirited man, a maverick of sorts, who wasn't afraid to blaze his own path at an institution that required strict conformity from its employees. Flake granted Lester Bush access to Bennion's papers, knowing that he was skirting the edges of protocol. University officials would likely have deemed it inappropriate, or at least unwise, to air the Brethren's private meeting minutes. Typically, collections of this nature end up at the LDS church archives in Salt Lake, where they are kept from the public. But the Bennion family had defied convention and donated them to BYU following the apostle's death. This allowed Bush to gain access to material that was supposed to remain private and confidential.[20]

Except for the apostles and perhaps Lowell Bennion, no one had ever seen these meeting minutes—certainly not Stephen Taggart, Fawn Brodie, or Sterling McMurrin. This made Bush's work all the more valuable. Energized by his discovery, Bush took copious notes, supplemented by additional research at the LDS church archives and the University of Utah. He assembled his notes into a massive document called "Compilation on the Negro" and made ten copies for his close friends; he also gave copies to Boyd Packer and Chad Flake.[21]

As Bush reviewed these rare documents, he realized why they were valuable—and controversial: there was no sign of a revelation to support the ban. There was nothing that linked the ban to Joseph Smith. But there was plenty of evidence that the founding prophet allowed Black men to be ordained to the priesthood. For Bush, this was a revolutionary moment. As he explained years later, "I believed I had undermined virtually the entire traditional case for the inspired origins of Mormon [racial] teachings."[22]

Bush's article, based on his research from the "Compilation on the Negro," rebutted all the essential teachings that general authorities had taught over the years about the ban. He not only challenged the work of Joseph Fielding Smith and Bruce R. McConkie, for example, but he criticized the work of

Fawn Brodie and Stephen Taggart, who also claimed that the ban originated with Joseph Smith. Bush said that it began under Brigham Young at a time when racism was rampant and four million Africans enslaved. Bush's conclusion was clear: the ban wasn't doctrinal or inspired. The implication was that it needed to go.[23]

Predictably, Bush's work angered the Brethren and they demanded to know who leaked the meeting minutes. Then-apostle Kimball asked BYU president Ernest Wilkinson to investigate. Kimball wasn't happy when he learned that "[a] librarian at BYU in 'special collections' released transcripts of meetings held by the Twelve concerning the negro question—meetings held in [1954]—which allegedly proved total lack of revelation past or present on the matter." Kimball demanded that Wilkinson shut off all access to the private collection.[24]

The Brethren had less luck suppressing Bush's article. But they tried. It had been circulating in draft form for at least two years. Apostles Packer and McConkie read it and general authority Marion D. Hanks and church president Harold B. Lee were apprised of its contents, as were other general authorities. Historians in the church's History Department had also seen it. All wanted it suppressed except for Hanks and the church historians, who warmly encouraged Bush to publish his trailblazing work. Hanks, who had long made clear how much he detested the ban, expressed appreciation to Bush for his work and praised him for his integrity. Hanks thought it was a mistake to send the manuscript to Packer, who was not known to be open to anything that was controversial or that challenged the prevailing church narrative.[25]

Bush learned this the hard way when Packer requested to meet with him. Former First Presidency secretary turned general authority Joseph Anderson joined them. In two tense but cordial meetings, Packer strongly implied that Bush shouldn't publish his work. As Bush recalled, Packer said it was "unfortunate that [Bush] had chosen to publish in *Dialogue*," alleging that it "would give the article notoriety and lead to its use against the Church." The Brethren strongly disliked the liberal journal and deemed it an enemy of the church. Packer suggested that *BYU Studies* publish it instead, drawing a hearty laugh from Bush, who noted that the conservative journal "wouldn't have touched [his essay] with a ten-foot pole." Packer reassured Bush that he would exert pressure on the editors to get the journal to publish it, but Bush didn't bite. When he realized that *BYU Studies* didn't interest Bush, Packer asked him to delay publication in *Dialogue* until he had a chance to thoroughly review the manuscript.[26] Bush agreed to the apostle's request, but he didn't anticipate what came next. After the meeting ended, someone from church headquarters—most likely Packer—asked BYU vice president Robert Thomas to get involved. Thomas contacted *Dialogue* editor Robert Rees and pleaded with him not to publish Bush's article. It would do irreparable harm to the church and BYU, Thomas stressed, and cause church historian Leonard Arrington to "lose his job." Just as troubling, Thomas claimed, the church would lose its tax exemption from the IRS. And finally, Thomas strongly implied that the Brethren would take "vindicative action" against both Rees and others involved in the project.[27]

Why Packer didn't caution Bush directly can only be a matter of speculation. Perhaps he wanted to avoid criticism by placing a buffer between Bush and the Brethren. Perhaps he didn't want to acknowledge the extent to which Bush's research would damage the church. Or perhaps he didn't want to admit that the Brethren were afraid of where all of this might lead. In any event, Rees refused Thomas's demands and published Bush's article, ignoring any potential fallout.[28] Bush's research created a firestorm at church headquarters. Apostle McConkie denounced it as "crap." Hanks said that it caused quite a stir among the Brethren. "Recent conversations suggest that this is so," he informed Bush.[29]

★ ★ ★

Sometime early in his presidency, Kimball decided to lift the ban. He had given it "a great deal of thought [and] a great deal of prayer," he wrote in his diary, having recognized that the ban was incompatible with his vision to globalize the church.[30] He knew that the church couldn't fulfill Jesus's command to take the gospel to "every nation, kindred tongue and people" as long as the ban remained in place.

But Kimball also knew that lifting the ban wouldn't be easy. David O. McKay had tried—and failed—and neither of his successors, Joseph Fielding Smith or Harold B. Lee, had shown any inclination to lift it. There were too many hard-liners in the Twelve. Apostle McConkie was the most formidable holdup, but senior apostles Mark E. Petersen and Ezra Taft Benson vigorously opposed Black priesthood ordination as well. Then there were less prominent apostles, men not generally known to rock the boat or cause problems but strong defenders of LDS racial teachings all the same. Delbert

L. Stapley, Boyd K. Packer, L. Tom Perry, David B. Haight, Marvin J. Ashton, and Howard W. Hunter fell into this camp, as did Thomas S. Monson and Gordon B. Hinckley. The only one in favor of lifting the ban was Hugh Brown, but he lacked clout within the new Kimball administration. After years of pressing for change, he had simply given up hope that the ban would be lifted during his lifetime. He died in 1975, leaving opponents of the ban without an advocate among the Twelve.

President Kimball had long been troubled by the ban. As early as 1963, he confessed to his son Edward that the ban was "a possible error."[31] He sometimes raised questions about it. "What do you think about whether the Negroes should receive the priesthood?" he asked a BYU professor. But most telling, Kimball supported Brown's ill-fated 1969 attempt to lift the ban. Kimball's diaries and private papers make it clear that he agonized over the ban, which had caused him intense moments of grief and despair. As church president, he once received a letter that began "Dear Bigot Kimball." When he related this experience to his fellow general authorities, his eyes welled up with tears and he said, softly, "I am not a bigot."[32]

His fellow general authorities didn't think he was a bigot, nor did the broader church body. How could they? Kimball was known to be the most impassioned advocate for Native American Latter-day Saints, having supported an Indian Placement Program that allowed young Native Americans to leave their reservations and live in Latter-day Saint homes during the school year, where they could receive better educational opportunities and be nurtured in Mormon teachings. Kimball pushed for the program despite tremendous opposition from fellow apostles. (Some condescendingly called it "Brother Kimball's program.")[33] He also frequently addressed racial intolerance in his sermons, cautioning Latter-day Saints to avoid that "ugly creature." "What a monster is prejudice," he emphasized. On another occasion he said, "Racial prejudice is of the devil. Racial prejudice is of ignorance. There is no place for it in the gospel of Jesus Christ." In fact, so sensitive and so concerned was Kimball about racial intolerance that some Latter-day Saints predicted that if the ban were to end, it would be under Kimball's direction.[34]

This isn't to say that Kimball had progressive views on race. He didn't. He exhibited many of the racial prejudices toward Black people that were common in his generation.[35] Nonetheless, Kimball's private papers reveal that his distaste for the ban had grown over time, catalyzed by stories of pain

200 SECOND-CLASS SAINTS

and anguish he heard from Black and biracial Latter-day Saints. This was especially evident during his visits to South America in the 1960s, when, as an apostle, he visited LDS meetinghouses. After meeting Fernandez, a "negro boy" in Uruguay, who begged the apostle to let him serve a mission, Kimball wrote, "My heart went out to him and I embraced him."[36] In another instance, he heard the pain and anguish of young Black Brazilian Latter-day Saints and "was touched as the Negro boys bore their testimonies." One, named Rodriquez, also pleaded with Kimball to serve a church mission, and, when he learned that he couldn't, said, "I accept the Church and I am willing to wait for the millennium wherein there will be a change of my body and when I can trade this life for another. Please remember me in your prayers." Likewise, at a stake conference in Brazil, the apostle met "a negro family" who paid tithing and were faithful members of the church. Referring to the father, Kimball agonized in his diary, "My heart went out to them and I thought of how many people . . . almost ignore their priesthood when this man would give his life for it."[37]

Kimball had wrestled with stories like these over the years and had searched the scriptures diligently to determine if they supported the church's race teachings. He once compiled a list of about twelve prominent verses on the cover page of his scriptures. Next to one of the verses, Moses chapter 7, verse 8, where it says "a blackness came upon all the children of Canaan," Kimball put a big question mark, signifying that he wasn't comfortable associating blackness with "negroes." As for Abraham chapter 2, the other proof text, which deals with Mormon conceptions of the preexistence, Kimball didn't reveal how he felt.[38] But when inquisitive Latter-day Saints asked him about the justification for the priesthood and temple ban, he simply repeated what Joseph Fielding Smith and others had said.[39]

Whether he really believed this or had simply rehashed a familiar line is open to debate. Likely he experienced cognitive dissonance, pledging support for the church's teachings on the one hand, but also acknowledging the lack of scriptural support on the other.[40] In public, Kimball maintained the church position, but in private he believed it "a possible error."[41]

Kimball's frustration with the ban had bubbled over in August 1974, when the NAACP sued the LDS church for discrimination against "a negro boy" in one of the LDS church-sponsored Boy Scout troops. The boy couldn't advance in Scout leadership because he didn't hold the Aaronic

Priesthood—a requirement for all church-sponsored troops.[42] Kimball agonized over this, knowing that he would have to defend the policy on the witness stand if the case went to trial. "He could not sleep," his secretary noted. "He could talk of little else in the meetings with his counselors." His anguish subsided only when the judge tossed out the case after the church changed its policy requiring troop members to have the priesthood as a precondition for Scout leadership.[43]

In the ensuing months, Kimball remained under near-constant pressure from the media, and his diary reflected his frustration. After meeting with a journalist early in his presidency he wrote, "I think we got off pretty well on the usual question of the Negro and the priesthood."[44] In some instances, Kimball demonstrated his weariness by refusing altogether to field questions about the ban. At the dedication of the Washington, D.C., Temple in September 1974, his refusal prompted the *New York Times* headline "Mormon Avoids Question on Blacks." Instead, Kimball and his colleagues referred journalists to a prepared PR statement.[45]

The Brethren may have been frustrated with the media, but they reserved their harshest criticism for Latter-day Saints. Support for the ban became a litmus test for their orthodoxy. Apostle McConkie asked a pointed question at the October 1974 general conference: "Am I valiant if I am deeply concerned about the Church's stand on who can or who cannot receive the priesthood and think it is time for a new revelation on this doctrine?"[46] The point of McConkie's question was to stifle criticism from Black Mormons in the Genesis Group and liberal Mormons everywhere who refused to accept the status quo.

Almost daily, it seemed, President Kimball had read about criticisms of the ban in the press. But those were easy to push aside. More difficult to ignore were the civil entanglements the ban caused for both BYU and the church. Though BYU had managed to avoid the IRS, the Brethren were clearly concerned about the church losing its tax exemption. In May 1975, President Kimball, along with his counselors, sent a letter to all the general authorities, regional representatives, stake presidents, mission presidents, and bishops instructing them to share it with rank-and-file Latter-day Saints. The letter made it clear that the church honored civil rights for "the Negro," but "matters of faith, conscience, and theology" were "not within the purview of civil law." The letter stated that the First Amendment gave churches discretion over doctrine. Then Kimball delivered the punch: "The position of the Church of Jesus Christ of Latter-day Saints with regard to the granting of the Priesthood to the Negro falls wholly within the category of religion. It has no bearing upon matters of civil rights. In no case or degree does it deny to the Negro his full privileges as a citizen of the nation."[47]

The letter clearly revealed the First Presidency's anxiety—an anxiety shared by BYU president Dallin H. Oaks. With the Bob Jones University case hovering over BYU, Oaks urged the university community "to take careful notice of these threats and to lend your voice and influence to counteract them. In my judgment," he explained, "the private sector is seriously threatened in America today and that threat is affecting or will shortly affect all non-governmental institutions, including those formed for religious, educational, cultural, social, and other charitable purposes." Oaks expressed dismay that the federal government was "moving to take over the formal accrediting function heretofore handled by private organizations." In other words, Oaks wanted the government out of BYU's business.[48]

Oaks was especially chagrined that fall when BYU law dean Carl Hawkins received a letter from the American Bar Association threatening to withhold accreditation of BYU's fledgling law school because of the church's racial teachings. It was a "very threatening letter," Hawkins noted angrily. "Somebody has decided to make a real issue of our discrimination, so that our accreditation is really in jeopardy."[49] BYU leaders had gone to great lengths to ensure that the church's racial teachings wouldn't be a barrier to accreditation. Before the Board gave approval to establish the law school in 1970, Ernest Wilkinson, then the president, received a letter from Millard Ruud, a consultant to the American Bar Association, who assured Wilkinson that "as long as there is no racial or religious bias in BYU Law School's admission policy" the law school could move forward.[50]

Now, five years later, someone at the Bar Association changed their mind. Through careful negotiations, Oaks and his assistants convinced the Bar Association that BYU wouldn't discriminate in hiring decisions against either women or people of color, and officials at the Bar Association backed down. Years later Oaks remarked on the delicate nature of these negotiations: "I marvel at our overcoming the accrediting authorities' reservations about approving a new law school whose sponsoring Church did not yet extend the blessings of holding its priesthood to all worthy male Church members."[51]

Meanwhile, President Kimball was hearing from Latter-day Saints about how the ban affected them personally and professionally. In the summer of 1975, Kimball received a sobering letter from a Latter-day Saint bishop in Rochester, New York, who was also the superintendent of a large school district. A Black teacher, who was not hired, sued the district, citing racial discrimination. The New York Division of Human Rights held a formal hearing and called the superintendent to testify.[52]

It did not go well. Asked whether he belonged to "any organization which had unusual attitudes toward blacks," the bishop said no. Then he was asked if he was "a member of the Mormon Church and held a responsible office in that church." He said yes. He was then asked if "negroes were allowed to hold major offices in the church." He replied that they could not. He said "that negroes were not given the Priesthood and that major positions of responsibility were filled by those who held the Priesthood." Then he was asked "if members of any other race were denied the Priesthood." He said no.[53]

At this moment, the bishop reported, a startling realization came over him: he belonged to a church that harbored racist teachings he couldn't defend.[54]

The experience left the bishop humiliated and devastated, for he had perjured himself on the witness stand. Anguished and crestfallen, he wrote President Kimball a long and pointed letter. He told Kimball about a conversation he had had with Apostle McConkie, who had recently visited Rochester: "I asked him if there was anything that local leaders could do either to hasten the day when negroes may hold the Priesthood based on individual faith and worthiness or to help bring about greater clarity as to why they cannot." McConkie's counsel was profoundly disappointing. He "replied that there is nothing we can do, that the matter is entirely in the hands of the Lord."[55]

What the Rochester bishop didn't know is that Kimball had already decided to lift the ban. He just needed to secure buy-in from his counselors and the Quorum of the Twelve. Kimball had even broached the idea with his counselors.[56] As church president, he had the authority to lift the ban unilaterally, but he was acutely aware of what usually happened when church presidents exerted their authority without support from the apostles. Doing so almost always caused chaos and division within the church ranks. This was particularly true when church president Wilford Woodruff proclaimed a revelation in 1890 to end polygamy without first securing the approval of the apostles, which sparked a huge backlash within the Quorum of the Twelve as well as a massive exodus from the church.[57] And it was certainly true more recently, in 1969, when President McKay tried to lift the ban without the Brethren's consent. Kimball knew that if the ban were to end, he would have to bring the Brethren along slowly and methodically. He wouldn't force or cajole them. What he did was something far more subtle and brilliant: he would use the newly announced Brazil temple as leverage. The road to the priesthood for Black Mormons went through Brazil.

★ ★ ★

Plans for a temple in São Paulo, Brazil, had been in the works for quite some time. In the spring of 1973, then-church president Harold B. Lee and Apostle Gordon B. Hinckley went to São Paulo to locate a possible site.[58] After Lee's death, construction of the temple fell to Kimball, who pushed Lee's vision forward enthusiastically. In May 1975, Kimball formally announced plans for the new temple.[59]

Kimball had been to Brazil several times and knew the country's history. "The racial problem is acute in Brazil," he wrote in his diary, after one of his visits. Kimball knew that the scope and frequency of interracial marriages in Brazil presented two significant problems for the church: first, church officials couldn't determine who had "negro" ancestry; second, interracial marriages would prevent a significant percentage of native Brazilians from entering the soon-to-be-built São Paulo Temple.[60]

Nothing vexed the Brethren more than determining ancestry. In September 1975, at a missionary meeting in São Paulo, the mission president, Roger Beitler, gave an entire lesson on the subject, aware of the difficulties his missionaries had in policing racial boundaries. "We don't know why the negro doesn't hold the priesthood and do not know when he will receive it," Beitler noted. "We must receive our negro brothers with no reservations. . . . We shouldn't make snap judgments about a person having negro blood." He instructed the missionaries to continue using "lineage lessons" to detect "negro ancestry" and to avoid speaking "to the press about the church's stand toward the negro."[61] General authority Bernard Brockbank was even more frank. He told missionaries that the "church in Brazil badly needs Priesthood leadership in order to fortify the existing organization, and Negro baptisms simply will not help alleviate the current need for more Priesthood."[62]

President Kimball was well aware of these issues. He was particularly worried about "how to issue a temple recommend" and about leadership for the Brazilian church.[63] Sometime in the summer of 1975, Kimball dispatched numerous general authorities on a fact-finding mission to gauge the leadership abilities of Black Brazilians. Catherine Beitler, Roger Beitler's wife, vividly recalls the first apostle who visited the mission home and stayed with them. She was in "awe" when she met Apostle L. Tom Perry for the first time in October 1975. She bombarded him with questions thinking that he, as a member of the Twelve, "would have the latest information from heaven." The jovial Perry sidestepped her questions, preferring to discuss the Boston Red Sox, his favorite baseball team, who were in the World Series that year.[64]

Neither Catherine Beitler nor her husband had any idea why there was a sudden influx of visitors from Salt Lake. They arrived unannounced and gave no indication of what they were up to. Some twenty-two general authorities had visited in a relatively short span. Catherine recorded each of their names in her diary. Even President Kimball visited twice. The most frequent visitor was Apostle McConkie, whom the Beitlers got to know well.[65] McConkie and his wife, Amelia, stayed in the mission home with the Beitlers, and they traveled together to missionary conferences. They discussed the challenges the church faced in Brazil and talked frequently about the construction of the new temple, then underway. The two couples became so close that Amelia offered to be the godmother to the Beitlers' daughter.[66]

Over the next several months word trickled back to President Kimball that some Latter-day Saints of "cursed ancestry" were going to extraordinary lengths to raise money for the temple. James E. Faust, who was living in Brazil at the time as president of the International Mission, reported, "They have made their monetary contributions for the construction of the temple and they've made their sacrifices just the same as everybody else." Faust added, "And I've advised President Kimball and Brother McConkie of the faithfulness of these people."[67]

President Kimball didn't need to be reminded; he knew they were faithful. What he needed was time—time to convince the hard-liners to lift the ban. And time to prepare a stubborn church body for the change

206   SECOND-CLASS SAINTS

to come. There was probably much truth to BYU professor Marvin Hill's observation that most Mormons "are fiercely prejudiced and that actually dictates what the leadership does."[68]

As the priesthood ban in Brazil consumed President Kimball's attention, matters at home also gripped him. Douglas Wallace, a forty-six-year-old Latter-day Saint attorney from Vancouver, Washington, baptized twenty-two-year-old Larry Lester, a Black man, and then ordained him to the Aaronic Priesthood. All of this took place in the swimming pool at the Travelodge Motel in Portland in front of the gaze of the media. And none of it had the sanction of church authorities. Wallace knew exactly what he was doing. He called the media in advance to publicize the event. He told reporters that he ordained Lester "to force a revision of Mormon doctrine regarding blacks." Reporters eagerly wrote about the event.[69]

Wallace continued the pressure campaign a few days later when he traveled to Salt Lake City to attend general conference. Once the proceedings began, he and two associates walked down the aisle of the Tabernacle and reportedly shouted, "Make way for the Lord! Don't touch the Lord." Ushers shooed them out, at which point Wallace continued his grandstanding outside, proclaiming that he wanted to put Kimball "on trial." For what, he didn't say. What became of Larry Lester? His ordination was declared "null and void" and his baptism in the Travelodge Motel swimming pool wasn't recognized by the Brethren.[70]

President Kimball, clearly agitated, captured the whole ordeal in his diary: "Totally without authority from anyone, [Wallace] baptized a black boy and then proceeded to ordain him to the priesthood. He was determined to come to General Conference where he hoped to have a confrontation with me. We got a restraining order to keep him out of the Conference. He was excommunicated from the Church." For Kimball, Wallace was nothing more than a "menace"—and an embarrassing reminder of why he disliked the ban.[71]

The Wallace affair was just one more incident among many that pecked away at Kimball's patience and strengthened his resolve to lift the ban. This was most evident in the fall of 1976, when Kimball met with an LDS economist named Jack Carlson, a man he had known for years, in his office at church headquarters. The two had a remarkably candid and frank discussion about how the ban was affecting the church. Carlson told Kimball that he was "afraid the Church is a strong horse riding full-force into the 21st Century, and the Church leaders are like a rider sitting backwards, looking

LIFTING THE BAN 207

the other way." He believed that Latter-day Saints wouldn't curry favor with the federal government as long as the church discriminated against Black people. Kimball "listened intently."[72]

Meanwhile, over general conference weekend in October 1976, a long-simmering issue came to a head. John Pea, a mixed-race Latter-day Saint from Hawaii, petitioned the First Presidency for the priesthood. This wasn't a typical case. Pea had been serving as the president of a Hawaii branch of the church when he discovered that he "had one-fourth or one-eighth Negro blood."[73] Hawaiians didn't seem to care about race or cursed lineages—the state had always been racially diverse—but the Brethren cared. Once Pea's lineage was discovered in 1936, then-apostle George Albert Smith released him from his calling as branch president and requested that he stay his hand from performing priesthood ordinances. Kimball had known about the man's plight for years.[74]

Pea and his family had lived with this humiliation all those years and remained active in the church, despite the fact that his sons couldn't serve missions or marry in the faith's temples. Now, forty years later, Pea asked for the priesthood—and, astonishingly, the Brethren agreed. The First Presidency reviewed the facts and concluded, as President Kimball explained, "that there was no justification for withholding the Priesthood." The church's genealogical department couldn't determine his ancestry, thereby contradicting Pea's own research. The First Presidency ordered his reordination at once and his approval for a temple recommend pending his ability to pass a "worthiness interview."[75]

President Kimball and his counselors had made a similar ruling a month earlier when they lifted the restriction on Herbert Augustus Ford of Ontario, Canada. Ford's grandmother was from St. Croix in the Virgin Islands and allegedly had a cursed lineage. Ford had been denied the priesthood ever since he came of age for priesthood ordination. It didn't help that the church patriarch muddled his lineage, declaring that he was "of the blood of Abraham, through Ephraim and Manassah." This meant that, unlike other Black Latter-day Saints, he wasn't burdened with a cursed lineage in his patriarchal blessing. What he was burdened with was an overzealous mission president who took one look at him, glared at his "olive complexion," and pronounced him cursed.[76]

For nearly half a century Ford had carried that burden. Kimball was determined to make it right. Throughout it all, Ford remained active and devoted to the church, which tugged at Kimball's sense of fairness. When

208   SECOND-CLASS SAINTS

the genealogy department researched the matter at Kimball's request, they cleared Ford of bearing a cursed lineage.[77]

Kimball was also deeply affected when Latter-day Saints made individuals suspected of having African ancestry unwelcome. During one unforgettable moment, he rebuked an entire congregation in Fillmore, Utah, for gossiping about Ross Marshall, a devout member of their stake, of whom it was rumored that he had a cursed lineage.[78]

But it wasn't just Kimball losing patience. In 1975 Thomas Fyans, the mission president in Mexico, contacted Apostle Howard W. Hunter about a "sister missionary" under his supervision who just discovered that she "had a grandfather who was black." Concerned that this disclosure might affect the remaining months of her mission, Fyans urgently sought guidance from Hunter. He asked the apostle if he should send her home. Hunter promptly wrote back inquiring whether she was an effective missionary and how much time she had left. Fyans said she was a very good missionary and that she had four months left in her mission. Hunter's reply left no doubt that he, too, had grown impatient with the ban: "What I would do, if I were you, Tom, I'd study that carefully, very carefully, [and] take a minimum of four months to do it."[79]

★ ★ ★

The priesthood and temple ban came back into the national spotlight when Morris Udall, a Mormon, ran for the 1976 Democratic presidential nomination.[80] Mormons hadn't fared well running for the nation's highest office, and Udall had no better luck. A decade earlier, the press had skewered George Romney for his ties to what many perceived was a racist church, and Ezra Taft Benson generated intense heat, both within and outside of the church, when word leaked that he sought a presidential ticket with a segregationist.[81] But unlike the other two presidential aspirants, Udall wasn't a practicing Mormon, having drifted away from the church during the Second World War. Neither was his brother, Stewart, who raised a lot of hackles at church headquarters when he published a sharply worded attack on the priesthood ban in *Dialogue*—the same journal that published Lester Bush's seminal work.[82]

Morris, or "Mo," as he was called, was a former congressman from Arizona and a one-time professional basketball player. He wasn't as outspoken about the ban as Stewart was, but he wasn't quiet about it, either. Like his younger

LIFTING THE BAN 209

brother, he found the church's treatment of Black people abhorrent. "For more than 25 years I have held and expressed a deep-seated and conscientious disagreement with the church doctrine on the role of blacks," Mo emphasized during the presidential campaign. "I continue to hope that in good time the Mormon church will find a way out of the dilemma, which distressed me and many other Americans both in and out of the church."[83] Ironically, though, Mo got hammered in the presidential primaries for the racial policies he loathed. Coleman Young, the Black mayor of Detroit, decided to make Mormon racism an issue in the campaign despite Udall's having left the church over that very issue. To a group of Black Baptist ministers in Detroit, Young impishly said, "I'm asking you to make a choice between a man from Georgia who fights to let you in his church, and a man from Arizona whose church won't even let you in the back door."[84]

Unlike with Romney, however, the Brethren didn't give much thought to Udall's presidential aspirations. Had he won the nomination they would have had to pay attention. But he didn't get very far in the primaries. Instead, the Brethren cultivated a relationship with the eventual nominee, Jimmy Carter, forsaking one of their own in favor of a Baptist peanut farmer. In October 1976, just a few weeks before the election, Carter, a deeply religious man (unlike Udall), met with President Kimball, who gave Carter a copy of his genealogy dating back to the Civil War. Less than a month later, Carter was elected the nation's thirty-ninth president.[85]

Kimball and Carter met again the following spring, when Kimball flew to Washington following the cornerstone-laying ceremony of the São Paulo Temple. This was a big deal. It was not only the first temple in South America; it was a key to Kimball's plan to lift the ban.

Carter was ready for the meeting. His staff had prepared him well. "The proper ecclesiastical form of address for Mr. Kimball is 'President,'" a staffer noted, adding, "When the Prophet speaks . . . his writings and letters are regarded somehow like scripture and the majority will rally to any call."[86] Carter wanted the Mormons to support the Equal Rights Amendment, which was then up for ratification, but Kimball was in no mood to discuss politics. The meeting lasted fifteen minutes and Kimball gave no indication of the weightier issues on his mind. He was simply too tired and too distracted to talk to Carter about anything substantive.[87]

It was the cornerstone ceremony from the previous day that occupied Kimball's mind. He wasn't even sure he would be able to make it. His health had spiraled downward in recent days and he had had moments of intense discomfort. Traveling in his entourage were his counselor, Marion Romney; his secretary, Arthur Haycock; and his personal physician, Dr. Ernest Wilkinson Jr., the son of the former BYU president. When President Kimball and his party deplaned at Congonhas Airport, a throng of people awaited him. As he slowly walked down the airport breezeway and came into plain sight, a special choir of young adults burst out singing "We Thank Thee O God for a Prophet."[88] Kimball heard this song often during his church presidency, and it sometimes made him uncomfortable. "This [song] always humbles me to the dust," he once said. "I try to feel that this is an honor for the President of the Church and that I am just representing him."[89] The humility was vintage Kimball.

About two thousand people attended the ceremony the following day, including the presidents of the four Brazil missions, a stake president from South Africa, and past mission presidents. James E. Faust conducted the meeting while President Kimball presided. Before the ceremony began, Kimball, sitting on the stand next to Faust and Romney, made eye contact with a forty-four-year-old convert named Helvécio Martins, a Black Brazilian businessman. "President Kimball was looking in my direction," Martins recalled. "He motioned with his finger for me to come and speak to him. I turned away, not believing his gesture could be meant for me, and continued my duties. Still, I couldn't help looking at him again. Smiling, the prophet repeated the signal, which I again could not believe was meant for me." As Martins struggled to comprehend the moment, Faust made eye contact with him and motioned him to come to the stand. Martins promptly did as directed and met the prophet. The two talked for a brief moment before President Kimball looked him straight in the eye and said, "Brother Martins, what is necessary for you is fidelity. Remain faithful and you will enjoy all the blessings of the gospel."[90] All the blessings of the gospel, of course, meant the priesthood. And it meant full access to the temple. The church president was planting a seed.

When the ceremony ended, Kimball walked up to Martins, stopped, took his hand in "a strong grip" while holding his arm with his other hand, and said, "Don't forget, Brother Martins, don't forget." Kimball then scurried away.[91]

Moments later Faust handed Martins a note asking if he would drive him to the airport that evening. Faust wanted to see if Martins understood

LIFTING THE BAN   211

Kimball's message. As the two drove through the winding streets, they reflected on the day's events. They discussed the cornerstone-laying ceremony, in particular, and Faust asked whether Martins remembered the president's counsel. Martins nodded affirmatively but "admitted that the experience perplexed" him. Faust then reiterated what Kimball had said, informing the bewildered Brazilian, "The promises of the Lord will be fulfilled only in the lives of faithful servants."[92]

Kimball himself followed up through Faust later that year. He wanted Faust to check with Martins to make sure he "understood the implications" of what he had told him. Martins said he understood. Kimball's secretary, Francis Gibbons, recalled that Kimball's "concern for those deprived of priesthood blessing due to racial origin was typified by his concern for Helvécio Martins."[93]

Why did Kimball target Martins for special treatment? It could have been anyone in Brazil, really, but Martins was special. The president had been eyeing Martins since at least 1974, when the two first met during a church conference. Perhaps one reason for Kimball's affection was Martins's devotion to the church. He and his family had suffered the indignity of the ban ever since they were baptized in 1972, but they had endured it with grace and courage. Beyond that, they had sacrificed to help build a beautiful building they wouldn't be permitted to enter: Rudá, Helvécio's wife, sold her jewelry to donate to the São Paulo Temple fund, and Helvécio worked night and day to raise money. The Martins family had also saved money for their son Marcus to serve a mission, in the hope that one day he might be able to do so. "All of this grieved Kimball," church historian Leonard Arrington noted.[94]

There were other factors that signaled the Brethren's affection for Martins. Apostle Ezra Taft Benson called him to be the public relations director for the church in Brazil, despite not having the priesthood. Indeed, everyone in upper church leadership who knew Martins had great affection for him. As Apostle David B. Haight aptly noted, he was "the strongest NEGRO or BLACK in the whole church."[95]

With the faithfulness of Martins and his family etched in his mind, Kimball began seriously laying the groundwork to overturn the 126-year-old ban.[96] At the April general conference that spring, he delivered an address on "continuous revelation"—a theme he addressed often during his presidency. He wanted to remind the Saints that God had always spoken

212   SECOND-CLASS SAINTS

to church prophets, without interruption, without pauses or gaps, and with purpose. "I say in the deepest of humility," Kimball assured his listeners,

> but also by the power and force of a burning testimony in my soul, that from the prophet of the restoration to the prophet of our own year, the communication line is unbroken, the authority is continuous, a light, brilliant and penetrating, continues to shine. The sound of the voice of the Lord is a continuous melody and a thunderous appeal. For nearly a century and a half there has been no interruption.[97]

Kimball's resolve to lift the ban was further reinforced a month later, when he met again with Jack Carlson; this time Carlson's wife, Renee, joined them, along with Arthur Haycock. Without wasting a precious minute, Carlson bluntly told Kimball to lift the ban: "Jack's advice was, you should do it fast. Take advantage of the fact that you are the Prophet."[98]

In Carlson's judgment, if Kimball didn't lift the ban, his likely successors— Apostles Petersen and Benson—wouldn't. Kimball listened intently as Carlson explained to him how Mormons were excluded from government positions within the Carter administration because of the ban and because of the church's opposition to the Equal Rights Amendment. The president asked the economist what he thought would transpire if he lifted the ban. President Kimball "was really serious about what the repercussions would be within the Church," Renee recalled, and "what it would be within the Quorum of the Twelve." He worried "what he would have to do to get them to go along with it." Kimball's frankness surprised Renee. "He was very candid," she noted. "There was no, 'I think I need to go pray.' It wasn't that [at] all. It was a very rational, political issue that he would have to steer through this committee." In addition, he wanted to know what impact Black priesthood ordination would have on the church in the South. Would they support a policy change? Would they invite Black members into their worship services as full equals? Would they honor a revelation if President Kimball produced one? All these questions lingered as the president talked with the Carlsons.[99]

The meeting lasted forty-five minutes.[100] Kimball moved quickly on Carlson's advice. A month later, in June 1977, he invited a select group of general authorities to provide him with their opinions on the ban. Apostles Packer, Monson, and McConkie submitted memos.[101] To Kimball's astonishment, all supported lifting the ban. Perhaps it's not surprising that Monson and Packer supported ending the restriction. After all, they had witnessed firsthand how the ban had ripped apart the Genesis Group and caused dissension within its ranks. But McConkie's support was entirely unexpected. He had a long history of writing and saying demeaning things about Black people. These views derived from his late father-in-law, Joseph Fielding Smith, one of McConkie's most important mentors, whose racist theories about Black people found their way into *Mormon Doctrine*. In any event, this was the first indication Kimball had that McConkie was willing to end the restriction. The apostle provided the president with a lengthy justification for conferring the priesthood on Black men, intuitively recognizing the impossibility of preserving the ban when the church was building a temple in biracial Brazil. Much of the memo discussed the idea that Black people would have to receive the priesthood before the Second Coming of Jesus Christ.[102]

The memo was classic McConkie: punchy, to the point, opinionated. In clear, straightforward prose, the apostle poked a gaping hole in the theological rationale for Black priesthood denial—a rationale that his own father-in-law had developed and articulated with stunning meticulousness for over a half century. McConkie expanded on a teaching of Joseph Smith to justify lifting the ban.[103] He posited that Black people would no longer be deemed outside of the house of Israel. Instead, they would be adopted into it through conversion. Their "negro blood" would be "purged out" of them "by baptism [and] the receipt of the Holy Ghost and personal righteousness," making them heirs to all the blessings of Abraham, including priesthood and temple blessings. Tellingly, though, McConkie sidestepped the issue of favored lineages—a favorite talking point of Joseph Fielding Smith. He neither denounced this concept nor supported it. Instead, he implicitly noted that lifting the ban would make all lineages equal, if not in theory at least in practice.[104]

It didn't matter that McConkie's bold pronouncement contradicted a memo that the First Presidency had sent Kimball just a few years earlier. ("In regard to the matter of becoming members of the House of Israel by adoption when we are baptized," First Presidency Secretary Joseph Anderson informed Kimball, "I am directed to tell you that this is not the doctrine of the church.")[105] Nor did it matter that McConkie contradicted himself. In 1967, he had explained to a group of LDS college students that "negroes" couldn't have patriarchal blessings and be "adopted into the House of Israel." It didn't matter, either, what he wrote in *Mormon Doctrine*, that "negroes are not equal with other races where the receipt of certain spiritual blessings are concerned."[106]

What mattered now was that McConkie was creating new doctrine to accommodate the sweeping changes that President Kimball envisioned. What also mattered was that President Kimball gave him the latitude to support such sweeping changes. The president's impulse to expand Mormonism across the globe needed a new theology to match the evolving times, and McConkie provided it. The president and the apostle seemed to have a sense of where the church needed to go. Undoubtedly, McConkie's many visits to Brazil led him to the conclusion that Mormonism would be halted in its tracks unless Black people could experience the full rituals of the church. Kimball's universalist message, then, hovered over every inch of McConkie's memo. Salvation had to be brought to everyone, McConkie wrote, including Black people. All nations had to hear the gospel. For McConkie, Kimball's universalist vision didn't just ring in his ears; it was a loud, pulsating voice that told him now was the time to bring Black people fully into the fold.[107]

When Kimball read McConkie's memo he was astonished. The apostle had never given any indication that he was prepared to lift the ban. A great burden had been lifted from the president's shoulders. Kimball acknowledged McConkie's "special support" precisely because he needed it.[108] Having the church's foremost theologian in his corner was vital to his efforts, but more important, McConkie's support would carry tremendous weight with the Twelve. What McConkie said mattered—Kimball knew it and the Brethren knew it.[109]

★ ★ ★

In December 1977, about six months after McConkie agreed to lift the ban, general authority (and future apostle) Neal A. Maxwell made a confidential phone call to Leonard Arrington. He wanted the church historian to locate two statements that Joseph Fielding Smith had made—one wherein he stated that "darkies are wonderful people" and another in which he predicted that Black people would receive the priesthood. Arrington took this as evidence that Maxwell was marshaling resources to present to Kimball to lift the ban. The church historian's instincts were correct; change was in the air. Just after the New Year in January 1978, Arrington presciently wrote, "I predict the Church will take a small step toward recognizing the dignity and worthiness of members of the Church of the black race."[110]

The new year brought Kimball renewed energy and focus. He once told his son Edward, "Revelation[s] will probably never come unless they are desired. I think few people receive revelations while lounging on the couch or while playing cards or while relaxing." Kimball continued, "I believe most revelations would come when a man is on his tiptoes, reaching as high as he can for something which he knows he needs, and then there are bursts upon him [that provide] the answer to his problems."[111]

The year 1978 was when Spencer W. Kimball was on his tiptoes, preparing the church for what lay ahead. His wife, Camilla, was worried about him. Throughout January and February, he had been spending long hours in the temple praying and seeking guidance. Her husband looked "haggard and tired," she noted. Arthur Haycock assured her everything was fine.[112]

One of the first things Kimball did in the new year was to dispatch BYU professor (and future general authority) Merrill Bateman to Africa on a secret fact-finding mission. Ghanaians and Nigerians had written to James Faust in his capacity as president of the International Mission requesting church literature and missionaries.[113] Bateman was the ideal candidate to be sent abroad. He knew Ghana and Nigeria well, having been to those countries many times over the years, both as an employee of the Mars Corporation and as an economics professor. Now he would visit BYU graduates from Nigeria and Ghana and report back to the First Presidency on their commitment to the church. President Kimball wanted to know if Africans were ready for the priesthood. And he also wanted to know if they had the leadership skills to run their own branches and wards.[114]

Bateman's special mission was strictly confidential. No one could know that he was there for "religious purposes," noted John Baker, a friend and confidant of Bateman's.[115]

As Bateman embarked for Africa, the church's genealogy department was overwhelmed with requests to determine cursed lineages, particularly in South Africa and Brazil. This had been going on for a long time and had caused tremendous grief in the church, especially when a cursed ancestry was revealed, which prompted the affected parties to write the genealogy department to confirm the finding. In the spring of 1978 the department became overwhelmed with such requests, and the president responded by shutting it down. In February, Kimball made an important policy change that would ripple throughout the church: he announced that the genealogy department would no longer consider cases of "negro blood" when there was insufficient evidence to deny people the priesthood. Stake presidents, mission presidents, bishops, and branch presidents would have to determine lineage on their own.[116] This was the first clear sign that the winds were shifting because it meant that church headquarters would no longer police racial boundaries.[117]

A month later, on March 9, Kimball held a special meeting in the temple. The Brethren sniffed change. They reminded the president of something he already knew: if church policy was to be changed, it would have to be by the unanimous consent of the Twelve, after much prayer and deliberation with the First Presidency. In other words, the ban could be lifted only through revelation behind the united front of upper leadership.[118]

That spring, several apostles continued to resist Kimball, causing him grief. Throughout much of March he had difficulty sleeping. On March 23, he said he had a "wakeful night." He struggled with the ban and felt it "should be lifted," his secretary, Francis Gibbons, wrote. Kimball shared the experience with his counselors, and the three discussed frankly and openly how lifting the ban would affect the apostles and the broader church body.[119] These were all the same questions he had ruminated over with the Carlsons the year before. N. Eldon Tanner and Marion G. Romney, Kimball's loyal counselors, said they would sustain him to the bitter end if he decided to admit Black men to the priesthood, even though earlier both men had had strong misgivings about lifting the ban. Romney had always defended it with conviction; Tanner felt the same. But both came around sometime that spring.[120]

Now Kimball had at least five important apostles in his corner: his counselors and Apostles McConkie, Packer, and Monson. But what about the others? "He sensed resistance from some," Kimball's son Edward candidly explained. But he "did not push, lobby, pressure, or use his office to seek compliance. Instead, he increased his visits to the temple, imploring the Lord to make his will known, not only to him but also to the [apostles]." Gibbons captured the moment when he stated that President Kimball struggled "with how to resolve the matter in a way that the entire leadership would stand behind."[121]

Kimball's diary is tantalizingly silent on which apostles resisted him, but in private he told Edward that it was Mark Petersen, Ezra Taft Benson, and Delbert Stapley.[122] On April 20, Kimball met again with the Twelve, this time imploring them to pray with him in the temple about lifting the ban.

LIFTING THE BAN

It was clear they weren't ready to make a change because some continued to give him resistance. After the meeting ended, Kimball did something unexpected but consistent with effective management practices: he met with the apostles individually to get their perspectives, listening patiently as they expressed their concerns and voiced their positions. The determined church president resolved to win them over one by one.[123]

We don't have an account of what was said at these private meetings, but the holdouts likely feared that removing the barrier to priesthood ordination would lead to interracial marriage, which President Kimball also feared.[124] Most likely, they would have discussed Brazil and the problem of building a temple there when a number of faithful Black and biracial Latter-day Saints wouldn't be permitted to enter. Apostle McConkie understood this problem well: "There have been discussions . . . about patriarchal blessings for Negroes and about problems we might encounter in Brazil after the dedication of the São Paulo Temple." Apostle LeGrand Richards similarly noted, "This situation that we face down there in Brazil—Brother Kimball worried a lot about it—how the people are so faithful and devoted."[125]

Another issue they likely discussed was patriarchal blessings for individuals of Black African descent. They never quite figured out how to address this. The church's lineage theology, in fact, was in shambles. Some church patriarchs declared a cursed lineage on Black and biracial people; some no lineage at all; and some the lineage of Ephraim, which was generally reserved for priesthood holders—the men who ran the church. The Twelve met in 1958 and again in 1970 to resolve the issue, but they couldn't agree.[126] Their differences were on full display when they met with church patriarchs in 1973 during general conference weekend in Salt Lake. There, anxious patriarchs expressed concern about giving blessings to Black people. "If the spirit is to indicate a lineage of Cain, is it not possible to stipulate that?" asked one. Apostle Richards recognized the precariousness of the moment and told the patriarch not to pronounce a lineage through Cain. It will only "discourage people," he insisted. Apostle Stapley counseled patriarchs to say that Black members "were descendants of Abraham"; Eldred Smith, the presiding church patriarch, rebuffed him and said not to declare any lineage at all. This caused confusion among patriarchs and Black people whom they blessed, most especially in Brazil, where patriarchs had been declaring lineages "from many tribes," including the tribes reserved for temple and priesthood blessings. To address the problem, the Brethren

218   SECOND–CLASS SAINTS

dispatched Apostle L. Tom Perry to São Paulo in 1976, but it's not clear that he resolved anything.[127]

On May 4, 1978, the Brethren met again to discuss the ban. At that meeting something unexpected happened. Apostle Richards, a voluble and affable elderly man, asked the president if he could share an experience he had had during the meeting. In Richards's words, "I saw during the meeting a man seated [in a chair] above the organ, bearded and dressed in white, having the appearance of Wilford Woodruff." Richards then pointed toward a portrait of Woodruff hanging in the room. "I saw him just as clearly as I see any of you Brethren."[128] What Richards's vision meant is open to interpretation. Perhaps it meant that if Woodruff had the courage to end polygamy in 1890 at the risk of dividing the church, Kimball and the Twelve could end a priesthood restriction that had brought the church similar grief. Perhaps this was the moment that moved the doubters and naysayers to fall into line.

Whatever the reason, the Brethren soon decided that they wanted to see what past prophets and apostles had said about the ban. At the end of May, it was reported that the apostles were studying Lester Bush's massive four-hundred-page "Compilation on the Negro" as well as his *Dialogue* article.[129] Apostle Petersen gave a copy of Bush's article to President Kimball, though it's likely that he already knew about it since it made a lot of noise at church headquarters when it was published. Kimball marked it up in red ink. Petersen also gave him a draft copy of Newell Bringhurst's article on Brigham Young and the priesthood ban, although it's not clear whether the president read it since his copy was not marked up. In addition, Kimball asked Homer Durham, a general authority supervising the Historical Department, to research past statements from the apostles regarding the priesthood ban. He produced a document he titled "Prophets Tell of Promise of Priesthood to All Races," in which he selectively culled past statements of Mormon prophets affirming that Black men would receive the priesthood.[130]

All of this was a strong push to win over the last remaining holdouts. Kimball had already made up his mind at that point to lift the ban. On May 30, he moved into the final stages of the revelatory process by writing a "tentative statement in longhand removing racial restrictions on the priesthood." He said he had a "good, warm feeling" about it. Now he had to get each of the apostles to agree to it.[131]

On June 1, the Twelve and the First Presidency met in the temple. It wasn't by accident that Apostle Petersen was away on a church assignment in Ecuador, for there is no indication in the months leading up to this meeting that he consented to lifting the ban.[132] Nor is there evidence that Apostle Stapley was prepared to accept what was coming. He was in the hospital and had given no indication that he saw a place for Black men in the church as priesthood holders.[133]

The Brethren knew what was about to happen. They had been prepped for it for months, and in the case of those closest to Kimball, his counselors, for well over a year.[134] The day began as usual during the Brethren's weekly meeting in the Salt Lake Temple. There was no indication in Kimball's diary that June 1 would be one of the most consequential days in LDS church history. Indeed, the day's events went conspicuously unmentioned.

The meeting began at 9:00 a.m. and lasted well over two hours. After the Brethren conducted their usual business and took communion, President Kimball asked them to forgo lunch and stay to discuss additional business. He told them he wanted to lift the ban. At that moment, there appeared to be one holdout, Ezra Taft Benson, who had shown no willingness to end the restriction in previous deliberations on the subject. Benson reportedly wanted to "table" the discussion, but Kimball demurred.[135] In any event, the prophet knew that a revelation required unanimity from the Twelve, so he asked the apostles if they had "anything to say," hoping to enlist their support to win over Benson. Perhaps it's fitting that the apostles who came to the president's aid were the ones who determined first that the ban had to end. McConkie spoke first, followed by Packer and Monson. These headstrong men now dominated the room as they expressed to Benson and the rest of the Twelve the wisdom of lifting the ban. McConkie gave a ten-minute oration on why Black people "must receive the priesthood before the Millennium." He also discussed the points from his memo to President Kimball, reiterating that there were no scriptural barriers to granting Black men the priesthood.[136]

Packer spoke next, also for ten minutes, delivering "equally persuasive reasons." He quoted from the Doctrine and Covenants to support the change. Then Monson offered his opinion. After they finished, each of the apostles spoke. "There was a wondrous and marvelous spirit of unity in the meeting," McConkie observed. All that was left now was to pray. The Brethren gathered in a prayer circle—a special Mormon temple ritual—and

Salt Lake Temple, Salt Lake City, Utah, ca. 1910, the sacred Mormon edifice where the First Presidency and Quorum of the Twelve Apostles lifted the priesthood and temple ban on June 1, 1978. Courtesy of Utah State Historical Society.

listened intently as President Kimball prayed. Kimball's prayer, which lasted about ten minutes, confirmed their decision to lift the ban.[137] Each said they felt the Holy Spirit prick their hearts while the president prayed. This included even Benson, who explained that he "would have voted against" the proposal to ordain Black men had he not "experienced the feeling that I did in this room this morning." All of the apostles called it the most intense experience of their lifetime and believed that it was a genuine communication from God. "Not one of us who was present on that occasion was ever quite the same after that," Gordon Hinckley soberly recalled. Benson said it was "the sweetest spirit of unity and conviction" he had "ever experienced."[138]

In the days following the revelation, Kimball was a nervous wreck. He was "as agitated as he had ever been," his wife observed.[139] Worried, she called Arthur Haycock. She wanted to know why her husband was "so distressed and concerned," to which Haycock said he knew what was troubling her husband, but he wasn't at liberty to say. He assured her that all would be well. She'd have to be patient.[140]

Why was Kimball so distressed after the momentous revelation? Plainly put, he didn't know if the rest of the general authorities would accept it. This included the church patriarch, the First Quorum of the Seventy, and the presiding bishopric. He worried himself sick over it.

On June 7, President Kimball appointed a committee consisting of Apostles McConkie, Packer, and Hinckley to draft a statement announcing

Spencer W. Kimball (seated), the twelfth president of the Church of Jesus Christ of Latter-day Saints and leader who initiated the lifting of the priesthood and temple ban, with his secretary, D. Arthur Haycock, Salt Lake City, Utah, n.d. Courtesy of Utah State Historical Society.

222 SECOND-CLASS SAINTS

the revelation. Each produced a separate statement, which Francis Gibbons melded together into a single document for consideration by the First Presidency.[141] The president himself carefully read the statement that Gibbons provided, studying every word, every phrase, for tone and effect. Then, with his counselors, Kimball made "slight editorial amendments," to what became the basis for the announcement of "the new revelation."[142]

The next day, the First Presidency met with the Quorum of the Twelve Apostles and discussed the wording of the statement and how they should release it. They made additional changes to it, all minor.[143] Some apostles expressed a desire to wait until the October general conference to announce the news; others, like McConkie, believed that it should be shared right away. "It will leak, and we have to beat Satan," the apostle feared. "He'll do something between now and then to make it appear that we're being forced into it."[144] The First Presidency concurred with McConkie and agreed to release it the next day after they secured the support of the rest of the general authorities.

Only moments after the meeting ended, the president telephoned Apostle Petersen, still in Ecuador, to apprise him of the revelation. Petersen agreed to support it but "felt that the revelation's coming was more striking than the decision itself." In other words, the fact that the Twelve achieved a consensus to lift the ban shocked him. He knew, as did President Kimball and the rest of the apostles, that one dissenter would have thwarted the entire revelation. In any event, with everyone on board, Petersen wasn't going to oppose it: "I told President Kimball that I fully sustained both the revelation and him one hundred percent." But he did have one request: he asked the president to add a disclaimer discouraging interracial marriage when church leaders published the revelation in the *Church News*. Kimball agreed.[145]

Hours later the First Presidency visited Apostle Stapley in the hospital to give him the news. "I'll stay with the Brethren on this," he reassured Kimball. This was hardly a ringing endorsement, but it was the best Stapley could muster. He died two months later.[146]

Petersen's and Stapley's support for the revelation, however tepid, thrilled Kimball. It meant that there was full unanimity among the Twelve. Now he had to win over the rest of the general authorities, and there were no assurances that he would do so. Some, like Eldred Smith, the church patriarch, had strong views about Black people and were not afraid to express

LIFTING THE BAN   223

them.[147] On this and other issues, Smith had clashed with the Brethren over the years, demonstrating an independence of mind rarely seen among general authorities.[148] Little wonder Kimball was anxious. He didn't know if Patriarch Smith would support the revelation.

★ ★ ★

On June 9, 1978, the First Presidency summoned the general authorities to the Salt Lake Temple for a special meeting with the First Presidency and Quorum of the Twelve. The meeting was highly confidential. No one could know about it, not even their secretaries, the First Presidency instructed. All of the general authorities in the Salt Lake area were invited. This included the First Quorum of the Seventy, the church patriarch, and the presiding bishopric. The only general authorities excused were the ones overseas on church assignments.[149]

The meeting began at 7:00 a.m. The air was rife with suspicion and intrigue. Why a special meeting, the general authorities wondered? Was there a "particular current problem"? Was the Second Coming near? Would Black men get the priesthood? No one knew for sure what the meeting was about, but there was plenty of speculation.[150] As they ambled into the temple, Apostle Packer stopped Marion Hanks, shook his hand, and whispered, "It is good for us to be here." Then, choking back tears, Packer said, "This is an important day."[151]

After speaking with Packer, Hanks took his seat. He knew something unusual was about to happen. Packer, well known at church headquarters for his gruffness, was "uncommonly cordial" that day, which took Hanks by surprise. He suspected the cause was the lifting of the ban: "I knew that from looking into Boyd Packer's eyes, he and I having discussed the matter on many occasions and he having hinted periodically that something of consequence would happen one day before too long."[152]

As the prelude music played and the Brethren filed into the temple, Hanks leaned over to fellow general authority Paul Dunn, who sat next to him, and whispered, "This is about the Negro."[153]

The meeting opened with the Brethren singing "We Thank Thee, Oh God, for a Prophet"—a song that Eldon Tanner specifically requested for the occasion. Then Ezra Taft Benson, the president of the Quorum of the Twelve, "offered a beautiful invocation."[154] Hanks observed that the senior apostle said three times in his prayer "this momentous event." Benson's

224   SECOND-CLASS SAINTS

prayer only added to the intrigue. Finally, the church president spoke. Kimball said that he had spent many days and nights in the temple during the past year "struggling with the challenge of the priesthood for all members of the Church." He had discussed the matter repeatedly with his counselors, with the Quorum of the Twelve, and with others. Then the president broke the news: the decades-old ban would be lifted. He had had a revelation. The room was eerily silent as he described the details of what had transpired the previous week. Kimball asked Francis Gibbons to read the statement the First Presidency and the Twelve had prepared. Gibbons got out only two lines before Hanks "started to weep." His mind immediately harked back to all of the Black men he knew who had been harmed by the ban. Some were still alive; others had passed on. Ruffin Bridgeforth and Monroe Fleming came to mind, and most especially his dear friend Len Hope. "I thought of his death and funeral and of the loss of their faithful children because they could not hold the priesthood," Hanks tearfully noted.[155]

Neal Maxwell also wept, soaking a handkerchief with his tears. (Later that evening he told his wife not to wash it. He wanted a keepsake from that special occasion.) James Faust, who had done so much to lay the groundwork for the revelation by working with Brazilian Latter-day Saints and apprising President Kimball and Apostle McConkie of their faithfulness, also reacted to the announcement with joy. He had been hoping for a policy change for some time.[156]

After Gibbons finished reading the statement, Franklin Richards, the most senior of the lower-ranking general authorities, took some of the luster out of the room by prattling on about what the statement omitted. He backed the revelation, he said, but the statement that Gibbons read "left out women." What did he mean by this? Should they, too, get the priesthood? Richards didn't say. Faust spoke next. He told the audience "about the Brazil Temple and the inability of the people there to qualify because there was mixed blood in most of them." Hanks called it "an impressive statement."[157]

Following Faust's remarks, McConkie recounted the events of the previous week and shared with the group the new theology he had created. Then Hanks rose. One report stated that he was "so overcome that he could not speak."[158] After gathering his composure, he spoke in such a low voice that his colleagues could barely hear him. "I thank God that I have lived long enough to see this day," he somberly stated.

> There have been two thoughts in my mind—the first of faces and lives I have grieved for and prayed for, and secondly that the cynics and the critics will have at us again for this, but having with complete loyalty sustained the position of the Church through the years I cared not for what any critic might do. The good news has been delivered and I am full of joy and rejoicing.[159]

Following Hanks's remarks, all the general authorities agreed to support the revelation, even Eldred Smith, which pleased Kimball. After the sustaining vote, Paul Dunn witnessed something that he would remember for the rest of his life. He saw President Kimball put his hand on Tanner's leg and say, softly, "Eldon, go tell the world."[160]

Tanner promptly left the meeting and handed the statement to Heber Wolsey, now managing director of public communications for the church, instructing him to share it with the media. Wolsey got about halfway through it when he began to weep, influenced, no doubt, by the scars he had incurred defending the church over the years.[161] Now there was joy as he read these words:

> [God] has heard our prayers, and by revelation has confirmed that the long promised day has come when every faithful, worthy man in the Church may receive the holy priesthood, with power to exercise its divine authority, and enjoy with his loved ones every blessing that flows therefrom, including the blessings of the temple. Accordingly, all worthy male members of the Church may be ordained to the priesthood without regard for race or color.[162]

Moments later Tanner returned to the meeting and told President Kimball, "It's done." The meeting adjourned at 9:35 a.m., the general authorities stunned and shocked at what they had just witnessed.[163]

Later that evening Hanks wrote in his diary:

> I have anguished for a lifetime, fasted and prayed a multitude of times, defended the Church under harassment on many university campuses, faced people on many fronts in all walks of life and suffered, wept on my pillow many times, grieved with a few choice souls who had broken hearts over this, read all I could, written much at the behest of prophets and apostles, and now feel that the matter is done and I could only weep and rejoice and thank God.[164]

226 SECOND–CLASS SAINTS

Kimball's diary entry that evening was much more subdued; likely he was exhausted by the day's events: "This morning at seven o'clock by prior arrangement I met in the upper room of the Salt Lake Temple with all of the General Authorities to consider with them the matter of giving the Priesthood to all worthy male members of the Church."[165]

He continued, "Immediately following the release of this announcement the telephones started to ring and rang continuously the balance of the afternoon. People, members and nonmembers, called from around the world to learn if what they had heard on the radio and TV was true." Kimball closed his entry noting it "was a very busy day."[166]

What the revelation meant for the church and for the general authorities was yet to be determined. Were Black people still cursed? Had they been less valiant? Could faithful Black and White Latter-day Saints marry each other with the church's blessing? Could Black people receive the lineage of Ephraim in their patriarchal blessings? The revelation didn't say, and the Brethren remained tight-lipped. There would be plenty of time later to sort out these important questions.

For now, the Brethren wanted to bask in the glorious news. As Gibbons explained, the revelation "seemed to relieve them of a subtle sense of guilt they had felt over the years."[167]

8

Debris in the Streets, 1978–1985

In the days following the announcement, the usually taciturn President Spencer W. Kimball was exuberant. Camilla, his wife of nearly sixty years, noticed a stark change in his demeanor. Kimball's colleagues in the church hierarchy likewise found him more relaxed than usual. His barber found him "happy, buoyant, and warm." "The prophet has a great weight off his shoulders," he observed. Kimball had encountered several missionaries in the barbershop and asked them whether they heard the news. "Isn't it beautiful?" he asked, repeating the question several times.[1]

Kimball had worked hard on the revelation and justifiably took pride in it. He had "wrestled over it" for years and had spent many days and sleepless nights agonizing over whether his colleagues in the Twelve would agree to lift the ban.[2] The fact that he did it and his predecessor, David O. McKay, couldn't brought him great satisfaction. Admittedly, McKay presided over the church during the tumultuous civil rights years when announcing a revelation to lift the ban would have looked suspicious. The Brethren were always worried about how things looked to the public; they never wanted to give the impression that they would be caving to pressure. The timing had to be right.[3]

With the revelation, however, came new challenges. Would the church membership support it? Would Black people flock to the church? Were they ready to run their own congregations? Would the church body welcome them? And important questions remained about LDS racial teachings. The revelation didn't address cursed lineages, the preexistent hypothesis, or interracial marriage.

228   SECOND-CLASS SAINTS

The silence on these important doctrinal issues was strange, even bizarre. And yet President Kimball soon learned that he wouldn't be able to control the narrative simply by having people read "Official Declaration 2," the name of the statement that the Twelve and First Presidency released to the public. Apostle Bruce R. McConkie was a big reason why. Within days after the revelation, he began to embellish details of it. But some Latter-day Saints also became restless. They asked to see the revelation, and when they learned that one didn't exist, an enterprising Latter-day Saint created one.

In addition, rumors swirled around the events of June 1 with a stunning intensity. In the ensuing months, a rumor began to circulate that the IRS had pressured the church to lift the ban. Latter-day Saints also wanted to know if the revelation for racial equality meant that there would be one for gender equality. Would women, too, get the priesthood?

These issues and others posed significant problems for the Brethren. But most pressing was how to address the church's now-defunct racial teachings. The revelation put the Brethren in a difficult position, for now they had the daunting task of confronting a past they would all rather forget. Most problematic were the racial theories in Joseph Fielding Smith's *The Way to Perfection*, McConkie's *Mormon Doctrine*, and the First Presidency statements of 1949 and 1969. The Brethren didn't want to get into the business of correcting current and former church leaders. The revelation left a pile of "debris in the streets," and they were forced to clean it up.[4]

* * *

June 9, 1978, proved a glorious day for members of the Genesis Group. Apostle Thomas S. Monson called Monroe Fleming and Ruffin Bridgeforth shortly after the revelation was announced and broke the news.[5] "I expected it would come," Fleming rejoiced. "I had faith." The policy change meant that Fleming would no longer feel like he was "a guest in [his] father's house." Fleming, age seventy-eight, had been in the church for twenty-five years and would finally be able to hold the priesthood. The feeling was overwhelming.[6]

Bridgeforth, too, could scarcely control his emotions. He called June 9 the greatest day of his life. "I knew if the priesthood was to come in my lifetime," he exulted, "it would come under President Kimball and it has." Upon further reflection, Bridgeforth added, "We are getting close to the end times—the latter days—because I think that we perhaps have reached a state of brotherhood."[7] Robert Stevenson, one of a handful of Black BYU students in 1978, also thought the end of the ban marked "a closeness to the last days."[8]

Other Genesis members also felt jubilation, anticipation, and overwhelming joy. Joseph Freeman, who would become the first Black Latter-day Saint to be ordained to the priesthood, exclaimed, "The yearning desire I'd had since joining the Church—to be found worthy to act in the name of the Lord, to know that I would have my family forever, to be able to bless and baptize my own children, to lead as a priesthood patriarch in our home—this tremendous blessing was now to be mine!"[9]

When Darius Gray learned of the news, he closed his eyes, took a deep breath, and said, "God is good."[10] For her part, Genesis member Mary Bankhead rejoiced that her grandson could attend the deacon's quorum with White boys and not feel like a stranger. James Dawson, one of two Black members in the famed Mormon Tabernacle Choir, jubilantly proclaimed that the revelation was a pivotal moment in Mormon history: "My faith is strengthened and I am very happy."[11]

Overseas, the excitement was just as palpable. When Helvécio Martins returned home from work on June 9, his wife, Rudá, rushed to the door, sobbing, as she exclaimed, "I have news, amazing news! The First Presidency just announced the prophet's revelation: the priesthood will now be given to all men, regardless of race! Helvécio, you will hold the priesthood!"[12]

Upon hearing these long-anticipated words, Martins fell to his knees and wept. After a few moments, he gathered his composure and retreated to his bedroom, where he joined his wife in prayer—a prayer of gratitude, a prayer of humility—for the couple knew that their life in the church would change forever.[13] The priesthood meant that the Martinses' son could serve a mission and the family could be bound together for eternity in a special "sealing ritual" in the temple. (A year later the couple were sealed. They wept again.)[14] Six months later Apostle David B. Haight called Martins into the stake presidency—the first Black priesthood holder to be called to such a position.[15]

Two days later, William Grant Bangerter, who had replaced James Faust as the president of the International Mission, called a special meeting to inform all the mission presidents in Brazil.[16] The meeting was emotional. As Bangerter explained, "This revelation means a lot to the people of Brazil because of the mixture of this race within the people of Brazil and because of the numerous black members of the church which are in Brazil."[17] Following the meeting, Roger Beitler rushed home to share the news with his wife, Catherine. He read the First Presidency's statement to her and both began to weep. "As Roger read the letter to me, he started crying and I started crying," Catherine wrote in her diary.[18]

What did the revelation mean? "It means the Lord loves us! It means He answers prayers!" Catherine said.[19] No longer would their missionaries be asked to speculate on someone's lineage; no longer would they inform Brazilians that they couldn't bear the priesthood or attend the temple because of their "cursed blood"; and no longer would they use those demeaning lineage lessons. The revelation meant that they could toss them in the garbage and never look back.

Meanwhile, after years of relentless negative publicity, President Kimball basked in the positive reaction to the revelation. Heber Wolsey, the LDS director of public communications and a friend of Kimball's, informed him "that the Church received in one week about a million dollars worth of publicity, almost all bad," during the BYU protests in the late 1960s. "Since June 9 . . . it is estimated that some $2–3 million worth of publicity has been received by the Church, almost all good."[20]

Wolsey's glowing report thrilled Kimball. The president collected dozens of these news accounts for his private files. *Time* and *Newsweek* ran upbeat stories about the revelation, which pleased the Mormon prophet. Nearly every major newspaper in the United States carried the announcement "as the front-page news," the LDS *Church News* enthusiastically reported.[21]

The news reports praised the church for shedding its parochial past and moving toward the development of a universal church. The *Salt Lake Tribune* editorialized that "a burden had been lifted from all Utahns," characterizing the now-defunct priesthood ban as "an irritating barrier to better human relationships." Newspapers outside of Utah extolled the church for "scrapping a 148-year-old racist tradition" and for "dissolving a black bias" that had stunted the growth of the church.[22] An African American newspaper praised the new direction for eliminating a "racist policy" and blazing a new path opening the Mormon church to all people.[23]

Especially welcoming was the response of President Jimmy Carter, who sent Kimball a warm congratulatory telegram. Carter wanted the tone to be just right, so he asked Jim Jardine, a devout Mormon working in his administration, to write it. Jardine read a draft to general authority Neal A. Maxwell, who gave it a thumbs-up. Similarly, Sterling McMurrin, the sharp-tongued critic who for years had pestered the Brethren to lift the ban, sent the aged leader a note, calling the revelation "a gracious, compassionate, courageous, and humane act," which "lifted a tremendous burden from the conscience of the members of the church."[24]

Lowell Bennion was another enthusiastic supporter of the revelation. He had tried for nearly thirty-five years to convince the Brethren to end the ban, and he welcomed the news. "Dad was not an emotional man," Lowell's son Douglas noted, but after learning of the revelation, "that was [one] time there was emotion in his voice." Even Fawn Brodie praised the revelation. She once called the ban "the ugliest thesis in Mormon existing theology," but when the Brethren lifted it she was pleased. Lowry Nelson, who had been a burr under the Brethren's saddle for nearly four decades, also spoke out. What did he think? The revelation was long overdue. That was the best he could muster.[25]

The revelation was an opportunity to heal old wounds and repair old relationships. To Hugh Brown's grandson, Edwin Firmage, Apostles N. Eldon Tanner, Gordon B. Hinckley, and James E. Faust tearfully remarked, "Your grandfather would love to have seen this day." Reaching out to Firmage constituted the apostles' tacit acknowledgment of Brown's bitter, hard-fought battles with the hard-liners. Their words to Firmage were an olive branch to the Brown family, who had expressed great anguish at Brown's being dropped from the First Presidency.[26]

Most important, the revelation opened new possibilities for Black Latter-day Saints. Many asked for new patriarchal blessings. They wanted their lineage declared.[27] Others made immediate plans to be sealed in the temple. "We are looking forward to having the Priesthood in our home and to be married in the temple," Black couple Frank and Sharon Stewart cheerfully explained to President Kimball. "It has given [us] such a boost to be more righteous. [We] had always worried for our future. But now we have a real goal to work for." Mary Lee Allen, a Black woman, informed Kimball that she had been waiting "for this day" for "more than 23 years." The announcement left her "overjoyed."[28]

But not all praised Kimball's revelation. The president received about thirty letters from critics condemning him for lifting the ban. A couple in Florida suspected that the new policy was "a giant step backward for

232 SECOND-CLASS SAINTS

the church."[29] Another critic called Kimball a "senile old BASTARD," a "STUPID FOOL" who would destroy the church. The letter concluded, "Our CHURCH shall curse the day you were born and PRAY for your destruction."[30] Kimball took the criticism in stride.

For liberal Mormons, the revelation was bittersweet. Many had left the faith over the ban and now felt a sense of justice, if not relief, that LDS racial policies had changed. "It is about time you decided to ordain our BLACK brethren," a critic told Kimball. The "liberals in the church have won and the bigots have lost." Another expressed tremendous anguish over having been excommunicated "for advocating giving blacks the priesthood." He was "now happy that the church was following the admonition to bring the gospel to every kindred, nation, and tongue."[31]

The NAACP had strong feelings about the ban as well and even took some credit for lifting it. James Dooley, the president of the Salt Lake branch, met with the First Presidency in the spring of 1978 and asked them to pray about lifting the ban. After President Kimball ended the restriction, Dooley was elated. "I've never said this to anybody," he confessed years later, "but I'd rather take some credit" for Kimball's revelation.[32]

Yet other members of the Black community were more circumspect. "Don't expect me to thank Spencer Kimball. I'll thank Spencer Kimball when he announces he has had a revelation that Mormons will not practice racial hiring. Then I will be elated," sighed Marvin Davis, an African American in Salt Lake.[33]

For Mormon feminists, the revelation was also bittersweet. If Kimball could receive a revelation to end race discrimination, they reasoned, he could also end sex discrimination by granting women the priesthood. That sentiment prompted them to write to President Kimball thanking him "for listening to the Lord and ending white racism in the church." Now they hoped he would "pray and work to eliminate sex discrimination."[34] They requested that he seek a revelation asking God if it was time to ordain women to the priesthood. After giving the matter some thought, Kimball demurred. He couldn't bring himself to ordain women, in part because of long-entrenched Mormon teachings regarding gender roles but also because of the contentious debate over the Equal Rights Amendment, which Kimball was "greatly exercised over." To a reporter he affirmed, "[The] church will not extend the priesthood to women now that it has ordained its first black." Perhaps N. Eldon Tanner, Kimball's trusted counselor, spoke

DEBRIS IN THE STREETS 233

for the rest of the First Presidency when he said, "I am not currently praying that women will someday hold the Priesthood."[35]

Nevertheless, most Latter-day Saints praised June 1, 1978, as a day of joy. A survey in conservative Utah County found that "71 percent of the 245 . . . residents [polled] were 'very happy' with the revelation and another 14 percent were 'pleased,' though they expressed reservation." These numbers were probably accurate, as Mormon historians Leonard Arrington and Davis Bitton speculated that the "announcement was received, almost universally, with elation" throughout the church.[36]

★ ★ ★

It didn't take long for the revelation to take on a mystical quality. The transition started out innocently enough. After the First Presidency and the Quorum of the Twelve met with the general authorities to obtain their support for the revelation, Henry Taylor, who was in attendance, reported, "Along the east wall of the Council Room are hung oil paintings of the twelve men who have been the Presidents of the Church and prophets of the Lord. The facial expression of the brethren in the portraits are serious and sober." He continued, "One of the brethren in giving his feelings regarding the recent revelation, remarked: 'I feel that our former presidents are pleased with what we have done today. As I look at their portraits, I think I can see them smiling with approval.'"[37] Other accounts suggest that it was President Kimball himself who expressed that sentiment.[38]

But it was Max Pinegar, president of the Language Training Center, which trains LDS missionaries for their mission assignments, who set off a firestorm. Pinegar heard the details of the revelation from his twin brother, Rex, a general authority, who was at the June 9 meeting. That evening, Max called a special meeting to discuss the revelation with the missionaries. He repeated the anecdote about the smiling Brethren but stressed that he didn't want to give the impression that "past Church prophets had appeared to the [general] authorities in [a] vision." He cautioned the missionaries to stay on script—to follow President Kimball's counsel to let the First Presidency statement speak for itself.[39]

Soon, all hell broke loose. On June 16, Apostle Bruce R. McConkie shared details of the revelation in a private family gathering at his house. The apostle's sister, Margaret Pope (also known as May), and her husband, Bill, were there, as were other family members. There the apostle explained

234   SECOND-CLASS SAINTS

the events of June 1 in vivid detail. He compared the revelation to the "day of Pentecost" at Kirtland, Ohio, when founding prophet Joseph Smith claimed to see angels, prophetic personages, and even Jesus Christ himself. The family pressed him for details. They wanted to know if there was a "rushing of great wind" as indicated in the Doctrine and Covenants, and all he would say is "Just like Kirtland." Were there "angelic choirs" in the temple that day? "Just like Kirtland." "Were there visitors beyond the veil?" "Just like Kirtland." May's heart was pounding as she was scribbling names down as fast as her brother spoke, listing the possible angels and past prophets who may have visited the Brethren on the day of the revelation. McConkie stopped her: "I didn't say they didn't come, May. I just said I wasn't telling." He instructed his family not to embellish any part of the story.[40]

The apostle certainly knew what he was doing when he compared the priesthood revelation to what happened at Kirtland, for it was there that Joseph Smith encountered the otherworld and then described it in evocative detail in the Doctrine and Covenants. All of this occurred at the dedication of the Kirtland Temple in April 1836, where the prophet claimed to have seen Moses, Elias (Noah), Elijah, and other angelic beings. Most dramatically, Smith said he saw Jesus, describing his hair as "white like the pure snow; his countenance shone above the brightness of the sun; and his voice . . . as the sound of the rushing of great waters."[41] For Latter-day Saints, this was familiar language. Smith's divine epiphany was etched in the hearts and minds of every church member from the time of their youth up to their adult years, when they learned about this foundational story in Sunday School.

No wonder May couldn't sleep that night. She knew exactly what her brother meant when he compared the revelation to Kirtland and was simply overwhelmed by it.

The next day McConkie's brother-in-law Bill Pope related some of these stories at a stake conference at BYU (with the apostle's permission). Pope told the audience that his wife had stayed up until 2:00 a.m. typing her notes so that he could have an accurate account of Apostle McConkie's remarks. Before a crowd of hundreds of people, Pope began by explaining, "Brothers and sisters, this is a great day in the Church." On the day of Pentecost, the Apostle Paul had a spiritual experience that resembled "cloven tongues of fire." Pope said that Apostle McConkie, who had often pondered that statement, now knew what Paul meant, for the priesthood revelation "was the most spiritual experience that he had ever had."[42]

DEBRIS IN THE STREETS

Pope wasn't finished. The next day he spoke at another church meeting, this time in his home ward in Provo. He again recounted the events of June 1, adding several embellishments to the story. Annie Whitton, who was in attendance, recorded the details of Pope's sermon:

> In the prayer circle revealed by the Lord, the windows of heaven were open. It was in the days of Pentecost and the Kirtland temple era. Many members of the early church appeared, including Pres. [Joseph] Smith, [John] Taylor, and [Brigham] Young. Tongues of cloven fire fell upon all the thirteen men instantaneously, confirming a positive answer to President Kimball's prayer. Elder McConkie was not able to describe the scene in words. He said it was the greatest spiritual experience of his life.[43]

Whitton's account was confirmed by another congregant, BYU religion professor George Pace.[44]

The story was embellished further by the apostle's son Joseph Fielding McConkie, a religion professor at BYU. On June 25, during a priesthood quorum meeting at his ward in Orem, Utah, the younger McConkie said that "all the former presidents of the church were present in the temple at the 6/1 meeting." Joseph, echoing his father, said that the revelation was "just like the Pentecost" at Kirtland. The younger McConkie said that all of the apostles "saw and heard the same thing."[45]

Similarly, Apostle McConkie's nephew began sharing details of the revelation with fellow Mormons. He told them "that Elder McConkie has seen the Savior," adding that "the experience in the temple must have been tremendous." Furthermore, he recounted how previous church leaders had visited the temple on the day of the revelation. All of the most important leaders were there: Joseph Smith, Brigham Young, John Taylor, and "many others."[46]

The McConkies and the Popes were not the only ones to promote the notion of otherworldly visitors at the temple. Apostle Boyd K. Packer, McConkie's confidante and close friend, contributed to the embellishment. According to one account, he declared in a church "testimony meeting" that "Jesus himself had appeared at the June 1 meeting" and he "could [now] testify that Jesus was a person of body, parts, and passions—a person of flesh and blood." Packer said that Jesus appeared to the Twelve and the First Presidency to express "his desire to have them accept the blacks into the priesthood."[47] This stood in marked contrast to the more sober account Packer had given to Kimball's son Edward, whom he told that "the Brethren

236 SECOND-CLASS SAINTS

met, with portraits of the presidents on the walls, and said one could almost sense those prophets giving their approval."[48]

Quickly platitudes about the approval of past church leaders had transformed into stories of heavenly beings and angelic choirs. The stories spread to Latter-day Saints from California to Maine.[49] This was gossip run amok. Latter-day Saints heard these stories second- and third-hand, then passed them on to other Latter-day Saints. The story grew from a pebble into a boulder within a matter of days, getting more vivid with each telling.[50]

When President Kimball learned about the fantastical stories circulating, he asked McConkie to recount what he had told his family. In a detailed, twelve-page memo to the church president, the apostle wrote, "On this occasion in the upper room of the temple something akin to the day of Pentecost occurred." McConkie also said that the Brethren heard "the voice of the Lord." But he didn't mention anything about heavenly choirs, angelic beings, Joseph Smith, or Jesus appearing.[51]

McConkie was wise to keep some of these details from the president. Spencer Kimball wasn't a man who liked to embellish things. The Brethren's sacred experience in the temple didn't need to be dressed up. He ordered the apostle to remove the claim that the Brethren had heard a voice during the revelation.[52] Kimball didn't feel comfortable with that detail, nor did other apostles, who also felt that McConkie embellished the account. Apostle David B. Haight said that McConkie had "overstated the experience." Apostle LeGrand Richards concurred, as did Apostle Gordon B. Hinckley, who noted years later, "[The revelation] was a quiet and sublime occasion. . . . No voice audible to our physical ears was heard."[53]

Meanwhile, a twenty-three-year-old Mormon convert named David John Buerger became intrigued by the various stories that were circulating. Buerger was something of a gadfly. He had joined the church in 1973 and became enamored with, to borrow a popular Mormon cliché, "the mysteries of the Kingdom": the visions of early LDS apostles, esoteric Mormon teachings, and complex theological precepts.[54] Now he had something more immediate worth exploring. Buerger heard about Max Pinegar's address from his friend Gary Bergera, who was there and took notes and then acquired Jay Bell's notes on Bill Pope's BYU address. Buerger called Pope to confirm the details. Furthermore, Buerger obtained the notes that a BYU professor took of Joseph Fielding McConkie's account of the revelation to his priesthood quorum. Buerger then compiled the three accounts into a document called "The 1978 Negro Revelation" and sent it to Apostle McConkie.[55] He told McConkie that he found each source credible and wanted the apostle to verify them. "If the enclosed copy of my synopsis is not accurate," he asked, "would you please indicate where its details are at fault, and, if possible, provide a correct rendition of your experience?"[56]

McConkie rarely responded to letters of this kind, but on this occasion the stakes were too high to ignore it.[57] He told his interlocutor that the accounts then circulating weren't true. The revelation came about by "the power of the Holy Ghost revealed to President Kimball," McConkie emphatically stated. "Aside from this, and for all practical purposes, everything else in the document you enclosed is false. . . . The rumors going around in my judgment are not in the best interests of the church." The apostle, having been rebuked for his embellishments, was now doing damage control.[58]

McConkie also contacted Annie Whitton, who had been describing otherworldly visitors accompanying the revelation and asked her not to spread "such unfounded rumors."[59] Naturally, the apostle's instructions confused and stunned Whitton. She had heard the details from Bill Pope and later confirmed them with May Pope. Whitton then circulated her account to family and friends. Now McConkie was saying that she got the details wrong. This caused Whitton a great deal of anxiety.[60]

Promoting false teachings or "false doctrine," in Mormon parlance, is a serious matter, and Whitton was accused of doing that very thing by a respected apostle. McConkie's rebuke perplexed her, indeed devastated her, and she promptly told him so. "I express my deep regrets at the embarrassment to which I may have exposed both you and the Church," she said mournfully. But then Whitton went on the defensive. She told McConkie that May Pope had approved the contents of the document and even added a few details of her own. Whitton was incredulous that she could be accused of "spreading such unfounded rumors" when the details of her story came from McConkie's own family. None of it made sense to Whitton, who believed her account "to be the complete truth."[61]

Whitton's anguished letter troubled McConkie. He promptly responded that the blame didn't belong with her, but with his sister, who was known to tell tall tales.[62] Joseph Fielding McConkie also took potshots at May. "Margaret doesn't tell an accurate story," the younger McConkie told David Buerger. "She's never told an accurate story in her life."[63]

238   SECOND-CLASS SAINTS

The apostle asked again Whitton to "quell the rumors" swirling around "the new revelation."[64] He made the same request of the Popes and his son. According to one account, the apostle "was angry about how the Popes had spread this story around" and asked them to correct the record.[65] The Popes did as they were told and published a mea culpa in the BYU student newspaper on August 3. "There have been many false rumors and stories attributed to us concerning the new revelation," they wrote. "This revelation came by the Holy Ghost. There were no messengers involved. All other such stories are false."[66] All of this might have blown over had it not been for *Time* magazine, which published a tantalizing story about the revelation. It was one thing to have fanciful accounts of the revelation circulate within the Latter-day Saint community and quite another to have them appear in one of the nation's most popular magazines. Respected journalist Richard Ostling interviewed President Kimball for his story, the first interview the president had given since the revelation. Ostling wrote, "How did the word come [of the priesthood revelation]? By one account 13 Apostles (top leaders) experienced a common revelation at a prayer meeting on June 1. In other renditions it came complete with a visitation from Joseph Smith, the prophet of Palmyra, N.Y., who founded the faith in 1830."[67]

Kimball wasn't pleased when he read Ostling's article, especially the part about Joseph Smith appearing in the temple. The president had worked very hard to ensure that the media had a correct account of how the revelation occurred. Don LeFevre, the church PR spokesman, told the *New York Times* "that revelation does not necessarily entail a thunderbolt and a personal appearance by the Almighty," but rather is "a strong feeling that one choice is correct, followed by a feeling of peace," which "can be taken as sufficient evidence that Divine guidance has been offered." That is precisely how President Kimball wanted the story to be told.[68]

For this reason, McConkie's antics troubled the president. He not only undercut how Kimball wanted to explain the revelation, but he gave an account of the priesthood revelation that was just plain false. In response, the frustrated president asked his son Edward, a law professor at BYU, to refute Ostling's article for conveying "a mistaken impression." Edward produced a carefully scripted rebuttal explaining that the revelation was far less dramatic than it had been portrayed.[69]

President Kimball made slight edits to the letter and then shared it with his counselors. But N. Eldon Tanner and Marion G. Romney didn't think

DEBRIS IN THE STREETS

239

Edward should send it. Nothing good would come of it, they reasoned. "Church members did not need it and the others will not be influenced by it."[70]

This was wise counsel. Why bring attention to something that most people might not know about? Better to focus on clearing up confusion among the faithful. When McConkie went to address LDS religion teachers that August, Church Education System director Joe Christensen asked him to set aside his prepared remarks and "give those assembled some guidance relative to the new revelation."[71] McConkie seized the moment, recognizing it as an opportunity to set the record straight before a crowd that frequently told faith-promoting stories without ever vetting them.[72]

Before a gathering of approximately a thousand seminary and institute teachers, the apostle delivered one of the most cited and consequential sermons of his forty-year ministry.[73] That he spoke extemporaneously on a topic of significant interest only heightened McConkie's stature as a leading Mormon theologian. He took as inspiration "All are alike unto God," derived from a well-known verse in the Book of Mormon (2 Nephi 26:33) that church leaders rarely sermonized on while the ban was in place.[74]

McConkie took dead aim at the elephant in the room. "The Lord could have sent messengers from the other side to deliver" the news, the apostle stated, "but he did not." Some Latter-day Saints

> would like to believe that the Lord himself was there, or that the Prophet Joseph Smith came to deliver the revelation. . . . Well, these things did not happen. The stories that go around to the contrary are not factual or realistic or true, and you as teachers in the Church Education System will be in a position to explain and to tell your students that this thing came by the power of the Holy Ghost.[75]

After correcting the record, McConkie told the educators that Black men had to receive the priesthood before the Second Coming of Jesus Christ so that missionaries could preach to all "peoples and races and cultures to be offered the saving truths of the gospel." "We have revelation that tell[s] us that the gospel is to go to every nation, kindred, tongue, and people before the Second Coming," the apostle affirmed.[76]

The entire sermon bore President Kimball's unmistakable influence, from his desire to expand Mormonism to his insistence that the revelation came about by the Holy Spirit. Notably, McConkie didn't say anything about "the day of Pentecost" or "cloven tongues of fire," and neither did he liken the revelation to the divine epiphanies at Kirtland or discuss the intriguing notion that the apostles had heard the voice of God. He simply focused on the revelation coming by the Holy Spirit, which is what Kimball had asked the apostles to do all along.

Equally important, McConkie stressed that the church had entered a new era. "Forget everything that I have said, or what President Brigham Young or President George Q. Cannon or whomever has said in the days past that is contrary to the present revelation. We spoke with a limited understanding and without the light and knowledge that now has come into the world." He continued, "It doesn't make a particle of difference what anybody ever said about the Negro matter before the first day of June of this year, 1978. It is a new day and a new arrangement, and the Lord has now given the revelation that sheds light out into the world on this subject."[77]

McConkie was backpedaling. He—and many other apostles and church presidents—had long argued that Black people wouldn't receive the priesthood until after the Second Coming of Jesus Christ, when their curse would be removed.[78] It wasn't just leaders who taught this. Church apologists echoed similar views, proclaiming that "Negroes will not receive the Priesthood until a great while after the second advent of Jesus Christ."[79] Now McConkie, a proud man, was admitting that he had been wrong.

★ ★ ★

The revelation was codified into the LDS canon at the October 1978 general conference after N. Eldon Tanner called for a sustaining vote. The Brethren called it "Official Declaration 2."[80] McConkie was the only church leader to discuss the revelation at the conference. In a "carefully-worded" sermon on revelation, the apostle related the various ways that revelation had occurred in church history: "We cannot speak of revelation without bearing testimony of the great and wondrous outpouring of divine knowledge that came to President Spencer W. Kimball setting forth that the priesthood and all of the blessings and obligations of the gospel should now be offered to those of all nations, races, and colors."[81]

McConkie offered few details on what had occurred. The revelation was the most important event in the history of the church in the twentieth century—President Kimball compared it to the revelation that ended polygamy—yet it barely registered a blip from the Brethren at the faith's most important and well-attended conference.[82] Naturally, this confused

Latter-day Saints who wanted answers—answers about racial teachings that continued to hover over the church like a dense fog. Lester Bush, for one, wanted to know "what view the Church now takes on all the traditional doctrines which formerly sustained the priesthood restriction on blacks" and if the church still accepted "the Cain/Ham genealogy." He asked if there was still a connection between skin color and moral purity in a premortal life, specifically how racial teachings in the Book of Mormon and Pearl of Great Price should be interpreted in light of the end of the priesthood ban. Robert Vernon, Spencer Kimball's neighbor, asked directly, "Does the Church now reject the 'descendants of Cain,' 'curse of Ham,' and 'pre-existent sin' arguments?"[83]

The lack of clarity also confused Mormon fundamentalists. They believed that the church had strayed from Joseph Smith's teachings on polygamy and now had strayed even further by ordaining Black men to the priesthood. In a one-page ad in the *Salt Lake Tribune*, a fundamentalist group identifying itself as "Concerned Latter-day Saints" asked in big bold letters, "[Is] LDS soon to repudiate a portion of their Pearl [of] Great Price?"[84] Joseph Jensen, the leader of the group, said they paid $2,676 to publish the ad to warn Latter-day Saints "that they are moving more and more toward changes that will suit the world rather than God."[85]

But it wasn't just the theology that concerned Latter-day Saints and fundamentalist critics. Some asked to see a written copy of the actual revelation and were angry when the Brethren didn't produce one. "Why don't they publish that revelation and let the Lord speak in his own words?" inquired Eugene Wagner. "All we saw was a statement of the First Presidency, and that is not how a revelation looks."[86] Fundamentalist critic Ogden Kraut, who had left the mainstream LDS church years earlier to practice polygamy, was even more blunt. "Where is this revelation?" he asked Kimball. "If such a revelation is to be thrust upon four million members of the Church, as official doctrine, they are entitled to read it."[87]

Why did the Brethren not produce a written revelation? It was a good question. After all, Mormon prophets had produced dozens of written revelations throughout the church's history, most of which were canonized as sacred scripture in the Doctrine and Covenants.[88] More important, the statement had been vague about the church's past teachings. Was it still the doctrine of the church that Black people were cursed? The Brethren remained tight-lipped; that was by design.

242 SECOND-CLASS SAINTS

President Kimball cautioned BYU professors, reporters at the church-owned *Deseret News*, and the upper church leadership not to "editorialize about the revelation." He didn't want them to pontificate on the rationale behind it.[89] This explains why the general authorities didn't talk about the revelation much in public, at least during the early years, and why their authorized biographers didn't provide details. Tanner's biography, published in 1982, doesn't discuss the revelation at all. Others mentioned it only in a paragraph or two. Ezra Taft Benson probably spoke for a majority of his colleagues when he said it was just too private to talk about.[90]

Years later church spokesman Jerry Cahill offered a more compelling reason why Kimball cautioned the Brethren not to run off-script from the church's approved statement: they "would have been subjected to questions like 'Did you see God?' from insensitive reporters. The announcement was wisely left to speak for itself."[91]

All of this might be true, but there is more to the story. The Brethren didn't want to be asked if the church still believed in McConkie's teachings in *Mormon Doctrine* or his father-in-law's in *The Way to Perfection*, both of which were still in print. And, of course, there were a number of church leaders who still held racist views about Black people. Religion scholar Forrest Wood was on to something when he asked, "Was the world supposed to believe that Mormon president Spencer W. Kimball's claim to a divine revelation, in which he alleged that God told him to declare black men eligible to enter the priesthood, instantly eradicated racist thinking and habits among church members?"[92]

In any event, the Brethren's silence allowed others to fill in the gaps. A spurious document titled "A Revelation" did just that. The document, which began to circulate at the October general conference, purported to be the revelation that Kimball had received at the June 1 meeting in the temple. It looked authentic. It followed closely the phraseology in the Doctrine and Covenants, adopting well-known Mormon phrases like "Hearken, Oh ye people," "verily I say unto you," and "fullness of my gospel." All of it squared with Mormon teachings. Most of it, in fact, resembled what President Kimball and Apostle McConkie had said about the revelation over the past several months. "A Revelation" counseled Latter-day Saints to take the gospel to "my long-suffering and persecuted children, known among you as Negroes." It stated that Black people could receive the priesthood and be adopted into the house of Israel. And finally, it counseled against interracial marriage: "[A]ll of my negro children cleave unto their own in the matter of marriage, and this because of the prejudice of men and the hardness of their hearts." The document closed by invoking another familiar Mormon idiom, "Alpha and Omega," signifying that God was "the beginning and the end."[93]

We don't know who wrote the document or how widely it circulated within the church, but Kimball got a copy of it, read it closely, then scribbled across the top, "This is fake."[94]

★ ★ ★

The president had more important things to worry about than a spurious revelation circulating. He still struggled to control the narrative. Within weeks of the revelation, a newspaper in Boise, Idaho, suggested that a litany of lawsuits, political pressure, the excommunication of dissidents, and the Brazil Temple had all "led up to the Mormon Church's change in doctrine to allow blacks to its priesthood." Another account explained, "[In] 1978, at a time when the Church was under intense social, economic and governmental pressure on race issues, its leaders announced that they had received a divine message giving African-American and African black men status equal to that of white men in the Church."[95]

The most astonishing claim, however, was that there was nothing divine about the revelation; rather, the IRS, at President Carter's direction, pressured the church to lift the ban.[96] At first glance, this was plausible. After all, the Carter administration had cracked down on religious institutions that harbored discriminatory policies. It makes for a tantalizing story, which goes something like this: the president of the United States met in secret with Kimball and threatened that the IRS would revoke the LDS church's tax exemption if the ban wasn't lifted. One account even states that Carter discussed the ban with Kimball on June 1, only hours prior to the revelation. The Brethren denied all of this—as well they should. There was no truth to any of it.[97]

President Carter certainly knew about the ban. Jack Carlson informed President Kimball that Carter hated the way the church treated Black people. And John Fitzgerald, who detested the church's race policies, wrote Carter and the Justice Department several blistering letters asking them to force the church to ordain Black men to the priesthood.[98] But there is no evidence that Carter influenced the priesthood revelation. His diaries reveal that he met with Mormon leaders to discuss the LDS church's missionary program, which he had long admired. Years later Carter flatly denied that he meddled with Mormon racial teachings. "We never threatened them," he insisted, "but I expressed my opinion to LDS leaders."[99]

The more interesting part of the story is how the rumors began in the first place. Stories of IRS involvement began to circulate in 1979, a year after the revelation, when Mormon dissidents Jerald and Sandra Tanner received a tip from a disgruntled LDS lawyer who worked at the church's law firm Kirton McConkie.[100] What the attorney revealed became the basis for a story the Tanners published in their December 1979 newsletter:

> We . . . learned from a source within the [Mormon] Church that the Church leaders were very concerned that they were going to lose their tax exemption status on property they own in the United States. In the months just prior to the revelation, Church leaders were carefully watching developments in a case in Wisconsin in which an organization was about to lose its tax-exempt status because of racial discrimination. The Church leaders finally became convinced that the tide was turning against them and that they would lose their tax exempt status in Wisconsin and eventually throughout the United States because of their doctrine of discrimination against Blacks. . . . This was probably only one of many factors which entered into the decision to admit blacks into the priesthood. It may very well have been the "straw that broke the camel's back."[101]

The Tanners were not the only ones to give the story credence. Myron Sorensen, also of Kirton McConkie, had earlier told a group of LDS church historians that "Wisconsin had taken away the Church's tax-exemption status and tithing could not be listed as [a] tax-exempt deduction." He added that "Hawaii was moving to this policy also because of the discrimination against blacks."[102] Leonard Arrington, the LDS church historian, was so convinced by Sorensen's statement that he passed it along to his children just two weeks after the revelation. Years later Arrington repeated this claim in his memoir.[103]

True enough, there was a Wisconsin statute that prohibited private institutions from discriminating "on the basis of race." And true enough, the statute stated that organizations that discriminated could lose their tax-exempt status. But the law wasn't passed until 1979 and didn't take effect until after January 1981, so the LDS church couldn't have lost its tax exemption in 1978.[104] Instead, people likely heard about the Wisconsin law in advance and feared the worst.

DEBRIS IN THE STREETS 245

What this meant, of course, is that critics were seeking secular explanations for the lifting of the ban. They wanted to attribute it to political expedience when, in reality, there were a number of less sinister explanations for the church's actions. First and foremost, the ban conflicted with President Kimball's vision to expand Mormonism to all people. Second, bishops and mission presidents had been unwittingly conferring priesthood ordination on persons with African lineage and the Brethren knew it. And third, by the 1970s the church's genealogical department had been overwhelmed by the number of requests to sort out lineage questions. None of these reasons had anything to do with legal challenges, bad PR, or alleged threats from the IRS. They were all just minor annoyances the Brethren had learned to live with through the years as they sought to uphold a doctrine that their predecessors had bequeathed to them.

★ ★ ★

Besides the revelation raising sticky questions about the timing of the ban, it opened up a messy scholarly debate over its origins. Historian Newell Bringhurst published an article in the *Utah Historical Quarterly* in the winter of 1978 showing that the ban had begun under Brigham Young. General authorities and some church historians took exception to Bringhurst's article, as they had Lester Bush's five years earlier, despite overwhelming evidence that church leaders ordained Black men to the priesthood during the early days of the church.[105]

General authority G. Homer Durham, who served as the managing director of the LDS Historical Department, took matters into his own hands. He wanted "evidence to show that Joseph Smith had been responsible for fastening the Priesthood denial to blacks upon the Church."[106] To this end, Durham requested a meeting with Ronald Esplin, one of the research historians under his direction. He asked Esplin to produce a private report examining the key documents and issues surrounding the ban. Only Durham would see it. Durham instructed Esplin not to "mention it to anybody."[107]

Esplin understood the assignment. He was, he wrote, "personally convinced that Brigham Young received the doctrine from Joseph Smith." "If you take Bringhurst's article," he explained, it would lead "one to conclude that it came from Brigham Young." But "if you take Brigham Young at face value you can't believe that. It came before his time." For Esplin, it was inconceivable "that Brigham Young would have announced some radically new doctrine in relationship to the priesthood and Blacks." Therefore, he speculated that Young had learned about the ban "at the feet of Joseph Smith where he learned the great doctrines of salvation."[108]

This was shoddy reasoning, but he had to please his boss. At Durham's insistence, Esplin published his findings in *BYU Studies*.[109] But Esplin couldn't locate any documents tying the ban to Smith, nor did he engage Bringhurst's and Bush's evidence that a handful of Black men had been ordained to the priesthood during Smith's tenure. Nonetheless, the loyal church historian mustered support from some of his associates in Salt Lake. William Hartley, Esplin's colleague in the LDS Church Historical Department, postulated that Esplin's conclusions were "correct about Joseph being the author." He predicted that the interpretation will "prevail among scholars."[110]

Hartley's prediction wasn't accurate; knowledgeable scholars didn't take Esplin's claims seriously. Even Esplin himself recognized the fragility of his position when he assisted Leonard Arrington in writing a church-sanctioned biography of Brigham Young. Both refused to discuss the priesthood ban in the book, ignoring the abundance of evidence which suggested it began with Brigham Young.[111] Not surprisingly, LDS scholars condemned Esplin's work. Bush assailed the article as superficial, complaining that it had a "complete lack of documentation," while Bringhurst called it "misleading," citing misrepresentation of key documents. LDS sociologist Armand Mauss, himself an accomplished scholar on the priesthood ban, called Esplin's article "a classic example of how to draw *a priori* conclusions from a non-existent data base."[112]

These criticisms forced the beleaguered historian into a defensive posture. Esplin reluctantly admitted to Durham that his "evidence is circumstantial and impressionistic."[113] BYU history professor James Allen, one of the editors of *BYU Studies*, noted that he and his colleagues felt tremendous pressure to publish the article despite admitting that Esplin's work was "highly circumstantial." "As you may well guess," Allen informed Bush, "certain people thought it was a fine piece, and wanted to have something like that said." That certain person, of course, was Homer Durham.[114]

Durham's meddling wasn't unusual. He had acted on orders from higher-ups. At the time, there were frequent clashes between some of the Brethren and church historians, which ultimately led to the dissolution of the Church Historical Department in 1982. Ezra Taft Benson and Boyd Packer were the most energetic in insisting that church historians focus on faith-promoting episodes in church history, while Kimball and others sided with the church historians who argued that church history should be told, warts and all.[115] Esplin and Durham were caught up in this tug of war, pressured by the Benson-Packer faction to produce a narrative that was faith-promoting, which meant, of course, affirming that the ban originated with Joseph Smith.[116]

All of this seemed like a lot of drama over an academic dispute, but to the Brethren it mattered. Their seminal 1949 statement had clearly stated that the ban began with Joseph Smith. And the two most popular LDS books in the twentieth century—Joseph Fielding Smith's *The Way to Perfection* and McConkie's *Mormon Doctrine*—said the same. It was perilous to question any of this, lest it undermine the Brethren's authority. Apostle David B. Haight put it well: "Every time [the ban] was raised before, all we could think of was defending our position. Nobody would ask the question seriously, we just needed to defend our position."[117]

Bringhurst and Bush, of course, challenged that position, which made some of the Brethren testy, not only because they didn't like to be challenged but because the historians implied that racism was responsible for the ban. Apostle Mark E. Petersen, for instance, spoke "very harshly" about Bush's *Dialogue* article and even targeted him for discipline in 1983.[118] Petersen also targeted Mauss. The apostle was angry that Mauss had published an explicit *Dialogue* article called "The Fading of the Pharaoh's Curse: The Decline and Fall of the Priesthood Ban against Blacks in the Mormon Church." Bringhurst managed to avoid Petersen's wrath because he wasn't a practicing Latter-day Saint. Nevertheless, his seminal 1981 book, *Saints, Slaves, and Blacks*, was met with stony silence at church headquarters.[119] Clearly, the Brethren wanted to talk as little as possible about the ban. They hoped that it would fade into the past while they focused on the future, but Bringhurst, Bush, and Mauss wouldn't let them.

★ ★ ★

The revelation also raised a host of unanswered questions about interracial marriage. From its earliest days, every church president had rejected "intermarriage" between Black and White people, fearing that interracial intimacy, love, and sex would prevent couples from experiencing the salvific ordinances in Mormon temples.[120] All of that was moot now that Black members could attend the temple. Yet, inexplicably, the revelation didn't change the Brethren's position. In fact, they felt so strongly about interracial marriage that when they announced the new priesthood revelation in the *Deseret News*, they placed a half-page disclaimer next to it discouraging such unions. Apostle McConkie reaffirmed the prohibition in a new printing of *Mormon Doctrine*, and other apostles attested to that stance.[121]

In opposing interracial marriage, the Brethren swam against the tide of popular opinion. A 1978 Gallup Poll revealed that 66 percent of Americans favored interracial marriage; five years later that number swelled to 71 percent.[122] Without question, the Brethren's opposition to interracial marriage smacked of racism. This was perhaps most evident at BYU, where they tried to limit the number of Black students. Frank Arnold, the BYU men's basketball coach, reported to a faculty member in 1981 that he belonged to a committee designed "to keep the quota on blacks very low. He said the Brethren are very fearful of . . . large numbers of blacks on campus, presumably whether they are Mormons or not."[123]

In 1981 only forty Black students attended the church school—less than 1 percent of the student body.[124] Most notably, BYU didn't place quotas or restrictions on any other minority or ethnic group, which underscored the Brethren's stark opposition to White and Black students being involved in interracial relationships.[125] It was clear that not much had changed since the 1960s.

Some Black Latter-day Saints outside of BYU scoffed when the Brethren told them that they could receive their temple ordinances but were *still* discouraged from dating and marrying White members. Their concerns were both moral and practical. With so few Black members in the church, the dating pool was quite limited. Who would they marry if they couldn't find a Black LDS partner? Was it permissible to marry a Black person outside of the church, or was it better to cross the color line and marry a White person within the church? The Brethren didn't say.[126]

The lack of direction from church headquarters put Black members in a quandary. Melvin Mitchell, a Black Latter-day Saint, complained, "It's very hard for black men to date in the church [and] from what I understand, it's very hard for black women also."[127] Nathleen Albright, a Black Latter-day Saint woman, was confused by the "double message" in the *Church News* announcing the priesthood revelation and the statement opposing interracial marriage. Praying, she asked God if it was "okay" to marry a White man she had fallen in love with. The answer was yes.[128]

DEBRIS IN THE STREETS 249

Church spokesman Don LeFevre further muddied the waters when he declared that there is "no ban on interracial marriage" in the church, adding that "if a black partner contemplating marriage is worthy of going to the Temple, nobody's going to stop him. . . . [O]bviously, he may go with the blessings of the Church." But for Black Latter-day Saints there was nothing obvious about it. LeFevre's statement contradicted the statement in the *Church News* as well as admonitions in church literature. The Brethren themselves appeared conflicted about interracial marriage, further proof that it was still a divisive topic in the church.[129]

In January 1978, some six months before President Kimball lifted the ban, Apostle Packer and general authority Marion Hanks gave conflicting counsel to Robert Stevenson, a Black man, when he sought their advice about marrying Susan Bevan, a White woman. In a meeting at Packer's office to discuss the marriage, the apostle, who had recently condemned interracial unions in a devotional address at BYU, discouraged Stevenson.[130] He told him that he "could accomplish [his] mission in life and be more effective without being married to a white woman." Hanks, on the other hand, called the prospective marriage a delightful idea. "I think that you'll be more effective and you'll be able to break down racial barriers," he enthused. "I think it's the best thing in the world that you marry Susan." Stevenson followed Hanks's advice.[131]

Another Black Latter-day Saint who received conflicting advice was Mary Sturlaugson, a BYU student who had endured much since she converted to Mormonism in 1976. Shortly after her baptism a White Latter-day Saint man approached her to tell her why "her race does not have the priesthood." The man smugly explained, "In the preexistence we all had an opportunity to hear and accept the gospel. But while we were listening to the gospel, your race was off playing basketball! We have come to this earth and we still have the gospel—and your race still has that basketball!" Other Latter-day Saints told her that her skin color "was the curse given to Cain."[132]

Naturally, these harsh words challenged Sturlaugson's faith, but she persevered and became the first Black woman to serve a mission after President Kimball lifted the ban. Now, following her mission, she faced the biggest crisis of her life: whether to marry John Eyer, a White man whom she loved, or follow the counsel of her church leaders and avoid interracial marriage. Troubled, she sought advice from Apostle LeGrand Richards, who

250   SECOND-CLASS SAINTS

cautioned against the marriage. Then she received counsel from general authorities Dean Larsen and Hartman Rector Jr., who reaffirmed Richards's position. Likewise, her bishop and stake president told her not to marry Eyer. Anguished and in despair, she sought counsel from President Kimball, who for years had preached against interracial marriage.[133] In Kimball's office at church headquarters, she told the president she loved a man that her church said she couldn't marry. Tears rolled down her cheeks as she shared her vision of life with Eyer. After listening patiently, Kimball got up out of his chair, walked to Sturlaugson, and embraced her, whispering, "My child, it is not wrong. It is not wrong. The only reasons we counsel against [interracial marriage is] because of the problems the children could face. As far as its being incompatible with the Lord's gospel, or with your Father in Heaven, it is not." As they parted that day, Kimball hugged Sturlaugson again and told her, "Be of good cheer, the Lord loves you dearly." A short while later she married Eyer.[134]

★ ★ ★

The ink was barely dry on Official Declaration 2 when journalist Richard Ostling asked President Kimball if the church still believed that Black people had been less valiant in a pre-earth life. Kimball cringed at such questions and wanted to avoid them. He wasn't a man to make waves, and the journalist had forced him to go on record to comment on a teaching that many of the Brethren *still* counted as doctrine. We don't have a transcript of the interview, but Ostling wrote, "Kimball says flatly that Mormonism no longer holds to such a theory."[135] Apostle LeGrand Richards provided a different answer to the same question: "Some time ago, the Brethren decided that we should never say that." Richards didn't say that Brethren no longer believed in the preexistence theory, only that the Brethren shouldn't teach it publicly.[136]

Nothing proved harder to explain, though, than Mormon teachings on whiteness, which critics called "an embarrassment to the church." The First Presidency had declared in 1944 that God hadn't revealed whether Black people would be whitened in the resurrection, but many of the Brethren continued to teach it.[137] As an apostle, Kimball taught this idea many times, most vividly at the 1960 general conference, when he asserted that dark-skinned Lamanites became "as light as Anglos" when they left their reservations to live in the homes of Latter-day Saints as part of the church's Indian

Placement Program. Kimball theorized that Native Americans had been "growing white and delightsome" and offered as evidence that children in the program "are often lighter than their brothers and sisters in the hogans on the reservation."[138]

This is one of those sermons that Kimball wished he could have back. According to his son Edward, the sermon embarrassed his father because of its connection of skin color to moral purity. Moreover, Latter-day Saints demanded to know if skin hues really did lighten over time.[139] And just like questions about the preexistence and "curse of Cain," Kimball preferred to avoid this one too. Of course, he brought this anguish on himself. More important, though, Kimball was embarrassed by the sermon because, as he would later learn and regret, Mormon whiteness teachings offended Black and Brown Latter-day Saints. Such teaching suggested that God disapproved of their dark skin, but worse, it meant that they had to aspire to whiteness to earn his favor. Naturally, Native American Latter-day Saints too found Mormon whiteness teachings offensive. They "don't want to have their skin color changed; they like being brown," according to general authority George Lee, himself a Native American. "So we try not to teach them that." Black Latter-day Saints, understandably, found the teaching demeaning as well.[140]

In 1979, Kimball's controversial sermon came back to haunt him. John Dart, a journalist from the *Los Angeles Times*, read Kimball's sermon and asked several hard questions that the Mormon prophet struggled to answer. He asked Kimball to explain why Mormons had racialized themselves and demanded proof that skin pigment actually changed. The president couldn't provide any. He said he wasn't aware of any scientific studies that would corroborate the teaching that dark-skinned Native Americans would become "white and delightsome." "You need scientists to prove it, I guess."[141]

The president's diary is frustratingly silent on this interview, but it must have bothered him because two years later, a special committee of apostles amended the Book of Mormon. They changed the phrase "white and delightsome" to "pure and delightsome" in a not so subtle attempt to shift the conversation from skin color to moral purity. This change was part of a massive effort to cross-reference all four Standard Works of scripture in the LDS canon as well as provide headings for sections and chapters. Apostles McConkie, Monson, and Packer led the committee and were aided by a handful of BYU religion professors. Ironically, though, as the committee

252   SECOND-CLASS SAINTS

evaluated each verse, they cross-referenced passages from some of the racialized verses in Mormon scripture (e.g., Moses 5:40, 7:22) with verses in
the Bible that discussed the "mark upon Cain" (Gen. 4:15). This had the
obvious implication of tying the "mark upon Cain" to Black skin. Almost
certainly a detail of this nature would have escaped President Kimball, but
certain apostles couldn't free themselves from the notion that Black people
were cursed.[142]

Lineage designations in patriarchal blessings also remained a problem.
Following the priesthood revelation, Apostle James E. Faust and others
taught that Black people could be adopted into the house of Israel and
enjoy all the privileges of the church.[143] The revelation didn't address the
lineage question, nor did the church's official handbook for patriarchs, published in 1981, which avoided the subject altogether. Without a firm policy,
patriarchs continued to proclaim a variety of lineages on Black Latter-day
Saints, including even cursed lineages. Some Black Latter-day Saints poked
fun at the teaching, masking a painful microaggression with humor. In 1980,
when a White Latter-day Saint asked Keith Hamilton, a newly baptized
Black convert, what his lineage was, Hamilton acidly replied, "The seed of
Cain."[144]

The revelation was supposed to make these problems vanish. But they
didn't.[145] Apostle McConkie was the most adamant in refusing to let go of
Mormon racial teachings, stubbornly insisting that Black members were
only adopted into the house of Israel. In McConkie's reckoning, all lineages
had some of the blood of Abraham in them—except those of Black people.
"I believe the seed of Cain has none," he proclaimed. In addition, he continued to discuss royal lineages and preferential treatment that some had
earned in a pre-earth life, despite assuring Latter-day Saint religious educators that "all are alike unto God." McConkie never grappled with the theological implications of this paradox. Nor did he expunge the offensive racial
theories in his revised edition of *Mormon Doctrine*, published in 1979. The
new edition included information about the priesthood revelation but left
intact all the passages about Black people being less valiant and cursed.[146]

Moreover, the following year, in 1980, McConkie referred to Black
people as "the seed of Cain" in a general conference sermon.[147] Then, in
1981, he published a revised version of his "All Are Alike unto God" address and included all the forbidden language that President Kimball asked
him to take out—this in a revised essay called "The New Revelation on

DEBRIS IN THE STREETS

253

the Priesthood." The apostle likened the priesthood revelation to the day of Pentecost at the Kirtland Temple dedication, but most controversial, he said that the Brethren heard "the voice of God" when they prayed, and that President Kimball "heard the voice and we heard the same voice." McConkie also claimed that the "ancient curse is no more," implying that God had removed it in 1978. He then repeated statements from his June 1977 memo in which he declared that "the seed of Cain and Ham and Canaan" could now "inherit by adoption all the blessings of Abraham, Isaac, and Jacob."[148]

President Kimball accepted McConkie's premise that Black people could be adopted into the house of Israel, but he became enraged when he discovered that McConkie had rejected his counsel to exclude accounts of hearing God's voice during the revelation.[149] Shortly after McConkie's piece appeared, Edward Kimball found his elderly father, then in declining health, agitated and angry. Edward's mother, Camilla, had been reading "The New Revelation on the Priesthood" to her husband, and the president became visibly upset when she read the words "We all heard the same voice, received the same message." The president, too feeble to summon McConkie to a meeting to reprove him, asked Edward to have McConkie remove the phrase stating that all the Brethren "heard the voice of God audibly."[150]

The president couldn't let the matter go. Two weeks later he had his home nurse read McConkie's address to him and he burst out, "This is all bunk. That didn't happen." Spencer's outburst shocked Camilla, who thought he meant that the revelation was bunk. She was "devastated" upon hearing this. This would be tragic "misinformation" if it got out, she reasoned, trying to calm herself down. Edward quickly intervened to assure his mother that his father simply meant that the Brethren didn't hear the voice of God during the revelation, not that the revelation itself was bunk. The feeble Mormon prophet confirmed this.[151]

Meanwhile, Edward had the unpleasant task of meeting with Apostle McConkie. It wasn't a meeting that Edward relished.[152] It must have been awkward having the son of a church president relay an uncomfortable message to a respected church apostle. But it needed to be done.

The meeting occurred on May 12, 1982, in McConkie's office at church headquarters. President Kimball's secretary, Francis Gibbons, joined them. Edward was nervous as Gibbons began by explaining that the First

254 SECOND-CLASS SAINTS

Presidency "considered the discussion important and asked him to record it." Edward then explained why he was there. His father had asked him to express his concerns about the address directly to the apostle. McConkie, though, knew exactly what the meeting was about. Edward planned to write a book on his father's efforts to lift the ban. McConkie had received a draft of one of the chapters from Arthur Haycock, the First Presidency secretary, who shared it without Edward's permission. McConkie winced when he read Edward's claim that the apostle "exaggerated" the details of the revelation because he wanted "to say something dramatic."[153]

Edward's blunt language put McConkie on the defensive throughout the meeting. The apostle said he didn't believe that anyone "could reasonably interpret what he had written as asserting that the Presidency and the Twelve had heard an audible voice because he made clear that it was the power of the Spirit that impressed the assembled men." He went on to explain that at the end of his article "he was showing his concern that the events not be exaggerated by supposing that there was a visitation by [a] heavenly messenger." Edward interrupted, reminding the apostle that "excluding a visitation did not exclude an audible voice." McConkie apparently conceded the point because he agreed to revise the manuscript in a subsequent printing. For the remainder of the meeting, though, McConkie quibbled with Edward over his draft. He was annoyed that Edward included so many details that didn't appear to be "faith-promoting." Clearly, McConkie was nitpicking, obviously perturbed that he had to justify to the president's son what he considered to be a minor phrase in something he had written.[154]

The meeting ended after a little more than an hour. As soon as Edward left the church office building, he went to his car and wrote down the details in his diary. He then scurried off to his parents' home, where he gave his father an account of the meeting.[155]

The stubborn apostle never removed the "voice of God" phrasing from the text. McConkie was his own man.[156]

★ ★ ★

President Kimball's bold vision to universalize the church led to a systematic expansion of missionary service in predominantly Black areas in Brazil, Sub-Saharan Africa, and various cities in the United States. Under the president's direction, missions opened in Puerto Rico (1979), the Dominican

DEBRIS IN THE STREETS

Republic (1981), the West Indies (1983), Haiti (1984), and Jamaica (1985).[157] In 1978, the number of Black Mormons was very small, according to Don LeFevre, the church spokesman, who confessed that he had "no idea" how many Black members there were. Kenneth L. Woodward of *Newsweek* speculated that "most estimates [ranged] between 1,000 and 5,000 out of a total LDS membership of 4.2 million, though precise numbers are difficult to determine since the church does not keep records on race." In 1988 *Los Angeles Times* journalist Russell Chandler estimated that there were between "100,000 and 125,000 black members throughout the world," comprising "at least 50 times as many as 10 years ago."[158]

In the United States, the number of Black Mormons was much smaller.[159] Most estimates cited "several thousand," although such numbers are just "guestimates," Chandler surmised.[160]

While these numbers were an improvement, the church didn't experience the rapid expansion that everyone expected, especially in Africa, where growth rates paled in comparison to those of Catholics, Mennonites, Lutherans, and even the Reorganized Church of Jesus Christ of Latter Day Saints. A number of factors limited the LDS church's growth in Africa. The church hadn't been there as long as others, and more important, it was less likely to accommodate local customs and practices in worship services, preferring a one-size-fits-all approach dictated from church headquarters in Salt Lake City. "Based on the standard of many other churches, it simply is not true to describe Mormon growth in Africa as spectacular, amazing, or in any of the other standard superlatives," scholar Philip Jenkins has insightfully explained. "A balanced comment would place Mormon growth as moderate at best and limited to some small areas."[161]

Scholars speculate that there may have been some three hundred or four hundred members in Africa prior to the priesthood revelation, but in 1988 that number increased by only a modest amount. Still, there were signs of encouragement. Missionaries assigned to Sub-Saharan Africa reported enthusiastic interest in Mormonism, and Mormon writers began to flood LDS publishing houses with faith-promoting accounts of missionary work there. Newell Bringhurst estimates that there were over seventeen hundred Nigerians and Ghanaians on the rolls of the church by November 1979.[162]

In Brazil, the growth rate was much higher. Some missions there reported up to nine hundred baptisms per month, many of which were from the northern part of the country, where missionaries had avoided proselytizing before the revelation. Now the church expanded its proselytizing efforts, reaching millions of potential new converts.[163] The rapid growth rate concerned President Kimball, who told William Grant Bangerter, the International Mission president, that he "hoped that we would not fill up the Church with Black people," which he promptly conveyed to the mission presidents. Catherine Beitler recounts in her diary what Bangerter told them: "Don't go baptize a lot of [Negroes]—we will turn into the Assembly of God Church. We want leaders; we want the church to be a white Church."[164]

It might seem extraordinary that Kimball wanted to limit the number of Black Brazilians in the church when he had worked so hard over the previous few years to ordain them to the priesthood and permit them into the faith's temples. Yet he felt uneasy about moving too fast too soon, especially in northern Brazil, where Black people were in the majority. To be sure, this caution was born out of Kimball's strong racial prejudices, but he was also concerned about baptizing too many Black Brazilians without experienced leaders to train them and bring them along.

Other factors also affected growth rates. Many Black members felt "uneasy in the largely white, middle-class wards that dominate the church in the United States," observed Ruffin Bridgeforth, adding that five years after the ban ended "there [hasn't] been a great number of black people come into the church." "That's because many blacks remain bitter toward the church even though the ban preventing" them from the priesthood had been lifted.[165] Jim Sinquefield, another Black member, put it even more starkly. He explained that "many blacks despise the church for its previous policy and that attitude keeps black membership low."[166]

The church's refusal to condemn its racial teachings, coupled with the prejudice of many White Latter-day Saints, made it difficult for Black members to remain in a predominantly White church.[167] One Black Latter-day Saint complained that "there's supposed to be a feeling of equality" in the church, but White members did not always feel that way. "Their true feeling is manifested in their actions. Now they do a pretty good job of covering up, [but] being a black, I can make this determination pretty easily."[168] When asked in a questionnaire in the early 1980s if they felt like "an oddity in [their] ward/branch," more than a quarter of Black Latter-day Saints answered "very often" or "sometimes." When asked if "prejudice" was a problem in the church, nearly 17 percent said "very often" and about

28 percent "sometimes."[169] Taken together, nearly half of Black Latter-day Saints felt uncomfortable in the church.

At the same time, Black members balked at Mormon racial theories. Nearly 30 percent of those interviewed were "concerned" about Mormon racial teachings, while 7 percent were "appalled."[170] Many Black Latter-day Saints, however, had not heard of the curse and preexistence teachings until *after* they had converted because church leaders instructed missionaries to avoid the topic when teaching prospective converts.[171] The church didn't have a standard set of instructions or a recommended source to which missionaries could turn when asked about the ban. Thus, left to their own devices, missionaries gave a range of answers when pressed to explain the restriction. Some appealed to the divine curse theory, others to the preexistence, still others simply said that Black people weren't ready for priesthood ordination.[172] These confused responses caused considerable frustration in the church, especially for Black converts. Compounding matters further, Black converts encountered antiblack racism in *Mormon Doctrine* and *The Way to Perfection*, which were still in print. These books reinforced to them that the Brethren *still* believed that Black people were inferior.

President Kimball made modest attempts to temper Mormon racial teachings during the final years of his life, but when he died in 1985, the work was far from finished. The task would now fall to his successor, Ezra Taft Benson. Given Benson's track record, few believed that he was up to it.

9

The Stigma Still Goes On,
1985–2000

On November 11, 1985, newly installed church president Ezra Taft Benson held his first press conference at LDS church headquarters. With his counselors Gordon B. Hinckley and Thomas S. Monson by his side, Benson tried to blunt the harsh statements he had made in the past about Black people. He wanted to signal a new tone—a message of inclusion and hope—that contrasted sharply with his previous sermons as an apostle. "My heart has been filled with an overwhelming love and compassion for all members of the Church and our Heavenly Father's children everywhere," Benson asserted at the press conference. "I love all our Father's children of every color, creed, and political persuasion. My only desire is to serve as the Lord would have me do."[1]

With these memorable words, Benson offered an olive branch to critics who claimed that he was unfit to be the church president. The reporters in the room that day were keenly aware of the provocative, highly charged things that he had said about people of color in the past, and they were concerned about or at least intrigued by what his presidency might mean for a church that was now evangelizing in Black African countries.[2]

Some Latter-day Saints worried too. Rumors circulated that Benson would appoint his ultraconservative son, Reed, into the Quorum of the Twelve. Other reports said that he would align the church with the Republican Party and publicly endorse Ronald Reagan's presidency.[3] None of that happened, though, because Benson had been reined in. In 1980, Benson gave a polarizing sermon at BYU, in which he claimed that a "living prophet is more important than a dead prophet." His colleagues rightly viewed this as an affront to early church leaders. President Spencer

THE STIGMA STILL GOES ON

W. Kimball required Benson to apologize to all the general authorities, and after that humiliating experience Benson no longer expressed his extremist views in public.[4]

But that hardly meant his presidency would be free from controversy. Nor was that of his successor, Gordon B. Hinckley, who also faced significant challenges regarding the church's race teachings. Liberal Mormons found it unconscionable that the church refused to repudiate them.

★ ★ ★

On a brisk wintery day in February 1986, Coretta Scott King spoke to Utah lawmakers at the state capitol in Salt Lake City. In the nearly two decades after her husband's assassination, she had carried forward his message of racial equality, brotherly love, and economic justice. Now she crisscrossed the country trying desperately to convince lawmakers to honor her husband's legacy by naming a holiday after him.[5] Utah was, perhaps, her toughest sell. The vast majority of lawmakers were conservative Mormons who had twisted themselves into knots trying to figure out how they could oppose the King federal holiday without appearing to be blatantly racist. They came up with a litany of excuses to justify their opposition. It cost too much money, they said. What did he do for Utah? Why celebrate a "Black" holiday? But all this masked their contempt for King, whom they saw as a communist and womanizer. That's precisely what Benson and Cleon Skousen had said about King. The legislature opted to call the holiday "Human Rights Day," an obvious affront to Dr. King's life and legacy.[6]

Coretta Scott King left Utah sorely disappointed that she couldn't convince lawmakers that her husband was a decent man worthy of a holiday.

Latter-day Saints in Arizona fought over the King holiday as well. Governor Evan Mecham, a friend of Benson and Skousen's, a member of the John Birch Society, and a practicing Latter-day Saint, rescinded the holiday in 1987, causing an uproar. Some Mormons opposed the King holiday; others, like Benson's grandson, Steve, supported it.[7] The stark division among Latter-day Saints prompted the national news media to describe how Mecham had divided them. *Newsweek* magazine called it "Arizona's Holy War"; the *Washington Post* declared that "Mormons [were] spilt by turmoil over church member Mecham."[8]

The dust-up in Arizona prompted Arizonian Julian Sanders, a staunch Latter-day Saint and also a member of the John Birch Society, to ask

President Benson to issue a public statement opposing the King holiday. In the letter, Sanders reminded Benson that he had once called King "a liar, adulterer and thief" and compared the civil rights leader to an "anti-Christ." Sanders was also angry that John Lyons, an LDS spokesman in Mesa, had implied that the church favored the King holiday. "Here, Brother Lyons would have us believe that the CHURCH obviously supports the prostituted moderates and liberals who united in collective wisdom to force upon us a TAX-PAID HOLIDAY honoring the MASTER DECEIVER of the ages!" Sanders demanded to know "the true position of the CHURCH."[9]

Officials at the LDS Public Affairs Department avoided wading into this thicket, as did President Benson. Even after the president's outspoken grandson Steve leaked Sanders's letter to the *Arizona Republic* in an effort to embarrass his grandfather, whom he called a "race baiter," the church ducked the issue by reiterating through a church spokesman President Benson's 1985 press release affirming his love for "all of our Father's children of every color, creed, and political persuasion."[10]

For their part, Black Latter-day Saints looked at opposition to the King holiday with a combination of dismay and disgust. Black Latter-day Saint Catherine Stokes found Utah's refusal to recognize the King holiday troubling. "Martin's message was the same message as Jesus Christ, but for some reason people don't seem to recognize it," she observed.[11] Another Black Latter-day Saint, Chester Hawkins, blamed the John Birch Society's influence on Benson for the state's refusal to honor the King holiday. "Ezra Taft Benson kind of messed up the whole ballgame," Hawkins sighed. "The black people knew him, about him and the John Birch Society. They thought they had enough of that bunch." Hawkins didn't think it was fair to blame the entire church for Benson's racism, but he acknowledged that "so many people got the impression that the John Birch Society was running the Church."[12]

The King holiday affair seemed to be a touchstone for the animus that many Black Latter-day Saints felt for the church's reluctance to support civil rights in the 1960s. Apostle Bruce R. McConkie was another source of anguish for them. When he died in April 1985, some Black people assessed his legacy unfavorably. They didn't share Apostle Boyd K. Packer's enthusiasm that McConkie's "sermons and writings [would] live on." They didn't want his sermons and writings to live on, at least the ones that focused on race and lineage.[13]

THE STIGMA STILL GOES ON   261

Frustration over McConkie's landmark book *Mormon Doctrine* had been building for some time. Following his passing, some Black and biracial Latter-day Saints felt empowered to condemn it. George Rickford, an Englishman of Black African and European ancestry, recalled the first time he read *Mormon Doctrine*. He was meeting with LDS missionaries at his home in Leicester, England, when they had him read a passage titled "Negroes." "Very slowly," Rickford recalled, "as if through a thick fog it dawned upon me what they were trying with such embarrassment and sadness to say. 'George,' they seemed to say, 'you'd be more than welcome to join our Church, but there is no possibility of you ever holding the priesthood.'" Rickford exploded in anger. "Words like discrimination, prejudice, bigotry flowed from me," he angrily recalled. "How could they call themselves the Church of Jesus Christ and subscribe to such things?" In an impulsive moment, Rickford threw the missionaries out of his house and told them never to come back.[14]

Annette Reid, another Black Latter-day Saint, shared a similar antipathy toward *Mormon Doctrine*. She welled up with tears whenever she heard McConkie's name. It's as though she blamed him and him only for all the times she heard that Black people descended from Cain, that they straddled a fence in a pre-earth life, or just the basic, garden-variety racism she endured at church. Fairly or unfairly, she attributed these teachings to McConkie, because she believed that most members gleaned their views about the priesthood and temple ban from *Mormon Doctrine*.[15]

Reid resolved to tell Apostle McConkie how much she despised his book the first chance she got: "I had vowed that when I ever met Bruce R. McConkie I would ask him about his explanation in his *Mormon Doctrine*." The opportunity arose in the early 1980s when she served a church mission in Utah. There she met McConkie at a stake conference and was seated next to him at dinner. She sought to take advantage of the occasion to confront him directly, mustering the courage to tell him how much his racial teachings had harmed her. But then she had a sudden and swift change of heart. She couldn't go through with it. "I could just sense the weariness from him, and I just couldn't be angry with him," she ruefully explained.[16]

As McConkie began his sermon, however, Reid's attitude changed again. Suddenly and abruptly, her resolve to confront him over his racist teachings reemerged without warning. All of the emotions she had experienced

262 SECOND-CLASS SAINTS

in the past came roaring back with stunning intensity. "All these years I've been building up this animosity," she explained, and now she could no longer conceal her pain. After the conference had ended, she decided to confront him through a letter. This would allow her to control her emotions, to conceal the resentment she felt while softening it with small doses of tact and affection. In the letter she included a poem she wrote called "See Me as I Am," which mirrored the same anguished tone as Ralph Ellison's *Invisible Man*, the famous book he published in 1952 lamenting that White Southerners saw him only as a disadvantaged Black man. With Ellison's penetrating words looming over her, Reid implored the apostle to see her first and foremost as a human being, not as a Black person, not as someone whom God had cursed, but as a sister in the gospel—a fellow traveler in the body of Christ.[17]

The apostle, tired and beleaguered from years of travel, and perhaps already debilitated from the cancer that would ultimately claim his life, wrote Reid a tender response.[18] "I really loved your singing the other night and I'm grateful for the letter you wrote," McConkie began. Then, in a rare moment of vulnerability and openness, Mormonism's foremost theologian confessed to the troubled missionary that he had to repent for some things he had said about Black people.[19] McConkie never gave specifics, and Reid never asked, but his letter soothed her anguished heart just when her anxiety over Mormon racial teachings had threatened to consume her.

Another Latter-day Saint, Robert Stevenson, who became BYU's first Black student body vice president years earlier, was just as candid in denouncing McConkie's controversial book. "I would have liked to have seen a greater retraction of a lot of the McConkie stuff," he said shortly after the apostle died. Stevenson wanted the book to be "openly retracted so that there's no doubt in anybody's mind that these men were speaking" without inspiration. He lamented that "*Mormon Doctrine* is still in print" and claimed that the book continued to plague the Black LDS community. The "stigma still goes on," he mourned.[20]

Whether in the final years of his life McConkie recognized the pain he had caused Black people is doubtful. After all, he didn't expunge the racist teachings in *Mormon Doctrine*, nor did he express remorse for teaching them. Indeed, the apostle's last published book—a hefty tome called *A New Witness for the Articles of Faith*—reinforced much of the racial theology in *Mormon Doctrine*. All the familiar language was there: "favored families,"

THE STIGMA STILL GOES ON   263

"chosen seed," and biblical curses. The book was published shortly after he died and indicated that he hadn't changed any of his views about Black people.[21]

It wasn't just Black Latter-day Saints who challenged the apostle. McConkie had been dead for only a year when his antiblack teachings became a source of controversy among some BYU faculty. For those who knew Eugene England, a liberal BYU professor, it wasn't surprising that he frequently got himself into trouble on the race issue. He once likened the ban to carrying a "Mormon Cross," clearly agitated that the Brethren had asked members to accept a doctrine that seemed unbearable and unfair. Because of statements like this, England had to constantly defend himself over something he had said or written about the priesthood ban.[22] The Brethren should have seen controversy coming when they approved him for a faculty position in 1977. Not only was he a protégé of Lowell Bennion, but he was the cofounder of *Dialogue*, the liberal Mormon journal the Brethren deemed subversive. In addition, England fancied himself a feminist, antiwar activist, and critic of Mormon culture, which is to say that he never fit the mold of what the Brethren thought a BYU professor should be.[23]

Perhaps it's not surprising that he clashed with McConkie, one of the most doctrinally orthodox and theologically conservative general authorities. Their feud began in 1979, when England gave a provocative address at BYU called "The Lord's University." In it, he speculated that God had advanced in knowledge and power, drawing a sharp rebuke from McConkie, who claimed such words bordered on the heretical.[24] Before thousands of students and faculty at a BYU devotional assembly, McConkie delivered a controversial sermon titled "The Seven Deadly Heresies," in which he identified England's teachings as one of the heresies. While England's name went unmentioned, McConkie made a clear reference to the professor when he denied that "God is progressing in knowledge and learning new truths."[25]

Not long afterward, England sent McConkie a copy of a revised version of "The Lord's University." The apostle responded with a bombastic, ten-page, single-spaced letter rebuking him for teaching false doctrine. "This may be the most important letter you have or will receive," McConkie informed England, adding that he held "over him" the "scepter of judgment." McConkie brusquely reminded England that it was his "province" as an apostle "to teach what the doctrine is" and "your province to echo what I say or remain silent."[26]

A year after the apostle died the professor returned fire. In a controversial 1986 address, England excoriated McConkie's antiblack teachings.[27] Unfazed by potential repercussions, England branded Mormon racial teachings "racist" and "unscriptural." He took dead aim at Brigham Young's teachings in the *Journal of Discourses* and McConkie's in *Mormon Doctrine*. England pointed out that Young was wrong when he wrote that "interracial mixing with blacks should bring death" to Black people and also noted that McConkie erred when he predicted that "blacks would never receive the priesthood in this life." Just as important, England scoffed at how McConkie had stigmatized Black people by claiming that "dark skin or black ancestry is a sign of a mistake in the pre-existence."[28]

Even after McConkie's death, it took courage for England to criticize him publicly in such a direct manner before an audience of Mormon scholars, who, while liberal, still maintained loyalty to the church and its leaders. While it's true that the ban had ended eight years earlier, the theological rationale for it remained as robust and hearty as ever, at least among McConkie's most devout followers. This included the apostle's friend Robert Matthews, the BYU religion dean, who obtained a copy of England's paper and then wrote a thirteen-page critique assailing the professor for his faulty interpretations of Mormon doctrine. Matthews, whose PhD was from BYU, was a company man—an effective teacher of Mormon theology, a diligent administrator, but one lacking the nimbleness of mind and flexibility of spirit required to embrace England's speculative theology.[29] Besides, Matthews had to defend his friend, Apostle McConkie. England had spoken ill of the prophets and apostles—or so Matthews alleged. This was frowned upon in the Mormon community. No one in the church was supposed to speak ill of "the Lord's anointed."[30]

The previous year Apostle Dallin H. Oaks had warned members not to criticize the Brethren who have been "called of God," adding, "It does not matter that the criticism is true."[31] England either didn't hear this counsel or simply chose to ignore it, but the result was the same: Matthews made him pay.

The BYU dean scolded England for embracing heretical views and criticizing the Brethren. Matthews, for instance, rejected England's claim that polygamy and LDS racial theology were tragic mistakes. Moreover, he chastised England for alleging that "the Lord has allowed this dispensation to be wrong all along": "Such a statement is at best divisive among the members and unsupportive of the Brethren." He saved his most aggressive lines for last in defending McConkie. "He did not, and does not, say that the Brethren and the Church had been wrong all along in denying the blacks the priesthood in the first place, or that the Church had fostered a wrong theology that now would need to be changed." Matthews continued, "I knew Elder McConkie rather well, and I know for a fact that in 1980, two years after the 1978 revelation, he did not think or propose that the Church had been wrong in its policy towards the blacks but only that they had misunderstood when the change would come."[32]

After reading Matthews's devastating critique, England realized that it could cost him his job. He knew that Matthews had clout at BYU. He knew that the Brethren liked and trusted him. Recognizing his perilous position, England defended himself in a spirited reply. He denied that he would "knowingly teach or write contrary to official Church doctrine or practice." He also scoffed at Matthews's claims of heresy. And naturally, England took issue with the way that Matthews characterized his assessment of McConkie, writing, "I do not believe the Church was wrong in its policy or that Elder McConkie said they were, and I did not state or imply such."[33]

What did all this mean? The Matthews-England tiff marked the beginning of a theological culture war in which Matthews and his conservative allies strove to preserve McConkie's antiblack teachings while liberals like England urged the Brethren to discard them.[34] For England, the church had to seek its better angels—to live up to the Book of Mormon precept that all were "alike unto God"—if it hoped to expand worldwide and bring persons of color into the church.[35]

★ ★ ★

Not long after the Matthews-England kerfuffle, another feud erupted at BYU. In 1993, McConkie's son Joseph coauthored a book with his friend and colleague Robert Millet. Both taught religion at BYU, both were allies of Robert Matthews, and both were ardent defenders of Apostle McConkie's teachings.[36] In *Our Destiny: The Call and Election of the House of Israel*, published by Bookcraft, an LDS-affiliated publishing house, Millet and McConkie quoted extensively from Apostle McConkie's writings to defend their position that Latter-day Saints bore special Israelite privileges and leadership responsibilities in the church, based on their Northern European heritage and premortal behavior. Among the authorities they cited was William J. Cameron, a White supremacist and anti-Semite, whose writings in the 1920s was widely embraced by Latter-day Saint authors and general authorities of that era.[37]

Cameron was best known for peddling conspiracy theories in Henry Ford's newspaper, the *Dearborn Independent*, which he edited. His writings consist of a pungent mix of anti-Semitism and antiblack racism.[38] He also printed one of the most virulent anti-Jewish tracts of the era, a forgery called *Protocols of the Elders of Zion*, which influenced not only Adolf Hitler and the Ku Klux Klan but also J. Reuben Clark and Ezra Taft Benson.[39] The track claimed that a cabal of Jewish leaders had hatched a plot to control the world's money supply and spread socialism and communism throughout the world. Cameron published several iterations of *Protocols* in the *Dearborn Independent*, unaware or unconcerned that the *Protocols* had been forged.[40]

Despite Cameron's checkered past, Millet and McConkie called him a "wise man." They quoted a lengthy passage from him stating that God favored a "divine selection" of people: "'By what right does God choose one race or people above another? . . . It is much better than asking by what right God degrades one people beneath another, although that is implied.'"[41]

This was familiar language to Latter-day Saints. Since the early twentieth century, Mormonism's most prominent theologians, B. H. Roberts and Joseph Fielding Smith, had claimed that God favored White people because they were racially pure.[42] Such ideas were also prevalent in how Mormon leaders depicted Jesus Christ with a glimmering whiteness in church-sanctioned art and literature. Here the Brethren ignored the olive-colored skin hues typical of most Middle Eastern Jews because Black and Brown skin didn't conform to their notions of racial purity.[43]

It's unlikely that Millet and McConkie knew that Cameron was controversial, much less that he was a racist. None of their other writings demonstrates a familiarity with Cameron's racist views. It seems likely that they only knew Cameron from a 1938 LDS publication called *God's Covenant Race*, which also conveyed the notion that Northern Europeans occupied a privileged status in God's racial hierarchy.[44]

On the other hand, the BYU duo knew that Mormon racial teachings were controversial. Joseph Fielding McConkie referred to Black people as "descendants of Cain," and he unapologetically stated that Black priesthood denial was justified because it was biblically based.[45] Millet wasn't as bombastic or as aggressive, but he too defended the church's race teachings. A few years before he published *Our Destiny*, he wrote an essay lamenting that some Latter-day Saints felt uneasy about the church's lineage theology: "Too many even among the Latter-day Saints cry out that such sentiments are parochial and primitive, that they lead to exclusivism and racism."[46]

Millet's article formed the foundation of *Our Destiny*, so it's not surprising that the book was controversial. The book was barely off the press when it ignited a firestorm. This started when Steven Epperson, a newly hired BYU history professor, reviewed *Our Destiny* in which he criticized the core ideas of Mormon lineage theology. No one at BYU was more qualified to appraise the book than Epperson. He was fiercely independent, impressively erudite, and well-versed in Mormon theology.[47] In addition, he published a well-received book entitled *Mormons and Jews: Early Mormon Theologies of Israel*.[48]

That Epperson published his review in *BYU Studies*, the premier journal at the church-owned university, made the stakes even higher. Epperson didn't hold back. He scolded Millet and McConkie for their "dogmatic priestly writing style," "authoritative pronouncements," and anti-Jewish theology. But he also scolded them for quoting Cameron, whose "weekly publication [of] columns in the 1920s and 1930s contained 'some of the most vile anti-Semitism ever to be published in this country,'" adding that Cameron's writings became "'the bible of the German anti-Semites, including Adolf Hitler.'" And Epperson called their statements on "lineage and station" deeply problematic, "at best specious and irrelevant in today's Church." He opined that *Our Destiny* "would unwittingly" turn the church back to a bygone era.[49]

Epperson had even harsher things to say about the book in private. In his diary, he called *Our Destiny* "a regressive, repulsive book, a piece of clap-trap straight out of the 1920s and '30s." He hoped that his review would "destroy the arguments" and predicted that it would "kick up a hornet's nest."[50] Years later he reflected, "I'll be frank: I thought it was some real weird shit."[51]

Rarely do BYU professors write blistering critiques of their colleagues' work, yet unlike England, Epperson didn't criticize the Brethren, at least

268   SECOND-CLASS SAINTS

directly. He confined his review to the arguments in *Our Destiny* without commenting on its main sources. This was a clever tactic, but it didn't fool anyone, least of all Millet and McConkie, or BYU administrators, or the Brethren, who didn't take Epperson's review in the spirit of scholarly collegiality. Epperson's review, in fact, *did* kick up a hornet's nest, as he predicted it would. The uproar trickled down from the Board of Trustees to BYU administrators, who called for a thorough review of Epperson's own book, which didn't have anything to do with his critique of *Our Destiny*.[52] Epperson's review had demonstrated troubling signs of unorthodoxy, so they went fishing for evidence to oust him.

Adding to Epperson's grief, Joseph Fielding McConkie threatened a libel suit against him. McConkie's uncle Oscar, whose law firm Kirton McConkie did legal work for the church, sent Epperson a chilling letter pledging to sue him for calling his nephew a racist.[53]

This was all quite stressful for Epperson, but he wasn't surprised. He anticipated, he later recalled, that the review would "entail some risks that could include repercussions about being able to continue at BYU since my three-year review was coming up." But he thought that BYU was a serious university, with serious scholars, and that issues raised in his critical review might be weighed against differences of perspective undergirded by academic freedom.[54]

However, Epperson's faith in academic freedom was misplaced, or at least overly optimistic. Less than two years after he published the review, BYU fired him. University administrators cited his inability to obtain an ecclesiastical endorsement—a requirement for employment—but by that point he was clearly a marked man.[55] He criticized Mormon racial theology, which meant that he had also, at least indirectly, criticized Apostle McConkie.

A year later, in 1998, England too was out. That seemed almost inevitable given the professor's long history of activism and independence. He clashed with BYU president Merrill Bateman and the Board of Trustees over academic freedom, and Bateman forced him to resign, which the Board supported.[56] Epperson's and England's dismissals from BYU showed that the Brethren wouldn't tolerate protestors or agitators—or anyone, for that matter, who held unorthodox views of church history and doctrine. This extended to other BYU faculty as well, namely, feminists and social scientists whom the Brethren also dismissed from the university; and it extended to LDS scholars outside of BYU who were "blackballed" from speaking

THE STIGMA STILL GOES ON

on campus. Under President Benson's direction, the Brethren formed the Strengthening Church Members Committee, comprised of apostles and church bureaucrats who kept "secret files" on liberal Mormon scholars. The Brethren also discouraged BYU faculty from publishing in *Sunstone* and *Dialogue*. They feared "alternate voices," Apostle Oaks explained, believing that feminists, intellectuals, and gay-rights supporters threatened the church. To that end, the Brethren targeted professors like England and Epperson for sanction. They didn't want Latter-day Saint scholars publishing their research in liberal journals or participating in symposia and conferences that challenged the church's uncomplicated, faith-promoting narrative.[57]

★ ★ ★

The Mormon laity were largely shielded from these academic debates, but the Brethren knew that LDS racial doctrine posed a problem, and they made subtle attempts to address it. In 1990, when the church revised the temple ceremony, leaders dropped a depiction of Satan with dark skin. At roughly the same time, Deseret Book, the church's publishing house, removed from print Joseph Fielding Smith's *The Way to Perfection*—one of the most controversial (and successful) books the church had ever published.[58]

Removing *The Way to Perfection* from print was, without question, significant progress, but Deseret Book didn't take the equally controversial *Mormon Doctrine* out of print. Given Apostle McConkie's recent death his legacy was still too significant to roll back his teachings. As Mormon bookseller Curt Bench perceptively noted, many Latter-day Saints considered *Mormon Doctrine* the "Fifth Standard Work." Bench explained that a number of Latter-day Saints still believed that the book's "statements on 'negroes' [and] the 'curse of Cain'" represented "the Church's real position."[59] Plus, the McConkie family fiercely protected the apostle's legacy and undoubtedly would have balked had the Brethren removed the book from print.[60]

Rather than confront McConkie's antiblack theology, then, the Brethren embarked on a public relations blitz to soften the church's racial teachings. In 1988, the First Presidency issued a statement repudiating "efforts to deny any person his or her inalienable dignity and rights on the abhorrent and tragic theory of the superiority of one race or color over another."[61]

This statement revealed a profound paradox. McConkie had asserted in *New Witness for the Articles of Faith* that God did indeed privilege "the superiority of one race or color over another," and Millet and the younger

270 SECOND-CLASS SAINTS

McConkie argued precisely the same point in *Our Destiny*. But the Brethren refused to rejigger the faith's lineage theology; they preferred to skirt around the edges without directly confronting McConkie's teachings. In 1995, for example, Apostle Russell M. Nelson sermonized in general conference that Latter-day Saints were "children of the covenant" whose right it was "to receive the gospel, blessings of the priesthood, and eternal life." He claimed, "The literal seed of Abraham and those who are gathered into his family by adoption receive these promised blessings." Nelson avoided discussing Black adoption into the house of Israel or emphasizing the privileged lineage of White Latter-day Saints, and he did not address an ongoing and persistent problem when he failed to clarify how to declare lineage for Black Latter-day Saints.[62]

Lineage declarations continued to befuddle Black Latter-day Saints throughout Benson's presidency. Guidelines in the church's handbook for patriarchs contained no counsel on how to pronounce lineage for Black people. Thus some patriarchs told Black members that they were adopted into the house of Israel through the lineage of Ephraim, some through "Abraham, Isaac, and Jacob," while others, disturbingly, through Ham and Cain. In 1987, for example, a biracial Latter-day Saint teenager from Arizona received his patriarchal blessing and wasn't assigned a specific lineage but was offered blessings "by reason of adoption into the House of Israel." Three years later, as he prepared for his LDS church mission, he received an addendum to his blessing, and the patriarch informed the young man that his lineage "was that of Cain and that he would be entitled to the blessings of Israel only by way of adoption into the House of Israel."[63]

The patriarch's lineage designation caused the young man anguish. He declared that he "lived believing he was truly a descendant of Cain" and grew weary trying "to prove himself worthy of the fullness of the Lord's blessings." These issues were not just confined to patriarchs in the United States. In the United Kingdom, patriarchs declared the lineage of "Ham" on Black Latter-day Saints, but in South Africa Black people "were to be assigned to the lineage of Ephraim as a matter of church policy."[64]

All of this occurred, ironically, at the same time that some Christians began attempting to atone for their racism.[65] In 1994, a year after *Our Destiny* was published, Pentecostals issued their "Racial Reconciliation Manifesto," in which they dissolved the Pentecostal Fellowship of North America, an organization permitting only White members, and created in its place the

Pentecostal and Charismatic Churches of North America, a multiethnic and multiracial organization. Most significant, Pentecostal leaders apologized for the "sin of racism" and admitted that their church's teachings and theologies had harmed "generations born and unborn."[66]

The following year, in 1995, the Southern Baptist Convention, the faith's most important body, apologized for the church's role in supporting slavery and segregation. "We apologize to all African Americans for condoning and/or perpetuating individual and systemic racism in our lifetime," the manifesto read, adding that the church couldn't heal until "we ask forgiveness from our African American brothers and sisters."[67] At nearly the same time that Pentecostals and Baptists issued their statements, the South African government formed the Truth and Reconciliation Commission to address the long years of abuse the government heaped on Black South Africans through apartheid, which ended in the early 1990s. The commission addressed human rights violations and held accountable British Africans and Afrikaners who pillaged land from the Black population. The commission came at the urging of Catholics, Baptists, and moderate and liberal evangelicals from around the world, all of whom condemned apartheid.[68]

It's likely that the Brethren followed these events closely, but they weren't about to apologize for the church's race teachings. To do so would be tantamount to admitting a critical theological error, which might undermine the Brethren's prophetic authority. Even today they view themselves as "living oracles" and have repeatedly claimed that God won't allow them to lead the church astray.[69] But there's another reason why they wouldn't apologize for past teachings. The First Presidency and the Quorum of the Twelve Apostles function like a big family. Some of the Brethren are close with each other, some clash, but at the end of the day they're still family. They protect their own.[70]

In this context, it's easy to understand why the Brethren refused to apologize for their predecessors' teachings about race and lineage. Still, that doesn't mean they ignored them. Some of the general authorities began to distance themselves from Apostle McConkie's teachings. They delivered sermons in general conference intended to bolster the church's image while at the same time offering subtle repudiations of Mormon lineage theology. Apostle James E. Faust was perhaps the most emphatic in this regard. He believed that "no race or class seems superior to any other in spirituality and faithfulness." All races are "equal before the Lord."[71]

Other Mormon leaders rejected racial hierarchies as well. Chieko Okazaki, a Japanese American counselor in the Relief Society general presidency, promoted racial inclusivity in her books and sermons. "Hooray for our differences," she wrote in a popular book, adding that "without them there would be no harmony." She counseled Latter-day Saints to "lighten up" and treat all races and ethnicities equally.[72] Similarly, in his aptly titled book *Tolerance*, general authority John Carmack declared that Latter day-Saints "do not believe that any nation, race, or culture is a lesser breed or inferior in God's eyes. Those who believe in or teach such doctrine have no authority from either the Lord or his authorized servants." It may be that Carmack had Apostle McConkie and his followers in mind when he observed "there are still widely held beliefs and attitudes that certain races, cultures, and nationalities are superior to others." "There is no superior race or inferior race," he asserted."[73]

Perhaps the most vivid expression of racial inclusion occurred in 1992 in the church's ad campaign. It depicted a racially diverse group of teenagers with this caption: "God created the races—but not racism. We are all children of the same Father. Violence and hatred have no place in His family."[74]

All this was part of a concerted effort to burnish the church's image with communities of color, and Latter-day Saints responded. Gabriela Ferguson, a Latter-day Saint in California, "noticed a difference in attitudes about racial equality in and out of the Church." "In the community," she explained, "it starts to be like 'we're better than you because of what race we are.' But in the Church, it's not like that because we're all taught the same values. In our ward we have Samoans, Mexicans, blacks, whites, but we realize that because of the gospel, we're all the same."[75] Another Latter-day Saint, Lee Copeland, observed "subtle yet significant changes in the attitudes of Church authorities toward nonwhite races." The "racial stereotypes of the last century are beginning to disappear."[76]

That the church assumed a kinder, gentler approach toward people of African descent during Benson's tenure as church president was surprising, to say the least. In 1987, for example, a Salt Lake City ward sponsored the first annual Ebony Rose Black History Conference, which featured Mary Bankhead, one of the oldest surviving Black Latter-day Saints and a descendent of a pioneer Black family.[77] The following year BYU held a daylong "LDS Afro-American Symposium," which featured prominent Black Latter-day Saints. Apostle Oaks delivered the keynote address, speaking

THE STIGMA STILL GOES ON   273

enthusiastically about the priesthood revelation and the "church's world-wide growth, particularly in countries with large populations of blacks." University officials also authorized the first annual Black History Month, paying particular attention to Black Latter-day Saints.[78]

Most notably, in the aftermath of the Los Angeles riots in 1992, Latter-day Saints worked tirelessly with Black churches to help those most affected by the damage—Blacks, Whites, and Asians.[79] Church members brought food and water to these beleaguered people and even drove them to work. Some LDS bishops canceled their worship services to assist with recovery efforts, which endeared Latter-day Saints to their neighbors. Rev. Cecil Murray, an African Methodist Episcopal minister, praised the church for its kindness and generosity and instructed his parishioners to be friendly to the LDS missionaries, whom they had largely ignored in the past.[80]

This was all positive PR. The *Ensign* and *Church News*—the two most important news sources for Latter-day Saints—published a string of favorable stories illustrating the growth in Black converts and their significant contributions to the church. One story highlighted BYU student-teachers working in majority Black schools in Washington, D.C. Another featured racially integrated wards, such as the one in Scarsdale, New York. Still others focused on Black Latter-day Saint families in Roswell, Georgia, East Saint Louis, and Los Angeles. Even the *New York Times* acknowledged the church's efforts, touting its accomplishments in a story called "Spreading the Word in the South Bronx."[81]

All of this coincided with accounts the church published about missionary growth in countries with large Black and biracial populations. In 1988, church officials announced that the number of converts in Brazil had swelled to 300,000, up from 50,000 ten years earlier. "On the Caribbean islands," a church news reporter enthused, "Church membership has grown more than tenfold in the past decade to about 30,000. In isolated locales on the northern coast of South America with high concentrations of black population, Church growth has been similarly explosive." Conversions lagged among African Americans in the United States, but the reporter wrote, "Many congregations are becoming significantly integrated; a few are now predominantly black."[82]

The church's growth in Black communities was largely a function of its growth in general, especially in Sub-Saharan Africa, where baptisms occurred at a "lively pace" after President Kimball lifted the ban. In Nigeria and Ghana, hundreds converted to Mormonism, creating jubilance and excitement in the church.[83] From 1985 to 1994, the year that Benson died, church membership ballooned from 5.9 million members to 9 million— a 42 percent increase. Then, in 1996, two years after his death, the First Presidency made an astonishing announcement: more members lived abroad than within the United States.[84]

With the church realizing its global potential, general authorities organized the first stake in Sub-Saharan Africa during the Benson years and called the first Black general authority, Helvécio Martins.[85] Armand Mauss opined that "Elder Martins' call was connected to a hope that the Church leaders

Helvécio Martins of Rio de Janeiro, Brazil, the first Black general authority, 1990. Courtesy of *Salt Lake Tribune*.

THE STIGMA STILL GOES ON 275

would take a further step by denouncing the numerous myths and folklore created to explain more than a century of discrimination against Saints of African descent." For others, his call represented a "political move"—a result "'on the part of Church leaders to distance themselves from public criticism and to respond to pressure from within the ranks.'" Sandra Tanner speculated that Martins's selection as a general authority "was intended to neutralize highly-publicized charges of racism directed at the church."[86]

Whatever the reason, having Martins in leadership would diversify the mainly all-White general authority ranks. It would also remind critics that the church was serious about welcoming Black people into the church. Thomas S. Monson called Martins into the governing body in March 1990, at about the same time that the church had changed its temple ceremony portraying Satan with dark skin and leaders removed *The Way to Perfection* from print. The timing of this wasn't coincidental. The Brethren were sending a message that the church was preparing itself to be a global church.

Perhaps it's fitting that Martins could claim distinction as the church's first Black general authority. For many years, he had been loyal to the church, and now the Brethren rewarded him. "All that Rudá and I could do was cry," Martins wrote in his autobiography, incredulous that Monson had called him. "I could not find any other words to say to President Monson except, 'Why me?'" Martins immediately recognized, however, that his call made him a symbol in the church, and he didn't like it. When the media emphasized his "nationality and race," or when well-intentioned members identified him as "the Brazilian General Authority," or when some said that he was the church's "representative for the black race in the councils of the Church" he chafed. "Whenever I have the opportunity to dispel [these misperceptions]," he explained, "I do so, for I was not called by the Lord to represent any specific race, nationality, or ethnic group of his children. I was called by prophecy [and] revelation . . . to represent God's children—be they white, black, yellow, or any other color—wherever they live on earth."[87]

Latter-day Saints eagerly embraced Martins in his new calling and often hugged him when they saw him in public.[88] When I saw him in a grocery store in Provo, Utah, just after he was ordained a general authority, I shook his hand, pleased to tell him that I supported him in his new calling. And yet, despite the church's modest success in Africa, and despite the church's conciliatory tone toward Black people in general conference and church publications, and despite the church calling its first Black general authority, trouble loomed on the horizon. *Mormon Doctrine* remained in print and

276 SECOND-CLASS SAINTS

continued to cause anguish for Black Latter-day Saints. After Benson died in 1994, he was replaced by senior apostle Howard W. Hunter, who served for a mere nine months as church president before he too died.[89] That left his successor, Gordon B. Hinckley, with the daunting task of addressing the damage caused by *Mormon Doctrine*.

★ ★ ★

Hinckley was the right man for the job when he became the fifteenth church president in March 1995. He too was a company man—literally and figuratively. He spent his early career working for the church in public relations until his call to the Quorum of the Twelve Apostles in 1961. As an apostle, he served on a number of important committees, including as adviser to the Genesis Group, where he learned firsthand the challenges that Black Latter-day Saints experienced. Perhaps most important, he presided as the church's de facto president during much of the 1980s and early 1990s, first as a counselor to President Kimball after he and his other counselors fell ill, then during President Benson's administration when Benson's health declined.[90]

Under Hinckley's energetic leadership the church improved its image considerably, not least by meeting with the media to explain difficult church teachings. Hinckley felt comfortable dealing with the media and seemed to enjoy the give and take.[91] He gave interviews to numerous heavy hitters during his presidency, none more hyped than a 1996 sit-down with veteran *60 Minutes* reporter Mike Wallace.[92]

Wallace was pleased when he landed the interview. He had been "trying for decades to get some top Mormon leader, any top Mormon leader," as he put it, to speak with him on camera.[93] For twenty-five minutes, the pair discussed a range of topics, including polygamy, women and the priesthood, and church finances. The interview was frank and free-flowing and Wallace clearly admired the Mormon leader.[94] The tone abruptly changed, however, when Wallace asked Hinckley about Mormon racial teachings, specifically if "blacks had the mark of Cain." Hinckley bristled at the question and responded defensively, "It's behind us. Look, that's behind us. Don't worry about those little flicks of history." Wallace shot back, "Skeptics will suggest, 'Well, look, if we're going to expand, we can't keep the blacks out.'" An agitated Hinckley paused, collected his thoughts, then called Wallace's assertion "pure speculation."[95]

THE STIGMA STILL GOES ON

For the millions of people watching the broadcast it was obvious that Mormon racial teachings made Hinckley uncomfortable. He wasn't used to questions about the priesthood ban or questions that forced him to defend the church's antiblack teachings. On another occasion, when a reporter asked Hinckley why the church denied Black members the priesthood, he testily responded, "I don't know. I don't know," then changed the subject.[96] He told another reporter, "[W]e've rectified whatever may have appeared to be wrong at that time."[97]

Hinckley knew these questions would come but hated fielding them, especially from Latter-day Saints, and especially when members called the church's teachings racist or when they called for a retraction of *Mormon Doctrine*.

No one challenged Hinckley more than David Jackson, an outspoken African American convert from Orange County, California, who demanded that the church president remove *Mormon Doctrine* from print and apologize for the church's racial theology. If anyone could force the church to confront its racial heritage, it was Jackson. His patriarchal blessing called him "a rare person" with a special purpose in life, promising that he would "play an important role in the church."[98] Jackson circled these words in his blessing and interpreted them to mean that God had called him to "expose the root of the church's Black Doctrine to the public."[99]

Born in Birmingham, Alabama, in 1942, Jackson was a lukewarm Baptist before he converted to the LDS church in November 1990, along with his wife, Betty, and their son, Andy.[100] The Jacksons weren't in the church very long before David stumbled upon McConkie's *Mormon Doctrine* while researching the priesthood ban for a church "fireside" his bishop asked him to give. "It was then," Jackson recalled, "that I discovered derogatory information about people of African descent according to Mormon history and scriptures."[101] Deeply troubled about how *Mormon Doctrine* depicted Black people, Jackson contacted LDS scholar Armand Mauss, who sent him a copy of his book *Neither White nor Black* and an unpublished article he had written that discussed the lingering effects of Mormon racism.[102]

Jackson gasped when he read what Mauss had sent him. He found dozens of offensive statements on race compiled in the book, including excerpts from Brigham Young's *Journal of Discourses*, the 1949 First Presidency statement, Joseph Fielding Smith's *The Way to Perfection*, and McConkie's *Mormon Doctrine*. But it was McConkie who ruffled Jackson the most. The apostle's

278 SECOND-CLASS SAINTS

sanctimonious tone angered Jackson, as did his appeal to biblical curses and the preexistence to justify the priesthood and temple ban. Jackson found these assertions "beyond belief" and refused to accept them.[103]

Flush with anger over McConkie's teachings, in October 1995 Jackson took the bold step of asking President Hinckley to remove *Mormon Doctrine* from church-owned bookstores and to issue a public repudiation of LDS racial teachings. Included in the letter were scriptural references from the Pearl of Great Price, statements by Brigham Young, as well as the 1949 First Presidency proclamation. What followed next can only be described as a mixture of courage and brashness: Jackson asked Hinckley to include an addendum to Official Declaration 2 in the Doctrine and Covenants, "repudiating any interpretation of doctrine that ties racial characteristics of any kind to spiritual conditions or spiritual worthiness in this life or in the preexistence." He informed Hinckley that he'd write it himself. In addition, Jackson asked the president to read the statement in general conference. He titled it "Official Declaration 3."[104]

The full statement said:

> I, therefore, as president of the Church of Jesus Christ of Latter-day Saints, do hereby, in the most solemn manner, declare that these charges of practicing or teaching racism are false. We are not teaching racism through our scriptures nor permitting any person to enter into this practice. Some cases have been reported in which the parties alleged that racism was taught or scriptures were interpreted negative to people of African descent. There is nothing in my teaching to the Church that employs racism which can be reasonably construed to inculcate or encourage racism and when the elders of the church have used language which appears to convey any such teachings, he [*sic*] has been properly reproved. And I publicly declare that my advice to the Latter-day Saints is to refrain from any teachings that may show racism to any people of color based on racial characteristics of any kind to spiritual conditions or spiritual worthiness either in this life or in the preexistence.[105]

Jackson's attempt to influence President Hinckley met with predictable obstinance at church headquarters. Members are not supposed to write proclamations for the church president or counsel him on how to run the church. Michael Watson, Hinckley's secretary, provided a terse response:

> I have been asked to acknowledge your letter of October 9, 1995, which was addressed to President Gordon B. Hinckley regarding the challenges which may be faced by those of African descent.

THE STIGMA STILL GOES ON

Your bishop, Arlen Dean Woffinden, has been advised in a letter from the office of the First Presidency that a member of his ward has raised this question. If you will contact Bishop Woffinden and identify yourself as the member who raised the question, he will be pleased to read the answering letter to you.[106]

Hinckley's refusal to send him the letter directly frustrated Jackson, and when he demanded to see a copy his bishop refused.[107] The First Presidency had instructed the bishop not to share it, because they feared that Jackson would circulate it.[108]

We know the contents of the letter because Jackson's bishop read it to Dennis Gladwell—a fellow ward member of Jackson's—who then relayed its contents to Jackson. In Gladwell's words, the "office [of the First Presidency] seemed to disavow any doctrine that explained curses or skin color by sins or omissions in the pre-existence by stating that the Lord had not yet spoken completely on the subject." The letter also reaffirmed that the church doesn't believe in a doctrine of racial superiority, and it distanced the church from any authority claiming "that the Church was not responsible for the personal opinions of its members."[109] The fact that church leaders didn't want anyone to know that they had problems with *Mormon Doctrine* was telling.

In 1997, Jackson tried again to get the church to address Mormon racial teachings. He, Mauss, Gladwell, and general authority Marlin Jensen, a friend of Gladwell's, consulted on a statement for the twenty-year anniversary of the priesthood revelation that they hoped might influence Hinckley to repudiate the church's race teachings. The statement was positive and upbeat, devoid of anything controversial that might anger Hinckley or his colleagues. Gladwell constructed it, with Jensen's input.[110] It read:

> Prior to the Revelation in 1978, many of the brethren and others outside of the Church, speculated as to why the priesthood was withheld. A variety of views and statements were published, which collectively focused on two possible explanations: events or choices in the pre-existence and/or a linkage to the curse of Cain or Ham through lineage. It is clear today that the brethren who espoused these views based their opinions on the way they interpreted the scriptures at the time. These interpretations and all previous teachings on the subject were overcome by the brilliant spiritual outpouring in 1978. As Elder Bruce R. McConkie testified, "We spoke with lesser light and knowledge in those days." On this 20th anniversary of the Revelation, we reaffirm again that God is no respecter of persons, that He invites all to come unto

280 SECOND-CLASS SAINTS

Him, and that all men and women are equal before God and have equal right and access to eternal life and exaltation.[111]

The hard-charging Jackson didn't like the statement, however. He thought it wasn't aggressive enough. It didn't "remove people of African descent from the lineage of Cain," condemn the general authorities who taught racist teachings, or refute *Mormon Doctrine* or the 1949 First Presidency statement. As Jackson explained, McConkie's writings had been "the chief components in the continuous promotion of the Negro Doctrine that still exists today," and he insisted that the apostle's teachings needed to be forcefully condemned.[112]

Meanwhile, as the June 1998 twenty-year anniversary approached, Jackson's hope to get Hinckley to condemn Mormon racial teachings was abruptly compromised when *Los Angeles Times* reporter Larry Stammer leaked the group's plans. An informant contacted Stammer and shared the substance of Mauss, Gladwell, and Jackson's work with Jensen, which became the basis for an article Stammer published titled "Mormons May Disavow Old View on Blacks." The story caught the Brethren off guard.[113] The day the story broke a church spokesman told a reporter at the news station KSL Channel 5—owned by the church—that it was "totally erroneous." A church press release noted that church leaders had "read the story" and were "surprised at its contents. The matter it speaks of has not been discussed by the First Presidency and the Quorum of the Twelve."[114]

Over seventy news outlets reported the story, which embarrassed President Hinckley and quashed any hope that Jackson would secure a retraction of Mormon racial teachings. The church's swift response disavowing the story compelled Stammer to write a follow-up in which he noted that "the Mormon plan to disavow racist teachings" had been "jeopardized by publicity." The leak also stunned Mauss and Gladwell, who accused Jackson of leaking it—an allegation he vehemently denied.[115] Still angry over the incident some fifteen years later, Jackson stood by his denial. Rather, he said, the leaker was Darrick Evenson, a disaffected Latter-day Saint and longtime critic of LDS racial teachings. Evenson learned about the matter from Mauss, who shared details of the group's deliberations with the Miller-Eccles group, an LDS study group that Evenson attended.[116]

By now it didn't matter where the blame lay; the damage had been done. In September 1998, a few months after the story broke, President Hinckley said that he didn't intend "to make further changes in reinterpreting historic

Mormon teachings," which meant that he had no intention of removing *Mormon Doctrine* from print or making a statement in general conference addressing the church's antiblack theology.[117]

Hinckley's failure to act had devastating consequences for the Jackson family: it pushed them out of the church. Nevertheless, it's wrong to assume that all Black Latter-day Saints opposed the priesthood and temple ban or left the church in defiance of it. Some accepted it and found peace in the church. Nowhere was this better illustrated than when Motown legend and Grammy-winning singer Gladys Knight left the Baptist Church and joined the Mormons. Knight had been apprised of the church's race teachings when she converted in 1997, but she took them on faith. When her son and daughter-in-law, already members, introduced her to the church, she was pleased that her baptism "didn't affect" her career. Still, she lamented, "[S]ome people questioned why I joined this church, considering its history with blacks." Knight rebuffed such critics. "[W]e have to stop judging what others look like. The more you get into the gospel," she insisted, "the

Grammy-winning artist and Mormon convert Gladys Knight singing at the LDS church's "Be One" Celebration, the fortieth anniversary of the priesthood and temple revelation, Conference Center, Church of Jesus Christ of Latter-day Saints, Salt Lake City, June 1, 2018. Courtesy of *Salt Lake Tribune*.

282 SECOND-CLASS SAINTS

more you can get rid of that. Now it's time for people of color to come to His church. It's just our time."[118]

Another Black Mormon convert who made peace with the ban was former professional basketball player Thurl Bailey, who joined the church in 1995 after he married a White LDS woman. Bailey was introduced to Mormonism when he played professional basketball for the Utah Jazz. He later joked that, during his playing days, he had been given "70 Book of Mormons" by members eager to convert him.[119] But as he heard the missionary lessons, nudged on by his wife Sindi's gentle encouragement, Bailey took the ban on faith, believing that if he trusted God, God would "answer my questions about this issue."[120]

Still, Bailey's acceptance of Mormon racial teachings came grudgingly, especially as Utah Latter-day Saints needled him to justify his marriage to a White woman. "The conversion and the marriage—everyone always asks about that," Sindi sighed. The people who gave them the most pushback were Sindi's parents. Initially they treated Bailey poorly and encouraged their daughter to end the relationship. For much of their adult life, her parents were taught that interracial marriage was a sin, that it tainted blood lines, and now their daughter's marriage to a Black man forced them to accept something that seemed unnatural and impure. Gradually, though, Sindi's parents softened toward Bailey, and over time their relationship blossomed, hastened when Sindi's parents apologized for the way they treated their son-in-law. Today Bailey remains firmly ensconced in the faith, arguably the church's most prominent Black ambassador, along with Gladys Knight.[121]

If Knight and Bailey took Mormon racial teachings in stride, former Black Panther Eldridge Cleaver seemed astonishingly unaware of them when he converted to Mormonism in 1983. His baptism into the church demonstrated how far he had evolved from the fiery Marxism of his youth to the ultraconservative firebrand of his adult years. The famed author of *Soul on Ice* and *Soul on Fire* converted to Mormonism at roughly the same time he became a "bible-quoting conservative," as *Jet* magazine put it.[122] Cleaver was attracted to the church through the influence of general authority Paul Dunn, whose books he read and admired, and through the right-wing activism of Cleon Skousen, whose ultraconservative Freemen Institute seminars the former Black Panther attended and spoke at. Cleaver was enamored with how Mormon theology depicted Melchizedek, the

Former Black Panther Eldridge Cleaver after he converted to the Church of Jesus Christ of Latter-day Saints, ca. 1980s. Courtesy of *Salt Lake Tribune*.

Old Testament patriarch after whom Joseph Smith named a branch of the priesthood. After reading about Melchizedek in Latter-day Saint scriptures, Cleaver enthused that there was a "spiritual quality" about him that he found appealing.[123]

For those who knew him, it wasn't shocking that Cleaver's activity in the LDS church proved transitory and ambivalent. He dabbled in several religions prior to his Mormon conversion, and his attendance at LDS church services was spotty at best. In 1986, he quit attending altogether after he accused two Latter-day Saints of stealing $350,000 from his campaign funds when he ran for the U.S. Senate.[124] Ironically, though, given his long-standing denunciations of racial injustice, his inactivity in the church had nothing to do with LDS racial teachings. When Mormon historian Newell Bringhurst asked him in 1996 what he knew about Mormon racial theology, Cleaver informed the historian that he didn't know much. "You caused me to think a lot about the Church," Cleaver told him, adding, "I must go to Church and take some more classes and read some more."[125]

Cleaver never got the chance. He died two years later, thoroughly cleansed of the radicalism of his youth but genuinely curious about what his Mormon faith could offer him.

What these stories reveal is that Black Latter-day Saints experienced LDS racial teachings in different ways, with different stresses and anxieties and with various degrees of tolerance and resistance. Admittedly, few had ever pressed for change to the extent that David Jackson did, but neither did most Black people ever feel truly comfortable with Mormonism's exclusionary practices. What these stories also reveal is that the church was conflicted by its racial heritage. Latter-day Saints professed that Black members were coequals with White members in the church, but they also believed that they descended from a lesser lineage owing to some deed or sin they had committed before they were born.

In the twenty-first century, this conflicted narrative couldn't be sustained simply because a number of critics, both Black and White, demanded on social media that the Brethren own Mormon racial teachings, repudiate them, and apologize for them. The church needed its own racial reconciliation, critics asserted, but couldn't achieve one as long as some Latter-day Saints remained committed to defending Apostle McConkie's antiblack teachings.

10

Hard Doctrine, 2000–2013

With pressure mounting from critics for the church to "disavow [the] old view on Blacks," Alexander B. Morrison of the church's First Quorum of the Seventy stepped up to the microphone at the October 2000 general conference. No general authority had ever addressed antiblack racism in this setting. President Gordon B. Hinckley asked him to do so, and Morrison was a good choice.[1] He had lived in Sub-Saharan Africa on church assignment for many years and had witnessed the devastating effects of racism, poverty, and war on Black Africans. He published two books about his experiences there—*The Dawning of a Brighter Day* and *Visions of Zion*—in which he denounced antiblack racism. Now he condemned it in general conference.[2]

Morrison tiptoed around Joseph Fielding Smith's and Bruce R. McConkie's antiblack teachings. Instead, he condemned racism more broadly, what he called "the abhorrent and morally destructive theory that claims superiority of one person over another by reason of race, color, ethnicity, or cultural background." Morrison warned that "racism is an offense against God and a tool in the devil's hands," adding that the church "has from its beginnings stood strongly against racism in any of its malignant manifestations." He also emphasized that the church couldn't grow in Africa until members accepted Black people as equals.[3]

Morrison wasn't at all candid, of course, when he declared that the church had always "stood strongly against racism." This was patently false and contrary to the church's long history of exclusionary practices. Nevertheless, Morrison's sermon was a powerful indictment of racism and a blunt call to Latter-day Saints to accept Black Africans into the church.

President Hinckley also embarked on a public relations crusade to improve the church's image with the Black community. He formed friendships with Black Baptist ministers and NAACP members and he threw his weight behind the Martin Luther King Jr. federal holiday. Hinckley also tried to improve race relations within the church, keenly aware of the pain that Black members experienced after years of being told they were cursed. Yet it was clear that he couldn't achieve his lofty goals as long as high church leaders failed to repudiate Smith's and McConkie's antiblack writings, especially BYU religion professors and rank-and-file members who continued teaching them.

All of this tension bubbled over in the early twenty-first century when outspoken members demanded that the Brethren confront and condemn Mormonism's turbulent racial heritage. Some wrote letters to church headquarters; others posted angry comments on their blogs and websites assailing the Brethren for not coming to terms with the church's racial past. The pressure worked to extraordinary effect. In 2010 the Brethren removed *Mormon Doctrine* from print, and in 2013 they issued a forceful statement repudiating Smith's and McConkie's teachings on race, lineage, and priesthood.

★ ★ ★

More than twenty years after the end of the priesthood and temple ban, Black Latter-day Saints remained frustrated at the church's refusal to repudiate its racial theology. President Hinckley was the holdup. He wasn't interested in looking backward. His eyes were on church expansion overseas, including Sub-Saharan Africa and other predominantly Black regions. Twenty-one percent of church members in 1977 lived outside the United States; that number grew to 51 percent in 1999 under Hinckley's tenure. Much of this growth occurred in Africa, South America, the Philippines, and the Caribbean, and Hinckley didn't see the wisdom in dredging up old teachings from McConkie or Smith.[4]

Hinckley was especially tight-lipped on interracial marriage, giving no indication if his views had changed or modified. The elderly church president seemed to be more concerned with same-sex marriage than interracial marriage. Early in his presidency, he supported a church effort to fund a ballot initiative in Hawaii to oppose same-sex marriage, and he played a significant role in the church's seminal document "The Family:

HARD DOCTRINE

A Proclamation to the World" (1995), which reaffirmed marriage as being between a man and a woman.[5] The document, however, said nothing about interracial marriage, even though some of the Brethren continued to oppose it. Well into the twenty-first century, Hinckley's colleagues counseled Latter-day Saints to avoid interracial dating and marriage. A youth Sunday School manual reinforced this message, as did general authority books and sermons still in print.[6]

This was astonishingly out of touch in a church that was becoming more interracial. Nowhere was this issue more fraught than in Hawaii, where the church had a strong presence. The Hawaiian Islands had always been a racial melting pot, brimming with Chinese, Filipinos, and Japanese emigrants.[7] This diverse population made it all but certain that Hawaiian Latter-day Saints would marry outside their race. It was even more likely that Latter-day Saints would marry interracially since, by the early twenty-first century, nearly half of Hawaiians had entered into interracial marriages—the highest rate in the United States.[8]

Interracial LDS couples met at BYU-Hawaii, where 40 percent of the student population came from over sixty nations, making it far more diverse than BYU-Provo and BYU-Idaho—the two other LDS church–owned universities.[9] The Brethren were mindful of this, and they took significant measures to mitigate interracial relationships. When the school opened in 1955, the Brethren told university administrators to limit the number of White students from the mainland. And since they couldn't prevent interracial relationships, they counseled Hawaiian priesthood leaders that interracial marriages had to be "handled very discreetly." The Brethren didn't care whether Samoans married Tongans or Hawaiians married Asians; they had concerns only "when white girls and boys from Utah and Idaho were involved."[10]

Where did this leave the church? By the twenty-first century, the church's teachings on interracial marriage were nearly impossible to sustain. This was especially evident as most Americans, including Mormons, came to slowly embrace interracial relationships, both in theory and in practice.[11] And more Mormons were entering into interracial marriages, including future apostle Gerrit W. Gong, an Asian American, and future general authority Peter Johnson, an African American. Indeed, this was happening throughout the church at a rapid pace, as thousands of Latter-day Saints married outside their race in the Caribbean, Brazil, Africa, the United States, and elsewhere, making Mormon worship services truly interracial spaces.[12]

Despite this, some of the Brethren still refused to embrace interracial marriage, which caused friction with interracial couples who believed that the church's stance delegitimized their families. And it made it difficult for these families to worship at church or attend church activities because they were constantly being asked by White Latter-day Saints to justify their marriages.

Interracial couples pushed back. In 2004, Tamu Smith, a Black Latter-day Saint model and actress, took her children to a photo shoot for the cover of an LDS publication. The magazine's producers wanted to pair her with a Black man who would stand in for her White husband and Smith refused. "If they're not going to validate my family," she angrily responded, "then they're going to have to find someone else who is OK with that."[13]

Joy Smith, a White woman married to a Black man, experienced a similar humiliation in 2004 when she taught a lesson in Relief Society. She criticized the Brethren's teachings on interracial marriage, eliciting a wave of pushback from other women in the room. When Smith pointed out how "outmoded racist teachings persist," the Relief Society president told her she was "out of bounds" and released her from her calling.[14] Around the same time, church leaders told a Black LDS teenager named Channel Achenbach that when she became of marriage age, she shouldn't marry a White man because her "seed is cursed." Achenbach responded to such blatant racism by leaving the church.[15]

* * *

These teachings were deeply embedded in Mormon culture and extended beyond interracial marriage. In 1999, Genesis Group president Darius Gray told Armand Mauss that he received "countless calls from [Black] men and women all over the United States who were still dealing with racist folklore." These were people, Gray explained, "whose children were told that they were cursed" and had been "'neutral' in the pre-existence." Gray further explained that White members "pulled their children from Sunday School because they didn't want them in the same class as a Black child," adding that he received "about a 100" complaints a year from "Black Latter-day Saints" who encountered "various myths in LDS meetings from white LDS friends."[16]

Gray shared these stories with President Hinckley, who shuddered to think that Latter-day Saints would do this. During a chance visit to his house, Hinckley's daughter Virginia Pearce found him pacing his living

Darius Gray, a founding member of the Genesis Group and a prominent Black Latter-day Saint, n.d. Courtesy of *Salt Lake Tribune*.

room floor as he pondered Gray's report.[17] For years, Hinckley had denied that racism existed in the church and refused to address it. In 1999, a year after he clashed with David Jackson, the Mormon leader gave an interview with the *Los Angeles Times* underscoring his denial. "We're not bigoted," he protested.[18] Now Hinckley could no longer deny that there was a problem.

Gray wasn't the only one trying to counter antiblack racism in the church. Other Black Latter-day Saints shared stories of racism online. Some, like Tamu Smith and Zandra Vranes, masked their grievances in humor. Authors of the popular book *Diary of Two Mad Black Mormons*, these self-identified "Sistas in Zion" gently poked White members for their racial insensitivity. Others, like Darron Smith, provided unvarnished accounts of how he endured racial insults and slurs from fellow Mormons. Still others faced harassment at the faith's temples. "What's that N____ doing here?" asked a temple participant. Another said, "I can't believe they have a N____ woman working in the temple."[19]

Stories like these trickled back to Hinckley, who did his best to mitigate the problem. He spent the last decade of his life trying to improve the church's image with Black people by engaging in community outreach and forming relationships with Black leaders. It was his finest accomplishment as church president.

In media interviews, Hinckley commented that there could be a "black [LDS] president" one day, just as there could be a "black pope."[20] He was the first Mormon president to tour Sub-Saharan Africa, visiting Ghana, Zimbabwe, and Nigeria. He announced the construction of new temples in Ghana and Nigeria, the first on the African continent. And most telling, he accepted an invitation in 1998 to speak at the NAACP convention in Salt Lake City—another first for a Mormon president.[21] There, he received the NAACP's Distinguished Service Award amid a standing ovation. The NAACP leadership praised the eighty-seven-year-old for his work in Africa and thanked him for his efforts promoting ecumenical outreach to people of color around the world. In his acceptance speech, Hinckley told the 250 participants that God cared for neither race nor status and reaffirmed that all people were his personal "friends and neighbors." He added, "It matters not the race."[22]

Hinckley's award gave him a great deal of satisfaction and allowed him to exult for a brief moment.[23] His address not only generated much-needed positive press within the Black community, but it bridged what seemed like an irrevocable divide between the LDS church and the NAACP. Since the 1960s their relationship had been fractured at best, born out of distrust and suspicion on both sides—a result of Apostle Ezra Taft Benson's crusade against the civil rights movement and its leaders. But Hinckley, ever sensitive to public perceptions of the church, was determined to repair the damage that his predecessor had caused. He fostered new relationships with civil rights leaders and expressed support for racial justice causes. The result was that in a very short period, the Mormon president had managed to turn the LDS church and the NAACP from foes to friends.[24]

Hinckley helped to right another historical wrong in 2000 when he "lent his support" to a bill to rename Human Rights Day after Martin Luther King Jr., making Utah one of the last states in the country to honor the federal holiday. Hinckley instructed his counselor, James E. Faust, to contact Mormon media outlets and have them run stories in support of the name change. The president also instructed church lobbyists to contact key lawmakers to make the church's wishes known. Hinckley's "backing," noted NAACP leader Jeanetta Williams, "helped [to] sell the Legislature on the name change."[25]

Gordon B. Hinckley, the fifteenth president of the Church of Jesus Christ of Latter-day Saints, and Jeanetta Williams, president of the Salt Lake Branch of the NAACP, at Western Region 1 Leadership Conference of the NAACP, where Hinckley received the Distinguished Service Award, Salt Lake City, April 24, 1998. Courtesy of *Salt Lake Tribune*.

A year later, in 2001, Hinckley's goodwill was on full display again when he instructed the church's highly efficient and well-respected genealogy department to use its vast resources to digitize 500,000 Freedman's Bank records, helping to connect Black people with ancestors whose identities had either been stolen or obscured by slaveholders.[26]

Three years later, in 2004, Hinckley made another diplomatic gesture to the Black community when he met with Rev. Cecil Murray of the African Methodist Episcopalian Church in Los Angeles. Murray recounted:

> As we sat around the conference table, [Hinckley] apologized for the role the Church had played in participating in slavery. He says, "I have learned of

292   SECOND-CLASS SAINTS

the background of your church and the founding of your church, and I want to apologize for whatever role the Mormon Church has played—not only there—but has played in racism in America." I said, "I thank you very much for making that statement. It is certainly true that the Mormon Church has been a factor in discrimination, but you've done so much good—and now to hear these words—I would certainly say that your hearts are right."[27]

Hinckley's apology was stunning, the furthest a high-ranking Mormon leader had ever gone in addressing Mormon racism. He never said why he did it, but he was likely motivated by hearing from people like David Jackson and Darius Gray who reminded him how much Mormon racial teachings had affected Black members.[28]

With Hinckley aware of racism's pernicious effect, he and his colleagues embarked on an ambitious effort to remove racially offensive phrases in the Book of Mormon's chapter headings. Without fanfare or publicity, a committee expunged the phrases "skins of blackness" (2 Nephi 5) and "dark, filthy, and loathsome people" (Mormon 5) and replaced them with racially inclusive chapter headings.[29] Mormon experts praised the church's efforts. BYU linguistics scholar Royal Skousen correctly observed that "LDS officials don't want readers to focus on the kind of 'overt statements about race that were in [Apostle] McConkie's 1981 summaries.'" Another LDS scholar, Grant Hardy, astutely commented that "the church is clearly down playing the 'skin of blackness.'"[30]

Hinckley's efforts didn't go unnoticed by journalists, either. Observers praised Hinckley as the "new face of Mormonism" and commented that his outreach to the Black community made Mormonism a "colorblind faith." Other accounts praised the "new Mormon aim [to] reach out to blacks," publishing upbeat stories on the church's growth in Detroit, Los Angeles, Baltimore, New York City, and other cities with large African American populations.[31] Don Harwell, who replaced Darius Gray in 2003 as the president of the Genesis Group, speculated that the positive media attention meant "people are getting past stereotypes put on the church."[32]

In 2006, Hinckley endeared himself to Black Latter-day Saints as well when he delivered a landmark address in general conference condemning antiblack racism, inspired by Gray. Whereas Alexander Morrison had approached the topic gingerly, Hinckley was more direct. He had been "told," he said, of "racial slurs" and "denigrating remarks" among the church body. "I remind you," Hinckley warned the priesthood holders of the church, "that no man who makes disparaging remarks concerning those of another race can consider himself a true disciple of Christ. Nor can he consider himself to be in harmony with the teachings of the Church of Christ." Toward the end of his sermon, he reiterated that "there is no basis for racial hatred among the priesthood of this Church." Hinckley implored "any within the sound of [his] voice" who was "inclined to indulge" in racist behavior to "go before the Lord and ask for forgiveness."[33]

Some Black Latter-day Saints wept with joy when they heard this message, but Hinckley's remarks still fell short of what some ultimately wanted: a formal apology and/or a public retraction of *Mormon Doctrine*.[34] Their hopes were soon dashed, however, when President Hinckley died in 2008. His successor, Thomas S. Monson, didn't have Hinckley's media savvy, and it wasn't clear whether he shared his predecessor's commitment to fostering better race relations within the church. Still, many Black Latter-day Saints had hope. They took comfort knowing that Monson, like Hinckley, shunned dogmatism and seemed to avoid the ideological crusades of earlier leaders. They also took comfort knowing that Monson was a warm and affable man who cared deeply about people. And he was well-apprised of the church's problems with Black Latter-day Saints, having become "dear friends" with members of the Genesis Group after advising them during their early years. Added to that, as chairman of the Missionary Executive Committee in the late 1970s, Monson had assigned the first Black missionary to a two-year mission and he officiated over the first sealing of a Black family.[35]

And yet troubling signs loomed on the horizon. Racially offensive books continued to circulate at LDS bookstores, and the church's antiblack dogma continued to fester like an open sore. Well into Monson's presidency, in fact, Latter-day Saints could still purchase *Mormon Doctrine*, *Doctrines of Salvation*, and *Answers to Gospel Questions* at Deseret Book, the church-owned bookstore. The church, moreover, continued to use a 1981 Old Testament manual in its college religion courses that contained offensive passages about curses and divinely sanctioned lineages.[36]

★ ★ ★

Ever since the First Presidency declared in 1969 that the reasons for the priesthood and temple ban had "not [been] made known to man," the Brethren found themselves in an awkward position. When critics pointed to the antiblack writings of Brigham Young, Joseph Fielding Smith, and Bruce R. McConkie on various websites and social media platforms, the

294 SECOND-CLASS SAINTS

Brethren's claim not to know the reasons for the ban seemed disingenuous.[37] Nevertheless, they stuck to their position, and it became the dominant explanation for the ban in the postrevelation church.[38]

As one might expect, this position vexed some Black Latter-day Saints who found the church's position unconvincing. To them, it was difficult to understand how Mormon theology could provide answers to life's most important questions, yet the Brethren couldn't explain why their predecessors had denied millions of Black people the church's most sacred rites and rituals. Some Black Latter-day Saints filled in the gap with their own explanations. Darius Gray, for one, said that he had a spiritual experience that helped him make sense of it. His eyes got teary as he explained to me what had occurred to him during one early morning in 1998, when he awoke at 3:00 a.m. "bright eyed and alert." He said a "bucket of knowledge had poured into his head." The Holy Spirit prompted him to open his scriptures, and as he began reading the Spirit affirmed to him that the priesthood restriction was not imposed by God, "but of man." "God allowed the ban to happen," Gray intuited, to see how people would treat each other. Gray sought—and received—permission from President Hinckley to share his experience with his church friends and associates.[39]

Another Black Latter-day Saint, Keith Hamilton, took a different position. When I interviewed him in 2014, he told me that God instituted the ban through Brigham Young. Hamilton had expanded on this idea in a book he published. He could "bear witness," he wrote, that "the practice originated with God and that it was not the autonomous act of any man or council of men." Hamilton claimed that God had revealed that truth to him through "personal revelation."[40]

Meanwhile, as Mormon racial teachings continued to stoke controversy in the church, the Brethren made an important shift in how they characterized them. By the early 2000s, they began to call them folklore.[41] This was a subtle attempt to distance the church from Smith's and McConkie's antiblack teachings without directly repudiating them. Apostle Jeffrey R. Holland was the first high-ranking Mormon leader to label the church's race teachings this way. In a 2006 interview with PBS filmmaker Helen Whitney, he said that "the folklore must never be perpetuated."[42]

With similar candor, Holland confessed that he didn't know much about the "less valiant" position in the "pre-mortal councils"—the notion that

Black people had sinned before coming to earth, which stymied their privilege of holding the priesthood and receiving their temple ordinances. Even so, he branded such teachings obsolete and out of place in the postrevelation church and cautioned Latter-day Saints not to teach them. Holland explained:

> We don't pretend that something wasn't taught or practice wasn't pursued for whatever reason. But I think we can be unequivocal and we can be declarative in our current literature, in books that we reproduce, in teachings that go forward, whatever, that from this time forward, from 1978 forward, we can make sure that nothing of that is declared. That may be where we still need to make sure that we're absolutely dutiful, that we put [a] careful eye of scrutiny on anything from earlier writings and teachings, just [to] make sure that that's not perpetuated in the present. That's the least, I think, of our current responsibilities on the topic.[43]

Other general authorities and LDS spokespersons echoed Holland. General authority Sheldon Child flatly explained that "when you think about it, that's just what it is—folklore." The curse, the "less valiancy" positions, had "never really been official doctrine. . . . We have to keep in mind that it's folklore and not doctrine."[44] Church spokesperson Mark Tuttle reinforced Child's claim. "This folklore is not part of and never was taught as doctrine by the church," he boldly explained. "The church has no policy against interracial marriage, nor does it teach that everyone in heaven will be white." Thomas Valleta, the director of the Church Education System and the person responsible for college religious instruction in the church, likewise explained, "Such folklore is definitely not supposed to be taught in the seminary program. That [folklore] is certainly not true, and it's not in the curriculum."[45]

As the new reformulation made the rounds on the internet, liberal Mormons weren't having it. Black Latter-day Saint scholar Darron Smith called the new folklore line "bullshit." It was a "cop-out," he explained, for the church to call its racial teachings folklore when the church had always called it doctrine. For Smith, the reasons for the ban were clear: "It's called racism."[46] Others also dismissed the church's rebranding efforts. Former BYU anthropology professor David Knowlton found it personally satisfying to dismiss the troubled racial doctrine as "folklore," but he disagreed with church spokesman Mark Tuttle's characterization of LDS racial history.

He found Tuttle's position not only dishonest but also incompatible with his own personal experience in the church. "When I was a teenager," he explained on a Mormon blog site, "I was taught these ideas in Sunday School and Seminary as doctrines." "The trouble," he continued, "comes in the words 'never taught as doctrine.' Never is simply false. Besides that . . . the word raises questions about another word, 'doctrine.'"[47]

Armand Mauss also followed the unfolding development closely. Over the years, he had called Mormon racial teachings folklore and now took satisfaction that general authorities began to follow suit. Mormon scholars likewise picked up on the shift and began to call the curse and preexistent teachings folklore or "folk doctrine."[48] Not all church members, however, were as fast and loose with the church's race teachings. A number of Latter-day Saints viewed the ban as inspired doctrine. A 2016 survey revealed that 37 percent of Mormon men and 36 percent of Mormon women were "confident" that the ban "was inspired of God."[49]

Clearly, Mormon leaders' rebranding efforts had not taken hold among the faithful. That included a number of BYU religion professors who continued to teach the curse and preexistent theories, seemingly impervious to the shifting winds.

BYU religion dean Terry Ball should have known better. After all, he had been teaching at BYU since 1992 and likely knew that Black students found Mormon racial teachings offensive. It's difficult to imagine that he wouldn't have seen a 2008 editorial in the campus newspaper when a student complained that his religion professor likened Black skin to sin and taught "that blacks will be whites when they reach heaven."[50] And Ball likely would have read an open letter that a Black student wrote to BYU president Rex Lee in 1995 explaining, "[As] a recent convert to the Mormon church, I have begun to seriously doubt the sincerity of what the missionaries told me about racial equality. The racial discrimination, the constant rejection I have been facing since I came here, and the fact that there is no black professor at BYU to turn to during difficult times . . . make it increasingly hard for me to continue." And Ball certainly knew about Steven Epperson's critical review of his colleagues' book *Our Destiny*.[51]

But Ball brushed all of this aside when he delivered a devotional address at BYU in 2008. He asked the audience if they had "ever wondered" why they were "not born 500 years ago in some primitive aboriginal culture in

HARD DOCTRINE 297

some isolated corner of the world? Is the timing and placing of our birth capricious? For Latter-day Saints, the answer is no."[52] Ball's characterization of premortal agency and preferential birth caused uncomfortable flashbacks to general authorities like Joseph Fielding Smith who speculated that there "is a reason why one man is born black with other disadvantages, while another is born white with great advantages" and Alvin R. Dyer, who similarly asked:

> Why is it that you are white and not colored? Have you ever asked yourself that question? Who had anything to do with your being born into the Church and not born a Chinese or a Hindu, or a Negro? Is God such an unjust person that He would make you white and free and make a Negro cursed under the cursing of Cain that he should not hold the Priesthood of God?[53]

Implicit in Ball's address was that God privileged or punished individuals based on their skin color and premortal conduct. Liberal Mormons complained about this teaching for quite some time and pressed the Brethren to denounce it. In a 1998 essay published in *Sunstone*, Eugene England quoted Martin Luther King Jr. to emphasize that God judged people "by the content of their character, not the color of their skin." England regretted that a number of his students believed "that skin color is an indication of righteousness in the pre-mortal life," which they learned from "their parents or Seminary and Sunday School teachers."[54] In 2004, Mauss complained about extant teachings concerning "divinely disfavored lineage[s]," which Mormon theology traced back to the preexistence. He implored the Brethren to "cast off" the "curse of Cain."[55]

Black Latter-day Saints too continued to be troubled by Mormon preexistence teachings. Darron Smith lamented that Mormon students he taught offered "LDS racist folklore as a reasonable explanation for the priesthood ban on blacks."[56] Jesse Stott, an African American student living in Utah, grumbled that nothing hurt more than when White Latter-day Saints called him a "fence sitter." He'd rather be called the "n-word," he said. Similarly, a dark-skinned Mormon woman named Rebecca agonized when White members teased her about growing up in Mauritius, an island nation in the Indian Ocean. They told her that because she was "born on that small island" and because of an unspecified sin she had committed in the preexistence God had punished her with dark skin.[57]

298   SECOND-CLASS SAINTS

To the surprise of many critics, Ball wasn't the only BYU religion professor to publicly endorse such teachings. Three months after Ball's address,
his colleagues aired a controversial roundtable discussion on KBYU, the
university's TV station, in which they reaffirmed support for Mormon antiblack teachings. In a lesson titled "Priesthood Restriction through the Ages"
derived from the Pearl of Great Price, discussion leaders Joseph Fielding
McConkie and Robert Millet called Mormon racial teachings "hard doctrine" and went on to defend them.[58] Drawing from *Mormon Doctrine* and
other LDS works, both spoke approvingly of the divine curse and "less
valiant" teachings and spoke matter-of-factly about "chosen lineages." In
addition, they felt "very comfortable" believing that Joseph Smith had established the ban, despite massive evidence to the contrary.[59]

The entire broadcast was suspect. Calling Mormon racial teachings "hard
doctrine" not only undermined Holland's folklore position; it also undermined President Hinckley's outreach to the Black community. Having respected LDS religion teachers tout curses and hurl damaging speculative
theories about Black people on the university's TV station didn't present
a good image for the church. Former BYU history professor D. Michael
Quinn called the roundtable discussion "astonishing," while BYU English
instructor Margaret Young proclaimed the entire affair "awful." Shortly
after airing the segment, KBYU took it off the air, likely a result of complaints from people like Quinn and Young who found the entire segment
offensive.[60]

★ ★ ★

Meanwhile, as LDS church members continued to embrace the antiblack
teachings in *Mormon Doctrine*, the Brethren made a dramatic decision to
sideline the book. In 2010, they pulled it from LDS bookstores, marking a
quiet and unceremonious end to a controversial work. The church's newspaper, the *Deseret News*, didn't comment on the book's demise, preferring
to let it fade away without fanfare. But the *Salt Lake Tribune* reported, quoting Gail Halladay, the managing director for marketing at Deseret Book,
saying that "low sales" accounted for the book's demise. This was demonstrably false. Brisk online sales and anecdotal evidence indicate that *Mormon
Doctrine* was *still* a best-seller when it went out of print.[61] Moreover, Michael
Otterson, the managing director of public affairs for the church, confirmed
the popularity of the book in an interview with me. He provided another

HARD DOCTRINE

299

explanation why it was shelved: "[S]ome of the material was . . . dated, [which] no longer justified a reprinting."[62]

While Otterson's account is true—McConkie's book was indeed dated—it didn't tell the entire story of how the book came to an abrupt end. Early in Monson's presidency, a Black LDS doctor—a new convert—complained about the book to Deseret Book officials, and BYU professors and other concerned Latter-day Saints also made their views known.[63] In a letter to Deseret Book CEO Sheri Dew in 2009, with copies to Mark Willes, chairman of the Board, and Henry B. Eyring of the governing First Presidency, LDS attorney Stirling Adams wrote that he was mystified that *Mormon Doctrine* was still in print. He didn't mince words: "I'm writing to express my concern with the role Deseret Book has in distributing negative teachings about people with dark skin and their place before God and within our Church." Adams catalogued a number of egregious statements from *Mormon Doctrine* to make his point and told Dew that it was "unethical, for any book publisher, much less the church, to propagate them in 2009."[64]

Predictably, David Jackson and other liberal Mormons enthusiastically celebrated the death of *Mormon Doctrine*. Armand Mauss believed that its fate was sown a decade earlier when Jackson pestered Hinckley to rid the church of the book. Jackson himself took some credit for its demise by sharing with Hinckley how much the book had affected him personally.[65] Darius Gray could also take credit, for he had long complained about the book to the right authorities, and when it went out of print, he was ecstatic. "By not reprinting it," he enthused, "a weight will have been lifted off the body of the church. We have thankfully moved on." Another outspoken Latter-day Saint, Gregory Prince, concurred, stating that he was "delighted" by the news that *Mormon Doctrine* had been removed from print and that McConkie's book "has done some serious damage" to the reputation of the church.[66]

All of this was welcome news to those who had been harmed by the book, but there was still more work to be done. Shards of the old racial doctrine continued to fester in the Mormon community, particularly at BYU, where religion professors had taught it for years.[67] Among those in the Church Education System in the early 2000s, none paid a higher price for teaching Mormon racial doctrine than Randy Bott. He taught LDS church history and doctrine for over forty years, first as a seminary and institute teacher, then as a professor of religious education at BYU. Beloved by his students, he had been rated the "top professor" in the United States by rate-myprofessors.com.[68] And yet Bott was from the old school. He clung to the racist teachings of Smith and McConkie with tenacity, freely sharing them with students and colleagues when they inquired about the priesthood and temple ban. This is what got him into trouble with the Brethren, and it's what ended his distinguished career in religious education.

The voluble professor made the fateful mistake of discussing Mormon racial teachings with *Washington Post* reporter Jason Horowitz. In 2012, Horowitz visited BYU to research a story about the LDS church. He found a campus directory and "looked up professors who could help answer some of the religious questions that often came up in reporting on the church." He knocked on the office doors of several BYU religion professors, but they declined to speak with him, claiming they weren't authorized to do so. But Bott wasn't as circumspect. When Horowitz knocked on his door, the professor smiled, invited him in, and the two "had a long and fascinating chat about Mormon history, religion and beliefs." Bott "was gracious, helpful and articulate," Horowitz recalled. "At a certain point in our talk, I asked about the ban on blacks, and while he was at first somewhat reluctant, he eventually delved into the issue."[69]

Horowitz listened intently as Bott spoke candidly about divine curses, biblical counterfigures, and preferred lineages. Bott informed Horowitz that Black people couldn't hold the priesthood because they weren't ready. To emphasize the point, he said that "God has always been discriminatory." Bott then compared Black men to little children and explained that ordaining them to the priesthood before 1978 was akin to a "young child prematurely asking for the keys to her father's car." In other words, Bott stressed that Black men weren't ready to hold the priesthood any more than a child was ready to drive.[70]

Bott also asserted that Black people were better off without the priesthood because they weren't prepared for it spiritually or emotionally. If they had the priesthood and abused their authority, Bott reasoned, God would have punished them. A merciful God had actually "protected them from the lowest rungs of hell."[71]

The interview was a disaster. In comparing grown men to little children Bott had unwittingly borrowed language from White Southerners who, after the American Civil War, claimed that Black people lacked the moral and intellectual maturity for freedom.[72] But Bott's highly charged rhetoric wasn't the only problem with the interview. There was also the timing. It occurred during Mitt Romney's 2012 presidential campaign, when the Mormon candidate had already been dogged by questions about race that flared up during his first presidential run in 2008. At that time, Tim Russert of NBC News *Meet the Press* questioned Romney about belonging to a church that many perceived to be "a racist organization."[73]

As in his father's presidential campaign some forty years earlier, interlocutors criticized the younger Romney for belonging to a church that degraded Black people. Observers wanted to know if the church had "truly left its race problems behind" and wondered if Mormon "racial history [might] be a problem" for Romney's campaign.[74] For top-ranking Mormon leaders, Romney's constant grilling in the media was troubling enough, but the popular Broadway musical *The Book of Mormon*, which debuted in 2011, also made it difficult for the church to ward off charges of racism. It mocked the Mormon deity for "changing his mind about Black people" in 1978 and otherwise ridiculed the faith's core truth claims.[75]

Understandably, then, Bott's interview produced a "public relations headache" for the church. The Brethren were already on high alert in anticipation of questions the media might ask about sensitive issues in Mormon history, specifically its antiblack theology.[76] All of these fears were compounded by the fact that Americans already had a low opinion of Mormons. The church had spent millions of dollars on an "I'm a Mormon" ad campaign, but it didn't seem to help. Public opinion polls continued to show that Americans viewed Mormons unfavorably. And polls demonstrated that most Americans had a perfunctory understanding of the church and its teachings. In that context, it's easy to see why Bott's interview frustrated the Brethren: the professor drew attention to a highly sensitive subject that could sink the Romney campaign and negatively affect the church.[77]

Thus the church reacted swiftly to the *Post* story. The day it broke, the LDS Newsroom, the public relations arm of the church, produced two brief statements excoriating Bott. Michael Otterson told me that the church had to make a quick and forceful statement to mitigate the damage that the *Post* story caused. Both statements, he said, had been approved by the Quorum of the Twelve Apostles and the First Presidency.[78] The first,

"Church Statement regarding Washington Post Article on Race and the Church," declared that the "position attributed to BYU professor Randy Bott in a recent *Washington Post* article absolutely does not represent the teachings and doctrines of the church." The statement explained, "For a time in the Church there was a restriction on the priesthood for male members of African descent [but] it is not known precisely why, how, or when this restriction began in the Church." What "is clear is that it ended decades ago. . . . Some have attempted to explain the reason for this restriction but these attempts should be viewed as speculation and opinion, not doctrine. The Church is not bound by speculation or opinions given with limited understanding." It ended on a cautionary note: "We condemn racism, including any and all past racism by individuals both inside and outside the Church."[79]

The second statement, "The Church and Race: All Are Alike unto God," reaffirmed the church's commitment to racial equality—a theme the Brethren had been trumpeting since the 1980s: "The gospel of Jesus Christ is for everyone. The Book of Mormon states, 'black and white, bond and free, male and female . . . are alike unto God' (2 Nephi 26:33). This is the Church's official teaching."[80]

The church's rebuke of the popular professor undoubtedly injured Bott. It's not clear whether the Board of Trustees nudged him out or if he left voluntarily, but Bott retired from BYU that spring under a cloud of controversy. The interview also frazzled Horowitz, who found the backlash over his story puzzling. He expressed both genuine concern for Bott and also astonishment at the feedback he received from the story. "I received dozens of messages after the story's publication from African American Mormons, but also white Mormons, expressing relief and appreciation for prompting the church to address the ban," Horowitz explained. "I write a lot of stories about a lot of topics, and it is rare to get a response like that."[81]

Bott was under siege—that much was clear—but it wasn't just his church leaders who condemned the interview. Some of Bott's colleagues at BYU were combative and testy—and, frankly, embarrassed. "I am a professor at BYU," a colleague fumed,

> [and] I cringe with humiliation at the thought that Bott's business cards look like mine, and that I might have to clean up his (and Religious Education's) horrible, horrible mess when someone asks me at a conference what in the world made it possible for him to be gainfully employed at the same institution

where I work, in a department with a rather highly-regarded national reputation. Randy Bott, and the Religious Education department, have created a shameful situation that not only perpetuates false ideas among students, but also diminishes the value and esteem of their degrees once they graduate.[82]

Another colleague called the interview "extremely patronizing," to which another responded, "[If] we ever learn the reason [for the priesthood ban], that knowledge will come through the Lord's chosen prophets and apostles, not through BYU professors like me." Even BYU religion dean Terry Ball weighed in, writing, "The comments attributed to Professor Bott do not reflect the teachings in the classroom at Brigham Young University."[83]

Students didn't hold back, either. A BYU student newspaper declared that Bott's interview sparked "concern," even "outrage" across campus. One Black student pointedly noted, "Commenting on something we aren't for sure about, something so sensitive, can be considered offensive." Others defended Bott. One student felt sure that he had been misquoted because "[he]e's such a great and spiritual professor," adding, "He wouldn't go against the Church's principles." This is precisely what Bott told his students—that he had been misquoted—and he repeated this statement to a reporter from the *Deseret News*.[84]

Unfortunately, however, the facts don't support Bott. Not only did Horowitz tape the entire interview, but Bott posted similar thoughts about the ban on his "Know Your Religion" website, and he echoed the same sentiments to BYU students.[85] One student remarked, "I . . . ran into several people [at BYU] who perpetuated falsehoods and speculation around the priesthood and temple restriction. This included a BYU professor who told me one day after class almost word for word his opinion expressed in his unfortunate *Washington Post* interview."[86]

At the next general conference, the Brethren tried to mitigate the fallout from the *Post* story. In April 2012, Apostle D. Todd Christofferson delivered a carefully crafted sermon acknowledging that there "still persists some confusion about our doctrine and how it is established." He explained that "doctrinal exposition" comes "through the combined council of the First Presidency and Quorum of the Twelve Apostles," with "council deliberations" often including a weighing of canonized scriptures, the teachings of the church leaders, and past practices." "[N]ot every statement made by a church leader, past or present, necessarily constitutes doctrine. . . . [It] is commonly understood in the church that a statement made by one leader on a single occasion often represents a personal, though well-considered opinion, not meant to be official or binding for the whole church."[87]

Christofferson didn't mention Bott by name, but it was clear that he had the professor in mind. The apostle implied that Bott had gone rogue, but that wasn't true. The professor followed all the protocols that the apostle outlined in his sermon, including drawing on "past practice," the "council deliberations" from leaders, and current church-approved manuals supporting the priesthood and temple ban. Indeed, Bott's interview with Horowitz reflects an astute awareness of the First Presidency statements of 1949 and 1969, as well as authoritative books published by senior apostles in the decades after World War II.[88]

The tragedy of all this is that Bott was an unfortunate casualty of the Brethren's refusal to repudiate the church's antiblack teachings. Bott believed that how he had characterized the justifications for the priesthood and temple ban to Horowitz aligned with the church's *current* teachings— but he was wrong. Even more disconcerting, he was publicly humiliated in a church PR release, which affected not only him but also his colleagues. "We all taught what Randy taught," one confessed in private. "This could have happened to any one of us. We had no idea that the church's position had changed."[89]

★ ★ ★

Whether the Brethren felt remorse for scapegoating Bott isn't clear, but the following year, in 2013, they decided that they had had enough. The Brethren issued a statement repudiating Mormon racial teachings. The *Post* story convinced them that their strategy of condemning racism broadly without attributing it to the church's antiblack theology wasn't working— and indeed couldn't work as long as the Brethren sent mixed messages about the church's race doctrine. They recognized that there needed to be a firm, definitive statement from church headquarters denouncing the church's antiblack theology, lest there be more incidents like the one involving Bott.

In fact, the Brethren had been working on such a statement when the *Washington Post* story appeared. Under President Monson's direction, church leaders commissioned a series of essays in an effort to be more transparent about LDS church history and doctrine. They hoped these essays would refute criticism that the church was hiding its history. The Brethren carefully selected the essay topics in consultation with respected church scholars. Among them were a number of controversial subjects: polygamy and polyandry, DNA and the Book of Mormon, the historicity of the Book of Abraham, Women and Priesthood, and the priesthood and temple ban.[90]

The Brethren asked Paul Reeve, a practicing Latter-day Saint scholar from the University of Utah, to write the statement on race and priesthood.[91] Reeve's draft was read by several notable Latter-day Saints, among them Darius Gray, Armand Mauss, and Patrick Mason. Historians at church headquarters also reviewed the draft, which then went up the chain to the Quorum of the Twelve Apostles and the First Presidency for further review and editing. The result was a collaborative document titled "Race and the Priesthood," which the church posted on its website shortly after the *Washington Post* published the Bott interview.[92]

In the two-thousand-word essay, the Brethren denounced the curse and preexistent hypothesis, as well as racism and racial hierarchies: "Today, the Church disavows the theories advanced in the past that black skin is a sign of divine disfavor or curse, or that it reflects unrighteous actions in a premortal life." It also rejected the notion "that mixed-race marriages are a sin" and "that blacks or people of any other race or ethnicity are inferior in any way to anyone else." Just as important, the essay acknowledged that Black men held the priesthood during Joseph Smith's tenure as founding prophet and that the ban began with Brigham Young during "an era of great racial division in the United States." The statement closed by condemning racism while affirming that God loves everyone equally, "regardless of race."[93]

This was a powerful statement. The "Race and the Priesthood" essay repudiated the church's racial theology and promoted a racially inclusive gospel. But important questions remained. Was whiteness a sign of purity? Would Black people become "white and delightsome" in the resurrection? Did skin hues actually change over time, as Joseph Fielding Smith alleged? Did interracial marriage lead to "racial degeneration," as Bruce R. McConkie famously stated? The essay left those questions unresolved, preferring not to engage further in past teachings.[94]

For now, the Brethren had said what they wanted to say. Whatever was left unresolved by the "Race and the Priesthood" essay, what it accomplished was nothing short of extraordinary. In one brief statement, the Brethren bulldozed a gaping hole in the theological infrastructure of Black priesthood denial, boldly dismantling the scaffolding upon which it was based. And, just as important, they branded as theologically unsound the antiblack teachings of Smith and McConkie, sending a clear message to rank-and-file members that the curse and preexistent theories were no longer acceptable to teach in the postrevelation church. By declaring the "hard doctrine" dead, and by repudiating the racist teachings of the church's most prominent theologians, the Brethren had finally begun to confront entrenched racism in the church.[95]

Epilogue
Black (Mormon) Lives Matter,
2013–2023

In 1984, Baylor University sociologist Rodney Stark made a startling prediction. The Church of Jesus Christ of Latter-day Saints, he claimed, would be a major world religion by the late twenty-first century. Based on the church's remarkable growth rates from previous years, Stark argued that its membership would swell to 267 million by 2087, making the Utah-based church among the largest world religions. "Mormons," he wrote, "will soon achieve a worldwide following comparable to that of Islam, Buddhism, Christianity, Hinduism, and the other dominant world faiths."[1]

Stark's prediction proved overly optimistic. In 2021 the LDS church membership stood at 16 million members, well off Stark's ambitious prediction. While Latter-day Saints have not been as hard hit in membership decline as Southern Baptists, Catholics, and other denominations, the church's growth rate has not been above 2 percent since 2013. Like mainline Protestantism, Catholicism, and Evangelicalism, Mormonism's sputtering growth is a result of declining birth rates and changing attitudes about organized religion, among other factors.[2] Naturally, the changing landscape has affected the number of African converts in the LDS church, as well as African Americans. As of 2019, 3 percent of the 6 million members of the church in the United States are African Americans, and less than 6 percent of the 10-million-member international church identifies as Black. At Brigham Young University the numbers are equally limited. Fewer than 1 percent of the thirty-three thousand students are Black.[3] Not surprisingly, the lack of diversity at the LDS school has been a source of frustration for many students of color, one of whom complained that being at BYU is "like being a drop of soy sauce in a bowl of white rice."[4]

Some Mormon leaders and pundits predicted that Black people would convert to Mormonism in waves with the end of the priesthood and temple ban. But it didn't happen.[5] The church has struggled to attract Black people for a variety of reasons, not just because of sluggish growth rates but also because of cultural prejudices and a lack of diversity in the church body and among its leadership. The "Race and the Priesthood" essay notwithstanding, LDS leaders have studiously avoided difficult discussions of the church's residual antiblack theology, and they do not encourage teachers in youth and adult Sunday School classes to discuss it. Added to that, a number of Latter-day Saints continue to believe that the priesthood and temple ban was inspired by God. All of this leads to the startling conclusion that the church has not done enough to make itself inviting for people of color.[6]

Neither has the church apologized for those racial teachings used to justify its long-abandoned restriction on Black people. In 2015, Apostle Dallin H. Oaks starkly asserted, "[T]he church doesn't 'seek apologies' . . . and we don't give them."[7] Oaks made this astonishing statement just two years after First Presidency counselor Dieter F. Uchtdorf acknowledged in general conference, "[T]o be perfectly frank, there have been times when members or leaders in the Church have simply made mistakes. There may have been things said or done that were not in harmony with our values, principles, or doctrine."[8]

Uchtdorf's frank admission might be the closest thing that Black Latter-day Saints will ever get to an apology. But even so, the pain continues. I was present at a conference in 2017 when long-standing member Catherine Stokes, a well-respected Black Latter-day Saint, stood up after a presenter concluded their remarks and said, "I have been in this church for nearly four decades and racism in the church is stronger today than it was when I joined." I heard the pain in her voice as she spoke about racist teachings that continued to circulate within her ward and among her fellow Latter-day Saints.[9] In the same vein, Darius Gray recently told me that, initially, he didn't think an apology was necessary but has since changed his mind: "For the good of the church, we need an apology. The church can't heal until there's an apology."[10]

Never was this more acutely felt than in 2018 when an insensitive prankster, pretending to be a church PR spokesperson, devised a faux statement on LDS church letterhead with the catchy headline "President Nelson Meets with NAACP; Offers Apology for History of Racism." The full statement went on to explain:

> We have previously acknowledged that the false and racist explanations for the Priesthood and Temple restriction were wrong and disavowed them. Today, I am declaring that the ban itself was wrong. It was not of God but of fallible men, born of ignorance, pride and sin. . . .
>
> On behalf of the Church of Jesus Christ of Latter-day Saints, its current and past leaders and members, I offer this humble apology and plead for forgiveness in the merciful name of Jesus Christ, Amen.

Scores of Black Latter-day Saints praised the statement, and when they learned that it was a hoax, they were hurt "and in some cases traumatized by it." "I've spoken to black folks in tears because they thought this was real," commented Harvard graduate student Janan Graham-Russell, a Latter-day Saint of Black Haitian descent. Another Black Latter-day Saint, Zandra Vranes, "posted a tearful, 83-minute video on Facebook about how the hoax had retraumatized black members of the church." "May God have mercy on your soul," she told the prankster, a White disaffected Latter-day Saint named Jonathan Streeter.[11] Perhaps a headline from *Slate* magazine characterized it best: "A Fake Site Posted an Apology for the Mormon Church's History of Racism; Black Mormons Wish It Was Real."[12]

The fake apology not only made the church look bad, but it reminded all within earshot that prudence might dictate an *authentic* apology— something that both Black and White Latter-day Saints recognized was conspicuously missing in the "Race and the Priesthood" essay. Kristin Lowe, a White Latter-day Saint, remarked, "Racist statements and policies were once made by prophets and apostles, and we specifically need prophets and apostles to overturn them now. The language the church has used is not pointed enough, even though progress has been made in writings like the 'Race and Priesthood' Gospel Topics essay." Lowe went on to state that "Black and white members alike need to hear an admission of wrongdoing." She asked the Brethren to offer an apology in general conference.[13] When Black Latter-day Saint Julienna Viegas-Haws was asked what top ten things she would change about Mormonism, she listed "apologize for the [church's] racist past" as number 2, right behind "increase gender equality." Gina Colvin, an Indigenous Latter-day Saint from New Zealand, put it even more starkly: "The lives of faithful people both black and white were destroyed, upended, devastated by this doctrine. There are generations and generations of Black and Colored folk who have had to wonder who they are in God's eyes because church leaders sustained a discourse that blatantly positioned them as inferior. They need an apology. . . . They deserve an apology."[14]

The Brethren, however, were not inclined to give one. In 2015, Dallin Oaks stubbornly insisted that the word "apology" isn't in the scriptures, and in an address in 2018, he hinted that "most in the Church, including its senior leadership," rejected the idea of apologizing. He proclaimed that the leadership would like to concentrate "on the opportunities of the future rather than the disappointments of the past."[15] That might be so, but Oaks's bold statements didn't square well with recent church practices. In 2007, Henry B. Eyring of the First Presidency apologized on behalf of the church to the families whose ancestors were brutally murdered in the 1857 Mountain Meadows Massacre in southern Utah. And the church issued a public apology in 2012 for doing proxy baptisms in Mormon temples for Holocaust victims, despite telling Jewish leaders that they had stopped. So there was precedent for the church to apologize, even if Oaks claimed it wasn't scriptural and even if the Brethren preferred to focus on the future without confronting the injustices of the past.[16]

As one might suspect, Oaks's obstinance in refusing to apologize for the decades-old ban startled the church's Black members. They had every right to be startled.[17] During the church's nearly two-centuries-old history, Black Latter-day Saints had suffered indignity after indignity. The church's racial theology plunged them into a system of subordination that privileged whiteness. Mormon racial theology eerily resembled the White supremacist ideology in the United States that sustained slavery, segregation, and racism, bolstering a racial hierarchy that treated Black people as subhuman. In this context, the Mormon experience paralleled the larger American experience. Just as African Americans were denied basic rights and privileges common to most Americans, Black Latter-day Saints were denied basic rights and privileges common to White Latter-day Saints. Some light-skinned African American Latter-day Saints responded to these challenges by flouting the church's racial markers to pass as White in the hope of receiving the priesthood and the full benefits of church membership. Others, mostly dark-skinned Latter-day Saints, suffered the humiliation in silence, preferring either to accept their place in the church or worship at home in isolation.

These tragic policies led to a racial caste wherein White people dismissed Black people as less than equals.[18] Before 1978, LDS leaders prohibited Black people from performing or receiving important rituals in the church. This included blessing and naming their babies, receiving their salvific ordinances in Mormon temples, and being sealed to their families in sacred proxy rituals. In addition, Black people couldn't serve church missions, occupy positions of leadership in their wards and branches, teach lessons in youth or adult Sunday School, or give "talks" in LDS worship services. Most egregious, though, Black people were told that they could go to heaven only as servants to White people.

The priesthood and temple revelation was supposed to correct all of this. It was supposed to erase the "hard doctrine" that Black people had experienced during the 126-year-old priesthood and temple ban. But after 1978 a new set of problems arose. Like the many-headed hydra from Greek mythology, when one problem disappeared, another emerged. Tragically, the Brethren didn't repudiate the curse and preexistence theories when they lifted the ban; neither did they clarify racist tropes in the Book of Mormon, or provide instructions to patriarchs to correct offensive language that described Black people as "adopted into the house of Israel."

All of this led to a tragic and inexorable conclusion: the old racial doctrine continued to fester like an open wound. Microaggressions, large and small, affected Black Latter-day Saints in sacred worship spaces and in their everyday lives.[19] What's more, observant Black Latter-day Saints noticed disparities in Mormon theology that neither time nor inclination has healed. Darius Gray understood the problem well when he observed in 2012, "[W]e have Patriarchs who still aren't aware that lineage can and should be declared, regardless of race or ethnicity."[20] Here Gray implied that some Black Latter-day Saints are *still* denied a lineage declaration in their patriarchal blessings presumably because patriarchs are embarrassed to tell them that their lineage is cursed. Not surprisingly, White and Brown Latter-day Saints are spared this slight, creating a disparity in Mormon theology that the Brethren in the postrevelation church have yet to confront.

None of these slights, however, compares to the pain caused by whiteness teachings in the Book of Mormon. Since the 1980s, Mormon apologists have published dozens of books and articles defending a racial binary that equates whiteness with purity and darkness with sin. Darkness tropes in the Book of Mormon, they claim, are largely metaphorical, nothing more than archetypes of an individual's sinful nature. Here apologists draw on racial

312   SECOND-CLASS SAINTS

tropes from Western literature to bolster their position.[21] Yet, in doing so, they ignore scores of general authority sermons and writings affirming that dark skin would be whitened, either in mortality or in the resurrection. When Joseph Fielding Smith told church educators in 1954 "The Lord did put a mark on Cain" and that "we know of cases where it really has disappeared," he wasn't speaking metaphorically. Like his colleagues, Smith believed that the curse would be lifted, triggering a literal change in a Black person's appearance.[22]

Whether or not the apologists' claims are disingenuous is difficult to say. What's instructive is that the lived experience of persons of color suggests that the church's whiteness theology was and is a real thing that continues to afflict the church's marginalized communities, right down to the present day.

At the 2015 conference "Theology from the Margins: What It Means to Be a Non-White Mormon in America," Brown- and Black-skinned Latter-day Saints grimaced as they related how White Latter-day Saints informed them that they would be "white one day" when they repented of their sins. Their Black and Brown skin would gradually fade, and they would shed their curse just as the Book of Mormon prophets foretold.[23] To take just one example, in 2009 a White BYU student told her Black BYU roommate that she'd be White in the resurrection and therefore difficult to recognize in the next life. "You're so sweet," the White roommate enthused, "but I don't know how I'm going to recognize you in the celestial kingdom, because I just can't visualize you white. . . . So you'll [have to] recognize me. . . . You'll have to come find me."[24] These microaggressions were not isolated incidents. Latter-day Saints of color continue to be told that their Black and Brown skin will turn White pending their worthiness.[25]

Defending or explaining away this controversial teaching continues to hurt people of color. It is a stark reminder that the church hasn't achieved what scholar Jennifer Harvey called "the realization of reconciliation."[26] But there are other reminders. Since Helvécio Martins was called as a midlevel general authority in 1990, the church has had only a handful of Black men in its upper leadership, and none has been elevated to the Quorum of the Twelve Apostles or the First Presidency, the two highest governing bodies in the LDS church. Black women haven't fared much better; in the first decades of the twenty-first century, only a handful have served in the general presidencies of the Relief Society or Young Women's and Primary

BLACK (MORMON) LIVES MATTER   313

organizations. This is something the church will need to address if it hopes to be fully inclusive in its membership.[27]

For now, though, the church is left with the smoldering embers of the ban. The pain that it created continues to hover over the contemporary church, affecting all those who have felt its sting. Indeed, many of the subjects of this book—Elijah Abel, Jane Manning James, Abner Howell, Len and Mary Hope, Monroe Fleming, Ruffin Bridgeforth, Darius Gray, Eugene Orr, David Jackson, Catherine Stokes, Tamu Smith—and countless others were harmed by Mormon racial teachings. These teachings also harmed White and Brown Latter-day Saints, for each accepted a theology that conditioned them to see Black people as inferior to other races and ethnicities. And, just as tragic, when they spoke their consciences to criticize the church's racial theology, they were punished for it. Hugh B. Brown was dropped from the governing First Presidency; Lowell Bennion and Edgar Lyon lost their teaching positions in the Church Education System; and grassroots members like John Fitzgerald, Douglas Wallace, and Byron Marchant paid the ultimate penalty: they were excommunicated from the church.

Nevertheless, the Brethren's refusal to apologize for the ban is only part of the story. It must be balanced by the prodigious work that the church has done in recent years to right the wrongs of the past.[28] After Gordon B. Hinckley blazed the trail, Russell M. Nelson, the seventeenth LDS church president, has forged a close alliance with the NAACP in recent years, adhering to African American scholar Jemar Tisby's wise counsel that "racial justice often begins with relationships."[29] Since Nelson's presidency began in 2018, the church has undertaken a number of initiatives with the NAACP. First and foremost, the church has assisted in a number of humanitarian efforts, including pledging $2 million per year over a three-year period to "encourage service and help . . . those in need" in inner cities. The church has also pledged $1 million each year for up to three years to the United Negro College Fund to assist impoverished Black students to receive a college education. And the church has donated $250,000 to fund the Amos C. Brown Student Fellowship in Ghana to provide opportunities for Black students "to learn more about their heritage."[30]

No less important, the Brethren have been quick to denounce racist members who belittle Black people and/or demonstrate support for racist groups. When, for example, Ayla Stewart, a self-professed White Mormon nationalist, made headlines in 2017 for marching with neo-Nazis and Ku Klux Klansmen at a White supremist rally in Charlottesville, Virginia, the church denounced her swiftly and vigorously.[31] "White supremacist attitudes are morally wrong and sinful, and we condemn them," a church PR release stated. "Church members who promote or pursue a 'white culture' or white supremacy agenda are not in harmony with the teachings of the Church."[32]

At the same time, in some circumstances, the Brethren have been careful not to offend Black members. In 2016, when an Asian Latter-day Saint girl wrote a song called "White" for the Young Women's program in the church, Black Latter-day Saints complained, claiming that it depicted White people as pure and Black as sinful. "This song is very inappropriate," Janan Graham-Russell, a Black Latter-day Saint, explained. "I get the [doctrinal] idea but more care should be taken with anything involving the word 'white' and the LDS church because of its history and the present experiences of black members. It is symptomatic of not having honest conversations about race and what has been said about whiteness and blackness in our history." Other Black Latter-day Saints complained on their blogs, prompting LDS spokesman Eric Hawkins to announce, "The song is being pulled pending further review."[33]

The church also acted swiftly when a racist quote from Joseph Fielding Smith linking "dark skin" with a "curse" inexplicably appeared in a church Sunday School manual in 2020. Church spokeswoman Irene Caso promptly apologized for the error and noted that the outdated quote from the deceased apostle "doesn't reflect the church's current views on the topic."[34] Apostle Gary E. Stevenson even went so far as to apologize at an NAACP convention where he was speaking, acknowledging the "outdated commentary about race," and adding, "I'm deeply saddened and hurt by this error and for any pain that it may have caused our members and for others. We do condemn all racism, past and present, in any form, and we disavow any theory that advances that black or dark skin is a sign of a curse. We are brothers and sisters and I consider you friends. I love and appreciate you."[35]

The church's efforts in fighting racism were most prominent when the Brethren expressed sympathy for the Black Lives Matter protests sweeping the nation after the tragic death of George Floyd. In the immediate months after his murder in May 2020, Nelson and Oaks—the two most senior leaders in the church—both gave powerful sermons denouncing racial bigotry. Using the power of the pulpit, combined with their ecclesiastical authority, they boldly and firmly preached against the sin of racism. President Nelson stated at the October 2020 general conference, "I grieve that our Black brothers and sisters the world over are enduring the pains of racism and prejudice. Today, I call upon our members everywhere to lead out in abandoning attitudes and actions of prejudice. I plead with you to promote respect for all of God's children."[36] Oaks likewise counseled Latter-day Saints at the same conference to do all that they can "to root out racism." He made the same plea a few weeks later to BYU students during a devotional address. As he spoke, a large banner at the bottom of the TV screen displayed the words "BLACK LIVES MATTER."[37]

Two months after the October 2020 general conference, the Brethren amended the Church's *Handbook*, adding a new section on prejudice. The full statement read:

> All people are children of God. All are brothers and sisters who are part of His divine family (see "The Family: A Proclamation to the World"). God "hath made of one blood all nations" (Acts 17:26). "All are alike" unto Him (2 Nephi 26:33). Each person is "as precious in his sight as the other" (Jacob 2:21).
>
> Prejudice is not consistent with the revealed word of God. Favor or disfavor with God depends on devotion to Him and His commandments, not on the color of a person's skin or other attributes.
>
> The Church calls on all people to abandon attitudes and actions of prejudice toward any group or individual. Members of the Church should lead out in promoting respect for all of God's children. Members follow the Savior's commandment to love others (see Matthew 22:35–39). They strive to be persons of goodwill toward all, rejecting prejudice of any kind. This includes prejudice based on race, ethnicity, nationality, tribe, gender, age, disability, socioeconomic status, religious belief or nonbelief, and sexual orientation.[38]

Another encouraging sign is that the Brethren have been more tolerant of LDS scholars writing about Mormon history. In recent years, a number of scholars have examined the priesthood and temple ban afresh, daring to criticize narratives that were once considered taboo. Terryl Givens, a senior research fellow at BYU's Neal A. Maxwell Institute, wrote, "The door is open for an interpretation of . . . [the priesthood and temple ban] as having nothing divine about its implementation." Patrick Mason, holder of a distinguished chair in Mormon studies at Utah State University, asserted in a book published by the church's publishing house, Deseret Book, that the ban may have been a mistake instigated by "fallible human beings." In an award-winning book, Paul Reeve, a distinguished professor of Mormon studies at the University of Utah and principal author of the "Race and the Priesthood" essay, attributed the ban to Brigham Young's racism, as did Mormon scholar Russell Stevenson.[39] When Newell Bringhurst and I published a book on Black Latter-day Saints in 2015, we were astonished to learn that it was available at Deseret Book despite our claim that the priesthood ban resulted from "racial discrimination rather than divine revelation."[40]

Remarkably, it wasn't just LDS scholars who experienced a new era of freedom. LDS artists and painters have also benefited. "In the past several years," writes religious historian John Turner, "the church has introduced diverse images of the savior into its videos and online art exhibitions." A prominent example is work by Emile Wilson, a Latter-day Saint from Sierra Leone, who painted two pictures of a Black Jesus for an international art competition sponsored by the church. One of Wilson's paintings of Black Jesus hung conspicuously on the wall of the Church History Museum near LDS church headquarters, sandwiched between a sea of White Jesuses.[41] Turner writes, "These small steps suggest a growing willingness on the part of Mormon leaders to adapt their message and materials for local cultures.... The Mormon Jesus may not remain white much longer."[42]

This new openness also extended to the church's bookstore, Deseret Book, which now sells books in which Black Latter-day Saints provide graphic accounts of how they experienced racism at church.[43] Deseret Book even published a children's book to emphasize "the importance of representation in Church books and artwork for Black American children."[44]

If these gestures to promote racial diversity and openness represent real change in the church, the church's flagship university, BYU, offers a stark reminder of just how much work remains to be done. In February 2021, BYU released a staggering sixty-page report titled "Race, Equity, and Belonging." Commissioned by BYU president Kevin Worthen with support from the BYU Board of Trustees, the survey revealed that "BYU's BIPOC [Black, Indigenous, and people of color] students shared that their daily lives at BYU are too often marred by marginalizing comments, otherizing questions, and exhausting racial slights. These have come from roommates, classmates, church congregations, and faculty members." The report continued:

[Many] students reported feeling a sense of surprise, loneliness, and isolation when they realized that they see few other BIPOC students on campus and

BLACK (MORMON) LIVES MATTER

in their classes. They also reported that they find themselves serving as representatives of their respective races and educating students and faculty on issues relating to race and race relations. These experiences have left many disillusioned, brokenhearted, and struggling. Many described that these challenges to their sense of belonging and their ability to feel connected result in profound faith challenges.[45]

Given these challenges, perhaps it's not surprising that only 55 percent of non-White student respondents expressed a sense of "belonging" on campus compared to 76 percent of White respondents. Most revealing, though, the survey notes that students of color claimed they felt "unsafe because of racially insensitive statements, prejudicial attitudes, and discriminatory behaviors" in "some general education and religion classes." The report further states, "Many students reported that some of the most hurtful experiences they have had occurred in religion courses, where sensitive gospel topics such as the priesthood and temple ban and skin color in the Book of Mormon can be misunderstood or insensitively presented."[46]

The authors of the report, a racially diverse group of faculty from various departments across campus, offered twenty-six recommendations to root out systemic racism at the church-owned school. Most notable was the recommendation "Make changes to general education, religion and elective courses that educate students on race, unity, and diversity." The report also called on the university to foster "a more diverse campus for the benefit of students," as well as "[d]evelop diversity and inclusion training programs for students and employees." Another recommendation called for the university to create "a process that allows students to report instances of racial discrimination on campus. Through this process, such claims would be investigated and redressed, as appropriate." Several recommendations called for broader institutional reforms that dealt with hiring new administration to oversee, and work with, "an Office for Diversity and Belonging."[47]

But as challenging as these problems are, racism at BYU isn't the only problem that grips the postrevelation church. Right-wing extremism has worked its way into the pews and podiums, with scores of Latter-day Saints supporting efforts to limit the franchise for Black people and other racial minorities. A 2021 poll revealed that 46 percent of Latter-day Saints believe that Joseph R. Biden stole the election from Donald J. Trump, compared to 61 percent of White evangelical Protestants and 35 percent of Catholics.[48] This mirrors party affiliation, where a shocking 66 percent of Republicans believe that Biden gained the presidency fraudulently while 95 percent of Democrats and 72 percent of Independents reject this claim.[49]

Perhaps most troubling is that a small number of Latter-day Saints participated in the historic attack on January 6, 2021, when pro-Trump zealots stormed the U.S. Capitol in the hope of disrupting the peaceful transition of power. Violent insurrectionists beat scores of police officers and journalists, leaving five people dead and dozens injured. News images showed White Nationalist and dangerous militia groups hoisting Confederate flags and other symbols of oppression as they bludgeoned their way through the building.[50]

All of this alarmed the Brethren, who condemned the attack in a sharply worded statement. "With great concern," it read, "we observe the political and cultural divisions in the United States and around the world. We condemn violence and lawless behavior, including the recent violence in Washington, D.C. and any suggestion of further violence."[51] Three months later, at the church's April general conference, First Presidency counselor Oaks departed from the traditional Easter sermons to condemn right-wing extremists. "We should never assert that a faithful Latter-day Saint cannot belong to a particular party or vote for a particular candidate," he said, countering the late church president Ezra Taft Benson, who often said that members in good standing couldn't be Democrats. Oaks asked "local leaders to insist, that political choices and affiliations not be the subject of teachings or advocacy in any of our Church meetings."[52]

With hate groups and White Christian nationalism surging, the Brethren also warned that members should be careful about where they seek political information.[53] In a change to the *Church Handbook* in late 2020, they added an important new section advising members not to read literature that promotes "anger, contention, fear, or baseless conspiracy theories."[54] The *Church Handbook*'s warning is a sober acknowledgment that the church can't heal the wounds of racism as long as its members support political candidates or parties or embrace conspiracy theories that use race as a cudgel to divide Americans.

And yet, despite these significant challenges, there is hope. As of this writing, the church continues to engage in meaningful work with the NAACP to fight racism. And church leaders appear to be taking seriously the twenty-six recommendations that BYU faculty made in the "Race, Equity, and Belonging" report to address systemic racism at the church-owned school. Church leaders also continue to speak out loudly and boldly, calling racism a sin.[55] But most critically, the LDS church leadership finally repudiated the church's antiblack theology when they issued the "Race and the Priesthood" essay. This was the Brethren's way of "corporately confess[ing] the sin of racism," to borrow the words of Jemar Tisby, while also acknowledging that racism is "not just about individual behavior."[56]

These are all welcome measures. They reflect a church on the move, ever willing, even if only gradually and slowly, to embrace a central and unifying theme in Mormon scripture: that "all are alike unto God."[57]

Abbreviations

AAOH   African American Oral History Project, L. Tom Perry Special Collections, Harold B. Lee Library, Brigham Young University, Provo, Utah

AAOHU   African American Oral History Project, 1971–1973, J. Willard Marriott Library, University of Utah, Salt Lake City

ALM   Armand L. Mauss Papers, Utah State Historical Society, Salt Lake City

ARC   Adrian R. Chamberlain Papers, Morgan Library, Colorado State University, Fort Collins

ASB   Adam S. Bennion Papers, L. Tom Perry Special Collections, Harold B. Lee Library, Brigham Young University, Provo, Utah

AVW   Arthur V. Watkins Papers, L. Tom Perry Special Collections, Harold B. Lee Library, Brigham Young University, Provo, Utah

BW   Ezra Taft Benson–Robert Welch Correspondence, John Birch Society Papers, Appleton, Wisconsin

BY   Brigham Young Papers, Church History Library, the Church of Jesus Christ of Latter-day Saints, Salt Lake City, Utah

CAB   Claude A. Barnett Papers, The Associated Negro Press, 1918–1967, Subject Files on Black Americans, Library of Congress, Washington, D.C.

CDH   Chauncy D. Harris Papers, University of Chicago Library

CHL   Church History Library, the Church of Jesus Christ of Latter-day Saints, Salt Lake City, Utah

CLR   Governor Calvin L. Rampton Correspondence, Series 13856, Utah State Archives and Records Service, Salt Lake City

CM   Clarence Manion Papers, Chicago History Museum

CNO   Chieko N. Okazaki Papers, J. Willard Marriott Library, University of Utah, Salt Lake City

CRI   College of Religious Instruction Papers, L. Tom Perry Special Collections, Harold B. Lee Library, Brigham Young University, Provo, Utah

DJ   Duane Jeffery Papers, Special Collections, J. Willard Marriott Library, University of Utah, Salt Lake City

ABBREVIATIONS

DJB — David John Buerger Papers, Special Collections, J. Willard Marriott Library, University of Utah, Salt Lake City

DMQ — D. Michael Quinn Papers, Beinecke Rare Book and Manuscript Library, Yale University, New Haven, Connecticut

DOM — David O. McKay Papers, Special Collections, J. Willard Marriott Library, University of Utah, Salt Lake City

EBF — Edwin B. Firmage Papers, J. Willard Marriott Library, University of Utah, Salt Lake City

ECOH — Everett L. Cooley Oral History Project, J. Willard Marriott Library, University of Utah, Salt Lake City

EE — Eugene England Papers, Special Collections, J. Willard Marriott Library, University of Utah, Salt Lake City

EEC — Eugene E. Campbell Papers, L. Tom Perry Special Collections, Harold B. Lee Library, Brigham Young University, Provo, Utah

EJB — E. Jay Bell Papers, Special Collections, J. Willard Marriott Library, University of Utah, Salt Lake City

ELW — Ernest L. Wilkinson Papers, L. Tom Perry Special Collections, Harold B. Lee Library, Brigham Young University, Provo, Utah

ELWP — Ernest L. Wilkinson Presidential Papers, L. Tom Perry Special Collections, Harold B. Lee Library, Brigham Young University, Provo, Utah

EO — Eugene Orr Papers, Church History Library, the Church of Jesus Christ of Latter-day Saints, Salt Lake City, Utah

ETB — Ezra Taft Benson Papers, Church History Library, the Church of Jesus Christ of Latter-day Saints, Salt Lake City, Utah

FLT — F. LaMond Tullis Papers, Church History Library, the Church of Jesus Christ of Latter-day Saints, Salt Lake City, Utah

FMB — Fawn M. Brodie Papers, J. Willard Marriott Library, University of Utah, Salt Lake City

FSB — Frederick S. Buchanan Papers, J. Willard Marriott Library, University of Utah, Salt Lake City

GAP — Gregory A. Prince Papers, Special Collections, J. Willard Marriott Library, University of Utah, Salt Lake City

GAS — George Albert Smith Papers, Special Collections, J. Willard Marriott Library, University of Utah, Salt Lake City

GCW — George C. Wallace Collection, Alabama Department of Archives and History, Montgomery

GDC — Governor George D. Clyde Correspondence, Series 192, Utah State Archives and Records Service, Salt Lake City

GDW — George D. Watt Papers, Church History Library, the Church of Jesus Christ of Latter-day Saints, Salt Lake City, Utah

ABBREVIATIONS 323

GFR George F. Richards Papers, Church History Library, the Church of Jesus Christ of Latter-day Saints, Salt Lake City, Utah

GHD G. Homer Durham Papers, Special Collections, J. Willard Marriott Library, University of Utah, Salt Lake City

GOL Gustive O. Larson Papers, L. Tom Perry Special Collections, Harold B. Lee Library, Brigham Young University, Provo, Utah

GST George S. Tanner Papers, Special Collections, J. Willard Marriott Library, University of Utah, Salt Lake City

GTB George T. Boyd Papers, L. Tom Perry Special Collections, Harold B. Lee Library, Brigham Young University, Provo, Utah

GWR George W. Romney Papers, Bentley Historical Library, University of Michigan, Ann Arbor

HBB Hugh B. Brown Collection, Church History Library, the Church of Jesus Christ of Latter-day Saints, Salt Lake City, Utah

HBBR Hugh B. Brown Research File, L. Tom Perry Special Collections, Harold B. Lee Library, Brigham Young University, Provo, Utah

HBJ Heber J. Grant Papers, Church History Library, the Church of Jesus Christ of Latter-day Saints, Salt Lake City, Utah

HBLL Harold B. Lee Library, Brigham Young University, Provo, Utah

HCS Heber C. Snell Papers, Special Collections, Merrill-Cazier Library, Utah State University, Logan

HGI H. Grant Ivins Papers, Special Collections, J. Willard Marriott Library, University of Utah, Salt Lake City

HGW Heber G. Wolsey Papers, L. Tom Perry Special Collections, Harold B. Lee Library, Brigham Young University, Provo, Utah

HH Harold Hillam Papers, Church History Library, the Church of Jesus Christ of Latter-day Saints, Salt Lake City, Utah

HM Heber Meeks Papers, L. Tom Perry Special Collections, Harold B. Lee Library, Brigham Young University, Provo, Utah

HMM H. Michael Marquardt Papers, Special Collections, J. Willard Marriott Library, University of Utah, Salt Lake City

HN Hugh Nibley Papers, L. Tom Perry Special Collections, Harold B. Lee Library, Brigham Young University, Provo, Utah

IB Irene Bates Papers, Special Collections, J. Willard Marriott Library, University of Utah, Salt Lake City

IBU Interviews with Blacks in Utah, 1982–1988, Special Collections, J. Willard Marriott Library, University of Utah, Salt Lake City

IJAU Interviews with Japanese Americans in Utah, 1984–1988, Special Collections, J. Willard Marriott Library, University of Utah, Salt Lake City

ABBREVIATIONS

JAW	John A. Widtsoe Papers, Church History Library, the Church of Jesus Christ of Latter-day Saints, Salt Lake City, Utah
JAWL	John A. Widtsoe Letters, L. Tom Perry Special Collections, Harold B. Lee Library, Brigham Young University, Provo, Utah
JAWP	John A. Widtsoe Papers, Utah State Historical Society, Salt Lake City
JB	Juanita Brooks Papers, Utah State Historical Society, Salt Lake City
JBS	John Birch Society Papers, Appleton, Wisconsin
JBSR	John Birch Society Records, Brown University Archives, Brown University, Providence, Rhode Island
JC	James R. Clark Papers, L. Tom Perry Special Collections, Harold B. Lee Library, Brigham Young University, Provo, Utah
JCPL	Jimmy Carter Presidential Library, Atlanta, Georgia
JDW	J. D. Williams Papers, J. Willard Marriott Library, University of Utah, Salt Lake City
JFM	Joseph F. Merrill Papers, L. Tom Perry Special Collections, Harold B. Lee Library, Brigham Young University, Provo, Utah
JFS	Joseph Fielding Smith Papers, Church History Library, the Church of Jesus Christ of Latter-day Saints, Salt Lake City, Utah
JMOH	James H. Moyle Oral History Program, Church History Library, the Church of Jesus Christ of Latter-day Saints, Salt Lake City, Utah
JOFS	Joseph F. Smith Papers, Church History Library, the Church of Jesus Christ of Latter-day Saints, Salt Lake City, Utah
JRC	J. Reuben Clark Papers, L. Tom Perry Special Collections, Harold B. Lee Library, Brigham Young University, Provo, Utah
JWF	John W. Fitzgerald Papers, Special Collections, Merrill-Cazier Library, Utah State University, Logan
JWM	J. Willard Marriott Papers, Special Collections, J. Willard Marriott Library, University of Utah, Salt Lake City
JWML	J. Willard Marriott Library, University of Utah, Salt Lake City
KC	Kathleen Cleaver Papers, Stuart A. Rose Manuscript, Archives and Rare Book Library, Emory University, Atlanta, Georgia
KCS	Karl C. Sandberg Papers, J. Willard Marriott Library, University of Utah, Salt Lake City
KSP	Kenneth S. Pitzer Papers, Special Collections, Stanford University Libraries, Palo Alto, California
LEB	Lester E. Bush Papers, Special Collections, J. Willard Marriott Library, University of Utah, Salt Lake City
LFA	Lavina Fielding Anderson Papers, Special Collections, J. Willard Marriott Library, University of Utah, Salt Lake City
LGP	Lauritz G. Petersen Papers, L. Tom Perry Special Collections, Harold B. Lee Library, Brigham Young University, Provo, Utah

ABBREVIATIONS 325

LJA	Leonard J. Arrington Papers, Special Collections, Merrill-Cazier Library, Utah State University, Logan
LLB	Lowell L. Bennion Papers, Church History Library, the Church of Jesus Christ of Latter-day Saints, Salt Lake City, Utah
LN	Lowry Nelson Papers, Special Collections, J. Willard Marriott Library, University of Utah, Salt Lake City
LNC	Lowry Nelson Collection, L. Tom Perry Special Collections, Harold B. Lee Library, Brigham Young University, Provo, Utah
LOC	Library of Congress, Washington, D.C.
LR	LeGrand Richards Papers, Special Collections, J. Willard Marriott Library, University of Utah, Salt Lake City
LRK	Lynn Romney Keenan Collection of George W. and Lenore Romney Family Papers, L. Tom Perry Special Collections, Harold B. Lee Library, Brigham Young University, Provo, Utah
LS	Linda Sillitoe Papers, Special Collections, J. Willard Marriott Library, University of Utah, Salt Lake City
LSW	LaMar S. Williams Papers, Church History Library, the Church of Jesus Christ of Latter-day Saints, Salt Lake City, Utah
MDH	Marion D. Hanks Collection, Church History Library, the Church of Jesus Christ of Latter-day Saints, Salt Lake City, Utah
MGR	Marion G. Romney Papers, Church History Library, the Church of Jesus Christ of Latter-day Saints, Salt Lake City, Utah
MHP	Max H. Parkin Papers, Special Collections, J. Willard Marriott Library, University of Utah, Salt Lake City
MLB	Mary L. Bradford Papers, Special Collections, J. Willard Marriott Library, University of Utah, Salt Lake City
MLH	Matthew L. Harris Files, in author's possession
MLK	Martin Luther King Jr. Papers, The Martin Luther King Jr. Center for Nonviolent Social Change, Atlanta, Georgia
MSH	Marvin S. Hill Papers, Special Collections, J. Willard Marriott Library, University of Utah, Salt Lake City
MWP	M. Wilford Poulson Papers, L. Tom Perry Special Collections, Harold B. Lee Library, Brigham Young University, Provo, Utah
NAACP	NAACP Papers, part 24, Special Subjects, 1956–1965, Library of Congress, Washington, D.C.
PRC	Paul R. Cheesman Papers, L. Tom Perry Special Collections, Harold B. Lee Library, Brigham Young University, Provo, Utah
RCD	Reed C. Durham Papers, Special Collections, J. Willard Marriott Library, University of Utah, Salt Lake City
RDP	Richard D. Poll Papers, Special Collections, J. Willard Marriott Library, University of Utah, Salt Lake City

ABBREVIATIONS

REL   Rex E. Lee Papers, L. Tom Perry Special Collections, Harold B. Lee Library, Brigham Young University, Provo, Utah

RGV   Robert G. Vernon Papers, Special Collections, J. Willard Marriott Library, University of Utah, Salt Lake City

RKT   Robert K. Thomas Papers, L. Tom Perry Special Collections, Harold B. Lee Library, Brigham Young University, Provo, Utah

RLA   Richard Lloyd Anderson Papers, L. Tom Perry Special Collections, Harold B. Lee Library, Brigham Young University, Provo, Utah

RRPL   Ronald Reagan Presidential Library, Simi Valley, California

RWD   Roy W. Doxey Papers, L. Tom Perry Special Collections, Harold B. Lee Library, Brigham Young University, Provo, Utah

SBS   Sidney B. Sperry Papers, L. Tom Perry Special Collections, Harold B. Lee Library, Brigham Young University, Provo, Utah

SGE   S. George Ellsworth Papers, Merrill-Cazier Library, Utah State University, Logan

SH   Stephen Holbrook Papers, Utah State Historical Society, Salt Lake City

SLR   Stephen L. Richards Papers, Church History Library, the Church of Jesus Christ of Latter-day Saints, Salt Lake City, Utah

SLU   Stewart L. Udall Papers, Special Collections, University of Arizona Libraries, Tucson

SMM   Sterling M. McMurrin Papers, Special Collections, J. Willard Marriott Library, University of Utah, Salt Lake City

SWK   Spencer W. Kimball Papers, Church History Library, the Church of Jesus Christ of Latter-day Saints, Salt Lake City, Utah

TAB   Thomas A. Blakely Papers, Special Collections, J. Willard Marriott Library, University of Utah, Salt Lake City

TEL   T. Edgar Lyon Papers, Church History Library, the Church of Jesus Christ of Latter-day Saints, Salt Lake City, Utah

WAWF   William A. Wilson Folklore Archives, L. Tom Perry Special Collections, Harold B. Lee Library, Brigham Young University, Provo, Utah

WEB   William E. Berrett Papers, L. Tom Perry Special Collections, Harold B. Lee Library, Brigham Young University, Provo, Utah

WGB   William Grant Bangerter Papers, Church History Library, the Church of Jesus Christ of Latter-day Saints, Salt Lake City, Utah

WJG   William J. Grede Papers, Wisconsin Historical Society, Madison

USARS   Utah State Archives and Records Service, Salt Lake City

Notes

PREFACE

1. Kenneth L. Woodward, "Race Relations," *Newsweek*, June 19, 1978, 67; Molly Ivins, "Mormon Decisions on Blacks Promises Impact on Utah," *New York Times*, June 18, 1978. Edward L. Kimball, *Lengthen Your Stride: The Presidency of Spencer W. Kimball—Working Draft* (Salt Lake City: Benchmark Books, 2009), 361–68; Mary Jane Woodger, "Revelation Attitudes: The Coming Forth of Official Declaration 2," *Religious Educator* 3, no. 2 (2002): 185; Dallin H. Oaks, "For the Blessing of All His Children," keynote address, LDS African American Symposium, BYU, June 8, 1988, 1 Box 42, Folder 1, ALM; D. Michael Quinn, diary, June 9, 1978, Box 27, DMQ.

2. Spencer W. Kimball, diary, June 9, 1978, reel 39, SWK.

3. James C. Jones, "Racism," *Dialogue: A Journal of Mormon Thought* 52, no. 3 (Fall 2019): 206.

4. Melodie Jackson, "The Black Cain in White Garments," *Dialogue: A Journal of Mormon Thought* 51, no. 3 (Fall 2018): 210. Nephi is a prophet in the Book of Mormon; "Joseph" refers to church founder Joseph Smith Jr.; "Brigham" refers to Brigham Young, who succeeded Smith as church president; and "McConkie" refers to church apostle Bruce R. McConkie.

5. "President Oaks Full Remarks from the LDS Church's 'Be One' Celebration," LDS *Church News*, June 1, 2018, https://www.thechurchnews.com/2018/6/2/23221509/president-oaks-full-remarks-from-the-lds-churchs-be-one-celebration; Ahmad Corbitt, "Till We All Come in the Unity of the Faith," *Perspectives on Church History*, n.d., https://history.churchofjesuschrist.org/landing/perspectives-on-church-history?lang=eng; "Race and the Priesthood," *Gospel Topics Essays*, 2013, https://www.churchofjesuschrist.org/study/manual/gospel-topics-essays/race-and-the-priesthood?lang=eng. See also Matthew L. Harris and Newell G. Bringhurst, eds., *The Mormon Church and Blacks: A Documentary History* (Urbana: University of Illinois Press, 2015), 3–4, 81–83, 133–35, 143.

6. *Church History in the Fulness of Times* (Salt Lake City: Church of Jesus Christ of Latter-day Saints, 1992), 584–85; *Doctrine and Covenants: Student Manual* (Salt Lake City: Church of Jesus Christ of Latter-day Saints, 2001), 364–65. For hagiographic accounts of the ban, see Bruce R. McConkie, "The New Revelation on Priesthood," in *Priesthood* (Salt Lake City: Deseret Book, 1981), 126–37; Gordon B. Hinckley, "Member Meeting in Accra, Ghana," February 16, 1998, in *Discourses of President Gordon B. Hinckley*, 2 vols. (Salt Lake City:

328   NOTES

Deseret Book, 2005), 1:419–20; Juan Henderson, "A Time for Healing: Official Declaration 2," in *Out of Obscurity: The LDS Church in the Twentieth Century* (Salt Lake City: Deseret Book, 2000), 151–60; Marcus H. Martins, *Blacks and the Mormon Priesthood: Setting the Record Straight* (Orem, UT: Millennial Press, 2007); Brent L. Top, "Revelation on Priesthood," in *LDS Beliefs: A Doctrinal Reference*, ed. Robert L. Millet, Camille Fronk Olson, Andrew C. Skinner, and Brent L. Top (Salt Lake City: Deseret Book, 2011), 505–9. The one exception is Edward Kimball's biography of his father. This isn't an apologetic work, but it offers an apologetic defense of the ban at critical parts in the narrative—a result of editors who pushed Kimball to tell the story they wanted told. Edward L. Kimball, *Lengthen Your Stride: The Presidency of Spencer W. Kimball* (Salt Lake City: Deseret Book, 2005), ix–x; Kimball, *Working Draft*, v–vi; "Spencer W. Kimball and the Revelation on Priesthood," *BYU Studies* 47, no. 2 (2008): 5–78. Edward Kimball also conveyed to me that Deseret Book heavily edited his manuscript. Edward Kimball, interview with Matthew Harris, November 26, 2013, Kimball home, Provo, Utah.

7. Lucile C. Tate, *LeGrand Richards: Beloved Apostle* (Salt Lake City: Bookcraft, 1982), 291–92; Eleanor Knowles, *Howard W. Hunter* (Salt Lake City: Deseret Book, 1994), 235–36; Francis M. Gibbons, *Spencer W. Kimball: Resolute Disciple, Prophet of God* (Salt Lake City: Deseret Book, 1995), 293–96; Lucile C. Tate, *David B. Haight: The Life Story of a Disciple* (Salt Lake City: Bookcraft, 1987), 279; Francis M. Gibbons, *Ezra Taft Benson: Statesman, Patriot, Prophet of God* (Salt Lake City: Deseret Book, 1996), 281–82; Lee Tom Perry, *L. Tom Perry: An Uncommon Life—Years of Hastening the Work of Salvation* (Salt Lake City: Deseret Book, 2019), 79–80; Sheri L. Dew, *Go Forward with Faith: The Biography of Gordon B. Hinckley* (Salt Lake City: Deseret Book, 1996), 362; Heidi S. Swinton, *To the Rescue: The Biography of Thomas S. Monson* (Salt Lake City: Deseret Book, 2010), 392–96; F. Burton Howard, *Marion G. Romney: His Life and Faith* (Salt Lake City: Bookcraft, 1988), 239; Lucile C. Tate, *Boyd K. Packer: Watchman on the Tower* (Salt Lake City: Bookcraft, 1995), 225–27. G. Homer Durham's biography, *N. Eldon Tanner: His Life and Service* (Salt Lake City: Deseret Book, 1982), doesn't mention the revelation at all. See also Woodger, "Revelation Attitudes," 186: "many Latter-day Saints were surprised at the 1978 announcement."

8. McConkie, "The New Revelation on Priesthood"; "Official Declaration 2," Church of Jesus Christ of Latter-day Saints, https://www.churchofjesuschrist. org/study/scriptures/dc-testament/od/2?lang=eng. For McConkie's primary authorship of this document, see chapter 7.

9. LDS *Church News*, June 17, 1978, 4, 6.

10. Richard L. Bushman, *Joseph Smith: Rough Stone Rolling* (New York: Alfred A. Knopf, 2005), ch. 2; Steven C. Harper, *First Vision: Memory and Mormon Origins* (New York: Oxford University Press, 2019); Spencer W. Kimball, "Revelation Most Often, Not Dramatic," *Conference Report*, 1973, 23.

11. Book of Mormon, 1 Nephi, 17:45; Joseph Smith discourse between circa June 26 and circa July 2, 1839, in *The Joseph Smith Papers: Documents*, vol. 6: *February 1838–August 1839*, ed. Mark Ashurst-McGee, David W. Grua, Elizabeth A.

NOTES

329

Kuehn, Brenden W. Rensink, and Alexander L. Baugh (Salt Lake City: Church Historian's Press, 2017), 526.

12. Edwin B. Firmage, ed., *An Abundant Life: The Memoirs of Hugh B. Brown*, 2nd ed. (Salt Lake City: Signature Books, 1999), 125.

13. "Official Declaration 2," Church of Jesus Christ of Latter-day Saints, https://www.churchofjesuschrist.org/study/scriptures/dc-testament/od/2?lang=eng.

14. Harris and . Bringhurst, *Mormon Church and Blacks*, ch. 7.

15. See chapter 10.

16. "Race and the Priesthood."

17. Kimball, *Lengthen Your Stride*.

18. W. Paul Reeve, *Religion of a Different Color: Race and the Mormon Struggle for Whiteness* (New York: Oxford University Press, 2015); Newell G. Bringhurst, *Saints, Slaves, and Blacks: The Changing Place of Black People within Mormonism*, 2nd ed. (1981; Salt Lake City: Greg Kofford Books, 2018); Russell W. Stevenson, *For the Cause of Righteousness: A Global History of Blacks and Mormonism, 1830–2013* (Salt Lake City: Greg Kofford Books, 2014); Lester E. Bush Jr., "Mormonism's Negro Doctrine: An Historical Overview," *Dialogue: A Journal of Mormon Thought* 8, no. 1 (Spring 1973): 11–68; Max Perry Mueller, *Race and the Making of the Mormon People* (Chapel Hill: University of North Carolina Press, 2017).

19. Ralph Waldo Emerson, "Representative Men," in *Essays and Lectures*, ed. Joel Porte (New York: Library of America, 1983), 627.

20. Anthea Butler, *White Evangelical Racism: The Politics of Morality in America* (Chapel Hill: University of North Carolina Press, 2021), 9.

CHAPTER 1

1. W. Paul Reeve, *Religion of a Different Color: Race and the Mormon Struggle for Whiteness* (New York: Oxford University Press, 2015), 107–14, 128–34; Newell G. Bringhurst, *Saints, Slaves, and Blacks: The Changing Place of Black People within Mormonism*, 2nd ed. (1981; Salt Lake City: Greg Kofford Books, 2018), 36–38, 90–98; Max Perry Mueller, *Race and the Making of the Mormon People* (Chapel Hill: University of North Carolina Press, 2017), 87–89, 95, 97–98, 106–08, 146–49; Russell W. Stevenson, *For the Cause of Righteousness: A Global History of Blacks and Mormonism, 1830–2013* (Salt Lake City: Greg Kofford Books, 2014), 10, 13–15; Lester E. Bush Jr., "Mormonism's Negro Doctrine: An Historical Overview," *Dialogue: A Journal of Mormon Thought* 8, no. 1 (Spring 1973): 11–68; Angela Pulley Hudson, *Real Native Genius: How an Ex-Slave and White Mormon Became Famous Indians* (Chapel Hill: University of North Carolina Press, 2015), 65–68; Connell O'Donovan, "The Mormon Priesthood Ban and Elder Q. Walker Lewis: 'An Example for His More Whiter Brethren to Follow,'" *John Whitmer Historical Association Journal* 26 (2006): 47–99; Mark Lyman Staker, *Hearken, O Ye People: The Historical Setting of Joseph Smith's Ohio Revelations* (Salt Lake City: Greg Kofford Books, 2009), 64–65; Matthew L. Harris and Newell G. Bringhurst, eds., *The Mormon Church and Blacks: A Documentary*

330   NOTES

History (Urbana: University of Illinois Press, 2015), chs. 2–3. Only recently have scholars begun to recover these lost voices. See "Century of Black Mormons," edited by W. Paul Reeve, http://centuryofblackmormons.org.

2. Two recent studies of Young are John G. Turner, *Brigham Young: Pioneer Prophet* (Cambridge, MA: Harvard University Press, 2012); Thomas G. Alexander, *Brigham Young and the Expansion of the Mormon Faith* (Norman: University of Oklahoma Press, 2019).

3. Brigham Young address to the Utah Territorial Legislature, February 5, 1852, Box 48, Folder 3, BY. For the legislature legalizing slavery, see "An Act in Relation to Service," February 4, 1852, in Utah Territory, Legislative Assembly, *Acts, Resolutions, and Memorials* (Salt Lake City, 1852), ch. 17, 160–62. For Flake, Crosby, and Lay, see "Original Pioneer Party Contained 3 Negroes," *Deseret News*, May 31, 1947.

4. "Remarks by President Brigham Young, delivered in the Tabernacle Great Salt Lake City," October 9, 1859, in *Journal of Discourses*, ed. George D. Watt, 26 vols. (London: Latter-day Saints Book Depot, 1854–86), 7:290–91.

5. Reeve, *Religion of a Different Color*; Bringhurst, *Saints, Slaves, and Blacks*; and Amy Tanner Thiriot, *Slavery in Zion: A Documentary and Genealogical History of Black Lives and Black Servitude in Utah Territory, 1847–1862* (Salt Lake City: University of Utah Press, 2022) are the best expositions of early Black Latter-day Saints.

6. Reeve, *Religion of a Different Color*, 143; Bringhurst, *Saints, Slaves, and Blacks*, 66–67, 219, 111–12, 224; Thiriot, *Slavery in Zion*, 6–31, 38; Tonya S. Reiter, "Redd Slave Histories: Family, Race, and Sex in Pioneer Utah," *Utah Historical Quarterly* 85, no. 2 (Spring 2017): 108–26.

7. "'Aunt Jane' Laid to Rest," *Deseret Evening News*, April 21, 1908. For James, see Quincy D. Newell, *Your Sister in the Gospel: The Life of Jane Manning James—A Nineteenth Century Black Mormon* (New York: Oxford University Press, 2019); Quincy D. Newell, "The Autobiography and Interview of Jane Elizabeth Manning James," *Journal of Africana Religions* 1, no. 2 (2013): 251–91; Henry J. Wolfinger, "A Test of Faith: Jane Elizabeth James and the Origins of the Utah Black Community," in *American West Center Occasional Papers*, ed. Clark S. Knowlton (Salt Lake City: University of Utah Press, 1975), 126–72; Mueller, *Race and the Making of the Mormon People*, 133–52.

8. Jane Manning James, "Autobiography" (ca. 1902), folio 1 recto, MS 4425, 149, CHL. See also W. Paul Reeve, "'I Dug the Graves': Isaac Lewis Manning, Joseph Smith, and Racial Connections in the Two Latter-day Saint Traditions," *Journal of Mormon History* 47, no. 1 (January 2021): 29–67; Julie E. Hughes, "Respecting the Manning Family: Jane Manning James and Her Family in Wilton, Connecticut," *Journal of Mormon History* 49, no. 1 (January 2023): 69–91.

9. Newell, *Your Sister in the Gospel*, 34–35; Benjamin E. Park, *Kingdom of Nauvoo: The Rise and Fall of a Religious Empire on the American Frontier* (New York: Liveright, 2020), 141.

NOTES

331

10. "Joseph Smith—History," ch. 1, https://www.churchofjesuschrist.org/study/scriptures/pgp/js-h/1?lang=eng. Smith produced a number of accounts of his divine visitation. See Steven C. Harper, *First Vision: Memory and Mormon Origins* (New York: Oxford University Press, 2019).

11. The best account of Smith's life is Richard L. Bushman, *Joseph Smith: Rough Stone Rolling* (New York: Alfred A. Knopf, 2005). For controversial depictions of the Mormon prophet, see Fawn N. Brodie, *No Man Knows My History: The Life of Joseph Smith*, 2nd ed., revised and enlarged (New York: Alfred A. Knopf, 1977); Dan Vogel, *Joseph Smith: The Making of a Prophet* (Salt Lake City: Signature Books, 2004). For Smith's translations, see Michael Hubbard MacKay, Mark Ashurst-McGee, and Brian M. Hauglid, eds., *Producing Ancient Scripture: Joseph Smith's Translation Projects in the Development of Mormon Christianity* (Salt Lake City: University of Utah Press, 2020).

12. Newell, *Your Sister in the Gospel*, 38–46; Park, *Kingdom of Nauvoo*, 141–43; Hughes, "Respecting the Manning Family," 90–91.

13. James, "Autobiography," 145.

14. Jonathan A. Stapley, *The Power of Godliness: Mormon Liturgy and Cosmology* (New York: Oxford University Press, 2018), ch. 2.

15. George Q. Cannon, journal, August 22, 1895, Journal of George Q. Cannon, Church Historian's Press, https://www.churchhistorianspress.org/george-q-cannon/1890s/1895/08-1895?lang=eng; Newell, *Your Sister in the Gospel*, 105–6, 112–16; Mueller, *Race and the Making of the Mormon People*, 149–52; Harris and Bringhurst, *Mormon Church and Blacks*, 50–55; Tonya S. Reiter, "Black Saviors on Mount Zion: Proxy Baptisms and Latter-day Saints of African Descent," *Journal of Mormon History* 43, no. 4 (October 2017): 100–123.

16. For James's awareness on the limitations the curse placed on her, see her letter to church president John Taylor, December 27, 1884, in Wolfinger, "A Test of Faith," 148. For patriarchal blessings in general, see Irene M. Bates and E. Gary Smith, *Lost Legacy: The Mormon Office of Presiding Patriarch*, 2nd ed. (Urbana: University of Illinois Press, 2018).

17. Patriarchal Blessing of Jane Manning James by Hyrum Smith, May 11, 1844, CHL.

18. Joseph Smith, journal, January 2, 1843, in *The Joseph Smith Papers: Journals*, vol. 2: *December 1841–April 1843*, ed. Andrew H. Hedges, Alex D. Smith, and Richard Lloyd Anderson (Salt Lake City: Church Historian's Press, 2011), 212.

19. "Remarks by President Brigham Young, Delivered in the Tabernacle Great Salt Lake City," October 9, 1859, *Journal of Discourses*, 7:290–91; Young, *Journal of Discourses*, 10:10; "Messages of Governor Brigham Young," *Latter-day Saints Millennial Star* 15, no. 27 (July 2, 1853): 422. For Smith's and Young's views on slavery, see Kevin Waite, *West of Slavery: The Southern Dream of a Transcontinental Empire* (Chapel Hill: University of North Carolina Press, 2021), 125–34.

20. Joseph Smith, journal, January 25, 1842, in Hedges, Smith, and Anderson, *The Joseph Smith Papers*, 2:30.

NOTES

21. "History, 1838–1856, vol. D-1 [August 1, 1842–July 1, 1843]," 1434, Joseph Smith Papers, https://www.josephsmithpapers.org/paper-summary/history-1838-1856-volume-d-1-1-august-1842-1-july-1843/77. As mayor of Nauvoo, Smith also fined two Black men for attempting to marry White women. See Joseph Smith, journal, February 8, 1844, in *The Joseph Smith Papers: Journals*, vol. 3: *May 1843–June 1844*, ed. Andrew H. Hedges, Alex D. Smith, and Brent M. Rogers (Salt Lake City: Church Historian's Press, 2015), 175.

22. Woodruff, journal, February 5, 1852, Wilford Woodruff Journals and Papers, CHL, https://catalog.churchofjesuschrist.org/assets/a5c827b5-938d-4a08-b80e-71570704e323/0/361. George D. Watt, Young's clerk, omitted the "one-drop" reference in his transcription of the address but recorded Young as saying that men with "African blood . . . cannot hold one jot nor tittle of priesthood." Young's address to the Utah Territorial Legislature, February 5, 1852, Box 1, Folder 3, GDW (transcription by LaJean Carruth). Young also applied the one-drop rule to White people, or "Ephraimites"—meaning that they couldn't have any "negro blood" to be considered "pure whites." Council of Twelve Minutes, January 2, 1902, in *Minutes of the Quorum of the Twelve and First Presidency, 1900–1909*, 4 vols. (Salt Lake City: Smith-Pettit Foundation, 2010), 3:181.

23. Woodruff, journal, February 5, 1852. Watt transcribed Young's speech differently, stating that if Black and White people married, the couple and their "children would have to atone for the sin" by having their heads cut off. See Watt's transcription of Young's address to the Utah Territorial Legislature, February 5, 1852. For Young and McCary, see Connell O'Donovan, "Brigham Young, African Americans, and Plural Marriage: Schism and the Beginnings of Black Priesthood and Temple Denial," in *The Persistence of Polygamy: From Joseph Smith's Martyrdom to the First Manifesto, 1844–1890*, ed. Newell G. Bringhurst and Craig L. Foster (Independence, MO: John Whitmer Books, 2013), 48–86; Reeve, *Religion of a Different Color*, 107, 111. For polygamy, see Laurel Thatcher Ulrich, *A House Full of Females: Plural Marriage and Women's Rights in Early Mormonism, 1835–1870* (New York: Alfred A. Knopf, 2017).

24. For the 1888 law banning interracial marriage, see Chapter XLV, "Marriage: An Act Regulating Marriage," Sec. 2, in *Laws of the Territory of Utah, Passed at the Twenty-Eighth Session of the Legislative Assembly* (Salt Lake City: Tribune Printing and Publishing Co., 1888), 88; for the 1939 law, see "An Act Amending Section 40-1-2, Revised Statutes of Utah 1933, Relating to Prohibited and Void Marriages," in *Laws of Utah*, ch. 50, sec. 1 (Salt Lake City: Lorraine Press, 1939), 66. Turner, *Brigham Young*, 226; Peggy Pascoe, *What Comes Naturally: Miscegenation Law and the Making of Race in America* (New York: Oxford University Press, 2009), 85, 118–19, 134–50; Patrick Q. Mason, "The Prohibition of Interracial Marriage in Utah, 1888–1963," *Utah Historical Quarterly* 76, no. 2 (Spring 2008): 108–31.

NOTES

333

25. Ian Haney López, *White by Law: The Legal Construction of Race*, revised and expanded (New York: New York University Press, 2006), 82–83; Ariela J. Gross, *What Blood Won't Tell: A History of Race on Trial in America* (Cambridge, MA: Harvard University Press, 2008), 43–44, 100–110.

26. Robert Wald Sussman, *The Myth of Race: The Troubling Persistence of an Unscientific Idea* (Cambridge, MA: Harvard University Press, 2014), ch. 1; Franciso Bethencourt, *Racisms: From the Crusades to the Twentieth Century* (Princeton: Princeton University Press, 2013), 247–51; Matthew Desmond and Mustafa Emirbayer, *Race in America*, 2nd ed. (New York: W. W. Norton, 2020), 16–17. Scientists claim that if Americans trace their genealogy back at least two hundred years they will find 512 direct ancestors with at least one Black ancestor and one Native American. Peter Irons, *White Men's Laws: The Roots of Systemic Racism* (New York: Oxford University Press, 2022), xii; Daniel J. Fairbanks, *Everyone Is African: How Science Explodes the Myth of Race* (New York: Prometheus, 2015).

27. Susa Young Gates, *Surname Book and Racial History* (Salt Lake City: Genealogical Society of Utah, 1918); see also Francesca Morgan, *A Nation of Descendants: Politics and the Practice of Genealogy in U.S. History* (Chapel Hill: University of North Carolina Press, 2021), 64. The Relief Society was founded in Nauvoo, Illinois, in 1842 and is the oldest women's organization in the LDS church. It functions as an educational and philanthropic organization and operates under the direction of the male-oriented priesthood. Colleen McDannell, *Sister Saints: Mormon Women since the End of Polygamy* (New York: Oxford University Press, 2019), ch. 1.

28. Gates, *Surname Book and Racial History*, 3, 21, 38, 287; Sussman, *The Myth of Race*, ch. 5.

29. Lyman, Minutes of the General Board of the Relief Society, 1918, 9:69, CHL; Gates, *Surname Book and Racial History*, iv; James B. Allen, Jessie L. Embry, and Kahlile B. Mehr, *Hearts Turned to the Fathers: A History of the Genealogical Society of Utah, 1894–1994* (Provo, UT: BYU Studies, 1995), 69–70.

30. A. B. Wilkinson, *Blurring the Lines of Race and Freedom: Mulattoes and Mixed Bloods in English Colonial America* (Chapel Hill: University of North Carolina Press, 2020); Colin G. Calloway, *New Worlds for All: Indians, Europeans, and the Remaking of Early America*, 2nd ed. (Baltimore: Johns Hopkins University Press, 2013); Martha Menchaca, *Recovering History, Constructing Race: The Indian, Black, and White Roots of Mexican Americans* (Austin: University of Texas Press, 2002). Bethencourt, *Racisms*, provides a trenchant account of how race theorists in Africa, Asia, Europe, and the Americas struggled to define race during centuries of European expansion.

31. Sara Abel, *Permanent Markers: Race, Ancestry, and the Body after the Genome* (Chapel Hill: University of North Carolina Press, 2021); David Reich, *Who We Are and How We Got Here: Ancient DNA and the New Science of the Human Past* (New York: Pantheon Books, 2018); Jennifer Raff, *Origin: A Genetic History of the Americas* (New York: Twelve, 2022).

NOTES

32. Council of the Twelve Minutes, June 4, 1879, in *Minutes of the Quorum of the Twelve and First Presidency, 1835–1893*, 1:321; L. John Nuttall journal, May 31, 1879, 1:290–93, HBLL. For Abel, see Newell G. Bringhurst, "Elijah Abel and the Changing Status of Blacks within Mormonism," *Dialogue: A Journal of Mormon Thought* 12, no. 2 (Summer 1979), 23–36; Russell W. Stevenson, "'A Negro Preacher': The Worlds of Elijah Ables," *Journal of Mormon History* 39, no. 2 (Spring 2013): 165–254. Joel Williamson, *New People: Miscegenation and Mulattoes in the United States* (New York: Free Press, 1980), 24.

33. Joseph F. Smith, notes on Elijah Abel, ca. 1879, JOFS. For Abel's ordination and advance in church leadership, see Kirtland elders' certificates, 1836–1838, March 31, 1836, CR 100 401, 61, CHL; and his name listed among ministers of the gospel in Kirtland, Ohio, June 3, 1836, *Latter Day Saints' Messenger and Advocate* 2, no. 9 (June 1836): 335.

34. Smith, quoted in Council of the Twelve Minutes, August 26, 1908, in *Minutes of the Quorum of the Twelve and First Presidency, 1900–1909*, 3:420.

35. Council of the Twelve Minutes, June 4, 1879, in *Minutes of the Quorum of the Twelve and First Presidency, 1835–1893*, 1:321; Patriarchal Blessing of Elijah Abel by Joseph Smith Sr., ca. 1836, CHL.

36. Council of the Twelve Minutes, August 26, 1908, in *Minutes of the Quorum of the Twelve and First Presidency, 1900–1909*, 3:420; George F. Richards, diary, August 26, 1908, in *Minutes of the Quorum of the Twelve and First Presidency, 1900–1909*, 3:420. See also Harris and Bringhurst, *Mormon Church and Blacks*, 45–48.

37. Reeve, *Religion of a Different Color*, ch. 7, provides additional cases of light-skinned Latter-day Saints of African lineage who appeared White. See also Reeve's "Centuries of Black Mormons" for additional examples of light-skinned Latter-day Saints who enjoyed limited privileges in the church (https://exhibits.lib.utah.edu/s/century-of-black-mormons/page/welcome).

38. Hokulani K. Aikau, *A Chosen People, A Promised Land: Mormonism and Race in Hawaii* (Minneapolis: University of Minnesota Press, 2012); R. Lanier Britsch, "Mormons in the Pacific," in *The Oxford Handbook of Mormonism*, ed. Terryl L. Givens and Philip L. Barlow (New York: Oxford University Press, 2015), ch. 34; Marjorie Newton, *Mormon and Maori* (Salt Lake City: Greg Kofford Books, 2014); R. Robert Parsons, "Hagoth and the Polynesians," in *The Book of Mormon: Alma, the Testimony of the Word*, ed. Monte S. Nyman and Charles D. Tate Jr. (Provo, UT: Religious Studies Center, Brigham Young University, 1992), ch. 15.

39. Genesis 4:2–15; 9:22–27.

40. Stephen R. Haynes, *Noah's Curse: The Biblical Justification of American Slavery* (New York: Oxford University Press, 2002); David M. Goldenberg, *The Curse of Ham: Race and Slavery in Early Judaism, Christianity, and Islam* (Princeton: Princeton University Press, 2003).

41. Much scholarship has been devoted to the origins, historicity, and cultural influence of the Book of Mormon. See Terryl L. Givens, *By the Hand of Mormon: The American Scripture That Launched a New World Religion* (New York: Oxford

NOTES

335

University Press, 2002); Elizabeth Fenton and Jared Hickman, eds., *Americanist Approaches to the Book of Mormon* (New York: Oxford University Press, 2019); William L. Davis, *Visions in a Seer Stone: Joseph Smith and the Making of the Book of Mormon* (Chapel Hill: University of North Carolina Press, 2020).

42. 2 Nephi, 5:21.

43. Kathryn Gin Lum, *Heathen: Religion and Race in American History* (Cambridge, MA: Harvard University Press, 2022), 15–16; Haynes, *Noah's Curse*, 90–93.

44. 3 Nephi, 2:15.

45. 2 Nephi, 26:33.

46. Book of Moses, 5:23–26, 6:52–54, 7:22.

47. Abraham, 1:21–27. See also Terryl Givens, with Brian M. Hauglid, *The Pearl of Greatest Price: Mormonism's Most Controversial Scripture* (New York: Oxford University Press, 2019).

48. Orson Hyde, *Speech of Elder Orson Hyde Delivered before the High Priests Quorum in Nauvoo, April 27, 1845* . . . (Liverpool: James and Woodburn, 1845), 30; Orson Pratt, *The Seer* 1 (April 1853): 54–56. Neither Hyde's nor Pratt's teachings gained traction because church president Brigham Young rejected their ideas. See Wilford Woodruff journal, December 22–24, 1869, Wilford Woodruff Journals and Papers, https://catalog.churchofjesuschrist.org/assets?id=0c76d480-00aa-4210-9334-12a578908f1f&crate=0&index=220; Orson Hyde, speech to the Council of Fifty, March 22, 1845, in *The Joseph Smith Papers: Administrative Records, Council of Fifty Minutes, March 1844–January 1846*, ed. Matthew J. Grow, Ronald K. Esplin, Mark Ashurst-McGee, Gerrit J. Dirkmaat, and Jeffrey D. Mahas (Salt Lake City: Church Historian's Press, 2016), 360.

49. Armand L. Mauss, *All Abraham's Children: Changing Mormon Conceptions of Race and Lineage* (Urbana: University of Illinois Press, 2003), 238, called it "The Dubious Canonical Basis for Racial Restrictions." Mormon apologist Hugh Nibley also questioned the validity of the Pearl of Great Price as a proof text for the ban. Nibley, *Abraham in Egypt*, 2nd ed. (Salt Lake City: Deseret Book, 1981), 427–28.

50. Abraham, 1: 26–27, 3:22–28; B. H. Roberts, "To the Youth of Israel," *The Contributor* 6, no. 8 (1885): 297.

51. Woodruff sermon, "Eternal Variety of God's Creations," July 14, 1889, in *The Deseret Weekly* 39 (July 20, 1889): 114. For Roberts's and Woodruff's views in LDS periodicals, see George Q. Cannon, "Editorial Thoughts," *Juvenile Instructor* 26, no. 20 (October 15, 1891): 635–36; "Are Negroes Children of Adam?," *Latter-day Saints' Millennial Star* 65, no. 49 December 3, 1903, 776–78; "Negro and the Priesthood," *Liahona: The Elder's Journal* 5, no. 43 (April 11, 1908): 1162–67; First Presidency to Ben E. Rich (mission president), May 1, 1912, in *Minutes of the Quorum of the Twelve and First Presidency, 1910–1951*, 4:122–24.

52. Boyd Jay Petersen, "'One Soul Shall Not Be Lost': The War in Heaven in Mormon Thought," *Journal of Mormon History* 38, no. 1 (Winter 2012): 1–50; Charles R. Harrell, *This Is My Doctrine: The Development of Mormon Theology* (Salt Lake City: Greg Kofford Books, 2011), ch. 11.

53. First Presidency Minutes, March 11, 1900, in *Minutes of the Quorum of the Twelve and First Presidency, 1900–1909*, 3:35.

54. First Presidency to Milton H. Knudson, January 13, 1912, in *Minutes of the Quorum of the Twelve and First Presidency, 1910–1951*, 4:107.

55. Ibid.

56. Orson F. Whitney, "Saturday Night Thoughts" (1918–1919), reprinted in *Cowley and Whitney on Doctrine*, compiled by Forace Green (Salt Lake City: Bookcraft, 1963), 224–25; Melvin J. Ballard, "Three Degrees of Glory" (1922), 22, CHL.

57. Reid L. Neilson and Scott D. Marianno, "True and Faithful: Joseph Fielding Smith as Mormon Historian and Theologian," *BYU Studies Quarterly* 57, no. 1 (Winter 2018): 7–64.

58. Lowell L. Bennion, memoir, unpublished, 1976, 73, Box 8, Folder 4, LLB. For Smith's gruff side, see Ray R. Canning, oral history interview with Everett L. Cooley, November 16, 1983, 15–16, Box 4, Folder 8, ECOH; Reid L. Neilson and Scott D. Marianno, *Restless Pilgrim: Andrew Jenson's Quest for Latter-day Saint History* (Urbana: University of Illinois Press, 2022), 215–16. For Smith clashing with apostles, see Richard Sherlock and Jeffrey E. Keller, "The B. H. Roberts, Joseph Fielding Smith, and James E. Talmage Affair," in *The Search for Harmony: Essays on Science and Mormonism*, ed. Gene A. Sessions and Craig J. Oberg (Salt Lake City: Signature Books, 1993), ch. 6; Matthew Bowman, *The Mormon People: The Making of an American Faith* (New York: Random House, 2012), 179–80; Philip L. Barlow, *Mormons and the Bible: The Place of Latter-day Saints in American Religion*, updated ed. (New York: Oxford University Press, 2013), 136–41, 156–57, 170.

59. Grant, diary, December 31, 1938, HBJ; Clark, diary, June 1, 1948, Box 15, Folder 1, JRC.

60. Blessing of Joseph Fielding Smith by Patriarch Joseph D. Smith of Fillmore, Utah, May 11, 1913, Box 3, Folder 9, IB. Lloyd Ririe, a close friend of Joseph Fielding Smith's, told David John Buerger and Gary Bergera that Smith told him that his father said he was "to preserve the doctrines of the church." In Joseph Fielding Smith, "The Conservative Element," July 23, 1978, MLH.

61. Joseph Fielding Smith, *Doctrines of Salvation*, 3 vols., compiled by Bruce R. McConkie (Salt Lake City: Deseret Book, 1954–56); Joseph Fielding Smith, *Answers to Gospel Questions*, 5 vols. (Salt Lake City: Deseret Book, 1957–66).

62. Smith to Alfred M. Nelson, January 31, 1907, MS 14591, reel 1, CHL.

63. Joseph Fielding Smith, "The Negro and the Priesthood," *Improvement Era* 27, no. 6 (April 1924): 564–65.

64. Joseph Fielding Smith, *The Way to Perfection: Short Discourses on Gospel Themes*, 5th ed. (1931; reprint, Salt Lake City: Genealogical Society of Utah, 1945).

NOTES

337

65. Smith, *Way to Perfection*, 1–2; *Topical Outlines to the Way to Perfection* (Salt Lake City: Genealogical Society of Utah, 1936), 1.

66. Smith, *The Way to Perfection*, chs. 18–20.

67. This was a persistent theme in early Mormon discourse. See Reeve, *Religion of a Different Color*; Mueller, *Race and the Making of the Mormon People*; Joseph R. Stuart, "'A More Powerful Effect upon the Body': Early Mormonism's Theory of Racial Redemption and American Religious Theories of Race," *Church History: Studies in Christianity and Culture* 87, no. 3 (Fall 2018): 768–96.

68. Dozens of Latter-day Saints wrote Smith inquiring about Mormon racial teachings, clearly concerned about where Black people fit into the church's conception of soteriology. Some of these letters would be published, with Smith's replies, in Smith, *Answers to Gospel Questions*. Others can be found in Box 23, Folder 8, Box 27, Folder 3, Box 28, Folder 1, Box 38, Folders 5–9, JFS.

69. Smith, *Way to Perfection*, 43, 48, 101, 108–9.

70. Smith to Sperry, December 26, 1951, Box 3, Folder 3, WEB.

71. Smith, *Way to Perfection*, 48, 107–11. For Smith's awareness of Elijah Abel's priesthood ordination, see his letters to Eulis E. Hubbs, March 5, 1958, Box 9, Folder 7, JFS; Florence S. Preece, January 18, 1955, Box 24, Folder 28, SGE.

72. Smith, *Way to Perfection*, 107, 111. Smith wrote to J. Reuben Clark, April 3, 1939, Box 17, Folder 7, JFS: "In regard to the Negro, the doctrine of the Church is that they may be baptized and therefore enter the Celestial Kingdom, but not in exaltation."

73. Smith, *Way to Perfection*, 138–39; Smith, *Answers to Gospel Questions*, 2:54–55. For British Israelism ideas in church literature, see George S. Reynolds, *Are We of Israel?* (Salt Lake City: George Q. Cannon and Sons, 1895); Archibald F. Bennett, "The Children of Ephraim," *Utah Genealogical and Historical Magazine* 21 (January 1930): 67–85; James H. Anderson, *God's Covenant Race* (Salt Lake City: Deseret News Press, 1946).

74. For two seminal studies on this topic, see Mauss, *All Abraham's Children*, 29–31; Arnold H. Green, "Gathering and Election: Israelite Descent and Universalism in Mormon Discourse," *Journal of Mormon History* 25, no. 1 (Spring 1999): 195–228. See also Bethencourt, *Racisms*, 279–83.

75. Smith, *Way to Perfection*, 138; Reynolds, *Are We of Israel?*, 37, 55.

76. Christine Rosen, *Preaching Eugenics: American Religious Leaders and the American Eugenics Movement* (New York: Oxford University Press, 2005); Kelly J. Baker, *Gospel According to the Klan: The KKK's Appeal to Protestant America, 1915–1930* (Lawrence: University Press of Kansas, 2011).

77. Henry Louis Gates, *Stony the Road: Reconstruction, White Supremacy, and the Rise of Jim Crow* (New York: Penguin, 2019); Leon F. Litwack, *Trouble in Mind: Black Southerners in the Age of Jim Crow* (New York: Alfred A. Knopf, 1998); Donald Yacovone, *Teaching White Supremacy: America's Democratic Ordeal and the Forging of Our National Identity* (New York: Pantheon Books, 2022); James Q. Whitman, *Hitler's American Model: The United States and the Making of Nazi*

Race Law (Princeton: Princeton University Press, 2017). For popular histories, see Madison Grant, *The Passing of the Great Race* (New York: Charles Scribner's and Sons, 1916); Theodore Lothrop Stoddard, *The Rising Tide of Color against White World Supremacy* (New York: Charles Scribner's Sons, 1920).

78. Gates, *Stony the Road*, ch. 3; Karen L. Cox, *Dreaming of Dixie: How the South Was Created in American Popular Culture* (Chapel Hill: University of North Carolina Press, 2011), 38–43, 65–66; Eric Foner, *Forever Free: The Story of Emancipation and Reconstruction* (New York: Alfred A. Knopf, 2005), 220–22; M. M. Manring, *Slave in a Box: The Strange Career of Aunt Jemima* (Charlottesville: University of Virginia Press, 1998), ch. 3; George Makari, *Of Fear and Strangers: A History of Xenophobia* (New York: W. W. Norton, 2021), 156–61.

79. Howard R. Driggs, "Stories: True and False," *Improvement Era* 50, no. 12 (December 1915): 804; advertisement for "Little Black Sambo," *Improvement Era* 51, no. 12 (December 1948): 827; Howard R. Driggs, "The Immoral Story," *Improvement Era* 51, no. 11 (November 1916): 740; "The Funny Bone," *The Instructor* 69, no. 7 (July 1934): 340; "Uncle Remus," *Millennial Star* 83, no. 22 (June 2, 1921): 349–52; "The Funny Bone," *The Instructor* 53, no. 7 (July 1918): 392. For minstrel show advertisements, see "Three Nigger Minstrels from the Portsmouth (England) MIA Roadshow," *Millennial Star* 125, no. 10 (October 1963): 292; Norah Stephenson, "Leeds (England) District," *Millennial Star* 112, no. 10 (October 1950): 311; Earl J. Glade, "Student Progress—The Teacher's Reward," *The Instructor: Deseret Sunday School Union* 95, no. 2 (February 1960): 67; "North British Mission Holiday Festivities," *Millennial Star* 130, no. 2 (February 1968): 11; B. Y. Harbertson, "Achievement Standards Set by the 250th Quorum of Seventy," *Improvement Era* 43, no. 1 (January 1940): 39.

80. E.T.B., "Voices in America," *Improvement Era* 34, no. 9 (July 1931): 508; Preston W. Pond, "Boy Scout Dramas," *Improvement Era* 33, no. 10 (August 1930): 693; "Confidence," *The Contributor* 1, no. 3 (December 1879): 50; "The End of the Rainbow," *Improvement Era* 13, no. 8 (June 1910): 695; "The Funny Bone," *Juvenile Instructor* 59, no. 11 (November 1924): 626; G. W. Forsberg (president of the LDS Swedish Mission), "Youthful in Spirit," *Millennial Star* 94, no. 37 (September 15, 1932): 597.

81. Frank Steele, "Little Nigger Baby," *Juvenile Instructor* 55, no. 1 (January 1920): 44.

82. *Topical Outlines to the Way to Perfection*, 14.

83. Ibid., 15.

84. "Cain and His Posterity, Lesson 9, March 1, 1942, Gospel Doctrine," in "Gospel Doctrine Lesson," *The Instructor* 77, no. 1 (January 1942): 19–21. See also Smith, "For Those of Our Own Lineage," lesson 45, *in Birthright Blessings: Genealogical Training Class, Sunday School Lessons* (Salt Lake City: Deseret News Sunday Union Board, 1942), 135–39.

85. Smith recommended *The Way to Perfection* to Latter-day Saints. See his letters to J. Reuben Clark, April 3, 1939, Box 17, Folder 7, JFS; to Ida E. Holmes, February 9, 1949, Box 27, Folder 3, JFS; to Eulis E. Hubbs, March 5, 1958, Box 9, Folder 7, JFS; to Sidney B. Sperry, December 26, 1951, Box 3, Folder 3, WEB. See also Smith, *Answers to Gospel Questions*, 2:188. For Smith's colleagues

NOTES

339

recommending the book, see George Albert Smith, Box 78, Folder 7, GAS; Spencer W. Kimball, Box 64, Folder 5, SWK; J. Reuben Clark, "Negro and the Church" folder, Box 210, JRC; Boyd K. Packer, "The Curse upon Cain and Descendants," January 3, 1951, Box 63, Folder 11, LJA; Joseph F. Merrill to J. W. Monroe, January 26, 1951, Box 20, Folder 2, JFM.

86. For the publishing history of *The Way to Perfection*, see Stirling Adams's video, "Race, Lineage and the 1920s and 1940s Genealogical Society of Utah," *Dialogue: A Journal of Mormon Thought*, March 27, 2019, https://www.dialogue journal.com/2019/03/race-lineage-and-the-1920s-1940s-genealogical-soci ety-of-utah/.

87. Tope Folarin, *A Particular Kind of Black Man* (New York: Simon and Schuster, 2019), 24.

88. Lowell L. Bennion, oral history interview with Maureen Ursenbach Beecher, February 16, 1985, 84, JMOH; Bertrand F. Harrison, oral history interview with Everett L. Cooley, November 29, 1985, 11, Box 13, Folder 6, ECOH; Joseph Fielding Smith Jr. and John J. Stewart, *The Life of Joseph Fielding Smith: Tenth President of the Church of Jesus Christ of Latter-day Saints* (Salt Lake City: Deseret Book, 1972), 210–11.

89. John A. Widtsoe, notes on "The Negro," ca. 1941, Box 227, Folder 5, JAW.

90. John A. Widtsoe to S. Norman Lee, October 9, 1947, JAWL; Grant, diary, October 20, 1925, HJG. John A. Widtsoe, ed., *Discourses of Brigham Young* (Salt Lake City: Deseret Book, 1925).

91. Widtsoe, quoted in Council of Twelve Minutes, August 28, 1947, in *Minutes of the Quorum of the Twelve and First Presidency, 1910–1951*, 4:442.

92. John A. Widtsoe, "Were Negroes Neutrals in Heaven?," *Improvement Era* 47, no. 6 (June 1944): 385 (italics added).

93. John A. Widtsoe, *Gospel Interpretations: More Evidences and Reconciliations* (Salt Lake City: Bookcraft, 1947), 217, 235; Brendan Simms, *Hitler: A Global Biography* (New York: Basic Books, 2019), 91–92, 98–100.

94. George F. Richards, *Conference Report*, April 1939, 57–59; Widtsoe to Lee, October 9, 1947; Richards, journal, April 7, 1939, GFR.

95. Joseph Anderson, *Prophets I Have Known* (Salt Lake City: Deseret Book, 1973), 122. Anderson was McKay's secretary.

96. The best biography of McKay is Gregory A. Prince and William Robert Wright, *David O. McKay and the Rise of Modern Mormonism* (Salt Lake City: University of Utah Press, 2005).

97. McKay, transcript of a telephone conversation with Marion G. Romney, June 13, 1957, Box 39, Folder 3, DOM; see also Lowell L. Bennion, oral history interview with Maureen Ursenbach Beecher, March 9, 1985, JMOH.

98. Edward R. McKay to Sterling M. McMurrin, September 19, 1968, Box 291, Folder 11, SMM; L. Jackson Newell, ed., *Matters of Conscience: Conservations with Sterling M. McMurrin on Philosophy, Education, and Religion* (Salt Lake City: Signature Books, 1996), 199–200. McKay's friends noted his independent streak. Bennion, memoir, 62.

340   NOTES

99. "Minutes of Special Meeting by President McKay," McKay, diary, January 17, 1954, Box 32, Folder 3, DOM.

100. McKay to Bennion, November 3, 1947, Box 20, Folder 2, LLB. Bennion thanked McKay years later for writing the letter. Bennion to McKay, December 1, 1952, Box 20, Folder 2, LLB.

101. McKay to Bennion, November 3, 1947.

102. Much of this section derives from Lowry Nelson's autobiography *In the Direction of His Dreams* (New York: Philosophical Library, 1985).

103. Ibid., 334.

104. Meeks to Nelson, June 20, 1947, Box 20, Folder 1, LN. Meeks made a detailed report of the racial makeup of Cuba, which he sent to the First Presidency. The letter and the report can be found in "Report of Visit to Cuba," July 23, 1947, Box 2, Folder 10, HM.

105. Nelson to Smith, June 26, 1947, Box 20, Folder 1, LN. For Cuba's interracial population, see Ada Ferrer, *Cuba: An American History* (New York: Scribner, 2021), 69. For Cuba's long history of slavery, see David Brion Davis, *Inhuman Bondage: The Rise and Fall of Slavery in the New World* (New York: Oxford University Press, 2006).

106. One entry from Smith's diary reads, "My nerves are nearly gone but [I] am holding on the best I know how." George Albert Smith, diary, January 2, 1933, CHL. Smith suffered from the nerve condition neurasthenia. Francis M. Gibbons, *George Albert Smith: Kind and Caring Christian, Prophet of God* (Salt Lake City: Deseret Book, 1990), 264.

107. For Smith's counselors running the church during most of his presidency, see D. Michael Quinn, *Elder Statesman: A Biography of J. Reuben Clark* (Salt Lake: Signature Books, 2002); Prince and Wright, *David O. McKay*.

108. First Presidency to Nelson July 17, 1947, Box 20, Folder 1, LN.

109. Nelson to the First Presidency, October 8, 1947, Box 20, Folder 1, LN.

110. First Presidency to Nelson, November 12, 1947, Box 20, Folder 1, LN.

111. First Presidency statement, August 17, 1949, CHL; also in Lester E. Bush and Armand L. Mauss, eds., *Neither White nor Black: Mormon Scholars Confront the Race Issue in a Universal Church* (Midvale, UT: Signature Books, 1984), 221 (appendix). Another published statement, mistakenly dated 1951, is in John J. Stewart, *Mormonism and the Negro* (Orem, UT: Community Press, 1960), 16–17.

112. First Presidency statement of August 17, 1949, in Bush and Mauss, *Neither White nor Black*, 221.

113. Romney, *Conference Report*, April 1945, 90.

114. Several BYU faculty, for example, questioned the ban, and BYU president Ernest L. Wilkinson wanted his faculty to have copies of the 1949 statement. Wilkinson, memo to BYU religion professor Sidney B. Sperry, Box 2, Folder 9, SBS; see also Box 58, Folder 4, HN.

115. Widtsoe First Presidency statement, August 17, 1949: "Church Doctrine regarding Negroes," Box 6, Folder 5, JAWP; see also Box 64, Folder 6, SWK.

NOTES   341

CHAPTER 2

1. Lloyd to Smith, July 2, 1948, Box 49, Folder 19, RDP.
2. Anderson to Lloyd, July 6, 1948, Box 49, Folder 19, RDP.
3. Clark, diary, June 1, 1948, Box 15, Folder 1, JRC; McKay, diary, April 28, 1948, Box 26, Folder 1, DOM.
4. Allyson Hobbs, *A Chosen Exile: A History of Racial Passing in American Life* (Cambridge, MA: Harvard University Press, 2014); Gayle Wald, *Crossing the Line: Racial Passing in Twentieth-Century U.S. Literature and Culture* (Durham, NC: Duke University Press, 2000).
5. South African Mission History, ca. 1971, CHL. President Wright described his responsibilities as "great" and "frightening." South African Mission Minutes, 1853–1951, 14, CHL.
6. See Evan P. Wright, *A History of the South African Mission*, 3 vols. (Privately published, 1977–87), CHL.
7. Badger to First Presidency, August 17, 1908, in *Minutes of the Quorum of the Twelve and First Presidency, 1900–1909*, 4 vols. (Salt Lake City: Smith-Pettit Foundation, 2010), 3:420.
8. John Iliffe, *Africans: The History a Continent* (New York: Cambridge University Press, 1995), 279–84; John Reader, *Africa: A Biography of a Continent* (New York: Alfred A. Knopf, 1999), 490–91, 511–12.
9. Deborah Posel, "What's in the Name? Racial Categorisations under Apartheid and Their Afterlife," *Transformation: Critical Perspectives on South Africa* 47 (2001): 56; France Winddance Twine, *Racism in a Racial Democracy: The Maintenance of White Supremacy in Brazil* (New Brunswick, NJ: Rutgers University Press, 1997).
10. Wright, *A History of the South African Mission*, 3:419–20.
11. James B. Allen, Jessie L. Embry, and Kahlile B. Mehr, *Hearts Turned to the Fathers: A History of the Genealogical Society of Utah, 1894–1994* (Provo, UT: BYU Studies, 1995).
12. Elder Bruce R. Peterson, quoted in Wright, *A History of the South African Mission*, 3:281–82. President Wright provided missionaries with reference works to aid in tracing ancestry. See "Genealogical Meeting," December 26, 1952, in South African Mission Minutes, 8.
13. Wright to First Presidency, January 21, 1949, Box 64, Folder 6, SWK.
14. First Presidency to Wright, February 5, 1949, Box 64, Folder 6, SWK.
15. First Presidency to Wright, [March 1949], Box 64, Folder 6, SWK.
16. Wright to First Presidency, March 31, 1949, Box 64, Folder 6, SWK.
17. First Presidency to Wright, August 31, 1949, Box 64, Folder 6, SWK.
18. "Address Delivered by President Evan P. Wright at the Cape District Conference, Mowbray, C.P. South Africa," October 24, 1952, in Wright, *A History of the South African Mission*, 3:421–27; Wright to First Presidency, November 23, 1949, Box 64, Folder 6, SWK.
19. See Box 78, Folder 7, GAS.

NOTES

20. Council of Twelve, Minutes, October 29, 1936, in *Minutes of the Quorum of the Twelve and First Presidency*, 1910–1951, 4:364. Pea would later be re-ordained an elder during Spencer Kimball's tenure as church president. Kimball, diary, August 2, 1977, reel 39, SWK; D. Arthur Haycock, oral history interview with Brian D. Reeves, January 14, 1992, 29–31, JMOH.

21. Smith Jr., quoted in First Presidency Minutes, September 24, 1969, Box 70, Folder 6, DOM.

22. Alma, 37:4; Gregory A. Prince and William Robert Wright, *David O. McKay and the Rise of Modern Mormonism* (Salt Lake City: University of Utah Press, 2005), ch. 14; Francis M. Gibbons, *David O. McKay: Apostle to the World, Prophet of God* (Salt Lake City: Deseret Book, 1986), 234–35, 308–9, 327–28.

23. Prince and Wright, *David O. McKay*, 372; McKay, quoted in Aldren Whitman, "David McKay, Mormon President, Was Ardent Advocate of Universal Expansion," *New York Times*, January 19, 1970.

24. South African Mission Proselyting Plan, December 1951, compiled by Gilbert G. Tobler, Mowbray, C.P. South Africa, Discussion 13, 45–46, CHL.

25. Wright to the First Presidency, June 17, 1952, Box 64, Folder 6, SWK.

26. Ibid. Wright instructed his missionaries not to encourage South Africans to migrate to the United States. See mission meeting minutes, December 29, 1951, in South African Mission Minutes, 25.

27. Wright to the First Presidency, June 17, 1952.

28. T. Edgar Lyon, "Negro Problem," September 1, 1954, Box 26, Folder 1, TEL; also in Box 20, Folder 2, LLB.

29. Lyon recounted this story to church historian Leonard Arrington, in Arrington diary, July 17, 1962, Box 57, Folder 6, LJA.

30. Arrington diary, July 17, 1962.

31. Brooks to T. Edgar Lyon, February 20, 1962, Box 26, Folder 5, TEL. Brooks was an outspoken critic of the ban. Brooks to O. Boyd Mathias, May 27, 1957, Box 3, Folder 11, JB.

32. Lowell L. Bennion, "A Case Study," n.d., Box 20, Folder 2, LLB; Jeremy Talmage and Clinton D. Christensen, "Black, White, or Brown? Racial Perceptions and Priesthood Policy in Latin America," *Journal of Mormon History* 44, no. 1 (January 2018): 119–45.

33. McKay notes, June 13, 1957, Box 39, Folder 3, DOM.

34. First Presidency to Marion G. Romney, June 8, 1944, MGR. See also Robert Greenwell, "One Devout Mormon Family's Struggle with Racism," *Dialogue: A Journal of Mormon Thought* 51, no. 3 (Fall 2018): 155–80.

35. Bennion, "A Case Study"; McKay, diary, November 1, 1963, Box 55, Folder 3, DOM, in which he told a young man of suspected "negro lineage" to serve a church mission.

36. Lyon to Clinton R. Miller, January 19, 1955, Box 26, Folder 8, TEL.

37. For Moroni Abel and Elijah R. Abel, see "Century of Black Mormons," ed. W. Paul Reeve, http://centuryofblackmormons.org. The entire Abel family

NOTES 343

was listed as "mulattoe" in the Federal Census, June 1, 1860, MLH. Robert Abel, a descendent of Elijah Abel, informed the First Presidency "that Elijah Able's descendants have all had the Priesthood bestowed upon them." David O. McKay, diary, June 30, 1964, Box 56, Folder 6, DOM.

38. Darius Gray, oral history interview with Dennis and Elizabeth Haslam, December 4, 1971, 39, Box 1, Folder 7, AAOHU.

39. Council of the Twelve Minutes, June 4, 1879, August 26, 1908, in *Minutes of the Quorum of the Twelve and First Presidency*, 1:320–21, 3:420–21; George F. Richards, diary, August 26, 1908, in *Minutes of the Quorum of the Twelve and First Presidency*, 3:421–22; John Henry Smith, diary, August 26, 1908, in *Church, State and Politics: The Diaries of John Henry Smith*, ed. Jean Bickmore White (Salt Lake City: Signature Books, 1990), 608.

40. Council of the Twelve Minutes, January 25, 1940, Box 64, Folder 5, SWK; also in *Minutes of the Quorum of the Twelve and First Presidency*, 4:370.

41. Richards, diary, February 16, 1940, in *Minutes of the Quorum of the Twelve and First Presidency*, 4:370; Clark, diary, February 27, 1940, Box 11, Folder 1, JRC.

42. Clark, quoted in Council of the Twelve Minutes, January 25, 1940.

43. Council of the Twelve Minutes, October 9, 1947, in *Minutes of the Quorum of the Twelve and First Presidency*, 4: 443.

44. Iliffe, *Africans*, 125–26; Reader, *Africa*, 489–90.

45. J. Reuben Clark, memorandum, "The Afrikan Branches of the Church of Jesus Christ of Latter-day Saints" [1947], Box 207, JRC.

46. Council of the Twelve Minutes, October 9, 1947.

47. Clark, quoted in the Council of the Twelve Minutes, January 25, 1940.

48. Storrs to Lowell L. Bennion, December 29, 1957, Box 20, Folder 2, LLB. LDS missionaries in Brazil frequently commented in their diaries about the difficulty of discerning African ancestry. Reuben Ficklin diary, November 18 and December 11, 1955, April 23, 1956, and March 8, 1958, CHL; Harold Hillam diary, November 24, 1954, September 18, 1955, and October 14, 1956, HH.

49. Timmins, oral history interview with Gregory A. Prince, November 16, 2000, MLH. For Brazil's history of slavery and race mixing, see David Brion Davis, *Inhuman Bondage: The Rise and Fall of Slavery in the New World* (New York: Oxford University Press, 2006), ch. 5.

50. Mark L. Grover, "Religious Accommodation in the Land of Racial Democracy: Mormon Priesthood and Black Brazilians," *Dialogue: A Journal of Mormon Thought* 17, no. 3 (Fall 1984): 25–26.

51. First Presidency to Francis W. Brown, January 13, 1947, MLH; Rulon Stanley Howells, oral history interview with Gordon Irving, January 18, 1973, 62, JMOH.

52. Edward E. Telles, *Race in Another America: The Significance of Skin Color in Brazil* (Princeton: Princeton University Press, 2004), 38–39, 81. For the 1950 census, see https://www.researchgate.net/figure/Distribution-of-the-population-by-skin-colour-Brazil-1950-91_tbl1_51365772.

344 NOTES

53. McKay to Howells, June 29, 1935, Dorothy H. Ipsen Collection of Rulon S. Howell Missionary Papers, 1934–1949, CHL.

54. Howells, oral history interview with Irving, 63, 82.

55. Sorensen, oral history interview with Gordon Irving, 1973, 61, JMOH.

56. Grover, "Religious Accommodation," 32.

57. For Smith's encouragement of using patriarchs to determine lineage, see Digest of the minutes of the meeting of patriarchs of the church with the General Authorities, October 11, 1958, Box 64, Folder 4, SWK; see also Joseph Fielding Smith, *Answers to Gospel Questions*, 5 vols. (Salt Lake City: Deseret Book, 1957–66), 5:168.

58. William Grant Bangerter, *These Things I Know: The Autobiography of William Grant Bangerter* (Provo, UT: Privately published, 2013), 170; Howells, oral history interview with Irving, January 18, 1973, 62, 82.

59. Howells, oral history interview with Irving, 62; Elder Marvin, oral history interview with Mark L. Grover, April 28, 1988, Box 44, Folder 11, ALM.

60. "Lineage Lesson," Brazil North Mission, 1970, CHL.

61. "Lesson—9, Intermarriage between the Descendants of Cain and Israelites," 7–8, Priesthood Lineage, 1908–1969, Box 9, Folder 1, FLT.

62. First Presidency Minutes, July 7, 1962, Box 50, Folder 4, DOM; Matthew L. Harris and Newell G. Bringhurst, eds., *The Mormon Church and Blacks: A Documentary History* (Urbana: University of Illinois Press, 2015), 102–3; Grover, "Religious Accommodation," 28.

63. Bishop Melvin S. Droubay to Church Missionary Committee, April 27, 1969, Box 64, Folder 1, SWK; Len Hope Sr. and Mary Lee Pugh, membership records, n.d., CHL.

64. Richards and Clark to Smith, May 29, 1951, and Smith's response, June 8, 1951, Box 17, Folder 13, JFS. See also J. Reuben Clark diary, June 1, 1948, Box 15, Folder 1, JRC, in which he noted that Latter-day Saints submitted questions about LDS doctrine in "the question and answer column in the Church News," at which point they "were all submitted to Bro. Joseph Fielding Smith." For mission presidents asking the Brethren questions about race and priesthood ordination, see Spencer W. Kimball, diary, November 23, 1960, reel 23, SWK.

65. Ariel Smith Ballif, oral history interview with R. Lanier Britsch, July 27, 1973, 37, JMOH; Armand L. Mauss, "The Fading of the Pharaoh's Curse: The Decline and Fall of the Priesthood Ban against Blacks in the Mormon Church," *Dialogue: A Journal of Mormon Thought* 14, no. 3, (Fall 1981): 12; R. Lanier Britsch, *Unto the Islands of the Sea: A History of the Latter-day Saints in the Pacific* (Salt Lake City: Deseret Book, 1986), 502.

66. McKay, diary, October 11, 1956, Box 38, Folder 1, DOM; Smith to Richards and Clark, June 8, 1951; Britsch, *Unto the Islands of the Sea*, 502.

67. McKay, quoted in Bennion, "A Case Study."

NOTES

345

68. McKay, diary, February 17, 1955, Box 34, Folder 6, DOM; McKay report to the Council of the Twelve regarding his tour of the South Pacific Islands, February 24, 1955, scrapbook 142, Box 34, Folder 6, DOM. See also Ballif, oral history interview with Britsch, 37.

69. Mauss, "The Fading of the Pharaoh's Curse," 12; Marjorie Newton, *Southern Cross Saints: The Mormons in Australia* (Laie, HI: Institute for Polynesian Studies, 1991), 209–10; Brenton Griffin, "Racial Categories: Indigenous Australians and Mormonism, 1850s to the Present," *Dialogue: A Journal of Mormon Thought* 54, no. 2 (Summer 2021): 1–31.

70. First Presidency Minutes, February 12, 1969, Box 69, Folder 4, DOM; Prince and Wright, *David O. McKay*, 81–94; Russell W. Stevenson, *For the Cause of Righteousness: A Global History of Blacks and Mormonism, 1830–2013* (Salt Lake City: Greg Kofford Books, 2014), 89–91; Brown, oral history interview with Clinton D. Christensen, December 5, 2012, 2, JMOH; Bangerter, mission journal, October 25, 1960, WGB. For strictures to avoid teaching cursed lineages, see Heber J. Grant to L. H. Wilkin, January 28, 1928, in Lester E. Bush, ed., "Compilation on the Negro in Mormonism," 228–29 (1972), CHL; David O. McKay, diary, November 15, 1952, Box 30, Folder 6, DOM; Bruce R. McConkie, *Mormon Doctrine* (Salt Lake City: Bookcraft, 1958), 477.

71. Nelson, "The Last Judgment" (1978), Box 8, Folder 2, 24, LNC.

72. McMurrin to Nelson, July 28, 1972, Box 19, Folder 3, LN.

73. Juanita Brooks to Lowry Nelson, January 25, 1949, Box 20, Folder 4, LN; John C. Swensen to Lowry Nelson, December 12, 1947, Box 20, Folder 4, LN; William C. Carr to Lowry Nelson, March 26, 1948, Box 20, Folder 4, LN; Gustive Larson to Lowry Nelson, December 28, 1948, Box 11, Folder 16, GOL.

74. Nelson to Lester E. Bush, October 13, 1972, Box 3, Folder 29, LEB; Nelson to H. Grant Ivins, June 10, 1968, Box 2, Folder 25, HGI; Nelson to Leonard J. Arrington, October 2, 1952, Box 40, Folder 4, LJA.

75. Nelson to Gustive Larson, December 21, 1948, Box 11, Folder 16, GOL. See also Nelson to Robert A. Wilkinson, Box 19, Folder 6, LN. For the circulation of Nelson's correspondence, see Box 26, Folder 6, TEL; Box 10, Folder 12, MWP; Box 17, Folder 9, GTB; Box 36, Folder 2, GST; Box 35, Folder 1, RCD; Box 21, Folder 13, LJA; Box 341, Folder 9, SMM.

76. Nelson to McKay, March 20, 1952, Box 20, Folder 12, LN; Nelson to Lester E. Bush, October 13, 1972, Box 3, Folder 29, LEB.

77. Lowry Nelson, "Mormons and the Negro," *The Nation*, May 24, 1952, 488.

78. Kimball's copy of Nelson's article is in Box 64, Folder 6, SWK; Kimball to Edward L. Kimball, June 1963, Box 63, Folder 6, SWK; Anderson to Nelson, May 23, 1954, Box 210, "The Negro and the Church and Priesthood" folder, JRC.

79. Nelson, "Mormons and the Negro," 488.

346   NOTES

80. Ernest L. Wilkinson and Leonard J. Arrington, *Brigham Young University: The First One Hundred Years*, 4 vols. (Provo, UT: Brigham Young University Press, 1975–76), 2:287, 3:114–15, 4:185–86; Gary James Bergera and Ronald Priddis, *Brigham Young University: A House of Faith* (Salt Lake City: Signature Books, 1985), 162. For a biography of Doxey, see Box 13, Folders 3 and 5, RWD.

81. Roy W. Doxey, letter to the editor, "The Mormons and the Negro," *The Nation*, August 6, 1952, 120.

82. Nelson to Doxey, July 22, 1952, Box 20, Folder 12, LN.

83. Nelson, letter to the editor, *The Nation*, October 18, 1952, 368.

84. Nelson, "The Last Judgment" (1978), 24, Box 8, Folder 2, LNC.

85. Nelson to Harold T. Christensen, October 2, 1952, Box 20, Folder 12, LN; Nelson to L. H. Fitzpatrick, October 2, 1952, Box 20, Folder 5, LN. Wilkinson, memo to the First Presidency, re: "Teaching of the Negro Question in Institutes and Seminaries," November 21, 1953, Box 3, Folder 3, WEB.

86. Wilkinson, memo to the First Presidency, November 21, 1953; Wilkinson, memo to Sidney B. Sperry, November 29, 1951, Box 2, Folder 9, SBS; Wilkinson, memo to Dean Ariel S. Ballif, November 29, 1951, Box 3, Folder 3, WEB. Wilkinson's copy of the 1949 First Presidency statement is listed as having been produced on August 17, 1951 instead of the correct date of August 17, 1949. See, for example, Hugh Nibley's personal copy, Box 58, Folder 4, HN.

87. Wilkinson, memo to Nibley, June 23, 1952, Box 3, Folder 3, WEB; Bergera and Priddis, *Brigham Young University*, 24. Terryl L. Givens, *By the Hand of Mormon: The American Scripture That Launched a New World Religion* (New York: Oxford University Press, 2002), 118–24; Truman G. Madsen's foreword in *Nibley on the Timely and the Timeless: Classic Essays of Hugh W. Nibley* (Provo, UT: Religious Studies Center, Brigham Young University, 1978), xi.

88. Nibley articulated his views on "the Negro Question" in both public and private reflections. See Box 152, Folder 5, HN; Hugh W. Nibley, "The Best Possible Test," *Dialogue: A Journal of Mormon Thought* 8, no. 1 (Spring 1973): 77; Hugh W. Nibley, *Abraham in Egypt*, 2nd ed. (Provo, UT: Foundation for Ancient Research and Mormon Studies and Deseret Book, 2000), 578–79.

89. Wilkinson, memo to Berrett, re: "Status of the Negro in Our Church," January 3, 1955, Box 3, Folder 3, WEB; John J. Stewart (with a supplement by William E. Berrett), *Mormonism and the Negro* (Salt Lake City: Community Press, 1960).

90. Gustive Larson to Nelson, December 28, 1948, Box 11, Folder 16, GOL; William C. Carr to Nelson, March 26, 1948, Box 20, Folder 4, LN; Parley Christensen to Nelson, June 18, 1952, Box 20, Folder 11, LN; Lewis Max Rogers, interview with Everett L. Cooley, July 18, 1988, 32, Box 24, Folder 8, ECOH; Gaylon L. Caldwell, *Rocks Over Red Bridge: The Autobiography of Gaylon L. Caldwell* (Fairfield, CA: Self-published, 1990), ch. 12; Brigham D. Madsen, *Against the Grain: Memoirs of a Western Historian* (Salt Lake City: Signature Books, 2002), 107, 348.

91. Mary Lythgoe Bradford, *Lowell L. Bennion: Teacher, Counselor, Humanitarian* (Salt Lake City: Dialogue Foundation, 1995), ch. 3.

NOTES

347

92. Bennion, memoir, unpublished, 1976, 75, Box 8, Folder 4, LLB; Ulrich, quoted in *Conversations with Mormon Historians*, ed. Alexander L. Baugh and Reid L. Neilson (Salt Lake City: Deseret Book and Religious Studies Center at Brigham Young University, 2015), 546; Alder, quoted in Elise M. Alder, "Mormon Hero: Lowell Bennion," April 29, 1984, Box 1, Folder 2, Series 2, "Character Legends," HBLL.

93. Bennion, memoir, 64, 58, 61. For Bennion writing Sunday School manuals, see Bradford, *Lowell L. Bennion*, 69, 87, 118; and Peggy Fletcher, "Saint for All Seasons: An Interview with Lowell Bennion," *Sunstone*, February 1985, 11–12.

94. Bennion, memoir, 61–62, 64, 66, 73; Fletcher, "Saint for All Seasons," 9.

95. Bennion, memoir, 64.

96. Bennion, outline for his fireside sermon, "Negro Problem," April 1, 1951, Box 20, Folder 2, LLB; Bennion, memoir, 64, 67.

97. Bennion to McKay, December 1, 1952, Box 20, Folder 2, LLB.

98. Boyd, notes from an interview with David O. McKay, March 1955, Box 15, Folder 4, GTB; Rogers, interview with Cooley, 29–30.

99. Both men wrote extensively about their opposition to the priesthood and temple ban. See Box 26, Folder 4, TEL; Box 1, Folder 17, HCS.

100. L. Jackson Newell, ed., *Matters of Conscience: Conversation with Sterling M. McMurrin on Philosophy, Education and Religion* (Salt Lake City: Signature Books, 1996), 181–82. See also Box 184, Folder 6, and Box 223, Folder 8, SMM.

101. For transcripts and correspondence of the "Swearing Elders," see Box 1, Folders 1–9, TAB. See also Thomas A. Blakely, "The Swearing Elders: The First Generation of Modern Mormon Intellectuals," *Sunstone*, December 1985, 8–13; Madsen, *Against the Grain*, 218–19; William Mulder, oral history interview with Everett L. Cooley, March 8, 1988, 212–15, Box 26, Folder 6, ECOH.

102. Cache Valley Stake Presidency to Snell, September 1, 1963, Box 291, Folder 12, SMM; McMurrin, oral history interview with Robert L. Miller, June 11, 1986, 122–24, Box 291, Folder 12, SMM; Newell, *Matters of Conscience*, 189–90; Mark E. Petersen to Heber C. Snell, November 20, 1952, Box 3, Folder 5, HCS.

103. Smith to McMurrin, June 6, 1952, Box 291, Folder 3, SMM; McMurrin to McKay, March 31, 1954, Box 291, Folder 3, SMM. President McKay's son Lawrence noted that his father "put his arms around [McMurrin] and kept him in the church." David Lawrence McKay, oral history interview with Gordon Irving, March 30, 1984, 174, JMOH; Newell, *Matters of Conscience*, 191–93, 197–99.

104. Westwood to McKay, February n.d. 1952, Box 4, Folder 7, WEB; Ardis Westwood, "The Curse on the Negro Regarding the Priesthood," February 18, 1952, Box 4, Folder 7, WEB.

105. McKay to Wilkinson, February 20, 1952, Box 4, Folder 7, WEB.

106. Monroe to Merrill, January 24, 1951, Box 20, Folder 2, JFM.

107. Dallin H. Oaks, *Life's Lessons Learned* (Salt Lake City: Deseret Book, 2011), 67–68; T. Edgar Lyon, "Problems in Teaching Religion," 1954, Box 26, Folder 4, TEL; Lowell Bennion, "Problems Raised in the Minds of Students by the Denial of the Priesthood to the Negro," n.d., Box 20, Folder 2, LLB.

348   NOTES

108. Copies of church handouts on "the negro" can be found in Box 36, Folder 2, GST; Boyd K. Packer, "The Curses upon Cain and His Descendants," January 3, 1951, Box 63, Folder 11, LJA.

109. Sterling M. McMurrin to Lowry Nelson, August 2, 1952, Box 20, Folder 5, LN.

110. Kimball, diary, September 19, 1954, reel 12, SWK; Mathias to Kimball, April 29, 1954, Box 20, Folder 2, LLB.

111. Mathias wrote a research paper in graduate school titled "The Mormon Church and Its Negro Doctrine" and shared it with critics. John W. Fitzgerald to unknown correspondent, May 1, 1959, Box 8, Folder 26, JWF; Lowry Nelson to Mathias, January 15, 1954, Box 20, Folder 12, LN; Mathias to Leonard J. Arrington, 1958, Box 40, Folder 8, LJA; Juanita Brooks to Mathias, May 27, 1957, Box 3, Folder 11, JB; Mathias to George Ellsworth, September 5, 1962, Box 4, Folder 4, SGE. Mathias also contacted J. Reuben Clark about his trouble with Mormon racial theology. Mathias to Clark, February 18, 1953, Box 389, Folder 2, JRC. In 1965, Mathias "asked for, and received, excommunication from the LDS church." Mathias to Brigham D. Madsen, [1998], MLH.

112. Wolfgang Saxon, "Chauncy Harris, 89, Geographer of a Little-Known Soviet Union," *New York Times*, January 12, 2004.

113. Margaret Harris, "Text of Sermon on Mormonism Delivered by Margaret Harris, Chauncy Harris's Daughter to the Methodist Congregation of Cambridge, Massachusetts, c. 1970," 4, Box 90, Folder 7, CDH.

114. Harris to Bennion, January 19, 1954, Box 20, Folder 2, LLB. For more on Lee's address "Youth of a Noble Birthright," see chapter 4.

115. Harris to unnamed correspondent, March 10, 1952, Box 20, Folder 2, LN; Harris to E. DeAlton Partridge, January 30, 1956, Box 20, Folder 5, LN.

116. Harris to Nelson, November 14, 1953, Box 20, Folder 2, LN; Ernest L. Wilkinson to McKay, January 31, 1953, Box 9, Folder 7, ASB; Harris to Ernest L. Wilkinson, January 26, 1953, Box 89, Folder 4, CDH.

117. Harris to McKay, January 28, 1953, Box 89, Folder 4, CDH.

118. J. A. Rogers, "Was Ezra Taft Benson's Decision Influenced by His Mormonism?" *Pittsburgh Courier*, October 10, 1953.

119. Harris to First Presidency, November 13, 1953, Box 89, Folder 4, CDH.

120. Anderson to Harris, May 4, 1954, Box 89, Folder 4, CDH.

121. Unsigned First Presidency statement, November 16, 1953, Box 210, "The Negro and the Church and the Priesthood," folder, JRC.

122. "Minutes of Special Meeting by President McKay," January 17, 1954, Box 32, Folder 3, DOM; A. Hamer Reiser, oral history interview with William G. Hartley, August 9, 1974, 164–69, JMOH.

123. Sorensen, oral history interview with Irving, 46.

124. First Presidency and Council of the Twelve Minutes, November 4, 1965, Box 61, Folder 3, DOM; also in Box 64, Folder 8, SWK.

NOTES

349

125. Grover, "Religious Accommodation," 31n18.

126. "Excerpts from Minutes of Meeting of the Council of the Twelve and First Presidency," February 25, 1954, Box 64, Folder 8, SWK; also in Box 32, Folder 3, DOM.

127. I draw this conclusion based on my reading of hundreds of pages of First Presidency and Quorum of the Twelve meeting minutes.

128. For Lowell Bennion's close relationship with Apostle Bennion, see George T. Boyd, oral history interview with Robert L. Miller, November 15, 1985, Box 15, Folder 2, 28, ECOH.

129. Spencer W. Kimball, "Manuscript of the Council of the Twelve Minutes and First Presidency Statements on the Negro," [May 1954], Box 64, Folder 5, SWK.

130. The following account derives from Wallace Bennett and Leonard Arrington, both of whom attended the "Swearing Elders" meeting when Apostle Bennion spoke. Bennett to Adam S. Bennion, May 17, 1954, Box 10, Folder 3, LEB; Arrington, diary, May 13, 1954, Box 26, Folder 4, LJA. See also Ernest L. Wilkinson to Adam S. Bennion, June 1, 1954, Box 9, Folder 7, ASB; Sterling M. McMurrin, oral history interview with Robert L. Miller, January 7, 1986, Box 15, Folder 5, 122–23, ECOH. Years later Arrington misremembered the date of the Bennion Report and listed it as 1957. Arrington, diary, June 9, 1978, Box 33, Folder 4, LJA. Nicholas Udall, Spencer Kimball's nephew, incorrectly claimed the report was issued during George Albert Smith's administration. Edward L. Kimball, *Lengthen Your Stride: The Presidency of Spencer W. Kimball—Working Draft* (Salt Lake City: Benchmark Books, 2009), 319, n45.

131. Mathias to Bennion, July 19, 1954, Box 20, Folder 2, LLB.

132. "The Negro and the Priesthood" [May 1954], Box 20, Folder 2, LLB. Bennion shared copies of the report with his friends. See Box 24, Folder 29, SGE; Box 35, Folder 1, RCD; Box 40, Folder 2, LJA; Box 17, Folder 9, GTB.

133. "The Negro and the Priesthood," 3–4.

134. Ibid., 5.

135. Ibid., 2.

136. Ibid., 4.

137. Newell, *Matters of Conscience*, 199–200.

138. Ibid., 200. McMurrin thanked McKay for meeting with him and speaking freely about the ban. McMurrin to McKay, March 24, 1954, Box 291, Folder 3, SMM.

139. McMurrin, oral history interview with Gregory A. Prince, May 26, 1994, MLH.

140. Kimball to Ernest L. Wilkinson, November 9, 1970, Box 547, Folder 4, ELW. For more on the disclosure of the First Presidency and Quorum of the Twelve meeting minutes, see chapter 7.

CHAPTER 3

1. James T. Patterson, *Brown v. Board of Education: A Civil Rights Milestone and Its Troubled Legacy* (New York: Oxford University Press, 2001); Michael J. Klarman, *From Jim Crow to Civil Rights: The Supreme Court and the Struggle for Racial Equality* (New York: Oxford University Press, 2004).

2. W. E. B. Du Bois, *The Souls of Black Folk* (1903), in *DuBois: Writings*, ed. Nathan Huggins (New York: Library of America, 1986), 372.

3. Clark to Matson, April 12, 1948, Box 378, Folder 1, JRC; Stephen L. Richards, diary, January 23, 1952, SLR.

4. The Clark–Matson correspondence can be found in Box 378, Folder 1, JRC. The two exchanged several letters. Clark also kept several newspaper and magazine articles discussing blood banks. See "Clarkana," Box 295, "Negro" folder, JRC.

5. Rowena J. Miller (Clark's secretary) to O. Boyd Mathias, March 3, 1953, Box 389, Folder 2, JRC. For segregated blood banks at the church-owned hospital, see Susan E. Lederer, *Flesh and Blood: Organ Transplantation and Blood Transfusion in Twentieth-Century America* (New York: Oxford University Press, 2008), 197. For segregated blood banks in the Red Cross, see Thomas J. Sugrue, *Sweet Land of Liberty: The Forgotten Struggle for Civil Rights in the North* (New York: Random House, 2008), 64; Walter C. Alvarez, "Constitutional Inadequacy," *Journal of the American Medical Association* 119, no. 10 (July 4, 1942): 780–83.

6. F. Ross Peterson, "'Blindside': Utah on the Eve of *Brown v. Board of Education*," *Utah Historical Quarterly* 73, no. 1 (Winter 2005): 4–20; Tonya S. Reiter, "Not in My Neighborhood: The 1939 Controversy over Segregated Housing in Salt Lake City," *Utah Historical Quarterly* 90, no. 1 (Spring 2022): 4–18; D. Michael Quinn, *Elder Statesman: A Biography of J. Reuben Clark* (Salt Lake City: Signature Books, 2002), 342–44.

7. Candacy Taylor, *Overground Railroad: The Green Book and the Roots of Black Travel in America* (New York: Abrams Press, 2020), 322, 341; Christine Cooper-Rompato, "Utah in the *Green Book*: Segregation and the Hospitality Industry in the Beehive State," *Utah Historical Quarterly* 88, no. 1 (Winter 2020): 38–56.

8. W. Miller Barbour, "Breaking the Barriers: Anti-Negro Prejudice Lessens in Western Hotels," *Frontier*, November 1954, quoted from Lester E. Bush, ed., "Compilation of the Negro in Mormonism," 262 (1972), CHL.

9. Klarman, *From Jim Crow to Civil Rights*, 204–12; Jeffrey D. Gonda, *Unjust Deeds: The Restrictive Covenant Cases and the Making of the Civil Rights Movement* (Chapel Hill: University of North Carolina Press, 2015).

10. Lee, "Youth of a Noble Birthright" (1945), CHL. For evangelical and Fundamentalist Christians supporting segregation, see David L. Chappell, *A Stone of Hope: Prophetic Religion and the Death of Jim Crow* (Chapel Hill: University of North Carolina Press, 2004), 108–17; Daniel K. Williams, *God's Own Party: The Making of the Christian Right* (New York: Oxford University Press, 2010), ch. 2.

NOTES
351

11. Smith, diary, June 16, 1945, GAS; Clark, diary, August 30, 1944, Box 13, Folder 3, JRC; McKay, diary, February 25, 1949, Box 26, Folder 4, DOM. McKay also rejected integration in public schools. See his diary, April 2, 1956, Box 37, Folder 1, DOM.

12. First Presidency to Ezra Taft Benson, June 23, 1942, in *Minutes of the Quorum of the Twelve and First Presidency, 1910–1951*, 4 vols. (Salt Lake City: Smith-Pettit Foundation, 2010), 4:393.

13. Hanks, oral history interview with Jessie L. Embry, May 18, 1989, 7, 16, AAOH; Marion D. Hanks Recollections, compiled by Stephen J. Sorenson, December 2004, MDH; Hanks's recollection of the Hopes family [1985], MDH.

14. Hanks, oral history interview with Embry, 10.

15. Leone Rose to J. Reuben Clark, September 13, 1949, and Miller's reply, September 20, 1949, Box 380, Folder 8, JRC.

16. David H. Oliver, *A Negro on Mormonism* (Salt Lake City: Self-published, 1963), 23; Paul Cracroft, oral history interview with Everett L. Cooley, October 2, 1984, 41–43, Box 2, Folder 8, ECOH; Gladwin Hill, "Marked Decline in Racial Bias in Far West Revealed by Survey," *New York Times*, May 29, 1955; Lyman B. Power, "Philoshenanigans," *Utah Daily Chronicle*, October 12, 1955.

17. Smith, "Non-Segregation," 1956, Box 9, Folder 7, JFS.

18. "Elder Lee Conducts Course for Teachers," *Church News*, June 24, 1954, 4; William E. Berrett to T. Edgar Lyon, July 29, 1954, Box 26, Folder 4, TEL; Harold B. Lee to Geraldine Callister, April 30, 1968, Harold B. Lee Papers, MLH. See also William E. Berrett, "Race Problems, Church History and Philosophy 245—Advanced Theology Address," July 10, 1956, CHL.

19. William E. Berrett, interview with Mary L. Bradford, May 5, 1987, Box 4, Folder 9, MLB; see also Mary Lythgoe Bradford, *Lowell Bennion: Teacher, Counselor, Humanitarian* (Salt Lake City: Dialogue Foundation, 1995), 131; Ernest L. Wilkinson, diary, August 28, 1954, Box 99, Folder 2, ELW.

20. L. Brent Goates, *Harold B. Lee: Prophet and Seer* (Salt Lake City: Bookcraft, 1985), 317–18.

21. A copy of the sermon can be found in Box 5, Folder 2, MLB. For liberals opposing Smith's anti-evolution views, see George T. Boyd, notes from an interview with David O. McKay, March 1955, Box 15, Folder 4, GTB; William Lee Stokes to David O. McKay, February 11, 1957, MLH; Bertrand F. Harrison, oral history with Robert L. Miller, November 29, 1986, 19, Box 13, Folder 6, ECOH.

22. Lyon, diary, August 27, 1954, Box 4, Folder 2, TEL.

23. Peggy Petersen Barton, *Mark E. Petersen: A Biography* (Salt Lake City: Deseret Book, 1985).

24. Petersen to J. Reuben Clark, September 9, 1954, Box 210, "Negro and the Church," folder, JRC; "Race Problems—As They Affect the Church, Address by Elder Mark E. Petersen, Given at the Convention of Teachers of Religion on the College Level, Provo, Utah, August, 27, 1954," CHL; Bradford, *Lowell Bennion*, 131.

25. Petersen, "Race Problems," 1.

26. Ibid., 5.

27. Ibid., 9–11.

28. Ibid., 13–15.

29. Ibid., 15–16.

30. Ibid., 17.

31. Ibid., 19.

32. "Discussion after the Talk on Racial Prejudice by Elder Mark E. Petersen" transcript, [August 27, 1954], Box 4, Folder 7, WEB.

33. Ibid., 22. In 1944, the First Presidency said that it wasn't church doctrine that Black people would be White in the resurrection, but that didn't stop the Brethren from speculating. First Presidency secretary Joseph Anderson to W. N. Montgomery, August 3, 1944, "Manuscript of Council of the Twelve Minutes and First Presidency Statements on the Negro," 12, Box 64, Folder 5, SWK.

34. "Discussion after the Talk on Racial Prejudice by Elder Mark E. Petersen" transcript, 22. Smith also noted this in a private letter to a Latter-day Saint. Smith to Alfred J. Burdett, January 28, 1957, Box 39, Folder 9, JFS.

35. "Discussion after the Talk on Racial Prejudice by Elder Mark E. Petersen" transcript, 24–25.

36. Ibid., 25.

37. Ibid., 27.

38. Ibid., 28–29.

39. Ibid., 29–30.

40. Bennion, memo to Ernest L. Wilkinson, September 1, 1954, Box 20, Folder 2, LLB.

41. "Discussion after the Talk on Racial Prejudice by Elder Mark E. Petersen" transcript, 31. See also transcript of a telephone conversation between Bennion and David O. McKay, June 13, 1957, Box 39, Folder 3, DOM; Bennion, interview with Maureen Ursenbach Beecher, March 9, 1985, 127–28, JMOH; "Status of Man Holding Priesthood Who Marries Negro," 1963, Box 64, Folder 8, SWK.

42. "Discussion after the Talk on Racial Prejudice by Elder Mark E. Petersen" transcript, 33.

43. Ibid., 33.

44. Ibid., 34; Andrew Jenson, ed., *Latter-day Saint Biographical Encyclopedia*, 4 vols. (Salt Lake City: Andrew Jenson History Co., 1901–36), 3:577.

45. McKay, diary, January 17, 1954, Box 32, Folder 3, DOM; Smith to Florence Preece, January 18, 1955, Box 9, Folder 7, JFS; "Discussion after the Talk on Racial Prejudice by Elder Mark E. Petersen" transcript, 34.

46. "Discussion after the Talk on Racial Prejudice by Elder Mark E. Petersen" transcript, 34.

47. Ibid., 37.

NOTES

48. Lyon to Bennion, August 28, 1954, Box 71, Folder 5, TEL.
49. Bennion to Wilkinson, September 1, 1954, Box 20, Folder 2, LLB.
50. David H. Yarn, memo to Ernest L. Wilkinson, May 3, 1968, Box 556, Folder 12, ELW; Daniel H. Ludlow, memo to Ernest L. Wilkinson, re: "Mormonism and the Negro," February 18, 1969, Box 556, Folder 17, ELW.
51. For Kimball's copy, see Box 64, Folder 6, SWK; Tanner, quoted in First Presidency Minutes, March 20, 1963, Box 52, Folder 6, DOM; Hillam, diary, November 24, 1954, HH.
52. Bob Baker to George S. Tanner, February 11, 1957, Box 36, Folder 2, GST; Williams, "An Analysis of 'Race Problems—As They Affect the Church,'" October 19, 1958, Box 24, Folder 2, JDW; Wallace Turner, *The Mormon Establishment* (Boston: Houghton Mifflin, 1966), 250–54.
53. Falwell, quoted in Obery M. Henricks Jr., *Christians Against Christianity: How Right-Wing Evangelicals Are Destroying Our Nation and Our Faith* (Boston: Beacon Press, 2021), 24. See also Williams, *God's Own Party*, 43–47; Chappell, *A Stone of Hope*, 108–14; Jane Dailey, "Sex, Segregation, and the Sacred after Brown," *Journal of American History* 91, no. 1 (June 2004): 122–26.
54. James F. Burks, "Integration or Segregation," May 30, 1954, in *The Age of Jim Crow*, ed. Jane Dailey (New York: W. W. Norton, 2009), 279.
55. L. Nelson Bell, "Christian Race Relations Must Be Natural—Not Forced," August 17, 1955, in *Jerry Falwell and the Rise of the Religious Right*, ed. Matthew Avery Sutton (Boston: Bedford/St. Martin's, 2013), 53; Chappell, *A Stone of Hope*, 107.
56. "The Church and Segregation," May 3, 1954, in Dailey, *The Age of Jim Crow*, 288–89; Grant Wacker, *America's Pastor: Billy Graham and the Shaping of a Nation* (Cambridge, MA: Harvard University Press, 2014), 16.
57. Ronald V. Huggins, *Lighthouse: Jerald and Sandra Tanner—Despised and Beloved Critics of Mormonism* (Salt Lake City: Signature Books, 2022); Turner, *Mormon Establishment*, 253.
58. Jerald Tanner and Sandra Tanner, *The Negro in Mormon Theology* (Salt Lake City: Modern Microfilm, 1963).
59. Anderson to Petersen, October 21, 1963, Box 269, Folder 13, ELWP; Petersen to Wilkinson, October 25, 1963, Box 269, Folder 13, ELWP.
60. Clyde D. Sandgren, memo to Wilkinson, re: Letter from Mark E. Petersen, November 1, 1963, and Wilkinson, memo to Sandgren, November 4, 1963, Box 269, Folder 13, ELWP.
61. Petersen to Tanner, February 13, 1965, MLH.
62. Hanson to Petersen, July 31, 1968, Box 464, Folder 1, ELWP.
63. Nelson to Petersen, May 28, 1975, Box 20, Folder 11, LN.
64. Peterson to Nelson, May 30, 1975, Box 20, Folder 11, LN. Petersen also downplayed his authorship to other Latter-day Saints. See Petersen to Karl C. Sandberg, December 20, 1963, Box 1, Folder 9, KCS.
65. Nelson to John W. Fitzgerald, May 6, 1975, Box 20, Folder 11, LN.

NOTES

66. James R. Clark, "Cain and Satan—and Two Modern Problems: (1) Racial Segregation and (2) Subversive Groups," 1955–1956, Box 49, Folder 24, RDP.

67. Arthur M. Richardson, "That Ye May Not Be Deceived: A Discussion of the Racial Problem—Segregation or Integration?" [1955], copy in Box 26, Folder 4, TEL. See also Dean C. Jessee, "The Attitude of the Leaders of the Church of Jesus Christ of Latter-day Saints toward Segregation," [1955], Box 40, Folder 8, LJA.

68. *Improvement Era* 59, no. 11 (November 1956): 769.

69. Emma Marr Petersen, *Choose Ye This Day* (Salt Lake City: Bookcraft, 1956), 7, 45, 48–50.

70. As early as 1946, Clark professed that Latter-day Saints "should give to every man and every woman, no matter what the color of his and her skin may be, full civil rights." J. Reuben Clark, "Plain Talk to Girls," *Improvement Era* 49, no. 8 (August 1946): 492.

71. Petersen to Clark, September 9, 1954, Box 210, "Negro and the Church" folder, JRC; Kimball notation on front of draft 3 of Clark's undelivered general conference address, September 13, 1954, JRC. Kimball expressed his approval to Clark directly, but didn't provide a reaction to the address (see JRC).

72. Clark, undelivered address, Draft #3, September 13, 1954, JRC.

73. Clark, memo, n.d., Box 295, "negro" folder, JRC; Patterson, *Brown v. Board*, ch. 2.

74. Fitzpatrick to Lowry Nelson, September 12, 1952, Box 20, Folder 5, LN.

75. McMurrin to Lowry Nelson, August 2, 1952, Box 20, Folder 5, LN.

76. L. H. Kirkpatrick, "The Negro and the L.D.S. Church," *Pen Magazine,* Winter 1954, 12–13, 29, Box 64, Folder 6, SWK.

77. Wallace R. Bennett, "The Negro in Utah," *Utah Law Review* 3 (Spring 1953): 340–48.

78. Nelson to Kirkpatrick, October 2, 1952, Box 20, Folder 5, LN.

79. Fleming, oral history interview with Leslie G. Kelen, July 29, 1983, 16, Box 7, Folder 6, IBU.

80. Howell to Kate Carter, January 1965, in Kate B. Carter, *The Story of the Negro Pioneer* (Salt Lake City: Daughters of the Utah Pioneers, 1965), 56–57. When the team decided to eat in the kitchen area with Howell, the restaurant owner relented and let Howell eat in the dining area. See "Home Boys Victorious," *Salt Lake Tribune*, November 30, 1900.

81. Mary Lucille Bankhead, oral history interview with Leslie G. Kelen, January 14, 1983, 9, Box 1, Folder 4, IBU.

82. Richards to Howell, June 10, 1951, in Carter, *The Story of the Negro Pioneer*, 58–59; Kimball, quoted in Carter, *The Story of the Negro Pioneer*, 59.

83. Berrett, "Race Problems," July 10, 1956, 6, CHL.

84. Carter, *The Story of the Negro Pioneer*, 60.

85. Simeon Booker and Herman Burrell, "The Religion That Bars Negroes," *Negro Digest* 5, no. 11 (September 1947): 54.

NOTES

86. First Presidency and Quorum of the Twelve Minutes, October 23, 1955, Box 64, Folder 5, SWK.

87. Smith to First Presidency, March 30, 1955, Box 64, Folder 6, SWK.

88. Oliver, *A Negro on Mormonism*, 12. Oliver attended a meeting in which Apostle Petersen explained Smith's plan.

89. Clark, "Negro" statement, n.d., Box 64, Folder 6, SWK; First Presidency Minutes, January 14, 1964, Box 56, Folder 1, DOM.

90. Kimball and Smith's proposal later culminated in the Genesis Group, the LDS church's first Black support group (see chapter 6). For Till and Parks, see Devery S. Anderson, *Emmett Till: The Murder That Shocked the World and Propelled the Civil Rights Movement* (Jackson: University Press of Mississippi, 2015); Jeanne Theoharis, *The Rebellious Life of Mrs. Rosa Parks* (Boston: Beacon Press, 2013).

91. Clark, diary, December 2, 1957, Box 20, Folder 3, JRC.

92. First Presidency to Watkins, September 1, 1958, Box 6, Folder 2, AVW.

93. First Presidency Minutes, September 19, 1958, Box 42, Folder 3, DOM.

94. Matthew L. Harris, *Watchman on the Tower: Ezra Taft Benson and the Making of the Mormon Right* (Salt Lake City: University of Utah Press, 2020), 47–48, 73–76; William I. Hitchcock, *The Age of Eisenhower: America and the World in the 1950s* (New York: Simon and Schuster, 2018), 239.

95. Hanks to Duncan, February 25, 1957, Box 2, Folder 18, LS. For the bill, see Patrick R. Eckman, "Variety Features Utah House Session," *Salt Lake Tribune*, January 23, 1957.

96. Fitzgerald to McKay, December 22, 1958, Box 7, Folder 24, JWF; Wilkins to E. W. Pfeiffer, March 25, 1958, NAACP.

97. Report of Utah State Advisory Committee, to the United States Commission on Civil Rights, March 31, 1959, reel 7, part 27, Selected Branch Files, Papers of NAACP, 1–4, LOC.

98. Ibid., 4–5.

99. "Mormons and Civil Rights," *Time*, April 13, 1959, 96.

100. "Mormons and Civil Rights," *Deseret News*, April 15, 1959, "Clarkana," Box 295, "Negro" folder, JRC; and Box 44, Folder 3, DOM.

101. "Who Is to Blame?," *Salt Lake NAACP Newsletter*, June 1, 1959, copy in "Clarkana," Box 295, "Negro" folder, JRC. See also Albert B. Fritz [president of the Salt Lake Branch, NAACP], "Civil Rights and Negro Treatment in Utah," *Deseret News*, April 23, 1959.

102. Mrs. Rudger N. Price, "Time Magazine Article Incurs Ire of Reader," *Deseret News*, April 21, 1959; Orlando A. Rivera, "Pros and Cons on Civil Rights," *Deseret News*, April 23, 1959; Catherine A. Harmson, "Time Magazine Scored for Article on Utah," *Deseret News*, April 23, 1959. See also Lloyd V. Viall, "Says Negro Treated Better Here," and Harold C. Christensen, "Takes Issue with Christie Freed Article," *Deseret News*, April 27, 1959.

103. Miller, memo, notes of Petersen's call, April 17, 1959, "Clarkana," Box 295, "Negro" folder, JRC.

356   NOTES

104. Anonymous letter to McKay, October 6, 1959, Box 64, Folder 5, SWK.

105. Ibid.

106. First Presidency to Auxiliary Officers of the Church, October 27, 1959, Box 64, Folder 5, SWK.

107. Meeting minutes of J. Reuben Clark's remarks to mission presidents, March 30, 1960, 7, Box 169, April 1960 conference folder, JRC.

108. In 1959, Gerald Heywood served in the branch as a missionary and witnessed the mass defection of Latter-day Saints. Heywood to Lester Bush, December 1, 1968, in Bush, "Compilation on the Negro," 264.

109. Dunn, interview with Gregory A. Prince, June 5, 1995, MLH.

110. Bennion to Samuel G. Holmes, January 29, 1959, Box 15, Folder 11, LLB; Brigham D. Madsen, *Against the Grain: Memoirs of a Western Historian* (Salt Lake City: Signature Books, 1998), 219.

111. L. Jackson Newell, ed., *Matters of Conscience: Conversation with Sterling M. McMurrin on Philosophy, Education and Religion* (Salt Lake City: Signature Books, 1996), 192–94; Blake Ostler, "An Interview with Sterling McMurrin," *Dialogue: A Journal of Mormon Thought* 17, no. 1 (Spring 1984): 25; Sterling M. McMurrin, *The Philosophical Foundations of Mormon Theology* (Salt Lake City: University of Utah Press, 1959). For the Brethren's response to McMurrin's book, see Quinn, *Elder Statesman*, 205; Newell, *Matters of Conscience*, 354.

112. Transcription of notes from D. Arthur Haycock of a talk by Sterling McMurrin to the Salt Lake City chapter, March 8, 1960, in Box 220, Folder 2, SMM; also in D. Arthur Haycock, memo [to First Presidency], March 8, 1960, CHL. An audiotape of McMurrin's address can be found in AV 30, CHL.

113. "A Monthly Branch Report," *Salt Lake NAACP Newsletter*, March 31, 1960, part 25: Branch Department Files—Series C: Branch Newsletters and Printed Materials, 1956–1965, reel 8, Papers of the NAACP, LOC.

114. Transcription of notes from D. Arthur Haycock of a talk by Sterling McMurrin to the Salt Lake City chapter, March 8, 1960; Fawn McKay Brodie, *No Man Knows My History: The Life of Joseph Smith* (New York: Alfred A. Knopf, 1945).

115. Transcription of notes from D. Arthur Haycock of a talk by Sterling McMurrin to the Salt Lake City chapter, March 8, 1960.

116. "A Monthly Branch Report," *Salt Lake NAACP Newsletter*, March 31, 1960. For McMurrin's admirers, see Ted Curtis to McMurrin, March 21, 1960, Box 341, Folder 9; Jay B. Christensen to McMurrin, March 25, 1960, Box 220, Folder 2; John L. Sorenson to McMurrin, March 9, 1960, Box 341, Folder 9; and McMurrin to George T. Boyd, March 22, 1960, Box 220, Folder 2, all in SMM.

117. Bennion to McMurrin, March 14, 1960, and McMurrin's reply, March 22, 1960, Box 220, Folder 2, SMM. See also Bennion to McMurrin, March 23, 1960, Box 220, Folder 2, SMM.

118. McKay, diary, March 18, 1960, Box 45, Folder 2, DOM.

119. For details on this point, see chapter 4.

NOTES 357

120. Merle C. Bennion, oral history interview with Maureen Ursenbach Beecher, June 8, 1985, 75, JMOH; T. Edgar Lyon Jr., *T. Edgar Lyon: A Teacher in Zion* (Provo, UT: Brigham Young University Press, 2002), 266n61. Bennion's student Frederick Buchanan also noted that Tagg spied on Bennion and Lyon. Buchanan, diary, July 24, 1962, Box 253, Folder 8, FSB. This wasn't the first time that the Brethren used spies to monitor controversial faculty, nor would it be the last. In the late 1940s, BYU faculty member J. Reuben Clark III spied on Sterling McMurrin when he taught summer courses at BYU. See Ray R. Canning, oral history interview with Everett L. Cooley, November 2, 1983, 49–50, Box 4, Folder 8, ECOH. In 1966, Apostle Ezra Taft Benson established a "spy ring" at BYU to ferret out liberal professors. See Gary James Bergera, "The 1966 BYU Student Spy Ring," *Utah Historical Quarterly* 79, no. 2 (Spring 2011): 164–88.

121. Petersen, "Historical Sketch," unpublished manuscript, 1980, 14, Box 8, Folder 26, LGP; Petersen, unpublished autobiography [1985], 105–6, Box 12, Folder 15, LGP; Albert Payne, "Reasonable Conclusions to a Presentation on the L.D.S. Negro Problem to the Faculty of the Salt Lake Institute," March 14, 1962, Box 20, Folder 2, LLB; Sterling M. McMurrin, oral history interview with Robert L. Miller, July 28, 1984, 10, Box 15, Folder 5, ECOH.

122. Petersen to Smith, May 11, 1962, Box 192, Folder 2, ELWP; Petersen, diary, May 11, 1962, Box 12, Folder 8, LGP. Bennion demanded to see a copy of Petersen's report and confronted Tagg for "going behind our back." See Lauritz G. Petersen, diary, May 24, 1962, Box 12, Folder 8, LGP; Petersen to T. Edgar Lyon, May 22, 1962, Box 192, Folder 2, ELWP. See also William E. Berrett, "Confidential" memo to Ernest L. Wilkinson re: "Charges Made by Melvin Tagg, Institute Faculty Member," to Ernest L. Wilkinson, May 30, 1962, Box 192, Folder 2, ELWP; Lowell L. Bennion, oral history interview with Maureen Ursenbach Beecher, February 23, 1985, 105, JMOH; T. Edgar Lyon, oral history interview with Davis R. Bitton, 1974–75, 203, JMOH; Peggy Fletcher, "Saint for All Seasons: An Interview with Lowell L. Bennion," *Sunstone*, February 1985, 10.

123. William E. Berrett, "Confidential" memo to Ernest L. Wilkinson re: "Lowell Bennion: Nature of Complaints Reported by Ted Tuttle and Boyd K. Packer," July 5, 1962, Box 192, Folder 2, ELWP; Ernest L. Wilkinson, "Memorandum of Complaints against Lowell Bennion as Given to Me by Boyd Packer on [the] Telephone Today," July 3, 1962, Box 192, Folder 2, ELWP.

124. Bennion, memoir, 51; Bennion, oral history interview with Beecher, 106; George T. Boyd, recollection to Duane Jeffery, February 21, 1985, Box 45, Folder 7, DJ.

125. Norma Ashdown (Hugh B. Brown's secretary) to Frederick Buchanan, July 31, 1962, Box 92, Folder 6, FSB. Brown authorized Ashdown to tell inquisitors that he fully supported Bennion and that he considered him to be "one of the finest teachers in the Church."

358 NOTES

126. Bennion, memoir, 51; see also Ernest L. Wilkinson, diary, August 9, 1962, Box 100, Folder 7, ELW.

127. Merle C. Bennion, oral history interview with Beecher, June 8, 1985, 76–77.

128. Wilkinson, "Confidential" memo to William E. Berrett, "Re: Lowell Bennion and T. Edgar Lyon," July 25, 1962, Box 192, Folder 2, ELWP.

129. Packer, quoted in Ernest L. Wilkinson, memo to William E. Berrett, "Re: Meeting with Lowell L. Bennion and T. Edgar Lyon," October 4, 1962, Box 192, Folder 2, ELWP.

130. Lyon, diary, June 18, 1962, Box 5, Folder 3, TEL; Lyon to Heber C. Snell, September 18, 1962, Box 2, Folder 21, HCS.

131. Boyd, interview with David J. Whittaker, July 28, 1984, 76, Box 27, Folder 19, GTB; Tanner, diary, July 1, 1962, Box 14, Folder 10, GST; Boyd to Mary L. Bradford, November 18, 1987, Box 2, Folder 6, LS.

132. Bradford, *Lowell L. Bennion*, 169; Lyon, *T. Edgar Lyon*, 259. A number of these letters are in Box 192, Folder 2, ELWP; Box 20, Folder 2, LLB; and Box 71, Folder 5, TEL.

133. Hanks, interview with Ted Lyon Jr., August 4, 1992, 10, Box 2, Folder 11, TEL; Bennet to First Presidency, August 6, 1962, Box 192, Folder 2, ELWP; "Statement of Ernest L. Wilkinson, Chancellor of the Church School System, Re: Dr. Lowell L. Bennion and Dr. T. Edgar Lyon," [June 1962], Box 192, Folder 2, ELWP. Wilkinson secured permission for Bennion to write curriculum manuals, but the Brethren were lukewarm to it. Wilkinson to McKay, June 19, 1962, and the First Presidency's reply, June 20, 1962, Box 192, Folder 2, ELWP. See also First Presidency Minutes, June 20, 1962, Box 50, Folder 3, DOM. Bennion recognized Wilkinson's ruse and denied the "promotion." Instead he accepted an administrative position at the University of Utah. Bradford, *Lowell L. Bennion*, 171. Lyon took a position within the Church Education System writing church manuals. Lyon, *T. Edgar Lyon*, 260.

134. Bradford, *Lowell L. Bennion*, 170; Lyon, *T. Edgar Lyon*, 259–60.

135. Smith, diary, August 2, 1962, Box 4, Folder 1, JFS.

136. Mark E. Petersen, "Avoiding Sectarianism," in *Charge to Religious Educators* (Salt Lake City: The Church of Jesus Christ of Latter-day Saints, 1982): 114, 118, Box 19, Folder 8, GTB.

CHAPTER 4

1. Hugh B. Brown, oral history interview with Edwin B. Firmage, November 30, 1968, 39, Box 3, Folder 2, EBF.

2. Spencer W. Kimball, diary, October 29, 1964, reel 27, SWK; Hugh B. Brown, oral history interview with Edwin B. Firmage, November 12–13, 1968, 3–6, 39, Box 3, Folder 2, EBF; Edwin B. Firmage, ed., *An Abundant Life: The Memoirs of Hugh B. Brown*, 2nd ed. (Salt Lake City: Signature Books, 1999), 16–18.

NOTES

359

3. Charles Brown and Zola Brown Hodson, oral history interview with Eugene Campbell, June 7, 1973, Box 30, Folder 2, EEC. See also Edwin B. Firmage, "Hugh B. Brown in His Final Years," *Sunstone*, November 1987, 7.

4. First Presidency Minutes, January 3, 1962, Box 49, Folder 3, DOM; First Presidency Minutes, March 1, 1962, Box 49, Folder 5, DOM.

5. First Presidency Minutes, January 3, 1962; LaMar S. Williams, memo to the First Presidency and Council of the Twelve, re: "Missionary Work with Negroes," May 3, 1961, Box 1, Folder 7, LSW.

6. Christopher Cannon Jones, "'A Verry Poor Place for Our Doctrine': Religion and Race in the 1853 Mormon Mission to Jamaica," *Religion and Culture* 31, no. 2 (Summer 2021): 262–95.

7. First Presidency Minutes, October 13, 1961, Box 48, Folder 6, DOM.

8. Gregory A. Prince and William Robert Wright, *David O. McKay and the Rise of Modern Mormonism* (Salt Lake City: University of Utah Press, 2005), 81–85; Russell W. Stevenson, *For the Cause of Righteousness: A Global History of Blacks and Mormonism, 1830–2013* (Salt Lake City: Greg Kofford Books, 2014), 75–88.

9. Williams, memo to First Presidency and Council of Twelve, May 3, 1961, and First Presidency Minutes, October 11, 1962, Box 51, Folder 3, DOM. For the First Presidency blessing Williams in his new missionary assignment, see November 21, 1962, Box 1, Folder 8, LSW; First Presidency Minutes, March 1, 1961, Box 47, Folder 1, DOM.

10. Romney meeting with the First Presidency, December 5, 1961, Box 49, Folder 2, DOM.

11. First Presidency and Quorum of the Twelve Minutes, October 18, 1962, Box 51, Folder 5, DOM.

12. First Presidency Minutes, January 9, 1962, Box 49, Folder 3, DOM; "Memorandum of Subjects which President N. Eldon Tanner took up with President McKay," April 5, 1962, Box 49, Folder 6, DOM.

13. McKay, diary, January 9, 1962, Box 49, Folder 3, DOM; Williams, oral history interview with Gordon Irving, May 19, 1981, 38, JMOH; Williams, journal, October 29, 1961, LSW.

14. McKay, diary, January 9, 1962.

15. Brown to John W. Fitzgerald, March 13, 1962, Box 4, Folder 10, JWF.

16. Bennion, oral history interview with Maureen Ursenbach Beecher, March 9, 1985, 129, JMOH; Peggy Fletcher, "Saint for All Seasons: An Interview with Lowell Bennion," *Sunstone*, February 1985, 11.

17. Lyon notes, February 12, 1962, Box 26, Folder 1, TEL.

18. Ruffin Bridgeforth, interview with Mary L. Bradford, March 4, 1991, Box 1, Folder 7, LS.

19. Bennion to Romney, March 16, 1962, Box 17, Folder 4, LLB.

20. Buchanan, diary, February 23, 1962, Box 253, Folder 8, FSB.

21. Buchanan, diary, March 11, 1962, Box 253, Folder 8, FSB.

22. McKay, diary, October 11, 1962, Box 51, Folder 3, DOM.

360   NOTES

23. Wallace Turner, "Mormons Weigh Stand on Negro," *New York Times*, June 7, 1963; "Negro Issue Is Considered by Mormons: Church May Abandon Its Discrimination," *Chicago Tribune*, July 9, 1963. See also "Third Degree," *Newsweek*, June 17, 1963, 21.

24. McKay, diary, June 7, 1963, Box 53, Folder 5, DOM; Spencer W. Kimball to Edward L. Kimball, June 15, 1963, Box 64, Folder 5, SWK. When Harrison Salisbury, the director of national correspondence at the *New York Times*, sought to clarify the church's position, LDS church leaders "preferred to say nothing on the subject." Salisbury to Jerald Tanner, June 18, 1963, Box 19, Folder 4, HCS.

25. First Presidency Minutes, June 7, 1963, Box 53, Folder 5, DOM; Turner to Stephen Holbrook, July 9, 1963, Box 1, Folder 23, SH; Brown to Stewart L. Udall, July 22, 1963, Box 209, Folder 3, SLU; Brown, oral history interview with Richard Poll and Eugene Campbell, January 26, 1973, Box 51, Folder 23, RDP.

26. Smith, quoted in Jeff Nye, "Memo from a Mormon," *Look*, October 22, 1963, 78, Box 9, Folder 6, JFS; see also Joseph Fielding Smith, *Answers to Gospel Questions*, 5 vols. (Salt Lake City: Deseret Book, 1957–66), 2:185.

27. Smith, diary, February 22, 1962, Box 4, Folder 1, JFS; "President Smith Discusses Vital Issue," *Church News*, July 14, 1962; Smith to Joseph Henderson, April 10, 1963, MLH; Smith, *Answers to Gospel Questions*, 2:178, 185; 4:170–71.

28. Smith to J. Reuben Clark, April 3, 1939, Box 17, Folder 7, JFS.

29. Nye, "Memo from a Mormon," 74–75.

30. The civil rights movement forced Smith to tone down his earlier views. See Matthew L. Harris, "Joseph Fielding Smith's Evolving Views on Race: The Odyssey of a Mormon Apostle-President," *Dialogue: A Journal of Mormon Thought* 55, no. 3 (Fall 2022): 24–27.

31. Nye, "Memo from a Mormon," 78. In his book *Answers to Gospel Questions*, 4:170, Smith also denied having taught that "the Negro is an inferior being." For critics mocking Smith, see "Mormon Has No Animosity toward 'Darkies,'" *Jet*, October 24, 1962, 52; Lester Kinsolving, "But, We Like Darkies, Except . . . ," *San Francisco Chronicle*, March 23, 1970; "Stuff You Missed in Sunday School," n.d., https://missedinsunday.com/memes/race/darkies/; "Blacks and the Priesthood," *MormonThink*, n.d., http://www.mormonthink.com/black web.htm#racistcomments.

32. Doctrine and Covenants, 107:27. For Widtsoe and Bennion opposing the ban, see chapters 1–2.

33. Joseph Fielding Smith, *Doctrines of Salvation*, compiled by Bruce R. McConkie, 3 vols. (Salt Lake City: Deseret Book, 1954–56); Smith, *Answers to Gospel Questions*.

34. Daniel H. Ludlow, memo to BYU Religion Faculty, "Review of Priesthood Correlation in the 1960s," June 8, 1970, Box 3, Folder 11, SBS; L. Brent Goates, *Harold B. Lee: Prophet and Seer* (Salt Lake City: Bookcraft, 1985), 140–55, 363–72.

NOTES 361

35. Romney, oral history interview with Bruce Blumell, 1976, 18, JMOH.

36. Ernest L. Wilkinson, diary, April 23, 1959, Box 100, Folder 1, ELW; Harold B. Lee, "The Place of the Living Prophet, Seer, and Revelator" (July 8, 1964), in *Stand Ye in Holy Places: Selected Sermons and Writings of President Harold B. Lee* (Salt Lake City: Deseret Book, 1974), 159. For Lee's temper, see Ernest L. Wilkinson, diary, November 10, 1960, Box 100, Folder 4, ELW; Helen L. Goates, oral history interview with Carl Arrington, September 12, 1973, CHL, copy in Box 59, Folder 8, LJA.

37. Harold B. Lee, "Youth of a Noble Birthright" (1945), reprinted in Lee, *Youth and the Church* (Salt Lake City: Deseret Book, 1955), 168, 170; Clark, quoted in Lee, diary, May 6, 1945, CHL.

38. Joseph Fielding McConkie, *The Bruce R. McConkie Story: Reflections of a Son* (Salt Lake City: Deseret Book, 2003), 345.

39. Ibid., 286–87; Joseph Fielding McConkie, "Bruce R. McConkie: A Special Witness," *Mormon Historical Studies* 14 (Fall 2013): 205. Lavina Fielding Anderson, "The LDS Intellectual Community and Church Leadership: A Contemporary Chronology," *Dialogue: A Journal of Mormon Thought* 26, no. 1 (Spring 1993): 15, 19; Claudia L. Bushman, *Contemporary Mormonism: Latter-day Saints in Modern America* (Westport, CT: Praeger 2006), 148–49; Lavina Fielding Anderson and Janice Merrill Allred, eds., *Case Reports of the Mormon Alliance*, vol. 2: *1996* (Salt Lake City: Mormon Alliance, 1997), chs. 5–6.

40. "Enlarged 'Mormon Doctrine' Out," in LDS *Church News*, published in *Deseret News*, November 26, 1966; BYU *Daily Universe*, November 18, 1966.

41. Bruce R. McConkie, *Mormon Doctrine* (Salt Lake City: Bookcraft, 1958), 102, 107–8, 476–77, 554. See also Matthew L. Harris and Newell G. Bringhurst, eds., *The Mormon Church and Blacks: A Documentary History* (Urbana: University of Illinois Press, 2015), 71–72.

42. Benson to Joseph Fielding Smith, March 3, 1966, reel 6, ETB; Matthew L. Harris, *Watchman on the Tower: Ezra Taft Benson and the Making of the Mormon Right* (Salt Lake City: University of Utah Press, 2020), 3–5, 87–89; Ezra Taft Benson, *Title of Liberty: A Voice of Warning*, compiled by Mark A. Benson (Salt Lake City: Deseret Book, 1964), 1; Ezra Taft Benson, *An Enemy Hath Done This*, compiled by Jerreld Newquist (Salt Lake City: Parliament Publishers, 1969), 64, 305.

43. Harris, *Watchman on the Tower*, 46–47, 56–59, 72–73; Ezra Taft Benson, "Trust Not the Arm of Flesh," *Improvement Era* 70, no. 12 (December 1967): 55; Ezra Taft Benson, "To the Humble Followers of Christ," *Improvement Era* 72, no. 12 (June 1969): 43; Edward H. Miller, *A Conspiratorial Life: Robert Welch, the John Birch Society, and the Revolution of American Conservatism* (Chicago: University of Chicago Press, 2021); Matthew Dallek, *Birchers: How the John Birch Society Radicalized the American Right* (New York: Basic Books, 2023); Beverly Gage, *G-Man: J. Edgar Hoover and the Making of the American Century* (New York: Penguin, 2022).

362   NOTES

44. Kimball to Kimball, June 15, 1963, Box 64, Folder 5, SWK. For Kimball's experience visiting South America, see chapter 7.

45. Kimball to Kirk Davis, January 30, 1948, Box 64, Folder 1, SWK; Kimball to Victor L. Cline, May 28, 1956, Box 64, Folder 6, SWK. See also Kimball to Edward L. Kimball, June 15, 1963, Box 64, Folder 5, SWK.

46. Hanks, comments on the "Negro" to his Seminary students (1951), MDH; Hanks, "Recollections" (December 2004), compiled by Stephen J. Sorenson, MDH; Richard Hanks, email to Matthew Harris, August 13, 2019.

47. Glenn L. Pearson, *Book of Mormon: Key to Conversion* (Salt Lake City: Bookcraft, 1963), 6; John J. Stewart, *Mormonism and the Negro* (1960; Orem, UT: Community Press, 1967); John L. Lund, *The Church and the Negro: A Discussion of Mormons, Negroes and the Priesthood* (Salt Lake City: Paramount Publishers, 1967. A church magazine touted Stewart's book as "a complete and unprejudiced explanation of LDS Church doctrine regarding the Negro and those of negroid blood." *Improvement Era* 68, no. 12 (December 1965): 1064.

48. Basil Brown, quoted in "Romney Claims Mormon Race View Does Not Dictate His Position," *Minneapolis Spokesman*, December 12, 1963.

49. Romney, quoted in ibid.; Timothy N. Thurber, *Republicans and Race: The GOP's Frayed Relationship with African Americans, 1945–1974* (Lawrence: University Press of Kansas, 2013), 265–66.

50. "Underground War on Mormon Colour Bar," *London Times*, July 10, 1962; "Mormon Issue," *Time*, March 2, 1962; "Book of Mormon Enters Politics," *Christian Century*, March 28, 1962, 382.

51. Thomas C. Romney, *Mormon Colonies in Mexico* (1938; Salt Lake City: University of Utah Press, 2005); F. Burton Howard, *Marion G. Romney: His Life and Faith* (Salt Lake City: Bookcraft, 1988), 197.

52. Lee to Romney, December 18, 1972, Box 55, no folder listed, LRK; Richards to Spencer W. Kimball, February 26, 1974, reel 39, SWK.

53. J. A. Rogers, "Rogers Says," *Pittsburgh Courier*, October 10, 1953; Margie Taylor, "Is Salt Lake City Like Atlanta, Georgia?," *The Nation*, January 3, 1953, 20; Wes McClune to Claude Barnett, Associated Negro Press, April 30, 1953, CAB.

54. Kimball to Edward L. Kimball, June 1963, Box 63, Folder 6, SWK; Smith, *Answers to Gospel Questions*, 4:170.

55. First Presidency Minutes, January 3, 1962, Box 49, Folder 3, DOM.

56. P. L. Prattis, "Issues: Good and Bad," for the Associated Negro Press, May 29, 1963, CAB.

57. Sylvia Jukes Morris, *Rage for Fame: The Ascent of Clare Boothe Luce* (New York: Random House, 1997); Alan Brinkley, *The Publisher: Henry Luce and His American Century* (New York: Alfred A. Knopf, 2010).

58. "Clare Boothe Luce Says Romney '64 Deadlock Choice," *Arizona Republic*, September 1, 1963. Copies in Box 58, Folder 4, HN; Box 54, Folder 5, DOM.

59. Richard D. Poll, *Working the Divine Miracle: The Life of Apostle Henry D. Moyle*, ed. Stan Larson (Salt Lake City: Signature Books, 1999).

NOTES

60. D. Michael Quinn, *The Mormon Hierarchy: Wealth and Corporate Power* (Salt Lake City: Signature Books, 2017), 174, 451–66; D. Michael Quinn, "I-Thou vs. I-It Conversions: The Mormon 'Baseball Baptism' Era," *Sunstone*, December 1993, 30–44. The controversial "baseball baptisms" program was popular in Europe in the late 1950s and early 1960s. LDS missionaries required young men to be baptized before they could join an LDS-sponsored sports league. It was a ploy to get them baptized to boost convert quotas.

61. First Presidency Minutes, September 11, 1963, Box 54, Folder 4, DOM. Moyle died of a heart attack a week after he responded to Luce.

62. Moyle to Luce, September 13, 1963, Box 54, Folder 3, DOM; also in Box 509, Folder 3, ELW. A Mormon missionary also wrote Luce, trying to convince her that Mormons didn't treat Black people unkindly: "[It] is our understanding that the negro will, in due time of the Lord, have his dark skin coloring taken from him; that in keeping with God's divine justice his limitations will be removed." Unidentified writer to Clare Boothe Luce, May 24 [1964], Box 21, Folder 4, PRC.

63. Romney to Luce, September 23, 1963, Box 238, Folder "Mormon Church, 1963–66," GWR.

64. R. Greg Stokes, "Mormons, 'Curse of God' Give Utah Negroes Additional Problems," *Montreal Gazette*, December 7, 1963; "Worst Race Problem: Negroes in Utah Are Told They Bear a Curse," *Daytona Beach Morning Journal*, October 27, 1963. See also "Status of Utah Negroes Said among Worse in Nation," *Dallas Morning News*, October 31, 1963; "Racial Discrimination by Mormons Is Charged," *Ottawa Citizen*, November 14, 1963.

65. Williams to Hugh B. Brown, June 7, 1963, Box 24, Folder 2, JDW.

66. J. D. Williams, "Mississippi, Utah, and Civil Rights," *Pen Magazine* 51 (Autumn 1962): 26–39, Box 24, Folder 3, JDW. Nevada was the other western state without civil rights protections. See Elmer R. Ruso, "Civil Rights Movement in Nevada," in *Black Americans and the Civil Rights Movement in the West*, ed. Bruce A. Glasrud and Cary D. Wintz (Norman: University of Oklahoma Press, 2019), ch. 5; J. D. Williams, "The Separation of Church and State in Mormon Theory and Practice," *Dialogue: A Journal of Mormon Thought* 1, no. 2 (Summer 1966): 50; J. D. Williams, oral history interview with Everett L. Cooley, October 22, 1984, 36–37, Box 55, Folder 3, ECOH.

67. "Utah Advisory Committee," in *The National Conference and the Reports of the State Advisory Committee to the US Commission on Civil Rights, 1959* (Washington, D.C.: U.S. Government Printing Press, 1960), 379–80.

68. "An Act Amending Section 30-1-2, Utah Code Annotated 1953, Relating to Marriages Prohibited and Void . . . ," in *Laws of Utah* (Salt Lake City: Lorraine Press, 1963), chap. 42, sec. 1, p. 162; "Clyde Busy Signing Bills," *Daily Herald* (Provo, UT), March 19, 1963; Peggy Pascoe, *What Comes Naturally: Miscegenation Law and the Making of Race in America* (New York: Oxford University Press, 2009), 242–43.

364   NOTES

69. Kasai, oral history interview with Sandra T. Fuller, January 25, 1984, 71–72, Box 1, Folder 13, IJAU; Patrick Q. Mason, "The Prohibition of Interracial Marriage in Utah, 1888–1963," *Utah Historical Quarterly* 76, no. 2 (Spring 2008): 129–30; First Presidency Minutes, February 7, 1963, Box 52, Folder 4, DOM.

70. Albert Fritz to Governor George D. Clyde, April 16, 1963, Reel 63, Folder N, GDC.

71. Fritz, oral history interview with Leslie G. Kelen, May 15, 1984, 27–29, Box 4, Folder 6, IBU; Fritz to Richard D. Poll, November 2, 1963, Box 49, Folder 22, RDP.

72. Fritz, oral history interview with Kelen, 27–29; Sterling M. McMurrin, "A Note on the 1963 Civil Rights Statement," *Dialogue: A Journal of Mormon Thought* 12, no. 2 (Summer 1979): 60–63; McMurrin "taped monologue," ca. 1980, MLH.

73. Burnett, oral history interview with Leslie G. Kelen, September 20, 1983, 44, Box 4, Folder 3, IBU.

74. McMurrin, oral history interview with Gregory A. Prince, May 26, 1994, MLH; Harris and Bringhurst, *Mormon Church and Blacks*, 75.

75. Brown, *Conference Report of the Church of Jesus Christ of Latter-day Saints*, October 1963, 91.

76. Kimball, diary, October 6, 1963, reel 25, SWK; Brown, diary, October n.d., 1963, HBB; also in Box 52, Folder 12, RDP.

77. Burnett, oral history interview with Kelen, 44. See also "Mormon Leader Asserts Equality," *Utah Daily Chronicle*, October 7, 1963.

78. Brown to John W. Fitzgerald, October 21, 1963, Box 4, Folder 10, JWF; Spencer W. Kimball to Edward L. Kimball, November 1963, Box 63, Folder 6, SWK; Brown to Paul Cracroft, October 29, 1963, Box 171, Folder 2, EBF.

79. Martin Luther King Jr., "A Letter from a Birmingham Jail" (1963), in *A Testament of Hope: The Essential Writings and Speeches of Martin Luther King, Jr.*, ed. James M. Washington (New York: Harper One, 1986), 290–91. See also David J. Garrow, *Bearing the Cross: Martin Luther King, Jr. and the Southern Christian Leadership Conference* (New York: Perennial, 1986), 248–50, 291–92.

80. Kimball to Kimball, November 1963, Box 63, Folder 6, SWK.

81. J. Reuben Clark, "Plain Talk to Girls," *Improvement Era* 49, no. 8 (August 1946): 492.

82. Hugh B. Brown, *The Abundant Life* (Salt Lake City: Bookcraft, 1965), 208; Benson, *Title of Liberty*, 54; Stapley to George W. Romney, January 23, 1964, Box 313, Folder "Mormon Church, 1962–67," GWR. For the Birchers and Kennedy's assassination, see Miller, *A Conspiratorial Life*, 288–89.

83. Kimball to Kimball, November 1963.

84. "Romney Asked to Tell LDS Stand on Negroes," *Daily Herald* (Provo, UT), October 29, 1963.

85. Turner, interview with Romney, January 1964, at the Hotel Utah, Salt Lake City, in Wallace Turner, *The Mormon Establishment* (Boston: Houghton, Mifflin, 1966), 306–7.

NOTES

365

86. "Thousands across Nation Hold Sympathy Marches: Romney Leads a Protest," *New York Times*, March 10, 1965.

87. O. N. Malmquist, "Press for Civil Rights, Rebuff 'Hate Groups,' Romney Asks," *Salt Lake Tribune*, January 18, 1964; M. DeMar Teushher, "Romney Asks Devotion to U.S. Rights Cause," *Deseret News*, January 18, 1964.

88. Rick Perlstein, *Before the Storm: Barry Goldwater and the Unmaking of the American Consensus* (New York: Hill and Wang, 2001), 363; Alvin R. Felzenberg, *A Man and His Presidents: The Political Odyssey of William F. Buckley, Jr.* (New Haven: Yale University Press, 2017), 149, 157.

89. "Romney Supports Civil Rights Bill," *New York Times*, January 18, 1964; Richard Norton Smith, *On His Own Terms: A Life of Nelson Rockefeller* (New York: Random House, 2014), xxii–xxiii; Rick Perlstein, *Nixonland: The Rise of a President and the Fracturing of America* (New York: Scribner, 2008), 148.

90. Bennion to George T. Boyd, February 18, 1964, Box 1, Folder 4, MLB. For civil rights splitting the GOP, see John S. Huntington, *Far-Right Vanguard: The Radical Roots of Modern Conservatism* (Philadelphia: University of Pennsylvania Press, 2021), 176–77.

91. Stapley to Romney, January 23, 1964; McKay, diary, July 2, 1964, Box 57, Folder 1, DOM; Benson, *Title of Liberty*, 76.

92. McKay, diary, July 2, 1964.

93. Tanner, quoted in Glen W. Davidson, "Mormon Missionaries and the Race Question," *Christian Century* 82 (September 29, 1965): 1185; First Presidency Minutes, March 4, 1965, Box 59, Folder 3, DOM.

94. Kennedy, "Civil Rights Message" (June 11, 1963), and Johnson, "To Fulfill These Rights" (June 4, 1965), in *Ripples of Hope: Great American Civil Rights Speeches*, ed. Josh Gottheimer (New York: Basic Books, 2003), 227–32, 275–81; Anthony B. Pinn, "Race, Religion, and Theological Discourse," in *Religions in America: 1945 to the Present*, 3 vols., ed. Stephen J. Stein (New York: Cambridge University Press, 2012), 3:453–70; Henry Louis Gates Jr., *The Black Church: This Is Our Story, This Is Our Song* (New York: Penguin Press, 2021); Gary May, *Bending toward Justice: The Voting Rights Act and the Transformation of American Democracy* (New York: Basic Books, 2013), ch. 6.

95. William Mulder, "Revelation, Rights," *Utah Daily Chronicle*, April 5, 1965, Box 26, Folder 6, TEL; Lowell L. Bennion, "Religion and Social Responsibility," *Instructor* 100, no. 10 (October 1965): 391; Fritz, oral history interview with Leslie G. Kelen, May 5, 1984, 35, Box 2, Folder 6, IBU; "NAACP Protests Mormons' Silence on Civil Rights," March 11, 1965, NAACP.

96. Johnie M. Driver to Governor Calvin L. Rampton, March 6, 1965, Box 1, Folder 24, CLR; *Civil Rights Newsletter* 3, no. 3 (February 11, 1965), Box 24, Folder 3, JDW; "Utah Council of United Church Women," open letter, February 1, 1965, Box 1, Folder 24, CLR; "NAACP Protests Mormons' Silence on Civil Rights"; "NAACP Calls March for LDS Appeal," *Salt Lake Tribune*, March 7, 1965.

NOTES

97. "NAACP Presses Protests in Utah," *New York Times*, March 10, 1965; "Star Athlete Bares Testimony; Utah Discrimination Exposed," *Utah Daily Chronicle*, March 10, 1965; David O. McKay, diary, March 7, 1965, Box 59, Folder 3, DOM. For the Selma march, see May, *Bending toward Justice*, 85–90.

98. Ross, as noted in David O. McKay, diary, March 8, 1965, Box 59, Folder 3, DOM.

99. Fritz, quoted in Johnie M. Driver, "L.D.S. Church Leaders Should Speak Out for Moral Justice," March 9, 1965, NAACP; "NAACP Presses Protests in Utah," *New York Times*, March 10, 1965.

100. "A Clear Stand on Civil Rights," *Deseret News*, March 9, 1965.

101. Driver, "L.D.S. Church Leaders Should Speak Out for Moral Justice." Emphasis in the original.

102. Kimball, diary, March 9, 1965, reel 7, SWK; "NAACP Presses Protests in Utah"; "NAACP Calls March for LDS Appeal."

103. Sterling M. McMurrin, "Time Running Out," *Salt Lake Tribune*, March 12, 1965.

104. S.B. 44, "Civil Rights," May 11, 1965, in *Laws of the State of Utah, 1965, Passed by Regular Session of the Thirty-Sixth Legislature*, ch. 174, 634–35, USARS.

105. For the NAACP critical of Benson, see "Bedfellows: Benson and the Birchers," *NAACP Newsletter*, Salt Lake City Branch, April 1966, reel 7, part 27 (Utah), Selected Branch Files, *Papers of the National Association for the Advancement of Colored People*, LOC; Benson, conference address, "Not Commanded in All Things," April 6, 1965, unaltered version in David O. McKay scrapbook 79, DOM. First Presidency Minutes, May 3, 1965, Box 59, Folder 5, DOM: Benson, *An Enemy Hath Done This*, 310; "Attack on Housing Color Bar," *Deseret News*, September 24, 1966.

106. "Mormon 'Fight' over Civil Rights," *San Francisco Chronicle*, April 17, 1965; Brown to McMurrin, April 9, 1965, Box 301, Folder 12, SMM.

107. Ezra Taft Benson to Hugh B. Brown, October 8, 1963, HBB. Welch and Benson met in 1961 and became close friends. See BW. J. Edgar Hoover, *Masters of Deceit: The Story of Communism in America and How to Fight It* (New York: Holt, Rinehart and Winston, 1958), ch. 18; J. Edgar Hoover, *A Study of Communism* (New York: Holt, Rinehart and Winston, 1962), ch. 11; Benson to Hugh B. Brown, September 18, 1962, Box 3, Folder 4, HBBR. For Benson's praise of Welch, see Benson to Hugh B. Brown, July 31, 1963, HBB; Benson to Joseph Fielding Smith, July 31, 1963, MSS SC 1260, HBLL. Welch's anti–civil rights conspiracies are detailed in Robert Welch, *Birch Bulletin*, September 1965, 3–20; *What's Wrong with Civil Rights?* (Belmont, MA: American Opinion, 1965).

108. Gage, *G-Man*, 543–44; Welch, "What's Wrong with Civil Rights?," n.p.; Ezra Taft Benson to Robert Welch, August 11, 1965, BW; Benson to Welch, November 17, 1967, BW. For Benson's conspiracy views, see Harris, *Watchman on the Tower*, 57–59, 82–87; Matthew L. Harris, "Martin Luther King, Civil Rights, and Perceptions of a 'Communist Conspiracy,'" in *Thunder from the Right: Ezra Taft Benson in Mormonism and Politics*, ed. Matthew L. Harris

NOTES

367

(Urbana: University of Illinois Press, 2019), ch. 5. For Bircher conspiracy theories, see Miller, *A Conspiratorial Life*; Dallek, *Birchers*.

109. Adam Duncan informed the First Presidency that Benson's anti–civil rights message was "causing damage to the church and its' image." Duncan to First Presidency, November 1, 1963, HBB. Two members of King's inner circle were former members of the Communist Party. However, Hoover's wiretaps of King confirmed that both individuals were no longer active in the party. Still, Hoover continued to promote the idea that King was a communist. Gage, *G-Man*, 543–45; David J. Garrow, *The FBI and Martin Luther King, Jr.* (New York: Penguin, 1983), 40–43.

110. Johnson, letter to the editor, *Utah Daily Chronicle*, April 12, 1965, Box 4, Folder 2, EE; Judy Geissler, "Racial Bigotry: An Open Letter," BYU *Daily Universe*, May 7, 1969; Lon Wilcox, letter to the editor, BYU *Daily Universe*, May 12, 1969; Michael Vanhille, letter to the editor, BYU *Daily Universe*, May 12, 1969; W. Cleon Skousen, memo to Ernest L. Wilkinson, January 23, 1970, Box 177, Folder 16, ELW; Wimmer to King, December 2, 1966, and Head to King, May 20, 1967, MLK.

111. Martin Luther King Jr., *Strive toward Freedom* (1958), in *The Radical King*, ed. Cornell West (Boston: Beacon Press, 2015), 41–42; King, "Where Do We Go from Here?" (1967), in Washington, *A Testament of Hope*, 629–30; "Communism and Other Subversive Activities," 1964, NAACP.

112. Gary Gerstle, *American Crucible: Race and Nation in the Twentieth Century* (Princeton: Princeton University Press, 2001), 248; King, interview with *Playboy* magazine, 1965, in Washington, *A Testament of Hope*, 362.

113. NAACP resolution, July 10, 1965, NAACP.

114. For Tanner, see David O. McKay, diary, June 23, 1965, Box 60, Folder 2, DOM.

115. NAACP resolution, July 10, 1965.

116. David L. Chappell, *A Stone of Hope: Prophetic Religion and the Death of Jim Crow* (Chapel Hill: University of North Carolina Press, 2004), 107–8; Mark A. Noll, *God and Race in American Politics: A Short History* (Princeton: Princeton University Press, 2008), 130–32; John T. McGreevy, *Parish Boundaries: The Catholic Encounter with Race in the Twentieth-Century Urban North* (Chicago: University of Chicago Press, 1996), 147–49; Paul Hofmann, "Pope and Dr. King Confer on Rights," *New York Times*, September 19, 1964.

117. William D. Russell, "Martin Luther King: Satan or Saint?," *Saints' Herald* 110 (July 1, 1963): 434; RLDS First Presidency, "Our Position on Race and Color," *Saints' Herald* 110 (August 1, 1963): 506. See also Matthew L. Harris, "A Tale of Two Religions: RLDS and LDS Reponses to the Civil Rights Movement," *John Whitmer Historical Society Journal* 43, no. 1 (Spring–Summer 2023): 114–32.

118. Noll, *God and Race*, 131–32; Daniel K. Williams, *God's Own Party: The Making of the Christian Right* (New York: Oxford University Press, 2010), 70–72; Thomas S. Kidd, *Who Is an Evangelical: The History of a Movement in Crisis* (New Haven: Yale University Press, 2019), 101–3.

368 NOTES

119. Hugh B. Brown, quoted in "Mormon' Stand Draws Protest," *Arizona Daily Star*, March 12, 1965.

120. First Presidency Minutes, June 4, 1965, Box 60, Folder 1, DOM.

121. Lowell Bennion wrote, "I felt that [President McKay] would have changed the doctrine had he kept his health and vigor in his later years." In Peggy Fletcher, "Saint for All Seasons: An Interview with Lowell L. Bennion," *Sunstone*, February 1985, 11. For McKay's stroke, see Spencer W. Kimball, diary, February 19, 1965, reel 27, SWK.

122. Dunn, oral history interview with Gregory A. Prince, January 11, 1997, MLH; Brown, quoted in Davidson, "Mormon Missionaries and the Race Question," 1185.

123. Brown to Tanner, May 27, 1966, Box 82, Folder 1, EBF.

124. Benson, *Title of Liberty*, 39; Jack Anderson, "Reed Benson Spreads Birch Gospel," *Washington Post*, January 15, 1965; David O. McKay, diary, October 26, 1962, Box 51, Folder 5, DOM. For Watts, see Kevin Boyle, *The Shattering: America in the 1960s* (New York: W.W. Norton, 2021), 208–9.

125. Reed A. Benson, "Memo to the Utah Chapters" of the John Birch Society, September 2, 1965, BW; also in Box 27, Folder 7, JDW.

126. First Presidency Minutes, September 17, 1965, Box 60, Folder 6, DOM; "NAACP Chapter Claims Riot Report 'Malicious,'" *Ogden Standard-Examiner*, September 28, 1965; "NAACP Assails Rumors of Protest at LDS Meet," *Salt Lake Tribune*, September 29, 1965. For Latter-day Saints accepting Benson's conspiracy theories, see Harris, *Watchman on the Tower*, 79. Other members also opposed the memo. See Elder Bean to First Presidency, September 30, 1965, HBB.

127. For Reed's relationship with his father, see Sheri L. Dew, *Ezra Taft Benson: A Biography* (Salt Lake City: Deseret Book, 1987), 152, 240, 248, 277.

128. A general authority conveyed to Eugene England that Mormon racial theology might "stir up an issue" that could be "physically dangerous to the General Authorities." England, oral history with Davis Bitton, September 16, 1975, 15, JMOH. Apostle Kimball also feared that militant activists might harm the Brethren. Spencer W. Kimball to Edward L. Kimball, November 1963, Box 63, Folder 6, SWK.

129. Council of the Twelve Minutes, November 4, 1965, Box 64, Folder 8, SWK.

130. Ibid.

131. "Mormons: The Black Saints of Nigeria," *Time*, June 18, 1965, http://content. time.com/time/subscriber/article/0,33009,898887,00.html.

132. Michael A. Cohen, *American Maelstrom: The 1968 Election and the Politics of Division* (New York: Oxford University Press, 2016), 186–87; J. B. Haws, *The Mormon Image in the American Mind: Fifty Years of Public Perception* (New York: Oxford University Press, 2013), ch. 2.

133. Warren Weaver Jr., "Romney Denies Mormon Policy Curbs His Fight for Civil Rights," *New York Times*, February 21, 1967; Willmar Thorkelson,

"Newspaper Says Romney Will Have to Face Religious Issue," *Minneapolis, Minnesota Star*, January 28, 1967.

134. Lenore Romney, interview with *Look* magazine, November 1967, quoted in "Mrs. Romney Backs Mormons in Their Teachings on Negroes," *New York Times*, November 24, 1967.

135. Udall to McKay, May 16, 1967, Box 64, Folder 5, DOM.

136. Udall, interview with James W. Ure, 1999, in *Leaving the Fold: Candid Conversations with Inactive Mormons*, ed. James W. Ure (Salt Lake City: Signature Books, 1999), 71. Sterling McMurrin edited Udall's draft. McMurrin to Udall, December 14, 1966, Box 220, Folder 3, SMM.

137. Stewart L. Udall, "An Appeal for Full Fellowship for the Negro," *Dialogue: A Journal of Mormon Thought* 2, no. 2 (Summer 1967): 5–7.

138. Ibid., 6.

139. For Latter-day Saint letters to Udall, which total in the dozens, see Box 209, Folder 5, SLU. See also Wallace Turner, "Udall Entreats Mormons on Race," *New York Times*, May 19, 1967; Dan L. Thrapp, "Race Discrimination Becoming Hot Issue in Mormon Church," *Los Angeles Times*, August 27, 1967.

140. England, oral history with Bitton, 13.

141. First Presidency Minutes, May 24, 1967, Box 65, Folder 2, DOM.

142. Kimball to Udall, May 25, 1967, Stapley to Udall, May 26, 1967, Box 209, Folder 5, SLU.

143. Udall to Romney, May 16, 1967, Box 238, Folder "Mormon Church, 1963–1966," GWR.

144. "Statement in Response to Secretary Udall's Article in *Dialogue*" [1967], Box 238, Folder, "Mormon Church, 1963–1966," GWR; Udall, interview with Ure, in Ure, *Leaving the Fold*, 69.

145. Armand L. Mauss, "Mormonism and the Negro: Faith, Folklore, and Civil Rights," *Dialogue: A Journal of Mormon Thought* 2, no. 4 (Winter 1967): 38–39. Mauss was later embarrassed by this statement and no longer considered himself an apologist. Mauss, email to Matthew Harris, April 19, 2020.

146. Harold B. Lee, "Loyalty," address given to Seminary and Institute Faculty, Brigham Young University, July 8, 1966, 5, Box 14, Folder 4, GTB.

147. In the 1950s, Manion founded an ultraconservative radio and TV program called *Manion Forum*. Benson praised his work. See Box 60, Folder 5, CM. For Benson quoting Manion, see Benson, *Title of Liberty*, 76; Benson, *An Enemy Hath Done This*, 82–83. Benson also arranged for Manion to speak at Assembly Hall on Temple Square. See "Minutes of Visit with President David O. McKay by Elder Ezra Taft Benson," May 30, 1966, Box 63, Folder 6, DOM. Benson spoke at Billy Hargis's "Anti-Communism Leadership School," along with other prominent segregationists. Richard Gid Powers, *Not without Honor: The History of American Anticommunism* (New York: Free Press, 1995), 279; Hargis to Reed Benson, August 8, 1962, reel 2, ETB. Benson read the "Dan Smoot Report" and quoted him in his writings. Benson, *An Enemy Hath Done*

370 NOTES

This, 139–40; Benson, *Title of Liberty*, 73. For right-wing talk radio emerging during the Cold War, particularly the influence of Smoot, Hargis, and Manion, see Heather Hendershot, *What's Fair on the Air? Cold War Right-Wing Broadcasting and Public Interest* (Chicago: University of Chicago Press, 2011), chs. 2 and 5; Nicole Hemmer, *Messengers of the Right: Conservative Media and the Transformation of American Politics* (Philadelphia: University of Pennsylvania Press, 2016), 47–48, 60–61, 112–13.

148. Robert Welch arranged the ticket: see Welch to William J. Grede, April 7, 1967, Box 26, Folder 1, WJG; Ezra Taft Benson to Robert Welch, March 8, 1968, BW. Thurmond said that he never consented to it. Thurmond to Harry Feyer, August 14, 1967, Box 26, Folder 2, WJG. For Thurmond and civil rights, see Thurber, *Republicans and Race*, 224–25, 302–3; Huntington, *Far-Right Vanguard*, 153–54.

149. Benson, "Trade and Treason" (February 17, 1967), in Benson, *An Enemy Hath Done This*, 69–70. For riots in 1967, see Peter B. Levy, *The Great Uprising: Race Riots in Urban America during the 1960s* (Cambridge: Cambridge University Press, 2018). For Black Power, see Peniel E. Joseph, *Waiting 'til the Midnight Hour: A Narrative History of Black Power in America* (New York: Henry Holt, 2006).

150. McKay, diary, July 25, 1967, Box 65, Folder 4, DOM; Brown, diary, August 6–12, 1967, HBB; also in Box 52, Folder 14, RDP.

151. First Presidency Minutes, September 1, 1967, Box 66, Folder 1, DOM; Eric A. Eliason and Tom Mould, *Latter-Day Lore: Mormon Folklore Stories* (Salt Lake City: University of Utah Press, 2013), 269.

152. Mark E. Petersen, "Our Divine Destiny," BYU devotional address, February 20, 1968, *BYU Speeches*, https://speeches.byu.edu/talks/mark-e-petersen/div ine-destiny/; Petersen's general conference address, April 6, 1968, "America and God," *Improvement Era* 71, no. 6 (June 1968): 76–79. "By any means necessary" was a phrase that Malcolm X often used, as well as other Black Power advocates. Joseph, *Waiting 'til the Midnight Hour*.

153. Benson, quoted in McKay diary, September 22, 1967, Box 66, Folder 2, DOM.

154. Ezra Taft Benson, "Trust Not the Arm of Flesh," *Improvement Era* 70, no. 12 (December 1967): 55–58.

155. Ibid., 55, 58. Reed Benson to Robert Welch, November 2, 1967, BW.

156. Ezra Taft Benson, *Civil Rights—Tool of Communist Deception* (Salt Lake City: Deseret Book, 1968).

157. Benson, *An Enemy Hath Done This*, ch. 13; Dew, *Ezra Taft Benson*; Francis M. Gibbons, *Ezra Taft Benson: Statesmen, Patriot, Prophet of God* (Salt Lake City: Deseret Book, 1996).

158. A 1972 poll revealed that one out of three Latter-day Saints in Utah believed that there was "a black conspiracy to destroy the Mormon Church." See Wallace Turner, "Mormons Operating a Special Meeting Unit," *New York Times*, April 16, 1972. Latter-day Saints who supported Benson's conspiracy theories are well-documented. See, for example, W. Cleon Skousen,

NOTES 371

"The Communist Attack on the Mormons," March 1970, in "Special Report by National Research Group," American Fork, Utah, MLH; Willard Woods, "Martin Luther King Day," *Freemen Digest*, January 1984, 21–24; Tara Westover, *Educated: A Memoir* (New York: Random House, 2018), 248; Matthew L. Harris and Madison S. Harris, "The Last State to Honor MLK: Utah and the Quest for Racial Justice," *Utah Historical Quarterly* 88, no. 1 (Winter 2020): 5–21; "Latter-day Conservative" website, https://www.latterdayconservative.com/author/ezrataftbenson/.

159. McKay, quoted in Wallace Turner, "Head of Mormonism on Negroes, on Coast, Sees No Easing of Church Views," *New York Times,* November 17, 1964; Tanner, quoted in "The Swarming Mormons," *Seattle Magazine*, December 1967, 60.

CHAPTER 5

1. Hollis B. Bach to Wilkinson, April 11, 1968, Box 463, Folder 19, ELWP.
2. For two insightful accounts of the athletic protests, see Gary James Bergera, "'This Time of Crisis': The Race-Based Anti-BYU Athletic Protests of 1968–1971," *Utah Historical Quarterly* 81, no. 3 (Summer 2013): 204–29; J. B. Haws, *The Mormon Image in the American Mind: Fifty Years of Public Perception* (New York: Oxford University Press, 2013), ch. 3.
3. Quoted in Mike Barney, "SJS Blacks May Boycott Y Game," BYU *Daily Universe*, November 25, 1968.
4. Ernest L. Wilkinson and Leonard J. Arrington, *Brigham Young University: The First One Hundred Years*, 4 vols. (Provo, UT: Brigham Young University Press, 1976), 2:572–74, 3:745–47, 779–80.
5. Gary James Bergera, "Ernest L. Wilkinson's Appointment as Seventh President of Brigham Young University," *Journal of Mormon History* 23, no. 2 (Fall 1997): 128–54.
6. Gary James Bergera and Ronald Priddis, *Brigham Young University: A House of Faith* (Salt Lake City: Signature Books, 1985), 25–26, 99–101; Wilkinson and Arrington, *Brigham Young University*, 2:555, 3:280, 316–18; Gary James Bergera, "Student Political Activism at Brigham Young University, 1965–71," *Utah Historical Quarterly* 81, no. 1 (Winter 2013): 65–90.
7. Wilkinson to Petersen, April 14, 1968, Box 464, Folder 1, ELWP.
8. Marion Bowen to Wilkinson, July 1, 1953, and Wilkinson's reply, July 8, 1953, Box 3, Folder 3, WEB.
9. Wilkinson to Orson Haynie, August 15, 1952, and Wilkinson to Smith, August 15, 1952, Box 3, Folder 5, WEB.
10. Lee, quoted in Wilkinson diary, November 10, 1960, Box 100, Folder 4, ELW.
11. Jane Dailey, *White Fright: The Sexual Panic at the Heart of America's Racist History* (New York: Basic Books, 2020).

NOTES

12. David Lawrence McKay, oral history interview with Gordon Irving, March 30, 1984, 176, JMOH. For demographics of Black people in Utah, see Quintard Taylor, *In Search of the Racial Frontier: African Americans in the American West, 1528–1990* (New York: W. W. Norton, 1998), 135, 253; James B. Allen, *Still the Right Place: Utah's Second Half-Century of Statehood, 1945–1995* (Provo: Charles Redd Center for Western Studies at Brigham Young University and Utah State Historical Society, 2016), 461–62.

13. William B. Arthur, interview with Smith, July 14, 1962, in Jeff Nye, "Memo from a Mormon," *Look*, October 22, 1963, 78, in Box 9, Folder 6, JFS; Clark, diary, November 5, 1941, Box 11, Folder 2, JRC. For "darkies" as a racial slur, see Eric Foner, *Forever Free: The Story of Emancipation and Reconstruction* (New York: Alfred A. Knopf, 2005), 216. For the "negro twist" reference, see Joseph Fielding Smith to Wilkinson, September 10, 1963, Box 269, Folder 16, ELWP. For White depictions of Black people in the media, see Robert N. Entman and Andrew Rojecki, *The Black Image in the White Mind: Media and Race in America* (Chicago: University of Chicago Press, 2001); Karen L. Cox, *Dreaming of Dixie: How the South Was Created in American Popular Culture* (Chapel Hill: University of North Carolina Press, 2011), 165–66.

14. Kimball, diary, August 4, 1965, reel 27, SWK.

15. Thomas S. Monson, *On the Lord's Errand: Memoirs of Thomas S. Monson* (Salt Lake City: Self-published, 1985), 184; Bruce R. McConkie, "The New Revelation on Priesthood," in *Priesthood* (Salt Lake City: Deseret Book, 1981), 127; Bruce R. McConkie, "The Coming Tests and Trials of Glory," *Conference Report*, April 1980, https://www.churchofjesuschrist.org/study/general-conference/1980/04/the-coming-tests-and-trials-and-glory?lang=eng; Brown to Ernest Cook, May 6, 1968, HBB.

16. Examples of these articles can be found in Ezra Taft Benson–Robert Welch Correspondence, JBS Headquarters; Box 64, Folder 6, SWK; "Clarkana," Box 295, "Negro" Folder, JRC.

17. First Presidency Minutes, February 15, 1961, Box 47, Folder 1, DOM. See also Jessica Marie Nelson, "Race, Latter-day Saint Doctrine, and Athletics at Utah State University, 1960–1961," *Utah Historical Quarterly* 88, no. 1 (Winter 2020): 22–37.

18. "Church Schools and Students of Color" [1961], Box 3, Folder 3, WEB. Berrett's racism is well-chronicled in Rebecca de Schweinitz, "'There Is No Equality': William E. Berrett, BYU, and Healing the Wounds of Racism in the Latter-day Saint Past and Present," *Dialogue: A Journal of Mormon Thought* 52, no. 3 (Fall 2019): 59–83.

19. "Church Schools and Students of Color."

20. Ibid.

21. "Questions and Answers," n.d., Box 3, Folder 5, WEB.

22. Kimball, quoted in Abe Chunin, "The Negro Policy in Athletics at BYU," *Arizona Daily Star*, September 12, 1962.

NOTES

373

23. Peter B. Levy, *The Great Uprising: Race Riots in Urban America during the 1960s* (Cambridge: Cambridge University Press, 2018), 153; see also Elizabeth Hinton, *America on Fire: The Untold History of Police Violence and Black Rebellion since the 1960s* (New York: Liveright, 2021), 21–22.

24. Benson, memo to General Authorities, re: Martin Luther King, April 6, 1968, CHL; also in Box 63, Folder 1, SWK; and Box 12, Folder 23, JWM. Brown, *Conference Report*, April 5–7, 1968, 3; McKay, diary, April 5, 1968, Box 67, Folder 4, DOM. For Brown's response to the memo, see Edwin B. Firmage, oral history interview with Gregory A. Prince, June 6, 1995, and Charlie Brown, oral history interview with Gregory A. Prince, May 24, 1996, MHL. For context to this memo, see Matthew L. Harris, "Martin Luther King, Civil Rights, and Perceptions of a 'Communist Conspiracy,'" in *Thunder from the Right: Ezra Taft Benson in Mormonism and Politics*, ed. Matthew L. Harris (Urbana: University of Illinois Press, 2019), 137–38.

25. Benson to the First Presidency and Council of the Twelve Apostles, "re: Dangers Ahead," April 10, 1968, Box 67, Folder 4, DOM.

26. Ezra Taft Benson, "Americans Are Destroying America," *Improvement Era* 71, no. 6 (April 6, 1968): 68, 70. For Black Power militants, see Peniel E. Joseph, *Waiting 'til the Midnight Hour: A Narrative History of Black Power in America* (New York: Henry Holt, 2006).

27. Ezra Taft Benson, "Book of Mormon Warns America," May 21, 1968, in Ezra Taft Benson, *An Enemy Hath Done This*, compiled by Jerreld L. Newquist (Salt Lake City: Parliament Publishers, 1969), ch. 29; Matthew L. Harris, *Watchman on the Tower: Ezra Taft Benson and the Making of the Mormon Right* (Salt Lake City: University of Utah Press, 2020), 84.

28. Hugh B. Brown, "God Is the Gardener" (May 31, 1968), *BYU Speeches of the Year, 1967–68* (Provo, UT: Brigham Young University Press, 1968), 2. For the First Presidency's instructions not to publish Benson's address, see Dean A. Peterson, memo to Ernest L. Wilkinson, June 28, 1971, Box 577, Folder 8, ELWP; Benson to Wilkinson, June 23, 1971, Box 577, Folder 8, ELWP. For the controversy that Brown's address sparked, see First Presidency Minutes, July 19, 1968, Box 68, Folder 1, DOM.

29. "Negro Trackmen Shun Utah Meet: 8 on El Paso Squad Won't Compete at Brigham Young," *New York Times*, April 13, 1968; "Negroes to Boycott BYU Meet; Cougars Deny UTEP Charge," *Salt Lake Tribune*, April 12, 1968; "BYU Wins Triangular Track Meet," *El Paso Times*, April 14, 1968.

30. Morgan, quoted in Jack Olsen, "In an Alien World," *Sports Illustrated*, July 15, 1968, 41–42.

31. "Statement Issued by President Wilkinson," April 1968, Box 443, Folder 2, ELW; Ray to Wilkinson, April 22, 1968, Box 443, Folder 2, ELWP. See also Wilkinson, diary, April 13, 1968, Box 102, Folder 5, ELW.

32. Wilkinson to Ray, April 16, 1968, and Wilkinson to Ray, May 3, 1968, Box 443, Folder 2, ELWP.

374 NOTES

33. Millet, quoted in "Negroes to Boycott BYU Meet"; "Mormon Leaders Deny Having Negro Bias," *Denver Post*, April 14, 1968.

34. Fitzgerald to Millet, cc. to Wayne Banderberg, April 13, 1968, Box 27, Folder 24, JWF; also in Box 443, Folder 2, ELWP; and Box 64, Folder 1, SWK. See also Millet, memo to Wilkinson, April 18, 1968, Box 443, Folder 2, ELWP.

35. Wilkinson to Kimball, April 13, 1968, Box 64, Folder 1, SWK; Dyer, quoted in First Presidency Minutes, May 8, 1968, Box 67, Folder 5, DOM. A "jack Mormon" is someone critical of the church who doesn't adhere to all its teachings.

36. For George Wallace's request for Benson to join the ticket, see Wallace to David O. McKay, February 12, 1968, Box 2, Folder 3, GCW, and McKay's response, February 14, 1968, Box 67, Folder 2, DOM. Harris, *Watchman on the Tower*, 74–76; Tom Wicker, "Impact on Romney Move: His Withdrawal Could Prove to Be One of Decisive Actions of Election," *New York Times*, February 29, 1968.

37. First Presidency Minutes, March 1, 1968, Box 67, Folder 3, DOM. For fringe groups supporting Wallace's candidacy, see Michael A. Cohen, *American Maelstrom: The 1968 Election and the Politics of Division* (New York: Oxford University Press, 2016), 232, 236; John S. Huntington, *Far-Right Vanguard: The Radical Roots of Modern Conservatism* (Philadelphia: University of Pennsylvania Press, 2021), 192–95, 200–203; Dan T. Carter, *The Politics of Rage: George Wallace, The Origins of the New Conservatism, and the Transformation of American Politics* (New York: Simon and Schuster, 1995), 314, 343, 356, 366.

38. Mark L. Grover, "Religious Accommodation in the Land of Religious Democracy: Mormon Priesthood and Black Brazilians," *Dialogue: A Journal of Mormon Thought* 17, no. 3 (Autumn 1984): 30. Thanks to Stirling Adams for checking several Portuguese editions of *The Way to Perfection* at the L. Tom Perry Special Collections, BYU.

39. "Memorandum on a Trip to See President Joseph Fielding Smith," June 29, 1964, Box 7, Folder 9, JC; James R. Clark, comp., *Messages of the First Presidency*, 6 vols. (Salt Lake City: Bookcraft, 1965–75); First Presidency to Earl C. Crockett (acting BYU president), May 21, 1964, Box 42, Folder 11, RKT; Council of the Twelve Minutes, October 6, 1966, Box 64, Folder 4, SWK; Joseph Fielding Smith, *Answers to Gospel Questions*, 5 vols. (Salt Lake City: Deseret Book, 1957–66), 4:170. McKay refused to publish a controversial address by Eldred Smith in which the patriarch told BYU students that Black people would be servants to White people in the resurrection. McKay, diary, November 13, 1966, Box 63, Folder 7, DOM; Ernest L. Wilkinson to Smith, November 25, 1966, Box 378, Folder 3, ELWP. For Smith's address, see "A Patriarchal Blessing Defined," November 8, 1966, CHL; also in Box 211, Folder 6, ELW.

40. Hollis B. Bach to Ernest L. Wilkinson, May 24, 1968, Box 463, Folder 19, ELW.

NOTES

375

41. Executive Committee of the BYU Board of Trustees, "Problems re: So-called Civil Rights," April 25, 1968, Box 248, Folder 1, ELW; Ernest L. Wilkinson, memo to Clyde D. Sandgren, "Civil Rights Matters," May 16, 1968, Box 163, Folder 19, ELW.

42. Ernest L. Wilkinson, "Memorandum of Statement Made to Inspection Team from the Department of Health, Education, and Welfare," in Wilkinson, diary, May 16, 1968, Box 102, Folder 5, ELW.

43. Ibid.

44. Ibid. BYU administrators would use this same tactic years later when the federal government investigated BYU for its discriminatory policies against LBGTQ+ students. See Kevin Worthen (BYU president) to Catherine E. Lhamon (assistant secretary for civil rights, U.S. Department of Education), November 19, 2021, https://www2.ed.gov/about/offices/list/ocr/docs/t9-rel-exempt/brigham-young-university-request-11192021.pdf.

45. Wilkinson, "Memorandum of Statement Made to Inspection Team from the Department of Health, Education, and Welfare."

46. Bruce Ackerman, *We the People*, vol. 3: *The Civil Rights Revolution* (Cambridge, MA: Harvard University Press, 2014), 232–41; Hugh Davis Graham, "The Civil Rights Act and the American Regulatory State," in *Legacies of the 1964 Civil Rights Act*, ed. Bernard Grofman (Charlottesville: University of Virginia Press, 2000), 46–49.

47. Stephen C. Halpern, *On the Limits of the Law: The Ironic Legacy of Title VI of the 1964 Civil Rights Act* (Baltimore: Johns Hopkins University Press, 1995), ch. 3.

48. Bach to Wilkinson, May 24, 1968, Box 463, Folder 19, ELWP.

49. These statistics can be found in Box 42, Folder 11, RKT.

50. Wilkinson, diary, May 1, 1968, Box 102, Folder 5, ELW; Ezra Taft Benson to Wilkinson, March 27, 1968, Box 461, Folder 8, ELWP.

51. "Opinion of Wilkinson, Cragun & Barker regarding Application of Federal Civil Rights Acts to Brigham Young University," June 5, 1968, 35–36, Box 163, Folder 19, ELWP; see also Robert W. Barker to Clyde D. Sandgren, July 12, 1968, Box 163, Folder 19, ELWP. For context to *Jones v. Mayer*, see Ackerman, *Civil Rights Revolution*, 209–17.

52. Barker, memorandum for Ernest L. Wilkinson and Clyde D. Sandgren, "Privileged and Confidential," July 3, 1968, Box 463, Folder 19, ELWP.

53. Sterling M. McMurrin, *The Theological Foundations of the Mormon Religion* (Salt Lake City: University of Utah Press, 1965).

54. Sterling M. McMurrin, "The Negroes among the Mormons," address at the annual banquet of the Salt Lake City Chapter of the NAACP, June 21, 1968, 7, 9, Box 289, Folder 2, SMM; copies also in Box 14, Folder 30, JFS; Box 64, Folder 1, SWK.

55. McMurrin, "The Negroes among the Mormons," 7.

56. Wilkins to McMurrin, [June 1968], Box 290, Folder 4, SMM. For the dozens of letters both praising and criticizing the address, see Box 290, Folder 3, SMM.

NOTES

57. "Mormons Says Church to Lose 'Thousands' over Negro Stand," *Palo Alto Times*, June 22, 1968. See also "Member Loss Is Foreseen for Mormons," *Easton Express*, June 22, 1968; "LDS Church May Lose Thousands over Bias," *Las Vegas Review-Journal*, June 23, 1968; "Expert Says Racism Hurts Mormon Church," *Bridgeport Post*, June 23, 1968.

58. First Presidency Minutes, June 26, 1968, Box 67, Folder 6, DOM.

59. Dyer's call to the First Presidency caught the apostles off guard. Spencer Kimball noted, "We were all shocked and surprised and almost numbed." Kimball, diary, September 21, 1967, reel 30, SWK.

60. Four by Alvin R. Dyer: *The Meaning of Truth* (Salt Lake City: Deseret Book, 1961); *The Challenge* (Salt Lake City: Deseret Book, 1962); *Who Am I* (Salt Lake City: Deseret Book, 1966); *The Refiner's Fire* (Salt Lake City: Deseret Book, 1969).

61. Alvin R. Dyer, "For What Purpose?," address to a missionary conference, Oslo, Norway, October 30, 1961, CHL; also in Box 11, Folder 32, JFS.

62. McMurrin, oral history interview with Gregory A. Prince, October 30, 1994, Box 289, Folder 11, SMM; First Presidency Minutes, June 26, 1968.

63. First Presidency Minutes, June 26, 1968.

64. McMurrin to Llewelyn McKay, Edward McKay, and David Lawrence McKay, August 26, 1968, and Edward's reply, September 19, 1968, both in Box 291, Folder 11, SMM.

65. McKay, quoted in McMurrin, transcript of a taped monologue, ca. 1980, Box 22, Folder 2, GAP.

66. Wilkinson, diary, May 29, 1968, Box 102, Folder 5, ELW.

67. Brown to McMurrin, September 19, 1968, Box 291, Folder 11, SMM.

68. McMurrin, transcript of a taped monologue; Taggart to McMurrin, March 15, 1968, and McMurrin's reply, April 2, 1968, Box 290, Folder 7, SMM.

69. Wilkinson, memo to Sandgren, December 7, 1968, Box 463, Folder 20, ELWP.

70. Bach to Wilkinson, November 1, 1968, Box 463, Folder 19, and November 15, 1968, Box 163, Folder 19, ELWP.

71. Petersen to Stone, July 9, 1968, Box 464, Folder 1, ELWP.

72. Brinkerhoff to Hudspeth, November 5, 1968, Box 45, Records and Correspondence, 1966–1969, Preliminary Register of the Athletic Records and Correspondence, HBLL; "Y Students Favor Negro Recruitment," BYU *Daily Universe*, December 19, 1968.

73. Edwards, quoted in Ernest L. Wilkinson, memo to Board of Trustees, October 29, 1969, 9, "Compiled Information Concerning African Americans, BYU, and the Church," HBLL. See also Harry Edwards, *The Revolt of the Black Athlete* (New York: Free Press, 1969), 84–87, 97–108, 124.

74. Darron T. Smith, *When Race, Religion, and Sport Collide: Black Athletes at BYU and Beyond* (Lanham, MD: Rowman and Littlefield, 2016), 72–75.

75. Ernest L. Wilkinson, memo to the BYU Board of Trustees, "Confidential— For Use of Trustees Only," December 4, 1968, Box 10, Folder 19, JFS. See also Wilkinson, memo to Board of Trustees, October 29, 1969, 9.

NOTES

377

76. Wilkinson to Bach, December 17, 1968, Box 163, Folder 29, ELWP; Sandgren, memo to Wilkinson, September 19, 1969, "Proposed Letter to Hollis Bach," Box 163, Folder 29, ELWP.

77. Thomas, memo to Wilkinson, January 21, 1969, Box 556, Folder 12, ELWP.

78. Thomas, memo to Wilkinson, re: "Possible Effects on Academic Programs If Racial Issue Is Unresolved at BYU," January 30, 1969, Box 556, Folder 12, ELWP. Wilkinson also accepted this premise. He listed two consequences in his diary if BYU didn't comply with Title VI: loss of "federal funds" and loss of membership in the Western Athletic Conference. Wilkinson, diary, May 1, 1968, Box 102, Folder 5, ELW.

79. Hanks, diary, January 10, 1969, MDH.

80. Kimball, diary, February 5, 1969, reel 30, SWK; Digest of Minutes of Meeting of Brigham Young Board of Trustees, February 5, 1969, Box 489, Folder 14, ELWP.

81. "Memorandum of Discussion during BYU Board of Trustees Meeting Held on April 9, 1969," Box 488, Folder 13, ELWP; Wilkinson, memo to Board of Trustees, October 29, 1969, 10–11; Kimball, diary, April 9, 1969, reel 30, SWK.

82. Lee, quoted in Wilkinson memo to unknown recipient, July 18, 1970, Box 272, Folder 17, ELW; "Memorandum of Discussion during BYU Board of Trustees Meeting," April 9, 1969, Box 488, Folder 13, ELWP; Benson to Ernest L. Wilkinson, March 27, 1968, Box 461, Folder 8, ELWP. Benson had a long history of opposing federal aid to education. Benson to Wilkinson, January 19, 1959, reel 6, ETB; Benson to Dwight D. Eisenhower, January 19, 1959, reel 6, ETB.

83. "Memorandum of Discussion during BYU Board of Trustees Meeting Held on April 9, 1969"; Lee, quoted in Wilkinson memo to unknown recipient, July 18, 1970.

84. Wilkinson diary, September 9, 1968, Box 103, Folder 1, ELW; "Memorandum of Discussion during BYU Board of Trustees Meeting Held on April 9, 1969," Box 488, Folder 13, ELWP.

85. Hanks, diary, April 29, 1969, MDH.

86. Berrett, "The Negro Situation," address at the Church Education Coordinators Convention, March 6, 1969, Box 3, Folder 5, WEB.

87. Ibid.

88. Wilkinson to Bach, March 19, 1969, Box 515, Folder 5, ELWP; Digest of Minutes of Meeting of Brigham Young University Board of Trustees, March 5, 1969, Box 489, Folder 14, ELWP.

89. In 1968 and 1970, according to statistics that BYU filed with the U.S. Office for Civil Rights, 0.03% of the student body were "Negroes." In Box 42, Folder 11, RKT. See also Wilkinson, memo to the Board of Trustees, October 29, 1969, 3, Unnamed Black BYU student quoted in "No Flag Burning at Brigham Young—A University without Trouble," *U.S. New and World Report*, January 20, 1969, 59.

378   NOTES

90. Bach to Wilkinson, March 27, 1969, Box 515, Folder 4, ELWP; see also Digest of Minutes of Meeting of Brigham Young University Board of Trustees, April 9, 1969, Box 489, Folder 14, ELWP.

91. Bach to Wilkinson, June 23, 1969, Box 515, Folder 3, ELWP.

92. Lee, quoted in "Memorandum of Discussion during BYU Board of Trustees Meeting," April 9, 1968.

93. Wilkinson, memo to the Board of Trustees, October 29, 1969, 2, 31.

94. Digest of Minutes of Meeting of Brigham Young Board of Trustees, September 4, 1969, Box 489, Folder 14, ELWP.

95. Ibid.

96. Middlemiss, notes, March 24, 1969, Box 69, Folder 5, DOM.

97. Brown, diary, August 29, 1969, HBB; copy in Box 52, Folder 15, RDP.

98. David Lawrence McKay, oral history interview with Gordon Irving, March 30, 1984, 176, JMOH.

99. First Presidency Minutes, September 10, 1969, Box 70, Folder 5, DOM.

100. Ibid.

101. First Presidency Minutes, September 17, 1969, Box 70, Folder 6, DOM.

102. Dyer analysis of Taggart's manuscript, undated, in Clare Middlemiss notebook titled "Notes," MLH; First Presidency Minutes, September 30, 1969, Box 70, Folder 6, DOM.

103. Charles Brown commented that his father had "a very strong ego." Charles Manley Brown and Zola Brown Hodson, interview with Eugene Campbell, June 7, 1973, 12, Box 30, Folder 2, EEC.

104. First Presidency Minutes, September 24, 1969, Box 70, Folder 6, DOM; Tanner to Wahlquist, September 25, 1969, Box 54, Folder 1, LFA.

105. Paul Salisbury, interview with "President Hugh B. Brown at 8:00 a.m., in his office at 47 East South Temple, Salt Lake City," September 29, 1969, Box 172, Folder 9, EE.

106. L. Brent Goates, *Harold B. Lee: Prophet and Seer* (Salt Lake City: Bookcraft, 1985), 388–89; Francis M. Gibbons, *Ezra Taft Benson: Statesman, Patriot, Prophet of God* (Salt Lake City: Deseret Book, 1996), 261–62; Kimball, diary, September 25, 1969, reel 33, SWK.

107. Spencer W. Kimball, diary, August 31, 1965, reel 27, SWK; Salisbury, interview with Brown, September 29, 1969; Marjorie Hyer, "Mormon Church Dissolves Black Bias," *Washington Post*, June 10, 1978. For Fleming's work at the Hotel Utah and his association with general authorities, see Frances Fleming, oral history interview with Leslie G. Kelen, July 29, 1983, 36–37, 79–80, Box 7, Folder 6, IBU. Several apostles considered Fleming a friend and admired his "faithfulness to the Church." Edward L. Kimball and Andrew E. Kimball Jr., *Spencer W. Kimball: Twelfth President of the Church of Jesus Christ of Latter-day Saints* (Salt Lake City: Bookcraft, 1977), 345; Heidi S. Swinton, *To the Rescue: The Biography of Thomas S. Monson* (Salt Lake City: Deseret Book, 2010), 395.

NOTES

379

108. Fleming to Tanner, May 6, 1962, in "Solving the Racial Problem in Utah," 8, Box 3, Folder 13, HGI. Fleming also made his views known to friends. See Heber C. Snell, oral history interview with Frederick S. Buchanan, Lewis Max Rogers, and Dale LeCheminant, June 13 and October 18, 1973, 66, Box 56, Folder 7, ECOH; Fleming to Heber C. Snell, January 4, 1964, Box 2, Folder 10, HCS. For Fleming affirming his faith in the church, see "Seminary Students Hear Negro LDS Convert," *Leader-Garland Times* (Tremonton, UT), November 20, 1969.

109. Lee's daughter, Maurine Lee Wilkins, explained this to her friend Romano Bernhard. Bernhard, oral history with Gregory A. Prince, December 5, 1998, MLH. Wilkinson, diary, October 27, 1969, Box 103, Folder 3, ELW.

110. Salisbury, interview with Brown, September 29, 1969.

111. David Lawrence McKay, the president's son, explained that during the "last few years" of his father's life "old age came on and he didn't like to make decisions." McKay, oral history interview with Irving, March 30, 1984, 176.

112. Edwin B. Firmage, oral history interview with Gregory A. Prince, October 10, 1996, MLH; Ernest L. Wilkinson, diary, June 10, 1968, Box 102, Folder 5, and January 27, 1970, Box 103, Folder 4, ELW. For Lee as the most influential apostle in the 1950s and 1960s, see Marion G. Romney, oral history interview with Bruce D. Blumell, Glen L. Rudd, and others, October 6, 1976, 18, JMOH.

113. Wilkinson, diary, September 5, 1962, Box 101, Folder 1, ELW; Wilkinson, diary, November 10, 1960, Box 100, Folder 4, ELW; Helen Goates, oral history with Carl Arrington, September 12, 1973, JMOH.

114. Dyer, minutes of a meeting with Brown, October 8, 1969, Box 70, Folder 7, DOM.

115. Brown, diary, October 10, 1969, HBB.

116. Brown, "Questions from the Floor," University of Utah Institute of Religion, October 10, 1969, Box 28, Folder 4, EEC, emphasis in original.

117. Wilkinson, memo to the Board of Trustees, October 29, 1969, 17.

118. Pat Putnam, "No Defeats, Loads of Trouble," *Sports Illustrated*, November 3, 1969, 26; William Ashworth, "Inside Story of Fired Black Athletes," *Jet* 37, no. 6 (November 11, 1969): 62–69; "BYU's Racial Policy Is under Fire Again," *Riverton Ranger,* October 6, 1969.

119. Wilkinson, memo to the Board of Trustees, October 29, 1969, 6, 18, 23; Wilkinson, memo to the Board of Trustees, November 5, 1969, 9, "Compiled Information concerning African Americans, BYU, and the Church," HBLL; James, quoted in Wilkinson, diary, October 23, 1969, Box 103, Folder 3, ELW.

120. Wilkinson first informed the Board that BYU discriminated against Black students in a memo six months earlier. Wilkinson, memo to Board of Trustees, January 28, 1969, Box 556, Folder 12, ELWP.

121. Wilkinson, memo to the Board of Trustees, October 29, 1969, 15, 19–24, 27–31, 34; Wilkinson, diary, March 21, 1970, Box 103, Folder 4, ELW.

122. Digest of Minutes of Meeting of Brigham Young Board of Trustees, November 5, 1969, Box 489, Folder 14, ELWP; Goates, *Harold B. Lee*, 379; Sheri L. Dew, *Go Forward with Faith: The Biography of Gordon B. Hinckley* (Salt Lake City: Deseret Book 1996), 295; Wilkinson, diary, December 3, 1969, Box 103, Folder 3, ELW.

123. Wilkinson, memo to unknown recipient, July 18, 1970, Box 272, Folder 17, ELW.

124. Ernest L. Wilkinson to Hollis B. Bach, September 11, 1970, Box 550, Folder 5, ELWP.

125. Bach to Wilkinson, June 1, 1970, and August 28, 1970, both in Box 550, Folder 5, ELWP.

126. "Stanford to Bar Contests with Mormon Institutions," *New York Times*, November 13, 1969; "Stanford Drops Brigham Young," *Daily Defender*, November 13, 1969.

127. Statement from President Kenneth S. Pitzer, Stanford University, November 12, 1969, Box 4, Folder 4, KSP. See also Kenneth S. Pitzer to Charles A. Taylor (Stanford athletic director), November 11, 1969, Box 4, Folder 4, KSP. Lester Kinsolving, "Mormon Racial Change Predicted," *San Francisco Chronicle*, December 27, 1969.

128. Pitzer, memo to the Stanford Board of Trustees, December 24, 1969, Box 4, Folder 4, KSP; Wilkinson to Pitzer, December 19, 1969, Box 4, Folder 4, KSP.

129. Wilkinson, diary, December 3, 1969, Box 103, Folder 3, ELW.

130. Willard Wyman (special assistant to Kenneth Pitzer) to Brown, November 18, 1969, Box 558, Folder 5, ELWP; Willard Wyman, memo to unidentified correspondent, Subject: Church of Jesus Christ of Latter-day Saints, November 10, 1969, Box 4, Folder 4, KSP; Kenneth S. Pitzer to Ernest L. Wilkinson, December 30, 1969, Box 559, Folder 7, ELWP; Wilkinson, memo to unidentified correspondent, December 24, 1969, Box 558, Folder 4, ELWP.

131. Edwin B. Firmage, ed., *An Abundant Life: The Memoirs of Hugh B. Brown*, 2nd ed. (Salt Lake City: Signature Books, 1999), 142.

132. Tanner, "ULTRA CONFIDENTIAL MEMORANDUM" to Wilkinson, re: "Conference with President Tanner on December 3rd after Board of Trustees Meeting, December 8, 1969," Box 272, Folder 10, ELW.

133. Dew, *Go Forward with Faith*, 295. For Durham's draft, see "Declaration of the First Presidency and Council of the Twelve" [December 1969], Box 134, Folder 14, GHD. For Lee's role, see Goates, *Harold B. Lee*, 379–80. Maxwell's official biography doesn't address the issue. Bruce C. Hafen, *A Disciple's Life: The Biography of Neal A. Maxwell* (Salt Lake City: Deseret Book, 2010). Hanks, diary, December 10, 1969, MDH; Wilkinson to Hinckley, December 11, 1969, Box 508, Folder 12, ELW.

134. "Letter of First Presidency Clarifies Church's Position on the Negro," *Improvement Era* 73 (December 1969): 70–71.

135. Hanks, diary, December 10, 1969, MDH.

NOTES   381

136. Firmage, *An Abundant Life*, 142. For Tanner and Hanks recollections of the document, see Hanks, diary, December 13, 1969, MDH.

137. Brown, quoted in Lester Kinsolving, "LDS Leader Says Curb on Priesthood to Ease," *San Francisco Chronicle*, December 25, 1969; Kinsolving, "Mormon Racial Change Predicted."

138. Lee, quoted in Wilkinson, memo, December 27, 1969, Box 272, Folder 17, ELW; Wilkinson, diary, December 22, 1969, Box 103, Folder 3, ELW. See also First Presidency Minutes, December 26, 1969, Box 71, Folder 2, DOM.

139. McMurrin to Gregory A. Prince, October 30, 1994, Box 289, Folder 11, SMM.

140. Alvin R. Dyer, diary, December 26, 1969, Box 71, Folder 2, DOM; "Policy Statement of Presidency," LDS *Church News, Deseret News*, January 10, 1970, 12.

141. Brown, oral history interview with Eugene England [1970], Box 136, Folder 13, EE. Brown's grandson, Edwin Firmage, explains, "Grandfather's release from the First Presidency was absolutely, directly related to the race issue." Firmage, oral history interview with Gregory A. Prince, June 6, 1995, MLH; Firmage, *An Abundant Life*, 142–43.

142. Brown to J. Willard Marriott, January 30, 1970, Box 52, Folder 14, JWM.

143. Brown, oral history interview with England, 22; Brown, diary, January 19, 1970, HBB.

144. McMurrin to Brown, January 29, 1970, Box 301, Folder 12, SMM.

145. Ivins to Lowry Nelson, February 11, 1970, Box 2, Folder 27, HGI.

CHAPTER 6

1. [J. Wilson Bartlett], "To All Stake Presidents Interested in Truth and Liberty This Call Is Made," [April 1970], Box 5, Folder 22, DJB; Harold B. Lee, "To the Defenders of the Faith," *Improvement Era* 73, no. 6 (June 1970): 64.

2. Brown and Zina Brown, oral history interview with Eugene England, [1970], 22, Box 136, Folder 13, EE. See also Spencer W. Kimball, diary, April 1970, reel 34, SWK; Edwin B. Firmage, oral history interview with Gregory Prince, June 6, 1995, MLH; Ernest L. Wilkinson, diary, January 5, 1965, Box 101, Folder 5, ELW; Calvin L. Rampton monologues, vol. 3, nos. 20–29, February 27, 1984, 20, Box 8, no folder, ECOH.

3. Eugene Orr, interview with H. Michael Marquardt, November 7, 1971, Box 6, Folder 3, HMM.

4. Joseph Fielding Smith, quoted in "Racist Practice," *Honolulu Star-Bulletin*, January 31, 1970, copy in Box 9, Folder 7, JFS.

5. Kimball to Andrew E. Kimball Jr., January 16, 1970, reel 33, SWK. For Heber C. Kimball's prophecy, see Orson F. Whitney, *Life of Heber C. Kimball* (Salt Lake City: Privately published, 1888), 457.

6. Marsh to the Council of Twelve, January 20, 1970, Box 64, Folder 1, SWK.

7. Jacksonville stake presidency to Council of Twelve, January 21, 1970, Box 64, Folder 1, SWK.

NOTES

8. William F. Reed, "The Other Side of 'The Y,'" *Sports Illustrated*, January 26, 1970, 38.

9. James E. Hansen II, *Democracy's College in the Centennial State: A History of Colorado State University* (Fort Collins: Colorado State University, 1977), 472.

10. Wilkinson, diary, February 5, 1970, Box, 103, Folder 4, ELW.

11. Ibid.

12. Sheri L. Dew, *Go Forward with Faith: The Biography of Gordon B. Hinkley* (Salt Lake City: Deseret Book, 1996), 295.

13. Paul James, "Colorado State Fracas," KSL-TV editorial, February 6, 1970, Box 557, Folder 2, ELW; Paul James, *Cougar Tales* (Sandy, UT: Randall Books, 1984), 47–48. Details about the BYU-Colorado State fracas can be found in Box 1, Folders 15–17, ARC.

14. James, *Cougar Tales*, 47–48. See also Gary Bergera, "'This Time of Crisis': The Race-Based Anti-BYU Athletic Protests of 1968–1971," *Utah Historical Quarterly* 81, no. 3 (Summer 2013): 222–23.

15. Wilkinson, memo to Daniel H. Ludlow, February 11, 1970, Box 15, Folder 3, CRI; Executive Committee, Board of Trustees Minutes, February 19, 1970, Box 489, Folder 14, ELWP.

16. "Protest Not against Y, Says Watts," BYU *Daily Universe*, March 11, 1970; Daniel H. Ludlow, "Our Divine Destiny—A Third Dimension View," March 17, 1970, in *BYU Speeches of the Year, 1969–1970* (Provo, UT: BYU Extension Division, 1970), 9; Lee, quoted in "Time of Testing," BYU *Daily Universe*, September 28, 1970.

17. "Eldridge Cleaver Speaks at Jerry Rubin's Funeral," *Orlando Sentinel*, December 2, 1994; "Rubin's Speech: A Theatrical Put-On" and "Letter to the Editor," both in *Utah Daily Chronicle*, February 12, 1970.

18. William Koerner, "*Is All Well in Zion?*" (Salt Lake City: Self-published, May 1970), 15–16; Francis M. Gibbons, *Harold B. Lee: Man of Vision, Prophet of God* (Salt Lake City: Deseret Book, 1993), 424.

19. Gibbons, *Harold B. Lee*, 425.

20. Ibid., 424–25; Heidi S. Swinton, *To the Rescue: The Biography of Thomas S. Monson* (Salt Lake City: Deseret Book, 2010), 366.

21. Meeting Minutes with Ernest L. Wilkinson, Ben E. Lewis, Milton F. Hartvigsen, and Heber G. Wolsey, February 7, 1970, in Wolsey, memo to Wilkinson, February 19, 1970, Box 20, Folder 1, HGW.

22. Petersen to J. Willard Marriott, February 5, 1970, Box 52, Folder 14, JWM. See also L. Brent Goates, *Harold B. Lee: Prophet and Seer* (Salt Lake City: Bookcraft, 1985), 433–34.

23. Kimball, diary, February 18, 1970, reel 34, SWK.

24. Ibid.

25. "U.S. Journal: Provo, Utah," *New Yorker*, March 21, 1970, 120.

26. W. Cleon Skousen, "The Communist Attack on the Mormons," March 1970, National Research Group, American Fork, UT; Wallace Turner, "Conservative and Liberal Mormons Advise Church on Negro Exclusion Policy," *New York Times*, June 21, 1970.

NOTES 383

27. Lee and Smith allegedly called Skousen's writings "B.S." in reference to "Brother Skousen." See Michael G. Root report, 1972, and Susan Brimley report, 1974, in "Collection of Character Legends," WAWF. See also Smith to Mark E. Petersen, January 10, 1968, Box 443, Folder 11, ELWP.

28. J. Reuben Clark to W. Cleon Skousen, March 28, 1958, Box 403, Folder 12, JRC Papers; W. Cleon Skousen, *The Naked Communist* (Salt Lake City: Ensign, 1958). For evangelical and Protestant Cold War conspiracy theories, see Kevin M. Kruse, *One Nation under God: How Corporate America Invented Christian America* (New York: Basic Books, 2015). Ernest Wilkinson reported that Skousen sold 310,000 copies of *The Naked Communist*—a figure he learned from Skousen. Wilkinson, memo to Skousen re: "List of Books You Have Published," November 1, 1975, MLH.

29. "Church Sets Policy on Birch Society," *Deseret News*, January 4, 1963; David O. McKay, diary, January 23, 1963, Box 52, Folder 3, DOM. For Skousen's stint on the Birch Society's speakers' circuit, see *John Birch Society Bulletin*, June 1965, 31–32, Box 16, Folder 9, JBSR.

30. Ezra Taft Benson, *Civil Rights—Tool of Communist Deception* (Salt Lake City: Deseret Book, 1968). See also Matthew L. Harris, *Watchman on the Tower: Ezra Taft Benson and the Making of the Mormon Right* (Salt Lake City: University of Utah Press, 2020), 44–46, 63, 79.

31. Roy Fugal to Harold B. Lee and Spencer W. Kimball, March 27, 1970, Box 63, Folder 3, SWK.

32. See chapter 5; Harris, *Watchman on the Tower*, 77–78; and Matthew L. Harris, "Martin Luther King, Civil Rights, and Perceptions of a 'Communist Conspiracy,'" in *Thunder from the Right: Ezra Taft Benson in Mormonism and Politics*, ed. Matthew L. Harris (Urbana: University of Illinois Press, 2019), 134, 138.

33. Victor L. Brown, memo to General Authorities, re: "Security during General Conference," April 2, 1970, reel 34, SWK; Goates, *Harold B. Lee*, 413.

34. Kimball, diary, April 4, 1970, reel 34, SWK.

35. Kimball, diary, April 4 and April 5, 1970, reel 34, SWK.

36. A. Theodore Tuttle, "Principles and Promises," *Improvement Era* 73, no. 6 (June 1970): 81; Goates, *Harold B. Lee*, 413–14.

37. William W. Tanner, oral history interview with Chad Orton, April–July 1986, 15, CHL.

38. Douglass Moore, quoted in "Black Militant Sights LDS Ward as Target," *Salt Lake Tribune*, April 30, 1970; Kimball, diary, April 30, 1970, reel 34, SWK.

39. Don May, the radio news director at the University of Washington, called the Seattle Liberation Front "a racial coalition comprised of the SDS [Students for a Democratic Society], and non-students whom they call 'street people' from downtown Seattle." Ed Butterworth, memo to Ernest L. Wilkinson, March 9, 1970, Box 24, Folder 10, HGW. "Off BYU," March 1970, in Special Collections, University of Washington Libraries, https://digitalcollections.lib. washington.edu/digital/iiif/protests/40/full/full/0/default.jpg; https://depts.

washington.edu/civilr/images/BSU/weatherman%20leaflet%20byu%20de
monstration.jpg.

40. Heber G. Wolsey, memo to Ernest L. Wilkinson, March 13, 1970, Box 24, Folder 13, HGW.

41. Executive Committee Meeting Minutes, Board of Trustees, March 17, 1970, Box 24, Folder 10, HGW.

42. Wolsey to Odegaard, February 5, 1970, and Wilkinson to Odegaard, February 7, 1970, Box 24, Folder 7, HGW; Minutes of a meeting with Ernest L. Wilkinson, Ben E. Lewis, Milton F. Hartvigsen, and Heber G. Wolsey, February 7, 1970, in Wolsey, memo to Wilkinson, February 19, 1970, Box 20, Folder 1, HGW; "Statement from Ernest L. Wilkinson, President of Brigham Young University," March 9, 1970, Box 24, Folder 13, HGW.

43. Wolsey outlined some of his activities with Gray in a letter to LDS Church Commissioner Neal A. Maxwell, February 25, 1972, Box 19, Folder 2, HGW. See also Wolsey, oral history interview with Janice L. Hubbard, July 26, 2006, in Janice L. Hubbard, "Pioneers in Twentieth Century Mormon Media: Oral Histories of Latter-day Saints Electronic and Public Relations Professionals," master's thesis, Brigham Young University, 2007, 201–2.

44. Gray's employment at KSL is discussed in the Clare Middlemiss notes, June 26, 1968, Box 67, Folder 6, DOM.

45. Community member, quoted in Wolsey, "Minorities, Civil Rights, and BYU," devotional address at Brigham Young University, May 12, 1970, 2, Box 179, Folder 15, ELW.

46. Andrew David Louis, "BSA Denies Church's Rights," n.d., Box 19, Folder 2, HGW.

47. Wilkinson, diary, March 17, 1970, Box 103, Folder 4, ELW. For Schweppe's position on the tract, see Wilkinson, memo to Wolsey, March 26, 1970, Box 24, Folder 9, HGW; Wolsey, oral history interview with Hubbard, 200–201.

48. "BYU Policy Ad Runs in Seattle Newspapers," BYU *Daily Universe*, March 31, 1970. For copies of the newspapers, see Box 587, Folder 14, ELWP; Box 7, Folder 1, HGW.

49. Wolsey, "Minorities, Civil Rights, and BYU," 3–7.

50. Wilkinson, diary, March 21, 1970, Box 103, Folder 4, ELW. See also Wilkinson, memo to unknown recipient, May 22, 1970, Box 556, Folder 12, ELW.

51. Vaughn Hubbard to Ernest L. Wilkinson, April 2, 1970, Box 4, Folder 12, CRI. For others praising the tract, see Box 4, Folder 12, CRI; Box 24, Folders 9, 13, HGW.

52. Wilkinson, memo to Heber G. Wolsey and Daniel H. Ludlow, March 28, 1970, Box 15, Folder 3, CRI.

53. "Text of Odegaard's Statement on Campus Ferment," *Seattle Post-Intelligencer*, March 28, 1970, Box 9, Folder 7, JFS; Wilkinson to Schweppe, March 7, 1970, Box 24, Folder 9, HGW; Wolsey to Odegaard, February 6, 1970, Box 24, Folder 7, HGW.

NOTES

54. Wilkinson, diary, September 24, 1970, Box 103, Folder 5, ELW. See also Ernest L. Wilkinson and Leonard J. Arrington, *Brigham Young University: The First One Hundred Years*, 4 vols. (Provo, UT: Brigham Young University Press, 1976), 3:480.

55. Wilson, memo to John R. Hogness, March 10, 1970, Box 4, Folder 12, CRI.

56. Larry Brown, "U.W. Charged with Financing Race Bias," *Seattle Post-Intelligencer*, June 1970, Box 24, Folder 9, HGW.

57. Wilkinson to Kimball, March 5 and April 29, 1970, both in Box 63, Folder 3, SWK; Wilkinson, diary, April 16, 1970, Box 103, Folder 4, ELW.

58. Nelson to Wilkinson, April 13, 1970, Box 556, Folder 14, ELW; Wilkinson to Nelson, May 7, 1970, Box 19, Folder 5, LN.

59. Wolsey, "Minorities, Civil Rights, and BYU," 3–7.

60. Wilkinson, memo, Ludlow and Heber G. Wolsey, "Confidential," March 28, 1970, Box 15, Folder 3, CRI.

61. Thomas, memo to Daniel H. Ludlow, re: "New Curriculum in the College of Religion," June 8, 1970, Box 27, Folder 8, CRI.

62. Ludlow, memo to BYU Religion faculty, March 31, 1970, Box 25, Folder 7, CRI.

63. Ludlow, memo to Wilkinson, June 11, 1970, Box 15, Folder 3, CRI.

64. Ludlow, memo to BYU Religion faculty, March 31, 1970, Box 25, Folder 7, CRI.

65. Wilkinson to Schweppe, June 12, 1970, Box 42, Folder 11, RKT.

66. Bach to Wilkinson, June 1, 1970, Box 550, Folder 5, ELW.

67. Kimball, diary, June 18, 1970, reel 33, SWK.

68. Smith to Smith, June 15, 1970, Box 9, Folder 7, JFS.

69. Boyd K. Packer, memo to Harold B. Lee, July 6, 1970, Box 9, Folder 7, JFS. Ellery, quoted in "Improved Elks Conclude Meet at Service Today," *Salt Lake Tribune*, July 5, 1970.

70. Joseph Crespino, "Civil Rights and the Religious Right," in *Rightward Bound*, ed. Bruce J. Schulman and Julian Zelizer (Cambridge, MA: Harvard University Press, 2008), 90–105; Randal Balmer, *Bad Faith: Race and the Rise of the Religious Right* (Grand Rapids, MI: Eerdmans, 2021), ch. 6; Daniel K. Williams, *God's Own Party: The Making of the Christian Right* (New York: Oxford University Press, 2010), 163–64, 190.

71. Wilkinson, memo to the BYU Executive Committee and Board of Trustees, August 11, 1970, Box 550, Folder 4, ELWP.

72. In 2017, I was granted permission to review a portion of Kennedy's papers—a restricted collection at BYU—and found no evidence of IRS involvement with the LDS church. Kennedy's biographer, Martin B. Hickman, in *David Matthew Kennedy: Banker, Statesman, Churchman* (Salt Lake City: Deseret Book, 1987), avoids the subject altogether.

73. For Bob Jones losing its tax exemption status, see Williams, *God's Own Party*, 71, 197. BYU law librarian Galen Fletcher provided me with a copy of the friend

of the court brief. See also "Mormons Support Bob Jones' Case," *Sumter Daily Item*, July 31, 1981, and an unpublished report titled "Ronald Reagan and Tax Exemptions for Racist Schools," by David Whitman of Harvard's Kennedy School of Government (1984), Box 8, Folder 8, REL.

74. Executive Committee of the Board of Trustees Minutes, April 25, 1968, Box 164, Folder 1, ELWP; Wilkinson, quoted in First Presidency Minutes, January 8, 1968, Box 67, Folder 1, DOM.

75. Executive Committee of the Board of Trustees Minutes, September 4, 1969, Box 489, Folder 14, ELWP; BYU Forum Assembly Chairman LaVar Bateman to Robert K. Thomas, July 19, 1969, Box 40, Folder 5, RKT.

76. Bateman to Thomas, July 19, 1969.

77. Thomas, memo to Wilkinson, re: "Appearance of Roy Wilkins on Campus," August 28, 1970, Box 556, Folder 11, ELWP; Roy Wilkins, "The Mormons and the Negroes," *Los Angeles Times*, January 26, 1970.

78. "Speaker Lists Contributions," BYU *Daily Universe*, November 3, 1972; "Senator Edward W. Brooke at BYU," *Dialogue: A Journal of Mormon Thought* 11, no. 2 (Summer 1978): 119–20; Gary James Bergera and Ronald Priddis, *Brigham Young University: A House of Faith* (Salt Lake City: Signature Books, 1985), 302.

79. Wilkinson to Bach, September 11, 1970, Box 550, Folder 5, ELWP.

80. Stanley Pottinger (director, Office for Civil Rights) to Senator Wallace F. Bennett, September 2, 1970, Box 550, Folder 5, ELWP; Gordon C. Coffman (Wilkinson, Cragun and Barker) to Wilkinson, September 10, 1970, Box 550, folder 5, ELWP; Wilkinson to Barker, September 13, 1970, Box 550, Folder 5, ELWP; Wilkinson, memo to Robert K. Thomas and Robert Smith and all Deans, re: "Recruitment of Faculty," December 24, 1968, Box 517, Folder 6, ELW.

81. Minutes of the Combined, Concurrent Meeting of the Church Board of Education and Brigham Young University Board of Trustees, October 7, 1970, Box 570, Folder 11, ELWP. For information relating to the lawsuit, see Bruce C. Hafen, memo, to Oscar W. McConkie Jr. and Dallin H. Oaks, August 11, 1971, and Jay W. Butler and Ernest L. Wilkinson, memo, unnamed person, n.d., both in Box 24, Folder 13, HGW. A judge tossed out the University of Washington lawsuit a year later citing "lack of merit." Wilkinson and Arrington, *Brigham Young University*, 3:480–81.

82. Grant Ivins, "Second-Class Citizens," *Salt Lake Tribune*, April 10, 1970, Box 3, Folder 9, HGI.

83. Newell G. Bringhurst, *Fawn McKay Brodie: A Biographer's Life* (Norman: University of Oklahoma Press, 1999), 188–89; Terryl Givens, with Brian M. Hauglid, *The Pearl of Greatest Price: Mormonism's Most Controversial Scripture* (New York: Oxford University Press, 2019), 154–55.

84. Brodie to John W. Fitzgerald, December 4, 1970, Box 4, Folder 8, JWF. See also Brodie to Everett L. Cooley, December 17, 1970, Box 4, Folder 15, FMB.

NOTES 387

85. Fawn McKay Brodie, "Can We Manipulate the Past," address given at the Hotel Utah, October 3, 1970, 10, CHL. See also Bringhurst, *Fawn McKay Brodie*, 190–92; "Church 'Misreads' Past to Justify Doctrine, Author Charges," *Salt Lake Tribune*, October 4, 1970.

86. Pugsley to General Authorities, August 20, 1970, Box 9, Folder 7, JFS; "Attention L.D.S.," *Utah Daily Chronicle*, November 19, 1969, Box 9, Folder 7, JFS.

87. Snell to Pugsley, September 14, 1970, Box 1, Folder 16, HCS.

88. Joseph Fielding Smith's secretary, Arthur Haycock, instructed mission presidents and stake presidents to respond to the members' questions. See Haycock to Kenneth Gardiner (Hawaii mission president), October 26, 1970, Haycock to Darold Johnson (Chicago stake president), October 27, 1970, Haycock to William Day (Kentucky-Tennessee mission president), November 4, 1970, all in Box 22, Folder 18, JFS.

89. Unknown correspondent to Joseph Fielding Smith, Hugh B. Brown, N. Eldon Tanner, Robert L. Simpson, January 19, 1970, Box 9, Folder 7, JFS.

90. Wilkinson, diary, Mary 5, 1960, Box 100, Folder 4, ELW Papers. The Board agreed to hire qualified Black Latter-day Saints in 1968. Wilkinson, memo, re: "Recruitment of Negro Members as Faculty," December 24, 1968, quoted in "Minutes of the Department Chairmen's Meeting," BYU religion department, January 8, 1969, Box 28, Folder 3, CRI.

91. Wilkinson, diary, July 18, 1970, Box 103, Folder 4, ELW; Fay Botham, *Almighty God Created the Races: Christianity, Interracial Marriage, and American Law* (Chapel Hill: University of North Carolina Press, 2009).

92. Wynetta Martin, *Black Mormon Tells Her Story* (Salt Lake City: Hawkes, 1972), 68–70; "Wynetta Martin Joins BYU Faculty," BYU *Daily Universe*, December 4, 1970.

93. Wilkinson, diary, March 8, 1971, Box 104, Folder 1, ELW; Dallin H. Oaks, memo to Wilkinson, "Affirmative Action Programs Threatened or Required to Enforce Civil Rights," December 27, 1971, Box 557, Folder 16, ELW; Jon Larson, memo to "University Personnel Committee," April 2, 1975, Box 40, Folder 4, RKT; Martin Gerry to Dallin H. Oaks, August 12, 1976, Box 40, Folder 6, RKT; Dallin H. Oaks memo to his cabinet, August 17, 1976, Box 40, Folder 6, RKT; "Mormon College Challenges U.S. Sex Bias Rules," *Los Angeles Times*, October 18, 1975. For a discussion of how the Nixon administration addressed gender discrimination, see Bruce Ackerman, *We the People*, vol. 3: *The Civil Rights Revolution* (Cambridge, MA: Harvard University Press, 2014), 242–67.

94. Bergera and Priddis, *Brigham Young University*, 36–37; Bryan Waterman and Brian Kagel, *The Lord's University: Freedom and Authority at BYU* (Salt Lake City: Signature Books, 1998), 40–42.

95. J. B. Haws, *The Mormon Image in the American Mind: Fifty Years of Public Perception* (New York: Oxford University Press, 2013), 69–70.

388   NOTES

96. Gillispie to McKay, June 4, 1967, Box 4, Folder 16, JWF.

97. Reiser to Gillispie, July 5, 1967, and McKay and Brown to Lyman Perkes, July 5, 1967, Box 4, Folder 16, JWF.

98. Howell, address to the Olympus LDS Seminary in Salt Lake City, April 17, 1963, in Box 61, Folder 3, MHP; John Lamb, "My Responsibility," *Improvement Era* 69, no. 1 (January 1966): 36–37. See also "Testimony of Linda Howard," Petersburg Ward, Virginia, July 26, 1968, Box 35, Folder 6, RCD; Albert Fritz, oral history interview with Leslie G. Kelen, March 15, 1984, 14, Box 2, Folder 7, IBU.

99. Lamb, quoted in Wilford E. Smith, "The Limits of Divine Love," *Dialogue: A Journal of Mormon Thought* 3, no. 4 (Winter 1968): 99–100. For Whittingham, see John Lewis Lund, *The Church and the Negro: A Discussion of Mormons and the Priesthood* (Salt Lake City: Paramount, 1967), 68–72; Carey C. Bowles, *A Mormon Negro Views the Church* (Maplewood, NJ: Self-published, 1968), Box 40, Folder 5, LJA.

100. Darius Aiden Gray and Margaret Blair Young, *The Last Mile of the Way* (Salt Lake City: Bookcraft, 2003), 378–79.

101. "Autobiography of Ruffin Bridgeforth," July 28, 1961, Box 14, Folder 25, JB; Bridgeforth, oral history interview with Alan Cherry, March 16, 1985, AAOH.

102. Margaret Blair Young, in "Riots, Race, and Rumors in Utah, 1965," *Radio West*, October 8, 2020, https://radiowest.kuer.org/post/riots-race-and-rum ors-utah-1965.

103. For a brief biography of Gray, see Margaret Blair Young, "Darius Gray," *BlackPast*, August 18, 2016, https://www.blackpast.org/african-american-hist ory/gray-darius-aidan-1945/. An LDS bishop named Quinn McKay married Gray. Quinn McKay, "A Rural Utah, Mormon Boy—The Blacks and the LDS Church," 12–13, September 2006, CHL.

104. Orr, oral history interview with Clint Christensen and Dan Baker and Edith Baker, June 3, 2013, 11–12, 14, EO; Orr interview with Ronald Coleman, June 1972, in Ronald Coleman, "Mormonism and the Black Curse: A Black Perspective," master's thesis, California State University, Sacramento, 1973, 32.

105. Orr, oral history interview with Christensen and Baker and Baker, 2–3, 6. See also Eugene Orr, "In the Same Manner," in *My Lord, He Calls Me: Stories of Faith by Black American Latter-day Saints*, ed. Alice Faulkner Burch (Salt Lake City: Deseret Book, 2022), 45–46, 50.

106. Orr, quoted in "*Nobody Knows: The Untold Story of Black Mormons*—Script," *Dialogue: A Journal of Mormon Thought* 42, no. 3 (Fall 2009): 116.

107. Gray, quoted in Margaret Blair Young, "The Genesis Group: Support for Black Latter-day Saints," *Meridian Magazine*, August 17, 2012, https://latterdaysaint mag.com/article-1-11298/.

108. Orr, oral history interview with Christensen and Baker and Baker, 14; Gray, oral history interview with Elizabeth Haslam and Dennis Haslam, December

NOTES

389

1, 1971, 2, Box 1, Folder 7, AAOHU. See also "*Nobody Knows*," 116; Orr, "In the Same Manner," 50–51.

109. Orr, oral history interview with Christensen and Baker and Baker, 12; Orr, "In the Same Manner," 51.

110. Gray and Young, *The Last Mile of the Way*, 377; Orr, "In the Same Manner," 51.

111. Gray, oral history interview with Haslam and Haslam, 4.

112. Smith to Joseph Henderson, April 10, 1963, MLH.

113. Williams, oral history interview with Gordon Irving, May 6, 1981, 31, JMOH; Gray, oral history interview with Haslam and Haslam, 4–5.

114. Dew, *Go Forward with Faith*; Swinton, *To the Rescue*; Lucille C. Tate, *Boyd K. Packer: A Watchman on the Tower* (Salt Lake City: Deseret Book, 1995). For non-hagiographic depictions of Packer, see Armand L. Mauss, *Shifting Borders and a Tattered Passport: Intellectual Journeys of a Mormon Academic* (Salt Lake City: University of Utah Press, 2012), 72–73; Leonard J. Arrington, *Adventures of a Church Historian* (Urbana: University of Illinois Press, 1998), 119–21.

115. Monson, quoted in Goates, *Harold B. Lee*, 380.

116. Gray, oral history interview with Haslam and Haslam, 5.

117. Orr, interview with Michael Marquardt, November 14, 1971, Box 6, Folder 3, HMM; Orr, telephone interview with Matthew Harris, October 9, 2014; Orr, "In the Same Manner," 51.

118. Orr, interview with Marquardt, November 14, 1971; Orr, telephone interview with Harris. Hinckley provided similar rationales for Black priesthood denial in an interview with Ronald Coleman, June 1972, recounted in Coleman, "Mormonism and the Black Curse," 33. For Hinckley, see also "Apostle Calls Black Issue Exaggerated," *Salt Lake Tribune*, August 14, 1975.

119. Gray, oral history interview with Haslam and Haslam, 6–7; Orr, interview with Marquardt, November 14, 1971.

120. Gray, oral history interview with Haslam and Haslam, 8.

121. Ibid., 8–9; Orr, telephone interview with Matthew Harris; Orr, "In the Same Manner," 52.

122. Orr, interview with Marquardt, November 7, 1971, Box 6, Folder 3, HMM; Gray, oral history interview with Haslam and Haslam, 9.

123. For Bridgeforth's, Gray's, and Orr's patriarchal blessings, see Orr, interview with Marquardt, November 14, 1971; Darius Gray, "No Johnny-Come-Lately: The 182-Year Long BLACK Mormon Moment," presented at the 2012 FairMormon Conference, https://www.fairmormon.org/conference/aug ust-2012/no-johnny-come-lately-the-182-year-long-black-mormon-mom ent. See also Matthew L. Harris, "Mormons and Lineage: The Complicated History of Blacks and Patriarchal Blessings, 1830–2018," *Dialogue: A Journal of Mormon Thought* 51, no. 3 (Fall 2018): 83–129.

124. Council of Twelve Minutes, May 14, 1970, and May 21, 1970, Box 63, Folder 3, SWK. For the tension related to declaring cursed lineages on Black Latter-day Saints, see "Patriarchs' Meeting Minutes," April 6, 1973, Box 4, Folder 3, IB.

390 NOTES

125. Orr, interview with Marquardt, November 7, 1971.

126. Lee, quoted in Swinton, *To the Rescue*, 367.

127. Williams, oral history interview with Irving, 31; Gray, oral history interview with Haslam and Haslam, 13–14; Joseph Fielding Smith to First Presidency, March 30, 1955, Box 64, Folder 6, SWK.

128. Gray, oral history interview with Haslam and Haslam, 14; Bankhead, oral history interview with Leslie G. Kelen, January 14, 1983, 10, Box 1, Folder 4, IBU.

129. Sinquefield, oral history interview with Alan Cherry, March 30, 1985, 12, AAOH. For details of the first Genesis meeting, see Gray and Young, *The Last Mile of the Way*, 385–89; Orr, "In the Same Manner," 51; Dew, *Go Forward with Faith*, 296.

130. Council of the Twelve Minutes, March 16, 1972, Box 63, Folder 6, SWK.

131. Packer and Monson, quoted in Helen Kennedy, oral history interview with Alan Cherry, April 11, 1986, 15, AAOH; Gray, oral history interview with Haslam and Haslam, 13; Alan Cherry, oral history interview with Jessie Embry, April 24, 1985, 103, AAOH.

132. Bridgeforth, as quoted in Wallace Turner, "Mormons Operating a Special Meeting Unit for Blacks," *New York Times*, April 6, 1972.

133. Orr, oral history interview with Christensen and Baker and Baker, 27; Orr, telephone interview with Matthew Harris; Gray and Young, *The Last Mile of the Way*, 374.

134. Gray, oral history interview with Haslam and Haslam, 21.

135. Orr, oral history interview with Christensen and Baker and Baker, 45; Orr, "In the Same Manner," 46–47.

136. Orr, oral history interview with Christensen and Baker and Baker, 17. Orr also acknowledged his activism in an interview with Ronald Coleman, June 1972, in Coleman, "Mormonism and the Black Curse," 32.

137. Bridgeforth, quoted in Kennedy, oral history interview with Cherry, 14.

138. Orr, oral history interview with Christensen and Baker and Baker, 29; Orr, telephone interview with Matthew Harris; Orr, interview with Marquardt, November 14, 1971.

139. Genesis Special Interest Group letter to President Spencer Kimball, September 19, 1976, EO; Orr, oral history interview with Christensen and Baker and Baker, 27; Joseph Freeman, *In the Lord's Due Time* (Salt Lake City: Bookcraft, 1979), 103.

140. Bridgeforth, quoted in Peggy Olsen, "Ruffin Bridgeforth: Leader and Father to Mormon Blacks," *This People*, Winter 1980, 16.

141. Packer, quoted in Tate, *Boyd K. Packer*, 227.

142. Ruffin Bridgeforth, "A Brief History of the Genesis Group," n.d., Box 63, Folder 10, LJA; Orr, telephone interview with Matthew Harris; Young, "Darius Gray"; Gray and Young, *The Last Mile of the Way*, 389.

NOTES   391

CHAPTER 7

1. "The Chosen," *Newsweek,* July 17, 1972, 50; Wallace Turner, "Mormons' New Chief: Harold Bingham Lee," *New York Times,* July 8, 1972.

2. Lee, quoted in Ernest L. Wilkinson, memo to Robert K. Thomas and Ben E. Lewis, October 30, 1969, Box 509, Folder 3, ELW.

3. Harold B. Lee, "Youth of the Church" (1945), reprinted in Harold B. Lee, *Decisions for Successful Living* (Salt Lake City: Deseret Book, 1973).

4. For Fitzgerald's letters to the *Salt Lake Tribune,* see the volume he compiled titled "Conflict" (1973), Box 16, Book 3, JWF. Bruce R. McConkie, *Mormon Doctrine,* 2nd ed. (Salt Lake City: Bookcraft, 1966).

5. Haycock, memo to Lee, June 18, 1973, Box 5, Folder 7, LJA.

6. Edward L. Kimball, *Lengthen Your Stride: The Presidency of Spencer W. Kimball— Working Draft* (Salt Lake City: Benchmark Books, 2009), 330; Leonard J. Arrington, *Adventures of a Church Historian* (Urbana: University of Illinois Press, 1998), 180.

7. Lee, quoted in Ernest L. Wilkinson, memo to unknown recipient, November 29, 1973, Box 272, Folder 17, ELW.

8. D. Arthur Haycock (Kimball's secretary), quoted in Heidi S. Swinton, *In the Company of Prophets* (Salt Lake City: Deseret Book, 1993), 84.

9. Francis M. Gibbons, *Spencer W. Kimball: Resolute Disciple, Prophet of God* (Salt Lake City: Deseret Book, 1995), 273–74; Wilkinson, diary, June 10, 1968, Box 102, Folder 5, ELW.

10. Kimball, diary, March 2, 1950, reel 7, SWK.

11. Arrington, diary, October 2, 1978, Box 33, Folder 6, LJA; Kimball, *Lengthen Your Stride,* 8–9, 11, 13–15.

12. Spencer W. Kimball, "When Will the World Be Converted?," *Ensign,* October 1974, https://www.churchofjesuschrist.org/study/ensign/1974/10/when-the-world-will-be-converted?lang=eng. See also Kimball, *Lengthen Your Stride,* 37–38, 161–62.

13. Kimball, "When Will the World Be Converted?"; Swinton, *In the Company of Prophets,* 85.

14. Hinckley to Kimball, April 4, 1974, in Kimball, diary, April 4, 1974, reel 39, SWK.

15. William Grant Bangerter, "A Special Moment in Church History," *Conference Report,* October 1977, https://www.churchofjesuschrist.org/study/general-conference/1977/10/a-special-moment-in-church-history?lang=eng.

16. Kimball, *Lengthen Your Stride,* 162–63; Martin B. Hickman, *David Matthew Kennedy: Banker, Statesman, Churchman* (Salt Lake City: Deseret Book, 1987), 336–37.

17. Kennedy, interview with Edward L. Kimball, January 24, 1991, Box 63, Folder 5, SWK; Hickman, *David Matthew Kennedy,* 342–43.

18. Unnamed LDS man to Kimball, November 6, 1974, Box 64, Folder 5, SWK.

NOTES

19. Lester E. Bush, "Mormonism's Negro Doctrine: An Historical Overview," *Dialogue: A Journal of Mormon Thought* 8, no. 1 (Spring 1973): 11–68. For the importance of Bush's article, see Devery S. Anderson, "A History of Dialogue: Part II: Struggle toward Maturity, 1971–1982," *Dialogue: A Journal of Mormon Thought* 33, no. 2 (Summer 2000): 23.

20. Lester E. Bush, "Writing 'Mormonism's Negro Doctrine: An Historical Overview' (1973): Context and Reflections, 1998," *Journal of Mormon History* 25, no. 1 (Spring 1999): 229–71. My characterization of Chad Flake derives from my own experience with him and that of others who knew him.

21. Bush to Davis Bitton, September 27, 1973, Box 1, Folder 1, LEB.

22. Bush, "Writing 'Mormonism's Negro Doctrine,'" 249.

23. Bush, "Mormonism's Negro Doctrine," 25–28.

24. Kimball to Wilkinson, November 9, 1970, Box 547, Folder 4, ELW; Lester E. Bush to Chad J. Flake, October 1, 1973, Box 1, Folder 1, LEB; Flake to Bush, October 1973, Box 2, Folder 49, LEB.

25. Bush to Davis Bitton, September 27, 1973, Box 1, Folder 1, LEB; Marvin S. Hill to Leonard J. Arrington, October 14, 1971, Box 40, Folder 4, LJA; Reed C. Durham to Bush, December 17, 1973, Box 2, Folder 41, LEB; Arrington to Packer, February 9, 1973, Box 19, folder 8, LJA; Bush, "Writing Mormonism's Negro Doctrine," 245–46.

26. Packer to Bush, May 9, 1973, Box 3, Folder 36, LEB.

27. Bush, "Writing Mormonism's Negro Doctrine," 262.

28. To soften the blow, Rees asked several respected LDS scholars to contribute essays critiquing Bush's essay. Bush, "Writing Mormonism's Negro Doctrine," 260–63.

29. Hanks to Bush, July 10, 1975, Box 2, Folder 58, LEB; Matthew L. Harris and Newell G. Bringhurst, eds., *The Mormon Church and Blacks: A Documentary History* (Urbana: University of Illinois Press, 2015), 95.

30. Kimball, diary, April 1, 1974, reel 39, SWK.

31. Kimball to Kimball, June 15, 1963, Box 64, Folder 5, SWK.

32. Kimball, *Lengthen Your Stride*, 337; Paul H. Dunn, oral history interview with Gregory A. Prince, May 21, 1996, MLH.

33. Kimball, *Lengthen Your Stride*, 356n8; Matthew Garrett, *Making Lamanites: Mormons, Native Americans, and the Indian Placement Program, 1947–2000* (Salt Lake City: University of Utah Press, 2016), 224–29, 233–34.

34. Spencer W. Kimball, "The Evil of Intolerance," *Conference Report*, April 1954, 103–8; Edward L. Kimball, ed., *The Teachings of Spencer W. Kimball* (Salt Lake City: Bookcraft, 1982), 237; LaMar S. Williams, oral history interview with Gordon Irving, May 19, 1981, 37, JMOH.

35. Kimball, interview with Harris, November 26, 2013; Edward Kimball, "Draft of the Priesthood Revelation," June 1978, unpublished manuscript, MLH.

36. Kimball, diary, May 20, 1964, reel 26, SWK.

37. Kimball, diary, May 27, 1964, reel 26, SWK; Kimball, diary, November 21, 1967, reel 30, SWK.

NOTES

38. Kimball's personal scriptures—the Book of Mormon, Doctrine and Covenants, and Pearl of Great Price—are from the 1954 edition. Thanks to rare books dealer Reid Moon for sharing Kimball's scriptures with me.

39. Kimball to Kirk Davis, August 1, 1948, Box 64, Folder 6, SWK; Kimball to Victor B. Cline, May 28, 1956, SWK.

40. Edward Kimball perceptively notes, "Spencer knew that the restriction did not come from explicit scriptures but rather from interpretations by various Church leaders." Kimball, *Lengthen Your Stride*, 310.

41. Kimball to Edward L. Kimball, June 15, 1963.

42. France A. Davis, oral history interview with Leslie G. Kelen, August 4, 1983, Box 1, Folder 23, IBU; Terry Lee Williams, oral history with Leslie G. Kelen, April 4, 1986, Box 7, Folder 5, IBU; James E. Dooley, oral history interview with Leslie G. Kelen, September 20, 1983, Interview 4, tape 100, ECOH.

43. Gibbons, *Spencer W. Kimball*, 278; "Mormons Pressed on Scouts Policy," *New York Times*, August 3, 1974.

44. Kimball, diary, April 1, 1974, reel 39, SWK.

45. Wallace Turner, "Mormon Avoids Question on Blacks," *New York Times*, September 9, 1974; "Statement on Blacks," Public Communications Department, Church of Jesus Christ of Latter-day Saints, September 9, 1974, Box 64, Folder 5, SWK.

46. Bruce R. McConkie, "Be Valiant in the Fight of Faith," *Conference Report*, October 1974, https://www.churchofjesuschrist.org/study/general-confere nce/1974/10/be-valiant-in-the-fight-of-faith?lang=eng.

47. First Presidency to General Authorities, Regional Representatives of the Twelve, Stake Presidents, Mission Presidents, and Bishops, May 6, 1975, Box 64, Folder 5, SWK.

48. Dallin H. Oaks, "Three Threats to the Private Sector," devotional address at BYU, August 15, 1975, Box 76, Folder 2, REL.

49. Hawkins to Rex E. Lee, September 19, 1975, Box 76, Folder 2, REL. See also James White (consultant on legal education to the American Bar Association) to Oaks and Hawkins, September 9, 1975, Box 76, Folder 2, REL.

50. Ruud to Wilkinson, December 21, 1970, and Ruud to Wilkinson, February 10, 1971, Box 269, Folder 7, ELW. See also Jay Butler, memo to Wilkinson, "Re: Conference with Millard H. Rudd," January 4, 1971, Box 272, Folder 25, ELW; Wilkinson, diary, January 6, 1971, Box 104, Folder 1, ELW; Minutes of the Combined Concurrent Meeting of the Church Board of Education at Brigham Young University, January 6, 1971, Box 252, Folder 6, ELWP.

51. Dallin H. Oaks, "Unfolding in Time," *Clark Memorandum,* Spring 2013, 18.

52. LDS bishop to Kimball, June 2, 1975, Box 64, Folder 5, SWK. I have opted to omit the bishop's name.

53. Ibid.

54. Ibid.

55. Ibid.

56. Edward L. Kimball, meeting with Francis Gibbons and Bruce McConkie, May 12, 1982, recounted in Edward L. Kimball's diary, May 12, 1982, MLH.

57. Thomas G. Alexander, *Things in Heaven and Earth: The Life and Times of Wilford Woodruff, A Mormon Prophet* (Salt Lake City: Signature Books, 1991); Ken Driggs, "After the Manifesto: Modern Polygamy and Fundamentalist Mormons," *Journal of Church and State*, 32, no. 2 (Spring 1990): 367–89.

58. L. Brent Goates, *Harold B. Lee: Prophet and Seer* (Salt Lake City: Bookcraft, 1985), 514, 574.

59. Kimball, diary, March 19, 1974, reel 39, SWK; Mark L. Grover, "The Mormon Priesthood Revelation and the São Paulo, Brazil Temple," *Dialogue: A Journal of Mormon Thought* 23, no. 1 (Spring 1990): 39–53.

60. Kimball, diary, November 21, 1967, reel 30, SWK.

61. Beitler, quoted in Zone Conference notes, Brazil South Mission, September 1975, CHL.

62. Brockbank, quoted in Gary Crocker, "Lineage in the Field," April 1973, MLH.

63. Apostle David B. Haight recounted Kimball's concerns about temple recommends to Quinn McKay. McKay, oral history interview with Gregory A. Prince, May 21, 1999, MLH. See also Quinn McKay, "A Rural, Utah, Mormon Boy—The Blacks and the LDS Church," May–September 2006, 16, CHL.

64. Catherine Humphrey (formerly Beitler), interview with Matthew L. Harris, June 8, 2018, Boise, Idaho; also Humphrey email to Harris, August 16, 2018, and November 5, 2020.

65. Humphrey, diary entries, 1975–77, MLH; Humphrey, email to Harris, August 16, 2018.

66. Humphrey, email to Harris, November 4, 2020.

67. Faust, oral history interview with Gordon Irving, December 30, 1977, 26, JMOH.

68. Hill to Lester E. Bush, May 6, 1976, Box 2, Folder 58, LEB.

69. Douglas Wallace, quoted in "Mormons Nullify Black's Ordination," *Denver Post*, April 3, 1976. See also "Member Ordains Black to Priesthood," *Salt Lake Tribune*, April 3, 1976.

70. Wallace, quoted in Kimball, *Lengthen Your Stride*, 339. Wallace later disputed that he said "Make way for the Lord." Wallace to Spencer W. Kimball, March 21, 1980, Box 6, Folder 11, JWF.

71. Kimball, diary, August 3, 1977, reel 39, SWK.

72. Royal Shipp, oral history interview with Gregory A. Prince, October 22, 1994, MLH.

73. D. Arthur Haycock, oral history interview with Brian Reeves, January 14, 1992, 30, JMOH.

74. Council of Twelve Minutes, October 29, 1936, in *Minutes of the Quorum of the Twelve and First Presidency, 1910–1951*, 4 vols. (Salt Lake City: Smith-Pettit Foundation, 2010), 4:364.

75. Kimball, diary, October 4, 1976, reel 39, SWK.

NOTES 395

76. Transcript of an interview of Herbert Augustus Ford and Mary Ford with Thomas Waywell, high councilman adviser to the stake president on genealogy for the Hamilton, Ontario, Stake, October 21, 1973, 8, 14, Box 32, Folder 5, DJB.

77. Theodore Burton and William Grant Bangerter (genealogical department) to Elden Olsen (stake president), September 30, 1976, Box 32, Folder 5, DJB.

78. Kimball, diary, April 17, 1977, and August 2, 1977, reel 39, SWK; Utah Stake Record, recorded by Max Day and signed by President Lloyd George, April 17, 1978, CHL; "Negro Family in Fillmore, Utah," n.d., Box 61, Folder 3, MHP. See also Robert Greenwell, "One Devout Mormon Family's Struggle with Racism," *Dialogue: A Journal of Mormon Thought* 51, no. 3 (Fall 2018): 155–80.

79. Fyans, oral history interview with Gregory A. Prince, June 3, 1995, MLH.

80. Newell G. Bringhurst and Craig L. Foster, *The Mormon Quest for the Presidency* (Independence, MO: John Whitmer Books, 2008), ch. 3.

81. Matthew L. Harris, *Watchman on the Tower: Ezra Taft Benson and the Making of the Mormon Right* (Salt Lake City: University of Utah Press, 2020), 74–75; J. B. Haws, *The Mormon Image in the American Mind: Fifty Years of Public Perception* (New York: Oxford University Press, 2013), 37–47.

82. For Stewart Udall, see chapter 4.

83. Udall, quoted in Donald W. Carson and James W. Johnson, *Mo: The Life and Times of Morris K. Udall* (Tucson: University of Arizona Press, 2001), 146.

84. Young, quoted in Jules Witcover, *Marathon: The Pursuit of the Presidency, 1972–1976* (New York: Viking, 1977), 338.

85. Frank Moore (staffer in Carter administration), memo to Jimmy Carter, "Meeting with Spencer W. Kimball and Marion G. Romney," March 11, 1977, White House Central File, "Spencer W. Kimball," JCPL; Kimball, diary, October 7, 1976, reel 39, SWK.

86. Moore, memo to Carter, re: "Meeting with Spencer W. Kimball and Marion G. Romney," March 11, 1977.

87. Ibid. Neither Kimball nor Carter discusses the event in their diaries. Jimmy Carter, *White House Diary* (New York: Farrar, Straus and Giroux, 2010); Kimball, diary, March 11, 1977, reel 39, SWK. For Mormons and Equal Rights Amendment, see Colleen McDannell, *Sister Saints: Mormon Women since the End of Polygamy* (New York: Oxford University Press, 2019), 109–18.

88. James E. Faust and William Grant Bangerter, "The History of the South American East Area Office of the Church of Jesus Christ of Latter-day Saints, July 9, 1975, to December 27, 1978," São Paulo, Brazil, CHL (see the entries for March 8–9, 1977).

89. Edward L. Kimball and Andrew E. Kimball Jr., *Spencer W. Kimball: Twelfth President of the Church of Jesus Christ of Latter-day Saints* (Salt Lake City: Bookcraft, 1977), 349–50.

90. Helvécio Martins, with Mark L. Grover, *The Autobiography of Helvécio Martins* (Salt Lake City: Aspen Books, 1994), 65–66.

396   NOTES

91. Ibid., 66.
92. Ibid., 67.
93. Gibbons, *Spencer W. Kimball*, 293.
94. Martins and Grover, *The Autobiography of Helvécio Martins*, 56–59; Kimball, *Lengthen Your Stride*, 331; Arrington, *Adventures of a Church Historian*, 182.
95. Martins and Grover, *The Autobiography of Helvécio Martins*, 59; Haight, quoted in Faust and Bangerter, "The History of the South American East Area Office."
96. Gibbons, *Spencer W. Kimball*, 292–93.
97. Spencer W. Kimball, "Revelation: The Word of the Lord to His Prophets," *Conference Report*, April 1977, https://www.churchofjesuschrist.org/study/ general-conference/1977/04/revelation-the-word-of-the-lord-to-his-proph ets?lang=eng.
98. Renee Carlson, oral history interview with Gregory A. Prince, June 2, 1994, Box 63, Folder 5, SWK.
99. Ibid.
100. Kimball, diary, May 20, 1977, reel 39, SWK.
101. Kimball, *Lengthen Your Stride*, 345; Leonard J. Arrington, diary, June 27, 1978, Box 33, Folder 4, LJA; D. Michael Quinn, diary, June 28, 1978, Box 27, DMQ.
102. McConkie, memo to Spencer W. Kimball, re: "Doctrinal Basis for Conferring the Melchizedek Priesthood upon the Negroes," [June 1977], MLH. For McConkie's views on Black people and the Second Coming, see Bruce R. McConkie, *The Millennial Messiah: The Second Coming of the Son of Man* (Salt Lake City: Deseret Book, 1982), 243; Bruce R. McConkie, "The New Revelation on Priesthood," in *Priesthood* (Salt Lake City: Deseret Book, 1981), 136.
103. Oscar W. McConkie, the apostle's brother, said that at President Kimball's request "Bruce had written a memo indicating [that] there was no scriptural impediment to giving the priesthood." Oscar W. McConkie, telephone interview with Edward L. Kimball, August 23, 1991, Box 63, Folder 5, SWK.
104. McConkie, memo to Spencer W. Kimball, re: "Doctrinal Basis for Conferring the Melchizedek Priesthood upon the Negroes," 4–5. McConkie's assertion that Gentile "blood" could be purged by baptism derived from Joseph Smith. See Smith's writings of June 27, 1839, in "History, 1838–1856, volume C-1 [November 2, 1838–July 31, 1842]," 8, Joseph Smith Papers, http://www. josephsmithpapers.org/paper-summary/history-1838-1856-volume-c-1-2- november-1838-31-july-1842/543. Smith applied the term "Gentile blood" more broadly; McConkie associated it with "Negro" converts.
105. Anderson to Kimball, May 28, 1971, Box 64, Folder 2, SWK.
106. McConkie, "Patriarchal Order," 1967, 21, transcript at CHL; Bruce R. McConkie, *Mormon Doctrine* (Salt Lake City: Bookcraft, 1958), 477.
107. McConkie, memo to Spencer W. Kimball, re: "Doctrinal Basis for Conferring the Melchizedek Priesthood upon the Negroes," 3–4.
108. Kimball, quoted in Boyd K. Packer, "Bruce R. McConkie, Apostle," April 23, 1985, 7, Box 141, Folder 1, DJ.

NOTES

397

109. Oscar W. McConkie, interview with Duane E. Jefferey, August 1, 1995, Box 141, Folder 1, DJ; D. Michael Quinn, diary, June 9, 1978, Box 27, DMQ.
110. Arrington, diary, January 1, 1978, Box 63, Folder 2, LJA.
111. Kimball to Kimball, March 11, 1963, Box 63, Folder 6, SWK.
112. Kimball, *Lengthen Your Stride*, 346.
113. Russell W. Stevenson, "'We Have Prophetesses': Mormonism in Ghana, 1964–79," *Journal of Mormon History* 41, no. 3 (July 2015): 244–45; Russell W. Stevenson, *For the Cause of Righteousness: A Global History of Blacks and Mormonism, 1830–2013* (Salt Lake City: Greg Kofford Books, 2014), 89–92; James P. Bell, *In the Strength of the Lord: The Life and Teachings of James E. Faust* (Salt Lake City: Deseret Book, 1999), 122–23.
114. Kimball, *Lengthen Your Stride*, 341; Gregory A. Prince, *Leonard Arrington and Writing of Mormon History* (Salt Lake City: University of Utah Press, 2016), 318–19.
115. Baker, oral history interview with Gregory A. Prince, October 26, 1994, Box 63, Folder 5, SWK; Bateman, interview with Edward L. Kimball, June 28, 1996, Box 63, Folder 5, SWK.
116. First Presidency to Stake and Mission Presidents, Districts Presidents, Bishops, and Branch Presidents, February 22, 1978, Box 61, Folder 3, MHP.
117. D. Michael Quinn, *The Mormon Hierarchy: Extensions of Power* (Salt Lake City: Signature Books, 1997), 870.
118. Kimball, *Lengthen Your Stride*, 346; McConkie, "New Revelation on Priesthood," 134.
119. Gibbons, *Spencer W. Kimball*, 293; Kimball meeting with Gibbons and McConkie, May 12, 1982, in Edward L. Kimball, diary, May 12, 1982, MLH.
120. Marion D. Hanks, diary, June 9, 1978, MDH; Kimball meeting with Gibbons and McConkie, May 12, 1982, Edward Kimball, diary, May 12, 1982.
121. Kimball meeting with Gibbons and McConkie, May 12, 1982; Edward Kimball diary, May 12, 1982; Kimball, *Lengthen Your Stride*, 347.
122. Kimball, interview with Harris, November 26, 2013.
123. Eleanor Knowles, *Howard W. Hunter* (Salt Lake City: Deseret Book, 1994), 235; Gibbons, *Spencer W. Kimball*, 293–94; Kimball, *Lengthen Your Stride*, 356; Lucile C. Tate, *David B. Haight: The Life Story of a Disciple* (Salt Lake City: Bookcraft, 1987), 279; Francis M. Gibbons, *Ezra Taft Benson: Statesman, Patriot, Prophet of God* (Salt Lake City: Deseret Book, 1996), 281; Lee Tom Perry, *L. Tom Perry: An Uncommon Life—Years of Hastening the Work of Salvation* (Salt Lake City: Deseret Book, 2019), 80.
124. Kimball, diary, January 5, 1965, reel 27, SWK; Kimball, *The Teachings of Spencer W. Kimball*, 302–3.
125. McConkie, memo to Spencer W. Kimball, June 30, 1978, MLH; Richards, interview with Wesley P. Walters and Chris Vlachos, August 16, 1978, Box 1, Folder 1, LR.
126. Council of Twelve Minutes, October 11, 1958, Box 64, Folder 4, SWK; Council of Twelve Minutes, May 14 and May 21, 1970, Box 63, Folder 3, SWK.

127. "Patriarchs' Meeting," April 6, 1973, Box 4, Folder 3, IB; Perry, Quarterly Stake Conference Report by General Authorities of the Santo Andre Stake Conference, May 15–16, 1976, CHL.

128. Richards, quoted in Lucile C. Tate, *LeGrand Richards: Beloved Apostle* (Salt Lake City: Bookcraft, 1982), 291–92.

129. "President Bill Pope Discourse on June 17, 1978, BYU 3rd Stake, DeJong Concert Hall, BYU," notes taken by Jay Bell, Box 32, Folder 12, DJB. See also "The '400 Page Document,'" Box 32, Folder 12, DJB.

130. Lester E. Bush, "'Mormonism's Negro Doctrine' Forty-Five Years Later," *Dialogue: A Journal of Mormon Thought* 51, no. 3 (Fall 2018): 7; Newell G. Bringhurst, "An Ambiguous Decision: The Implementation of Mormon Priesthood Denial for the Black Man—A Re-examination," *Utah Historical Quarterly* 46, no. 1 (Winter 1978): 45–64; Petersen, memo to Kimball, "Discussion Re: *Utah Historical Quarterly*," May 25, 1978, Box 63, Folder 2, SWK; Gibbons, *Spencer W. Kimball*, 294; Durham, "Prophets Tell of Promise of Priesthood to All Races," [May 1978], Box 63, Folder 11, LJA.

131. Kimball, *Lengthen Your Stride*, 349; Gibbons, *Spencer W. Kimball*, 294.

132. Kimball, interview with Harris, November 26, 2013.

133. As late as 1975, Apostles Petersen and Stapley visited LDS church missions and told missionaries that the ban wouldn't end in their lifetime. Wally Taylor, email to Matthew Harris, October 22, 2020. Taylor served in the Seattle, Washington, Mission when Petersen and Stapley visited. Church patriarch Eldred G. Smith stated that President Kimball "always had enough members to form a quorum, but he made sure that the members present would give him the decision he wanted." Smith, oral history interview with Seth L. Bryant, March 7, 2007, MLH.

134. Gibbons, *Spencer W. Kimball*, 292–94; Kimball, *Lengthen Your Stride*, 344n8, 345; F. Burton Howard, *Marion G. Romney: His Life and Faith* (Salt Lake City: Bookcraft, 1988), 239; Sheri L. Dew, *Go Forward with Faith: The Biography of Gordon B. Hinckley* (Salt Lake City: Deseret Book, 1996), 362; Lucile C. Tate, *Boyd K. Packer: Watchman on the Tower* (Salt Lake City: Bookcraft, 1995), 226; Joseph Fielding McConkie, *Bruce R. McConkie: Reflections of a Son* (Salt Lake City: Deseret Book, 2003), 379; Swinton, *To the Rescue*, 393; Knowles, *Howard W. Hunter*, 235; Tate, *David B. Haight*, 279.

135. Kimball conveyed to his son Edward that Benson was a holdout. Edward Kimball, interview with Harris, November 26, 2013. Apostle L. Tom Perry conveyed to a stake president that Benson wanted to "table" the discussion about lifting the ban. The stake president conveyed this to me in a phone interview, August 19, 2021. Benson's diaries at the LDS Church History Library are not available to confirm this detail.

136. Kimball, *Lengthen Your Stride*, 350; Leonard J. Arrington, diary, June 27, 1978, Box 33, Folder 4, LJA; "The Revelation on the Priesthood as Related by

NOTES 399

Elder Bruce R. McConkie and Told by Bill Pope, Address to BYU Third Stake Conference, Provo, Utah, June 17, 1978," Box 22, Folder 24, EJB. This same address is catalogued as "Bill J. Pope address, circa 1978," CHL. Pope was McConkie's brother-in-law.

137. McConkie, "The Receipt of the Revelation," 4–5; Leonard J. Arrington, diary, June 27, 1978, Box 33, Folder 4, LJA; Kimball, *Lengthen Your Stride*, 350; Tate, *Boyd K. Packer*, 225–26. Packer had studied the priesthood ban intensely over the previous year. He asked Henry Christiansen of the church's genealogical department to prepare a document for him listing scriptures on race and lineage, statements from Joseph Smith, First Presidency and Quorum of the Twelve meeting minutes, and signed statements of the First Presidency. He compiled them in 1977 and donated them to the LDS Church History Library. My thanks to Jonathan Stapley for this information.

138. Kimball, *Lengthen Your Stride*, 359; Kimball, interview with Harris, November 26, 2013; Hinckley, "Priesthood Restoration," LDS Church Fireside, May 15, 1988, *Ensign*, October 1988, https://www.churchofjesuschrist.org/study/ens ign/1988/10/priesthood-restoration?lang=eng; Dew, *Ezra Taft Benson*, 457.

139. Kimball, *Lengthen Your Stride*, 355.

140. Haycock, quoted in Swinton, *In the Company of Prophets*, 83.

141. Bruce R. McConkie, memo to Spencer W. Kimball, re: "Draft of Document," June 1, 1978, MLH; Gibbons and McConkie, May 12, 1982, in Edward Kimball, diary, May 12, 1982; Leonard J. Arrington, diary, June 27, 1978, Box 33, Folder 4, LJA.

142. McConkie, "The Receipt of the Revelation," 7–8; Swinton, *In the Company of Prophets*, 83.

143. McConkie, "The Receipt of the Revelation," 8; Gibbons, *Spencer W. Kimball*, 295.

144. Leonard J. Arrington, diary, June 27, 1978, and June 12, 1978, Box 33, Folder 4, LJA Papers; recording Bruce R. McConkie related in a family memo to Jay Todd, June 26, 1978, Box 22, Folder 24, EJB.

145. Petersen, quoted in Peggy Petersen Barton, *Mark E. Petersen: A Biography* (Salt Lake City: Deseret Book, 1985), 176; McConkie, "The Receipt of the Revelation," 8–9; Quinn, *Mormon Hierarchy*, 870; "Interracial Marriage Discouraged," *Church News*, supplement to *Deseret News*, June 17, 1978, 4.

146. Stapley, quoted in Kimball, *Lengthen Your Stride*, 357; McConkie, "The Receipt of the Revelation," 9.

147. In one of his addresses, Smith declared that Black people would be "servants" to White people in an afterlife. See Eldred G. Smith, BYU devotional address, "A Patriarchal Blessing Defined," November 8, 1966, CHL; also in Box 211, Folder 6, ELW. The Brethren refused to publish the address. David O. McKay, diary, November 13, 1966, Box 63, Folder 7, DOM; Ernest L. Wilkinson to Eldred G. Smith, November 25, 1966, Box 378, Folder 3, ELWP.

148. Matthew L. Harris, "Mormons and Lineage: The Complicated History of Blacks and Patriarchal Blessings, 1830–2018," *Dialogue: A Journal of Mormon Thought* 51, no. 3 (Fall 2018): 110–18; Irene M. Bates and E. Gary Smith, *Lost Legacy: The Mormon Office of Presiding Patriarch*, 2nd ed. (Urbana: University of Illinois Press, 2018), ch. 9.

149. Henry D. Taylor, "Worthy Male Members to Receive the Priesthood Regardless of Race or Creed," BYU Sixth Stake Conference address, October 29, 1978, 1, CHL; also in Box 22, Folder 24, EJB.

150. James Faust wrote, "I had no premonition that such a change was imminent." Faust to Philip Morgan, April 28, 1981, MLH. See also Paul H. Dunn, oral history interview with Gregory A. Prince, June 5, 1995, MLH; Neal A. Maxwell, quoted in "Apostles Talk about Reasons for Lifting the Ban," *Provo Daily Herald*, June 5, 1988; Henry Dixon Taylor, *Autobiography of Henry Dixon Taylor* (Provo, UT: Brigham Young University Press, 1980), 286; Bell, *In the Strength of the Lord*, 124.

151. Hanks, diary, June 9, 1978, MDH.

152. Ibid.

153. Ibid.

154. Taylor, "Worthy Male Members to Receive the Priesthood Regardless of Race or Creed," 1; McConkie, "The Receipt of the Revelation," 9.

155. Hanks, diary, June 9, 1978.

156. Bruce C. Hafen, *A Disciple's Life: The Biography of Neal A. Maxwell* (Salt Lake City: Deseret Book, 2002), 417; Bell, *In the Strength of the Lord*, 124; Faust to Morgan, April 28, 1981.

157. Hanks, diary, June 9, 1978.

158. Leonard J. Arrington, diary, June 27, 1978, Box 33, Folder 4, LJA.

159. Hanks, diary, June 9, 1978.

160. Ibid.; McConkie, "The Receipt of the Revelation," 9–10; Dunn, oral history interview with Prince, June 5, 1995; Taylor, "Worthy Male Members to Receive the Priesthood Regardless of Race or Creed," 3.

161. McConkie, "The Receipt of the Revelation, 10.

162. Taylor, "Worthy Male Members to Receive the Priesthood Regardless of Race or Creed," 2–3; "Official Declaration 2," Church of Jesus Christ of Latter-day Saints, https://www.churchofjesuschrist.org/study/scriptures/dc-testament/od/2?lang=eng.

163. McConkie, "The Receipt of the Revelation," 10; Kimball, *Lengthen Your Stride*, 359.

164. Hanks, diary, June 9, 1978.

165. Kimball, diary, June 9, 1978, reel 39, SWK.

166. Ibid.

167. Gibbons, quoted in Quinn, *Mormon Hierarchy*, 870. See also McConkie, "New Revelation on Priesthood," 132.

NOTES   401

CHAPTER 8

1. Leonard J. Arrington, diary, June 12, 1978, Box 63, Folder 11, LJA.

2. Sheri L. Dew, *Go Forward with Faith: The Biography of Gordon B. Hinckley* (Salt Lake City: Deseret Book, 1996), 362.

3. Kimball said that the revelation came in 1978 "because conditions and people have changed. It's a different world than it was 20 or 25 years ago." Quoted in *Salt Lake Tribune*, June 13, 1978.

4. Marvin Perkins, an African American Latter-day Saint, referred to extant LDS racial teachings as "debris in the streets." Quoted in Peggy Fletcher Stack, "Black Mormon Panelists: LDS Church Must Face Its Racial History," *Salt Lake Tribune*, June 18, 2013.

5. Heidi S. Swinton, *To the Rescue: The Biography of Thomas S. Monson* (Salt Lake City: Deseret Book, 2010), 395.

6. Fleming, quoted in "Black Mormon no longer feels like a guest in your father's house," *Arizona Daily Star* (Tucson, AZ), June 11, 1978. See also Marjorie Hyer, "Mormon Church Dissolves Black Bias," *Washington Post*, June 19, 1978.

7. Ruffin Bridgeforth, quoted in Kenneth L. Woodward, "Race Relations," *Newsweek,* June 19, 1978, 67. See also Kenneth A. Briggs, "Mormon Church Strikes Down Ban against Blacks in Priesthood," *New York Times*, June 10, 1978.

8. David Liggett, "Policy Change 'Scary Thing,' Former ASBYU Officer Says," BYU *Daily Universe*, June 13, 1978.

9. Joseph Freeman, *In the Lord's Due Time* (Salt Lake City: Bookcraft, 1979), 2–3.

10. Gray, quoted in Edward L. Kimball, *Lengthen Your Stride: The Presidency of Spencer W. Kimball—Working Draft* (Salt Lake City: Benchmark Books, 2009), 363.

11. "Mormon Black Priest Decision Praised; Females Still Barred, *Lakeland Ledger*, June 11, 1978; Woodward, "Race Relations," 67.

12. Helvécio Martins, with Mark L. Grover, *The Autobiography of Helvécio Martins* (Salt Lake City: Aspen Books, 1994), 69–70.

13. Ibid.

14. "Historical Record, Section B—Historical Events," 1979, CHL.

15. James E. Faust and William Grant Bangerter, "The History of the South American East Area Office of the Church of Jesus Christ of Latter-day Saints, July 9, 1975, to December 27, 1978, São Paulo, Brazil," CHL (see entry for May 21, 1979); Martins and Grover, *The Autobiography of Helvécio Martins*, 83–84; "First Black Is Called to Stake Presidency," *LDS Church News*, December 16, 1978.

16. William Grant Bangerter, *These Things I Know: The Autobiography of William Grant Bangerter*, compiled by Cory William Bangerter (Provo, UT: Self-published, 2013), 303–4.

17. Bangerter, quoted in "The History of the South American East Area Office," June 9, 1978.

18. Beitler, diary, June 10, 1978, MLH.

402   NOTES

19. Ibid.

20. Wolsey to Kimball, June 21, 1978, Box 63, Folder 1, SWK.

21. Woodward, "Race Revelations", 67; Richard N. Ostling, "Mormonism Enters a New Era," *Time*, August 7, 1978, 10–13, in Box 63, Folder 2, SWK. Kimball collected news clippings from dozens of newspapers (see Box 63, Folders 1–2, SWK). See also "Reaction to Revelation Varies," LDS *Church News*, July 15, 1978, 4; "New Priesthood Policy Stirs Media Interest," *Sunstone*, September–October 1978, 4.

22. "A Burden Is Lifted," *Salt Lake Tribune*, June 11, 1978. See also Tom Foley, "Scrapping a 148-Year-Old Racist Tradition," *New York Daily World*, July 7, 1978; Marjorie Hyer, "Mormon Church Dissolves Black Bias," *Washington Post*, June 10, 1978; Briggs, "Mormon Church Strikes Down Ban against Blacks in Priesthood"; "Mormon Church President Kimball Opens Way for Blacks in Priesthood," *San Francisco Chronicle*, June 10, 1978.

23. "Revelation Ends Racist Policy of Mormon Church," *Amsterdam News*, June 17, 1978.

24. Bruce C. Hafen, *A Disciple's Life: The Biography of Neal A. Maxwell* (Salt Lake City: Deseret Book, 2002), 418. "Carter Praises LDS Church Action," *Deseret News*, June 10, 1978; McMurrin to Kimball, June 20, 1978, Box 290, Folder 2, SMM.

25. Douglas Bennion, quoted in Mary Lythgoe Bradford, *Lowell L. Bennion: Teacher, Counselor, Humanitarian* (Salt Lake City: Dialogue Foundation, 1995), 258; Brodie, quoted in Newell G. Bringhurst, "Fawn M. Brodie as a Critic of Mormonism's Policy toward Blacks—A Historiographical Reassessment," *John Whitmer Historical Association Journal* 11 (1991): 35–36, 45; Lowry Nelson, *In the Direction of His Dreams: Memoirs* (New York: Philosophical Library, 1985), 349.

26. Firmage, oral history interview with Gregory A. Prince, October 10, 1996, MLH; Firmage, oral history interview with Stan Larson, September 13, 2010, 15, Box 67, Folder 25, ECOH.

27. Matthew L. Harris, "Mormons and Lineage: The Complicated History of Blacks and Patriarchal Blessings, 1830–2018," *Dialogue: A Journal of Mormon Thought* 51, no. 3 (Fall 2018): 125–26.

28. Stewarts to Kimball, June 14, 1978, Box 63, Folder 1, SWK; Allen to Kimball, June 13, 1978, Box 63, Folder 1, SWK.

29. Mr. and Mrs. R. Wilson to Kimball, June 11, 1978, Box 64, Folder 3, SWK.

30. Unknown letter writer to Kimball, June 16, 1978, Box 64, Folder 3, SWK.

31. Unknown letter writer to Kimball, June 10, 1978, Box 64, Folder 3, SWK; Unknown letter writer to Kimball, June 11, 1978, Box 63, Folder 1, SWK.

32. Dooley, oral history interview with Leslie G. Kelen, December 6, 1983, 30, Box 19, Folder 4, ECOH. See also NAACP Newsletter, vol. 8, [June] 1978, copy in Box 220, Folder 5, SMM.

NOTES 403

33. Davis, quoted in Molly Ivins, "Mormon Decision on Blacks Promises Impact on Utah," *New York Times*, June 18, 1978.

34. Wayne Carle to Kimball, June 10, 1978, Box 63, Folder 1, SWK; Ruth Ehringer to Kimball, June 11, 1978, Box 64, Folder 3, SWK. See also Robert Bryson, "Church Officials Applaud LDS Action on Blacks," *Salt Lake Tribune*, June 10, 1978; Joanna Brooks, Rachel Hunt Steenblik, and Hannah Wheelwright, eds., *Mormon Feminism: Essential Writings* (New York: Oxford University Press, 2016), 123–24, 144–45.

35. Kimball, diary, August 16, 1979, reel 39, SWK; "Prophet Says Priesthood Not Extended to Women," BYU *Daily Universe*, June 13, 1978; "Not for Women," *Deseret News*, June 13, 1978; Tanner to Philip Morgan, April 21, 1981, MLH.

36. "Priesthood Policy Survey Well Received in County," BYU *Daily Universe*, June 22, 1978; Lester E. Bush, "Introduction," *Dialogue: A Journal of Mormon Thought* 12, no. 2 (Summer 1979): 9; Dallin H. Oaks, "For the Blessing of All His Children," keynote address, LDS African American Symposium, BYU, June 8, 1988, Box 42, Folder 1, ALM; Leonard J. Arrington and Davis Bitton, *The Mormon Experience: A History of the Latter-day Saints* (New York: Alfred A. Knopf, 1979), 324.

37. Henry D. Taylor, "Worthy Male Members to Receive the Priesthood Regardless of Race or Creed," BYU Sixth Stake Conference, October 29, 1978, 1, CHL.

38. Marion D. Hanks, diary, June 9, 1978, MDH.

39. "The Max L. Pinegar LTM Discourse," June 9, 1978, Box 32, Folder 12, DJB.

40. Bill Pope, "The Revelation on the Priesthood as Related by Elder Bruce R. McConkie and Told by Bill Pope," BYU Third Stake Conference, June 17, 1978, Box 22, Folder 24, EJB. (A partial transcript of this address is catalogued as "Bill J. Pope address, circa 1978," CHL.) See also Leonard J. Arrington, diary, June 27, 1978, Box 33, Folder 4, LJA.

41. Doctrine and Covenants, 110: 2–3; Dean C. Jessee, Mark Ashurst-McGee, Richard L. Jensen, eds., *The Joseph Smith Papers: Journals*, vol. 1 (Salt Lake City: Church Historian's Press, 2008), 219–23.

42. Pope, "The Revelation on the Priesthood as Related by Elder Bruce R. McConkie."

43. Annie Whitton, "An Account of the Revelation Which Extends the Priesthood to All Worthy Members," June 18, 1978, MLH.

44. George Pace, "Circumstances Surrounding the Receiving of the Revelation Which Granted All Worthy Male Members the Priesthood," June 18, 1993, Box 33, Folder 4, LJA.

45. Notes taken by BYU professor Clayton White, who heard Joseph Fielding McConkie speak on June 25, 1978, Box 32, Folder 12, DJB.

46. "Some Circumstances Relating to the Revelation Granting the Priesthood to the Negroes," June 25, 1978, MLH.

47. Leonard J. Arrington, diary, August 28, 1978, Box 33, Folder 5, LJA.

404 NOTES

48. Packer, interview with Kimball, June 8, 1978, Box 63, Folder 5, SWK.

49. I grew up in Maine in the 1980s and heard these stories as a teenager. They were reaffirmed to me during my LDS mission to Idaho in the late 1980s. The Arrington papers confirm that this story circulated widely.

50. Leonard J. Arrington, diary, July 5, 1978, Box 33, Folder 4, LJA; "Some Circumstances Relating to the Revelation Granting the Priesthood to the Negroes."

51. Bruce R. McConkie, "The Receipt of the Revelation Offering the Priesthood to Worthy Men of All Races and Colors," June 30, 1978, 6, MLH.

52. Kimball, *Lengthen Your Stride*, 608.

53. Gordon B. Hinckley, "Priesthood Restoration," *Ensign*, October 1988, https://www.churchofjesuschrist.org/study/history/topics/restoration-of-the-aaronic-priesthood?lang=eng; Haight sermon at Priesthood Leadership meeting, Pullman-Lewiston Bi-stake Conference, May 16, 1993, notes by Terrance Day, Box 41, Folder 1, ALM; Merrill J. Bateman, interview with Edward L. Kimball, June 28, 1996, Box 63, Folder 5, SWK; Leonard J. Arrington to Edward L. Kimball, January 6, 1996, Box 63, Folder 5, SWK.

54. Buerger later published on these very topics. See David John Buerger, *The Mysteries of Godliness: A History of Mormon Temple Worship* (San Francisco: Smith Research Associates, 1994).

55. These documents can be found in Box 32, Folder 12, DJB.

56. Buerger to McConkie, July 5, 1978, Box 32, Folder 12, DJB. For "The 1978 Negro Revelation," see Box 32, Folder 6, DJB.

57. McConkie to "Honest Truth Seekers," July 1, 1980, Box 141, Folder 1, DJB.

58. McConkie to Buerger, July 6, 1978, Box 32, Folder 12, DJB. Joseph Fielding McConkie told Buerger that his father was "embarrassed" about the rumors. David John Buerger, "An Interesting Conversation," July 10, 1978, Box 32, Folder 12, DJB.

59. McConkie to Whitton, cc. Bill and Margaret Pope, July 31, 1978, MLH.

60. Whitton, "An Account of the Revelation Which Extends the Priesthood to All Worthy Male Members"; McConkie to Whitton, August 21, 1978, MLH.

61. Whitton to McConkie, August 6, 1978, MLH.

62. McConkie to Whitton, August 21, 1978.

63. McConkie, quoted in Buerger, "An Interesting Conversation," July 10, 1978.

64. McConkie to Whitton, August 21, 1978.

65. D. Michael Quinn, diary, September 21, 1978, Box 27, DMQ.

66. Bill Pope and Margaret Pope, "Denies Rumor," BYU *Daily Universe*, August 3, 1978.

67. Ostling, "Mormonism Enters a New Era," 54–55.

68. Ivins, "Mormon Decision on Blacks Promises Impact on Utah."

69. Kimball to the editors of *Time*, August 2, 1978, Box 63, Folder 2, SWK. Kimball drafted the letter and recorded August 2 as the date, but the article didn't appear until August 7. Kimball either got the date wrong or read a version of Ostling's article in draft form.

NOTES

70. For Tanner and Romney's response to Edward Kimball's letter, see Box 63, Folder 2, SWK.

71. Bruce R. McConkie, "The New Revelation on Priesthood," in *Priesthood* (Salt Lake City: Deseret Book, 1981), 129.

72. For "Mormon Folklore" stories, see Eric A. Eliason and Tom Mould, eds., *Latter-day Lore: Mormon Folklore Stories* (Salt Lake City: University of Utah Press, 2013). The church leadership has cracked down on CES teachers for teaching folklore. See Christopher James Blythe, *Terrible Revolution: Latter-day Saints and the American Apocalypse* (New York: Oxford University Press, 2020), 266.

73. McConkie, "New Revelation on Priesthood," 129. Bruce Van Orden, a seminary teacher at the time, heard McConkie's sermon and confirmed the large gathering. Van Orden, email to Matthew Harris, January 1, 2021.

74. Bruce R. McConkie, "All Alike unto God," Church Religious Educator's Symposium, August 18, 1978, CHL; Book of Mormon, 2 Nephi, 26:33.

75. McConkie, "All Alike unto God," 4–5.

76. Ibid., 2.

77. Ibid., 2–3.

78. Bruce R. McConkie, *Mormon Doctrine* (Salt Lake City: Bookcraft, 1958), 477.

79. Joseph Fielding Smith, *The Way to Perfection*, 5th ed. (Salt Lake City: Genealogical Society of Utah, 1945), 107; "Remarks by President Brigham Young, delivered in the Tabernacle Great Salt Lake City," October 9, 1859, in *Journal of Discourses*, ed. George D. Watt, 26 vols. (London: Latter-day Saints Book Depot, 1854–86), 7:290–91; Wilford Woodruff, journal, February 7, 1852, Wilford Woodruff Journals and Papers, CHL, https://catalog.churchof jesuschrist.org/assets/a5c827b5-938d-4a08-b80e-71570704e323/0/362; John L. Lund, *The Church and the Negro: A Discussion of Mormons, Negroes, and the Priesthood* (Salt Lake City: Paramount, 1967), 45.

80. N. Eldon Tanner, "Revelation on Priesthood Accepted," *Conference Report*, October 1978, https://www.churchofjesuschrist.org/study/general-con ference/1978/10/revelation-on-priesthood-accepted-church-officers-sustai ned?lang=eng; "Official Declaration 2," Church of Jesus Christ of Latter-day Saints, https://www.churchofjesuschrist.org/study/scriptures/dc-testament/ od/2?lang=eng.

81. Bruce R. McConkie, "Thou Shall Receive Revelation," *Conference Report*, October 1, 1978, https://www.churchofjesuschrist.org/study/general-confere nce/1978/10/thou-shalt-receive-revelation?lang=eng.

82. Edward L. Kimball, interview with Spencer W. Kimball, June 1978, in Edward L. Kimball, "Draft of the Priesthood Revelation," June 1978, unpublished manuscript, MLH.

83. Bush to Marion D. Hanks, January 24, 1979, Box 1 Folder 4, LEB; Robert G. Vernon, "Questions on Church Negro Doctrine," June 28, 1978, Box 12, Folder 6, RGV. See also C. B. McBride to Bruce R. McConkie, September 7, 1979, Box 5, Folder 10, HMM.

406   NOTES

84. "LDS Soon to Repudiate a Portion of Their Pearl of Great Price?," *Salt Lake Tribune*, July 23, 1978, Box 63, Folder 2, SWK. See also Newell G. Bringhurst, "Fundamentalist Mormon Beliefs on Race and African Americans," in *The Persistence of Polygamy: Fundamentalist Mormon Polygamy from 1890 to the Present*, ed. Newell G. Bringhurst and Craig L. Foster (Independence, MO: John Whitmer Books, 2015), ch. 11.

85. Jensen, quoted in "Fundamentalists Reject Black Priesthood," *Salt Lake Tribune*, August 1, 1978. For other ads denouncing the revelation, see Jerald Tanner and Sandra Tanner, "The Changing World of Mormonism," *Salt Lake Tribune*, February 24, 1980; Joseph Jensen, "Shall We Excommunicate Joseph Smith?," *Salt Lake Tribune*, March 30, 1980; Jensen's ad in the *Salt Lake Tribune*, January 17, 1982.

86. Wagner, letter to the editor, *Salt Lake Tribune*, June 24, 1978.

87. Kraut to Kimball (with a copy to the First Presidency and Quorum of the Twelve), July 4, 1978, CHL.

88. A number of these revelations can be found at the Joseph Smith Papers website, https://www.josephsmithpapers.org/. See also Fred C. Collier, ed., *Unpublished Revelations of the Prophets and Presidents of the Church of Jesus Christ of Latter-day Saints*, 2 vols., 3rd ed. (Salt Lake City: Collier's, 2011).

89. Ellis T. Rasmussen (BYU dean of religious education), memo to All Religious Instruction Faculty, June 9, 1978, Box 32, Folder 6, DJB; Kimball, *Lengthen Your Stride*, 361; Paul Swenson, "Muting the Message," *Utah Holiday*, July 1978, 18.

90. Dew, *Go Forward with Faith*, 362; Lucille C. Tate, *LeGrand Richards: Beloved Apostle* (Salt Lake City: Bookcraft, 1982), 291–92; Hafen, *A Disciple's Life*, 417; Sheri L. Dew, *Ezra Taft Benson: A Biography* (Salt Lake City: Deseret Book, 1987), 456–57; Eleanor Knowles, *Howard W. Hunter* (Salt Lake City: Deseret Book, 1994), 235–36; Lucile C. Tate, *Boyd K. Packer: A Watchman on the Tower* (Salt Lake City: Bookcraft, 1995), 225–26; Swinton, *To the Rescue*, 392–95; F. Burton Howard, *Marion G. Romney: His Life and Faith* (Salt Lake City: Bookcraft, 1988), 239; James P. Bell, *In the Strength of the Lord: The Life and Teachings of James E. Faust* (Salt Lake City: Deseret Book, 1999), 124; Lucille C. Tate, *David B. Haight: The Life Story of a Disciple* (Salt Lake City: Bookcraft, 1987), 278–82. Kimball, *Lengthen Your Stride*, ch. 23; G. Homer Durham, *N. Eldon Tanner: His Life and Service* (Salt Lake City: Deseret Book, 1982).

91. Cahill to Edward L. Kimball, December 13, 1995, Box 63, Folder 5, SWK.

92. Forrest G. Wood, *The Arrogance of Faith: Christianity and Race in America from the Colonial Era to the Twentieth Century* (New York: Alfred A. Knopf, 1990), 111.

93. "A Revelation," [October 1978], Box 63, Folder 2, SWK.

94. Ibid.

95. David Briscoe, "Pressure Led to LDS Change in Black Policy," *Idaho Statesman*, June 17, 1978; David Farber, *The Rise and Fall of Modern American Conservatism: A Short History* (Princeton: Princeton University Press, 2010), 151.

96. "The Church and the IRS," *Mormon Matters*, September 26, 2009, https://www.mormonmatters.org/the-church-and-the-irs/; "The Mormon Church's

NOTES 407

Etch-a-Sketched Doctrine on Blacks," *Politicus USA*, June 10, 2012, https://www.politicususa.com/2012/06/10/voice-god-irs.html. See also Samuel D. Brunson, "Revoke Its Exemption: Pushing for Change in the Mormon Church," *Journal of Mormon History* 47, no. 4 (October 2021): 66n67.

97. Lance Gurwell, "Critics Still Question Revelation on Blacks, Mormons Defend 1978 Racial Action," *Chicago Tribune*, June 2, 1988; Bruce L. Olsen, "Distorted History," *Salt Lake Tribune*, April 5, 2001. Olsen worked in the church's PR department.

98. Fitzgerald to Carter, November 24, 1976, and March 7, 1977, Box 4, Folder 15, JWF. Carter referred Fitzgerald to the Department of Justice, and the Mormon dissident urged them to use the IRS to crack down on Mormons. Fitzgerald to Attorney General and Assistants, December 8, 1978 and the reply (signed by George McNemar), December 21, 1978; and Fitzgerald to Attorney General and Assistants, January 1, 1979, both in Box 7, Folder 30, JWF.

99. Carter to Matthew Harris, March 2013, MLH. In May 2014, I visited the Carter Presidential Library and found no evidence that Carter pressured Kimball to lift the ban. For Carter's visits with Mormon leaders, see Jimmy Carter, *White House Diary of Jimmy Carter* (New York: Farrar, Straus, and Giroux, 2010), 35, 41, 61.

100. Sandra Tanner, email to Matthew Harris, December 2, 2020.

101. Jerald Tanner and Sandra Tanner, "Death of the Anti-Black Doctrine," *Salt Lake City Messenger*, no. 41 (December 1979): 4.

102. Sorensen, quoted in Leonard J. Arrington, diary, June 12, 1978, Box 63, Folder 11, LJA. It is unknown if Sorensen is the same person who spoke to the Tanners.

103. Arrington to his children, June 15, 1978, Box 33, Folder 4, LJA; Leonard J. Arrington, *Adventures of a Church Historian* (Urbana: University of Illinois Press, 1998), 183.

104. Mike Wagner (deputy administrator at the Wisconsin Department of Revenue), email to Matthew Harris, September 30, 2013. The original bill, 1979 Assembly Bill 446, was signed by the governor on April 30, 1980, and took effect on January 1, 1981. For the statute, see https://docs.legis.wisconsin.gov/1979/related/acts/225.

105. William H. Hartley to Armand L. Mauss, [1979], Box 1, Folder 4, ALM; Newell G. Bringhurst, "An Ambiguous Decision: The Implementation of Mormon Priesthood Denial for the Black Man—A Re-examination," *Utah Historical Quarterly* 46, no. 1 (Winter 1978): 45–64; Lester E. Bush, "Mormonism's Negro Doctrine: An Historical Overview," *Dialogue: A Journal of Mormon Thought* 8, no. 1 (Spring 1973): 11–68.

106. Durham, quoted in Leonard J. Arrington, diary, June 9, 1978, Box 33, Folder 4, LJA.

107. Leonard J. Arrington, diary, June 12, 1978, Box 63, Folder 11, LJA; D. Michael Quinn, diary, June 6, 1978, Box 27, DMQ.

NOTES

108. Arrington, diary, June 12, 1978; Quinn, diary, June 6, 1978; Esplin, memo to G. Homer Durham, June 8, 1978, Box 63, Folder 11, LJA.

109. Ronald K. Esplin, "Brigham Young and Priesthood Denial to the Blacks: An Alternate View," *BYU Studies* 19, no. 3 (Spring 1979): 394–402.

110. Durham, memo to Leonard J. Arrington, June 5, 1979, Box 5, Folder 6, LJA; Hartley to Armand L. Mauss, [1979], Box 1, Folder 4, ALM.

111. Leonard J. Arrington, *Brigham Young: American Moses* (New York: Alfred A. Knopf, 1985); Gregory A. Prince, *Leonard Arrington and the Writing of Mormon History* (Salt Lake City: University of Utah Press, 2016), 401.

112. Bush to William H. Hartley, October 8, 1979, Box 1, Folder 4, LEB; Bringhurst to Esplin, July 13, 1979, Box 6, Folder 3, HMM; Mauss to Lester E. Bush, September 29, 1979, Box 3, Folder 23, LEB. See also D. Michael Quinn, diary, June 12, 1978, Box 27, DMQ.

113. Esplin, memo to Durham, June 8, 1978.

114. Allen to Bush, April 22, 1980, Box 2, Folder 5, LEB.

115. Ezra Taft Benson, "God's Hand in Our Nation's History," *BYU Speeches*, March 28, 1977, https://speeches.byu.edu/talks/ezra-taft-benson/gods-hand-nations-history/; Boyd K. Packer, "The Mantle Is Far, Far Greater Than the Intellect," *BYU Studies* 21, no. 3 (1981): 1–18; Arrington, *Adventures of a Church Historian*, ch. 14.

116. Kimball had many meetings relating to the Church History Department where he discussed with Packer, Benson, McConkie, Petersen, and Durham his views on LDS church history. Kimball, diary, January 18, 1978, February 1–2, 1978, February 24, 1978, May 31, 1978, reel 39, SWK.

117. Haight shared these views with Quinn McKay, October 1980. McKay, oral history interview with Gregory A. Prince, May 21, 1999, Box 63, Folder 5, SWK. See also Quinn McKay, "A Rural Utah, Mormon Boy—The Blacks and the LDS Church," May–September 2006, CHL.

118. Lester E. Bush, "Writing 'Mormonism's Negro Doctrine: An Historical Overview,' (1973): Context and Reflections, 1998," *Journal of Mormon History* 25, no. 1 (Spring 1999): 267.

119. Armand L. Mauss, *Shifting Borders and a Tattered Passport: Intellectual Journeys of a Mormon Academic* (Salt Lake City: University of Utah Press, 2012), 176; Armand L. Mauss, "The Fading of the Pharaoh's Curse: The Decline and Fall of the Priesthood Ban against Blacks in the Mormon Church," *Dialogue: A Journal of Mormon Thought* 14, no. 3 (Fall 1981): 10–45. Newell G. Bringhurst, "An Unintended and Difficult Odyssey," *Sunstone*, March 2003, 23–27; Newell G. Bringhurst, *Saints, Slaves, and Blacks: The Changing Place of Black People within Mormonism*, 2nd ed. (1981; Salt Lake City: Greg Kofford Books, 2018), xxv–xxvii.

120. Matthew L. Harris and Newell G. Bringhurst, eds., *The Mormon Church and Blacks: A Documentary History* (Urbana: University of Illinois Press, 2015), 109–12.

NOTES   409

121. "Interracial Marriage Discouraged," *Church News* supplement to *Deseret News*, June 17, 1978, 4; "Mixed Marriages Discouraged," *Salt Lake Tribune*, June 18, 1978; Bruce R. McConkie, *Mormon Doctrine* (Salt Lake City: Bookcraft, 1979), 527; Wesley Walters and Chris Vlachos, interview with LeGrand Richards, August 16, 1978, 4, Box 1, Folder 1, LR; Thane Young, "Mixed Messages on the Negro Doctrine: An Interview with Lester Bush," *Sunstone*, May–June 1979, 15; Boyd K. Packer, "Follow the Rule," *BYU Speeches*, January 14, 1977, https://speeches.byu.edu/talks/boyd-k-packer/follow-rule/.

122. Renee C. Romano, *Race Mixing: Black-White Marriage in Postwar America* (Cambridge, MA: Harvard University Press, 2003), 246.

123. Marvin S. Hill recollection, 1981, Box 43, Folder 3, MSH. Hill opined that it was "illegal" to have such quotas. Hill was on the committee that Arnold chaired.

124. Deanna Anderson, "Black Club at BYU Has Few Potential Members," *Deseret News*, November 13–14, 1981.

125. David M. Sorenson and the Ad Hoc Committee on Minority Students, Re: Financial Aid for Minority Students, February 19, 1981, MLH.

126. Jessie L. Embry, *Black Saints in a White Church: Contemporary African American Mormons* (Salt Lake City: Signature Books, 1994), 168–79.

127. Mitchell, oral history interview with Alan Cherry, March 12, 1988, 4, AAOH.

128. Albright, oral history interview with Alan Cherry, October 23, 1985, 7–10, AAOH.

129. LeFevre, quoted in George Raine, "Blacks Eligible for LDS Temple Rites," *Salt Lake Tribune*, June 14, 1978.

130. Packer, "Follow the Rule."

131. Stevenson, oral history interview with Alan Cherry, May 31, 1987, 11, AAOH; David Liggett, "Policy Change 'Scary Thing,' Former ASBYU Officer Says," BYU *Daily Universe*, June 13, 1978.

132. Mary Sturlaugson Eyer, *He Restoreth My Soul* (Salt Lake City: Deseret Book, 1982), 55.

133. Edward L. Kimball, ed., *The Teachings of Spencer W. Kimball* (Salt Lake City: Bookcraft, 1982), 302–3; Spencer W. Kimball, "Love v. Lust," *BYU Speeches*, January 5, 1965, https://speeches.byu.edu/talks/spencer-w-kimball/love-vs-lust/; Kimball, diary, January 5, 1965, reel 27, SWK.

134. Mary Sturlaugson Eyer, *Reflections of a Soul* (Salt Lake City: Randall Book, 1985), 27.

135. Ostling, "Mormonism Enters a New Era," 55.

136. Walters and Vlachos, interview with LeGrand Richards.

137. Robert Gottlieb and Peter Wiley, *America's Saints: The Rise of Mormon Power* (New York: G. P. Putnam's Sons, 1984), 174; Joseph Anderson (First Presidency secretary) to W. N. Montgomery, August 3, 1944, "Manuscript of Council of the Twelve Minutes and First Presidency statements on the Negro," 12, Box 64, Folder 5, SWK; Matthew L. Harris, "Whiteness Theology and the

410   NOTES

Evolution of Mormon Racial Teachings," in *The LDS Gospel Topics Series: A Scholarly Engagement*, ed. Matthew L. Harris and Newell G. Bringhurst (Salt Lake City: Signature Books, 2020), 257–60, 265–66.

138. Spencer W. Kimball, "The Day of the Lamanites," *Improvement Era* 63, no. 12 (December 1960): 923.

139. Kimball, interview with Matthew Harris, November 26, 2013, Kimball home, Provo, Utah. For the Indian Placement Program, see Matthew Garrett, *Making Lamanites: Mormons, Native Americans, and the Indian Placement Program, 1947–2000* (Salt Lake City: University of Utah Press, 2016).

140. Lee, quoted in John Dart, "Indians Hope to Shift Mormon View of Their Skin Color," *Los Angeles Times*, March 2, 1979. For Native American Latter-day Saints' discomfort with Mormon whiteness teachings, see Elise Boxer, "'The Lamanites Shall Blossom as the Rose': The Indian Student Placement Program, Mormon Whiteness, and Indigenous Identity," *Journal of Mormon History* 41, no. 4 (October 2015): 132–76; Ignacio Garcia, "Empowering Latino Saints to Transcend Historical Racialism," in *Decolonizing Mormonism: Approaching a Postcolonial Zion*, ed. Gina Colvin and Joanna Brooks (Salt Lake City: University of Utah Press, 2018), ch. 8. For Black Latter-day Saints' response to Mormon whiteness teachings, see Harris, "Whiteness Theology," 261–62.

141. Kimball, quoted in John Dart, "'Curse Idea Upsets Some Indian Mormons," *Los Angeles Times*, February 10, 1979.

142. The scriptural committee changed the phrase back to its original form as it appeared in the 1830 edition. See Douglas Campbell, "'White' or 'Pure': Five Vignettes," *Dialogue: A Journal of Mormon Thought* 29, no. 4 (Winter 1996): 120; Royal Skousen, *The Book of Mormon: The Earliest Text*, 2nd ed. (New Haven, CT: Yale University Press, 2022), 756. See also Tate, *Boyd K. Packer*, ch. 17; Swinton, *To the Rescue*, 387–90; Joseph Fielding McConkie, *The Bruce R. McConkie Story: Reflections of a Son* (Salt Lake City: Deseret Book, 2003), 381–85.

143. James E. Faust, "Patriarchal Blessings," Brigham Young University devotional, March 30, 1980, https://speeches.byu.edu/talks/james-e-faust_patriarchal-blessings; James E. Faust, *Gospel Principles* (Salt Lake City: Church of Jesus Christ of Latter-day Saints, 2009), 273; Daniel H. Ludlow, "Of the House of Israel," *Ensign*, January 1991, https://www.churchofjesuschrist.org/study/ens ign/1991/01/of-the-house-of-israel?lang=eng.

144. "Information and Suggestions for Patriarchs" (1981), in H. Michael Marquardt, comp., *Later Patriarchal Blessings of the Church of Jesus Christ of Latter-day Saints* (Salt Lake City: Smith-Pettit Foundation, 2012), 565–66. Leonard Arrington discusses the anxiety that patriarchs felt when they blessed Black Latter-day Saints. Arrington, diary, June 25, 1978, Box 33, Folder 4, LJA. Keith N. Hamilton, *Last Laborer: Thoughts and Reflections of a Black Mormon* (Salt Lake City: Self-published, 2011), 68.

NOTES

411

145. David Briscoe and George Buck, "Black Friday," *Utah Holiday*, July 1978, 38–40. See also "Mormon Revelation Solves Black Problem," *Denver Post*, July 7, 1978.

146. Bruce R. McConkie, "The Promises Made to the Fathers," in *Studies in Scripture*, vol. 3: *Genesis to 2 Samuel*, ed. Kent P. Jackson and Robert L. Millet (Salt Lake City: Randall Book, 1985), 53. McConkie, *Mormon Doctrine*, 108–9, 114–15, 343, 526–28; Bruce R. McConkie, *The Mortal Messiah* (Salt Lake City: Deseret Book, 1979), 22–23; Bruce R. McConkie, *The Millennial Messiah* (Salt Lake City: Deseret Book, 1982), 182–83, ch. 16; Bruce R. McConkie, *A New Witness for the Articles of Faith* (Salt Lake City: Deseret Book, 1985), 33–42, 510–12.

147. Bruce R. McConkie, The Coming Tests and the Trial of Glory," *Conference Report*, April 1980, https://www.churchofjesuschrist.org/study/general-con ference/1980/04/the-coming-tests-and-trials-and-glory?lang=eng.

148. McConkie, "New Revelation on Priesthood," 128.

149. Edward L. Kimball, diary, April 25, 1982, MLH.

150. Ibid.; Kimball, *Lengthen Your Stride*, 608.

151. Edward L. Kimball, diary, May 10, 1982.

152. Kimball, interview with Matthew Harris, November 26, 2013.

153. Edward L. Kimball, diary, May 12, 1982; Kimball, "Draft of the Priesthood Revelation."

154. Edward L. Kimball, diary, May 12, 1982.

155. Ibid.

156. Kimball, *Lengthen Your Stride*, 372n87.

157. Ibid., 385; Spencer W. Kimball, "The Uttermost Parts of the Earth," *Ensign*, July 1979, https://www.churchofjesuschrist.org/study/ensign/1979/07/the-uttermost-parts-of-the-earth?lang=eng.

158. LeFevre, quoted in Marjorie Hyer, "Mormon Church Dissolves Black Bias," *Washington Post*, June 10, 1978. Woodward, "Race Revelations," 55; Russell Chandler, "Door Is Opened: Mormonism: A Challenge for Blacks," *Los Angeles Times*, August 12, 1988.

159. Kimball, *Lengthen Your Stride*, ch. 24; Dallin H. Oaks, paraphrased in "LDS Afro-American Symposium," *Ensign*, August 1988, https://www.churchofjesu schrist.org/study/ensign/1988/08/news-of-the-church/lds-afro-american-symposium?lang=eng.

160. Chandler, "Door Is Opened"; Heidi S. Swinton, "Without Regard for Race," *This People*, Summer 1988, 20–22; Embry, *Black Saints*, 69.

161. Philip Jenkins, "Letting Go: Understanding Mormon Growth in Africa," in *From the Outside Looking In: Essays on Mormon History, Theology, and Culture*, ed. Reid L. Neilson and Matthew J. Grow (New York: Oxford University Press, 2016), 344.

162. Rendell N. Mabey and Gordon T. Allred, *Brother to Brother: The Story of Latter-day Saint Missionaries Who Took the Gospel to Black Africa* (Salt Lake City: Bookcraft, 1984); E. Dale LeBaron, ed., *"All Are Alike unto God": Fascinating*

Conversion Stories of African Saints (Salt Lake City: Bookcraft, 1990); Alexander B. Morrison, *The Dawning of a Brighter Day: The Church in Black Africa* (Salt Lake City: Deseret Book, 1990); Newell G. Bringhurst, "Mormonism in Black Africa: Changing Attitudes and Practices, 1830–1981," *Sunstone*, May–June 1981, 18.

163. Kimball, *Lengthen Your Stride*, 373; Mark L. Grover, "Mormons in Latin America," in *The Oxford Handbook of Mormonism*, ed. Terryl L. Givens and Philip L. Barlow (New York: Oxford University Press, 2015), 524–26; Mark L. Grover, "The Maturing of the Oak: The Dynamics of LDS Growth in Latin America," *Dialogue: A Journal of Mormon Thought*, 38, no. 2 (Summer 2005): 94–95.

164. Bangerter, diary, September 28, 1978, excerpts in "The History of the South American East Area Office of the Church of Jesus Christ of Latter-day Saints, July 9, 1975, to December 27, 1978, São Paulo, Brazil," CHL; Beitler, diary, June 22, 1978, MLH.

165. Bridgeforth, quoted in "Ban Still Sour Memory for LDS Blacks: Policy Reversed 5 Years Ago," *Salt Lake Tribune*, June 9, 1983.

166. Sinquefield, quoted in "Ban Still Sour Memory for LDS Blacks." See also Robin Witt, "More LDS Blacks: While Membership Increases, Some Still Voice Reservations," *Sacramento Bee*, August 11, 1979; Michael White, "LDS Priesthood Ban Still Sour Memory in Minds of Many American Blacks," *Deseret News*, June 12, 1983.

167. Leonard J. Arrington, diary, June 12, 1978, Box 63, Folder 11, LJA; Swinton, "Without Regard for Race," 22; Newell G. Bringhurst and Darron T. Smith, eds., *Black and Mormon* (Urbana: University of Illinois Press, 2004), 7.

168. John W. Phoenix, oral history interview with Alan Cherry, October 10, 1986, 11, AAOH.

169. Embry, *Black Saints*, 131. For the questionnaire, see "African American Oral History Project Spirituality Surveys," ca. 1980, Boxes 472–73, AAOH.

170. Embry, *Black Saints*, 70.

171. Ibid., 63; Darron T. Smith, "The Persistence of Racialized Discourse in Mormonism," *Sunstone*, March 2003, 32; Margaret Ramirez, "Mormons Steeped in Racism," *Chicago Tribune*, July 26, 2005; Gloria Talley Wilkinson, "The Path We Take—Do I Belong?," in *My Lord, He Calls Me: Stories of Faith by Black Latter-day Saints*, ed. Alice Faulkner Burch (Salt Lake City: Deseret Book, 2022), 38.

172. A mission handbook published in 1982 and 1989 is devoid of any references to past LDS racial teachings. However, most missionaries gleaned their views of Mormon racial teachings from Smith's *The Way to Perfection* and McConkie's *Mormon Doctrine*. Some missionaries even created their own manuals to explain the restriction, claiming that denying Black people the priesthood was an "act of mercy" because they weren't ready. See Reed Simonson, *"If Ye Are Prepared . . . ": A Reference Manual for Missionaries*, 1991, 243, CHL.

NOTES

CHAPTER 9

1. Don L. Searle, "President Ezra Taft Benson Ordained Thirteenth President of the Church," *Ensign*, December 1985, https://www.churchofjesuschrist.org/study/ensign/1985/12/president-ezra-taft-benson-ordained-thirteenth-president-of-the-church?lang=eng.

2. Matthew L. Harris, *Watchman on the Tower: Ezra Taft Benson and the Making of the Mormon Right* (Salt Lake City: University of Utah Press, 2020), 104–5; J. B. Haws, "LDS Church Presidency Years, 1985–1994," in *Thunder from the Right: Ezra Taft Benson in Mormonism and Politics*, ed. Matthew L. Harris (Urbana: University of Illinois Press, 2019), 208–10.

3. Bob Hudson, "Rumor Mongers Leave Unfulfilled," *Daily Herald* (Provo, UT), April 7, 1986; "Support for Candidate Possible Some Day, LDS Apostle Says," *Salt Lake Tribune*, February 22, 1974; Russell Chandler, "Possibility of Benson Heading Mormons Worries Some with Different Views," *Los Angeles Times*, April 1, 1976; T. R. Reid, "Thousands Mourn Leader of Mormons; Benson, Likely Successor, Presides over Service," *Washington Post*, November 10, 1985. Benson and Reagan were friends. Benson to Reagan, May 29, 1984, and Reagan to Benson, July 17, 1984, Box 7, "Latter-day Saints (Mormons)" file, RRPL.

4. Ezra Taft Benson, "Fourteen Fundamentals in Following the Prophet" (1980), *BYU Speeches*, https://speeches.byu.edu/talks/ezra-taft-benson/fourteen-fundamentals-following-prophet/. For Benson's apology, see "Apology" [1980], Ezra Taft and Flora A. Benson file, 1980–1992, Public Affairs Department, CHL; Harris, *Watchman on the Tower*, 102–3. Kimball rebuked Benson many times before the 1980 sermon. Kimball, diary, February 22, 1974, and November 5, 1974, reel 39, SWK.

5. David L. Chappell, *Waking from the Dream: The Struggle for Civil Rights in the Shadow of Martin Luther King, Jr.* (New York: Random House, 2014), 34, 68–89, 98–101, 110–11. For King's address to Utah lawmakers, see Paul Rolly, "King's Widow Gets Cheers, No Holiday," *Salt Lake Tribune*, February 7, 1986; Michael Call, "Widow Says King Set Everyone Free," *Daily Herald* (Provo, UT), February 7, 1986.

6. "The Inside of 'Mr. FBI'—Interview: W. Cleon Skousen," BYU *Daily Universe*, May 4, 1972; Ezra Taft Benson, "Our Immediate Responsibility" (October 25, 1966), in Ezra Taft Benson, *An Enemy Hath Done This*, ed. Jerreld L. Newquist (Salt Lake City: Parliament, 1969), 310. See also Matthew L. Harris and Madison S. Harris, "The Last State to Honor Dr. King: Utah and the Quest for Racial Justice," *Utah Historical Quarterly* 88, no. 1 (Winter 2020): 5–21; Harris, *Watchman on the* Tower, 107–10.

7. Harris and Harris, "The Last State to Honor Dr. King," 13–14; Karen Coates, "The Holy War Surrounding Evan Mecham," *Dialogue: A Journal of Mormon Thought* 22, no. 3 (Fall 1989): 66–80.

8. "Arizona's Holy War: Mecham's Predicament Splits the Mormons," *Newsweek*, February 1, 1988, 28; Scott McCartney, "Mormons Split by Turmoil over Church Member Mecham," *Washington Post*, March 12, 1988.

9. Sanders to Benson, October 1, 1989, MLH; Benson, "Our Immediate Responsibility," October 25, 1966, Benson, *An Enemy Hath Done This*, ch. 27.

10. Steve Yozwiak, "Holiday Opponent Says King Exceeded Lucifer," *Arizona Republic*, October 5, 1989; Steve Yozwiak, "Bigotry Rides Again: The Lucifer Epistle," *Arizona Republic*, October 6, 1989; Steve Benson, "Ezra Taft Benson: Mormonism's Prophet, Seer, and Race Baiter," *Blackfax: A Journal of Black History and Opinion* 13 (Winter 2008): 20–24; "Sanders Letter Angers His Ally, King Slurs Draw Rebuke," *Phoenix Gazette*, October 6, 1989.

11. Stokes, oral history interview with Alan Cherry, March 6, 1988, 21, AAOH.

12. Hawkins, oral history interview with Alan Cherry, March 1, 1985, 22–23, AAOH.

13. Boyd K. Packer, "Bruce R. McConkie, Apostle," April 23, 1985, Box 141, Folder 1, DJ.

14. George Rickford and June Rickford, oral history interview with Matthew Heiss, May 15, 1999, appendix, 5–6, JMOH. Years later Rickford had a change of heart and joined the LDS church (6–8).

15. Reid, oral history interview with Alan Cherry, February 20, 1985, 28, AAOH.

16. Ibid.

17. Ibid.; Ralph Ellison, *Invisible Man* (New York: Random House, 1952).

18. Joseph Fielding McConkie, *The Bruce R. McConkie Story: Reflections of a Son* (Salt Lake City: Deseret Book, 2003), 399–400.

19. Reid, oral history interview with Cherry, 28.

20. Stevenson, oral history interview with Alan Cherry, May 31, 1987, 29, AAOH. Grace Lichtenstein, "Mormon School Elects a Black to Student Office," *New York Times*, April 4, 1976.

21. Bruce R. McConkie, *A New Witness for the Articles of Faith* (Salt Lake City: Deseret Book, 1985), 35, 39; Bruce R. McConkie, "The Promises Made to the Fathers," in *Studies in Scripture*, vol. 3: *Genesis to 2 Samuel*, ed. Kent P. Jackson and Robert L. Millet (Salt Lake City: Randall Book, 1985), 47–62.

22. England to Bishop Alger, April 15, 1968, Box 171, Folder 27, EE; Eugene England, "Are All Alike unto God? Prejudice against Blacks and Women in Popular Mormon Theology," *Sunstone*, April 1990, 20; Eugene England, "The Mormon Cross," *Dialogue: A Journal of Mormon Thought* 8, no. 1 (Spring 1973): 78–86.

23. England asserted that he might be "too unorthodox a Mormon" to teach at BYU. England to Marion D. Hanks, March 21, 1974, Box 171, Folder 9, EE. See also Terryl L. Givens, *Stretching the Heavens: The Life of Eugene England and the Crisis of Modern Mormonism* (Chapel Hill: University of North Carolina Press, 2021); Kristine Haglund, *Eugene England: A Mormon Liberal* (Urbana: University of Illinois Press, 2021).

NOTES   415

24. McConkie, along with Mark E. Petersen, were the apostles most exercised over maintaining orthodoxy in LDS doctrine. Armand L. Mauss, *The Angel and the Beehive: The Mormon Struggle with Assimilation* (Urbana: University of Illinois Press, 1994), 80–81; England, "The Lord's University," Box 54, Folder 5, EE. See also Haglund, *Eugene England*, 63; Givens, *Stretching the Heavens*, 162–66.

25. Bruce R. McConkie, "The Seven Deadly Heresies," *BYU Speeches*, June 1, 1980, https://speeches.byu.edu/talks/bruce-r-mcconkie/seven-deadly-heresies/.

26. McConkie to England, February 19, 1981, Box 171, Folder 28, EE.

27. Eugene England, "On Fidelity, Polygamy, and Celestial Marriage," *Dialogue: A Journal of Mormon Thought* 20, no. 4 (Winter 1987): 138–54.

28. Ibid., 149.

29. Matthews, memo to Eugene England, November 7, 1986, Box 6, Correspondence from Eugene England Folder, 6/34, RLA. I base this assessment on my own personal interactions with Matthews as one of his students at BYU. For a similar assessment of Matthews, see Michael Hicks, *Wineskin: Freakin' Jesus in the '60s and '70s: A Memoir* (Salt Lake City: Signature Books, 2022), 186–87. See also Robert J. Matthews, interview with Alexander L. Baugh, 2015, in *Conversations with Mormon Historians*, ed. Alexander L. Baugh and Reid L. Neilson (Salt Lake City: Deseret Book, 2015), 383–405.

30. Boyd K. Packer, *Let Not Your Heart Be Troubled* (Salt Lake City: Bookcraft, 1991), 117–18; Dallin H. Oaks, "Criticism," May 4, 1986, *Ensign*, February 1987, https://www.churchofjesuschrist.org/study/ensign/1987/02/critic ism?lang=eng.

31. Oaks, quoted in "Elder Decries Criticism of LDS Leaders," *Salt Lake Tribune*, August 18, 1985.

32. Matthews, memo to England, November 7, 1986.

33. England to Matthews, n.d., Box 6, Correspondence from Eugene England Folder, 6/34, RLA.

34. McConkie's writings informed Matthews's work. See Robert J. Matthews, *A Bible! A Bible! How Latter-day Revelation Helps Us Understand the Scriptures and the Savior* (Salt Lake City: Bookcraft, 1990); Robert J. Matthews, *Behold the Messiah: New Testament Insights from Latter-day Revelation* (Salt Lake City: Bookcraft, 1994).

35. England, "Are All Alike unto God?"; Eugene England, "'No Respecter of Persons': A Mormon Ethics of Diversity," *Dialogue: A Journal of Mormon Thought* 27, no. 4 (Winter 1994): 79–102; Eugene England, "Becoming a World Religion: Blacks, the Poor—All of Us," *Sunstone*, June–July 1998, 49–60.

36. Leonard Arrington called Joseph Fielding McConkie a "hard liner." Arrington, diary, February 11, 1982, Box 66, Folder 10, LJA.

37. Robert L. Millet and Joseph Fielding McConkie, *Our Destiny: The Call and Election of the House of Israel* (Salt Lake City: Bookcraft, 1993), 22.

NOTES

38. Douglas Brinkley, *Wheels for the World: Henry Ford, His Company, and a Century of Progress* (New York: Viking, 2003), 258–62; Nell Irvin Painter, *The History of White People* (New York: W. W. Norton, 2010), 325–26.

39. Linda Gordon, *The Second Coming of the KKK: The Ku Klux Klan of the 1920s and the American Political Tradition* (New York: Liveright, 2017), 11; Brendan Simms, *Hitler: A Global Biography* (New York: Basic Books, 2019), 41, 94; Benson to Clark, December 9, 1957, and Clark to Benson, undated reply, reel 4, ETB.

40. Thomas Milan Konda, *Conspiracies of Conspiracies: How Delusions Have Overrun America* (Chicago: University of Chicago Press, 2019), 233; Michael Barkun, *A Culture of Conspiracy: Apocalyptic Visions in Contemporary America* (Berkeley: University of California Press, 2013), 4–5.

41. Millet and McConkie, *Our Destiny*, 22.

42. B. H. Roberts, "To the Youth of Israel," *The Contributor* 6, no. 8 (1885): 296–97; B. H. Roberts, *The Seventy's Course in Theology* (Salt Lake City: Deseret News, 1907), 163–66; Joseph Fielding Smith, *The Way to Perfection: Short Discourses on Gospel Themes*, 5th ed. (1931; Salt Lake City: Genealogical Society of Utah, 1945), chs. 15–16.

43. John G. Turner, *The Mormon Jesus: A Biography* (Cambridge, MA: Harvard University Press, 2016), ch. 9. See also Edward J. Blum and Paul Harvey, *The Color of Christ: The Son of God and the Saga of Race in America* (Chapel Hill: University of North Carolina Press, 2012), ch. 6.

44. James H. Anderson, *God's Covenant Race* (Salt Lake City: Deseret News, 1938).

45. McConkie, *The Bruce R. McConkie Story*, 377; Joseph Fielding McConkie, *Answers: Straightforward Answers to Tough Gospel Questions* (Salt Lake City: Deseret Book, 1998), 29–30.

46. Robert L. Millet, "The House of Israel: From Everlasting to Everlasting," in *A Witness of Jesus Christ: The 1989 Sperry Symposium on the Old Testament*, ed. Richard D. Draper (Salt Lake City: Deseret Book, 1990), 179.

47. Millet frequently quoted McConkie in his writings. Robert L. Millet, "The Just Shall Live by Faith," in *Studies in Scripture*, vol. 6: *Acts to Revelation*, ed. Robert L. Millet (Salt Lake City: Deseret Book, 1987), 56; Robert L. Millet, "'As Delivered from the Beginning': The Formation of the Canonical Gospels," in *Apocryphal Writings and the Latter-day Saints*, ed. C. Wilfred Griggs (Provo, UT: Religious Studies Center, Brigham Young University, 1986), 213. Like Robert Matthews, Epperson was my teacher at BYU, and I formed impressions of him both inside and outside of class.

48. Steven Epperson, *Mormons and Jews: Early Mormon Theologies of Israel* (Salt Lake City: Signature Books, 1992). For background on Epperson, see Scott Abbott, *Dwelling in the Promised Land as a Stranger: Personal Encounters with Mormon Institutions* (Newburgh, IN: BCC Press, 2022), 135–36.

49. Steven Epperson, "Some Problems with Supersessionism in Mormon Thought," *BYU Studies Quarterly* 34, no. 4 (1994–95): 125–36 (quotes at 125–26, 133–34).

NOTES

417

50. Epperson, diary, January 6, 23, 1994, MLH.

51. Epperson, email to Matthew Harris, January 21, 2021.

52. James D. Gordon, an assistant academic vice president at BYU, asked respected BYU religion professor Richard Lloyd Anderson to review the book. Gordon, memo to Anderson, October 3, 1996, and Anderson's review, December 29, 1996, Box 6, Drafts from Epperson Review, 6/95, RLA.

53. Abbott, *Dwelling in the Promised Land*, 149; Epperson, email to Harris, January 21, 2021.

54. Epperson, email to Harris, January 21, 2021.

55. Bryan Waterman and Brian Kagel, *The Lord's University: Freedom and Authority at BYU* (Salt Lake City: Signature Books, 1998), 391–93; Abbott, *Dwelling in the Promised Land*, 137–46.

56. Givens, *Stretching the Heavens*, 254–55, 258–60; Haglund, *Eugene England*, 18–23.

57. Peter Steinfels, "Secret Files," *New York Times*, August 22, 1992; Waterman and Kagel, *The Lord's University*, chs. 5–8; D. Michael Quinn, *The Mormon Hierarchy: Extensions of Power* (Salt Lake City: Signature Books, 1997), 311; Dallin H. Oaks, "Alternate Voices," *Ensign*, May 1989, https://www.churchofjesuschrist. org/study/general-conference/1989/04/alternate-voices?lang=eng; Boyd K. Packer, "All-Church Coordinating Council," May 18, 1993, MLH.

58. Curt Bench, email to Matthew Harris, January 14, 2021, speculates that Deseret Book removed *The Way to Perfection* from print sometime in late 1989 or early 1990. For revisions in the temple ceremony, see Keith E. Norman, "A Kinder, Gentler Mormonism: Moving beyond the Violence of Our Past, *Sunstone*, August 1990, 10; David John Buerger, *The Mysteries of Godliness: A History of Mormon Temple Worship* (San Francisco: Smith Research Associates, 1994), 169–70.

59. Bench to Armand L. Mauss, November 8, 1997, Box 41, Folder 9, ALM; Curt Bench, "Fifty Most Important Mormon Books," *Sunstone*, October 1990, 56.

60. Dennis B. Horne, *Truth Will Prevail* (blog), September 28, 2016, http://www. truthwillprevail.xyz/2016/09/mormon-book-bits-35-dennis-b-horne.html; and Joseph Fielding McConkie, interview with Devan Jensen (2005), "From Father to Son: Joseph F. McConkie on Gospel Teaching," *Religious Educator* 6, no. 1 (2005): 23–32.

61. "Church Issues Statement on Racial Equality," *Ensign*, February 1988, https:// www.churchofjesuschrist.org/study/ensign/1988/02/news-of-the-church/ church-issues-statement-on-racial-equality?lang=eng.

62. Russell M. Nelson, "Children of the Covenant," *Conference Report*, April 1995, https://www.churchofjesuschrist.org/study/general-conference/1995/04/ children-of-the-covenant?lang=eng.

63. Matthew L. Harris, "Mormons and Lineage: The Complicated History of Blacks and Patriarchal Blessings, 1830–2018," *Dialogue: A Journal of Mormon Thought* 51, no. 3 (Fall 2018): 127.

64. Ibid., 127–28.

65. Andrea Smith, *Unreconciled: From Racial Reconciliation to Racial Justice in Christian Evangelicalism* (Durham, NC: Duke University Press, 2019); Jennifer Harvey, *Dear White Christians: For Those Still Longing for Racial Reconciliation*, 2nd ed. (Grand Rapids, MI: Eerdmans, 2020).

66. "Racial Reconciliation Manifesto," October 17–19, 1994, in Paul Harvey and Philip Goff, eds., *The Columbia Documentary History of Religion in America since 1945* (New York: Columbia University Press, 2005), 388; Anthea Butler, *White Evangelical Racism: The Politics of Morality in America* (Chapel Hill: University of North Carolina Press, 2021), 91.

67. "Resolution on Racial Reconciliation on the 150th Anniversary of the Southern Baptist Convention," *SBC*, June 1, 1995, https://www.sbc.net/resou rce-library/resolutions/resolution-on-racial-reconciliation-on-the-150th-anniversary-of-the-southern-baptist-convention/; John Dart, "Southern Baptists Vote to Issue Apology for Past Racism," *Los Angeles Times*, June 21, 1995; Thomas S. Kidd and Barry Hankins, *Baptists in America: A History* (New York: Oxford University Press, 2015), 245.

68. Richard A. Wilson, *The Politics of Truth and Reconciliation in South Africa: Legitimizing the Post-Apartheid State* (New York: Cambridge University Press, 2001); Melani McAlister, "Theology, the State, and the Apartheid Struggle," in *At Home and Abroad: The Politics of American Religion*, ed. Elizabeth Shakman Hurd and Winnifred Fallers Sullivan (New York: Columbia University Press, 2021), 260–67.

69. M. Russell Ballard, "Stay in the Boat and Hold On!," *Conference Report*, October 2014, https://www.churchofjesuschrist.org/study/general-confere nce/2014/10/stay-in-the-boat-and-hold-on?lang=eng. See also *Teachings of the Living Prophets* (Salt Lake City: Church of Jesus Christ of Latter-day Saints, 1982), ch. 5; Brent L. Top, Larry E. Dahl, and Walter D. Bowen, *Follow the Prophets: Timely Reasons for Obeying Prophetic Counsel in the Last Days* (Salt Lake City: Bookcraft, 1993), ch. 6.

70. Two seminal works explore conflict in the upper church leadership: Gregory A. Prince and William Robert Wright, *David O. McKay and the Rise of Modern Mormonism* (Salt Lake City: University of Utah, 2005); Gary James Bergera, "Tensions in David O. McKay's First Presidencies," *Journal of Mormon History* 33, no. 1 (Spring 2007): 179–246.

71. James E. Faust, "Heirs to the Kingdom of God," *Conference Report*, April 1995, https://www.churchofjesuschrist.org/study/general-conference/1995/04/ heirs-to-the-kingdom-of-god?lang=eng. See also Howard W. Hunter, "The Gospel—A Global Faith," *Conference Report*, October 1991, https://www.chur chofjesuschrist.org/study/general-conference/1991/10/the-gospel-a-global-faith?lang=engl; M. Russell Ballard, "Equality through Diversity," *Conference Report*, October 1993, https://www.churchofjesuschrist.org/study/general-conference/1993/10/equality-through-diversity?lang=eng.

72. Chieko N. Okazaki, *Lighten Up!* (Salt Lake City: Deseret Book, 1993), 5, 22; and Box 37, Folder 3, CNO.

NOTES 419

73. John K. Carmack, *Tolerance* (Salt Lake City: Bookcraft, 1993), 62–64.

74. Craig Dimond, "Mormonad," *Ensign*, July 1992, https://www.churchofjesu schrist.org/study/new-era/1992/07/mormonad?lang=eng.

75. Ferguson, quoted in Shellie M. Frey, "L.A. Lesson: We're All Sisters," *Ensign*, October 1992 https://www.churchofjesuschrist.org/study/new-era/1992/10/l-a-lesson-were-all-sisters?lang=eng.

76. Lee Copeland, "Calcutta to Kaysville: Is Righteousness Color-Coded?," *Dialogue: A Journal of Mormon Thought* 21, no. 3 (Fall 1988): 97.

77. Armand L. Mauss, *All Abraham's Children: Changing Mormon Conceptions of Race and Lineage* (Urbana: University of Illinois Press, 2003), 245.

78. "LDS Afro-American Symposium" program, June 8, 1988, Box 42, Folder 1, ALM; Dallin H. Oaks, "For the Blessing of All His Children," June 8, 1988, Box 42, Folder 1, ALM. For BYU and Black history month, see Mauss, *All Abraham's Children*, 247.

79. Elizabeth Hinton, *America on Fire: The Untold History of Political Violence and Black Rebellion since the 1960s* (New York: Liveright, 2021), ch. 9.

80. Mauss, *All Abraham's Children*, 246–48; "LDS Assist in Aftermath of Riots," *Church News*, May 9, 1992, https://www.thechurchnews.com/1992/5/9/23259556/lds-assist-in-aftermath-of-riots.

81. Alan Cherry, "Silent Songs We've Never Heard," *This People*, Summer 1988, 24–27; Heidi Swinton, "Without Regard for Race," *This People*, Summer 1988, 19–23; David Gonzales, "Spreading the Word in the South Bronx," *New York Times*, November 16, 1994; John L. Hart, "East St. Louis Branch Blossoms Again," *Church News*, February 1994, https://www.thechurchnews.com/archi ves/1994-02-05/east-st-louis-branch-blossoms-again-140692.

82. Lee Warnick, "I Knew the Time Had Come," *Church News*, June 4, 1988, https://www.thechurchnews.com/archives/1988-06-04/i-knew-that-the-time-had-come-153292. See also *Church Almanac* (Salt Lake City: Deseret News, 1998), 119.

83. Alexander B. Morrison, *The Dawning of a Brighter Day: The Church in Black Africa* (Salt Lake City: Deseret Book, 1990); E. Dale LeBaron, *"All Are Alike unto God"* (Salt Lake City: Deseret Book, 1990).

84. Laurie F. Maffly-Kipp, "Global Mormonism in Political Context," *Mormon Studies Review* 8 (2021): 25; David G. Stewart Jr., "The Dynamics of LDS Growth in the Twenty-First Century," in *The Palgrave Handbook on Global Mormonism*, ed. R. Gordon Shepherd, A. Gary Shepherd, and Ryan T. Cragun (New York: Palgrave Macmillan, 2020), ch. 6.

85. Haws, "LDS Church Presidency Years," 213. "Helvécio Martins of the Seventy," *Church News*, May 1990, https://www.churchofjesuschrist.org/study/ensign/1990/05/news-of-the-church/elder-helvecio-martins-of-the-seventy?lang=eng.

86. Mauss and Tanner, quoted in Mark L. Grover, "Helvécio Martins: First Black General Authority," *Journal of Mormon History* 36, no. 3 (Summer 2010): 28–29.

420 NOTES

87. Helvécio Martins, with Mark L. Grover, *The Autobiography of Helvécio Martins* (Salt Lake City: Aspen Books, 1994), 111–12, 117.

88. Ibid., 118.

89. Eleanor Knowles, *Howard W. Hunter* (Salt Lake City: Deseret Book, 1994).

90. Sheri L. Dew, *Go Forward with Faith: The Biography of Gordon B. Hinckley* (Salt Lake City: Deseret Book, 1996), 381–85, 400–401; J. B. Haws, *The Mormon Image in the American Mind: Fifty Years of Public Perception* (New York: Oxford University Press, 2013), 154.

91. Dew, *Go Forward with Faith*, 545; Haws, *Mormon Image*, 158–60.

92. W. Jeffrey Marsh, "When the Press Meets the Prophet," in *Out of Obscurity: The LDS Church in the Twentieth Century* (Salt Lake City: Deseret Book, 2000), 256–58; Dew, *Go Forward with Faith*, 537–45.

93. Wallace, quoted in Marsh, "When the Press Meets the Prophet," 247.

94. Dew, *Go Forward with Faith*, 543–44. Wallace later wrote the preface for Hinckley's book *Standing for Something: 10 Neglected Virtues That Will Heal Our Hearts and Homes* (New York: Times Warner, 2000).

95. Hinckley, interview with Mike Wallace, April 7, 1996, transcript at http://www.cbsnews.com/8301-1856"0_162-3775068.html?pageNum = 2.

96. Hinckley, interview with Helmut Nemetschek of ZDF television, Germany, at the Church Administration Building, Salt Lake City, January 29, 2002, transcript in MLH.

97. Hinckley, interview with David Ransom of the Australian Broadcasting Corporation, aired on *Compass*, November 9, 1997, transcript in *Sunstone*, December 1998, https://sunstonemagazine.com/wp-content/uploads/sbi/articles/112-70-72.pdf.

98. Jackson, patriarchal blessing, September 15, 1991, MLH.

99. Jackson, email to Matthew Harris, August 23, 2013.

100. This section draws on a forty-one-page document that Jackson compiled called "The Narrative of Events," January 2013, MLH.

101. Jackson to Armand L. Mauss, December 1, 1992, MLH; Jackson, "Narrative," 3; Jackson, email to Matthew Harris, December 4, 2011.

102. Jackson to Mauss, December 1, 1992, MLH; Armand L. Mauss and Lester E. Bush, eds., *Neither White nor Black: Mormon Scholars Confront the Race Issue in a Universal Church* (Midvale, UT: Signature Books, 1984).

103. Jackson, "Narrative," 2.

104. Jackson to Hinckley, October 9, 1995, MLH (appending a copy of "Official Declaration 3").

105. Ibid.

106. Watson to Jackson, October 25, 1995, MLH.

107. Jackson, email to Matthew Harris, December 4, 2011; Jackson, "Narrative," 10.

108. Jackson, "Narrative," 10–11; Jackson to Sterling Brennan, October 31, 1995, MLH; Brennan to Jackson, April 27, 1996, MLH.

109. Dennis Gladwell, "Implications of the 1978 Revelation," October 1996, 29, unpublished report in MLH.

NOTES

421

110. Gladwell drafted the statement unsolicited. Jensen read it, but he didn't have the authority to approve it. Gladwell, email to Matthew Harris, November 1, 2013.

111. "Anniversary Statement of 1978 Revelation" [spring 1998], MLH.

112. Jackson, fax to Marlin Jensen, May 14, 1998, MLH.

113. Larry Stammer, "Mormons May Disavow Old View on Blacks," *Los Angeles Times*, May 18, 1998.

114. A church spokesman said the story was "totally erroneous." KSL Channel 5, May 18, 1998, http://www.ksl.com/TV/newsslocb.htm. See also "*Los Angeles Times* Story on Blacks and the Priesthood: First Presidency Statement," press release from the LDS Public Affairs Department, May 18, 1998, Box 10, Folder 3, LDS Press Releases, CHL.

115. Mauss to Marlin Jensen and Bill Evans, May 28, 1998, Box 14, Folder 5, ALM; Armand L. Mauss, "Casting Off the 'Curse of Cain': The Extent and Limits of Progress since 1978," in *Black and Mormon*, ed. Newell G. Bringhurst and Darron T. Smith (Urbana: University of Illinois Press, 2004), 91–92; Larry B. Stammer, "Mormon Plan to Disavow Racist Teachings Jeopardized by Publicity," *Los Angeles Times*, May 24, 1998.

116. Jackson, "Narrative," 22–23. Also recounted in a telephone conservation with Matthew Harris, December 1, 2011; Evenson, email to Matthew Harris, October 30, 2013: "I was the one who gave the story to Stammer." Also in Evenson to Jackson, April 24, 1998, MLH. Evenson wrote a critical book on the priesthood ban: Darrick T. Evenson, *Black Mormons and the Priesthood Ban* (Salt Lake City: Self-published, 2002).

117. Hinckley, quoted in Larry B. Stammer, "Mormon Leader Defends Race Relations," *Los Angeles Times*, September 12, 1998.

118. Knight, quoted in Jamie Armstrong, "How Gladys Knight Became a Latter-day Saint," *LDS Living*, June 4, 2016, https://www.ldsliving.com/How-Gladys-Knight-Became-a-Mormon/s/76709.

119. LDS Living Staff, "Former NBA Star Thurl Bailey Shares Incredible Conversion Story: I Was Given around 70 Book of Mormons," *LDS Living*, May 17, 2016, https://www.ldsliving.com/Former-NBA-Star-Thurl-Bailey-Shares-Incredible-Conversion-Story/s/82134.

120. Bailey, quoted on the back cover of Luckner Huggins, *A Son of Ham: Under the Covenant* (Salt Lake City: Privately published, 2004); Paul Swenson, "Gladys and Thurl: The Changing Face of Mormon Diversity," *Sunstone*, July 2001, 15.

121. Doug Robinson, "Thurl Bailey's Wonderful Life," *Deseret News*, February 26, 2003; Swenson, "Gladys and Thurl," 14–16; Sarah Sanders Petersen, "In Mormon Channel Interview, Thurl Bailey Talks about Playing for the Utah Jazz, Conversion to LDS Church," *Deseret News*, April 13, 2016.

122. "Eldridge Cleaver Announces Bid for U.S. Senate Seat," *Jet*, February 24, 1986, 25. See also Newell G. Bringhurst, "Eldridge Cleaver's Passage through Mormonism," *Journal of Mormon History* 28, no. 1 (Spring 2002): 80–110.

NOTES

123. Peter Gillins, "Ex-Radical Mulling Mormonism," *Salt Lake Tribune*, January 23, 1981; Eldridge Cleaver, "My Autobiography," n.d., 48, Box 90, KC.
124. Vern Anderson, "Eldridge Cleaver: LDS Membership Transitory," *Salt Lake Tribune*, August 17, 1996.
125. Cleaver to Bringhurst, August 20, 1996, MLH.

CHAPTER 10

1. Larry Stammer, "Mormons May Disavow Old View on Blacks," *Los Angeles Times*, May 18, 1998. Hinckley told Darius Gray that he instructed Morrison to give the sermon. Gray, interview with Matthew L. Harris, April 22, 2014. General authorities condemned racism more broadly in their sermons, but without mentioning Black people. See Edward L. Kimball, ed., *The Teachings of Spencer W. Kimball* (Salt Lake City: Bookcraft, 1982), 236–37; *Gospel Ideals: Selections from the Discourses of David O. McKay* (Salt Lake City: Improvement Era, 1953), 541; Marion D. Hanks, "Without Prejudice, without Bigotry," BYU devotional address, March 30, 1965, in *Brigham Young University Speeches* (Provo, UT: Brigham Young University Press, 1965), 1–6; Hugh B. Brown, "He Lives—All Glory to His Name," *Improvement Era* 69, no. 6 (June 1966): 495; N. Eldon Tanner, "Judge Not, That Ye Be Judged," *Ensign*, April 1972, https://www.churchofjesuschrist.org/study/general-conference/1972/04/judge-not-that-ye-be-not-judged?lang=eng.
2. Alexander B. Morrison, *The Dawning of a Brighter Day: The Church in Black Africa* (Salt Lake City: Deseret Book, 1990); Alexander B. Morrison, *Visions of Zion* (Salt Lake City: Deseret Book, 1993).
3. Alexander B. Morrison, "No More Strangers," *Ensign*, September 2000, https://www.churchofjesuschrist.org/study/ensign/2000/09/no-more-strangers?lang=eng.
4. Victor L. Ludlow, "The Internationalization of the Church," in *Out of Obscurity: The LDS Church in the Twentieth Century* (Salt Lake City: Deseret Book, 2000), 212–13. For statistical reports as of December 1999, see *Church Almanac* (Salt Lake City: Deseret News, 2000), 576–78; David G. Stewart Jr., "The Dynamics of LDS Growth in the Twenty-First Century," in *The Palgrave Handbook of Global Mormonism*, ed. R. Gordon Shepherd, A. Gary Shepherd, and Ryan T. Cragun (New York: Palgrave Macmillan, 2020), 169–73.
5. "The Family: A Proclamation to the World," September 23, 1995, https://abn.churchofjesuschrist.org/study/scriptures/the-family-a-proclamation-to-the-world/the-family-a-proclamation-to-the-world?lang=eng. For Hinckley's role in "The Proclamation," see William N. Eskridge Jr. and Christopher R. Riano, *Marriage Equality: From Outlaws to In-Laws* (New Haven, CT: Yale University Press, 2020), 93–94. See also Taylor G. Petrey, *Tabernacles of Clay: Sexuality and Gender in Modern Mormonism* (Chapel Hill: University of North Carolina Press, 2020), ch. 4.

NOTES   423

6. "Lesson 31: Choosing an Eternal Companion," *Aaronic Priesthood Manual* (2011), CHL; Russell M. Nelson, "Children of the Covenant," *Ensign*, April 1995, n38, https://www.churchofjesuschrist.org/study/general-conference/1995/04/children-of-the-covenant?lang=eng; Donald Harwell and Jerri Harwell, oral history interview with Clinton D. Christensen, November 19, 2013, 28, CHL (regarding Apostle David Bednar's opposition to interracial marriage). For books still in print opposing interracial marriage, see Joseph Fielding Smith, *Doctrines of Salvation*, compiled by Bruce R. McConkie, 3 vols. (Salt Lake City: Deseret Book, 1954–56); Joseph Fielding Smith, *Answers to Gospel Questions*, 5 vols. (Salt Lake City: Deseret Book, 1957–66); Bruce R. McConkie, *Mormon Doctrine* (Salt Lake City: Bookcraft, 1979); Harold B. Lee, *Decisions for Successful Living* (Salt Lake City: Deseret Book, 1973).

7. Hokulani K. Aikau, *A Chosen People, A Promised Land: Mormonism and Race in Hawaii* (Minneapolis: University of Minnesota Press, 2012).

8. Rebecca Trounson, "Hawaii Leads Nation with 40 Percent Interracial Marriage Rate," *Star Advertiser* (Honolulu, HI), February 16, 2012.

9. Marcus H. Martins, "Multinational Single-Student Wards at BYU-Hawaii," in *All God's Children: Racial and Ethnic Voices in the LDS Church*, ed. Cardell K. Jacobson (Springville, UT: Bonneville Books, 2004), 115; R. Lanier Britsch, *Unto the Islands of the Sea: A History of the Latter-day Saints in the Pacific* (Salt Lake City: Deseret Book, 1986), 185–86.

10. First Presidency Minutes, May 29, 1969, Box 70, Folder 1, DOM; Quorum of the Twelve Minutes, October 6, 1966, Box 64, Folder 4, SWK; "Minutes of Special Meeting by President McKay," David O. McKay, diary, January 17, 1954, Box 32, Folder 3, DOM; Amanda Hendrix-Komoto, "Mahana, You Naked! Modesty, Sexuality, and Race in the Mormon Pacific," in *Out of Obscurity: Mormonism since 1945*, ed. Patrick Q. Mason and John G. Turner (New York: Oxford University Press, 2016), 186.

11. Jeffrey M. Jones, "Record-High 86% Approve of Black-White Marriages," *Gallup Poll*, September 12, 2011, https://news.gallup.com/poll/149390/record-high-approve-black-white-marriages.aspx; Laura Seitz, "Mixed Marriages on the Rise," *Deseret News*, April 13, 2007; Jane Dailey, *White Fright: The Sexual Panic at the Heart of America's Racist History* (New York: Basic Books, 2020), 254–55.

12. Shepherd, Shepherd, and Cragun, *The Palgrave Handbook of Global Mormonism*, passim; Caroline Kline, *Mormon Women at the Crossroads: Global Narratives and the Power of Connectedness* (Urbana: University of Illinois Press, 2022), 118–20.

13. Tamu Smith, quoted in Shane Johnson, "White Wash," *Salt Lake Weekly*, December 16, 2004.

14. Joy Smith, quoted in Johnson, "White Wash." See also Darron T. Smith, "Unpacking Whiteness in Zion: Some Personal Reflections and General Observations," in *Black and Mormon*, ed. Newell G. Bringhurst and Darron T. Smith (Urbana: University of Illinois Press, 2004), 148–49.

424   NOTES

15. Achenbach, quoted in Gerrard Kaonga, "Black Mormon Told They Can't Marry White Members Because 'Seed Is Cursed,'" *Newsweek*, January 16, 2023, https://www.newsweek.com/mormon-stories-podcast-channel-achenbach-racism-marriage-seed-cursed-1774116.

16. Mauss, transcript of a phone interview with Gray, May 25, 1999, Box 42, Folder 3, ALM.

17. Margaret Young and Darius Gray heard this report from Virginia Pearce and related it to me in a meeting at BYU, December 13, 2011. See also Margaret Blair Young and Darius Aidan Gray, "Race and Mormons," in *The Oxford Handbook of Mormonism*, ed. Terryl L. Givens and Philip L. Barlow (New York: Oxford University Press, 2015), 378.

18. Hinckley, quoted in Teresa Watanabe, "Leading a World Faith Explosion with Roots in Small-Town America," *Los Angeles Times*, May 9, 1999.

19. "Sistas in Zion," https://www.facebook.com/sistasinzion/; Darron T. Smith, "Black and Mormon: The Darron Smith Story," *Mormon Stories*, March 30, 2006, https://mormonstories.org/podcast/mormon-stories-022-023-and-024-black-and-mormon-the-darron-smith-story/.Smith; Zandra Vranes, *Diary of Two Mad Black Mormons: Finding the Lord's Lesson in Everyday Life* (Salt Lake City: Ensign Peak, 2014). Robert A. Rees, "Black African Jews, the Mormon Denial of Priesthood to Blacks, and Truth and Reconciliation," *Sunstone*, October 2004, 65.

20. Hinckley, interviews with Larry King: "Gordon Hinckley: Distinguished Religious Leader of the Mormons," *Larry King Live*, September 8, 1998, http://www.lds-mormon.com/lkl_00.shtml; "A Conversation with Gordon B. Hinckley, President of the Church of Jesus Christ of Latter Day Saints," *Larry King Live*, December 26, 2004, http://transcripts.cnn.com/TRANSCRIPTS/0412/26/lkl.01.html.

21. Peg McEntee, "Families Can Save Us, Hinckley Says; LDS Leader Addresses NAACP in S.L., a First for a Mormon Church President," *Salt Lake Tribune*, April 25, 1998; Russell W. Stevenson, *For the Cause of Righteousness: A Global History of Blacks and Mormonism, 1830–2013* (Salt Lake City: Greg Kofford Books, 2014), 196–97.

22. In *Discourses of President Gordon B. Hinckley*, vol. 1: *1995–1999* (Salt Lake City: Deseret Book, 2005), 533, 537–38.

23. On April 6, 2000, I heard Hinckley discuss his enthusiasm for the award when he spoke at the Palmyra, New York, Temple dedication.

24. For Benson and civil rights, see chapter 4.

25. Matthew L. Harris and Madison S. Harris, "The Last State to Honor MLK: Utah and the Quest for Racial Justice," *Utah Historical Quarterly* 88, no. 1 (Winter 2020): 15–16.

26. LDS Church Public Affairs, "Freedman's Bank Records," News Release and Fact Sheet, February 19, 2001, CHL; Carrie A. Moore, "New CD-ROM to Open Doors," *Deseret News*, February 27, 2001.

NOTES

27. Murray, quoted in Margaret Blair Young and Darius Gray's film script, "*Nobody Knows: The Untold Story of Black Mormons*—Script," *Dialogue: A Journal of Mormon Thought* 42, no. 3 (Fall 2009): 124–25. See also Margaret Blair Young, "Pastor to Pastor: President Hinckley's Apology for Racism in the Church," *Patheos Mormon: Hosting the Conversation on Faith*, September 17, 2012, http://www.patheos.com/Mormon/Pastor-to-Pastor-Margaret-Blair-Young-09-18-2012.

28. Hinckley didn't apologize for the ban, of course, only the church's role in fostering racism more broadly. Gray said he conveyed to Hinckley on many occasions that racism was a problem in the church. Gray, telephone interview with Matthew Harris, April 22, 2014.

29. Carrie A. Moore, "Doubleday Book of Mormon Is on the Way," *Deseret News*, November 11, 2004.

30. Skousen and Hardy, quoted in Peggy Fletcher Stack, "Church Removes Racial References in Book of Mormon Headings," *Salt Lake Tribune*, December 20, 2010.

31. Amy Shebeck, "Colorblind Faith," *Chicago Reporter*, September 26, 2007; William Lobdell, "New Mormon Aim: Reach Out to Blacks," *Los Angeles Times*, September 21, 2003; Andy Newman, "For Mormons in Harlem, a Bigger Space Beckons," *New York Times*, October 2, 2005; Miriam Hill, "Mormons Gain in Inner Cities Church Is Attracting More Blacks and Hispanics," *Philadelphia Inquirer*, December 10, 2005; H. Allen Hurst, "Black Saints in a White Church; Mormon Church Grows in Urban Areas Despite Racist Reputation," *Baltimore Afro-American*, December 23, 2005.

32. Harwell, quoted in Hurst, "Black Saints in a White Church."

33. Gordon B. Hinckley, "The Need for Greater Kindness," *Ensign*, April 2006, https://www.churchofjesuschrist.org/study/general-conference/2006/04/the-need-for-greaterkindness?lang=eng.

34. Carrie A. Moore, "Much Has Changed for LDS Blacks since '78," *Deseret News*, June 7, 2008; Peggy Fletcher Stack, "Mormon and Black: Grappling with a Racist Past," *Salt Lake Tribune*, June 6, 2008.

35. Monson to Bill Morton, April 13, 1981, MLH; Heidi S. Swinton, *To the Rescue: The Biography of Thomas S. Monson* (Salt Lake City: Deseret Book, 2010), 367–68, 395–96.

36. "Out of the Best Books? Publications Continue to Promote Folklore," *Sunstone*, March 2003, 34–35; *Old Testament Student Manual* (Salt Lake City: Church of Jesus Christ of Latter-day Saints, 1981, 2010). In 2009, I did a review at several LDS-owned bookstores, and many of Smith's and McConkie's books were still in print.

37. "Letter of First Presidency Clarifies Church's Position on the Negro," *Improvement Era* 73, no. 12 (December 1969): 70–71. For two influential websites, see "Blacks and the Priesthood," *MormonThink*, http://www.mormonthink.com/blackweb.htm; "Racial Doctrines and Policies," *Mormon Stories*, https://www.mormonstories.org/truth-claims/mormon-doctrine/race-skin-color/.

426 NOTES

38. See, for example, Dallin H. Oaks, *Life's Lessons Learned: Personal Reflections* (Salt Lake City: Deseret Book, 2011), 68–69; Robert L. Millet, *Getting at the Truth: Responding to Difficult Questions about LDS Beliefs* (Salt Lake City: Deseret Book, 2004), 63.

39. Gray, interview with Harris, April 22, 2014. Gray later shared the experience publicly: Darius Gray, "Challenges We Face Are 'Not a Curse, but a Calling,'" *Affirmation*, November 23, 2014, https://affirmation.org/darius-grays-keyn ote-speech-2014-affirmation-conference/.

40. Keith N. Hamilton, *Last Laborer: Thoughts and Reflections of a Black Mormon* (Salt Lake City: Self-published, 2011), 132. Hamilton, interview with Harris, August 4, 2014.

41. Matthew L. Harris and Newell G. Bringhurst, eds., *The Mormon Church and Blacks: A Documentary History* (Urbana: University of Illinois Press, 2015), 3–4.

42. Holland, interview with Helen Whitney, March 4, 2006, transcript at http://www.pbs.org/mormons/interviews/holland.html.

43. Ibid. Holland also decried antiblack teachings to missionaries. See Margaret Young, "All God's Critters: Some Thought on the Priesthood Restriction and Differing Opinions, Part II" (blog), *By Common Consent*, July 23, 2011, http://bycommonconsent.com/2011/07/23/all-gods-critters-some-thoughts-on-the-priesthood-restriction-and-differing-opinions/.

44. Child, quoted in Carrie A. Moore, "LDS Marking 30-Year Milestone," *Salt Lake Tribune*, June 7, 2008. Marlin Jensen of the First Quorum of the Seventy also characterized LDS racial teachings as folklore. See his interview with Helen Whitney, March 7, 2006, http://www.pbs.org/mormons/interviews/jensen.html.

45. Tuttle, quoted in Peggy Fletcher Stack, "Mormon and Black: Grappling with a Racist Past," *Salt Lake Tribune*, June 6, 2008; Valletta, quoted in Amy K. Stewart, "Being a Black Student at BYU Can Be Difficult," *Deseret News*, February 27, 2008.

46. Smith, quoted in Stack, "Mormon and Black."

47. David Knowlton, "What Is Doctrine?" (blog), *By Common Consent*, June 9, 2008, http://bycommonconsent.com/2008/06/09/what-is-doctrine/.

48. Armand L. Mauss, "Mormonism and the Negro: Faith, Folklore, and Civil Rights," *Dialogue: A Journal of Mormon Thought* 2, no. 4 (Winter 1967): 18–39; Armand L. Mauss, *Shifting Borders and a Tattered Passport: Intellectual Journeys of a Mormon Academic* (Salt Lake City: University of Utah Press, 2012), 98. Mauss also recounted his desire to see Mormon racial teachings branded "folklore" in several emails to me. For scholars' use of the term "folklore," "folk doctrine," or "folk traditions," see Jana Riess, *The Next Mormons: How Millennials Are Changing the LDS Church* (New York: Oxford University Press, 2019), 112, 117; David E. Campbell, John C. Green, and J. Quin Monson, *Seeking the Promised Land: Mormons and American Politics* (New York: Cambridge University Press, 2014), 60; Joanna Brooks, *Mormonism and White Supremacy: American Religion and the Problem of Racial Innocence* (New York: Oxford University Press, 2020),

NOTES 427

174; Terryl L. Givens, *Wrestling the Angel—The Foundations of Mormon Thought: Cosmos, God, Humanity* (New York City: Oxford University Press, 2015), 175.

49. Riess, *The Next Mormons*, 120.

50. Tristan Call, letter to the editor, BYU *Daily Universe*, January 23, 2008.

51. Anonymous letter to Rex Lee, [1995], Box 117, Folder 7, EE. For Epperson's review, see chapter 9.

52. Terry B. Ball, "To Confirm and Inform: A Blessing of Higher Education," *BYU Speeches*, March 11, 2008, http://speeches.byu.edu/?act=viewitem&id=1764.

53. Smith, *Doctrines of Salvation*, 1:61; Alvin R. Dyer, "For What Purpose?," LDS missionary conference address, Oslo, Norway, March 18, 1961, CHL.

54. Eugene England, "Becoming a World Religion: Blacks, the Poor—All of Us," *Sunstone*, June–July 1998, 52, 58.

55. Armand L. Mauss, "Casting Off the 'Curse of Cain': The Extent and Limits of Progress since 1978," in Bringhurst and Smith, *Black and Mormon*, 83.

56. Darron T. Smith, "These House-Negroes Still Think We're Cursed: Struggling against Racism in the Classroom," *Cultural Studies* 19, no. 4 (July 2005): 450.

57. Stott, quoted in Jessica Ravitz, "Mormon and Black: Jesse Stott Is Not Neutral," *Salt Lake Tribune*, June 8, 2008; Riess, *The Next Mormons*, 112.

58. Millet, then the dean of religious education at BYU, and McConkie, professor of ancient scripture at BYU, led the discussion. They were accompanied by BYU professors E. Dale LeBaron, Camille Fronk Olson, Richard D. Draper, Andrew C. Skinner, and Michael D. Rhodes. I received a DVD copy of "Priesthood Restriction through the Ages" from Fronk Olson.

59. Camille Fronk Olson was the exception to the rule. Prior to the discussion, she informed Robert Millet that she didn't think the Pearl of Great Price justified the traditional LDS rationales for the ban. Olson, conversation with Matthew Harris, November 20, 2013, BYU.

60. Quinn, email to Matthew Harris, November 25, 2013; Young, email to Matthew Harris and Newell G. Bringhurst, August 1, 2008. Within days after the segment aired in 2008, I viewed it on KBYU. Approximately a week later, however, the station pulled it from the air. When I called and asked why, I didn't receive a clear answer. "We don't know why," an employee told me. The roundtable discussion on Mormon scriptures was part of a recurring program on KBYU.

61. Peggy Fletcher Stack, "Landmark 'Mormon Doctrine' Goes Out of Print," *Salt Lake Tribune*, May 21, 2010. In 2010, a channel 2 KUTV report affirmed "strong book sales" of *Mormon Doctrine* in LDS bookstores in Salt Lake County. See "Publisher Stops Printing Popular LDS Book," May 20, 2010, http://www.kutv.com/news/features/local/index.shtml. Also, managers at several Deseret bookstores in Utah and Idaho told me that *Mormon Doctrine* ranked among their best sellers. Deseret Book corporate offices had "no comment" when I asked them why it went out of print (telephone conversation of October 15, 2013). LDS bookseller Curt Bench also confirmed the high sales of *Mormon Doctrine*. Bench to Armand Mauss, November 8, 1997, Box 41, Folder 9, ALM.

428 NOTES

62. Otterson, interview with Harris, December 12, 2013, LDS Church Headquarters; Otterson, email to Harris, February 24, 2014.

63. This account derives from conservations I had with two BYU professors (November 15, 2013 and August 4, 2014), as well as another individual, who contacted Deseret Book and asked them to remove the book from print. In 2009, at the Mormon History Association conference, several people approached Darius Gray and Margaret Young and offered "to sign a petition or whatever it takes to get [*Mormon Doctrine*] off the shelves." Margaret Young, "MHA with Darius—Part 2" (blog), *By Common Consent*, May 27, 2009, https://byco mmonconsent.com/2009/05/27/mha-with-darius-part-2/.

64. Adams to Dew (with copies to Mark H. Willes and Henry B. Eyring), May 29, 2009, MLH. Otterson explained that numerous Latter-day Saints had complained about *Mormon Doctrine*. Otterson, interview with Harris.

65. Mauss, *Shifting Borders and a Tattered Passport*, 110; David Jackson, "The Narrative of Events," January 2013, 37, MLH.

66. Gray and Prince, quoted in Stack, "Landmark 'Mormon Doctrine' Goes Out of Print."

67. Hyrum L. Andrus, *Distinct Doctrines and Teachings of the Pearl of Great Price* (Salt Lake City: Deseret Book, 1960), 252–53; W. Cleon Skousen, *Treasures from the Book of Mormon*, vol. 2 (Salt Lake City: Publisher's Press, 1971), ch. 13; Joseph Fielding McConkie, *Answers: Straightforward Answers to Tough Gospel Questions* (Salt Lake City: Deseret Book, 1998), 29–30; Richard D. Draper, S. Kent Brown, and Michael D. Rhodes, *The Pearl of Great Price: A Verse-by-Verse Commentary* (Salt Lake City: Deseret Book, 2005), 126. For racial teachings circulating at church, see Riess, *The Next Mormons*, ch. 6; Harris and Bringhurst, *Mormon Church and Blacks*, 132.

68. Tad Walch, "BYU Professor Sits atop National Rankings," *Deseret News*, December 11, 2008; "Beehives and Buffalo Chips," *Daily Herald* (Provo, UT), December 12, 2008.

69. Horowitz, email to Matthew Harris, December 4, 2013; Horowitz, phone interview with Harris, November 20, 2013.

70. Bott, quoted in Jason Horowitz, "The Genesis of a Church's Stand on Race," *Washington Post*, February 28, 2012.

71. Ibid. Bott appears to have derived this teaching from Mormon apologist John J. Stewart. See his *Mormonism and the Negro* (1960; Orem, UT: Community Press, 1967), 50–51.

72. Historians place such defenses as part of a "lost cause" myth of the Civil War. See David W. Blight, *Race and Reunion: The Civil War in American Memory* (Cambridge, MA: Harvard University Press, 2002).

73. Romney, interview with Russert on *Meet the Press*, NBC News, December 16, 2007, http://www.presidency.ucsb.edu/ws/index.php?pid=77749.

74. Max Perry Mueller, "Has the Mormon Church Truly Left Its Race Problem Behind?," *New Republic*, November 15, 2011; Daniel Burke, "Will Mormons'

NOTES 429

Racial History Be a Problem for Mitt Romney?" *Washington Post*, January 31, 2012. See also Max Perry Mueller, "'Twice-Told Tale': Telling Two Histories of Mormon-Black Relations during the 2012 Presidential Election," in *Mormonism and American Politics*, ed. Randall Balmer and Jana Riess (New York: Columbia University Press, 2016), ch. 10.

75. Book of Mormon lyrics, quoted in John G. Turner, "Why Race Is Still a Problem for Mormons," *Washington Post*, April 12, 2012. See also J. B. Haws, *The Mormon Image in the American Mind: Fifty Years of Public Perception* (New York: Oxford University Press, 2013), 242–48.

76. Nathan B. Oman, "Race, Folklore, and Mormon Doctrine," *Deseret News*, February 29, 2012; Harris, interview with Otterson.

77. Scott Keeter, "Public Opinion about Mormons," *Pew Research Center*, December 7, 2007, http://www.pewresearch.org/2007/12/04/public-opin ion-about-mormons/. See also Campbell, Green, and Monson, *Seeking the Promised Land*, 169; Peggy Fletcher Stack, "Mitt, Mormonism, and the Media: An Unfamiliar Faith Takes the Stage in the 2012 U.S. Presidential Election," in Balmer and Riess, *Mormonism and American Politics*, ch. 13. For the "I'm a Mormon" ad campaign, see Haws, *Mormon Image*, 246–48. Harris, interview with Otterson.

78. Otterson, interview with Harris.

79. "Church Statement regarding 'Washington Post' Article on Race and the Church," *Church Newsroom*, February 29, 2012, https://newsroom.churchof jesuschrist.org/article/racial-remarks-in-washington-post-article.

80. "Race and the Church: All Are Alike unto God," *Church Newsroom*, February 29, 2012, https://newsroom.churchofjesuschrist.org/article/race-church.

81. Horowitz, email to Harris, December 4, 2013.

82. Anonymous professor, quoted in Dave Banack, "The Bott Affair: Winners and Losers" (blog), *Times and Seasons*, March 6, 2012, http://timesandseasons.org/ index.php/2012/03/the-bott-affair-winners-and-losers/.

83. Margaret Young, Daniel Peterson, and Terry Ball, quoted in Kate Bennion, "*Washington Post* Article on Black Priesthood Ban Spurs Concern, Outrage," BYU *Daily Universe*, February 29, 2012. See also Haws, *Mormon Image*, 272; Rachel Cope, "Teaching Official Declaration 2" (blog), *Juvenile Instructor*, February 29, 2012, http://www.juvenileinstructor.org/teaching-official-decl aration-2/.

84. BYU students, quoted in Bennion, "*Washington Post* Article on Black Priesthood Ban Spurs Concern, Outrage"; Joseph Walker, "LDS Church Condemns Past Racism 'inside and outside the Church,'" *Deseret News*, February 29, 2012; Tamarra Kemsley, "BYU Professor Lambasted for Interview," BYU *Student Review*, February 29, 2012.

85. Horowitz, phone conversation with Harris, November 20, 2013. Bott dismantled his "Know Your Religion" website when the *Washington* Post story surfaced. Bott retitled it "Blacks and the Priesthood" and dated it April 3, 2008.

In 2021 and again in 2022, I contacted Bott requesting an interview, but he didn't respond.

86. Devan Mitchell, "A Black Mormon Man's Thoughts on Race, Priesthood, and the Church's Essay," *LDS Living*, June 8, 2017, http://www.ldsliving.com/A-Black-Mormon-Mans-Thoughts-on-Race-Priesthood-and-the-Churchs-Essay/s/85553.

87. D. Todd Christofferson, "The Doctrine of Christ," *Ensign*, May 2012, https://www.thechurchnews.com/archives/2012-04-01/elder-d-todd-christofferson-the-doctrine-of-christ-52441.

88. Matthew L. Harris, "Mormonism's Problematic Racial Past and the Evolution of the Divine-Curse Doctrine," *John Whitmer Historical Association Journal* 33, no. 1 (Spring–Summer 2013): 109.

89. Harris and Bringhurst, *Mormon Church and Blacks*, 137.

90. Matthew L. Harris and Newell G. Bringhurst, "Why the Gospel Topics Essays?," in *The LDS Gospel Topics Series: A Scholarly Engagement*, ed. Matthew L. Harris and Newell G. Bringhurst (Salt Lake City: Signature Books, 2020), 1–25.

91. Reeve later authored a book titled *Religion of a Different Color: Race and the Mormon Struggle for Whiteness* (New York: Oxford University Press, 2015), which won the Mormon History Association's "Best Book Award" in 2016. Reeve also wrote *Let's Talk about Race and Priesthood* (Salt Lake City: Deseret Book, 2023).

92. Reeve provides details about the drafting and editing process in his interview with Rick Bennett of *Gospel Tangents*, June 6, 2018, https://gospeltangents.com/2017/02/paul-reeve-wrote-the-race-essay/. Mauss, Gray, and Mason affirmed their participation in emails to me.

93. "Race and the Priesthood," December 2013, https://www.churchofjesuschrist.org/study/manual/gospel-topics-essays/race-and-the-priesthood?lang=eng.

94. Ibid. See also Matthew Harris, "Whiteness Theology and the Evolution of Mormon Racial Teachings," in Harris and Bringhurst, *The LDS Gospel Topics Series*, ch. 10.

95. Matthew L. Harris, "Confronting and Condemning 'Hard Doctrine,' 1978–2013," *Mormon Studies Review* 7 (2020): 21–28.

EPILOGUE

1. Rodney Stark, "The Rise of a New World Faith," *Review of Religious Research* 26, no. 1 (September 1984): 18.

2. Jana Riess, *The Next Mormons: How Millennials Are Changing the LDS Church* (New York: Oxford University Press, 2019), 6, 254n14–15; Stephen Bullivant, *Nonverts: The Making of Ex-Christian America* (New York: Oxford University Press, 2022), 18–41; Thomas S. Kidd, *America's Religious History: Faith, Politics, and the Shaping of a Nation* (Grand Rapids, MI: Zondervan, 2019), 257–58; David G. Stewart Jr., "The Dynamics of LDS Growth in the Twenty-First Century," in *The Palgrave Handbook of Global Mormonism*, ed. R. Gordon Shepherd, A.

NOTES 431

Gary Shepherd, and Ryan T. Cragun (New York: Palgrave Macmillan, 2020), 165–66, 174–75.

3. "A Portrait of Mormons in US," *Pew Research Center: Religion and Public Life*, July 24, 2009, https://www.pewforum.org/2009/07/24/a-portrait-of-morm ons-in-the-us/; "Facts and Figures," Brigham Young University, January 31, 2019, https://www.byu.edu/facts-figures. For LDS demographic statistics on Black members outside the United States, see Brady McCombs, "Mormons Grapple with Race Decades after the Ban on Black Leaders," *AP News*, June 1, 2018; David G. Stewart Jr. and Matthew Martinich, *Reaching the Nations: International Church Growth Almanac* (Henderson, NV: Cumorah Foundation, 2014).

4. BYU student, quoted in Nathan Winward "Commentary: Does Brigham Young University Value Diversity?," *Salt Lake Tribune*, April 21, 2019.

5. Edward L. Kimball, *Lengthen Your Stride: The Presidency of Spencer W. Kimball—Working Draft* (Salt Lake City: Benchmark Books, 2009), ch. 24; Newell G. Bringhurst, "The Image of Blacks within Mormonism as Presented in the Church News, 1978–1988," *American Periodicals* 2 (Fall 1992): 113–23; Philip Jenkins, "Letting Go: Understanding Mormon Growth in Africa," in *From the Outside Looking In: Essays on Mormon History, Theology, and Culture*, ed. Reid L. Neilson and Matthew J. Grow (New York: Oxford University Press, 2016), 338–50.

6. Joanna Brooks, *Mormonism and White Supremacy: American Religion and the Problem of Racial Innocence* (New York: Oxford University Press, 2020), 199.

7. Oaks, quoted in Peggy Fletcher Stack, "No Apology? Really? Mormons Question Leader Dallin H. Oaks' Stance," *Salt Lake Tribune*, January 30, 2015.

8. Dieter F. Uchtdorf, "Come, Join with Us," *Conference Report*, October 2013, https://abn.churchofjesuschrist.org/study/general-conference/2013/10/come-join-with-us?lang=eng.

9. Stokes, quoted from a Sunstone panel session, July 29, 2017.

10. Gray, telephone conservation with Matthew Harris, May 15, 2021.

11. Graham-Russell and Vranes, quoted in Benjamin Wood, "No, the Mormon Church Did Not Apologize for Having a History of Racism; Hoaxer Says He Meant Fake Message to Spark Discussion," *Salt Lake Tribune*, May 17, 2018.

12. Ruth Graham, "A Fake Site Posted an Apology for the Mormon Church's History of Racism; Black Mormons Wish It Was Real," *Slate*, May 18, 2018, https://slate.com/human-interest/2018/05/fake-apology-for-mormon-chur chs-history-of-racism-angers-black-members.html. Streeter later apologized for the prank. Peggy Fletcher Stack, "Creator of Fake LDS Apology Does His Own Apologizing, Acknowledges Causing 'Tremendous Pain for Black Mormons,'" *Salt Lake Tribune*, May 23, 2018.

13. Kristin Lowe, "General Conference Would Be a Good Time for the LDS Church to Apologize to the Black Community," *Religious News Network*, September 28, 2020, https://religionnews.com/2020/09/28/general-confere nce-lds-church-apologize-to-the-black-community-racism/.

432   NOTES

14. Julienna Viegas-Haws, "What Do Progressive Mormons Want? A Dialogue about Change," *Salt Lake Tribune*, August 7, 2015; Gina Colvin, "Mormons, Mandela, and the Race and Priesthood Statement," *KiwiMormon*, December 8, 2013, http://www.patheos.com/blogs/kiwimormon/2013/12/mormons-mandela-and-the-race-and-priesthood-statement/. See also Kristy Money and Gina Colvin, "LDS Church Should Go Further to Disavow Racist Priesthood Ban," *Salt Lake Tribune*, December 21, 2014.

15. Dallin H. Oaks, "President Oaks' Full Remarks from the LDS Church's 'Be One' Celebration," *LDS Church News*, June 1, 2018, https://www.thechurchn ews.com/leaders-and-ministry/2018-06-01/president-oaks-full-remarks-from-the-lds-churchs-be-one-celebration-10994. For Oaks's assertion that the word "apology" is not in the scriptures, see Stack, "No Apology? Really?"

16. Richard E. Turley Jr. and Barbara Jones Brown, *Vengeance Is Mine: The Mountain Meadows and Its Aftermath* (New York: Oxford University Press, 2023), xiv; Carrie A. Moore, "LDS Church Issues Apology over Mountain Meadows," *Deseret News*, September 12, 2007; Molly Slossum, "Mormon Church Apologizes for Posthumous Baptism of Jews," *Reuters*, February 14, 2012, https://www.reuters.com/article/us-mormons-apology-wiesenthal/mormon-church-apologizes-for-posthumous-baptism-of-jews-idUKTR E81E03S20120215.

17. Stack, "No Apology? Really?"

18. I am influenced by Isabel Wilkerson, *Caste: The Origins of Our Discontents* (New York: Random House, 2020).

19. Caroline Kline, *Mormon Women at the Crossroads: Global Narratives and the Power of Connectedness* (Urbana: University of Illinois Press, 2022), 118–19, 142–45; Janan Graham-Russell, "Choosing to Stay in the Mormon Church Despite Its Racist Legacy," *The Atlantic*, August 28, 2016, https://www.theatlantic.com/politics/archive/2016/08/black-and-mormon/497660/; James C. Jones, "Racism," *Dialogue: A Journal of Mormon Thought* 52, no. 3 (Fall 2019): 203–8; Melodie Jackson, "The Black Cain in White Garments," *Dialogue: A Journal of Mormon Thought* 51, no. 3 (Fall 2018): 209–11; Darron T. Smith, "Negotiating Black Self-Hate within the LDS Church," *Dialogue: A Journal of Mormon Thought* 51, no. 3 (Fall 2018): 29–44; LaShawn Williams, "Building Community and Identity among Black Latter-day Saints: Toward Completing the Flock through Conference Connections," in Shepherd, Shepherd, and Cragun, *The Palgrave Handbook of Global Mormonism*, 713–16.

20. Darius Gray, "No Johnny-Come-Lately: The 182-Year-Long BLACK Mormon Moment," *FAIR Conference*, August 2–3, 2012, https://www.fairlatt erdaysaints.org/conference/august-2012/no-johnny-come-lately-the-182-year-long-black-mormon-moment.

21. John A. Tvedtnes, "The Charge of 'Racism' in the Book of Mormon," *FARMS Review* 15 (2003): 183–97; Brant A. Gardiner, *Second Witness: Analytical and Contextual Commentary on the Book of Mormon*, 6 vols. (Sandy, UT: Greg

Kofford Books, 2007–8), 2:114–22; Rodney Turner, "The Lamanite Mark," in *Second Nephi: The Doctrinal Structure.*, ed. Monte S. Nyman and Charles D. Tate Jr. (Provo, UT: Religious Studies Center, Brigham Young University, 1989), 133–57; Ethan Sproat, "Skins as Garments in the Book of Mormon: A Textual Exegesis," *Journal of Book of Mormon Studies* 24 (2015): 138–65; Gerrit M. Steenblik, "Demythicizing the Lamanites' 'Skin of Blackness,'" *Interpreter: A Journal of Latter-day Saint Faith and Scholarship* 49 (2021): 167–258.

22. Smith, quoted in "Discussion after the Talk on Racial Prejudice by Elder Mark E. Petersen" transcript, 22, August 27, 1954, Box 4, Folder 7, WEB. Smith also applied this racial trope to Native Americans. Joseph Fielding Smith, *Answers to Gospel Questions*, 5 vols. (Salt Lake City: Deseret Book, 1957–66), 3:122–23. See also Matthew L. Harris, "Whiteness Theology and the Evolution of Mormon Racial Teachings," in *The LDS Gospel Topics Series: A Scholarly Engagement*, ed. Matthew L. Harris and Newell G. Bringhurst (Salt Lake City: Signature Books, 2020), 255–60, 264–66. Max Perry Mueller perceptively notes that Book of Mormon narrators taught that the Mormon gospel could heal "racial divisions" by "restoring" the human family "to its original raceless, white form." Max Perry Mueller, *Race and the Making of the Mormon People* (Chapel Hill: University of North Carolina Press, 2017), 42. Mueller also notes that Mormon leaders considered the whitening as both symbolic and literal (ch. 3).

23. Quoted in Peggy Fletcher Stack, "Sunstone Conference Asks What It's Like to Be Mormon and Not White," *Salt Lake Tribune*, March 16, 2015.

24. Quoted in Margaret Young and Darius Gray's film *Nobody Knows: The Untold Story of Black Mormons* (2008), transcript published in "Nobody Knows: *The Untold Story of Black Mormons*—Script," *Dialogue: A Journal of Mormon Thought* 42, no. 3 (Fall 2009): 120–21.

25. Harris, "Whiteness Theology," 261–64, 267–71.

26. Jennifer Harvey, *Dear White Christians: For Those Still Longing for Racial Reconciliation*, 2nd ed. (Grand Rapids, MI: William B. Eerdmans, 2020), 85.

27. In April 2022, the LDS church called its first Black woman into the General Primary presidency. Becky Bruce, "Latter-day Saints Call First Black Woman to Serve in a General Presidency," *KSL News*, April 3, 2022, https://kslne wsradio.com/1966550/latter-day-saints-call-first-black-woman-to-serve-in-a-general-presidency/.

28. Amos C. Brown, "Follow the LDS Church's Example to Heal Divisions and Move Forward," op-ed, *Salt Lake Tribune*, January 20, 2022; Megan McKellar, "Interview with the Reverence Amos C. Brown about Overcoming Prejudice Featured in September Issue of the Liahona," *Church News*, August 19, 2021, https://www.thechurchnews.com/living-faith/2021-08-19/reverend-brown-liahona-overcoming-prejudice-racism-naacp-222816.

29. Jemar Tisby, *How to Fight Racism: Courageous Christianity and the Journey toward Racial Justice* (Grand Rapids, MI: Zondervan, 2021), 87.

30. Sarah Jane Weaver, "First Presidency, NAACP Announce Major Education and Humanitarian Initiatives," *Church News*, June 14, 2021, https://www.the-churchnews.com/2021/6/14/23217787/first-presidency-naacp-announce-education-humanitarian-initiatives; Sheri Dew, *Russell M. Nelson: Insights from a Prophet's Life* (Salt Lake City: Deseret Book, 2019), 356–57; Richard E. Turley Jr., *In the Hands of the Lord: The Life of Dallin H. Oaks* (Salt Lake City: Deseret Book, 2020), 363.

31. Seyward Darby, *Sisters in Hate: American Women on the Front Lines of White Nationalism* (New York: Little, Brown, 2020), 109–11, 161–62, 166, 171; Conor Gaffey, "How a Charlottesville Speaker Forced the Mormon Church to Condemn White Supremacists," *Newsweek*, August 17, 2017, http://www.newsweek.com/charlottesville-mormons-white-supremacists-651747.

32. "Church Releases Statement Condemning White Supremacist Attitudes," *Church News*, August 15, 2017, https://www.churchofjesuschrist.org/church/news/church-releases-statement-condemning-white-supremacist-attitudes?lang=eng.

33. Graham-Russell and Hawkins, quoted in Peggy Fletcher Stack, "LDS Church Yanks Song 'White' after Lyrics Fell Flat with Mormons of Color," *Salt Lake Tribune*, December 13, 2016. See also Andrew Spriggs, "Whiteness in the 2017 LDS Mutual Theme," *Wheat and Tares*, December 9, 2016, https://wheatandtares.org/2016/12/09/whiteness-in-the-2017-lds-mutual-theme/.

34. Irene Caso (church spokeswoman), quoted in Peggy Fletcher Stack, "Error Printed in LDS Church Manual Could Revive Racial Criticisms," *Salt Lake Tribune*, January 18, 2020.

35. Stevenson, quoted in Sean Walker, "'We Are All Part of the Same Divine Family,' Elder Stevenson Tells the NAACP," *KSL.com*, January 20, 2020, https://www.ksl.com/article/46706963/we-are-all-part-of-the-same-divine-family-elder-stevenson-tells-salt-lake-naacp. In a 2017 general conference sermon, Apostle Quentin L. Cook made an oblique reference to Smith when he said, "Anyone who claims superiority under the Father's plan because of characteristics like race, sex, nationality, language, or economic circumstances is morally wrong and does not understand the Lord's true purpose for all of our Father's children." Quentin L. Cook, "The Eternal Everyday," *Ensign*, October 2017, https://www.churchofjesuschrist.org/study/ensign/2017/11/saturday-afternoon-session/the-eternal-everyday?lang=eng.

36. Russell M. Nelson, "Let God Prevail," *Conference Report*, October 2020, https://abn.churchofjesuschrist.org/study/general-conference/2020/10/46nelson?lang=eng.

37. Dallin H. Oaks, "Love Your Enemies," *Conference Report*, October 2020, https://abn.churchofjesuschrist.org/study/general-conference/2020/10/17oaks?lang=eng; Dallin H. Oaks, "Racism and Other Challenges," *BYU Speeches*, October 27, 2020, https://speeches.byu.edu/talks/dallin-h-oaks/racism-other-challenges/.

NOTES   435

38. *LDS General Handbook*, revised and amended, December 2020, https://abn.churchofjesuschrist.org/study/manual/general-handbook/38-church-policies-and-guidelines?lang=eng#title_number220.

39. Terryl L. Givens, *Wrestling the Angel—The Foundations of Mormon Thought: Cosmos, God, Humanity* (New York: Oxford University Press, 2015), 175; Patrick Q. Mason, *Planted: Belief and Belonging in an Age of Doubt* (Salt Lake City: Deseret Book, 2015), 110–11; W. Paul Reeve, *Religion of a Different Color: Race and the Mormon Struggle for Whiteness* (New York: Oxford University Press, 2015), 144–46; Russell W. Stevenson, *For the Cause of Righteousness: A Global History of Blacks and Mormonism, 1830–2013* (Salt Lake City: Greg Kofford Books, 2014), 17. See also W. Paul Reeve, *Let's Talk about Race and Priesthood* (Salt Lake City: Deseret Book, 2023).

40. Matthew L. Harris and Newell G. Bringhurst, eds., *The Mormon Church and Blacks: A Documentary History* (Urbana: University of Illinois Press, 2015), 4.

41. John G. Turner, *The Mormon Jesus: A Biography* (Cambridge, MA: Harvard University Press, 2016), 281; Emile Wilson, "Christ Praying in Gethsemane," 2016, https://history.churchofjesuschrist.org/media/christ-praying-in-gethsemane-emile-wilson?lang=eng#1.

42. Turner, *The Mormon Jesus*, 281; Peggy Fletcher Stack, "Art Competition Features an Uncommon Mormon Savior: A Brown Jesus," *Salt Lake Tribune*, July 13, 2016; Aleah Ingram, "Stunning Piece from Cambodian Artist Featured on 10th International LDS Art Competition," *LDS Daily*, July 12, 2016, https://www.ldsdaily.com/world/stunning-piece-from-cambodian-artist-featured-in-10th-international-lds-art-competition/.

43. Eddie LeRoy Willis, *Panther to Priesthood* (Salt Lake City: Deseret Book, 2022); Wain Myers, *From Baptist Preacher to Mormon Teacher* (Springville, UT: Cedar Fort, 2015); Alive Faulker Burch, ed., *My Lord, He Calls Me: Stories of Faith by Black Latter-day Saints* (Salt Lake City: Deseret Book, 2022).

44. Chantel Bonner and Mauli Junior Bonner, *A Child of God* (Salt Lake City: Deseret Book, 2021); Burch, *My Lord, He Calls Me*, 222.

45. "Report and Recommendations of the BYU Committee on Race, Equity, and Belonging," February 2021, 6file:///C:/Users/User/AppData/Local/Temp/race-equity-belonging-report-feb-25-2021.pdf.

46. Ibid., 22, 25.

47. Ibid., 18–49. The recommendations are conveniently summarized in Sara Smith Atwood, "Rooting Out Racism," *Y Magazine*, Spring 2021, 10–11.

48. David Noyce, "Latest from Mormon Land: Oh Say, What Is Truth? Lots of Latter-day Saints Believe Trump's 'Big Lie,'" *Salt Lake Tribune*, June 14, 2021.

49. "The 'Big Lie': Most Republicans Believe the 2020 Election Was Stolen," *PRRI Research*, May 12, 2021, https://www.prri.org/spotlight/the-big-lie-most-republicans-believe-the-2020-election-was-stolen/.

50. Jana Riess, "At the Capitol, We Saw the Best and the Worst of US Mormonism," *Religious News Service*, January 8, 2021, https://religionnews.com/2021/01/

436 NOTES

08/at-the-capitol-we-saw-the-best-and-the-worst-of-us-mormonism/; Scott D. Pierce, "FBI Arrests Arizona Man Who Was Dressed as a Book of Mormon Figure during Insurrection at U.S. Capitol," *Salt Lake Tribune*, July 16, 2021. See also Mark Bowden and Matthew Teague, *The Steal: The Attempt to Overturn the 2020 Election and the People Who Stopped It* (New York: Atlantic Monthly Press, 2022). For the Confederate flag as a symbol of oppression, see John M. Coski, *The Confederate Battle Flag: America's Most Embattled Emblem* (Cambridge, MA: Harvard University Press, 2006).

51. "Church Leaders Condemn Violence and Lawless Behavior during Times of Unrest," *LDS Newsroom*, January 15, 2021, https://newsroom.churchofjesu schrist.org/article/church-leaders-condemn-violence-and-lawless-behavior-during-times-of-unrest.

52. Dallin H. Oaks, "Defending Our Divinely Inspired Constitution," *Conference Report*, April 2021, https://abn.churchofjesuschrist.org/study/general-confere nce/2021/04/51oaks?lang=eng; Matthew L. Harris, *Watchman on the Tower: Ezra Taft Benson and the Making of the Mormon Right* (Salt Lake City: University of Utah Press, 2020), 88.

53. Kathleen Belew, *Bring the War Home: The White Power Movement and Paramilitary America* (Cambridge, MA: Harvard University Press, 2018); Keeanga-Yamahtta Taylor, "From Color-Blind to Black Lives Matter: Race, Class, and Politics under Trump," in *The Presidency of Donald J. Trump: A First Historical Assessment*, ed. Julian E. Zelizer (Princeton: Princeton University Press, 2022), ch. 11; Philip S. Gorski and Samuel L. Perry, *The Flag and the Cross: White Christian Nationalism and the Threat to American Democracy* (New York: Oxford University Press, 2022).

54. *LDS General Handbook*, revised and amended, December 2020, https://www. churchofjesuschrist.org/study/manual/general-handbook/38-church-polic ies-and-guidelines?lang=eng#title_number226.

55. D. Todd Christofferson, "The Doctrine of Belonging," *Conference Report*, October 2022, https://www.churchofjesuschrist.org/study/general-confere nce/2022/10/28christofferson?lang=eng; Dallin H. Oaks, "Helping the Poor and Distressed," *Conference Report*, October 2022, https://www.churchofjesu schrist.org/study/general-conference/2022/10/18oaks?lang=eng.

56. Tisby, *How to Fight Racism*, 95, 158.

57. Book of Mormon, 2 Nephi 26:33.

Index

For the benefit of digital users, indexed terms that span two pages (e.g., 52–53) may, on occasion, appear on only one of those pages.

Aaronic Priesthood
    partial ban lifting, 38–39, 95–98, 118
    See also Nigeria
Abel, curse and, 10, 15
    See also Bible; Cain; Canaan
Abel, Elijah, 313
    biographical sketch, 8
    descendants ordained, 342–43n.37
    held priesthood, 1, 17, 54, 73, 75, 121–22, 189–90
    investigated, 8–9
    ordination in error, 9–10, 28–29, 73
    patriarchal blessing, 8–9
    physical features, 8–9
    Joseph Fielding Smith on, 73
    status debated, 13
    temple blessings, 1
    See also Ball, Joseph T.; Smith, Joseph, Jr.
Adams, Stirling
    Mormon Doctrine, 299
Africa
    Merrill Bateman mission, 215–16
    expansion after ban, 254–55, 273, 286
    Gordon Hinckley visits, 290
    lineage, 30, 34, 42–43, 55–56
    missions, 195
    stake organized, 274–75
    temples, 290
    See also missions; Nigeria; South Africa
Anderson, Joseph
    answers First Presidency mail, 28–29, 45, 55
    See also First Presidency
apology for ban, 271, 280–81, 293, 308
    fake, 308–10
    Darius Gray on, 308

    lack of, 304, 308, 313
    to NAACP, 314
    Dallin Oaks on, 308, 310
    other apologies, 310
    requested, 278, 309–10
    See also Gospel Topics Essays
apostolic committee (Bennion Report)
    consult minutes, 57
    influence on David O. McKay, 60
    secretive element, 57–58
    studies ban, 56–61
Are We of Israel?
    influence on Joseph Fielding Smith, 17–18
Arrington, Leonard J., 197–98
    on ban, 214
    Brigham Young biography, 246
    research on ban, 214
    See also historians/scholars
art
    diversity, 316
    racist themes, 18
    See also literature
Ashton, Marvin J.
    supports ban, 198–99
Australia
    Indigenous ordinations, 43–44

Bach, Hollis B.
    BYU discrimination investigation, 138–40, 143–44, 145, 148–49, 174–75, 177
    See also Wilkinson, Ernest
Badger, Ralph
    mission president, 29–30
    writes to First Presidency, 29–30

438 INDEX

Bailey, Thurl
  converts to Mormonism, 282
  interracial marriage, 282
Ball, Joseph T.
  held priesthood, 1
  presiding minister, 1
  See also Abel; Elijah; Smith, Joseph, Jr.
Ball, Terry
  on Randy Bott, 303
  whiteness theology, 296–97
Ballard, Melvin J.
  on premortal curse, 13
ban inexplicable, 301–2
  dominant narrative, 293–94
  Gordon Hinckley, 277
  1969 statement, 156, 293–94
  See also "curse" on Black people,
    "fence-sitters," Pearl of Great
    Price, premortal existence
Bangerter, William Grant
  Brazil, 229–30, 255–56
  determining lineage, 41
  mission president, 41, 44, 229–30
  See also Brazil; Faust, James E.
Bankhead, Mary, 272–73
  ban lifted, 229
  Genesis Group, 187
Barker, Robert
  BYU discrimination investigation,
    136–37, 139–40
Bateman, Merrill
  BYU president, 268–69
  career, 215
  secret Africa mission, 215–16
Beitler, Catherine, 255–56
  ban lifted, 229–30
  and church leaders, 204–5
Beitler, Roger
  on ban, 204–5
  ban lifted, 229–30
  mission president, 204–5
Bennion, Adam S.
  chairs ban committee, 57
  collection on ban, 195–96, 197
  and "Swearing Elders," 58
  See also apostolic committee (Bennion
    Report); Bennion, Lowell
Bennion, Lowell L., 23
  advocates for Black family, 37
  ban as practice, 89

ban being lifted, 89, 90, 96–97,
    149, 231
  and church leaders, 90–91
  on civil rights, 112
  curriculum writer, 49–50, 358n.133
  drafts Bennion Report, 58–59
  fired, 63, 90–92, 313
  general conference sermon, 49–50
  opposes ban, 48–49, 50, 52, 58–59,
    72–73, 74
  spied on, 89
  teaching career, 48–49
  University of Utah, 358n.133
  See also apostolic committee (Bennion
    Report)
Bennion Report. See apostolic
    committee (Bennion Report)
Benson, Ezra Taft, 223–24, 266
  ban hardliner, 198–99, 212, 216–17,
    398n.135
  ban revelation, 242
  on BYU difficulties, 146–47
  and Hugh Brown, 119
  bypass Joseph Fielding Smith, 159
  censored, 115–16
  church president, 258
  on civil rights, 83–84, 93, 115–16, 120,
    123, 124, 130, 133–34, 367n.109
  on communism, 101–2, 124, 133–34
  conference sermon, 124–25, 134
  criticized, 54–55
  death, 275–76
  and First Presidency, 134
  "Fourteen Fundamentals," 258–59
  and historians, 246–47
  John Birch Society, 119, 123, 124
  and Martin Luther King Jr., 115–16,
    117, 133
  partisanship, 318
  past statements, 258, 259–60
  presidential run, 135–36, 370n.148
  public relations, 164
  and segregation, 66, 179–80
  spiritual experience, 219–21
  See also John Birch Society; Benson,
    Reed; conspiracy theories
Benson, Reed, 258–59
  John Birch Society, 119
    See also John Birch Society; Benson,
      Ezra Taft; conspiracy theories

INDEX

439

Benson, Steve
  leaks letter, 260
  Martin Luther King Jr. Day, 259
  See also Benson, Ezra Taft
Berrett, William E.
  ban apologetics, 147
  and Lowell Bennion, 91
  Black student admissions, 131–33
  "The Church and the Negroid
    People," 48
  on segregation, 81–82
  supports ban, 50
  See also BYU; Wilkinson, Ernest L.
Bible
  curse in, 10, 69–70, 85
  used to support ban, 169–71, 179–80,
    267, 300
  See also Book of Mormon; Pearl of
    Great Price; scriptures
biology
  race and, 6–7, 29, 31, 59
  See also blood; DNA
Black church leaders
  Helvécio Martins, 274–76, 312–13
  lack, 312–13
Black Lives Matter
  antiracism sermons, 314–15
  George Floyd murder, 314–15
Black Pete. *See* Kerr, Peter
Black Power, 124, 148–49
  Jerry Rubin, 162–63
  sports protests, 144–45
  threats, 166
  See also Cleaver, Eldridge
blood
  interracial transfusions, 63
  purged, 396n.104
  segregated blood banks, 63
  tests for race, 63–64
  See also blood atonement; lineage; "one
    drop" rule; whiteness theology
blood atonement
  interracial marriage and, 5
Bob Jones University
  IRS targets, 175–76, 202
  refuses federal funds, 146
  segregated, 138
  See also tax exemption
Book of Abraham. *See* Pearl of Great
    Price

Book of Mormon (musical)
  ban reversal, 301
Book of Mormon
  after ban lifted, 240–41
  changes, 251–52, 292
  curses in, 10
  inclusion in, 11, 265, 302, 319,
    433n.22
  racism, 172, 310, 311–12
  See also Lamanites; Pearl of Great
    Price; Nephites; scriptures
Book of Moses. *See* Pearl of Great Price
Bott, Randy
  casualty, 304
  colleagues on, 302–3
  general conference response, 303–4
  misquoted, 303
  racist teachings, 299–300
  retires, 302
  and Romney campaign, 300–1
  Southerner language, 300–1
  statements regarding, 301
  students on, 303
  teaching career, 299–300
  Washington Post article, 300–4
  See also Brigham Young University
    (BYU); Horowitz, Jason
Boyd, George T.
  opposition to ban, 50
  See also Bennion, Lowell; Lyon, T.
    Edgar
Brazil, 224
  ban complexity, 38–39, 40–41
  ban lifted, 229–30
  determining lineage, 40, 41, 56, 204–5
  expansion after ban, 254–56, 273
  fundraising, 205
  Germans, 40
  interracial marriage, 40, 59, 204, 216–
    17, 229–30
  Spencer W. Kimball and, 203–6
  lineage lessons, 41–42, 204–5
  David O. McKay visit, 56
  mission, 29, 41
  patriarchal blessings, 41, 56
  Portuguese speakers, 40
  temple, 203–5, 209–10, 212–13, 216–17,
    224
  See also Bangerter, William Grant;
    Faust, James E.; missions; slavery

440   INDEX

Bridgeforth, Ruffin, 96, 182, 223–24, 256,
        313
    ban lifted, 228–29
    converts to Mormonism, 182
    Genesis Group, 187, 190–91
    navigates ban, 182
    seeks priesthood, 181, 184–87, 188
    on Special Interest Group, 190
    See also Genesis Group; Gray, Darius;
        Orr, Eugene
Brigham Young University (BYU)
    accreditation, 176, 177, 202
    anti-discrimination statement, 136–37
    avoid government funds, 146
    Black faculty, 154–55, 174, 176, 177,
        179–81, 202
    Black speakers, 176
    Black students, 127, 128–30, 131–33,
        134–35, 137, 138, 144, 145, 148–49,
        154–55, 169–71, 175–76, 202, 248,
        307–8, 316
    discrimination investigation, 127, 136–
        40, 143–44, 145, 176, 179–81
    donations threatened, 144
    forbidden topics, 136
    history, 128
    interracial dating/marriage, 131, 132,
        171, 248
    opposition to ban, 47, 340n.114
    racism after ban, 316–17
    racist curriculum, 172, 173–74
    racist teachings after ban, 296, 298,
        299–300
    —sports protests, 132–33, 144, 146–47,
        154, 159
        Arizona, 167, 177
        Arizona State, 153
        Black Student Union, 167, 169,
            171–72
        Colorado State, 160–62
        and communism, 165
        complaints, 161–62, 164
        end, 181
        New Mexico, 146, 167
        responses, 163–64
        San Jose State, 144–45
        San Diego State, 177
        Seattle Liberation Front (SLF), 167,
            171–72
        spread, 160–61

    Stanford, 146, 155
    UTEP, 127, 134, 135–36, 139, 144–45,
        146, 153
    University of Utah, 153
    violence, 160–61
    Washington, 167–69, 171–72
    Western Michigan, 177
    Wyoming, 153, 167
    See also Bach, Hollis; *BYU Studies*;
        Church Education System;
        Wilkinson, Ernest L.
Bringhurst, Newell G.
    ban article, 218, 247
    and Ronald Esplin, 246
    Mormon Church and Blacks, 315–16
    Saints, Slaves, and Blacks, 247
British Israelism
    Our Destiny, 265–66
    Joseph Fielding Smith, 17–18
    See also Cameron, William J.; lineage
Brodie, Fawn M.
    on ban, 178, 188–89, 196–97
    ban lifted, 231
    No Man Knows My History, 88
    See also historians/scholars
Brooks, Juanita
    confronts ban, 36–37
    See also historians/scholars
Brown, Hugh B.
    ban being lifted, 89, 93–94, 95–98, 99–
        100, 118–19, 122, 127–28, 146–47,
        149, 150, 151, 152, 155–56, 157,
        186–87, 198–99, 231
    ban origins, 188–89
    and Lowell Bennion, 90–91, 96
    and Ezra Taft Benson, 133, 134
    biographical sketch, 93
    civil rights statement, 108, 115–16
    death, 198–99
    depression, 152–53
    dropped as counselor, 157–58, 313
    and Alvin Dyer, 150–51, 152
    isolated, 99–100
    Martin Luther King Jr. statement, 133
    and David O. McKay, 93, 95–96, 97–98,
        99–100, 142
    and Sterling M. McMurrin, 142–43
    New York Times interview, 97–98
    reputation, 93
    and Joseph Fielding Smith, 157–58

INDEX

statement upholding ban, 156–57
University of Utah speech, 152–53
See also civil rights; First Presidency;
    McKay, David O.; Tanner, N.
    Eldon
Brown v. Board of Education, 62
    LDS leaders respond, 62–63, 69,
        79–80
    Protestant reactions, 75–76
Buerger, David John
    ban revelation accounts, 236–37
    and Bruce R. McConkie, 236–37
    research interests, 236–37
    See also historians/scholars
Bush, Lester E.
    apostles study, 218
    Adam Bennion papers, 195–96, 197
    "Compilation on the Negro," 196–97,
        216–17
    Dialogue article, 195–96, 197–98,
        216–17
    and Ronald Esplin, 246
    Spencer Kimball and, 218
    targeted, 247
    See also *Dialogue*; historians/scholars;
        Packer, Boyd K.
BYU Studies
    Lester Bush article, 197–98
    Our Destiny review, 267
    Ronald Esplin article, 246
    See also BYU

Cain, 5
    after ban lifted, 240–41
    and ban, 1–2, 31, 279–80
    curse origins, 13, 15
    lineage, 187, 270
    "mark" on, 10, 21, 70, 72, 311–12
    seed, 5, 11, 19, 42, 101–2, 149–50, 216–
        17, 252, 267, 270
    See also Abel; Bible; "curse" on Black
        people; Ham, "mark" on Black
        people; Pearl of Great Price
California
    tax exemption bill, 175
Callis, Charles A.
    opposes ban, 39
Cameron, William J.
    author, 265–66
    conspiracy theories, 266

    God's Covenant Race, 266
    and Hitler, 266, 267
    Mormons cite, 265–66
    Protocols of the Elders of Zion, 266
    See also British Israelism, conspiracy
        theories, lineage
Canaan
    cursed, 10, 85
    See also Abel; Bible; Ham
Caribbean
    expansion after ban, 254–55, 273
    mission, 29
    See also missions
Carlson, Jack
    on ban, 206–7, 212–13, 243–44
    and Spencer Kimball, 206–7, 212–13
Carter, Jimmy
    ban lifted, 230–31, 243–44
    elected president, 209
    and Spencer Kimball, 209
    See also tax exemption
Christofferson, D. Todd
    on Randy Bott, 303–4
Church Education System (CES)
    opposition to ban, 44, 48–49, 50, 51–
        52, 67, 90, 91
    summer seminar, 67–74
    warned on orthodoxy, 92
    See also Brigham Young University
        (BYU)
church growth, 33
    ban complicates, 39
    Black membership, 307–8
    declines, 307–8
    Rodney Stark predictions, 307–8
    See also Hinckley, Gordon B.; Kimball,
        Spencer W.
church records
    document race, 42
civil rights, 93
    and ban being lifted, 118, 201–2
    BYU investigation, 136–40, 169–71,
        174
    Civil Rights Acts, 111, 112, 115–16,
        136–37, 138, 148, 180–81
    church exempt, 115, 117–18, 154–55,
        177
    J. Reuben Clark on, 79, 80
    and communism, 101–2, 115–16, 120,
        133–34

442 INDEX

civil rights (*cont.*)
 conflicting Mormon views, 110, 115–16
 Emmett Till murder, 83
 events in South, 109
 general conference statement, 108–9,
  113
 lack in Utah, 63, 84–85, 106–8
 moral issue, 112
 Mormon silence on, 63, 83–84, 110,
  112–13, 115, 122–23
 Mormon support, 80, 84, 156–57, 201–2
 opposition, 118
 Mark E. Petersen on, 69
 protests in Utah, 112–15, 119
 RLDS response, 117–18
 Rosa Parks, 83
 voting rights bill, 83–84
 See also civil rights; McMurrin,
  Sterling M.; NCAACP
Clark, J. Reuben, 100, 130, 266
 on blood purity, 63
 on civil rights, 79, 80, 83, 354n.70
 compassion, 38–39
 on interracial marriage, 86–87
 Lowry Nelson letter, 25
 opposes "one drop," 39, 87
 reputation, 25
 supports Black congregation, 83
 supports segregation, 64–66, 78–80, 87
 writer, 25, 26
 See also First Presidency; Grant,
  Heber J; McKay, David O.; Smith,
  George Albert
Cleaver, Eldridge
 church inactivity, 283–84
 death, 284
 evolution of, 282–83
 influences, 282–83
 religious journey, 283–84
 See also Black Power
communism
 civil rights and, 101–2, 115–16, 120,
  123, 133–34
 Ezra Taft Benson on, 101–2, 115–16,
  133–34
 and protests, 164–65
 Cleon Skousen on, 164–65
 See also Benson, Ezra Taft; civil rights;
  conspiracy theories; Hoover, J.
  Edgar; King, Martin Luther, Jr.

conspiracy theories
 Ezra Taft Benson, 101–2, 119, 123, 125,
  134, 163, 165
 Reed Benson, 119
 Book of Mormon, 134
 William J. Cameron, 265–66
 church handbook, 318
 civil rights, 101–2, 123, 124, 165,
  370–71n.158
 communism, 124, 134, 164–65
 government, 165
 J. Edgar Hoover, 101–2
 John Birch Society, 101–2, 123, 125,
  165
 Wiliam Koerner, 163
 Martin Luther King, 123
 Mormon chapels, 165
 protests, 164–65
 responses, 134
 Cleon Skousen, 163, 164–65
 See also Benson, Ezra Taft; Cameron,
  William J; Hoover, J. Edgar;
  Skousen, Cleon
Crosby, Oscar
 vanguard pioneer company, 1–2
Cuba
 mission to, 24
curriculum
 racial text, 7–8, 172, 173, 293, 295
curse on Black people, 4
 after ban lifted, 226, 227, 240–41, 288,
  297–98, 300, 310
 in Bible, 10
 in Book of Mormon, 11
 David O. McKay on, 23
 disavowed, 305
 Lowry Nelson on, 24
 origins debated, 13
 in Pearl of Great Price, 11
 premortal existence, 11
 Joseph Fielding Smith on, 16–17
 Brigham Young on, 4–5
 See also "mark" on Black people

demands for priesthood, 181
 Eugene Orr, 159
 John Pea, 207
Deseret Book
 books out of print, 269
 Mormon Doctrine, 269, 298–99

INDEX 443

publishing freedom, 316
racist publications, 125, 293
See also historians/scholars
devil. *See* Satan
Dialogue
Lester Bush article, 195–96,
197–98
call to lift ban, 121–22
church leaders on, 197–98
Armand Mauss plea, 122–23
See also historians/scholars
DNA, 8
See also biology
Doxey, Roy W.
ban apologetics, 46–47
response to Lowry Nelson, 46
Dunn, Paul H.
and Eldridge Cleaver, 282–83
on ending ban, 87, 118, 225
questions ban, 73
Durham, G. Homer
ban committee, 156
ban research, 218, 245–47
Historical Department, 246–47
Dyer, Alvin R.
Assistant to Twelve, 141–42
author, 141–42
on ban, 141–42
on ban critics, 135
and Hugh Brown, 150–51, 152
First Presidency, 141–42
and Sterling McMurrin, 141–42
meets with McKay sons, 149–50
preserves ban, 150
Taggart manuscript, 150
whiteness theology, 297
See also First Presidency

England, Eugene
BYU professor, 414n.23
criticizes ban, 263, 264–65
on curse, 297
"The Lord's University," 263–64
and Robert J. Matthews, 264–65
and Bruce McConkie, 263–65
resigns from BYU, 268–69
See also BYU; historians/scholars
Ephraim, 207, 217
favored lineage, 16, 17–18, 226, 270
See also lineage; patriarchal blessings

Epperson, Steven
Fired, 268
libel suit, 268
Mormons and Jews, 267–68
Our Destiny review, 267–68, 296
See also BYU; McConkie, Joseph
Fielding; Millet, Robert
Equal Rights Amendment (ERA)
Mormon opposition, 212
Mormon support sought, 209
women and priesthood, 232–33
Esplin, Ronald K.
ban research, 245–46
criticized, 246
See also Bush, Lester; Durham, G.
Homer
Evans, Richard L.
on Black BYU students/athletes,
145–47
public relations, 164
Evenson, Darrick T.
leaks repudiation, 280, 421n.116
See also Jackson, David

faith, loss of
due to ban, 50, 60
Faust, James E., 210, 271
ban lifted, 223–24
Brazil, 215, 224
and Helvécio Martins, 210–11
mission president, 215
See also Brazil
"fence-sitters," 23–24, 188–89
after ban lifted, 226, 250, 288, 297
folklore, 294–95
general conference, 22
Lowry Nelson letters, 25
lack of scriptural support, 15, 21, 45–46,
102
vs. "less valiant," 12, 23–24, 26, 46, 294–
95, 298
Mormon Doctrine, 261
1949 First Presidency statement, 26
premortal existence, 12, 13, 15
John A. Widtsoe on, 21
See also curse on Black people;
folklore, "mark" on Black people;
premortal existence
Fiji
ban, 37–38, 43–44, 87

444 INDEX

First Presidency
  antiprejudice statement, 315
  and Ezra Taft Benson, 115–16, 134
  censors materials, 136
  classifying Black people, 31
  disagreement, 29
  equated with God, 27
  invited to mission, 31
  letters about ban, 179
  mission correspondence, 31–32, 34,
    42–43
  Lowry Nelson letters, 25
  Nigeria mission, 94–95
  segregation at church, 66
  statements on ban, 2, 26, 47, 55, 135–36,
    156, 157, 228, 247, 277–78
  words as scripture, 27
  See also Anderson, Joseph; Brown,
    Hugh B.; Clark, J. Reuben;
    Gibbons, Francis; Hinckley,
    Gordon B.; Kimball, Spencer W.;
    Lee, Harold B.; McKay, David O.;
    Tanner, N. Eldon
Fitzgerald, John W., 182
  on ban, 135, 407n.98
  on civil rights, 84–85
  excommunicated, 192, 313
  letters in *Tribune*, 192
Flake, Green
  vanguard pioneer company, 1–2
Fleming, Monroe, 223–24, 313
  ban lifted, 228
  Hotel Utah, 151
  and NAACP, 119–20
  potential ordination, 151
  See also Brown, Hugh B.
Folarin, Tope
  experiences Mormon racism, 20
folklore
  vs. doctrine, 295–96
  Jeffrey Holland on, 294–95
  past teachings as, 294–95
  repudiated, 294–95
  See also curse on Black people; "fence-
    sitters," "mark" on Black people;
    premortal existence
Ford, Herbert Augustus
  church activity, 207–8
  denied priesthood, 207
  lineage, 207–8

Freeman, Joseph
  first ordained, 229
  Special Interest Group, 190
fundamentalist Mormons
  ads, 241
  ban in error, 241
  ban revelation text, 241
Fyans, J. Thomas
  lineage question, 208
  mission president, 208

genealogy. *See* Africa; Brazil; lineage;
    missions; South Africa
general conference
  antiracism sermons, 285, 292–93, 314–15
  ban revelation, 240–41
  church leaders as scripture, 27
  civil rights statement, 108–9
  "fence-sitters," 22
  Martin Luther King Jr. statement,
    99–100
  lineage theology, 269–70
  non–general authority speaker, 49–50
  protests, 107–8, 119–20, 123–24, 165–66
  right-wing extremism, 318
  rumor of ban lifting, 89, 96, 97
  shelved sermon, 78
  threats, 166
  Douglas Wallace stunt, 206
  whitening of skin, 251
Genesis Group, 201
  ban lifted, 228
  cautioned, 188
  created, 187
  earlier proposals, 82–83
  early members quit, 190–91, 212–13
  first fireside, 187
  first meeting, 187–88
  oversight, 188
  preliminary meetings, 183, 187
  preliminary suggestions, 184
  proxy baptisms, 187–88
  purpose, 187–88
  Special Interest Group, 190–91
  See also Bridgeforth, Ruffin; Gray,
    Darius; Hinckley, Gordon B.;
    Monson, Thomas S.; Orr, Eugene;
    Packer, Boyd K.
Gibbons, Francis M., 253–54
  on ban, 211, 216

INDEX 445

ban revelation, 221–22, 223–24, 226
See also First Presidency
Gillispie, David
   complains about ban, 181
Gladwell, Dennis, 279
   writes statement, 279, 280
Gospel Topics Essays
   genesis, 304–5
   race, 304–5, 318–19
   subjects, 304–5
Graham-Russell, Janan
   on fake ban apology, 309
   on use of "White," 314
Grant, Heber J.
   on Brigham Young statements, 21
   upholds ban, 23
   See also Clark, J. Reuben; First Presidency
Gray, Darius, 182, 313
   on ban apology, 308
   ban lifted, 229
   converts to Mormonism, 182–83
   criticism, 169
   discrimination at BYU, 182–83
   Genesis Group, 187, 190–91
   and Gordon Hinckley, 288–89, 425n.28
   Gospel Topics Essay, 305
   KSL, 182–83
   on lineage, 311
   on *Mormon Doctrine*, 299
   on racism, 188–89, 288
   reason for ban, 294
   response to protests, 168–69, 182–83
   seeks priesthood, 181, 184–87
   See also Bridgeforth, Ruffin; Genesis
      Group, Hinckley, Gordon B.; Orr,
      Eugene
Grover, Mark
   on patriarchal blessings, 41

Haight, David B.
   ban justification, 247
   ban revelation, 236
   supports ban, 198–99
Ham
   curse, 10, 11, 13, 19, 48, 75, 177–78,
      240–41, 279–80
   patriarchal blessings, 4, 187, 270
   See also Bible; Cain; scriptures
Hamilton, Keith, 252
   Ban origins, 294

handbook, church
   conspiracy theories, 318
   prejudice, 315
   See also patriarchal blessings
Hanks, Marion D., 91–92
   ban moderate, 102
   biographical sketch, 102
   BYU discrimination investigation,
      145–46
   and Lester Bush, 197, 198
   ending ban, 149, 156–57, 197, 223,
      224–25
   interracial marriage, 249
   supports Black Mormons, 66
   supports civil rights, 84, 112
   questions on ban, 192–93
   temple meeting, 223–24
Harris, Chauncy
   critic of ban, 53–54
   loses faith, 53–54
Hawaii
   BYU-Hawaii, 287
   interracial marriage, 287
   priesthood ordinations, 32, 38–39
   See also missions
Haycock, D. Arthur, 192–93, 212
   ban aftermath, 221
   meets with Black members, 184
   supervises Sterling McMurrin, 88
   See also First Presidency; Kimball,
      Spencer W.
Hinckley, Gordon B., 153
   antiracism sermon, 292–93
   apology for enslavement, 291–92
   apostle, 276
   ban committee, 156
   ban revelation, 236
   ban revelation committee, 221–22
   church expansion, 286, 290
   church president, 276
   counsels Eugene Orr, 189–90
   death, 293
   First Presidency, 276
   and Darius Gray, 288–89
   improves church image, 276
   on interracial marriages, 107, 286–87
   and David Jackson, 278–82
   journalists on, 292
   "mark" of Cain, 276
   Martin Luther King Jr. Day, 290

446 INDEX

Hinckley, Gordon B. (*cont.*)
  meets with Black members, 185–87
  and Cecil Murray, 291–92
  NAACP, 290, 313
  oversees Genesis Group, 188, 190–91, 276
  60 Minutes, 276–77
  on racist teachings, 276–77
  same-sex marriage, 286–87
  public relations, 164, 276, 286, 289–92
  supports ban, 198–99
  visits Africa, 290
  See also Benson, Ezra Taft; First Presidency; Genesis Group; Gray, Darius; NAACP
historians/scholars
  ban origins, 245, 315–16
  Historical Department, 246–47
  Newell Bringhurst, 245
  Lester Bush article, 195–96, 197–98, 216–17
  Mormonism and the Negro, 143, 149–50, 151, 196–97
  See also Deseret Book
Holland, Jeffrey R.
  "fence-sitters," teachings as folklore, 294
  repudiating racism, 294–95
  teachings as folklore, 294
  See also folklore
Hoover, J. Edgar, 101–2
  on civil rights, 116, 367n.109
  See also Benson, Ezra Taft; conspiracy theories
Hope, Mary and Len, 223–24, 313
  move to Utah, 66
  segregation at church, 66
Horowitz, Jason
  Backlash, 302
  Washington Post article, 300–4
  See also Bott, Randy
Howell, Abner, 96, 313
  on ban, 181–82
  discriminated against, 354n.80
  reputation, 81
  surveys Black Mormons, 82
  visits South, 81–82
Howells, Rulon S.
  on designating lineage, 41

mission president, 40
  See also Brazil
Hunter, Howard W.
  death, 275–76
  impatient with ban, 208
  supports ban, 198–99
  See also First Presidency
Hyde, Orson
  on premortal curse, 11–12
  Brigham Young and, 335n.48

Indigenous people
  ordination questions, 42–44
  whitening of skin, 250–51
  See also lineage
interracial marriage, 28, 42, 64–66, 86, 95
  after ban lifted, 226, 227, 247–50, 282, 286
  approved, 305
  blood atonement and, 5
  BYU, 129–30, 248
  censored teachings, 136
  Church News statement, 247–48
  and civil rights, 118
  conflicting advice, 248–50, 288
  differing impact, 85, 287
  Hawaii, 287
  influence on ban, 5, 11, 31, 35, 216–17
  David O. McKay on, 23
  Lowry Nelson letter, 25
  in Mormon magazines, 86–87
  Pearl of Great Price, 11
  Mark E. Petersen on, 69, 71, 77
  popular opinion, 248
  Joseph Fielding Smith on, 52
  South Africa, 29–30
  statement discouraging, 222
  Utah laws, 6, 107–8
  Brigham Young on, 4–5, 264
  See also Brigham Young University (BYU); civil rights
IRS. *See* tax exemption
Ivins, H. Grant, 158
  ban editorial, 177–78

Jackson, David, 313
  converts to Mormonism, 277
  criticizes *Mormon Doctrine*, 277, 299
  and Gordon Hinckley, 278–82
  leaves Mormonism, 280–81

INDEX 447

and Armand Mauss, 277–78
plan leaked, 280
requests repudiation, 278, 279–81
writes statement, 278, 279
See also Evenson, Darrick; Jensen, Marlin
James, Jane Manning, 313
biographical sketch, 2–3
patriarchal blessing, 4
and Joseph Smith, 4
status debated, 13
travels to Nauvoo, 4
James, Paul, 153, 161
See also Brigham Young University (BYU)
Jensen, Marlin K.
writes statement, 279
See also Evenson, Darrick: Jackson, David
John Birch Society, 101–2, 259
civil rights, 115–16, 123
and Ezra Taft Benson, 119, 123, 124, 260
opposition to, 130–31
rumor campaign, 119, 123
See also Benson, Ezra Taft; Benson, Reed; conspiracy theories; Welch, Robert

Kennedy, David
secretary of the treasury, 175–76
special church ambassador, 195
Kerr, Peter ("Black Pete")
held priesthood, 1
Kimball, Camilla, 215, 253
ban aftermath, 221, 227
See also Kimball, Spencer W.
Kimball, Edward L., 215
book on ban, 253–54
on Spencer Kimball, 216, 251
corrects Bruce McConkie, 253–54
refutes article, 238
See also Kimball, Spencer W.
Kimball, Spencer W., 45, 75, 97–98, 109, 145–46, 166, 172–73, 174–75
Leonard Arrington on, 193–94
ban aftermath, 221, 226, 227
ban as error, 199
ban as test, 160
ban committee, 212–13

ban lifted, 219–21, 223–24, 226
ban lifting critics, 231–32
ban revelation interview, 238
ban revelation statement, 221–22, 223–24
on Bennion committee, 57–58, 61
and Brazil, 203–6
on BYU difficulties, 146–47
Lester Bush and, 197, 218
and Jack Carlson, 206–7, 212–13
and Jimmy Carter, 209
church president, 193
on civil rights, 109–10, 115
discussion about ban, 52–53, 102
emotions, 193
ending ban 151, 152, 198–204
globalizing Mormonism, 193–95, 214, 245, 254–55
health, 193–94
and historians, 246–47
international visits, 199–200
interracial marriage, 216–17, 249–50
on Kennedy assassination, 110
and Harold Lee, 152
and Bruce McConkie, 212–13, 214, 221–22, 236, 253
and media, 201
NAACP suit, 200–1
and Native Americans, 199
Pearl of Great Price, 200
physical description, 193
public relations, 164
rebukes congregation, 208
on revelation, 211–12
on segregation sermon, 78
statement lifting ban, 218
strategic, 203–4, 214, 216–17
supports Black congregation, 82, 187
and Stewart Udall, 122
xenophobia, 130
whitening of skin, 250–51
women and priesthood, 232–33
See also First Presidency; Romney, Marion G.; Tanner, N. Eldon; whitening of skin; Wolsey, Heber
King, Martin Luther, Jr.
assassination, 133
and Ezra Taft Benson, 115–16, 117, 133
Black Mormons on, 260
civil rights as moral issue, 112

INDEX

King, Martin Luther, Jr. (*cont.*)
on communism, 116–17, 120
holiday, 259–60, 286, 290
J. Edgar Hoover on, 116
legacy, 259, 297
linked to communists, 93, 116–17, 123
march on Washington, 109
and George Romney, 110
See also Benson, Ezra Taft; communism;
conspiracy theories; Hoover, J.
Edgar
Kirton McConkie, 244, 268
Knight, Gladys
on past teachings, 281–82
Koerner, William, 162–63
Ku Klux Klan, 18, 266
LDS rhetoric and, 62–63

Lamanites
cursed in Book of Mormon, 10, 71
see also Book of Mormon; Nephites
lawsuits
discrimination, 200–1, 203
NAACP, 200–1
Lay, Hark
vanguard pioneer company, 1–2
Lee, Harold B., 145–46, 197
administrator, 159
ban committee, 156
ban hardliner, 151, 155, 157, 172–73, 192,
198–99
biographical sketch, 100
on Black BYU students/athletes, 129–
30, 146–47, 148, 154
bomb threat, 166
church president, 192
on civil rights, 122–23
correlation, 100
death, 193
on ending ban, 119–20, 192
and Marion D. Hanks, 102
influence, 152
prays about ban, 192–93
public relations, 164
reputation, 100
support for Black members, 187
supports segregation, 64–66, 179–80
welfare program, 100
See also Brigham Young University
(BYU); interracial marriage

Lester, Larry
unauthorized baptism/ordination, 206
Lewis, Enoch Lovejoy
held priesthood, 1
Lewis, Q. Walker
held priesthood, 1
lineage, 213
adoption, 213–14
after ban lifted, 226, 227, 240–41, 252,
298, 311
determining, 29–31, 34–35, 55–56, 87,
207, 215–16, 245
missionary lessons, 34, 41–42, 230
patriarchal blessings, 31–32, 41, 72, 270
policy change, 215–16
See also curse on Black people;
folklore; "mark" on Black people;
patriarchal blessings
literature
racist themes, 18–19
See also art
Lloyd, David
concerns over interracial marriage, 28
Luce, Clare Boothe
Mormon response to, 105–6
reputation, 105
on George Romney, 105
Ludlow, Daniel H.
identifies racist scriptures, 173–74
on prophecies, 161–62
on protests, 161–62
See also Brigham Young University
(BYU)
Lyon, T. Edgar
ban question, 35–36, 90, 96
and Lowell Bennion, 74
curriculum, 90–91
fired, 63, 90–92, 313
opposes ban, 50, 52
on passing as white, 37–38
summer seminar, 68
See also Bennion, Lowell; Brigham
Young University (BYU);
Church Education System

"mark" on Black people, 1–2, 4, 10, 19,
21, 31, 127, 249, 251–52, 264, 276,
311–12
See also curse on Black people; folklore;
lineage; premortal existence

INDEX

449

Martin, Wynetta
  BYU professor, 179–80
  converts to Mormonism, 180
  memoir, 180
  Tabernacle Choir, 180
  See also Brigham Young University
      (BYU)
Martins, Helvécio
  ban lifted, 229
  and James Faust, 210–11
  general authority, 274–76, 312–13
  and Spencer Kimball, 210, 211
  Armand Mauss on, 274–75
  promises to, 210–11
  public relations director, 211
  reputation, 211
  sacrifices, 211
  sealed in temple, 229
  stake presidency, 229
  Sandra Tanner on, 274–75
  on tokenism, 275
  See also Brazil
Martins, Marcus
  mission, 211, 229
  See also Martins, Helvécio; Martins,
      Rudá
Martins, Rudá, 275
  ban lifted, 229
  sacrifices, 211
  sealed in temple, 229
  See also Martins, Helvécio; Martins,
      Marcus
Mason, Patrick Q.
  ban origins, 315–16
  Gospel Topics Essay, 305
  See also historians/scholars
Mathias, Boyd
  on Bennion committee, 58
  concern over ban, 52–53
  loses faith, 52–53
Matthews, Robert J.
  defends Bruce McConkie, 264–65
  and Eugene England, 264–65
  intellect, 264
  See also Brigham Young University
      (BYU)
Mauss, Armand L.
  and Ron Esplin, 246
  folklore, 296
  Gospel Topics Essay, 305

and David Jackson, 277–78
on Helvécio Martins, 274–75
on lineage teachings, 297
on *Mormon Doctrine*, 299
plea in *Dialogue*, 369n.145
targeted, 247
writes statement, 279, 280
See also Bush, Lester; historians/
    scholars
Maxwell, Neal A., 211
  ban committee, 156
  ban lifted, 223–24
McCary, William
  held priesthood, 1
  priesthood ban and, 5
McConkie, Bruce R., 130
  "All Are Alike unto God," 239
  apostle, 192
  ban committee, 212–14, 219, 224–25
  ban revelation, 221–22, 240–41
  on ban critics, 201
  ban hardliner, 100, 198–99, 203, 212–13
  biographical sketch, 100
  Lester Bush and, 196–97, 198
  corrected by Ed Kimball, 253–54
  death and legacy, 260, 262, 263, 264,
      265 , –69
  embellishes ban revelation, 228, 233–
      34, 236–40, 252–53
  ending ban, 212–13
  and Eugene England, 263–65
  on lineage, 252–53
  "The New Revelation on Priesthood,"
      252–53
  New Witness for the Articles of Faith, A,
      262–63, 269–70
  presentation on ban, 219
  and Annette Reid, 261–62
  repents for teachings, 262
  repudiated, 286, 305
  reputation, 100, 214
  reversal on ban, 213–14, 240, 279–80
  and "Swearing Elders," 50–51
  teachings as folklore, 294
  visits Brazil, 205
  whiteness theology, 269–70
  –*Mormon Doctrine*
    after ban lifted, 228, 242, 247–48,
        252, 257, 262, 264, 269, 293,
        298–99

450 INDEX

McConkie, Bruce R. (*cont.*)
Curt Bench on, 269
criticized, 277–78, 299, 428n.64
impact, 261, 269, 275–76, 277–78,
279–80
reviews, 100–1
sales, 100–1, 427n.61
second edition, 192
supports ban, 100–1, 212–14, 247
taken out of print, 278, 280–81, 286,
293, 298–99
third edition, 252
See also folklore; Kimball, Spencer W.;
McConkie, Joseph Fielding; Pope,
Bill; Pope, Margaret; Smith, Joseph
Fielding (b. 1876); Whitton, Annie
McConkie, Joseph Fielding
embellishes ban revelation, 235, 236–37
Our Destiny controversy, 265–69
racial teachings after ban, 298
threatens libel suit, 268
See also Epperson, Steven; McConkie,
Joseph Fieldling; Millet, Robert
McKay, David O.
ban as policy, 56, 60
ban being lifted, 93, 95–98, 125–26,
149–50, 151, 198–99, 203–4, 227,
368n.121
and Lowell Bennion, 90–91
Bennion Report, 60
and Ezra Taft Benson, 135–36
biographical sketch, 22
and Hugh B. Brown, 93, 95–96, 97–98,
99–100
censors J. Reuben Clark, 79–80
on civil rights, 84–85
committee on ban, 56
conflicted on ban, 22–23, 26, 35, 43–44,
102, 342n.35
death, 159
on determining lineage, 55–56
failing health, 142, 147, 149–50, 152
on interracial marriage, 107
and Sterling McMurrin, 51, 60, 88–89,
141, 142–43
missionary work under, 33, 43
Nigeria, 94
nixes Black congregation, 83
supports segregation, 64–67
visits Brazil, 56

visits South Africa, 55–56
response to Chauncy Harris, 54
See also Africa; Brigham Young
University (BYU); Brown, Hugh
B.; civil rights; Clark, J. Reuben;
Dyer, Alvin R.; McKay, Lawrence;
McKay, Llewelyn; McMurrin,
Sterling M.; Nigeria; Smith,
Joseph Fielding (b. 1876); Tanner,
N. Eldon; Wilkinson, Ernest L.
McKay, David Lawrence
ending ban, 149–50, 151
See also Brown, Hugh B.; McKay,
David O.; McMurrin, Sterling M.
McKay, Llewelyn
ending ban, 149–50, 151
See also Brown, Hugh B.; McKay,
David O.; McMurrin, Sterling M.
McMurrin, Sterling M.
author, 87–88, 140
ban lifted, 230–31
ban origins, 143, 188–89
civil rights statements/editorials, 108,
115
commissioner of education, 140
and Alvin R. Dyer, 141–42
education, 87–88
ending ban, 149
and David O. McKay, 51, 60, 88–89,
140, 142–43
NAACP addresses, 87, 88–89, 140–42,
143
NAACP-Mormon meeting, 108
organizes "Swearing Elders," 50–51
orthodoxy questioned, 87–88
reputation, 87
and Joseph Fielding Smith, 51
See also civil rights; McKay, David O.;
NAACP
Meeks, Heber
Lowry Nelson letter, 24
report on Cuba, 340n.104
See also Cuba; Nelson, Lowry
Millet, Robert L.
on lineage, 267
Our Destiny controversy, 265–69
racial teachings after ban, 298
See also Brigham Young University;
Epperson, Steven; McConkie,
Joseph Fielding

INDEX

missions
avoid Black people, 40, 41–42, 72, 81
and ban, 29, 34, 257
Black countries, 94
determining lineage, 30–32, 34, 41,
204–5, 230
expand, 33
handbook, 412n.172
lineage lessons, 34, 41–42, 230
and NAACP, 117
not to gather, 342n.26
write headquarters, 31–32, 34, 42–43
See also Africa; Brazil; Caribbean;
Cuba; lineage; Nigeria; patriarchal
blessings; South Africa
Missouri
ban origins, 88, 143, 178, 188–89
Monson, Thomas S.
avoids Black neighbors, 130–31
ban committee, 212–13, 219
church president, 293
ending ban, 212–13
Gospel Topics Essays, 304–5
lack of media savvy, 293
meets with Black members, 185–87
oversees Genesis Group, 188, 190–91,
212–13, 293
supports ban, 198–99
See also First Presidency; Genesis
Group
Mormon Doctrine. See McConkie,
Bruce R.
Mormonism and the Negro (Stewart), 48,
362n.47, 428n.71
See also Berrett, William E.
Morrison, Alexander
Africa, 285
antiracism sermon, 285–86
author, 285
disingenuous, 285
See also Africa; Hinckley, Gordon B.
Moyle, Henry D.
biographical sketch, 105
controversies, 105
and Clare Boothe Luce, 105–6
See also First Presidency; McKay, David
O.
Mulder, William
on civil rights, 112
organizes "Swearing Elders," 50–51

Murray, Cecil, 273
and Gordon Hinckley, 291–92
musicians
discrimination, 66–67
See also art; literature

NAACP, 93, 95, 118, 286
apology to, 314
attacks Mormon missions, 117
ban lifting, 232
on civil rights statement, 108, 109
cooperation with Mormons, 108, 313,
318–19
and Gordon Hinckley, 290
protest rumors, 119–20
Sterling McMurrin addresses, 87, 88–
89, 140–42, 143
sues Mormons, 200–1
on Utah civil rights, 63, 107–8, 112,
115–16
See also Brown, Hugh W.; civil rights;
Hinckley, Gordon B.; McKay,
David O.; McMurrin, Sterling
M.; Nelson, Russell M.
Nelson, Lowry, 48, 54
ban lifted, 230–31
on BYU protests, 172–73
on civil rights, 80–81
critics, 46
letters on ban, 24, 25, 45
opposes ban, 44
publishes essays, 45–47
religious beliefs, 24
See also Cuba; historians/scholars;
Meeks, Heber; Smith, George
Albert
Nelson, Russell M.
antiracism sermon, 314–15
lineage theology, 269–70
and NAACP, 313
See also First Presidency
Nephites
white skin, 10
see also Book of Mormon; Lamanites
neutral. *See* fence-sitters
newspapers/periodicals (non-LDS)
on ban, 54–55, 75, 85–86, 97–98, 104–5,
106, 121, 141, 155, 164, 177–78,
192, 201
ban apology hoax, 309

452 INDEX

newspapers/periodicals (non-LDS) (*cont.*)
ban lifted, 230, 238
Black membership, 254–55
Randy Bott article, 300–4
Genesis Group, 188
on Gordon Hinckley, 292
interracial marriage statement, 222,
247–48
—*Deseret News*, 242
civil rights editorial, 113
See also Wolsey, Heber G.
Nibley, Hugh W.
opposes ban, 47–48, 71
Pearl of Great Price, 335n.49
See also Brigham Young University
(BYU)
Nigeria
Aaronic Priesthood, 95–97, 118
and George Romney campaign,
94–95
interracial marriage, 95
mission, 94–95, 117, 119–20
Mormon converts, 94, 120
segregation, 94–95
See also Africa; McKay, David O.;
Williams, LaMar
1949 statement. *See* First Presidency

Oaks, Dallin H.
"Afro-American Symposium,"
272–73
antiracism sermon, 314–15
on apologies, 308, 310
and ban, 52
on criticizing church leaders, 264
government intrusion, 202
on right-wing extremism, 318
threats to church, 268–69
See also Brigham Young University
(BYU); First Presidency
Official Declaration 2. *See* revelation
"one drop" rule, 5, 16–17, 28–29, 52, 70,
72
apostles investigate, 38–39
debated, 38
identification and, 8
opposition to, 21, 38–39
upheld, 39
women, 36–37
See also civil rights; South (US)

Orr, Eugene, 182, 313
boldness, 183, 184, 185–86, 189–90
demands priesthood, 159–60
Genesis Group, 187, 190–91
Gordon Hinckley counsels, 189–90
seeks priesthood, 181, 184–87, 189
speaks up, 183
Special Interest Group, 190
See also Bridgeforth, Ruffin; Genesis
Group; Gray, Darius
Ostling, Richard N.
Spencer Kimball interview, 238, 250
Otterson, Michael
Randy Bott article, 301–2
on *Mormon Doctrine*, 298–99
See also First Presidency; public
relations
Our Destiny. See Brigham Young
University (BYU); *BYU Studies*;
Epperson, Steven; McConkie,
Joseph Fielding; Millet, Robert

Pacific Islands
ban complexity, 38–39, 43
See also Fiji; Hawaii
Packer, Boyd K.
ban committee, 212–13, 219
ban revelation committee, 221–22
and ban critics, 90
and Lowell Bennion, 91, 185
embellishes ban revelation, 235–36
ending ban, 212–13, 223
and historians, 246–47
interracial marriage, 249
meets with Black members, 185–87
Lester Bush and, 197–98
oversees Genesis Group, 188, 190–91,
212–13
researches ban, 399n.137
supports ban, 198–99
See also Bennion, Lowell; Genesis
Group
Papua New Guinea
ordination questions, 44
patriarchal blessings, 72
Elijah Abel, 8–9
adoption, 213–14, 270, 310
after ban lifted, 226, 231, 252
Black curse, 4, 310
handbook, 252, 270

INDEX

lineage, 31–32, 41, 72, 187, 207, 217, 311
    See also Cain; curse on Black people;
        Ephraim; folklore; Ham; lineage;
        "mark" on Black people
Pea, John
    priesthood relinquished, 32, 207
    re-ordained, 342n.20
    requests priesthood, 207
Pearl of Great Price
    Hugh Nibley and, 335n.49
    papyri acquired, 178
    relationship to ban, 11–12, 23, 59, 174,
        200, 240–41, 427n.59
    See also Abel; Cain; folklore; premortal
        existence; scriptures
periodicals, LDS
    Black members, 273
    curse explored, 12, 15, 85–86
    interracial marriage, 288
    racist content, 18–19, 125
    See also curriculum
Perry, L. Tom, 205, 217–18
    supports ban, 198–99
Petersen, Emma Marr
    novel supporting segregation, 78
    See also Petersen, Mark E.
Petersen, Lauritz G.
    And ban critics, 90
Petersen, Mark E.
    attacks *Brown v. Board*, 62–63, 69
    author, 68–69
    ban hardliner, 198–99, 212, 216–17,
        398n.133
    on BYU difficulties, 146–47
    criticized, 77
    demands orthodoxy, 92
    denies giving speech, 77
    influence on colleagues, 75
    on interracial marriage, 69, 70, 71, 222
    on "one drop" rule, 70
    opposes Brazil missions, 40
    personality, 68–69
    public relations, 164
    racist addresses, 62–63, 68–74
    regrets past views, 76
    speech leaks, 76–77
    supports ban revelation, 222
    supports segregation, 70–71, 78
    See also Bennion, Lowell; Brigham
        Young University (BYU); civil

rights; Lyon T. Edgar; Smith,
    Joseph Fielding Smith (b. 1876)
Pharaoh
    and priesthood/temple ban, 11
Philippines
    Indigenous ordinations, 43–44
physical features
    determining race, 1–2, 8–9, 31, 72–73,
        129–30, 131, 207
    See also curse on Black people;
        folklore; lineage; "mark" on Black
        people; patriarchal blessings
Pinegar, Max
    embellishes ban revelation, 233, 236–37
    See also McConkie, Bruce R.
policy vs. doctrine, 56, 60, 89, 99, 142,
    149–51, 152
    See also McKay, David O.; McMurrin,
        Sterling M.
polygamy
    and priesthood ban, 5
Pope, Bill
    apology, 238
    embellishes ban revelation, 234–35,
        236–37
    See also McConkie, Bruce R.
Pope, Margaret
    apology, 238
    embellishes ban revelation, 233–34, 237
    known to exaggerate, 237
    See also McConkie, Bruce R.
Pratt, Orson
    on premortal curse, 11–12
    Brigham Young and, 335n.48
praying about ban 186–87, 192–93, 198,
    212, 216–17, 219–21, 223–24, 232
    See also Kimball, Spencer W.; McKay,
        David O.
pre-existence. *See* premortal existence
premortal existence
    adds theological complexity, 12
    after ban lifted, 227, 240–41, 257, 265–
        66, 297, 310
    controversy over, 11–13
    and curse, 11–12, 21, 26, 42, 45–46, 52,
        59, 69, 70, 72–73, 78, 150, 156,
        177–78, 185–86, 279–80
    disavowal of curse, 305
    Lowry Nelson letter, 25
    Mark E. Petersen on, 69, 70

454 INDEX

premortal existence (*cont.*)
 Joseph Fielding Smith on, 16
 See also curse on Black people;
  "fence-sitters," folklore; lineage;
  "mark" on Black people; Pearl of
  Great Price
presidential campaigns
 Ezra Taft Benson, 123, 135–36, 208
 George Romney, 104–6,
  121–22, 208
 Mitt Romney, 300–1
 Morris Udall, 208–9
priesthood ordinations
 black men, 1, 8–9, 17, 23, 26, 32, 37–38,
  39, 73, 245
 future promise, 27
 racist apologetics, 300
 reversed, 28, 32, 37
 See also Aaronic Priesthood
Protestantism
 racism in, 10, 11
 supports segregation, 75
public relations, 97–98
 apologetic strategies, 98, 136, 156, 160,
  163–64
 ban lifted, 230
 Black community, 286, 289–90, 313
 and Randy Bott, 301–2
 campaign, 164
 church magazines, 180
 counter BYU protests, 173
 crises, 126, 134–35
 department created, 164
 "I'm a Mormon," 301
 on racial teachings, 269, 272
 service, 273
 See also Brigham Young University
  (BYU); Gray, Darius; Otterson,
  Michael; Wolsey, Heber G.
Pugsley, Sharon
 Tribune ad, 178–79

Quinn, D. Michael, 298

race
 biology and, 6–7, 29, 31
 Susa Young Gates on, 6–7
 racial purity, 6–7

theology of, 11–12
 See also biology; DNA; lineage;
  patriarchal blessings; premortal
  existence
"Race Problems—As They Affect the
 Church." *See* Petersen, Mark E.
Rees, Robert A.
 Lester Bush article, 197–98
 See also *Dialogue*
Reeve, W. Paul
 ban origins, 315–16
 Gospel Topics Essay, 305, 315–16
Reid, Annette
 correspondence with Bruce
  McConkie, 261–62
 Mormon Doctrine, 261
Relief Society
 racial curriculum, 7–8
Republican Party, 258–59
 George Romney and, 111
 opposes civil rights, 111
revelation, 149–50, 151, 164
 active process, 215
 ban revelation text, 241, 242–43
 lack of regarding ban, 156, 196
 lifting the ban, 219–21, 223–24, 225,
  228, 240, 241
 needed to overturn ban, 54, 99, 105–6,
  181–82, 216
 Official Declaration 2, 240
 pressure and, 243
 —embellished, 242
  Jesus appeared, 235–36, 242
  past prophets appeared, 233, 235, 237,
   238, 239
  Pentecost, 233–35, 236, 239–40
  voice of God, 236, 254
 See also civil rights; Kimball, Spencer
  W.; McConkie, Bruce R.; policy
  vs. doctrine; Pope, Bill; Pope,
  Margaret; scriptures; temple
  meetings; Whitton, Annie
Richards, George F.
 ban hardliner, 39
 fence-sitters, 22
Richards, LeGrand, 217–18
 ban revelation, 236
 "fence-sitters," 250

INDEX

interracial marriage, 249–50
vision, 218
Richards, Stephen L.
  supports change, 56
RLDS Church
  Black members, 192–93
  success in Africa, 255
Roberts, B. H.
  on premortal curse, 11–12
  whiteness theology, 266
Romney, George W., 96
  and ban, 103, 104
  connections, 104
  gubernatorial run, 104–5
  and Clare Boothe Luec, 105–6
  and Nigerian mission, 94–95
  nomination as apostle, 104
  presidential run, 93, 94–95, 104, 121,
    122, 135–36
  and Delbert Stapley, 111
  supports civil rights, 103–4, 110–11, 121
  and Stewart Udall, 122
  See also presidential campaigns;
    Republican Party; Romney, Mitt
Romney, Marion G.
  on First Presidency, 27
  reversal on ban, 216
  supports ban, 216
  See also First Presidency; Kimball,
    Spencer W.
Romney, Mitt
  and Randy Bott, 300–1
  presidential campaign, 300–1
  See also presidential campaigns; public
    relations; Republican Party;
    Romney, George
Rubin, Jerry
  Black Power ties, 162–63
  integrating Mormonism, 162–63
  threat to church leaders, 162–63
  See also Black Power

Satan
  Black people as followers, 12
  endowment, 269
  linked with Cain, 11
scriptures
  after ban lifted, 251–52

relationship to ban, 10, 13, 20–21, 22,
  23–24, 52, 59, 70, 78, 99, 200
support segregation, 63, 69–70
See also Bible; Book of Mormon;
  "fence-sitters;" Pearl of Great
  Price; revelation
security
  headquarters, 163, 368n.128
  Harold B. Lee boosts, 163
  Temple Square, 165–66
seed of Cain. See Cain
segregation, 24
  as act of mercy, 70
  blood banks, 63
  early Mormonism, 2–3
  J. Reuben Clark sermon, 78
  laws, 18
  Mormon Doctrine, 100–1
  Mormon meetings/buildings, 55, 66–
    67, 71, 81, 82, 83, 310
  Mormon support, 64–66, 72, 77–78
  Nigeria, 94–95
  novel defending, 78
  opposition, 64
  Pentecostalism, 270–71
  Mark E. Petersen on, 69–71
  play defending, 77–78
  South (US), 75, 160
  Southern Baptist Convention, 271
  South Africa, 30
  Utah, 64, 85
  See also Brown v. Board of Education;
    civil rights; slavery
Sinquefield, Jim
  on low Black membership, 256
  on Genesis Group, 187–88
Skousen, W. Cleon, 162–63
  author, 165
  and Eldridge Cleaver, 282–83
  critics, 165
  protests and Communism, 164–65
  See also Benson, Ezra Taft; communism;
    conspiracy theories; Hoover, J.
    Edgar; John Birch Society
slavery
  Bible and, 10
  Brazil, 40
  Cuba mission, 24

456 INDEX

slavery (*cont.*)
  lineage and, 34–35
  Joseph Smith on, 4–5
  Brigham Young on, 4–5
  See also civil rights; slavery
Smith, Darron T.
  folklore vs. doctrine, 295–96
  racism, 289, 297
Smith, Eldred G., 37–38
  ban hardliner, 399n.147
  controversial sermons, 374n.39
  on Spencer Kimball, 398n.133
  on lineage, 217–18
  supports ban lifting, 225
  See also patriarchal blessings
Smith, George Albert
  ban as custom, 32–33, 150–51, 152
  counsels mission presidents, 30, 32
  interracial marriage, 28–29
  mental health, 340n.106
  Lowry Nelson letter, 24
  See also Clark, J. Reuben; First
    Presidency; Nelson, Lowry
Smith, Joseph Fielding (b. 1838)
  and Elijah Abel, 9–10
  origins of priesthood/temple
    ban, 13
  reminiscences, 8–9
  See also Smith, Joseph Fielding
    (b. 1876)
Smith, Joseph Fielding (b. 1876),
    90, 130
  on Elijah Abel, 73
  advanced age, 159
  author, 15
  on ban as custom, 150–51
  ban hardliner, 39, 51–52, 60–61,
    98, 99–100, 151, 159–60, 172–73,
    198–99
  and Lowell Bennion, 91, 92
  biographical sketch, 13–14
  on Black BYU students, 129–30,
    146–47
  Black people as "inferior race," 17
  books after ban, 293
  and Hugh B. Brown, 98, 157–58
  Lester Bush and, 196–97

church president, 159
compassion, 36
consults encyclopedia, 42–43
on curse, 16–17
death, 192
directness, 14
doctrinal hardliner, 336n.60
First Presidency, 122
Genesis Group, 187
influence on ban, 2, 13, 15, 17, 19–20,
  52, 99–100, 150, 184–85, 200, 212–
  13, 336n.61, 344n.64
influences on, 17–18
Look articles, 98–99
and Sterling McMurrin, 141
meeting sought, 184–85, 187
opposes "Swearing Elders," 51
opposition to, 20–21, 98
patriarchal blessing, 15
patriarchs and lineage, 344n.57
publishing history, 19–20
repudiated, 286, 305–6, 434n.35
scripturist, 14–15, 42–43
and Heber Snell, 51
summer seminar, 68
supports Black congregation,
  82–83
supports segregation, 67, 179–80
teachings as folklore, 294
translated writings, 19–20
whiteness theology, 266
on whitening of skin, 71, 311–12
See also Brigham Young University
  (BYU); Church Education
  System; folklore; McConkie
  Bruce R.; McKay, David O.;
  scriptures; *Way to Perfection, The*
Smith, Joseph, Jr.
  on Black opportunities, 4–5
  Black priesthood and, 1, 8–9, 26, 73, 75,
    121–22, 196, 245, 305
  founds Mormonism, 3–4
  and Jane Manning James, 4
  as originator of ban, 13, 15, 54, 59–60,
    88, 245–47
  racist views, 5
  on slavery, 4–5

INDEX

457

See also Abel, Elijah; Missouri;
  scriptures; priesthood ordinations;
  Young, Brigham
Smith, Tamu, 313
  Diary of Two Mad Black Mormons, 289
  interracial marriage, 288
  See also Vranes, Zandra
Snell, Heber C.
  opposes ban, 50
  and Joseph Fielding Smith, 51
  See also Church Education System
Snow, Lorenzo
  on curse origins, 13
Sorensen, Asael T., 56
  determining lineage, 41, 56
  mission president, 41
  See also Brazil
South (US)
  ban complexity, 38–39, 87
  interracial marriage, 59
  Mormon similarity to, 81–82, 84–85
  segregation, 64–66, 75, 81–82, 84–85,
    160
  See also civil rights; segregation;
    slavery
South Africa
  Afrikaners to preside, 39
  apartheid, 30
  ban lessons, 34
  Black church groups, 39
  determining lineage, 30–31, 32, 35,
    55–56
  mission, 29–30
  not to gather, 342n.26
  patriarchal blessings, 31–32
  seating at church, 29–30
  Truth and Reconciliation
    Commission, 271
  See also Africa; missions
spiritual gifts, 2–3
Stapley, Delbert L., 217–18
  on BYU difficulties, 146–47
  on civil rights, 110, 111
  death, 222
  and George Romney, 111
  supports ban, 198–99, 216–17, 398n.133
  supports segregation, 179–80

and Stewart Udall, 122
supports ban revelation, 222
See also Kimball, Spencer W.
Stark, Rodney
  Membership predictions, 307–8
Stokes, Catherine, 313
  on Martin Luther King Jr. Day, 260
  on persistent racism, 308
Streeter, Jonathan
  ban apology hoax, 308–10
Strengthening Church Members
    Committee, 268–69
Sturlaugson, Mary
  converts to Mormonism, 249
  interracial marriage, 249–50
  and Spencer Kimball, 249–50
  mission, 249–50
  racism, 249
"Swearing Elders"
  criticize church teachings, 50–51
  discussion topics, 50–51
  guest speakers, 50–51

Tagg, Melvin
  spies on Lowell Bennion, 89–90
Taggart, Stephen
  Mormonism and the Negro, 143, 149–50,
    151, 196–97
  reputation, 143
  See also historians/scholars
Tanner, Sandra and Jerald, 151
  on Helvécio Martins, 274–75
  publish Mark E. Petersen speech, 76
Tanner, N. Eldon, 75, 145–46
  administrator, 159
  on BYU difficulties, 146–47
  on civil rights, 112
  ending ban, 150–51
  mission president, 94–95
  reversal on ban, 216
  supports ban, 216
  women and priesthood, 232–33
  See also First Presidency; Kimball,
    Spencer W.; McKay, David O.
tax exemption
  ban lifting rumors, 228, 243–44
  Bob Jones University, 175–76, 202

INDEX

tax exemption (*cont.*)
  discrimination and, 175
  Sandra and Jerald Tanner, 244
  threatened, 160, 197–98, 201–2
  See also Carter, Jimmy
Taylor, John,
  and Elijah Abel, 8–9
temple meetings, 219
  lifting the ban, 219, 223
  prayer circle, 219–21
  spiritual experiences, 219–21
  See also Kimball, Spencer W.;
      McConkie, Bruce R.; Pope,
      Bill; Pope, Margaret; revelation;
      Whitton, Annie
temple rites, 4, 26, 311
  Elijah Abel, 8–9
  after ban lifted, 231, 247–48
  baptisms for the dead, 187–88
  David O. McKay, 22–23
  Satan removed, 269, 275
  See also Brazil
theology
  evolves, 214
  Mormon vs. other religions, 12
  premortal existence, 16
  of race, 11–12, 88, 216–17,
    224–25
Thomas, Robert K.
  on BYU curriculum, 173
  Lester Bush article, 197–98
  See also Brigham Young University
    (BYU)
Trump, Donald J.
  Mormon support, 317–18
  See also Black Lives Matter;
    presidential campaigns

Udall, Morris
  presidential campaign, 208–9
Udall, Stewart
  chastised, 122
  Dialogue article, 121–22, 208
Utah
  civil rights, 63, 80, 84–85, 106–7, 112–
    13, 115
  discrimination, 84–85
  interracial marriage laws, 6, 107

segregation, 64
  See also civil rights; NAACP

Vranes, Zandra
  Diary of Two Mad Black Mormons, 289
  on fake apology, 309
  See also Smith, Tamu

Wallace, Douglas
  excommunicated, 206, 313
  general conference stunt, 206
  unauthorized baptism/ordination, 206
Wallace, Mike
  Gordon Hinckley interview, 276
  See also newspapers/periodicals
    (non-LDS)
Way to Perfection, The
  after ban lifted, 228, 242, 257
  British Israelism, 17–18
  curriculum, 19
  deficiencies of, 54
  First Presidency and, 16
  goals of, 16
  influence on ban, 2, 16, 32, 46, 52,
    59–61, 69–70, 102, 103–4, 135, 247,
    277–78
  Portuguese edition censored, 136
  taken out of print, 269, 275
Welch, Robert, 101–2
  Benson presidential run, 370n.148
  on Martin Luther King Jr., 116
  See also curse on Black people; Deseret
    Book; folklore; "mark" on Black
    people; McConkie, Bruce R.;
    premortal existence; Smith,
    Joseph Fielding (b. 1876)
white, passing as, 28, 29, 34–35, 36, 37–38
  avoidance, 38
  See also lineage; patriarchal blessings;
    physical features; whiteness
    theology; whitening of skin
whiteness theology, 11, 18, 74, 77, 250–51,
    266, 305, 312, 314
  Bennion Report and, 59
  Book of Mormon, 311–12
  BYU devotional, 296–97
  countering, 272
  Hitler, 21–22, 77

INDEX

Harold B. Lee, 100
Bruce McConkie, 269–70
Our Destiny, 269–70
See also Cain; Ephraim; lineage;
patriarchal blessings; whitening
of skin
whitening of skin, 17, 70, 189, 199–200,
305, 312, 352n.33
Book of Mormon, 11, 71
Spencer Kimball on, 250–51
Harold B. Lee on, 100
patriarchal blessings, 4
Joseph Fielding Smith on, 71, 311–12
See also Book of Mormon; Indigenous
people; whiteness theology
Whitney, Orson F.
on curse, 13
Whitton, Annie
ban revelation account, 235, 237–38
See also McConkie, Bruce R.; Pope,
Bill; Pope, Margaret; revelation
Widtsoe, John A.
biographical sketch, 20–21
on German thought, 21–22
opposes colleagues, 20–21, 22, 102
Wilkins, Roy
BYU invitation, 176
on Sterling McMurrin, 141
on Utah civil rights, 84–85
See also NAACP
Wilkinson, Ernest L., 130, 197
ban committee, 156
on ban opposition, 47, 51–52, 73, 135
and Lowell Bennion, 91, 92
on Black faculty, 179–80
on Black students, 128–29, 148, 155
BYU expansion, 128
BYU protests, 134–35, 145–46, 153,
160–62, 167–68, 172–73
conservative values, 128
defends BYU curriculum, 173, 174
discrimination investigation, 127, 137–
39, 140, 143–44, 145, 147, 148, 177
on interracial marriage, 128–29, 171
memo on discrimination, 153–54
and Mark E. Petersen, 76–77
on student protests, 148–49
supports ban, 157

ties to church leaders, 128
and Heber Wolsey, 169–72
See also Berrett, William E.; Brigham
Young University (BYU);
Church Education System;
McKay, David O.
Williams, J. D.
opposes ban, 75
Williams, LaMar
advice to Black members, 185
Nigeria, 94–96, 119–20
See also Aaronic Priesthood; Africa;
First Presidency; McKay, David
O.; missions, Nigeria
Wolsey, Heber G.
ban lifted, 230
ban revelation statement, 225
pamphlet, 169–72
response to protests, 163–64, 167–71,
182–83
on using media, 173
See also Brigham Young University
(BYU); Gray, Darius; public
relations; revelation
women and priesthood, 224, 228
and ERA, 232–33
Spencer Kimball on, 232–33
request made, 232–33
Eldon Tanner on, 232–33
Woodruff, Wilford
Black people neutral, 12
reports "one drop" rule, 5
vision of, 218
Wright, Evan P.
First Presidency correspondence, 31–
32, 34
mission president, 341n.5
special blessing, 30
See also First Presidency; South Africa

Young, Brigham
and Elijah Abel, 8–9
ban originator, 1–2, 13, 26, 196–97, 245,
294, 305, 315–16
biography, 246
censored, 21
compared to Joseph Smith, 4–5
1852 territorial legislature, 5

INDEX

Young, Brigham (*cont.*)
 halts Black ordinations, 1–2
 on interracial marriages, 4–5, 264
 racist views, 4–5, 277–78
 removal of ban, 21
 on slavery, 4–5
 See also Smith, Joseph, Jr.

Young, Levi Edgar
 attends "Swearing Elders," 50–51
Young, Margaret, 298
 See also Brigham Young University
  (BYU)
Young, Susa Young
 on race, 6–7